The Theology of Ministry in the "Lima Document": A Roman Catholic Critique

Conrad T. Gromada

The Theology of Ministry in the "Lima Document": A Roman Catholic Critique

Conrad T. Gromada

International Scholars Publications
San Francisco - London
1995

Library of Congress Cataloging-in-Publication Data

Gromada, Contrad T.,1939-
   The theology of ministry in the "Lima document" : a Roman Catholic critique / Conrad T. Gromada.

      p. cm.
   Includes bibliographical references and index.
   ISBN 1-883255-97-X: $64.95 - ISBN 1-883255-96-1 (pbk.): $44.95
   1. Ministry and Christian Union. 2.Baptism, Eucharist, and ministry.
   3. Sacraments and Christian union. 4.Catholic Church- Doctrines.
   5.Catholic Church- Relations. I. Title. II. Series: Catholic Scholars
   Press (Series)
   BX9.5.S2G76 1995
   262' .1--dc20   94-43272
                                                           CIP

Editorial Inquiries:
 International Scholars Publications
 7831 Woodmont Avenue #345
 Bethesda,MD.20814

To order: (800) 55-PUBLISH

To Joseph and Jean Gromada
through whom I received both
the gift of life
and
the gift of a way of life

TABLE OF CONTENTS

FOREWORD

I am happy to recommend this text of Dr. Conrad Gromada presented to Catholic Scholars Press for publication. I was the director of Dr. Gromada's doctoral dissertation on ministry in the *Lima Document* (BEM) which serves as the basis for the book.

Dr. Gromada's work, "The Theology of Ministry in the *Lima Document*: A Roman Catholic Critique," is a very insightful piece of scholarship. He has provided the reader with a complete and accurate history of the different stages, transitions and influences which led to the actual text on ministry in BEM. In this serious and methodical exposition, he appeals not only to published but also unpublished sources. Additionally, he identifies and highlights individual theologians and theological perspectives which shaped the history and eventual direction of the ecumenical discussions on ministry. Anyone undertaking research on ministry in an ecumenical context or Ministry in the *Lima Document* must surely refer to this work.

Fortunately, his work is no mere history. It includes a well argued Roman Catholic appraisal of Lima's ecumenical perspective on ministry. Gromada is brave. He does not take the low road of glossing over serious issues in the "cause of unity." No, he understands that true dialogue welcomes difficult issues, disagreements, etc. However, he is thoroughly aware of the legitimate pluralism in Roman Catholic theology itself on the issues and questions of ministry in the church. In the end one finds his theological evaluation marked by balance, insight and comprehensiveness.

Gromada's style is clear and the text flows smoothly. The readers should have little difficulty following its evidence and argument. I am happy to note that he has updated the bibiliography of secondary literature including important works published in the last five years.

George S. Worgul, Jr. S.T.D., Ph.D.
Duquesne University
Pittsburgh, Pennsylvania

ACKNOWLEDGMENTS

The Lima Document, as it is commonly known, is actually Faith and Order Paper No. 111, *Baptism, Eucharist and Ministry*. This landmark document of the World Council of Churches' Commission on Faith and Order focuses on three essential issues which the Christian churches face in their quest for unity. Ministry, or rather, the Official Ministry of Pastoral Leadership in the Church, is an issue of particular difficulty and interest theologically, as well as psychologically, sociologically and historically. This present study, however, deals with ministry theologically, specifically from my own theological tradition, Roman Catholicism.

Dr. George S. Worgul, Jr. first suggested the topic to me. To Dr. Worgul I owe my deepest gratitude. As the promoter and supervisor of this research project he shared many ideas and approaches with me, especially the method which I eventually used in organizing the massive amount of material from the Archives of the World Council of Churches in Geneva, Switzerland. It was he who first encouraged me to do my primary research there.

On the way to Switzerland in 1985 I spent many wonderful hours in the company of Brother Jeffrey Gros, F.S.C., who at that time was the Director of the Commission on Faith and Order of the National Council of Churches of Christ in the U.S.A. He and his staff were kind enough to open their files to me as I made my initial inquiry into the topic. Jeff himself offered me room and board on several visits to New York City and helped in the making of important contacts. Also on the way to Geneva I visited for a few days with Father Jean-Marie-Roger Tillard, O.P. at the Collège dominicain de théologie d'Ottawa. He had served on various Faith and Order committees which produced the texts I have examined here. Father Tillard was also very hospitable and helpful.

I am grateful to the personnel at the Château de Bossey in Cartigny, near Geneva, who provided me with wonderful hospitality during the time of my work in the WCC Archives in Geneva. At Bossey I had the good fortune to spend many happy hours with Fr. Elias Mallon, an Atonement Father and the Vatican representative to the WCC. At WCC Dr. Günther Gassmann, the Director of Faith and Order, and his special assistant, Mrs. Renate Sbengen were very helpful. Most helpful, however, was Frère Max Thurian, the famous theologian of Taizé who graciously met with me several times during my visits to WCC headquarters. It is to Ans van der Bent, the chief librarian at WCC, that I owe a special debt of gratitude in his opening to me the Archives of Faith and Order and in his offering me many helpful hints.

From Geneva I travelled to the monastery of Chevtogne, Belgium, where I met for a few days with Father Emmanuel Lanne, O.S.B., the editor of *Irénikon*, who, like Fr. Tillard, had been a long-time theological participant in the committees of Faith and Order, especially those which produced the various ministry texts under study here. For his hospitality and insights I am very grateful. I also had the opportunity to meet briefly with Fr. Basil Meeking, the assistant to Cardinal Willebrands, of the Vatican's Secretariat for Promoting Christian Unity. Fr. Meeking was encouraging to me in my work. In Rome, I was the recipient of the wonderful hospitality of the Brothers of Christian Instruction, especially, Brother Henri Bernier. While in Rome I had the good fortune to confer with the staff at the Centro Pro Unione, run by the Atonement Fathers and to meet with Michael A. Fahey, S.J. and the late Edward J. Kilmartin, S.J. both of whom were teaching and doing research at the Pontifical Oriental Institute at the time. They too were helpful and encouraging.

Back in the United States I met with Robert Wright of General Theological Seminary in New York, who had served on the committee which produced the Lima text and with William H. Lazareth who had been the Director of Faith and Order in Geneva at the time of the Lima meeting in 1982 and during the years preceding Lima. Both Robert Wright and William Lazareth were helpful and encouraging. Finally I met with Geoffrey Wainwright at Duke University in North Carolina. He too had been intimately involved with the evolution of the text of Lima. In fact he served on the committee that finalized the text at Lima. He was helpful and encouraging as well.

Special thanks are due to my wife, Annette, whose patience and encouragement, during the time of this writing have been extraordinary. I am very grateful as well to my parents, Joseph and Jean Gromada, now deceased, who helped me during these many years in ways beyond reckoning, but in one special way in regard to this project, offering me the possibility of benefitting from the wonders of a word processor. To Richard Brobst I owe a special debt of gratitude for his hospitality and friendly support. That goes for Tom McCarthy as well. And there is the personal support and theological expertise of my good friends and colleagues,

Jack Dreese, M. Edmund Hussey and Giles H. Pater. I am deeply grateful to my two brothers, Henry and Joe, and their wives, Ruth and Karen, and their families whom I dearly love and upon whose support I have depended for too many years to tell. There is also James W. Malone, the bishop of Youngstown, who epitomizes for me the exercise of *episkopé* while perfecting the practice of gentility.

In recent days I am most grateful to Catholic Scholars Press and in particular, Dr. Robert West. And there are my colleagues at Ursuline College in Pepper Pike, Ohio (near Cleveland) on whose support I can always depend, especially Larry Mazzeno, Mary Kay Oosdyke, Dee Christie and, most assuredly, Christine Schwartz, the Director of Computer Services. Without Chris' tireless efforts to prepare the camera-ready manuscript this final text would not have been possible.

There are countless others without whose friendship and encouragement I may never have been able to sustain the effort required to complete this project.

Conrad T. Gromada
Ursuline College
Pepper Pike, Ohio

ABBREVIATIONS

ARCIC   Anglican-Roman Catholic International Commission

BEM   "The Lima Document," *Baptism, Eucharist and Ministry*

CD   *Christus Dominus*, Vatican Council II's Decree on the Pastoral Office of Bishops in the Church

DM   The document on Ministry, the Ministry section of "The Lima Document"

FO   Faith and Order, Commission of Faith and Order of the World Council of Churches

GS   *Gaudium et spes*, Vatican Council II's Pastoral Constitution on the Church in the Modern World

G.W.   Geoffrey Wainwright of Duke University

LG   *Lumen gentium*, Vatican Council II's Dogmatic Constitution on the Church

M   Ministry text

NT   The New Testament

PO   *Presbyterorum ordinis*, Vatican Council II's Decree on the Ministry and Life of Priests

T.I.   *Theological Investigations*, by Karl Rahner, S.J.

UR   *Unitatis redintegratio*, Vatican Council II's Decree on Ecumenism

WCC   The World Council of Churches

INTRODUCTION

Since the earliest days of Christianity when two or three gathered together in the name of Christ there was a need for "church order." The New Testament books themselves reflect varieties of church order, from the structured Pauline communities of the Pastoral epistles to the charismatic Johannine churches. Through the centuries the official ministries which have been charged to maintain church order have been often themselves the lightening rods of disorder, or rather disunity among the various churches of Christianity. For that reason the Faith and *Order* Movement from its inception has dedicated much effort to the issue of the ministry in the churches, that is, the official ministry of order.

It is not surprising, therefore, that in January, 1982, the Commission on Faith and Order of The World Council of Churches issued a challenge to the churches in terms of the three crucial signs of unity among them, baptism, eucharist and ministry. The document (widely known as "The Lima Document") treats these issues under one cover for publication. The ministry text, however, has a quite separate history, a history which deserves individual attention.

The Roman Catholic Church does not choose to be a member of The World Council of Churches. In the wake of Vatican Council II, however, many individual Roman Catholic theologians have served on the WCC's Commission on Faith and Order. Their influence has been felt in many ways. That influence is evident in "The Lima Document."

In order to understand more clearly the meaning of the text on ministry in "The Lima Document" and in order to serve Roman Catholic participation in the ongoing theological dialogue which the document calls for we undertake this study. We intend to trace the evolution of the text from its beginnings in the Faith and Order Movement, a movement which precedes by two decades the establishment of the World Council of Churches in 1948. The careful tracing of the text will enable us to clearly establish its precise meanings. We intend, fir of all then, to determine as accurately as possible the theology of ministry (that is, ordained ministry) in "The Lima Document." Secondly, we will compare its theology of ministry with the teachings on ministry in the Roman Catholic tradition. These teachings will include both official stances taken in recent years by the Vatican as well as the positions of many contemporary Roman Catholic theologians. Thirdly, in light of the first two efforts, we will offer our own suggestions for the development of a theology of ministry (among many theologies) in the Roman Catholic tradition. Such development is needed in order to ensure the fullest and most fruitful participation by Roman Catholic theologians in the ecumenical effort to achieve greater visible unity among the churches.

Chapter One will give an historical overview in order to situate the evolution of the text on ministry within the development of the Faith and Order movement. The next three chapters will trace the textual evolution itself. In these chapters twelve documents, including the final Lima text, have been singled out as the ones making the most significant contributions to the textual evolution. The fifth and final chapter will give the Roman Catholic tradition's theological response to the ministry section of the Lima text. It will include the official response of the Vatican, the contributions of many Roman Catholic theologians to this issue and the theological position of this present writer.

There is no one Roman Catholic theology of ministry just as there is no one New Testament theology of ministry. There are various theologies of ministry and corresponding theologies of church order. The tensions which arise in such a pluralistic theological situation can be either healthy or unhealthy tensions, tensions which testify to the magnificent multifaceted beauty of Christianity or tensions which rend the very fabric of its being. May this present effort contribute to the situation of healthy tension.

CHAPTER I

THE ORIGIN AND EVOLUTION OF "MINISTRY" IN THE FAITH AND ORDER MOVEMENT

The text on Ministry in the "Lima Document" is the result of a long process of ecumenical discussion and debate. This chapter will trace the development of the Document on the Ministry (DM) produced by the Faith and Order Commission (FO) of the World Council of Churches (WCC) in January, 1982 at its meeting in Lima, Peru. This analysis will proceed in two stages. First, it is necessary to locate briefly FO which produced the Ministry text within the origins of the modern ecumenical movement. Second, it is necessary to carefully analyze the discussions and texts which were the precursors of the final "Lima document." This analysis will follow a chronological order.

The result will be a clear understanding of the competing points of view expressed through the various stages of the evolution of the text. An identification of many of those persons who represented those points of view will also emerge. Knowing those persons can help to identify more clearly their precise influence on DM because of contributions they may have made to the topic of ministry in other places. Tracing the concrete personal process of convergence toward a final consensus statement will aid in the interpretation of the often subtle nuances of meaning contained in the final text.

THE ORIGINS OF FAITH AND ORDER IN THE MODERN ECUMENICAL MOVEMENT.

The origins of the Faith and Order movement is irrevocably marked by the Anglican impetus with its presuppositions concerning a particular notion of unity and a specific structure of the ministry held to be essential for that unity.[1]

"In the Chicago Quadrilateral of 1886 and the corresponding Lambeth Quadrilateral (1888) the Anglican Church accepted the idea of an organic, corporate unity of Christianity as its charter for unity."[2] The 1886 text noted:

> We do hereby affirm that the Christian unity now so earnestly desired . . . can be restored only by the return of all Christian Communions to the principles of unity exemplified by the undivided Catholic Church during the first ages of its existence; which principles we believe to be the substantial deposit of Christian Faith and Order committed by Christ and His Apostles to the Church unto the end of the world, and therefore incapable of compromise or surrender by those who have been ordained to be its stewards and trustees for the common and equal benefit of all men.
>
> As inherent parts of this sacred deposit, and therefore as essential to the restoration of unity among the divided branches of Christendom, we account the following to wit:
>
> 1. The Holy Scriptures of the Old and New Testament as the revealed Word of God.
> 2. The Nicene Creed as the sufficient statement of the Christian Faith.
> 3. The two Sacraments — Baptism and the Supper of the Lord — ministered with unfailing use of Christ's words of institution and of the elements ordained by Him.
> 4. The Historic Episcopate, locally adapted in the methods of its administration to the varying needs of the nations and peoples called of God into the unity of His Church.[3]

It is in this Anglican effort at broadly defining and formulating a concept of church unity with its presuppositions of organic unity and the historic episcopate that one can locate the roots of the twentieth century's ecumenical movement.

The individuals who were the pioneers of the modern ecumenical movement and in particular its Faith and Order component were an Anglican bishop, Charles Henry Brent, and an Anglican layman, Robert Gardiner. Brent had labored in the slums of Boston for twelve years when he was called in 1901 by the Protestant Episcopal Church in the USA to become a bishop in the Philippines. He became as

---

[1]"These two presuppositions were coolly received by the non-Anglicans participating in the work of Faith and Order" (Günther Gassmann, "The Development of the Ecumenical Discussion on the Ministry," FO/73:33, September 1973, p.1) at its first World Conference at Lausanne (August 3-31, 1927). In this connection it should be kept in mind that the 1896 encyclical of Pope Leo XIII, *Apostolicae curae*, declared Anglican clerical orders to be invalid precisely on the grounds of an organic unity requiring a clearly proven unbroken succession in the episcopacy.

[2]Gassmann, FO/73:33, p.1.

[3]Ruth Rouse and Stephen Charles Neill, eds., *A History of the Ecumenical Movement, 1517-1948*, (Philadelphia: The Westminster Press, 1954), pp. 264-265.

well "a specialist on the opium traffic and represented the American government at international conferences concerned with the suppression of this traffic in opium."[4] He was shocked by the ineffectiveness of the churches in the face of major societal problems, especially in mission countries. He believed this was due mainly to the churches' being divided one from the other.

In 1910, at the World Missionary Conference in Edinburgh, Bishop Brent became convinced there could be concrete results in the struggle for church unity precisely because such unity, along with the tireless efforts needed for its achievement, was God's will.[5] After Edinburgh and "'en route' to the Philippines, he attended the 1910 general convention of the American Episcopal Church in Cincinnati, Ohio, where his words in praise of the Edinburgh meeting resulted in the formation of a commission for the purpose of organizing an international meeting of Christian churches."[6] The work of this commission was delayed by World War I. Its labors were finally realized in the First World Conference of Faith and Order in 1927 under the presidency of Bishop Brent.

The commission's secretary was Robert Gardiner. Starting from scratch with no salary or staff, with no international or ecumenical experience, with not even a list of addresses of churches to be invited Gardiner dedicated himself to the task. Gardiner made successful contacts with several churches of the Orthodox tradition as well as with the Papal Secretary of State, Cardinal Gasparri.

During the war, international contacts were very difficult to make. At the end of the war, in 1919, a Faith and Order delegation was sent to Europe consisting of five American Episcopalians, headed by Bishop Anderson of Chicago. The delegation was welcomed in many countries and with especially great cordiality in

---

[4]W.A. Visser 't Hooft, "The 1927 Lausanne conference in retrospect," in *Lausanne 77: Fifty Years of Faith and Order*, FO Paper No. 82. (Geneva: The World Council of Churches, 1977), p. 5.

[5]"It is significant that Roman Catholic ecumenists relatively seldom dealt with the problem of mission. The divisions of the Church in its missionary outreach had been, for the non-Roman Churches, a primary impetus in the formation of the ecumenical movement, and the call for common witness was one of major themes from the Edinburgh Missionary Conference onwards. Roman Catholic Christians obviously felt this urgency less; they started rather from the view that the Church by its very nature had to be one." (Lukas Vischer, "The Ecumenical Movement and the Roman Catholic Church," *A History of the Ecumenical Movement, 1948-1968*, volume 2, edited by Harold E. Fey, Philadelphia: The Westminster Press, 1970, p. 316, footnote 1.)

[6]*New Catholic Encyclopedia*, s.v. "Brent, Charles Henry," by E. Delaney.

the Orthodox churches of the Balkans and the Near East. It was at this very same time that "the Patriarchates, especially the Ecumenical Patriarchate of Constantinople, were hopeful that a new era was opening up for them and a new freedom to develop with work in the future."[7] When the American delegation was received in Constantinople in 1919 a spokesman for the Holy Synod declared:

> Our joy is all the greater when we remember that, before it knew of your Church's most noble decision, but inspired by the same longing and with the same sacred goal in view, our Church had already studied the question of a league of different churches and of a possible coming together on their part, so that, with God's blessing and help, the way leading to unity might in future be made easier.[8]

This declaration proved to be a preliminary indication of what would appear in January 1920 in the Orthodox Encyclical,[9] namely, the call for a League of Churches parallel to the League of Nations being formed at that time. Even though the proposal was oriented more toward collaboration in practical and social tasks, it did not exclude the interests of the Faith and Order project.

The reception at the Vatican for the American Episcopalian delegation was personally cordial but rigid and closed-minded on many concrete issues and proposals. This spirit of rigidity and this lack of openness were in sharp contrast to what had been experienced by Gardiner in 1914 with Cardinal Gasparri. Cardinal Mercier of Malines, however, a life long correspondent with Gardiner until Gardiner's death in 1924 and sponsor of the conversations at Malines between Roman Catholics and Anglicans, was supportive of the efforts to secure Roman Catholic participation in the Faith and Order movement as it approached its first world conference. Unfortunately, Mercier's support was to no avail in regard to any official Vatican response.[10]

A preliminary conference took place in Geneva in 1920 in which seventy churches were represented. The Orthodox presence demonstrated that Gardiner's efforts to make the Faith and Order movement more than a western or pan-Protestant reality were relatively successful. The Continuation Committee of the conference was international in character and the responsibility for its forward movement would no longer be borne by the Americans.

Financial difficulties prevented the Continuation Committee from meeting

---

[7] *Lausanne 77: Fifty Years*, p. 7.

[8] Ibid., p. 8.

[9] Ibid.

[10] Ibid., pp. 8-9.

between 1920 and 1925. Brent maintained the leadership role, while new people were gradually gaining prominence. Two separate views of what the agenda should be for a World Conference of Faith and Order were emerging from the Committee. One view was represented by Bishop Palmer of Bombay, an Anglican who was elected at the 1920 meeting "chairman of the Subjects Committee, which was responsible for establishing the programme of the conference and directing the preparatory studies."[11] For Palmer there was a sense of urgency to bring about formal and concrete unity among the churches. The second view on what should be the agenda for a Faith and Order World Conference was sympathetic to Archbishop Söderblom's[12] emphasis on service but, unlike Söderblom, not to the neglect of doctrine. This view, perhaps more realistically than that of Palmer and others, held that the majority of the churches were not ready for comprehensive union negotiations but needed nonetheless to come together to freely express the difficult doctrinal issues that divided the churches. They agreed with Söderblom to this extent, that action in common on behalf of those in need can be a good starting point for rallying the Church as the one people of God, visible to all.

The pioneers, Brent and Gardiner and their friends, did not have in mind a specific goal of formal and concrete unity although they were not entirely sympathetic with the vision of the "Life and Work" movement represented by Söderblom. This movement was developing in parallel fashion during these same years before and after World War I.

The first World Conference on Faith and Order met in Lausanne, Switzerland in 1927. The tensions were keenly felt by the participants. Yet these many tensions provided a new opportunity for churches "to discover the ecumenical dimension of the Church."[13] A spirit of genuine dialogue and diplomacy marked the meeting. It clarified the need to confront head-on the "Protestant" and "Catholic" conceptions of the Christian faith. It celebrated an already existing unity despite deep differences. It affirmed the need to manifest visibly the unity of the Church. It furthered the process of correlating orthodoxy with orthopraxis; and in this ground-breaking event

---

[11]Ibid., p. 10.

[12]Nathan Söderblom (1866-1931), Lutheran Archbishop of Uppsala, Sweden, 1914-31. A leading force in European Protestantism he sought ecumenical cooperation in solving social problems without consideration of doctrinal differences. Largely because of him the Universal Christian Council on Life and Work was founded. This movement formed one of the two main streams that in 1948 merged in the World Council of Churches.

[13]Ibid., p. 19.

it became clear that the real *raison d'être* of the ecumenical movement was not to strengthen the Church against its enemies but rather to respond to the calling of the Church to be the People of God, the Body of Christ, in which all nations and races are reconciled.[14]

MINISTRY AS A TOPIC IN FAITH AND ORDER MEETINGS.

The issue of official ministry emerged as an unavoidable and crucial topic to be faced in the ecumenical enterprise. The non-episcopal churches were interested in intercommunion but they gradually realized that intercommunion would require their acceptance of the broad outlines of church constitution reflected in the Anglican and the Orthodox traditions.

> Most representatives of the Protestant churches collaborating with the Faith and Order movement were in fact striving toward this goal (of full communion between the churches) even if they did not regard a solution of the question of ministry as essential to it. However they were brought to realize that agreement on the question of the ministry is necessary in the interests of achieving an intercommunion which would also include the Anglican tradition.[15]

LAUSANNE, 1927.

Any agreements regarding official ministry achieved at Lausanne in 1927 focused on the foundations or sources of ministry. It was agreed that the official ministry of the church was: a gift of God; rooted in the authority of Jesus Christ; intimately joined with the preaching of the Gospel, administration of the sacraments and government of the Church; involved with a call by the Holy Spirit and an acceptance by the Church; and manifested by a commissioning through an act of ordination by prayer and the laying on of hands.[16]

There were disagreements and differences on the actual forms and patterns of organizing the ministry. The meeting referred "to the existence of differences in the understanding of the nature of the ministry, the nature of the ordination and the

---

[14]Ibid., p. 20.

[15]Gassmann, FO/73:33, p. 2. In addition, it is interesting to note that five years before Lausanne, "in 1922, after much negotiation with members of the Orthodox Churches, the ecumenical patriarch of Constantinople recognized the validity of Anglican orders." (*New Catholic Encyclopedia*, vol. 1, p. 530)

[16]*Proceedings of the World Conference: Lausanne, August 3-21, 1927*, ed. by H.N. Bate, New York: George H. Doran Company, 1927, section 5, no. 34.

grace conferred thereby, the function and authority of bishops and the nature of Apostolic Succession."[17]

EDINBURGH, 1937.

Unlike the Lausanne conference, the Second World Conference on Faith and Order in Edinburgh in 1937 was preceded by extensive preparatory work. This work led to a clarification of what had already been stated in 1927. Only one common agreement among the churches was added, namely, that the official ministry has as a presupposition, the royal priesthood of all Christians.

The Edinburgh meeting acknowledged with Lausanne that the churches agreed that the ministry instituted by Christ was a gift of God and that ordination is performed by the laying on of hands. Nonetheless it made clear that there were differing interpretations about what Lausanne had stated. Edinburgh restated even more clearly the differences that remained. Two views of apostolic succession were presented side by side: episcopal succession and presbyteral succession. The former view, taken by Episcopal, Anglican, Old Catholic, Orthodox and other churches of the East, held that continuity from apostolic times is to

> be thought of both as the succession of bishops in the principal sees of Christendom, handing down and preserving the Apostle's doctrine, and as a succession by laying-on of hands.[18]

The latter view held that continuity consists in

> a succession of ordination by presbyteries duly constituted and exercising episcopal functions, and in the succession of presbyters in charge of parishes, with special emphasis on the true preaching of the Word and the right administration of the Sacraments.[19]

This view was held by communions of the Presbyterian and Reformed tradition. This latter view also included

> other communions (who), while unaccustomed to use the term "Apostolic Succession, " would accept it as meaning essentially, or even exclusively, the maintenance of the Apostles' witness through the true preaching of the gospel, the right administration of the Sacraments, and the perpetuation of the Christian life in

---

[17]Ibid., no. 36 (and elaborated upon in the Appendix, nos. 44 - 47).

[18]*The Second World Conference on Faith and Order: Held at Edinburgh, August 3-18, 1937*, ed. by Leonard Hodgson. New York: The Macmillan Company, 1938, p. 246.

[19]Ibid., p. 247.

the Christian community.[20]

Although there is a repetition and brief explanation of the Lausanne formula for a "united church of the future" the Edinburgh Report

> makes it clear that on the way to full intercommunion and 'corporate unity' it will be necessary to reconcile differences between churches which hold that a) the threefold form of ministry of bishops, priests and deacons was instituted by Christ, b) the historic episcopate is essential for organic unity, c) the office of bishop is not essential to the Church, d) no specially ordained ministry whatsoever is required by the Church (Ed 140).[21]

The Edinburgh Conference's sober cataloguing of the real differences between the churches on the question of official ministry was frank and accurate. The ecumenical movement was still young.

AMSTERDAM, 1948.

The Edinburgh Conference of 1937 approved a proposal made by the Life and Work movement (at its Oxford, 1936 meeting) to form a world council of churches of which Faith and Order become an integral part along with Life and Work. Meetings were held in 1938 and 1939 to discuss a constitution for the proposed world council and other organizational matters in Faith and Order. The onset of war in Europe in 1939 interrupted these plans until 1946, when the Provisional Committee met at Geneva. At Geneva the First Assembly of the World Council of Churches was proposed for the summer of 1948 in Amsterdam.

The Amsterdam assembly did not specifically address the question of ministry. There was, however, a statement describing "our deepest difference," namely, "Catholic" and "Protestant" conceptions of the one Church of Christ which indirectly touched the question. This statement probably insured that "it would no longer be right to deal with the question of the ministry in isolation"[22], since the issues of visibility and continuity are among the most important issues underlying the meaning of official ministry.

---

[20]Ibid., p. 248. It seems clear that this divergence of views is rooted in the positions which became fixed at the time of the Protestant Reformation.

[21]Ibid., p. 3.

[22]Ibid., p. 4.

LUND, 1952.

The report of the Third World Conference of Faith and Order, held in Lund, Sweden in 1952 briefly treated official ministry in two places: in the broader context of continuity and in the context of worship. In the section entitled, "Continuity and Unity," it states that

> while the vast majority of Christians would agree that some form of commissioned ministry was essential to the continuing life of the Church, serious and at present irreconcilable disagreement arises on the question whether some particular form of ministerial order is essential to the continuity of the Church.[23]

In the section entitled, "Ways of Worship," it states that "some Churches emphasize the ministerial priesthood as definitely distinct from the priesthood of all believers."[24]

The Lund Conference marked a dramatic shift in the methodology of ecumenical dialogue. A methodology which emphasized a side by side comparison of the churches' traditional statements on issues was abandoned. It was replaced by a method which concentrated on a search for common christological and pneumatological roots. It also emphasized the common eschatological implications (and therefore, unfinished character) of the present convictions of the churches. This methodological shift was applied to the issue of official ministry. Lund articulated an urgency to make a "fresh starting-point (approaching) ministry, not as an isolated phenomenon but in the light of a profound Christological and eschatological approach to the doctrine of the Church."[25]

The orientation towards cooperative study rather than comparison of views appears in Lund's treatment of Apostolic Succession. After citing various denominational justifications of their respective forms of church order by way of various scriptural interpretations a footnote states that "recent biblical study has, however, led to a considerable growth together on the whole question."[26]

---

[23]*A Documentary History of the Faith and Order Movement 1927-1963*, ed. by Lukas Vischer, St. Louis: The Bethany Press, 1963, paragraph 36, p. 94.

[24]Ibid., paragraph 108, p. 109.

[25]Ibid., paragraph 38, pp. 95-96.

[26]Ibid., paragraph 37, footnote 1, p. 95.

EVANSTON, 1954.

The Second General Assembly of WCC took place in Evanston, Illinois, September 15-31, 1954. It

> deepened the christological approach of Lund and broadened its eschatological basis. Its biblically substantiated description of the Church and the fullness of its life and the manifold gifts of grace working in it indicate further presuppositions for future discussion of the ministry.[27]

Among the many exhortations to repentance for the disunity of the One Church of Christ, the Assembly stated on behalf of each and every member church of the WCC that

> we must seek to acknowledge beyond the bounds of our own church each ministry that preaches the gospel of reconciliation as a means whereby Christ performs His saving deeds. Especially need we to discover the meaning of the ministry of the laity for Christian unity."[28]

NEW DELHI, 1961.

The Third General Assembly of WCC took place in New Delhi, India from November 18 to December 6, 1961. The need for a generally accepted ministry was taken up in the context of its formula for unity. The Assembly had been preceded by several meetings in which the crucial question was faced: What kind of unity does God demand of His Church? The discussion of this question resulted in a definition of such unity, the New Delhi formula:

> We believe that the unity which is both God's will and his gift to his Church is being made visible as all in each place who are baptized into Jesus Christ and confess him as Lord and Saviour are brought by the Holy Spirit into one fully committed fellowship, holding the one apostolic faith, preaching the one Gospel, breaking the one bread, joining in common prayer, and having a corporate life reaching out in witness and service to all, and who at the same time are united with the whole Christian fellowship in all places and all ages in such wise that ministry and members are accepted by all, and that all can act and speak together as occasion requires for the tasks to which God calls his people.[29]

The above theological consensus had been described as "the ecumenical

---

[27]Gassmann, pp. 4-5.

[28]A *Documentary History*, paragraph 28, p. 140.

[29]*The Fourth World Conference on Faith and Order: Montreal 1963*, FO Paper No. 42, The Report edited by P.C. Rodger and L. Vischer, London: SCM Press Ltd., 1964, p. 82.

equivalent of the Lambeth Quadrilateral."[30]   And it was presented to the Central Committee of WCC at its 1960 meeting at St. Andrews, Scotland in this way:

> By its very nature such a unity is visible, but it does not imply a single centralized ecclesiastical institution — which is very generally set aside as being undesirable. It is compatible with a large degree of institutional and liturgical diversity, but it is neither "federal" nor merely "spiritual".[31]

Günther Gassmann has contended that with this formula for unity "the recognition of ministries — and in my opinion therefore the ministry itself — is thus given special importance and responsibility for the unity of the Church in both vertical and horizontal dimensions."[32]

The Working Committee of FO met in Paris, France from July 30 to August 3, 1962. In planning the agenda for the Montreal Conference of FO in 1963 it recognized that ecclesiology was "the core of many contemporary ecumenical problems."[33] Section III presented for consideration by the Conference a paper entitled, "The Redemptive Work of Christ and the Ministry of His Church."[34]

Three possible aims were listed for this Section:

> 1. To discuss the relation of Christ's ministry to the Church's ministry, and the status and function of the ordained ministry within Christ's Body. Special attention will be given to the priestly and apostolic vocation of the ordained ministry and its relation to the tasks and gifts of all believers.
> 2. To examine how a deeper understanding of Christ and his Church may affect the present understandings of the ministry in various churches. Questions ought also to be formulated which will enable the churches to understand how current doctrines and practices impede or enhance the ministry of Christ to the world.
> 3. To discuss the necessity and the variety of new forms of ministry, to evaluate their significance for the traditional doctrines of ordination and to relate these doctrines to such specific problems as:
>   (a) the place of the diaconate;
>   (b) the ordination of women.[35]

---

[30]*Evanston to New Delhi, 1954-1961: Report of the Central Committee to the Third Assembly of the World Council of Churches*, Geneva: WCC, 1961, p. 43.

[31]Ibid.

[32]Gassmann, p. 5.

[33]FO Paper No. 36, p. 32.

[34]Ibid., p. 34.

[35]Ibid.

MONTREAL, 1963.

The fourth World Conference on Faith and Order in Montreal marked the first time since 1937 that the question of official ministry was discussed in detail, "although it had not explicitly been a theme in the work of the preparatory committees."[36] The report of Section III, "The Redemptive Work of Christ and the Ministry of His Church," provides us with a text in which can be detected some seminal elements which would find their way, during the next twenty years, into the Lima document. In fact, this text will provide the actual starting point for the textual evolution of DM which will be undertaken in this study.

Although Montreal did little to overcome the longstanding differences in the churches' understanding of the official ministry, it

> did establish vital bridgeheads for the future by at last lifting the question of the ministry out of its isolation in the Church's theology and practice and its concentration on controversial aspects and placing it in the new context that had been developed in the preceding fifteen years of ecumenical work.[37]

For this reason, supplying the text and giving a short synopsis of its sections may prove valuable at this stage of our study.

> 77. Ministry and order have not been on the agenda of a World Faith and Order Conference since Edinburgh 1937. Section III at Montreal has been given the task of discussing again, after this interval, our understanding of the place of ministers of Jesus Christ in the life of the Church. During these twenty-five years there has been a notable recovery of the biblical teaching about the royal priesthood of the whole people of God. There have been times in the past when the word "layman" was understood to refer to someone who had a merely passive role in the life of the Church, and the word "ministry" referred exclusively to the full-time professional service of the Church. That time is past. A recovery of a true doctrine of the laity has brought with it the recognition that ministry is the responsibility of the whole body and not only of those who are ordained. This recovery is one of the most important facts of recent church history, and we express our gratitude in this connection for the work of the Department on the Laity of the World Council of Churches, and especially for the paper entitled Christ's Ministry and the Ministry of the Church (Laity Bulletin No. 15, available from the W.C.C.) which has been the starting point of our discussion.

> 78. It is a significant fact that the work of the Laity Department led it to raise the question of the function and authority of the ordained ministry, and it is with this question that we have tried to deal, even though the title given to us, if strictly interpreted, refers to the whole work of the Church in the world. We agree with the Department on the Laity that the narrower question can only be answered in the

---

[36]Gassmann, p. 5.

[37]Ibid., p. 6.

context of the broader, and we have tried always to bear this context in mind. But we confess frankly that we have not attempted to deal with the total ministry of the church in the world. For this we refer again to the work of the Laity Department.

79. Any fuller account of the doctrine of the ministry would have to be placed within the context of man's total existence in the world of which Christ is Redeemer and Lord.

80. In addressing ourselves to the narrower question we have faced difficulties even in defining our subject. We all acknowledge that the Church has always had and (so far as we know) always must have what we may call "a special ministry". But there is no universally agreed language by which to describe this special ministry in distinction from the ministry of the Church as a whole. There is no agreement as to the relation and distinction between them, and there is no agreement as to what is, and what is not, included in the "special ministry". Even a preliminary definition of terms implies some provisional opinion on questions of substance. Not merely in spite of, but precisely because of, this confusion we believe that the time is ripe to study afresh the special ministry of those who are ordained to be the servants of the servants of God, and its relation to the general ministry of all Christian people.

81. Recognizing the many unresolved differences of belief among us, we believe we ought to approach this question in the first place not merely by comparing our different confessional views, but by seeking to penetrate "behind our divisions to a deeper and richer understanding of the mystery of the God-given unity of Christ with His Church" (Lund Report). In this report we invite member churches to start to think together again about the special ministry, and we propose the following brief theses for study.

82. For the purpose of the present document we have agreed to use the words "special ministry" and "ministers" to describe that which is the focal concern of our study.

The Introduction of the report (para. 77-82) notes that "during these twenty-five years (since Edinburgh 1937) there has been a notable recovery of the biblical teaching about the royal priesthood of the whole people of God."[38]

83. The redemptive work of Christ has its origin in the mission given by the Father to the Son, and willed by the Son with the Father in the Holy Spirit. In accordance with the purpose of god, prepared and foretold under the covenant with Israel, and by the power of the Holy Spirit, the Son became man, proclaimed the Kingdom of God with power, was crucified, died, rose again, and lives eternally as Lord. In this Person, this history and this work, God was in Christ, reconciling the world to himself. That which the Lord Jesus Christ has thus accomplished, he has accomplished once for all.

84. In order that his redemptive work might be proclaimed and attested to the ends of the earth, and that its fruits might be communicated to man, Christ chose

---

[38] *The Fourth World Conference*, paragraph 77, pp. 61-62.

apostles, witnesses of his resurrection, and committed to them the word of reconciliation. Having clothed them with the Holy Spirit he sent them to gather all nations into the Church and to build it upon the one foundation which is no other than himself, and to inaugurate the ministry of the accomplished reconciliation for the salvation of all men. Thus the whole Church and its special ministry have their origin in the sending of the apostles.

85. The unique witness of the apostles to Christ is preserved by the Church in the New Testament. Their mission is continued by the Church and in its ministry.

86. The Church, the people chosen by God, is the community of those who have been gathered in faith by the apostolic preaching and by the power of the Spirit and have been plunged into the waters of baptism. It belongs to Christ, as his own body confesses him, worships him and obeys him, as the redeemer of the world. Taken from the world and set in the world, it constitutes there the royal priesthood declaring the wonderful deeds of God, and offering to him as a sacrifice both worship and daily life.

87. In order to build up the Church and to equip it for its mission, the Lord Jesus Christ has given ministers who, following the apostles and by the power of the Spirit, serve the accomplished reconciliation in, with, and for the body by announcing, attesting and communicating that reconciliation by the means which the Lord has given.

Paragraphs 83 to 87 are entitled, "The Work of Christ and the Mission of the Church." Here, as Gassmann puts it, "the approach of Lund and Evanston is adopted and the statements about the general and the special ministry of the Church are given a christological and ecclesiological basis (within a trinitarian framework)."[39] Christ's choosing of the apostles who are witnesses of the resurrection is the origin of the ministry of the whole Church and of its special ministers. The latter have been given to the Church so that it might be built up and equipped for its mission to the whole world. These ministers do what the apostles had done before them by the power of the Spirit.

88. All ministry in the Church is rooted in the ministry of Christ himself, who glorifies the Father in the power of the Holy Spirit. Christ stirs up, calls, strengthens and sends those whom he has chosen for the whole ministry of his Church and for the special ministry, making them the instrument of his message and of his work. Ministers are called to serve the work of the Lord by following him, by being conformed to him, and by announcing his name.

89. The special ministry thus reflects and serves the redemptive love of Christ.

(a) Christ is Prophet; his Church is called to be his witness, announcing to the world by word and deed the good news of the Word made flesh, of the

---

[39]Gassmann, p. 5.

accomplished reconciliation, and of the Kingdom which comes. That it may truly be so, the ministers are set in its midst to proclaim him.

(b) Christ is High Priest; his Church is called to be the true priesthood in the world, holding out to all men the gift of the reconciliation which he has purchased, and offering up on behalf of all men both the sacrifice of praise, thanksgiving and obedience, and the prayer of penitence and intercession. That it may truly be so, the ministers are set for the priestly service of the Gospel in the midst of the priestly people.

(c) Christ is King; his whole Church is called to be the sign of his kingdom in the midst of the world, the evidence to men that the devil is conquered and that God reigns. That it may truly be so, the ministers are set in the midst to be the servants of the King, guarding his people in their unity one with another and with him, leading them in their spiritual warfare, and equipping them with all the armour of God.

In these ways the ministers are the servants of the Servant of God, and thus share in his suffering and in his joy.

90. This ministry of Jesus Christ in his Church is made effective by the action of the Holy Spirit promised by the Lord to his people. To serve Christ in his Church means to wait always upon the Spirit of power, holiness and love. It is in this waiting upon the Spirit that the ministers of the Church preach the word, administer the sacraments, watch in prayer, lead God's people, and engage in deeds of brotherly help. In dependence upon the same Spirit the whole Church shares the responsibility for this stewardship of the riches of Christ.

91. The whole Church receives and supports those who have been given to it for the ordering of its mission, and they depend upon the spiritual gifts, the prayers and the generosity of the whole fellowship. Thus the whole body standing firm together is armed for its service.

Paragraphs 88 to 91 are entitled, "Christ, the Church and the Special Ministry." They describe the relationship of the ministry of the whole Church and of the special ministry to the prophetic, priestly[40] and kingly ministry of Christ where all ministry in the Church is rooted and from which it takes various forms under the inspiration of the Spirit. The mutual support between special ministers and the other members of the Church at large is stated.

92. The Holy Spirit dwells in the Church. He comes to each member in his baptism for the quickening of faith. He also bestows differing gifts (charismata) on groups and individuals. All his activities are to enable men to serve and worship God. All

---

[40]"Special ministry" is not directly associated with "priesthood" at this stage of development. Later in the text, paragraph 95 (section b), churches following various patterns, including those which follow the pattern of bishop, priest, deacon, are set side by side with churches which have the pattern of pastor, elder, deacon.

members of the Church are thus gifted for the common good.

93. The Spirit equips God's people in a threefold way:

(a) He enables them as children of their heavenly Father to live and work in the world without faithless anxiety. There they find their principal place of testimony and their principal sphere of service. There they live as first fruits of a new creation.

(b) The spirit builds up the body of Christ in love, truth and holiness, by equipping the members with the manifold and varied gifts which they need for the service of one another and for the mission of the Church.* [*We propose that the question of the diaconate and that of the ordination of women receive further attention in Faith and Order.]

(c) Among the differing gifts bestowed by the Spirit is the special ministry.

Paragraphs 92 and 93 emphasize the fact that all ministries in the Church, among which is the special ministry, are gifts of the Holy Spirit.

94. The call to the special ministry depends upon the presence and the action of the Holy Spirit in the Church. He is at the same time a free Spirit choosing whom he will, and an ever-present spirit guaranteeing to the Church that God does not cease to call men into the service of the Lord and to give them necessary gifts. He leads the Church to seek out and to recognize the presence amongst her members of these gifts and this calling, and to test the gift and the calling given to men by God. The divine initiative may make use of the voice of the community or may be addressed individually to the Christian. In any case, the exercise of the special ministry in the Church requires the acknowledgement and the confirmation of the Church.

95. This confirmation is given in ordination. According to the New Testament, this ordination consists in prayer with the laying on of hands. The orderly transmission of authority in ordination is normally an essential part of the means by which the Church is kept from generation go generation in the apostolic faith. All of us regard this continuity in the apostolic faith as essential to the Church. Some of us, including the Orthodox, believe that the unbroken succession of episcopal ordination from the apostles is a necessary guarantee of a valid ministry and of the safeguarding of the true faith, and that ordination is itself a sacrament. Others among us believe that it is the work of the Holy Spirit not only to preserve order in the Church but also to create new forms of order when existing forms have ceased to safeguard the true faith. Some believe that there is not sufficient authority in the New Testament to warrant the practice of ordination in the sense of setting men apart for a life-ministry in the Church. We recognize the gravity of these differences. At the same time we are all agreed in accepting the statement of the Third Assembly that the unity which we seek includes a ministry accepted and acknowledged by all. There are differences of belief and practice among us on what constitutes the special ministry. Some churches recognize seven orders in the special ministry, some three, some only one. But the threefold pattern (bishop, presbyter, deacon) is also found (e.g. in the form of pastor, elder, deacon) in churches which normally speak of only one order in the special ministry. There is need both for discussion between the churches about these differing traditions, and

also for self-examination within our churches about the way in which we have received and used the gift of ministry. For example, we must ask ourselves such questions as the following:

(a) Granted that there is an essential ministry given to the Church by the Lord, does the traditional pattern of ministry in our churches do justice to the variety of the gifts of the Spirit?

(b) Have churches which follow the pattern "bishop, priest, deacon" in fact preserved the specific character of each of these orders of ministry as taught in their formularies? Do churches which have the pattern "pastor, elder, deacon" (or some similar pattern) preserve the ministerial character of each? On what theological principles are elders (presbyters) or deacons included in, or excluded from, the special ministry?

(c) While in all our churches men and women are set aside for limited periods for some forms of ministry, ordination to the special ministry is almost universally regarded as being for life. What are the grounds for this?

(d) The following qualifications for the special ministry have by no means always been regarded as indispensable: academic training, full-time service, salary. Are they treated as indispensable in our churches today, and if so, on what grounds? How are these aspects of the ministry related to the fundamental theology of the ministry?

Paragraphs 94 and 95 are entitled, "The Call and Authorization of the Minister." Here the document cites the need for special ministry to be acknowledged and confirmed by the Church for its exercise and it cites the confirmation given by ordination whose New Testament pattern consists of prayer and the laying on of hands. Then it states that "the orderly transmission of authority in ordination is *normally* (emphasis added) an essential part of the means by which the Church is kept from generation to generation in the apostolic faith."[41] "The wider understanding of continuity hinted at . . . is not developed further. Instead some of the different views of Apostolic Succession, ordination and the structure of the ministry are expounded and confronted with some critical questions."[42]

96. The minister, like the apostle, is sent to the world to show forth by word and deed the dying and resurrection of Jesus Christ, and is also given to the Church to remind it of that dying and rising by which it lives, and which it has to communicate to the world.

97. The minister is sent to the world in which and for which Christ died. There he may be called to share the apostolic sufferings; afflictions, hardships, calamities.

---

[41] *The Fourth World Conference*, paragraph 95, p. 65.

[42] Gassmann, p. 6.

Certainly, he will share in the apostolic labours. He goes into the world on behalf of Christ, speaking to a divided and estranged mankind the word of reconciliation. In this obedience he will share in the apostolic joy.

98. The special responsibility committed to the minister in the Church is the equipment of the other members in the work of ministry that they may carry out the responsibility committed to them in baptism. This will call for a constant ministry of preaching, teaching and pastoral care. Ministers are given to the Church as the Lord's messengers, watchmen and stewards, and as such they have to give an account to him of their stewardship.

Paragraphs 96 to 98 first speak of the spiritual life of the minister in relationship to Christ and the Apostles. Then there is pointed out that "the special responsibility committed to the minister in the Church is the equipment of the other members in the work of ministry that they may carry out the responsibility committed to them in baptism."[43]

99. All baptized Christians are called to respond to, and participate in, the ministry of Christ directed toward the world. "He calls his Church to embody his ministry of reconciliation in its life as well as in its proclamation" (Report on "Christ and the Church", Faith and Order Findings, Part II, p. 56). Here we recognize the incalculable importance of the ministry of those members of the body who make constantly visible the presence of the Church in the midst of the world.

100 .In the changing world in which we live, the existing forms of ministry of the Church must be re-examined. This should be done not so that the ministry is conformed to the world, but that it may manifest the essential character of the ministry of Christ in the changing patterns of society. In speaking of "forms" in this section we are not touching at all upon such matters of fundamental tradition as - for example - the threefold order of the ministry in some churches: we are concerned with the changing place of the minister in society.

101. Churches faced with rapidly changing situations are struggling to find forms of ministry relevant to their situation, and this not by abandoning traditional forms of the special ministry, but by seeking to give a diversity and flexibility such as we recognize in the New Testament and in the Church of the first centuries.

(a) In many parts of Asia and Africa, in the past, the traditional Western forms of the special ministry have often been preserved in all their institutional rigidity. This has led to the serious results of leaving many congregations in those areas virtually without sacramental life because they cannot support an ordained pastor, and of forming congregations whose energies are more introverted than directed toward strengthening the Church's service and witness in the world. The Church has appeared as an institution centered in a building, rather than as a company moving out into the world.

(b) In many parts of the world, the traditional settled parish-congregation of recent

---

[43]*The Fourth World Conference*, paragraph 98, p. 67.

centuries has been changing rapidly. When there is a rapid development of urban and industrial society with its mobility of population and diversity of life, pastors serving within the existing parochial system find it increasingly difficult to minister effectively to the real communities in which men live and make their crucial decisions. In these cases there is need of new patterns of the special ministry; more dynamic, flexible, and relevant to the situation in which the ministry is at work.

102. There are several possibilities of more flexible forms of ministry in the light of experiments, for example:

(a) The Church may ordain a man who works in a secular employment but has shown pastoral gifts. He will serve the local congregation as a pastor, while continuing his secular work as e.g. farmer or village teacher.

(b) In some sectors of society which are impenetrable to existing forms of ministry (such as certain areas of industrial life, where groups of Christians are learning to work and witness in terms of the conditions of life there), the best way to ensure the full witness of the Gospel may be to ordain members of these groups to the ministry of word and sacraments after appropriate training, so that they may build up the body of Christ without being "professional clergy".

(c) In a frontier situation, where there is not Christian community among the people, the Church may select a minister and send him into some secular employment so that he becomes a part of the community and within it seeks to witness and to form the community of God's people, the Church.

(d) In highly specialized or diversified societies, the Church may consider the possibility of assigning to the professionally trained ordained minister a specific role to strengthen the witness and service of God's people in a particular sector of society, e.g. among industrial workers or other professional groups.

(e) In many pioneer situations in industrial and urban society a team ministry crossing denominational lines has been formed. Such a group ministry can be, within modern society, a visible manifestation of the solidarity of God's people. Thus the Church can perform a service among the people of today who genuinely seek fellowship in their perplexity and loneliness.

(f) In certain situations an itinerant ministry has enabled the Church to respond effectively to rapidly changing conditions.

103. When the Church is thus involved in a frontier situation, the question of unity becomes even more urgent. In cases of extreme need churches have learned the necessity and the blessing of inter-confessional assistance. Here again we recognize the insistence of God's calling of the Church into visible unity which alone can provide a unified ministry really effective in the new and revolutionary world in which we find ourselves.

104. The Church with all her ministries lives continuously in history as a pilgrim people among all the communities of mankind, in obedience to Christ and in a constant solidarity with the world. This means that the Church responds to the suffering and victorious ministry of Christ with repentance and renewal, with the

hope and joy which Jesus gives, always ready to be reshaped in the forms of its ministry according to his call at each stage of the pilgrim life.

The final paragraphs (99-104) of the report of Section III are entitled, "The Special Ministry in Today's World." There is no attempt to treat of nor to imply an abandonment of traditional forms of special ministry (such as the three-fold order in some churches). Rather, the report urges, in the face of Third World needs and of vast sociological changes in the West, a "seeking to give a diversity and flexibility (to the forms of special ministry) such as we recognize in the New Testament and in the Church of the first centuries."[44] What follows are several examples of possible new forms which the ministry could take in the light of recent experiments. The examples range from part-time ministries to team ministries cutting across denominational lines.

During the FO Conference at Montreal in 1963 the report of Section III moved forward the effort to address the "special ministry" (as it termed it) by stating that "we believe that the time is ripe to study afresh the special ministry of those who are ordained to be the servants of the servants of God, and its relation to the general ministry of all Christian people."[45]

The Working committee of FO, after the Montreal Commission meeting, proposed that "a study on the ministry be implemented as soon as possible."[46] The committee placed special emphasis on "the beginning we have made in seeking to state an understanding of the work of the ordained ministry within the larger context of the corporate ministry of the whole people of God."[47]

In addition, during its deliberations on "Women in the Ministry and the Ministries[48] account was taken of the fact that "there is in many churches an new emphasis on baptism as entry into the ministry of the whole Church and as the consecration of the whole people of God to a life of witness and service."[49] This same discussion made the point even more precisely, seeing "baptism as entry into the ministry of the whole Church and the participation of men and women in this

---

[44]Ibid., paragraph 101, p. 67.

[45]Ibid., paragraph 80, p. 62.

[46]FO Paper No. 41, p. 22.

[47]Ibid.

[48]Ibid., pp. 23-25.

[49]Ibid., p. 24.

ministry."[50]

After 1963, FO's discussions and meetings were filled with fits and starts in regard to developing a comprehensive approach to the topic of ministry for the remainder of the decade. Several papers were written by theologians and there were some efforts by isolated regional study groups, laying the groundwork for a more carefully organized beginning in 1967. It should be kept in mind that since 1963, the Baptism and Eucharist studies developed somewhat independently of the study on the Ministry. There was, however, constant agreement that all three topics eventually be placed together for ecumenical discussion *among* and approval *by* the member churches of WCC.

From this point forward the significant facts of each year need to be carefully delineated. Later in this present study specific references will be made to some of the statements or meetings or other events of each of those years. Here the effort will be to present the context for later specific references.

1964.

The FO Commission met at the University of Aarhus, Denmark, August 15-27, 1964. One of its four committees dealt with some major studies of FO and entitled its report, "Christ, the Holy Spirit and the Ministry." Specific recommendations were made under five headings:

(1) In the "Introduction" the reasons for continuing the study were given, in particular the mandate of the Fourth World Conference (Montreal 1963) and suggestions were given for the approach to such a study, e.g., the necessity of its being seen in the context of ecclesiology as a whole and its aim of building up the unity of the Church by bringing to bear representative views and experience.

(2) The ministry of Christ (and the Holy Spirit) was considered next. Parts of the Montreal Report were recommended as the starting point along with the need to expand the *triplex munus* (of prophet, priest, king) to include a treatment of such roles of Christ as Servant and Teacher. Some probing questions were asked regarding the continuity between the ministry of Christ and that of the Church.

(3) The ministry of the whole Church was discussed next. Some sources in addition to the Montreal Report were suggested. And attention was directed to: (a)

---

[50]Ibid., p. 25.

the significance of the liturgical life of the Church, (b) the vocation of the Church to transcend racial, national and cultural barriers (and how the many NT images of the Church may enable an expanded view of the ministry), (c) the role of the Holy Spirit in the reconciling ministry of Christ to the Church itself and, through the Church, to the world.

(4) By far, the longest of the five divisions of this committee report is the one on "Ministries in the Church." First the question is asked, What part should be played in the work of the whole Church "by a regularly commissioned ministry, whether this be described as 'ordained' or not?"[51] Then the committee report reiterates the need to follow the lead of Lund (1952) by proposing "that this subject should be studied not in the first instance by comparing the doctrine of ministry in various traditions, nor by immediately taking up familiar controversial problems, but from a consideration of what has always to be done in and by the Church."[52] The report proceeds by distinguishing between "matters of principle" and "particular questions." The section on "matters of principle" presents under five headings a series of many questions that need to be addressed:

1. The ministrations necessary for the life and mission of the Church
2. The principles of givenness and freedom
3. The forms and functions of the regular commissioned ministry
4. The qualifications for appointment to the ministry, and the nature of ordination
5. The authority of the ministry.[53]

A list of "particular questions" (a non-exhaustive list no doubt) is then given. The topics are:

1. Apostolic Succession
2. Priesthood
3. Diaconate
4. The ordination of women
5. The unification of ministries in recent plans for church union
6. Episcopal and patriarchal authority, and the problem of primacy.[54]

(5) Finally, under the rubric, "Methods of study," the committee concludes its report. It recommends the involvement of groups around the globe, with special reference to those already involved in Ministry as an ecumenical

---

[51]FO Paper No. 44, p. 49.

[52]Ibid.

[53]Ibid., pp. 49-52.

[54]Ibid., p. 52.

issue. It also recommends a survey of the various proposals of church union plans, the involvement of lay people in this study and the compilation of a glossary of terms.

1965.

A small consultation group of six people met at Présinge, near Geneva, March 18-22 in order to produce "a document on the basis of the report of Aarhus Committee II, which would be suitable for use in study groups."[55] A report of this meeting was made to the Working Committee of FO when it met at Bad Saarow (GDR), July 9-12, 1965. The report stressed "that a more extensive treatment of some of the issues involved still remained to be undertaken, and to this end it was planned to invite papers from (qualified) individuals."[56] Some regional groups were mentioned as interested in this study.

1966.

The FO Commission's Working Committee met, August 27-September 1, 1966, at the Lavra of St. Sergius, Zagorsk, USSR. It reported that the study guide produced in 1964 "has not proved sufficiently focused to elicit good discussion."[57] The report went on to say:

> Two other papers have been requested, one by Professor Robert Paul and one by Frère Max Thurian; these may help provide more material for discussion. However, the main problem has been groups. So far the only group really active is a double-barrelled Australasian one meeting in Melbourne and Dunedin.[58]

Disappointment was expressed at the poor results thus far on this study known as, "Christ, the Holy Spirit, and the Ministry." A question of where precisely to assign responsibility for future action was raised. Sufficient financial support for the project remained a concern. "It was agreed to attempt to solicit more responses from regional groups, to draw up a paper descriptive of the ministry in union negotiations,

---

[55]FO Paper No. 45, p. 9.
[56]Ibid.
[57]FO Paper No. 48, p. 10.
[58]Ibid.

and to evaluate available material for a report to the Commission."[59]

The two requested papers mentioned in the above report were printed as Mimeograph Papers of FO. The one by Robert S. Paul is numbered, "FO/66:35, June 1966" and that by Max Thurian is numbered, "FO/66:46, August 1966." They are both lengthy studies and were written in preparation for the FO Commission meeting in Bristol the following year. A paper highly critical of M. Thurian's study was written by Kenneth Grayston and was published as a FO Mimeograph Paper, "FO/67:4, January 1967."

1967.

It seems clear that the three papers by R.S. Paul, M. Thurian and K. Grayston were not given serious and thorough consideration at Bristol in 1967. In fact, in an interview with the present writer,[60] M. Thurian indicated that at Bristol 1967 the time was not ripe for an acceptance of his own text (and presumably that of R.S. Paul and that of K. Grayston) and a lengthy agenda plagued the meeting.

The report on ministry given in Aarhus in 1964 had called for study of the issue by regional groups. It was reported at Bristol that two regional groups, one meeting in Melbourne and the other in Dunedin, "working for over two years on the study, have done substantial papers and woven them together into reports."[61] Because there were only two such groups the aforementioned papers by R.S. Paul, M. Thurian and K. Grayston "did not receive wide attention."[62]

A small group met in Geneva in May of 1967 to draw up recommendations to put before the FO Commission at its meeting in Bristol in August of the same year. Prior to the meeting they were told that "our major task will be to draw up recommendations for the Faith and Order Commission concerning the future of the ministry study. So far it has not progressed well, with the only substantial work

---

[59]Ibid., p. 11.

[60]Personal interview of Frère Max Thurian by Conrad T. Gromada at the Faith and Order Secretariat at the headquarters of the World Council of Churches, Geneva, Switzerland, April 15, 1985 (and corroborated in subsequent interviews, April 29 - 30, 1985).

[61]FO/67:42, July 1967, p. 1.

[62]Ibid.

coming from regional groups in Melbourne and Dunedin."[63] The group that met in May made the observation that "a major problem in the prosecution of the study has seemed to be a lack of focus, with the result that: (a) interest has not been widespread; (b) results are difficult to collate and summarize."[64] The group went on to suggest that the focus of the study for the future should be the meaning of ordination.[65] It listed five factors that indicated this precise focus: (1) the need for a service (or ministry) to the permanent elements in the church (e.g., Word and Sacraments), and therefore, a service functionally shaped to meet this need; (2) the need to face and perhaps resolve the continuing contrast made between the ministry of the whole people of God and the "set apart ministry"; (3) concern for the ministry among the Orthodox, Roman Catholics and Anglicans who consider ordination to be in some way sacramental; (4) the "problem" presented in church union negotiations concerning the ordination of women; (5) the question of "re-ordination" in the ecumenical situation of increasing mobility between churches.[66]

This same report concluded with a list of questions regarding ordination and a proposal. The questions were listed under four headings: (i) ordination as biblical; (ii) its development in church history; (iii) ordination practices today; and (iv) ordination and the church today. The proposal was stated thus:

> That a study scheme, using some of the above questions, or some other, be devised for use by all groups. This would involve the examination of the questions in a particular order, with the aim of developing a statement on the meaning of ordination. This statement would incorporate first, any consensus reached; second the continuing differences; third, a statement concerning how much agreement is necessary for unity and proposals for ways to work toward such agreement[67]

The Report of Section III of the FO Commission's meeting at Bristol, England, July 29-August 9, 1967, contained the following proposal for the prosecution of the study on ordination in three parts: "the first is an outline which is proposed for use by a large number of regional groups; the second contains a number of questions which are proposed for study in depth by only a few groups; the third

---

[63]WCC Archive Memorandum, May 1967, M.B. Handspicker, Archive Box: "Dept. of F and O, VII, vom 1967 bis 1968;" File: "Department of faith and order, 1967."

[64]FO/67:42, p. 1.

[65]Ibid., p. 2.

[66]Ibid., pp. 2-4.

[67]Ibid., p. 7.

is an outline of the method and the timetable of study."[68] The first two parts, containing the list of questions for groups contain much of the material previously recommended. The third part, "The Method and Timetable of the Study" recommended that an international theological commission be nominated, that members of the commission form groups to work on reports for submission to FO by September 1969 and that after the reports have been circulated among their members they reconvene in the Spring of 1970. In addition, this Bristol Section III Report encouraged more regional study groups to be formed. It urged more efforts to enhance coordination and to avoid duplication of the work going on in other studies then in progress.

1968.

A working paper entitled, "The Meaning of Ordination," was the fruit of an April, 1968 consultation convened at FO/WCC in Geneva (with some revisions made subsequent to the meeting). Having been presented with an initial draft worked out by the Secretariat, the participants at the April consultation brought together the thinking of Protestant, Roman Catholic and Orthodox traditions on the subject of ordination. They traced the areas of agreement and pointed out problems concerning ordination being faced by all the churches in their ministry in the modern world. Areas where agreement is not yet attained were delineated. Possible fields where the churches could proceed together were pointed out.[69]

When the Working Committee of FO met July 21-23, 1968, in Sigtuna Sweden, the above-mentioned working paper was presented for consideration. Some comments recorded at this meeting included the need to involve sociologists and more theological experts in order to avoid facile labels like "Protestant," "Roman Catholic" and "Orthodox." The comments indicated the need to study some unresolved historical points in scripture and the early church, and to include references to indelible character. The meeting called for a rethinking of the concept of apostolic succession in Roman Catholic theology as well as the source of a bishop's jurisdiction.[70] It was agreed to "send out the paper to the regional groups

---

[68]FO Paper No. 50, 1968, p. 144.

[69]FO/68:21, June 1968, p. 1.

[70]FO Paper No. 53, pp. 22-23.

with not only an Orthodox, but also a Roman Catholic and a non-Lutheran-Reformed Protestant reaction to be added.[71]

1969.

The minutes of the FO Working Committee meeting of August 4-8, 1969, at Canterbury England, recorded the following statement:

> in accordance with the request of the Working Committee which met at Sigtuna (in July, 1968), Orthodox, Roman Catholic and Protestant responses to the working paper had been sought and produced . . . It was noted that approximately forty groups were now studying the paper in twenty countries.[72]

1970.

From August 3 to 8, 1970 the FO Working Committee met at Crêt-Bérard (near Geneva). One searches in vain to find any mention at this meeting of the study of the ordained ministry.

Shortly afterwards, August 9-13, 1970, at Cartigny (also near Geneva) a meeting was held to bring to a close the current work of "The Joint Theological Commission on Catholicity and Apostolicity." This Commission had held three formal meetings during 1967 and 1968. The 1970 meeting is pertinent to the present study because the matters discussed parallel FO's project on ministry and will have a bearing on the Roman Catholic theological critique which is the ultimate purpose of this present writer's effort.

In interviewing Frère Max Thurian[73] the present writer discovered that the Cartigny Ordination Consultation, held September 28 - October 3, 1970, was an important event in the evolution of FO's treatment of the ministry. This Consultation produced a report "which had benefited from the results of labors of 36 study groups and from the work of the Department of Studies in Mission and Evangelism."[74] The final product of the consultation (after some subsequent reworking by the FO

---

[71]Ibid., p. 23.

[72]FO Paper No. 54, p. 9.

[73]Thurian interview, April 15, 1985 (April 29 - 30, 1985).

[74]*Major Studies and Themes in the Ecumenical Movement*, compiled by Ans van der Bent, p. 16.

Secretariat) is a document entitled, "The Ordained Ministry."[75] In a cover letter to the participants of the Cartigny Consultation, Gerald F. Moede, the Chairman of the meeting, wrote that "this version of the work will be submitted to the Faith and Order Commission at its meeting this summer in Louvain, Belgium (August 1-12, 1971)."[76] An outline of this document indicates the overall approach that was being taken as the Louvain 1971 meeting of FO approached:

- Preface
I. The Source, Focus and Function of Ordained Ministry
   - The Priesthood of All
   - The Ordained Ministry
II. Tradition and Change
III. The Authentication of Ministry
   - An Evolution in Authentication
   - Relevant Questions
IV. The Ordained Person and the Community
   - The Ordination Service - in the community
   - Changing Manifestations of Community
   - The Larger Community
V. Who is to be Ordained?
   - Appointment and Discipline
   - The Social Milieu
   - The Ordination of Women
VI. Ordination, Ministry and Profession
VII. Mutual Acceptance of Ministry
   - The Way Ahead[77]

The final section of the document entitled, "The Way Ahead," reports that

certain elements of a possible slowly-emerging conception of ordained ministry can be discerned. Making no attempt to assess priority or give logical order, such elements as these can be included in an enumeration: a ministry called to focus on the apostolic mission of speaking the kerygma, administering the sacraments, building up and overseeing the community, accepted, confirmed, and prayed for by the Church; a ministry related to the world, instituted to serve it in all its joy and torment; a ministry able to change its form according to the mind of Christ as history evolves, in the interest of reconciliation and liberation of men; not necessarily bound to full-time occupation, salary, particular education, or life tenure; a ministry rooted in and related to Christ, but open to the future, free to emerge in different ways in the creation of and nourishment of Christian community in new kinds of situations, and potentially recognisable (sic) and

---

[75]FO/71:1, January 1971.

[76]WCC Archive letter, in File No. FO772.MCO, "Mimeographed documents in chronological order, 1970-72."

[77]FO/71:1, pp. 1-22.

confirmed in different ways by the Church in different times and places.[78]

This document emerging from the Cartigny Ordination Consultation concludes with a brief consideration of the question, "How can the canonical and juridical structures in which the ordained ministry has been moulded (*sic*) (and by which it has been partly determined) be helped to evolve in consonance with the theological agreement which is emerging?"[79] In answer, the report points out that exceptions and irregularities to perfect order abound throughout church history. It indicates that church unions already accomplished require repentance, love and acceptance. It suggests that the principles of "*Ecclesia supplet*" and "economy" might very well be appropriately applied. And it suggests that discussion should not focus too heavily on having to conform to past patterns of "ordering" the church.[80]

1971.

For the most part the document, "The Ordained Ministry" (FO/71:1, January 1971), was commended and approved at the FO Commission meeting, held at Louvain, Belgium, August 2-13, 1971. It was later reported "that important work on the subject had been done by Dr. Moede prior to Louvain."[81] The Working Committee, at its August 11 meeting at Louvain discussed a few highlights of the document and summarized the common understanding about the "ordained ministry" achieved up to that point. In addition the committee listed several areas requiring further consideration:

a)   the connection between the ministry of the whole people of God and the ministry of the ordained (Chapter I);

b)   the degree to which the different Churches accept the ministries of others (Chapter VII);

c)   the sacramental reality involved in ordination (Chapter I,5);

d)   the 'personal, existential relationship' of the minister with the Holy Spirit (Chapter I,7);

e)   the interior, personal, and spiritual life of the minister, including marriage and celibacy;

f)   the ministry of women in the Church, in particular with reference to ordination;

g)   the implications of possible ordination for a limited term;

---

[78]Ibid., p. 20.

[79]Ibid.

[80]Ibid., pp. 20-21.

[81]FO Paper No. 65, p.24.

h) the relationship between bishop, presbyter and deacon (e.g. the WCC
    Report on the Diaconate)

i) the question of the nature and embodiment of apostolic succession
    within the Church.[82]

G. Gassmann, in 1973, after summarizing the contents of the Louvain report, states that the statement on ministry was indeed a summary of all the new insights, questions and problems that began to emerge at Montreal in 1963. He noted that Roman Catholic participation in the discussions since Vatican II (1962-65) had further enhanced as well as complicated the whole issue. Gassmann says that the Louvain report

> combines the broad lines of a common understanding of ordination, which some Protestants may well find too 'catholic', with a steady concentration on the understanding, tasks and forms of the ministry in the modern world. Al (*sic*) exclusive claims on behalf of one particular form of ministry are relativized by the presentation of a series of findings of recent biblical and historical scholarship.[83]

The WCC Executive Committee, at its September, 1971 meeting in Sofia decided that the existing consensus statements on baptism and eucharist be "sent to all members of the WCC Central Committee, all member churches and national and regional councils for their official reactions and possible implementation."[84] It was clearly acknowledged that much more work was required on the ministry statement.

1972.

A draft entitled, "Ecumenical Agreement on Ministry," was published in June, 1972[85] in preparation for a Consultation to be held later that year in Marseille. As indicated in a personal interview of M. Thurian by the present writer[86] the draft was written by M. Thurian as a Staff member of the FO Secretariat. It was sent as "Document V" to members of the Working Committee in advance of their meeting in Utrecht, August 3-8, 1972. At the Utrecht meeting the discussion about future work on the matter of the ordained ministry included some of the following concerns: (1) insuring adequate participation by Roman Catholic and Orthodox theologians as

---

[82]FO Paper No. 59, pp. 223-224. The document itself will be considered in greater detail below when a textual tracing is made of the various drafts leading to the "Lima Document."

[83]FO/73:33, September 1973, p. 9.

[84]FO/72:18, October 1972, p. 3.

[85]FO/72:6.

[86]Thurian interview, April 15, 1985 (April 29 - 30, 1985).

well as by representatives of black theology and by conservative evangelicals; (2) addressing the question, "Was the ordained ministry primarily or exclusively for the church as a gathered community or had it also an obligation to be concerned with 'mission'?";[87] (3) giving adequate attention to the 'separated' ministry's indispensable relationship to ministry in the wider sense. After the discussion "it was agreed — that general approval be given to the proposals outlined for the continuing work on the study on Ecumenical Agreement on Ministry."[88]

The FO Consultation on the Ministry took place in Marseille, September 25-30, 1972. The report of that Consultation is entitled, "The Ordained Ministry in Ecumenical Perspective," and is a FO Mimeograph Paper, "FO/72:18, October 1972." In an interview with M. Thurian[89] the present writer asked why Thurian's preliminary proposal, mentioned above,[90] was not considered sufficient for acceptance by the Consultation at Marseille. His response indicated that his proposal was considered too closely linked to the FO tradition and therefore not sufficiently open to the new problems and issues confronting the churches in the social ferment of the late 1960's and early 1970's. The spirit of the times included a tendency to place more emphasis on *praxis* than on *theoria*. He further indicated that there was a strong conviction *au courant* that the churches could be united more readily in terms of social action than of doctrine.

G. Gassmann's assessment of the report was that it "produced a stricter and more systematic presentation and development of the material contained in the Louvain report. It takes up the results of the bilateral conversations."[91] He had noted the concurrent influence of those conversations. In highlighting the conversations which involved Roman Catholics he said the following:

> Whenever the Roman Catholic Church took part in these talks the problem of differing views concerning the ministry and its structures was dealt with - in many cases more intensively and more purposefully than had been possible in multilateral discussions.[92]

---

[87]FO Paper No. 65, p. 24.

[88]Ibid., p. 25.

[89]Thurian interview. April 15, 1985 (April 29 - 30, 1985).

FO/72:6. Thurian indicated that his own proposals were similar to those of the Orthodox theologian and Associate Director of the FO Secretariat, V. Borovoy.

[91]FO/73:33, p.11. The report of the Marseille Consultation is one of the documents which this present writer intends to consider more carefully in the tracing of the Lima text below.

[92]Ibid., p. 10.

In December, 1972 (or possibly January, 1973) letters were sent along with a copy of the Marseille report to members of the FO Commission, participants in the Marseille Consultation and other "colleagues" suggested to the FO Secretariat as persons "interested in the subject of the ordained ministry, and qualified to help us in our study of this subject."[93] They were asked by the Secretariat to make a response to the report by the end of August, 1973.

1973.

In September, 1973, at Salamanca, Spain, a Consultation was held which brought to a climax a FO study to devise an "ecumenical strategy" to coordinate the burgeoning efforts, official and unofficial, in the ecumenical movement at all levels of the Church's life. A carefully formulated statement emerged from the Consultation. Its description of "conciliar fellowship," was important:

> Jesus Christ founded one Church. Today we live in diverse churches divided from one another. Yet our vision of the future is that we shall once again live as brothers and sisters in one undivided Church. How can this goal be described? We offer the following description to the churches for their consideration: The one Church is to be envisioned as a conciliar fellowship of local churches which are themselves truly united. In this conciliar fellowship, each local church possesses, in communion with the others, the fullness of catholicity, witnesses to the same apostolic faith, and, therefore, recognizes the others as belonging to the same church of Christ and guided by the same spirit. As the New Delhi Assembly pointed out, they are bound together because they have received the same baptism and share in the same eucharist; *they recognize each other's members and ministries* (emphasis added). They are one in their common commitment to confess the Gospel of Christ by proclamation and service to the world. To this end, each church aims at maintaining sustained and sustaining relationships with her sister churches, expressed in conciliar gatherings whenever required for the fulfillment of their common calling.[94]

Conciliar fellowship provides a context and focus for ecumenical efforts which will impact on the Ministry study.

A small group met at Le Cénacle, in Geneva, October 22-27, 1973, to further refine the text from the Marseille Consultation of 1972. The 1972 text had been

---

[93]WCC Archive Files: (1) "Mimeographed documents in chronological order, 1970-72;" (2) "Faith and Order, Master File: 72:1-23, Mimeographed Papers, 1972."

[94] *Uppsala to Nairobi, 1968-75: Report of the Central Committee to the Fifth Assembly of the World Council of Churches*, ed. by David Enderton Johnson, New York: Friendship Press, 1975, p. 79.

"shared with a great number of groups and individual theologians for reaction and comment. In the light of the replies received, the text was revised at a second consultation held in Geneva in late 1973."[95] This "second consultation" is the October meeting at Le Cénacle. The product of this meeting was a Mimeograph Paper, "FO/73:40, November 1973." It retained the same title as the Marseille text, "The Ordained Ministry in Ecumenical Perspective."

1974.

A slightly revised text of the October, 1973 Le Cénacle meeting appeared as a FO Mimeograph Paper, "FO/73:40 (R), January 1974." This text was submitted to the FO Commission at its meeting in Accra, Ghana, July 23-August 4, 1974. During the discussion at Accra some felt that there was not enough emphasis on the ordination of women in the text. Others, on the other hand, "wondered whether it would be preferable to have in this document a briefer reference to the question of the ordination of women and to discuss the whole question in depth in another study."[96]

Among the other issues raised in discussion and later taken into account by a small committee for making revisions was that of the implication of the recognition of another church as genuine, namely, the genuineness of its ministry as well. A more "charismatic" approach to the gathered People of God was urged in order to diminish an emphasis on juridical realities that tend to dominate ecumenical dialogue on the topic of ecclesiology. A clarification was requested about the use of the term "special ministry" in place of "ordained ministry." Some asked questions about the references, in the document, to authority and to criteria for the legitimation of ministry. There was an insistence by some that all ministries be seen as charismatic. Others expressed the view that all ministries are not of equal value.

Reflecting on the Accra text on "a mutually recognized ministry" M. Thurian expressed to this present writer[97] the view that the Lutheran-Reformed approach to

---

[95]FO Paper No. 73, p. 60.

[96]Thurian indicated that his own proposals were similar to those of the Orthodox theologian and Associate Director of the FO Secretariat, V. Borovoy. This is confusing in the light of Orthodox objections.

[97]Thurian interview, April 15, 1985 (April 29 - 30, 1985).

ministry was more prominent than the "Catholic" approach. This prominence is evident in there being less emphasis on the three-fold ministry of the episcopate, the presbyterate and the diaconate than would prevail later at Lima.[98]

The final outcome of the Accra meeting included the following formal action:

That the draft documents on the agreements on Baptism, Eucharist and the Ordained Ministry in Ecumenical Perspective be revised in the light of the discussion and be referred to the Working Committee with a request that appropriate provision be made for final editorial revision and distribution.[99]

At this point the study of the ordained ministry came to be published for the first time along with and even under the same cover as the studies on baptism and the eucharist.[100] For "at its meeting in Berlin, the Central Committee of the World Council of Churches decided that all three texts should be published and communicated to the member churches."[101] The Preface of the booklet containing the three statements explains emphatically that "if the divided churches are to achieve the visible unity they seek in the ecumenical movement, one of the most important prerequisites is undoubtedly that they should agree about baptism, eucharist and ministry."[102]

After noting the broad spectrum of participation over many years in the study of these topics the FO Commission suggested the existence of an unnecessary gap between theological agreement and ecclesial life. The question was asked, "May it not be that the measure of agreement is greater than the churches are really ready to admit?[103] The main purpose of the three-in-one report is to "make it possible for the churches to achieve mutual recognition."[104]

The reader of the three statements is cautioned not to expect a complete theological synthesis, nor completely modern terminology. And there is a disclaimer about the documents having "the last word." A significant word, however, has been spoken and

for a time, the Commission will not do any further work on these themes. In its opinion, it is now up to the churches themselves to comment on its findings.

---

[98]Cf. paragraph 26, p. 36 of the ministry text in FO Paper No. 73.

[99]FO Paper No. 71, p. 34.

[100]FO Paper No. 73.

[101]Ibid., p. 61.

[102]Ibid., p. 5.

[103]Ibid., p. 6.

[104]Ibid.

Further discussion can only be constructive and fruitful if it has its basis in affirmations which really carry us further forward. We need discussion at a new level, and this new level can only be created by the churches themselves.[105]

1975.

The Fifth General Assembly of WCC took place in Nairobi, Kenya, November 23-December 10, 1975. The Assembly asked

that the churches study these texts and transmit their responses to the Faith and Order Commission by 31 December 1976, and that further study of these issues be taken on the basis of their replies. *In responding, the churches should not only examine whether the agreed statements reflect their present teaching and practice, but indicate the ways in which they are prepared to contribute to the common advance towards unity.* On the basis of the replies the study on baptism, the Eucharist, and the ministry should be continued and deepened.[106]

1976.

The Core Group of the FO Standing Commission met in Ariccia, Italy, April 4-10, 1976. In addition to reiterating the request for responses by the churches to the three texts by December 31, 1976 participants at this meeting asked

that an evaluative consultation on the Churches' responses be held in June, 1977, at which a paper should be prepared summarizing the theological issues requiring further study; such a paper should also include indications where positive reactions have been received that improve the three texts as well as to clarifying ways in which the texts contribute to the common advance towards unity. Special attention should be given to interpreting the reactions and reception of these agreed statements in relation to the goal of conciliar fellowship. Such a statement would have as its primary addressee the Central Committee of the World Council of Churches.[107]

1977.

By April, 1977 over ninety responses to the Accra text had been received

---

[105]Ibid., p. 7.

[106]*Breaking Barriers, Nairobi 1975: The Official Report of the Fifth Assembly of the World Council of Churches, Nairobi, 23 November-10 December, 1975*, ed. by David M. Paton, Grand Rapids: Wm. B. Eerdmans, 1976 pp. 68-69.

[107]FO/76:4, p. 15.

from the churches by the FO Secretariat.[108] The present writer interviewed M. Thurian[109] and J.M. Tillard,[110] participants in the evolution of the texts on baptism, eucharist and ministry. Both men indicated that no one response of the churches stood out as significantly altering or influencing in specific ways, the basic thrust of the theological content of the documents.

A celebration of the fiftieth anniversary of "Faith and Order" took place at Lausanne, Switzerland, May 26-June 5, 1977. At that time the FO Secretariat convened forty experts at Crêt-Bérard (near Lausanne) to evaluate the responses of the churches to the Accra text. This group produced a draft report.[111] The report first reviews the project carried forward by Accra and Nairobi regarding the agreed statements on baptism, eucharist and ministry. The report emphasizes that "conciliar fellowship" requires consensus on these three issues. Conciliar fellowship involves a common confession of the apostolic faith and a common witness to the world. It has as its aim that the churches "be able to recognize each other as living visibly in one faith and sharing one eucharistic fellowship."[112] "A new kind of reception" by the churches is indicated as essential. This reception demands a critical appropriation which is in response to the triune God's call of the divided churches to unity. The response can be given in two ways:

> one can receive the new agreement in the light of one's own tradition as a welcome enrichment of it, or one can rediscover one's own tradition in the light of the new consensus as a deeper and more adequate approach to what one's own heritage had been intending all along. In either case, it is by receiving afresh our own tradition while at the same time transcending its limitations that we are able to recognize the common faith of the whole Church in the ecumenical consensus achieved.
>
> Such response is never exclusively theological or doctrinal but involves the total life of the Church and a convergence in life and action.[113]

---

[108]FO/77:3, April 1977, "Churches on the Way to Consensus: A Survey of the Replies to the Agreed Statements, 'One Baptism, One Eucharist and a Mutually Recognized Ministry.'" In addition it should be noted that a later communique indicated more precisely who was responsible for this "survey": "Dr Bert Hoedemaker . . . had produced a detailed survey of all the replies received." (cf. FO Paper No. 83, p. 7.)

[109]Thurian interview, April 15, 1985 (April 29-30, 1985).

[110]Personal interviews of J.M. Tillard by Conrad T. Gromada at The Dominican House of Studies, Ottawa, Canada, March 26-28, 1985.

[111]*Towards an Ecumenical Consensus on Baptism, the Eucharist and the Ministry: A Response to the Churches*, FO Paper No. 84, Geneva: WCC, 1977.

[112]Ibid., p. 3.

[113]Ibid., p. 5.

The report calls for further responses from the churches in order to revise the statements in preparation for the Sixth Assembly of WCC (at Vancouver in 1983).

A second major section of this Crêt-Bérard Report outlines the present stage of the process in regard to each of the three topics. Under ministry there are listed four sub-headings that form a response to the churches' responses: (1) matters which already exhibit a common mind having been reached; (2) matters about which there is increasing agreement; (3) matters requiring further reflection and work as well as further guidance from the churches; (4) a treatment of the importance of context in any discussion on ministry. "Context" here has specific meanings. It can indicate the varying degrees of openness to consensus on the part of the churches. It can indicate the *de facto* mutual recognition of ministries among the churches. Or, finally, it can indicate the varying speeds at which the forms of mutual recognition will inevitably take place, depending on the particular churches involved.

The third and final section of the Crêt-Bérard report lists suggestions and recommendations for widening and deepening the agreement on baptism, eucharist and ministry. It calls for a commitment consisting of several concrete steps to be taken: (1) by member churches, (2) by ecumenical and confessional bodies, and (3) by the Faith and Order Commission itself. An Appendix is added to the report which acknowledges that "the issue of the ordination of women is clearly in need of further investigation and open discussion."[114] It is clear at this juncture that the issue of the ordination of women will not be treated comprehensively in the ministry statement under review. It was viewed as better placed in the WCC study on "The Community of Men and Women in the Church." The Appendix briefly summarizes, however, the replies of the churches on this issue, some new elements in recent ecumenical discussions and some specific questions which need to be addressed as the ordination of women is discussed.

The Standing Commission of the FO Commission met at Loccum (FRG), July 18-25, 1977. The Director of the FO Secretariat summed up the task of this meeting in regard to its handling of the Crêt-Bérard report:

> The intention of the report was to present 'a reply to the replies' from the the (*sic*) churches. It was addressed to the Central Committee in the hope that the Committee would adopt and send it to the member churches. It was necessary, therefore, for the Standing Commission to examine the report with this in mind and consider whether in its present form it was the right document to address to the

---

[114]Ibid., p. 17.

churches. It was proposed that a revision of the Statements should be prepared for the next Assembly of the World Council. This proposal had far-reaching consequences for the Faith and Order Commission since it laid on it new responsibility for action and initiative and forced on it a new style of working. Future work was to be done in more direct and close collaboration with the churches themselves. The report should go to the churches as a first communication, acknowledging the responses received and suggesting ways of continuing the exercise. The group in Crêt-Bérard had strongly pressed that in addition individual replies should be sent taking up the arguments made in the responses, countering some of the criticisms, and inviting a new input.[115]

After discussion some amendments to the text of the report were suggested, along with a request for a statement on the meaning of consensus as well as a proposed text of a cover letter to the churches, all for submission to the Central Committee of FO for approval. These suggestions were eventually agreed to and a tentative time-table was adopted for proceeding toward the Plenary Session of FO (then slated for 1981 and later changed to 1982 in Lima) and toward the next Assembly of WCC. The formation of a "support group" to the FO Secretariat was urged in order to give direct and adequate responses to the churches which had responded to the Accra text in the first place. This support group would also be charged with preparing a report on the issue for the FO Commission meeting in Bangalore in 1978. "This support group could consist of Bert Hoedemaker, Max Thurian, Nils Ehrenstrom plus, say, tow (*sic*) others, who might well be drawn from the Roman Catholic and Orthodox traditions."[116]

The Central Committee of WCC, meeting at Geneva, August 1977, "agreed that the Faith and Order Commission be authorized to send the report of the Standing Commission together with the text of the presentation by the director of the Faith and Order Secretariat to the member churches and pursue the study as proposed."[117] The director of the FO Commission and Secretariat, L. Vischer, made the proposal to the Central Committee of WCC precisely as follows:

> The three agreed statements should not be revised immediately. The Commission proposes, rather, that a revised text should be prepared for the next Assembly. The new text should aim at leading the churches a step forward on the road to real and full consensus. To achieve this, the revision must be undertaken in close consultation with the churches themselves. The "reply" to the "replies" which has been prepared and is to be sent to the churches - both to those which responded and

---

[115]*Minutes of the Meeting of the Standing Commission, held at Kloster Loccum, Federal Republic of Germany, July 18-25, 1977*, FO Paper No. 83, Geneva: WCC, p. 19.

[116]Ibid., p. 21.

[117]Ibid., p. 37.

> to those which did not - includes therefore a number of precise questions. The churches are asked to indicate to the Faith and Order Commission the direction they think the revision of the agreed statements should take.[118]

Vischer went on in his report to the WCC Central Committee to indicate that these consensus statements were intended not only for the expression of one faith but also for the achievement of one eucharistic fellowship. This fellowship is held together by a consensus which avoids a radical relativism and "leaves plenty of room for diversity of expressions."[119]

Vischer's report acknowledges the complexity of consensus-building and sees WCC as occupying a unique position of bridging the gaps between various levels of faith and life in the churches shaped both by their confessional stances and their sociological contexts. He is critical of the responses made by the churches to the Accra text because they often restrict themselves to confessional critiques and avoid concrete challenges to change their own practices. He asks the question, "Who speaks for the Church? Or more pointedly, what can the churches do to ensure that one day they will be in a position to speak together?"[120] And he is not hesitant to be critical of the texts themselves: "The three texts, especially the one on the ministry, had still too much the character of theological essays. Nor did they specify clearly enough the decisions the churches were being invited to make. They seemed to call rather for an expression of theological opinion."[121] Finally, he is intent on making it clear that "consensus is not merely a matter of producing and refining a document. Consensus has its basis and its roots in the fellowship. Consensus is the expression of an existing agreement. . . .The really important task is to strengthen the existing fellowship."[122]

Subsequently, toward the end of 1977 "the reply to the replies," the report of the FO Commission in response to the responses of the churches to the Accra text, was sent to them in order that "in close consultation with the churches, a revised version (of the Accra statements) be prepared before the Sixth Assembly of the World Council of Churches (in 1983)."[123] Some specificity of response was

---

[118]FO Paper No. 84, pp. 21-22.

[119]Ibid., p. 25.

[120]Ibid., p. 27.

[121]Ibid.

[122]Ibid., pp. 27-28.

[123]Ibid., p. 29.

requested in the cover letter. Further replies were requested by December 31, 1978.

1978.

The "support group" to the FO Secretariat, formed in 1977, made lengthy written replies to the churches which had sent official reactions to the Accra text. This same group met twice in early 1978 to prepare a discussion paper[124] for the FO Commission meeting in Bangalore, India, August 15-30, 1978. The paper attempted to answer each of the following four questions:

    i)   What are the purposes of these revised statements?
    ii)   What form should the revised statements take?
    iii) What is the relation between the emerging consensus on these matters
         and the liturgical forms of the churches?
    iv) By what procedure can the revision take place?[125]

At Bangalore, a committee dealt with the proposals of the discussion paper under the same four headings. Under the first heading, the purposes, a commitment was made to the process which had been continued at Accra. The statements were placed clearly in their broader context:

> The statements should be seen as aids to growing together into unity although they will not always be used as a basis for union. They presuppose, in any case, a sufficient agreement on basic Christian doctrine. They are not credal statements. So they do not of *themselves* necessarily express in a focal way all that is required for communion in one faith, but they could, if accepted by relating churches, lead to mutual acceptance of members and ministries and so to eucharistic sharing. Every effort, therefore, must continue to be made to ensure maximum participation in the process and adequate reception by the churches at all levels, for within each church there is a living and lively diversity which needs to be incorporated into the process.[126]

Under the second heading what emerged was a clear indication of that form which the Lima text would eventually take. This was especially true of the preliminary discussion paper's suggestion "that it would probably be valuable to make a distinction between fundamental affirmations for common teaching and a commentary which could perform several functions."[127] As regards the statement on ministry itself a clear direction for the future form of the text was indicated:

---

    [124]*Sharing in One Hope: Commission on Faith and Order, Bangalore 1978*, FO Paper No. 92, Geneva: WCC, 1978, pp. 247-251.

    [125]Ibid., p. 248.

    [126]Ibid., p. 252.

    [127]Ibid., p. 249.

> The Accra statement on *ministry* is of rather a different character to those on baptism and eucharist. It is more in the style of a commentary. Hence it would be important to formulate a statement on ministry of the same dimensions and kind as those on baptism and eucharist. A commentary would bring out the ecumenical importance of the degree of agreement thereby reached. The commentary could also discuss the practical and sociological questions concerning the varied styles and exercise of ordained ministry. The question of the ordination of women arises, and it would be helpful if the Commission would indicate ways in which this question should be included in the revised statements. Throughout, ordination and the ministry of the ordained would need to be set in the context of the total ministry of the whole Church.[128]

The Bangalore meeting accepted the suggestion about providing a commentary apart from the basic affirmations. It added, however, that such a commentary be much briefer than earlier envisioned. At Bangalore the hope was expressed "that the statement on ministry in the revised text will be of the same length as those on baptism and eucharist."[129] A workbook was also suggested in order to amplify explanations, cite examples of churches reaching consensus and provide helpful liturgical material. The need was expressed for an adequate introduction or preface to the statements which would include an explanation of "the process as *convergence towards consensus.*"[130]

As regards the content of the revised text the Bangalore meeting made many specific suggestions without attempting to take on the task of doing the actual revision. The suggestions which made reference to the topic of ministry included a need to give further consideration to: (1) the question of *episcopé* especially as it touched on the discussion between episcopal and non-episcopal churches; (2) the functions of ministry as discussed in the Accra text, p. 36; (3) the relationship between structures (orders) of ministry and practical functions (the exercise) of ministry; (4) the ordination of women. Regarding this fourth topic there was no clear resolution of how it should be handled in the context of the revised texts. There was agreement "that there should be a working group to consider the subject of the ordination of women in collaboration with those engaged in the study on The Community of Women and Men in the Church."[131]

The third heading of this Bangalore committee meeting treated the topic of

---

[128]Ibid.

[129]Ibid., p. 253.

[130]Ibid., p. 252.

[131]Ibid., p. 255.

relevant liturgical material. The workbook proposed in the preliminary discussion paper was seen as an appropriate location for such material. The suggestion for a compilation of an anthology of worship texts was also accepted. In addition there was urged the inclusion of examples of services of mutual recognition.

Under the fourth heading of the Bangalore discussion of the texts, "The Procedure for Revision," the group agreed to the timetable aimed at the FO Commission meeting (then planned for the summer of 1981) and the Sixth Assembly of WCC in 1983. As was suggested, working groups on the episcopacy and the ordination of women were to be formed. And the group strongly urged the maintaining of contacts with those churches involved in bilateral conversations.

A small Steering Group was formed to carry forward the work of the revision of the texts. It met in Geneva, November 25-27, 1978. L. Vischer, the director of the FO Secretariat, would later summarize the initial work of this group in the following manner:

> At its first meeting in November 1978, it discussed the way in which the revision could be achieved; it agreed on a number of proposals and decided to submit them for approval by the Standing Commission. . . . The Steering Group discussed in particular the question whether the revised version should be enlarged; it came to propose that the preface should be more substantial and include thorough reflection on the meaning of consensus; that sections should be added on the one apostolic faith and on the meaning of sacraments and that the text should be concluded by a section dealing with the issue of authority and reception.[132]

Continued consultation with the churches was planned as an important part of the continuing process of revision. Some specific questions were formulated to aid in the consultation. There was a recognition of the need for fresh research in the areas of baptism and confirmation, episcopate and episcopacy, and the ordination of women. It was urged that a study commission (to be appointed) should meet twice, once in 1979 and a second time in 1980, to deal with episcopate and episcopacy. The issue of the ordination of women should "be studied in the framework of the study on the Community of Women and Men in the Church; consultation to be convened in summer 1979."[133]

Special efforts were to be undertaken including the following: (1) a Consultation with Eastern Orthodox theologians; (2) a discussion at the next Forum on Bilateral Conversations, set for June 5-9, 1979; (3) the involvement of Roman

---

[132]*Minutes of the Meeting of the Standing Commission held at Taizé, France, August 20-24, 1979*, FO Paper No. 98, Geneva: WCC, 1980, p. 21.

[133]FO/79: 19, August 1979, p. 9.

Catholic participation (to be discussed with the Vatican's Secretariat for Promoting Christian Unity); (4) the seeking of an evaluation of the agreed statements by a group of women theologians. Several publications were envisioned in conjunction with the revised statements. One of these publications was a volume giving the theological background of the statements. Another was a handbook containing the agreed statements and all agreements reached in bilateral conversations. There were several other supporting booklets envisioned as well, e.g., those which provide relevant liturgical resources, or, e.g., catechetical aids. Finally, an updated timetable was made.[134] It included not only the "revision meetings" but also the various related consultations and meetings (to be held until 1983) which would serve to enhance the revision process.

1979.

In a paper prepared for the Consultation on Believers' Baptism held in Louisville, Kentucky, March 28-April 1, 1979, L.A. Hoedemaker of the Netherlands, reflected that "the consensus debate on baptism, eucharist and ministry has its firm place in the over-arching desire to realize visible communion, full mutual recognition, eucharistic fellowship and a conciliar life among churches and Christians."[135]

The Steering Group which had met, November 25-27, 1978, held its second meeting in Geneva, May 17-20, 1979.[136] At its first meeting the Steering Group had described its intentions for the second meeting in this way: "In preparation for this meeting a first proposal for the revision will be worked out. The Group will then work on the details and prepare a draft for consideration by the Standing

---

[134]Ibid., pp. 11-12.

[135]FO/79:1, February 1979, p. 3; also in *Louisville Consultation on Baptism, FO Paper No. 97, a reprint of Review and Expositor: A Baptist Theological Journal*, Vol. LXXVII, No. 1 (Winter, 1980), p. 9.

[136]"After the Bangalore meeting a small Steering Group for the revision of the texts was formed. In addition to the staff it comprised Protopresbyter Vitaly Borovoy, Metropolitan Emilianos, Dr L.A. Hoedemaker, Frère Max Thurian, Fr Richard Stewart and Dr Geoffrey Wainwright. It held two meetings, the first in November 1978 and the second in May 1979. A few consultants were invited to join the group at the second meeting." [From "Doc. 1" of the 1979 Taizé material in the WCC Archives Box, "Nairobi Follow-up (1976), Section II; Bangalore Follow-up 1978 (Aug. '79). Correspondence; Faith and Order, Standing Commission, Taizé, August 1979, Correspondence/documents."]

Commission."[137] L. Vischer summarized what actually happened:

> At its second meeting in May 1979, the Steering Group concentrated on the task of revising the two texts on baptism and the eucharist. First drafts were now ready and had been sent in advance to members of the Standing Commission. Work on the statement on the ministry was not yet as far advanced.[138]

A text on ministry, however, did emerge from this meeting[139] at which G. Wainwright indicated to this present writer[140] that an important turning point took place in regard to the text.[141]

The FO Secretariat invited all Eastern Orthodox churches to appoint delegates to a Consultation of Orthodox Theologians on the Revision of the Accra Text. The Consultation took place at Chambésy (near Geneva), May 31-June 2, 1979. In discussing the text on the ministry

> the discussion centered first on the relationship between the terms "ministry" and "priesthood". It was pointed out that the agreed texts, in speaking of ordained ministry, did not have in mind another reality than what the Orthodox called priesthood. The consultation was of the opinion that the terms used in the agreed statements were open to misunderstandings and should be clarified; possibly, a new section "vocabulary" could be included. The outline proposed by the steering group was felt to be workable . . ., but a number of important points were raised:
>
> a) The new text should take its starting point from the theme "Christ, the ministry and the community". The ministry/priesthood has been established together with the Church. No ministry without the community; no community without the ministry. Strong emphasis should be placed on the interaction between the two.
>
> b) Episcopacy should be dealt with extensively.
>
> c) Though it was recognized that the issue of primacy among the churches was an important problem and needs to be taken up in ecumenical discussion, doubts were expressed whether it should be included in a text on the ministry. Perhaps the text could state that primacy is an issue arising from the relationship between the local churches and, therefore strictly speaking, goes beyond the theme of priesthood.

---

[137]FO/79:19, August 1979, p. 11.

[138]FO Paper No. 98, p. 21.

[139]FO/79:18, July 1979.

[140]Personal interview of Geoffrey Wainwright by Conrad T. Gromada at Duke University, Durham, North Carolina, July 19, 1985.

[141]It was not made clear what Wainwright meant by "important turning point." Our analysis of the text (below), however, indicates several important developments which were introduced in it: 1) an explicit trinitarian focus; 2) an emphasis on pneumatology; 3) sacrificial language in reference to Christ; 4) a definition of significant terms; 4) a nuancing of the precise functioning of eucharistic presiding and its relationship to *episkopé* in the historical development of the Church; 5) the distinction between the apostolic succession of the whole Church and the fullness of the sign of this succession, viz., episcopal succession.

d) The ordination of women should not be included in the consensus affirmations. There can be a common affirmation that women should be given a more prominent place in the wide range of ministries in the Church, but the present debate on the ordination should be referred to only in the commentary.[142]

A few days after the Orthodox Consultation there began the Second Forum on Bilateral Conversations. It was held in Geneva, June 5-9, 1979. It took up four main topics and thus produced a four-fold report on: (1) the meaning of consensus; (2) authority in the church; (3) the eucharist in the Joint Statements; (4) ministry in the Joint Statements. The first topic, the meaning of consensus, has a direct bearing on the nature of the agreed statements. The report makes the point that "consensus is not to be identified with complete unanimity and uniformity of theological understanding."[143] Urging a deep trust between dialogue partners the report goes on to say:

> There is a legitimate necessity for unity in fundamental faith; there is also an equally necessary freedom in the diversity of its spiritual, liturgical and theological expression. Rather than the demand for cumulative precision, there should be a basic trust in the dialogue partner's *intentio fidei.*[144]

The second topic of the Forum's report was "Authority in the Church." In summarizing the work of the dialogues it was remarked that much of the results had been produced by churches possessing an episcopacy. For the future the report pointed out that

> it is a matter of urgency to engage the active participation in this dialogue of the Lutheran, Reformed and Free churches. It would be both undesirable and unproductive if further debate on the matter were to be confined to authority as it is exercised in churches which have bishops.[145]

The third topic, "The Eucharist in the Joint Statements," touched only sketchily on the relationship between ministry and eucharist.

The *fourth topic* was "Ministry in the Joint Statements." *It was treated under five headings.* Under the *first heading,* "The Ministry of Christ and the Ordained Ministry," the following is reported regarding the special or ordained ministry:

> All churches agree that this ministry has its commission and authorization from Christ. Beyond this, and to characterize it more closely, a variety of terms is used:

---

[142]FO Paper No. 98, pp. 82-83.

[143]*The Three Reports of the Forum on Bilateral Conversations,* FO Paper No. 107, Geneva: WCC, 1981, p. 18.

[144]Ibid.

[145]Ibid., p. 24.

sharing, representing, participating, reflecting, analogy, and continued presence. Further consideration should be given to whether something common lies behind such different terminology.

The reluctance of some churches to accept the concept of *priesthood* as appropriate for Christ's commissioned people of ministry indicates an issue needing further consideration.[146]

Under the *second heading*, "The Order of Ministry," the divisive nature of the presence or absence of the threefold order in the constitution of each church is stated. Under the *third heading*, "Apostolicity, Succession and Continuity," the following is reported:

Churches accustomed to identifying these characteristics in one element, e.g. the episcopate, have come now to realize that continuity is more widely based. Churches traditionally antipathetic to continuity increasingly regard this element as important. With special reference to ordination, churches increasingly advance the claim that the ordination they exercise is ordination into the ministry of the catholic Church and not only to a denominational ministry.[147]

The *fourth heading*, "Episcopal and Non-Episcopal Churches," states that "Non-episcopal churches do not regard themselves in merely negative terms, as *not* having episcopacy. They believe themselves rather as making a positive contribution to the understanding of what a Christian Church is."[148] And under the last heading, "Papacy and Collegiality," there is the acknowledgement that "Confessions which until recently were unable to talk about the papacy with any kind of objectivity now take it into discussion. Collegiality is a concept that contributes to this further discussion."[149]

The next Consultation sponsored by the FO Secretariat took place in Geneva, August 12-16, 1979. In reference to this Consultation it was later noted that "a special effort was made to make possible the rethinking of the section on ministry. A meeting on episcope and episcopate brought the awaited breakthrough (Geneva, August 1979)."[150] In preparation for the meeting which was officially entitled, "*episcopé* and *episcopos* in the ecumenical debate,"[151] Professor J.K.S. Reid of Great

---

[146]Ibid., p. 34.

[147]Ibid.; pp. 34-35.

[148]Ibid., p. 35.

[149]Ibid.

[150]*Mid-Stream: An Ecumenical Journal*, Volume XXIII, No. 3 (July, 1984), p. 225.

[151]The report is contained in *Episkopé and episcopate in Ecumenical Perspective*, FO Paper No. 102, Geneva: WCC, 1980.

Britain undertook the task of summarizing the theological debate up to that date, particularly noting the findings of bilateral conversations.[152]

> At the meeting itself, Professor R.E. Brown (USA) read a paper on the New Testament evidence on *episkopé* and *episkopos* and Professor J.D. Zizioulas (Great Britain) on the situation in the early Church. Finally the consultation turned its attention to the actual practice in the churches.[153]

The survey of NT evidence by Raymond E. Brown, a Roman Catholic, gave great encouragement to the group charged with the revision of the ministry statement, according to M. Thurian in one of his interviews with the present writer.[154]

The Memorandum issued as the fruit of this Consultation of August, 1979[155] posed seven questions to which it gave extended answers. The questions were as follows: (1) What is the relation of the episcopal ministry to the Church founded by Christ? (2) What is the relation of apostles to bishops and in what sense are bishops in apostolic succession? (3) How is *episkopé* to be exercised in the Church? (4) What is the relationship between bishops in the local church and bishops exercising *episkopé* over several local churches? (5) What are the functions of the bishop in exercising *episkopé* over several churches? (6) How can the past help us to shape the kind of *episkopé* we need today? (7) How can mutual recognition among the churches be achieved?

> In answer to the final question the participants in the Consultation stated:

> In some form, *episkopé* is being exercised in all churches. However, it is discharged in various ways. It is important to identify in each church the way in which *episkopé* is exercised. Often, the same reality exists in two churches though different designations are used. Often, the three dimensions mentioned under Question III (personal, collegial and communal) are present and operative under unexpected names. The debate around mutual recognition must not only take into account the theories which the churches defend about themselves, but must deal equally with their actual life and practice.

> Mutual recognition requires, in each church, a movement of renewal. Each tradition needs to re-examine its understanding and practice of *episkopé* in the light of Scripture and with a view to effective witness today.[156]

Finally, acknowledging that apostolic succession through episcopal ordination is what presents the most thorny issue for mutual recognition the

---

[152]Reid's report is a FO Mimeograph Paper, FO/79:17, July 1979.

[153]FO Paper No. 102, p. v.

[154]Thurian interview, April 15, 1985 (April 29 - 30, 1985).

[155]FO Paper No. 102, pp. 1-13.

[156]Ibid., p. 12.

Memorandum made the following remarks:

> Though apostolic succession does not offer any guarantee for maintaining the truth, non-episcopal churches may gain a new dimension in their life by introducing the sign. The step raises a serious difficulty; inasmuch as by accepting episcopal ordination non-episcopal churches give the impression of disavowing the ministry of earlier generations. The difficulty can only be overcome if the episcopal churches agree that the ministry of non-episcopal churches has been blessed by the Holy Spirit and that, though perhaps in an irregular way, a kind of succession has taken place in it. Some churches, for instance, have transmitted the ordained ministry through presbyteral ordination.[157]

The Standing Commission of FO met at Taizé, France, August 19-25, 1979. One of its main tasks was to concentrate on the revision of the agreed statements on baptism, eucharist and ministry. In order to carry out its tasks the Commission divided into four groups, two of which were devoted to the agreed statements. Group II reviewed the draft texts on baptism and eucharist. Group III, whose Moderator was Ms. Jeanne Audrey Powers, concentrated on the revision of the ministry text. This group "reviewed the Faith and Order Paper 73 (the Accra text), a suggested revision by Max Thurian, and the unedited draft developed by the Consultation on episkopé and episcopate held the preceding week."[158]

In his interview with the present writer[159] M. Thurian indicated that Lukas Vischer, as a final gesture before retiring from the office of director of the FO Secretariat at the end of 1979,[160] somewhat unexpectedly called for a stronger emphasis on the three-fold ministry in the revised text. He did this even though he knew it might be ecumenically problematic. Thus, as Thurian indicated, much of his own (Thurian's) emphases proposed in 1967 and 1972 but not heeded at Accra in 1974, found their way back into the revisions of the Accra statements now in 1979.

What follows is the official report of Group III at Taizé:

> The group recognized that the agreement among the churches on the ministry is at a far different stage than that on baptism and eucharist. In order to arrive at a new, more satisfactory text, considerable work needs yet to be done. New themes will need to be considered. The group heard an oral report on the consultation

---

[157]Ibid.

[158]"Report of Group 3" (in WCC Archive Box, "Nairobi Follow-up 1976), Section II; Bangalore Follow-up 1978 Aug. '79, Correspondence; Faith and Order, Standing Commission, Taizé, August 1979, Correspondence/documents").

[159]Thurian interview, April 15, 1985 (April 29 - 30, 1985).

[160]"The Standing Commission unanimously resolved to recommend to the World Council of Churches' Executive Committee that Dr William Lazareth be appointed director of the Commission on Faith and Order in succession to Dr Lukas Vischer." (FO Paper No. 98, p. 38.)

"Episcope and the episcopate" which had been held in the week immediately before the meeting of the Standing Commission. It felt encouraged by the findings of this consultation.

a.   *Outline of new revised statement on ministry.* The group confined its task to working out a general outline for the revised statement; it reads as follows:

Preface
I.   *The Christian Community and the Ministry*
      A.   The Christian Community
      B.   The Ministry of the Whole People of God
           (diversity of ministry, charismata)
      C.   The Ordained Ministry
           - essential functions (service)
           - authority
           - priesthood
II.   *The Ordained Ministries in the Christian Community*
      A.   Historical Development (apostles and ministry in the early Church)
      B.   The Diversity of Ordained Ministries (or C.)
      C.   Episcope and Episcopate (or B.)
      D.   Apostolic Succession
      E.   Ordination (meaning, act)
III. *The Practice of Ministry Today*
      A.   Conditions of Ordination
      B.   Change and Renewal
      C.   The Partnership of Women and Men in Ministry
IV.   *Towards the Recognition and Reconciliation of Ministries*

b.   *Form and style of the statement.* Four guidelines were commended in this respect:
      i)   that "consensus" and "commentary" be distinguished in keeping with the style of the baptism and eucharist documents
      ii)   that a "vocabulary" section in the preface be a means of initially defining terms to be used in the ministry document
      iii) that inclusive language with regard to human beings be used
      iv)   that positive and inclusive - rather than negative and exclusive - formulations be so stated.

c.   *Time schedule.* The group suggests that as soon as possible the staff should prepare a fully worked out new draft for consideration by the Steering Group at its next meeting. It also feels strongly that a special consultation should be called to consider this draft and to make sure that the widest possible variety of views has been taken into account; such a consultation could perhaps be held in May/June 1980.[161]

The Standing Committee "decided on further revision of the agreed

---

[161]Ibid., pp. 33-34.

52

statements and invited the Steering Group to continue its work."[162] "It was unanimously agreed that Frère Max Thurian should be named President of the Steering Committee for the revision of the agreed statements on baptism, eucharist and ministry."[163] And finally it was decided that

> while the Steering Committee is responsible for the revision of the consensus texts, the Standing Commission would be deeply appreciative if Lukas Vischer would attempt to supply a revision of the text on ministry, along lines outlined at the Taizé meeting.[164]

In carrying out this task:

> Four guidelines were commended:
> 1) that "consensus" and "commentary" be distinguished in keeping with the style of the baptism and eucharist documents
> 2) that a "vocabulary" section in the preface be a means of initially defining terms to be used in the Ministry document
> 3) that inclusive language with regard to human beings be used in this - and the other two - consensus document
> 4) that positive and inclusive - rather than negative and exclusive - formulations be so stated[165]

This task was indeed undertaken by Vischer as indicated in a letter to him from G. Wainwright on September 24, 1979 in which he writes, "I gather that you are taking rather direct responsibility for the revision of the Ministry text."[166]

In another letter, from a Staff member of the FO Secretariat to a theologian in Tübingen, inviting her to the January, 1980 meeting of the Steering Committee guiding the process of revision, it is indicated that "our primary effort during the meeting will be to develop the ministry text. We have now only the old document and a proposed new outline."[167]

---

[162]Ans van der Bent, *Major Studies*, p. 28.

[163]FO Paper No. 98, p. 38.

[164]Ibid., p. 39.

[165]"Report of Group 3" (in WCC Archive Box, "Nairobi Follow-up 1976), Section II; Bangalore Follow-up 1978 Aug. '79, Correspondence; Faith and Order, Standing Commission, Taizé, August 1979, Correspondence/documents").

[166]WCC Archive File, "BEM Steering Group Meetings (1979/1980), Correspondence/Documents," in WCC Archive Box, "Baptism - Eucharist - Ministry, After Bangalore (1978), Detailed replies to some comments by churches (1978); Steering Group (1979/80)."

[167]Ibid., Letter from Stephen Cranford to Dr. Erika Reichle, dated 18 September 1979.

1980.

The Steering Committee for the revision of the three texts, now under the presidency of M. Thurian, met at Geneva, January 15-19, 1980. A document entitled, "Revised draft of January 16, 1980 - Ministry,"[168] was provided for the fourteen participants at the time of the meeting. This document itself was revised and is entitled, "Final revised draft of 19/1/80 - Ministry."[169]

When M. Thurian later wrote to members of the Steering Committee he said,

> Concerning ministry, we saw that work remains to be done, especially on the question of authority (exousia), the *sacerdoce,* the collaboration of women and men in the ministry (Bill has promised a text on this issue), and finally on the variety and conditions of ministry.[170]

Another letter, written on behalf of Thurian from the FO Secretariat, clarifies what took place at the January meeting in Geneva and indicates the plans which were taking shape:

> Concerning the Ministry: The new text is not yet ready as the January meeting concentrated more on Baptism and the Eucharist. In June a few people will meet to give the text on which we are working its final form. In July we then hope to send out the revised text on the Ministry to the Faith and Order Commission members.[171]

However, in a letter dated, March 27, 1980, to members of the Steering Committee, Max Thurian indicated that "Lukas Vischer . . . is the author of the revised text."[172]

Geoffrey Wainwright, in an April 1, 1980 letter to the FO Secretariat, clarifies

---

[168]WCC Archive File, "BEM, last steps, drafts from 19 - V - 1979 to 14 - XI - 1981," in Archive Box, "Faith and Order, Archives, BEM, 79-82 corr 81, Lima 82."

[169]These two documents will be among the several texts examined in the next chapter of this present study.

[170]WCC Archive File, "BEM Steering Group Meetings (1979/1980), Correspondence/Documents," in Archive Box, "Baptism - Eucharist - Ministry; After Bangalore (1978); Detailed replies to some comments by churches (1978); Steering Group (1979/80)," Letter of February 7, 1980. The person, "Bill," referred to is presumably Dr. William Lazareth, the Director of the FO Secretariat, as of January 1, 1980.

[171]WCC Archive File, "BEM, After Bangalore (1978), Correspondence/Documents," in Archive Box, "Baptism - Eucharist - Ministry; After Bangalore (1978); Detailed replies to some comments by churches (1978); Steering Group (1979/80)," Letter from Mrs. Renate Sbeghen, Administrative Assistant, to Prof. J.K.S. Reid of Edinburgh, dated February 28, 1980.

[172]WCC Archive File, "BEM Steering Group Meetings (1979/1980), Correspondence/Documents," in Archive Box, "Baptism - Eucharist - Ministry; After Bangalore (1978); Detailed replies to some comments by churches (1978); Steering Group (1979/80)."

still further the work going on between scheduled meetings:

> I am in principle willing to draft some paragraphs on "conditions for ordination" in time for the June meeting. But my notes on the Ministry text are less full than my notes on Baptism and Eucharist. I remember being occupied on drafting business, while a session on Ministry was taking place. Could I therefore ask for Max's guidance on three points? First: I take it that we need to reduce greatly the amount of material found in paragraphs 50-63 of FO/73? Second: was it (finally???) decided that this was the place to deal with the question of women's ordination? Third: did you get a draft from Bill Lazareth on his contribution to the conversation, which we all found so illuminating at the time of the January meeting? If so, I should like to see it. Finally: by when would my draft on "conditions for ordination" be required? I am at the moment rather engaged on two presentations for the USA NCC consultation on the BEM texts (May 19th-22nd).[173]

In reply to his letter, Mrs. Sbeghen, at the FO Secretariat, indicated to Wainwright that

> the answers to your questions are the following: (1) Paras. 50-63 should be reduced considerably; in the new text these paragraphs should be summed up on approx. two pages. (2) Concerning the question of women's ordination, nothing needs to be mentioned in your draft because this item will appear under "variety of ministries". (3) We did not receive a contribution from Bill Lazareth, but you could perhaps get in touch with him and consult his notes. (4) There is no need to send the text in advance; we can copy it when you arrive.[174]

Meanwhile there was being planned a Forum on Baptism, Eucharist and Ministry, sponsored by the National Council of Churches in the USA at the suggestion of the WCC. In responding to the NCC of the USA's request for the three documents for use at the forum M. Thurian underlined the current situation in the evolution of the texts: "It is clear, of course, that the documents on baptism and eucharist are near to their final stage, while the ministry text must still go through several stages yet.[175] The forum was held at Marriottsville (near Baltimore), Maryland, May 19-22, 1980.

Geoffrey Wainwright was present at the forum as a participant but also as a member of the Steering Committee in order to report back to the Committee the insights of the meeting. In his summary of the proceedings he made the following remarks which have a direct bearing on the ministry text:

> A "catholicising" (sic) tendency was rather generally detected in the changes made since the 1974 statements, especially in those on eucharist and ministry. . . .

---

[173]Ibid., Letter to Mrs. Renate Sbeghen, Administrative Assistant, WCC Faith and Order.

[174]Ibid., Letter of April 10, 1980, from Renate Sbeghen to Prof. Geoffrey Wainwright.

[175]Ibid., Letter of March 4, 1980, from M. Thurian to Sister Ann Patrick Ware.

Both the variety and limits of the Marriottsville forum were noted. Of some 60 participants, only two were Orthodox, and only one was Episcopal, while the Roman Catholic Church sent no representative at all. Only one "black (sic) Church" was represented. Yet the wide representation of "mainline" Protestantism in a pluralist country was felt to be significant. This itself should give to the deliberations of the forum the weight of a "special consultation" along the lines of others held in connection with the revision of the documents. . . .

There was broad agreement among the participants that the statement on ministry was unacceptable in its revised and anticipated form. It appeared retrogressive in comparison with the 1974 statement. It had a "clerical" air. The Presbyterian group insisted on the ministry and mission of the whole Church as the indispensable context of the ordained ministries. A Southern Baptist rejected the apparent attempt to understand the ordained ministry primarily in relation to the sacraments. Several thought that the dimensions of diakonia/diaconate needed reintroducing. Many felt that there had been a narrowing of the understanding of apostolic succession in comparison with the 1974 text, and were suspicious of the distinction made in Section III ("Succession in the Apostolic Tradition") between "Apostolic tradition in the Church" and "Apostolic succession of ministry". The loss of the social and cultural influences on ministry and the ignoring of the diverse practical forms of its exercise, both historically and in the contemporary world, were regretted. An assurance was given that the questions of women's ministries and the ordination of women would be treated in the final text.[176]

The Steering Committee held its next meeting, June 3-7, 1980, in Geneva. Max Thurian indicated beforehand:

The main focus of the meeting will be the ministry document. Since last year's Standing Commission (meeting of August 19-25, 1979, at Taizé), we have had the task of drawing up a revised text on the ministry. A first draft was elaborated at our meeting in January. Now, after a certain lapse of time, the June meeting should criticize, comment and finally improve the draft.[177]

Lewis S. Mudge had been a participant at the forum in Marriottsville (near Baltimore) in May. As a consequence he was formally sent to the Steering Committee meeting in Geneva in June in order to present firsthand the results of a recent COCU study on the ministry.[178] Mudge, in commenting on the Geneva meeting wrote:

My own judgment is that it was highly worthwhile. The messages from Baltimore brought about a number of important changes in the ministry document which I

---

[176]"Report: NCC USA Forum on Baptism, Eucharist and Ministry," May 19 - 22, 1980, pp. 3-4. (From the files of the Commission on Faith and Order of the National Council of Churches of Christ in the U.S.A., 475 Riverside Drive, New York, N.Y. 10027.)

[177]WCC Archive File, "BEM Steering Group Meetings (1979/1980), Correspondence/Documents," Letter of March 4, 1980, from M. Thurian to G. Moede.

[178]Cf. Chapter VII of *In Quest of a Church Unity*, Princeton, New Jersey: Consultation on Church Union (COCU), [228 Alexander Street, Princeton, N.J. 08540].

think both satisfied the Roman Catholics and Orthodox present and have a good chance of meeting at least some of the problems articulated by North American Protestants.[179]

The fruit of the June, 1980 Steering Committee meeting is FO Mimeograph Paper, "FO/80:6, July, 1980."[180] This text is the final draft of the meeting, including revisions made subsequently by L. Vischer and M. Thurian. This is clear from a letter of July 23, 1980, in which is enclosed FO/80:6. In the letter M. Thurian writes to the members of the Steering Committee and other Consultants for the Revision of the BEM texts:

> As we planned at our meeting in June, Lukas and I have completed the ministry text. Most of the changes we have made arose from repetitions and awkward English style in some places. We also thought it better to put the chapter on reconciliation to the end. I hope that the new version will find your approval. The text is now being sent to all members of the Faith and Order Commission with the request that they send their comments and reactions before October 15. At our meeting in Rome (October 29 - November 1, with arrival on October 28 and departure on November 2), we shall study the comments received with a view to preparing the presentation of the text to the Standing Commission in January 1981.[181]

Comments on the revised texts were sought from the one hundred twenty members of the FO Commission as well as from many individual theologians. Upon more careful textual analysis it will become more evident how much influence any one reaction had on the proceedings of the next meeting of the Steering Committee, held in Rome, October 29 - November 2, 1980. It was an expanded Steering Committee meeting. It included a Consultation on the Ministry which involved more than a score of theologians and exegetes. The final draft of the Consultation, "FO/80:6(R), November 1980," is one of the major texts to be analyzed in the next chapter. That analysis will attempt to detect specific influences on the evolution of the text from particular theologians and any significant comments from the members of the FO Commission, who had been invited to respond to the earlier text of July, 1980.

---

[179] WCC Archive File, "BEM Steering Group Meetings (1979/1980), Correspondence/Documents," Letter of June 12, 1980 to Dr. Keith Bridston, WCC, 475 Riverside Dr., New York, N.Y. 10027.

[180] This text of June/July, 1980, is one of those texts to be given careful scrutiny in the next chapter of this present study.

[181] Ibid., Letter of M. Thurian.

1981.

The Standing Commission of the Commission on Faith and Order met at Annecy, France, January 3-10, 1981. This meeting stood to benefit greatly from the Consultation held in Rome just two months previous. At Annecy all three drafts, on baptism, eucharist - and ministry as well, were nearing a stage of mature formulation. At this stage all three texts, along with a proposed preface, had achieved formats and contents compatible enough to appear together in one homogeneous publication.

In its report to the Standing Commission at Annecy the Steering Committee responsible for the revision of the texts made seven relatively concise but substantial reflections and/or recommendations regarding: (1) the work that needs to be done before Lima in January, 1982; (2) four questions which need to be addressed to the churches; (3) distribution of the texts beyond the churches; (4) the role of the Assembly (Vancouver, 1983) in the reception process by the churches; (5) publications which should accompany the three texts; (6) financial means required for the entire process; and (7) a timetable up to 1985 when the FO Commission would again review the process and make further recommendations.[182]

Primary attention was given at Annecy to the text on ministry since the texts on baptism and eucharist had been thoroughly dealt with in previous Standing Commission meetings. In the plenary discussion on ministry the Standing Committee highlighted for the larger gathering some likely problem areas in the text (presumably the text from the previous November). These areas were the following:

i. The question of the threefold ministry (para 18);
ii. The relationship between charism and ordained ministry (paras 7, 28 and 40c);
iii. The ecclesiological implications of ordination (part VI);
iv. The use of the word "sign" (paras 31, 49b and 34b);
v. The use of the terms "apostle" and "apostolic";
vi. The question of whether a single set of terms is needed, in a given language, to describe the threefold ministry;
vii. The use of "technical" language in the texts and the difficulty of translating technical terms in various (particularly non-western) languages and cultures.[183]

The threefold ministry, however, proved to be the area in which most of the discussion was focused. The official report of the discussion cites the following

---

[182]*Minutes of the Meeting of the Standing Commission, 1981, Annecy*, Faith and Order Paper No. 106, Geneva: WCC, 1981, pp. 6-10.

[183]Ibid., p. 11.

points being made:

i.   The text should not only stress the symbolic value of the threefold ministry as a sign of unity, but also the practical value of realizing ministry's appropriate form.

ii.   The fact that the threefold ministry has been part of the Church's tradition is not a legitimate basis for maintaining it. The real question is: to what kind of ministry is God calling us for the effective proclamation of the Gospel in our time?

iii.   More exploration is needed to support the contention (para 18) that in some churches the threefold ministry functions even if different terms are used. The form can, and should, be distinguished from the function.

iv.   Faith and Order has generally affirmed the threefold ministry on the assumption 1) that what we seek is not simply a return to historical forms but a dynamic ministry which is appropriate for the Church's current mission, and 2) that episcopacy (oversight) resides in most communions regardless of their terminology. *Episcopé* and *diakoné* are of the essence of the Church, but that does not imply the endorsement of any one pattern for their manifestation.[184]

The "Annecy draft"[185] reflects the several revisions made as a result of the general discussion. This draft is a significant one to be reckoned with in the following chapter of this present study.

The discussion of the Standing Committee at Annecy proceeded from a discussion of the text on ministry to a consideration of the process of convergence and reception by the churches. It was agreed that "Faith and Order's role is to point toward convergences. It is the responsibility of the churches to acknowledge the reality of agreement or consensus achieved through the texts."[186] A lengthy debate ensued in which the opposing views dealt with the questions to be directed to the churches, namely, the questions posed in the preface to the three texts. One view was in favor of allowing the widest possible response while the other favored a more direct and focused response calling for some degree of commitment from each church. "Agreement was reached that the preface should try to elicit the strongest decision on, and 'reception' of, the texts possible, but that a 'questionnaire' form

---

[184]Ibid.

[185]FO/81:7, March 1981.

[186]FO Paper No. 106, p. 12.

should be avoided lest Faith and Order appear to be 'examining' the churches."[187] A formulation was offered for such an effort. That formulation is substantially the same one found near the end of the final text of the Lima preface the following year.

The Standing Committee at Annecy then considered the "next steps" to be taken with the three texts before Lima in January, 1982 and after Lima to a response by the churches, called for by December 31, 1984. The Director of FO was authorized to coordinate the preparation of three publications to accompany the actual texts. "These volumes would include: 1) a collection of theological essays, 2) a lay study guide, and 3) a collection of worship materials for baptism, eucharist and ministry (ordination)."[188] It is clear that the process of the reception of these texts by the churches had become paramount and that in the process the Vancouver Assembly of 1983

> must not lead to a polarization of issues: baptism, eucharist and ministry on the one hand and, for example, the "Church of the poor" on the other. Baptism, eucharist and ministry must be presented at the Assembly for what it is: a central aspect of the Church's witness to the modern world. "Ecclesiology" and "missiology" must not be divorced.[189]

Finally, at Annecy, it was decided that at the meeting in Lima, one year hence, the treatment of the texts on baptism, eucharist and ministry should be directed by

> one small (10 person) drafting group, with the possibility that, at the discretion of the staff, a second group be formed to deal with the issue of "reception". The following points were also stressed:
>
> i.   The plenary sessions at Lima must not be a drafting group of the whole. Any possible changes suggested by the plenary discussions would be formulated and brought back to plenary by the small drafting group.
>
> ii. The Lima meeting must complete a document ready for immediate circulation to the churches.
>
> iii. The Commission will not be voting on whether to "approve" the texts but simply on whether to authorize their distribution.[190]

As had been suggested by the Steering Committee it was decided that the three texts as corrected by the Standing Committee at Annecy and as edited in minor

---

[187] Ibid.

[188] Ibid., p. 13.

[189] Ibid., p 14.

[190] Ibid., p. 70.

ways[191] by the FO Staff "will be sent to the members of the Faith and Order Commission in March, 1981. Any suggested changes of specific phrasing should be sent to the Secretariat by October 1, 1981."[192]

Many suggestions for improving the Annecy draft on ministry are available in the archives of FO at WCC in Geneva. Some of those examined should prove to have a bearing on the final editing of the text in preparation for Lima. Any significant influence will be discussed in the textual analysis of the next chapter of this present study.

The Central Committee of WCC was to meet in August, 1981, in Dresden to receive progress reports from FO and to authorize the Plenary Commission of FO to decide on the manner of sharing the texts on baptism, eucharist and ministry with the churches.[193]

In a letter to six members of the FO Commission from W. Lazareth and M. Thurian the following was indicated:

> To assist Max Thurian in his work as Study Adviser, a small group is being asked to meet in November to complete the texts on Baptism, Eucharist and Ministry for the Lima Commission meeting. We will meet in Geneva from November 11 to 13. . . . Our task in November will be to incorporate, after discussing their appropriateness, the written corrections proposed by Commission members.[194]

This meeting produced a document, "Corrections of BEM for Lima," which suggests line by line revisions for the Lima text.[195] These corrections were forwarded to the small group which had been charged at Annecy in January, 1981 with the final editing at Lima in January 1982. This document of November, 1981 will be an integral part of the textual analysis of the next chapter of this present study of the evolution of the Lima Ministry text.

---

[191]"*Révision linguistique*," penned in by M. Thurian on the November, 1980 Timetable proposal, in WCC Archive File, "BEM, last steps, drafts from 19 - V - 1979 to 14 - XI -1981," in Archive Box, "Faith and Order, Archives, BEM, 79-82 corr. 81, Lima 82."

[192]FO Paper No. 106, p. 13.

[193]This had been proposed in Rome at the Standing Commission meeting of October/November, 1980 (cf. WCC Archive File, "BEM, last steps, drafts from 19 - V - 1979 to 14 - XI - 1981).

[194]WCC Archive File, "Circular letters, 1980 and 1981," in Archive Box, "Faith and Order: Documents 1980 - 1981; Circular Letters, 1980 - 1981," Letter of April 2, 1981. Those to whom the letter was sent are as follows: V. Borovoy, E. Timiadis, J. Vereb, G. Wainwright, M. Tanner, and M. West.

[195]FO Mimeograph Paper, "FO/81:18, November 1981."

SUMMARY OF THE FOREGOING CHAPTER.

In the preceding chronological report the FO Commission which produced the ministry text of Lima was situated in the historical development of the modern ecumenical movement. It was seen how the Anglican and, to some degree, the Orthodox participation in the formation of FO, kept the topic in the forefront of ecumenical discussion.

At Lausanne in 1927 and Edinburgh, ten years later, "ministry" appeared to be an almost insurmountable barrier to intercommunion between the episcopally and non-episcopally constituted churches. In 1948 with the formation of the WCC it was affirmed that "ministry" must be dealt with in the context of a discussion of the visibility and continuity of the church established by Christ.

At Lund in 1952, the methodological shift from a comparative method to that of a search for common christological and pneumatological roots broadened the context of the discussion of "ministry." A new emphasis on eschatology and new breakthroughs in biblical study on a broad ecclesial scale contributed to this widening of the context of the discussion.

At the WCC Assembly of 1961 a definition of church unity was adopted which placed additional emphasis on the importance of the issue of a recognizable official ministry. Preparations for the Montreal Conference of FO in 1963 continued to deepen this emphasis. Montreal 1963 marked the first time since 1937 that the issue of official ministry was discussed in detail in FO. In fact, Montreal's report, "The Redemptive Work of Christ and the Ministry of His Church," provides the first text to be analyzed in this present study.

Beginning with 1963 the foregoing chapter undertook to relate a year by year reporting of the events leading to Lima in 1982. Between 1963 and 1971 Frère Max Thurian emerged as a key figure in FO's efforts to deal with "ministry." Others were Kenneth Grayston and Robert S. Paul. However, the FO meeting at Bristol in 1967 did not give serious and thorough consideration to the efforts of these theologians. After Bristol more attempts at formulating a text were made. What stands out, however, is the Cartigny Ordination Consultation of September 28-October 3, 1970. The document which resulted from this Consultation formed the basis for the text of the Louvain meeting of 1971. This latter document is the second text to be analyzed in the next chapter.

Two other texts, one from a Consultation in 1972 and the other from a small group meeting of 1973, continued the overall approach of Louvain 1971. These two texts also will be analyzed in the present study. The widely distributed and therefore well-known document of Accra 1974, *One Baptism, One Eucharist and a Mutually Recognized Ministry*, was a revision of the 1973 text mentioned above. In fact, the four texts, mentioned here, of 1971, 1972, 1973 and 1974, can be analyzed together as a distinct unit among the texts to be dealt with in tracing the way to Lima.

In 1975 the Fifth General Assembly of WCC, at Nairobi, asked the member churches to study and make formal responses to the text on ministry (as well as on baptism and eucharist) from Accra by the end of 1976. On May 26, 1977 a group of forty experts were convened to evaluate the responses of the churches. By the end of 1977 the FO sent to the churches a reply to their replies to the 1974 Accra text. The FO then asked the churches for even more specific responses by the end of 1978.

During 1978 a clear direction was taken regarding the format of the final Lima text. That format made the distinction between the main text of basic affirmations and a commentary section. A small Steering Group was formed to carry forward the revision of the texts on ministry, baptism and eucharist. A text on ministry was produced at this Steering Group's second meeting in May, 1979. The text marked an important turning point in the process leading to Lima.

The next turning point took place in August, 1979 when the Standing Commission of FO met at Taizé. It considered a suggested text on the ministry and the results of a consultation held shortly before on *episcopé* and *episcopos*. The Taizé meeting made many far-reaching decisions which influenced the Lima text. At Taizé Max Thurian was named the President of a new Steering Committee for the revision of the three texts. Lukas Vischer was asked to supply a revision of the text on ministry in keeping with the outline suggested at Taizé. Vischer's efforts, with the help of Thurian and the rest of the members of the newly-formed Steering Committee, are seen most especially in the texts of January and July, 1980.

A final phase of the process was entered at the end of October, 1980 when a Consultation on Ministry, sponsored by FO, was held in Rome. Its final draft is a revision of the July, 1980 text mentioned above. The Consultation's efforts prepared the way for the meeting of the Standing Commission of FO, held at Annecy, in January, 1981. Another text emerged at Annecy which is the immediate precursor of the Lima text of one year later.

CHAPTER II

FROM MONTREAL 1963 TO ACCRA 1974

In this chapter we begin tracing the theological evolution of the significant ministry texts of the Faith and Order Commission which, over a span of twenty years, led to the Lima text on ministry in January, 1982. This effort will be accomplished using the section and subsection headings of the Lima text. In this first of three chapters devoted to this task the texts to be studied are as follows:

1) The Section III Report of the Fourth World Conference on Faith and Order, of July 12-26, 1963 at McGill University in Montreal. The report is entitled "The Redemptive Work of Christ and the Ministry of His Church."[1] Hereafter it will be referred to as Montreal/63.

2) The fifth Study Report of the meeting of the Faith and Order Commission, of August 2-13, 1971 in Louvain. The report is entitled "The Ordained Ministry."[2] Hereafter it will be referred to as Louvain/71.

3) The text resulting from the Consultation sponsored by the Faith and Order Commission, of September 25-30, 1972, in Marseille. The report is entitled "The Ordained Ministry in Ecumenical Perspective."[3] Hereafter it will be referred to as Marseille/72.

4) The text resulting from the Consultation sponsored by the Faith and Order Commission, October 23-27, 1973, in Geneva. The report is entitled "The Ordained Ministry in Ecumenical Perspective."[4] Hereafter it will be referred to as Geneva/73.

5) The text of the FO Commission at its meeting in Accra, Ghana, July 23-August 4, 1974. The text is entitled "One Baptism, One Eucharist, and a Mutually

---

[1]FO Paper No. 42, pp. 61-69.

[2]FO Paper No. 59, pp. 78-101.

[3]FO/72:18, October 1972, 28 pp.

[4]FO/73:40, November, 1973, 25 pp.

Recognized Ministry: Three Agreed Statements."[5] Hereafter it will be referred to as Accra/74.

In this time period most of the major theological themes which are found in the Lima text of 1982 are introduced and are expressed in increasingly nuanced ways, e.g., the primary role of the whole Trinity in ministry to salvation, the distinction between the Jesus of history and the Christ of faith and the important role of the Holy Spirit (pneumatology). The precise relationship between the church and the kingdom of God is expressed in increasingly clear terms. And the ordained ministry is set in the context of the ministry of all the baptized.

There is no clear definition of terms (glossary) provided in this phase of the development of texts.

The apostolic nature of the church is underscored. The functions of ordained ministry are named and the mutual dependence between that ministry and the whole community of the church is noted.

The topic of the ordained ministry's authority is not found in the earliest texts but it is introduced and developed during this time frame. There is also at the beginning of this time period a more tentative treatment of the priesthood in relationship to the ordained ministry. By the time of the Accra meeting in 1974 the topic is being fully discussed.

One is left with the impression that the issue of women's ordination, which was not treated in the earliest text, became overly emphasized by the time of the Accra meeting. After Accra, as we will see, there is a more careful, if not too careful, treatment of this important issue.

During this initial period of texts the threefold ministry is granted *an* importance but not *the* overriding importance found in the texts of subsequent stages. Consequently there is no material provided in this early stage in regard to guiding principles for the exercise of ordained ministry, the precise functions of bishops, presbyters and deacons, and the relationship of the threefold ministry to other charisms.

The effort to contextualize the issue of the succession of apostolic ministry within that of the succession of apostolic tradition is only begun during this stage. A movement toward accepting episcopal succession as a special sign of succession is to be noted. A heavier emphasis on episcopacy, however, is found in later stages.

---

[5]FO Paper No. 73. The statement on Ministry is on pp. 29-56.

The meaning of the act of ordination becomes increasingly clarified during this stage. The adjective, "sacramental," is used in reference to ordination. The universal and pneumatological nature of ordination is noted.

The texts of this period evidence a movement from sociology to theology in their treatment of the ordained ministry. And finally, it becomes clear during this period that the goal of visible unity of the churches is the controlling principle of this study by Faith and Order.

The divisions of the Lima text (which divisions control our study) are as follows:

I.   THE CALLING OF THE WHOLE PEOPLE OF GOD

II. THE CHURCH AND THE ORDAINED MINISTRY

   - One paragraph clarifying terminology

   A. The Ordained Ministry

   B. Ordained Ministry and Authority

   C. Ordained Ministry and Priesthood

   D. The Ministry of Men and Women in the Church

III. THE FORMS OF THE ORDAINED MINISTRY

   A. Bishops, Presbyters and Deacons

   B. Guiding Principles for the Exercise of the Ordained Ministry in the Church

   C. Functions of Bishops, Presbyters and Deacons

   D. Variety of Charisms

IV. SUCCESSION IN THE APOSTOLIC TRADITION

   A. Apostolic Tradition in the Church

   B. Succession of the Apostolic Ministry

V.   ORDINATION

   A. The Meaning of Ordination

   B. The Act of Ordination

   C. The Conditions for Ordination

VI. TOWARDS THE MUTUAL RECOGNITION OF THE ORDAINED MINISTRIES

I. THE CALLING OF THE WHOLE PEOPLE OF GOD.

The texts during this time period witness the conscious effort to introduce christology and pneumatology in some detail. There is a greater and greater consciousness of the historical Jesus *vis-à-vis* the Christ of faith. Treatment of the Trinity is introduced with greater and greater nuance. The themes of forgiveness, repentance and freedom are noted as major elements of the experience of communion with the Trinity. It is carefully noted that God's purpose for all human beings is membership in the Church. The Church's (not just Christ's) relationship to the Kingdom of God is clearly introduced, especially as that impacts on how the members of the Church are to struggle alongside all the oppressed of this world toward the freedom and dignity promised with the coming of the Kingdom. Regarding ordained ministry's relationship to other gifts of the Spirit, the note is added in Accra/74 that ordained ministry cannot be carried out independently of the general ministry of all the baptized or in some superior mode.

Louvain/71 [p. 89]

The neighborhood community of Christians will continue to be an important and living expression of the Church, and traditional groupings of people and pastor in a relatively homogeneous neighborhood. But the new forms of Christian community referred to above are also assuming importance, and are in need of an ordained ministry linked with the wider Church. It is not necessary for such communities to have the possibility of gathering around the eucharist as well? Are not such communities equally valid congregations of the Church even if they may be of limited duration?

Marseille/72 [p. 6]

The Lord Jesus Christ, through his Word and Spirit, forgives sins, delivers men from the lordship of the powers of destruction; he continues to gather worshipping communities out of this broken world, the one people of God, coming from the waters of baptism; by the power of the Spirit their life is hid with Christ in God. Thus "the neighborhood community of Christians will continue to be an important and living expression of the Church, and traditional groupings of people and pastor in a relatively homogeneous neighborhood, where such exist and are authentic, will continue to be meaningful and valid" (Louvain).

Geneva/73 [p. 3]

The Lord Jesus Christ, through his Word and Spirit, forgives sins, and delivers men from the lordship of the powers of destruction; he continues to gather worshipping communities out of this broken world, the one people of God, coming from the water of baptism.

Accra/74

3. The Lord Jesus Christ, through his Word and Spirit, forgives sins and delivers men from the lordship of the powers of destruction; He continues to gathering worshipping communities out of this broken world, the one people of God, coming from the water of baptism; He builds them up through Word and Sacrament.

The final phrase (in the Accra text immediately above), "He builds them up through Word and Sacrament," is added. Thus the Christological activity in terms of his preaching and sacramental ministry is emphasized. Nothing earlier than the Marseille/72 text serves as an antecedent reference to this paragraph in Accra/74.[6]

---

[6]Cf. Lima/82 §1.

Marseille/72 [p. 7]
The Church, as the Communion of the Holy Spirit, is called to prefigure and proclaim the Kingdom of God by being built up as the Body of Christ and by announcing the Gospel to the world.

Each member of this body is called to live his faith and to witness among men through his service of love and justice, and to account for his hope, sharing alongside men the common life of job and suffering, as well as the struggle of the oppressed toward that freedom and dignity promised with the coming of the Kingdom. Thus, in every place, the Christian community witnesses to the reconciliation which it experiences, and calls all men to be reconciled with God and among themselves.

Geneva/73 [p. 5]
The Church as the communion of the Holy Spirit is called to proclaim and prefigure the Kingdom of God by announcing the Gospel to the world and by being built up as the body of Christ. Within these two commissions each member of the body is called to live his faith and account for his hope. Each stands alongside men and women in their joy and suffering, and witnesses among them, through loving service; each struggles with the oppressed toward that freedom and dignity promised with the coming of the Kingdom.

Accra/74
11. The Church as the communion of the Holy Spirit is called to proclaim and prefigure the Kingdom of God by announcing the Gospel to the world and by being built up as the body of Christ. Within these two commissions each member of the body is called to live his faith and account for his hope. Each stands along-side men and women in their joy and suffering and witnesses among them through loving service; each struggles with the oppressed towards that freedom and dignity promised with the coming of the Kingdom.

Montreal/63

92. The Holy Spirit dwells in the Church. He comes to each member in his baptism for the quickening of faith. He also bestows differing gifts (charismata) on groups and individuals. All his activities are to enable men to serve and worship God. All members of the Church are thus gifted for the common good.

... Among the differing gifts bestowed by the Spirit is the special ministry.

Louvain/71 [p. 81]

But it does not appear that all the initiatives, all the charismata, or all the gifts from God should be subsumed under the name of ministry or claim ordination. The reasons for this will appear shortly. It is only necessary that the individual charismata of the nonordained servants be in no sense regarded as inferior to those of people who are specially commissioned; in the Church there are no second class citizens. This is simply to say that there is need for *diversified* ministry and service in the Church. For example, it is not necessary that all members of a team ministry be ordained; what is vital is that the whole People of God be built up and equipped for ministry. One of the new incentives of the present time then is brought about by the renewed understanding of this general and essential priesthood of the *whole* People of God.

Marseille/72 [p. 7]

The proclamation of the Gospel, the service to the world, and the edification of the community require a variety of activities, both permanent and provisional, spontaneous and institutional. For this purpose the Holy Spirit gives to the Church diverse and complementary gifts, among which there is the ordained ministry. This ordained ministry cannot be faithfully exercised without a close relationship with the other charismata.

Geneva/73 [p. 5]

This proclamation of the Gospel, service to the world and edification of the community require a variety of activities, both permanent and provisional, spontaneous and institutional. To fulfil these needs the Holy Spirit gives diverse and com-plementary gifts to the Church. These charismata, which constitute the general ministry of the whole people of God cannot be regarded as of less value than those given to the ordained ministers. In the Church there are no second class citizens. The ordained ministry, therefore, cannot be understood or carried out in isolation from this general ministry of the whole people.

Accra/74

12. This proclamation of the Gospel, service to the world and edification of the community require a variety of activities, both permanent and provisional, spontaneous and institutional. To fulfil these needs the Holy Spirit gives diverse and complementary gifts to the Church. These gifts are given by God to individuals for the common good of his people and their service and manifest themselves in acts of service within the Christian community and to the world. They are all gifts of the same Spirit. The ordained ministry, therefore, cannot be understood or carried out in isolation from the general ministry of the whole people.

Geneva/73 [p. 3]

Membership in the community of the Church involves fellowship with God the Father through Jesus Christ, in the Holy Spirit. It means being in a relationship of mutual in-dwelling with Jesus Christ. This fellowship makes possible a unique experience of community, based as it is upon communion with God and repentance, upon mutual forgiveness and acceptance, and resulting in freedom and new life. God's purpose is that all men should be brought into this community.

Accra/74

4. Membership in the community of the Church involves fellowship with God the Father through Jesus Christ, in the Holy Spirit. It means being in a relationship of mutual in-dwelling with Jesus Christ. This fellowship makes possible a unique experience of community, based as it is upon communion with God and repentance, upon mutual forgiveness and acceptance; it results in freedom and new life. God's purpose is that all men should be brought into this community.

The above paragraph from Geneva/73, almost identical to Accra/74 §4, is first found in the text of Geneva/73. The earliest of these five texts cited immediately above (from Montreal/63) refers to the ordained ministry as "the special ministry." Subsequent texts become increasingly wary of the use of this term. Subsequent texts also make an explicit effort to state in one way or another that "in the Church there are no second-class citizens." (Louvain/71)

II. THE CHURCH AND THE ORDAINED MINISTRY.

DEFINITION OF TERMS.

No separate section for the definition of terms was introduced until the text of Geneva 5/79. We will treat that material in the next chapter.

A. THE ORDAINED MINISTRY.

In tracing the evolution of the text using this subsection of the final Lima text as our guide we note three developments: 1) the strong awareness of the necessity of the ministry today being guided by the ministry of the apostles accompanied by a need to insure the continuity of that ministry; 2) the careful specification of the essential functions of the ordained ministry; 3) the underscoring of the interdependence of the community and the ordained minister.

Louvain/7 [p. 81-82]

But having made this crucial point, it must also be recalled that certain called and set-apart individuals have had a decisive role in the building up of the Church. The New Testament does report a setting apart to special ministry, distinctions of service *were* made. Throughout the Bible the concept of God's selectivity clearly emerges. There *is* a "scandal" of particularity — God called particular people for particular tasks and set them apart to serve the fellowship in distinct ways. Israel's history, its ever-deepening awareness of having been selected by God for particular service, the selection of prophets, priests and kings by God, the Incarnation itself, witness to selectivity and election. God had commonly called and employed individuals and groups to serve him in unique fashion — the selection of apostles con-

Louvain/71 [p. 81-82 cont.] tinued this tradition, and opened the door to the conception of a called and set apart ministry. That is to say, the existence of a set apart ministry is fully consistent with God's *modus operandi* in calling, sending, and empowering individuals for special responsibilities.

Montreal/63

83. The redemptive work of Christ has its origin in the mission given by the Father to the Son, and willed by the Son with the Father in the Holy Spirit. In accordance with the purpose of god, prepared and foretold under the covenant with Israel, and by the power of the Holy Spirit, the Son became man, proclaimed the Kingdom of God with power, was crucified, died, rose again, and lives eternally as Lord. In this Person, this history and his work, God was in Christ, reconciling the world to himself. That which the Lord Jesus Christ has thus accomplished, he has accomplished once for all.

84. In order that his redemptive work might be proclaimed and attested to the ends of the earth, and that its fruits might be communicated to man, Christ chose apostles, witnesses of his resurrection, and com-

Louvain/71 [p. 82 cont.]

In choosing and sending men to act and speak on his behalf, Christ continued this personal ministry, setting a precedent for the Church. It was the preaching and teaching of the apostles, their understanding of Jesus' life and ministry, which were the basis for kerygma and didache, of the New Testament canon, and the later creeds. The witness and ministry of the apostles, unique as it was, is in a real sense normative in the Church for all time, it is foundational. Thus ministry in the Church in subsequent ages is only truly ministry insofar as it is faithful to and empowered by the apostolic message, insofar as it is congruent with the message and ministry of the apostles. The apostolic ministry continues as a bond of unity for the Church in all times and places.

[pp. 85-86]

Marseille/72 [p. 10]

This apostolicity received is first historical embodiments in the early Christian communities and in the diversity of gifts which they were given. Within these communities, the apostles, as the eyewitnesses of the risen Lord, occupied a unique and fundamental place, which could not be handed on. (For a fuller discussion on the meaning of "apostles", see the report "Apostolicity and Catholicity of the Church".) In so far as they bore special, but not exclusive responsibility for proclaiming the message of reconciliation, establishing churches, and building them up in the apostolic faith, their ministry had to be continued. Such a ministry is essential to the Church in all times and circumstances. Because of the historical nature of the Church, it is inevitably exercised in diverse ways and through varied structures, but wherever it is car-

Geneva/73 [p. 5]

In order that his redemptive work might be proclaimed and attested to the ends of the earth, and that its fruits might be communicated to man, Christ chose apostles, and committed to them the word of reconciliation. Within the first Christian communities, the apostles exercised a unique and fundamental function, which could not be handed on. However, insofar as they bore special (but not exclusive) responsibility for proclaiming the message of reconciliation, establishing churches and building them up in the apostolic faith, their ministry had to be continued. Although there was a variety of gifts in the Early Church, the New Testament reports a setting apart to special ministry, distinctions of service were made. This special ministry was essential then — it is essential in all times and circumstances. Such a ministry is exercised by persons

Accra/74

13. In order that his redemptive work might be proclaimed and attested to the ends of the earth, and that its fruits might be communicated to man, Christ chose apostles and committed to them the word of reconciliation. Within the first Christian communities the apostles exercised a unique and fundamental function, which could not be handed on. However, in so far as they bore special (but not exclusive) responsibility for proclaiming the message of reconciliation, establishing churches and building them up in the apostolic faith, their ministry had to be continued. Although there was a variety of gifts in the Early Church, the New Testament reports a setting apart to special ministry, distinctions of service were made. This special ministry was essential then — it is essential in all times and circumstances. Such a minis-

Montreal/63 [cont.]
mitted to them the word of reconciliation. Having clothed them with the Holy Spirit he sent them to gather all nations into the Church and to build it upon the one foundation which is no other than himself, and to inaugurate the ministry of the accomplished reconciliation for the salvation of all men. Thus the whole Church and its special ministry have their origin in the sending of the apostles.

85. The unique witness of the apostles to Christ is preserved by the Church in the New Testament. Their mission is continued by the Church and in its ministry.

Louvain/71 [cont.]
The Churches also agree that the basic continuity with the apostolic community is provided by the whole People of God. As the Twelve were the image of the new Israel in Christ, so their successors are to be seen in the Church as a whole. The continuity of the ministry is not a continuity independent of, but within, the People of God.

Marseille/72 [p. 10 cont.]
ried out in faithfulness to the first apostles' mission and witness, it is an apostolic ministry and stands in succession to the apostles.

Geneva/73 [p. 5 cont.]
who are called within the community and given gifts and authority to transmit the living testimony of the apostles.

Accra/74 [cont.]
try is exercised by persons who are called within the community and given gifts and authority to transmit the living testimony of the apostles.

Montreal/63

78. It is a significant fact that the work of the Laity Department led it to raise the question of the function and authority of the ordained ministry, and it is with this question that we have tried to deal, even though the title given to us, if strictly interpreted, refers to the whole work of the Church in the world. We agree with the Department on the Laity that the narrower question can only be answered in the context of the broader, and we have tried always to bear this context in mind. But we confess frankly that we have not attempted to deal with the total ministry of the church in the world. For this we refer again to the work of the Laity Department.

Montreal/63

77. Ministry and order have not been on the agenda of a World Faith and Order Conference since Edinburgh 1937. Section III at Montreal has been given the task of discussing again, after this interval, our understanding of the place of ministers of Jesus Christ in the life of the Church. During these twenty-five years there has been a notable recovery of the biblical teaching about the royal priesthood of the whole people of God. There have been times in the past when the word "layman" was understood to refer to someone who had a merely passive role in the life of the Church, and the word "ministry" referred exclusively to the full-time professional service of the Church. That time is past. A recovery of a true doctrine of the laity has brought with it the recognition that ministry is the responsibility of the whole body and not only of

Louvain/71 [pp. 78–79]

Beside the pressing existential concern there are other reasons for taking up this question again. Perhaps most promising is the fact that the ministry discussion itself is undergoing an evolution in many Churches which makes a more comprehensive and balanced study possible. All Churches are being forced to ask, "How is the whole ministry of Christ being carried out in our tradition, in our ministry to the world?" All are being challenged to look at their total ministry afresh in the light of the Gospel. As a result of such reappraisal the last two decades have witnessed a new sensitivity to the ministry of the whole People of God, and of the place of the ordained ministry within this People. As the Churches have opened themselves to the questions men are asking, as they are taking more seriously the problem of

Marseille/72 [p. 3]

This process was described by the previous consultation on this subject at Cartigny (1970) thus:

There are other reasons for taking up this question again. Perhaps most promising is the fact that the ministry discussion itself is undergoing an evolution in many Churches which makes a more comprehensive and balanced study possible. All Churches are being forced to ask, "How is the whole ministry of Christ being carried out in our tradition, in our ministry to the world?" All are being challenged to look at their total ministry afresh in the light of the Gospel. As a result of such reappraisal the last two decades have witnessed a new sensitivity to the ministry of the whole People of God, and of the place of the ordained ministry within this People. As the Churches have opened themselves to the questions

Geneva/73 [p. 3]

The ordained ministry is to be understood as part of the community. An understanding of the ministry must therefore start from the nature of the Church, the community of believers. This conviction is now shared by most of the Churches. Thus the following considerations start from the Christian community; they then try to define the nature and functions of the ordained ministry in the light of this community.

Accra/74

2. The ordained ministry is to be understood as part of the community. An understanding of the ministry must therefore start from the nature of the Church, the community of believers. This conviction is now shared by most of the Churches. Thus the following considerations start from the Christian community; they then try to define the nature and functions of the ordained ministry in the light of this community.

Montreal/63

98. The special responsibility committed to the minister in the Church is the equipment of the other members in the work of ministry that they may carry out the responsibility committed to them in baptism. This will call for a constant ministry of preaching, teaching and pastoral care. Ministers are given to the Church as the Lord's messengers, watchmen and stewards, and as such they have to give an account to him of their stewardship.

Louvain/71 [p. 84]

The ordained minister fulfils a threefold function:

— gather together, "build up", and oversee the believers, and insure that the community be present in the world; that it be answerable for the yearnings, joys and sufferings of men, and that it may grow in the holiness of the Spirit, in order that it might be the promise of unity for the whole of humanity;

— unceasingly announce and show forth by his life, the good news of the reconciliation — the foundation

Marseille/72 [pp. 8-9]

With an apostolic responsibility toward all people and a pastoral responsibility toward the faithful, "ministers are given to the church as the Lord's messengers, watchmen and stewards, and as such they have to give an account to him of their stewardship." (Montreal, para. 98)

"The ordained minister fulfils a threefold function:

— gather together, build up, and oversee the believers, and insure that the community be present in the world; that it might be answerable for the yearnings, joys and sufferings of men, and that it may grow in the holiness of the Spirit, in order that it might be the promise of unity for the whole of humanity;

— unceasingly announce and show forth, by his life, the good news of reconciliation, the foundation of

Geneva/73 [p. 6]

The essential and specific function of the ordained minister is: to assemble and build up the Christian community, by proclaiming and teaching the Word of God, and (in) presiding over the liturgical and sacramental life of the eucharistic community.

The community and the minister are dependent on one another. Their undertoependency is a reminder that the minister does not exist in isolation, nor for himself, and that he cannot deal arbitrarily with the Christian people. For Christian life and ministry are received from an Other, from Christ living in his Church, and they are made alive by the Holy Spirit, who is sent constantly to extend God's Kingdom.

Accra/74

15. *The essential and specific function of the special ministry is: to assemble and build up the Christian community, by proclaiming and teaching the Word of God, and presiding over the liturgical and sacramental life of the eucharistic community.* The Christian community and the special ministry are related to one another. The minister cannot exist and fulfil his task in isolation. He needs the support and encouragement of the community. On the other hand, the Christian community needs the special ministry which serves to coordinate and unite the different gifts in the community and to strengthen and enable the ministry of the whole People of God. But above all, this relationship and mutual dependence manifests that the Church is not master of the Word and Sacrament, nor the source of its faith, hope and unity.

Louvain/71 [p. 84 cont.]
of man's liberation by God and of the unity of believers in the faith of the apostolic Church;

— preside over baptism and the eucharist — an action of grace on the part of the community and intercession for humanity in its entirety. [Cf. *The Eucharist in Ecumenical Thought*, above p. 69.]

Marseille/72 [pp. 8-9 cont.]
man's liberation by God and of the unity of believers in the faith of the apostolic church;

— preside over baptism and the eucharist — the thanksgiving of the community and the intercession for humanity in its entirety. (Louvain).

Accra/74 [cont.]
Christian life as well as the ministry are received from the living Christ in the Church.

Marseille/72 [p. 8]

This dependence on the one Lord and Saviour is expressed by the mutual dependency of the community and the minister. Their interdependence makes it clear that the Church is not master of Word and Sacraments, nor source of its faith, hope and unity. It also makes it clear that the minister does not exist on his own, nor for himself, and that he cannot deal arbitrarily with the Christian people. For Christian life and ministry are received from an Other: from Christ living in his church, and they are being made alive by the Holy spirit, who is sent constantly to extend God's Kingdom (Cf. Dombes 1972).

Montreal/63

88. All ministry in the Church is rooted in the ministry of Christ himself, who glorifies the Father in the power of the Holy Spirit. Christ stirs up, calls, strengthens and sends those whom he has chosen for the whole ministry of his Church and for the special ministry, making them the instrument of his message and of his work. Ministers are called to serve the work of the Lord by following him, by being conformed to him, and by announcing his name.

94. The call to the special ministry depends upon the presence and the action of the Holy Spirit in the Church. He is at the same time a free Spirit choosing whom he will, and an ever-present spirit guaranteeing to the Church that God does not cease to call men into the service of the Lord and to give them necessary gifts. He leads the Church to seek out and to recognize the presence amongst her members of these gifts and this calling, and to test the gift and the calling given to men by God. The divine initiative may make use of the voice of the community or may be addressed in-

Marseille/72 [p. 8]

"All ministry in the church is rooted in the ministry of Christ himself, who glorifies the Father in the power of the Holy Spirit. Christ stirs up, calls, strengthens and sends those whom he has chosen for the whole ministry of his Church and for the special ministry, making them the instrument of his message and of his work. Ministers are called to serve the work of the Lord by following him, by being conformed to him, and by announcing his name. The ordained ministry thus reflects ard serves the redemptive love of Christ" (Montreal, para. 88).

[pp. 7-8]

Whatever the diversity of charismata or of functions in a Christian community may be, the specific service of the ordained ministry is to ensure and to point out the dependency of the Church on Jesus Christ — Christ who is the source of the mission and foundation of the unity of the Church. As a member of the Christian community, the minister is also a "messenger" in it, whom it receives from Christ. His functions signify the priority of di-

Geneva/73 [p. 5]

That is to say, Christ, through the Holy Spirit, stirs up, strengthens and sends those whom he has called for this special ministry, making them instruments of his message and work. Persons called to this ministry are commissioned to serve the work of the Lord by following him, being conformed to him, and by announcing his name. The presence of this ministry in the community signifies the priority of divine initiative and authority in the Church's existence. Thus, whatever the diversity of functions in a Christian community may be, the specific service of the ordained minister is to assemble the community and to serve it by pointing to its fundamental dependence on Jesus Christ — Christ who is the source of its mission and the foundation of its unity.

Accra/74

14. Christ, through the Holy Spirit, stirs up, strengthens and sends those whom he has called for this special ministry making them ambassadors of his message and work. Persons called to this ministry are commissioned to serve the work of the Lord by following him, being conformed to him and by announcing his name. The presence of this ministry in the community signifies the priority of divine initiative and authority in the Church's existence. Thus, whatever the diversity of functions in a Christian community may be, the specific service of the ordained minister is to assemble the community and to serve it by pointing to its fundamental dependency on Jesus Christ — Christ who is the source of its mission and the foundation of its unity.

Montreal/63 [cont.]
dividually to the Christian. In any case, the exercise of the special ministry in the Church requires the acknowledgement and the confirmation of the Church.

Marseille/72 [pp. 7-8 cont.]
vine initiative and authority in the Church's existence, the continuity of the mission of God in the world, and the link of the communion and unity established by the Holy Spirit between the various communities of the Church.

The text of Marseille/72 added an important note emphasizing the continuity and necessity of the ministry of the apostles:

> In so far as they bore special, but not exclusive responsibility for proclaiming the message of reconciliation, establishing churches, and building them up in the apostolic faith, their ministry had to be continued. Such a ministry is essential to the Church in all times and circumstances.[7]

The Marseille/72 text, borrowing from other sources, also added two paragraphs to Montreal/63, §98 which have a direct bearing on the wording of Accra/74, §15. What follows first is the paragraph, quoted from the Louvain/71 text,[8] which specifies the essential functions of the ordained ministry:

> The ordained minister fulfils a threefold function:
> — gather together, build up, and oversee the believers, and insure that the community be present in the world; that it might be answerable for the yearnings, joys and sufferings of men, and that it may grow in the holiness of the Spirit, in order that it might be the promise of unity for the whole of humanity;
>
> — unceasingly announce and show forth, by his life, the good news of reconciliation, the foundation of man's liberation by God and of the unity of believers in the faith of the apostolic church;
>
> — preside over baptism and the eucharist — the thanksgiving of the community and the intercession for humanity in its entirely.[9]

Next what is quoted is from the Groupe de Dombes, 1972:

> This dependence on the one Lord and Saviour is expressed by the mutual dependence of the community and the minister. Their interdependence makes it clear that the Church is not master of Word and Sacraments, nor source of its faith, hope and unity. It also makes it clear that the minister does not exist on his own, nor for himself, and that he cannot deal arbitrarily with the Christian people. For Christian life and ministry are received from an Other: from Christ living in his church, and they are being made alive by the Holy Spirit, who is sent constantly to extend God's Kingdom.[10]

This paragraph is superseded by the following paragraph from Geneva/73, p. 6:

---

[7]Marseille/72, p. 10. This is echoed in Geneva/73, p. 5 and subsequently in Accra/74, §13.

[8]Louvain/71, p. 84.

[9]Marseille/72, pp. 8-9. This text is redone in Geneva/73, p. 6, as follows: "The essential and specific function of the ordained minister is: to assemble and build up the Christian community, by proclaiming and teaching the Word of God, and (in) presiding over the liturgical and sacramental life of the eucharistic community."

[10]Marseille/73, p. 8.

The community and the minister are dependent upon one another. Their interdependence is a reminder that the minister does not exist in isolation, nor for himself, and that he cannot deal arbitrarily with the Christian people. For Christian life and ministry are received from an Other, from Christ living in his Church, and they are made alive by the Holy Spirit, who is sent constantly to extend God's Kingdom.[11]

B. ORDAINED MINISTRY AND AUTHORITY.

Geneva/73 is the text most responsible for the material in this section of Accra/74. No material is found in the earliest of the texts of this period, namely, Montreal/63. The rootedness of authority is christological; the scriptural basis of this authority is cited in the text of Accra/74 with special emphasis on the commissioning by Christ of the apostles and on the ministry of Paul. It is a divine authority not given as an individual possession. Thus the exercise of authority in the Church involves community participation. Communion with the whole "community" of the Church can help insure that the exercise of authority will not be characterized by domination and will be characterized by genuine service.

---

[11]Geneva/73, p. 6.

Louvain/71

Ordination confers an authority (exousia) which is not that of the minister himself, but which demonstrates the authority of God received by the community; it also ratifies and manifests the fact that the minister is called and sent by God. But ordination is not the giving of a "thing" or a possession" or even an "office" *tout simple*; it arises from and results in a personal, existential relationship with the Holy Spirit, and it inseparably binds the ordained person with the aforementioned community; it is the sign and instrument of Christ in this community.

Marseille/72 [p. 13]

Ordination confers an authority (*exousia*) which is not that of the minister himself, but which demonstrates the authority of God received by the community; it also ratifies and manifests the fact that the minister is called and sent by God. But ordination is not the giving of a "thing" or a "possession" or even an "office" *tout simple*; it arises from and results in a personal, existential relationship with the Holy Spirit, and it inescapably binds the aforementioned community; it is the sign and instrument of Christ in this community." (Louvain)

[p. 9]

God expresses his faithfulness to the Church by the assistance which he grants to the ministry, without limiting his action to the activity of the minister alone. (Dombes) In faithfulness to the bonds of interdependence and reciprocity which unite minister and people he should exercise his ministry, not as autocrat, nor as impersonal functionary, but as companion of his people in listening for the Word of God. Particularly in this age of increasing

Geneva/73 [p. 6]

Ordination into the ministry implies authority in the exercise of this ministry. Since all ministry is rooted in Christ's ministry, this authority ultimately belongs to Christ who has received it from the Father (Matt. 28:18); it is in this sense a divine authority. On the other hand, since ordination is essentially a prayer for the gifts of the Holy Spirit for the continuing constitution and edification of the body, the authority of the ordained ministry is not to be understood as an individual possession of the ordained person but belongs to the whole community in and for which the minister is ordained. Authority in the name of God in its exercise must involve the participation of the whole community. The ordained minister manifests and exercises the authority of Christ precisely in the way Christ Himself revealed God's authority to the world; in and through *communion*. This in practice means that the ordained ministry is authoritative only in and through the concrete community to which it belongs. The ordained minister is not an autocrat nor an impersonal functionary. He is bound to the faithful

Accra/74

18. The exercise of such ministry has authority which ultimately belongs to Christ who has received it from the Father (Matt. 28:18); it is in this sense a divine authority. On the other hand, since ordination is essentially a setting apart with prayer for the gifts of the Holy Spirit for the continuing constitution and edification of the body, the authority of the ordained ministry is not to be understood as an individual possession of the ordained person but belongs to the whole community in and for which the minister is ordained. Authority in the name of God in its exercise must involve the participation of the whole community. The ordained minister manifests and exercises the authority of Christ in the way Christ himself revealed God's authority to the world: in and through *communion*.

19. This in practice means that the ordained ministry is authoritative only in and through the concrete community to which it belongs. The ordained minister is not an autocrat nor an impersonal functionary. He is bound to the faithful in interdependence and reciprocity,

Marseille/72 [p. 9 cont.]
education, liberation and popular participation in decision-making, it is important that the minister actualize his calling as a fellow-servant among the servant-people.

Geneva/73 [p. 6 cont.]
in interdependence and reciprocity, although his role is one of responsible leadership and judgment. Only if the authority of the ordained minister finds genuine acknowledgement in the communion of the community can this authority be protected from the distortion of domination.

Accra/74 [cont.]
although his role is one of responsible leadership and judgment. Only if the authority of the ordained minister finds genuine acknowledgment in the communion of the community can this authority be protected from the distortion of domination.

Geneva/73 [p. 19]

This conflict of roles is a challenge to the minister's authority. The minister has to ask himself ow far he is justified in forcing his will upon the congregation by virtue of the authority of his ordination. The congregation has to ask itself what are the limits of its response to the authority of its minister. Together they have to set their disagreements within the wider church and seek to resolve them there.

Accra/74

78. This conflict between different understandings of the role of the minister is a challenge to the minister's authority as well as to the mutual responsibility of the minister and the congregation in relation to each other. As all ministerial authority ultimately belongs to Christ, and the essential quality of all ministry is to be service, the minister has to ask himself how far he is justified in insisting upon his position over against the congregation by referring to his ordination. The congregation has to ask itself how far there are limits to its response to the authority of its minister; but above all, both parties have to look at their disagreements in the light of Christ's commission to his Church as a whole and their mutual responsibility to the will of Christ as well as to each other.

There is no material in the Montreal/63 text which corresponds to this section in the Accra/74 text. The Accra text finds its roots almost word for word in the text of Geneva/73.[12] The two paragraphs of the text of Marseille/72, however, the first of which is a paragraph from Louvain/71, contain much material later edited and found in some form in Accra/74.

C. ORDAINED MINISTRY AND PRIESTHOOD.

Several theological topics emerge in this section. The importance of tradition is emphasized. There is noted a reluctance on the part of the "churches of the Reformation" to use the word "priesthood" in reference to the ordained ministry. The overriding goal of unity demands the laying aside of this reluctance. The functions of ordained priests point to the priestly reality of Christ and of the baptized, a reality upon which the reality of ordained priesthood is based and a reality which exceeds that of ordained priesthood. Sacrifice and intercession are noted as characteristic of priesthood. The Accra text states that the ordained minister "fulfils his particular priestly service in strengthening, building up and expressing the royal and prophetic priesthood of the faithful through the service of the Gospel, the leading of the liturgical and sacramental life of the eucharistic community, and intercession." (Accra 21) It is important for ecumenical dialogue that cultic and intercessory aspects of the priesthood of the ordained are added in the Accra text. The ordained ministry is "of a completely new and different nature in relation to the sacrificial priesthood of the Old Testament." (Accra 22) This ministry is like that of Paul to the Gentiles, serving the mission in the world for the building up of the Church.

---

[12]Geneva/73, p. 6.

Montreal/63

86. The Church, the people chosen by God, is the community of those who have been gathered in faith by the apostolic preaching and by the power of the Spirit and have been plunged into the waters of baptism. It belongs to Christ, as his own body confesses him, worships him and obeys him, as the redeemer of the world. Taken from the world and set in the world, it constitutes there the royal priesthood declaring the wonderful deeds of God, and offering to him as a sacrifice both worship and daily life.

Louvain/71 [p. 81]

It is essentially through baptism and confirmation that Christians are made members of the Body of Christ and participants in his priesthood. Therefore, any service performed in the Church by a Christian, by virtue of his baptism and confirmation, supposes an offering of his whole person "as a living sacrifice, holy and acceptable to God" (Rom. 12:1), and consequently, has a priestly character. Thus the royal priesthood of necessity belongs to the people of God, and all forms of ministry within the Church assist, and in a sense must point to that corporate service. The call to be a part of, and to serve in Christ's Body is in no way based upon merit, but is simply an undeserved gift of God's grace. *Every* service is by Χάρις empowered by it, carried out *in* it. And since the Holy Spirit is gracious to every member, there is a *variety* of gifts; each baptized person undertakes an appropriate ministry within the many services.

Geneva/73 [p. 6]

Even if the New Testament never uses the terms "priest-hiereus" or "sacerdoce-hierateuma" to designate the ministry or the ordained minister, tradition has not been afraid of this usage. Although churches emerging from the Reformation avoid the word priesthood to designate the ordained ministry, churches of the catholic tradition employ this word in diverse forms: priestly ministry, ministerial priesthood, or, more recently, ministry of priesthood. The reconciliation in the use of terms makes it especially useful to discuss this question.

[pp. 67]

This manner of expressions always refers the function of the priests to a priestly reality upon which theirs is based, but which exceeds it — that is, the unique priesthood of Christ and the royal and prophetic, common and universal priesthood of the baptized (1 Peter 2:9, Rev. 1:6, 3:10, 20:6). The priesthood of Christ and the priesthood of the baptized community is a function of sacrifice and intercession. As Christ offers himself for all men the Christian offers

Accra/74

20. Even if the New Testament never uses the terms, "priest-hiereus" or "priesthood-hierateuma" to designate the ordained minister or the ministry, tradition has not been afraid of this usage. Although churches emerging from the Reformation avoid the word priesthood to designate the ordained ministry, churches of the catholic tradition employ this word in diverse forms: priestly ministry, ministerial priesthood, or, more recently, ministry of priesthood. The search for a reconciliation in ministries makes it especially useful to discuss this question of terms.

21. This manner of expression always refers the function of the priests to a priestly reality upon which theirs is based, but which exceeds it — that is, the unique priesthood of Christ and the royal and prophetic, common and universal priesthood of the baptized (1 Peter 2:9; Rev. 1:6, 3:10, 20:6). The priesthood of Christ and the priesthood of the baptized community is a function of sacrifice and intercession. As Christ offers himself for all men, the Christian offers his

Geneva/73 [pp. 6-7 cont.]

his whole being as a living sacrifice (Ro 12:1). As Christ intercedes to the Father for all men the Christian prays for the liberation of his human brothers. The minister, who participates, as every Christian, in the priesthood of Christ, and all the People of God, has been chosen, called and ordained to be given to the Church and to serve it, to organize and stimulate the royal and prophetic priesthood of the faithful, in order to edify the community of the body of Christ.

Accra/74 [cont.]

whole being "as a living sacrifice" (Rom. 12:1). As Christ intercedes to the Father for all men, the Christian prays for the liberation of his human brothers. The minister, who participates, as every Christian does, in the priesthood of Christ, and of all the People of God, fulfils his particular priestly service in strengthening, building up and expressing the royal and prophetic priesthood of the faithful through the service of the Gospel, the leading of the liturgical and sacramental life of the eucharistic community, and intercession.

Geneva/73 [p. 7]

The ordained ministry is then of a completely new and different nature in relation to the sacrificial priesthood of the Old Testament. This is not to say that the ministry does not have any proper priestly character. In fact he offers his life for the service of the mission in the world and of the edification of the church; the minister is, as St. Paul says about himself, "a minister of Christ Jesus to the Gentiles in the priestly service of the gospel of God, so that the offering of the Gentiles may be acceptable, sanctified by the Holy Spirit." (Rom 15:16)

Accra/74

22. The ordained ministry is then of a completely new and different nature in relation to the sacrificial priesthood of the Old Testament. As He offers his life for the service of the mission in the world and of the edification of the Church, the minister is, as St. Paul says about himself, "a minister of Jesus Christ to the Gentiles in the priestly service of the gospel of God, so that the offering of the Gentiles may be acceptable, sanctified by the Holy Spirit" (Rom. 15:16).

The three paragraphs in the Accra/74 text have no antecedents in Montreal/63, Louvain/71 or Marseille/72. The earliest text to treat directly this topic of the priesthood of the ordained ministry is that of Geneva/73. The Montreal and Louvain texts treat only the priesthood of all in the Church.

Note in §21 of the Accra text quoted above that the phrase, "the leading of the liturgical and sacramental life of the eucharistic community, and intercession," has been added. These cultic and intercessory aspects of the priesthood of the ordained minister significantly enhance the possibilities for ecumenical dialogue.

D. THE MINISTRY OF MEN AND WOMEN IN THE CHURCH.

This time period we are studying of the evolution of the ministry text demonstrates a movement from a mere footnote reference to an entire section devoted to the topic of the ordination of women. The arguments for and against women's ordination are given. One is left with the impression that there is an almost too impulsive favoring of the arguments for the ordination of women. This is especially evident in the statement in the Louvain text, quoted above, that "traditions have changed in the Church." (Louvain/71, p. 93) It is only with the texts which follow Accra/74 that the issue is placed in the larger context of "the ministry of men and women in the Church." and given a greater nuancing.

Louvain/71 [p. 93]
The Ordination of Women

Strong emotions are aroused when this subject is discussed. On the one hand, even in societies that no longer generally debar women from any office on grounds of sex alone, there are many men who find it deeply disturbing to be under the authority of a woman. On the other hand, more and more Christian women are expressing frustration in regard to the inability or unwillingness of Churches to consider them as fit candidates for ordination to presbyteral ministry. They feel depersonalized and deprived of the dignity of their adulthood in the Church, and this exclusion is leading in many cases toward feelings of bitterness and militancy.

Marseille/72 [p. 17]

Part of the difficulty no doubt arises from the predominance of male assumptions in Church organizations and of male imagery in theological concepts. But this male predominance, where it is a factor, is only an instance of our larger failure to think deeply about the relevance of our full, relationally understood, nature as sexual beings for our calling to the ministry of Christ's Church. It is equally superficial to take our sexual duality for granted and to say it makes a fundamental difference for ministry as to take it for granted and to say it makes no difference at all. In both perspectives the relational nature in which men and women share if they are to be fully human is slighted and the resulting patterns of ministry are impoverished through a lack of engagement of the full humanity of those who serve the Church.

Geneva/73 [p. 16]

Part of the difficulty in both cases may arise from the predominance of male imagery in theological reasoning and the predominance of male assumptions in Church organizations. This masculine predominance, where it is a factor, is an instance of our larger failure to think deeply about our nature as sexual beings who not only find fulfillment in relationship but who combine in our individual selves both masculine and feminine potentialities. A decision to ordain women is not enough if the predominance of male attitudes remains. Both men and women need to discover the full meaning of their sexual natures for the work of the ministry of Christ. The Church is entitled to the style of ministry which can be provided by women as well as that which can be provided by men. Indeed, an understanding of our mutual interdependence needs

Accra/74

67. Theological reasoning and church practice on both sides of this debate may be adversely influenced by continuing the predominance of male imagery in the modern social and cultural context. Although contemporary society, particularly in the West, affords greater equality to women than the society of biblical times, both proponents and opponents of the ordination of women are subject to assumptions of male dominance which are part of the fabric of language and custom. Such taken for granted conceptual patterns may distort theological reasoning and institutional practice both in churches which ordain women and in those which do not.

64. Both men and women need to discover the full meaning of their specific contribution to the ministry of Christ. The Church is entitled to the style of min-

Marseille/71 [p. 71 cont.]
Such issues as the feeling of some men that their security and authority are challenged, and the frustration that some women feel as they seek greater involvement and influence, are real but subsidiary in the present context. The real issue is that the Church is perpetuating a situation in which both men and women are diminished. Because of this, it is hard for both men and women to achieve a satisfactory understanding of their potential ministerial roles.

Geneva/73 [p. 16 cont.]
to be more widely reflected in all branches of ministry. If ministry demands the engagement of the full humanity of those involved in it, may it not also be enriched by the creative interaction of men and women in relationship?

Accra/74 [cont.]
istry which can be provided by women as well as that which can be provided by men. Indeed, an understanding of our mutual interdependence needs to be more widely reflected in all branches of ministry. If ministry demands the engagement of the full humanity of those involved in it, may it not also be enriched by the creative interaction of men and women in relationship?

Louvain/71 [cont.]
[p. 93]

Since those who advocate the ordination of women do so out of their understanding of the meaning of the Gospel and ordination, and since the experience of the Churches in which women are ordained has been positive and none has found reason to reconsider its decision, the question must be asked as to whether it is not time for all the Churches to confront this matter forthrightly. Churches which ordain women have found that women's gifts and graces are as wide and varied as men's, and that their ministry is fully as blessed by the Holy Spirit as the ministry of men. But even Churches which already ordain women must guard against discriminatory tendencies, since a real ambiguity can be observed in these Churches — the women ordained have usually been given positions of juridical and pastoral infer-

Marseille/72 [cont.]
[p. 16]

The perspective in which this issue must now be confronted brings into view the question of what the deeply relational character of humanity (Genesis 1:27) means for the form of our response to the Gospel. The duality of our sexual nature can be interpreted in different ways. Those traditions which ordain only men tend to view the differentiation of the sexes as a complementarity which justifies clear-cut institutional differentiation of male and female roles. Traditions which do ordain women tend to treat sexual differences as unimportant in this context, however relevant such differences may be in other areas of concern. Thus the debate reaches an impasse, borne of reading the same facts in different ways.

Geneva/73 [cont.]
[p. 16]
THE ORDINATION OF WOMEN

It seems clear that, without repudiating the efficacy of their ministries in the past, many churches are reading passages such as Genesis 1:27 and Galatians 3:28 with a sensitivity arising from new circumstances and new needs. The implications for the ordained ministry both of the relatedness of men and women as created in the image of God, and of the annulment of distinction between them in the perspective of redemption in Christ, need to be more fully explored. The different traditions read the same facts in different ways. Without denying the relatedness of the sexes in either creation or redemption, churches which ordain men only tend to see sexual differentiation as requiring a clearly defined separation of social roles. Churches

Accra/74 [cont.]
66. It seems clear that, without repudiating the efficacy of their ministries in the past many churches are reading passages such as Genesis 1:27 and Galatians 3:28 with a sensitivity arising from new circumstances and new needs. The implications for the ordained ministry both of the relatedness of men and women as created in the image of God, and of the transcending of the distinction between them in the perspective of redemption in Christ, need to be more fully explored. The different traditions read the same facts in different ways. Without denying the relatedness of the sexes in either creation or redemption, churches which ordain men only tend to see sexual differentiation as requiring a clearly defined separation of social roles. Churches which ordain both men and women, on the other hand, may risk the danger of un-

Louvain/71 [p. 93 cont.]
iority. The force of nineteen centuries of tradition
against the ordination of
women cannot be lightly
ignored. But traditions have
been changed in the Church.
This question must be faced,
and the item to face it is
now.

Geneva/73 [p. 16 cont.]
which ordain both men and
women, on the other hand,
may run the danger of
underestimating the social
significance of sexual difference.

Accra/74 [cont.]
derestimating the anthropological and social significance of difference between
the sexes.

Montreal/63

93. The Spirit equips God's people in a threefold way:

(a) He enables them as children of their heavenly Father to live and work in the world without faithless anxiety. There they find their principal place of testimony and their principal sphere of service. There they live as first fruits of a new creation.

(b) The spirit builds up the body of Christ in love, truth and holiness, by equipping the members with the manifold and varied gifts which they need for the service of one another and for the mission of the Church.* [*We propose that the question of the diaconate and that of the ordination of women receive further attention in Faith and Order.]

(c) Among the differing gifts bestowed by the Spirit is the special ministry.

Marseille/72 [cont.]

[p. 17]

For most communions, the role of women in the ministry is a matter of discipline and not of doctrine, although there are doctrinal positions relevant to the question. If agreement could be reached that the disciplinary status of the question predominates, the issue could be decided by a future ecumenical council. Short of that, differences of opinion on this subject may not, even now, need to be obstacles to the mutual recognition of ministry. Ecumenical considerations need not restrain a full and frank facing of this question.

Geneva/73 [cont.]

[p. 17]

For some churches these problems are not yet alive. While recording a position, they have not yet determined whether the decisive factors are doctrinal, or simply related to a longstanding traditional discipline. Nor are individuals within the different confessions in agreement about the doctrinal and disciplinary factors, or about their relation. Differences on this issue could raise possible obstacles to the mutual recognition of ministries. But these obstacles should not be regarded as insuperable. Openness to each other holds out the possibility that the Spirit may well speak to one Church through the insights of another. Ecumenical awareness and responsibility also demand that once a Church has decided what is timely and right, it should act in obedience to its own conviction. Since

Accra/74 [cont.]

69. For some churches these problems are not yet alive. While recording a position, they have not yet determined whether the decisive factors are doctrinal or simply related to a longstanding traditional discipline. Nor are individuals within the different confessions in agreement about the doctrinal and disciplinary factors or about their relation. Differences on this issue could raise possible obstacles to the mutual recognition of ministries. But these obstacles should not be regarded as insuperable. Openness to each other holds out the possibility that the Spirit may well speak to one Church through the insights of another. Ecumenical awareness and responsibility also demand that once a Church has decided what is timely and right, it should act in obedience to its own conviction. Since the opinion appears to be growing that doctrinal con-

Geneva/73 [p. 17 cont.]

the opinion appears to be growing that doctrinal considerations either favour the ordination of women or are neutral, the possibility is open that a future ecumenical council might deal with the question on mainly disciplinary grounds. Ecumenical considerations, therefore, should encourage, not restrain the full, frank facing of this question.

Accra/74 [cont.]

siderations either favour the ordination of women or are neutral, the possibility is open that a future ecumenical council might deal with the question. Ecumenical considerations, therefore, should encourage, not restrain, the full, frank facing of this question.

Geneva/73 [p. 19]

1. The need for a sharpened sense of ecumenical responsibility at this point cannot be over-stressed. The interrelatedness of the churches that has made the modern ecumenical movement both possible and necessary should have made us all aware that no church can wholly escape the impact of another church's action. It may not always be possible to implement changes in the structures of ministry through an ecumenical forum — desirable as this may be. Indeed, certain problems, even certain almost universal problems, may be amenable to solution only at a denominational or even local level. But in the process of making changes each church should seek to be as sensitive as possible to the potential ecumenical implications of its solutions to its problems, especially in so sensitive an area as the ministry.

Accra/74 [cont.]

80. The need for a sharpened sense of ecumenical responsibility at this point cannot be over-stressed. The interrelatedness of the churches that has made the modern ecumenical movement both possible and necessary should have made us all aware that no church can wholly escape the impact of another church's action. It may not always be possible to implement changes in the structures of ministry through an ecumenical forum — desirable as this may be. Indeed, certain problems, even certain almost universal problems, may be amenable to solution only at a denominational or even local level. But in the process of making changes each church should seek to be as sensitive as possible to the potential ecumenical implications of its solutions to its problems, especially in so sensitive an area as the ministry.

Montreal/63 makes one short reference to the question of the ordination of women in a footnote which states: "We propose that the question of the diaconate and that of the ordination of women receive further attention in Faith and Order."[13] Subsequent texts, leading up to Accra/74, evince much attention to the question of the ordination of women. Louvain/71 devotes two paragraphs to it, at the end of which it states:

> The force of nineteen centuries of tradition against the ordination of women cannot be lightly ignored. But traditions have been changed in the Church. This question must be faced, and the time to face it is now.[14]

Following Louvain more attention is given to the question in Marseille/72. The fifth and last of the paragraphs which it devotes to it states:

> For most communions, the role of women in the ministry is a matter of discipline and not of doctrine, although there are doctrinal positions relevant to the question. If agreement could be reached that the disciplinary status of the question predominates, the issue could be decided by a future ecumenical council. Short of that, differences of opinion on this subject may not, even now, need to be obstacles to the mutual recognition of ministry. Ecumenical considerations need not restrain a full and frank facing of this question.[15]

The discussion continues in the text of Geneva/73, the direct forerunner of Accra/74. These two texts, like the two before them, devote a section to the precise question of the *ordination* of women.[16] They provide the biblical and theological material which subsequent texts will use in their shorter but nonetheless poignant presentations of the pros and cons in regard to the ordination of women in the larger context of "the ministry of men and women in the Church."

---

[13]Montreal/63, p. 65.

[14]Louvain/71, p. 93.

[15]Marseille/73, p. 17. The full treatment in this text is on pp. 18-19.

[16]Geneva/73, pp. 16-17; Accra/74, §s 64-69.

III. THE FORMS OF THE ORDAINED MINISTRY.

A. BISHOPS, PRESBYTERS AND DEACONS.

In this time period of the evolution of the ministry text there is an acknowledgement of the importance and even divinely given nature of the three-fold ministry of bishop, presbyter, deacon (cf. Louvain/71). There is, however, a greater and greater willingness to accept a functional approach rather than an *a priori* or ontological one and a growing openness to a consideration of the three-fold ministry alongside other equally important ecclesial structures.

Montreal/63

95. This confirmation is given in ordination. According to the New Testament, this ordination consists in prayer with the laying on of hands. The orderly transmission of authority in ordination is normally an essential part of the means by which the Church is kept from generation go generation in the apostolic faith. All of us regard this continuity in the apostolic faith as essential to the Church. Some of us, including the Orthodox, believe that the unbroken succession of episcopal ordination from the apostles is a necessary guarantee of a valid ministry and of the safeguarding of the true faith, and that ordination is itself a sacrament. Others among us believe that it is the work of the Holy Spirit not only to preserve order in the Church but also to create new forms of order when existing forms have ceased to safeguard the true faith. Some believe that there is not sufficient authority in the New Testament to warrant the practice of ordination in the sense of setting men apart for a life-ministry in the Church. We recognize the gravity of these differences. At the same time we are

Louvain/71 [p. 86]

There are, however, different emphases in understanding how the identity given to the Church by Christ is to be faithfully maintained and the relationship of the ministry to this maintenance. To name three:

a) The threefold pattern of ministry, though it developed historically, is to be regarded as divinely given and is, therefore, indispensable for the existence of the Church. It is required for the building up of the communion, or at least as a sign that the People of God are one and the same People in all places and ages. The laying on of hands gives visible expression to this continuity.

b) There are certain functions of ministry which are given and which must be maintained in some way by the Church in every generation; as long as the functions, e.g. episcope, faithful preaching, administration of sacraments, and service to humanity are identifiable, the concrete patterns may change.

c) The succession is provided exclusively by the content of the Gospel. The Church is apostolic

Geneva/73 [p. 8]

Among the various ministerial structures the threefold ministry of bishop, presbyter-priest and deacon predominates. But it would be wrong to exclude other patterns of ministry which are found among the churches. Within the one faith allegiance it is possible to have, side by side, various styles of ecclesial life and ministerial structures, without making one the model for all the others. But a plurality of ecclesial cultures and ministerial structures does not diminish the one ministerial reality found in Christ and constituted by the Holy Spirit in the commission of the Apostles.

There is a unity in the diversity of ministerial structures, in that certain elements of ministry can always be identified in the very plurality and multiformity of ecclesial styles and structures. It would be difficult to imagine any structure of ministry which did not incorporate *episcope*, as that oversight over the church and the celebration of tho Christian mystery which belongs to the Gospel whether that church possesses the historic episcopate or not. *Diakonia*, as service in the world

Accra/74

25. The plurality of ecclesial cultures and ministerial structures does not diminish the one ministerial reality found in Christ and constituted by the Holy Spirit in the commission of the Apostles. Among the various ministerial structures the threefold ministry of bishop, presbyter-priest and deacon predominates. But it would be wrong to exclude other patterns of ministry which are found among the churches. Within the same community of faith it is possible to have, side by side, various styles of ecclesial life and ministerial structures, without making the one the model for all the others.

26. Both the episcopal and presbyteral functions of the Church must be understood as a sharing in the *diakonia*, that is, as costly service to the community of the Church and to the world through the proclamation and actualization of the Gospel. In the course of history, the function of *diakonia* has found expression in the office of deacon and the deaconess. For about 20 years now, many churches, independently from one another, have

Montreal/63 [cont.]
all agreed in accepting the statement of the Third Assembly that the unity which we seek includes a ministry accepted and acknowledged by all. There are differences of belief and practice among us on what constitutes the special ministry. Some churches recognize seven orders in the special ministry, some three, some only one. But the threefold pattern (bishop, presbyter, deacon) is also found (e.g. in the form of pastor, elder, deacon) in churches which normally speak of only one order in the special ministry.

Louvain/71 [p. 86 cont.]
insofar as it proclaims and serves again and again the same Christ and his liberating and reconciling message. As long as this message is proclaimed and lived ministries and means may change.

Geneva/73 [p. 8 cont.]
and in the proclamation of tho Gospel, is implicit in Christian ministry. Finally, *presbyteral function*, as an actualisation in the local situation of the full ministry of the Church, is essential to the meaning of ministry. In the ministry of the church all these elements are exercised by a person or persons, so representing a personal concretization of the mission of the whole Church.

Accra/74 [cont.]
been giving attention to the possible renewal of this office.

Montreal/63
95. [cont.]
There is need both for discussion between the churches about these differing traditions, and also for self-examination within our churches about the way in which we have received and used the gift of ministry. For example, we must ask ourselves such questions as the following:

(a) Granted that there is an essential ministry given to the Church by the Lord, does the traditional pattern of ministry in our churches do justice to the variety of the gifts of the Spirit?

(b) Have churches which follow the pattern "bishop, priest, deacon" in fact preserved the specific character of each of these orders of ministry as taught in their formularies? Do churches which have the pattern "pastor, elder, deacon" (or some similar pattern) preserve the ministerial character of each? On what theological principles are elders (presbyters) or deacons included in, or excluded from, the special ministry?

Louvain/71 [p. 86 cont.]
These differing views on the place of the ministry in the tradition of the Church influence the attitude of the churches to many of the questions which must be faced today, such as the ordination of women, the possibility of a nonprofessional ministry, and so forth. But there is evidence now that these three viewpoints are not mutually exclusive. For the third, in practice (for example) has developed a system of comprehensive and orderly oversight and administration of the sacraments intentionally faithful to the apostles (which the first sees as the basis of its position). On the other hand, the first is flexible in the actual practice of its ministries and sees the kerygma involved in the functions it maintains.

Montreal/63 [cont.]

(c) While in all our churches men and women are set aside for limited periods for some forms of ministry, ordination to the special ministry is almost universally regarded as being for life. What are the grounds for this?

(d) The following qualifications for the special ministry have by no means always been regarded as indispensable: academic training, full-time service, salary. Are they treated as indispensable in our churches today, and if so, on what grounds? How are these aspects of the ministry related to the fundamental theology of the ministry?

Louvain/71 [p. 86 cont.]

There is then, the continual need of relating the concept of ministry to the experience of it, getting at the mystery of it by employing a multiplicity of images and eventually, models. The New Testament used many structural images and eventually, models. The New Testament used many structural images — body, vine, building — but in almost every case growth and flexibility were assumed; *oikodome* (*sic*) was the principle for building up the body. An ever-growing openness to change, and a growing willingness to imitate this New Testament pattern can be discerned; it can be said that the vitality of the Church will be reflected by its openness to experiment with new forms and employ its ordained ministry in ever-new avenues of service.

Louvain/71 moves far beyond the text of Montreal/63 by stating that "the threefold pattern of ministry, though it developed historically, is to be regarded as divinely given and is, therefore, indispensable for the existence of the Church." (p. 86)   Geneva/73, however, like Montreal/63, states that "within the one faith allegiance it is possible to have, side by side, various styles of ecclesial life and ministerial structures, without making one the model for all the others." (p. 8) Accra/74 agrees with that text which immediately precedes it by repeating it. (Accra/74, §25) So overall Accra/74 maintains a functional approach to the threefold pattern of bishop/presbyter/deacon.[17]

B. GUIDING PRINCIPLES FOR THE EXERCISE OF THE ORDAINED MINISTRY IN THE CHURCH.

This section in the Lima text is not traceable to Accra and to the texts which precede it.

C. FUNCTIONS OF BISHOPS, PRESBYTERS AND DEACONS.

This section in the Lima text also is not traceable to Accra and to the texts which precede it.

D. VARIETY OF CHARISMS.

This section in the Lima text also is not traceable to Accra and to the texts which precede it.

---

[17]These texts relate for the most part to Lima 22.

IV. SUCCESSION IN THE APOSTOLIC TRADITION.

A. APOSTOLIC TRADITION IN THE CHURCH.

Part of the one paragraph in Lima/82 which constitutes this subsection finds its roots in Marseille/72. Geneva/73, which refashions the Marseille text, makes its way into the Accra/74 text, §28.

This section is marked by the great influence of the Marseille/72 meeting. While there is an effort to avoid heavily laden metaphysical words, e.g., "essential," there is a movement away from the sociological approach of Louvain/71. The aim of achieving ecumenical convergence is clearly becoming the overriding concern of these texts. And, finally, there is a movement toward the contextualizing of the issue of the succession of apostolic ministry within that of the succession of apostolic tradition.

Marseille/72 [p. 10]

Among the attributes of ministry, apostolicity has a central place. It is now generally agreed that this must be seen in the wider context of the apostolicity of the Church.

This apostolicity is rooted in God's sending his Son into the world. Christ is the true apostle. Through him the world is reconciled to the Father. The whole Church — the people of God, the Body of Christ — is called and sent to participate in this movement of reconciliation in the power of the Holy Spirit. Thus the entire Church has the apostolic mission and ministry of being an anticipatory sign of the coming Kingdom of God. This essential apostolicity is sustained by Christ's faithfulness and action of the Holy Spirit in the Church. There is then, an apostolic succession of the whole Church.

Montreal/63

87. In order to build up the Church and to equip it for its mission, the Lord Jesus Christ has given ministers who, following the apostles and by the power of the Spirit, serve the accomplished reconciliation in, with, and for the body by announcing, attesting and communicating that reconciliation by the means which the Lord has given.

Louvain/71 [pp. 81-82]

But having made this crucial point, it must also be recalled that certain are called and set-apart individuals have had a decisive role in the building up of the Church. The New Testament does report a setting apart to special ministry, distinctions of service *were* made. Throughout the Bible the concept of God's selectivity clearly emerges. There *is* a "scandal" of particularity — God called particular people for particular tasks and set them apart to serve the fellowship in distinct ways. Israel's history, its ever-deepening awareness of having been selected by God for particular service, the selection of prophets, priests and kings by God, the Incarnation itself, witness to selectivity and election. God had commonly called and employed individuals and groups to serve him in unique fashion — the selection of apostles con-

Marseille/72 [cont.]

Yet the apostolic succession in ministry can never be isolated from the apostolicity of the Church of which it is a part. The fullness of the apostolic succession of the whole Church involves continuity in the essential characteristics of the Church of the apostles; witness to the faith, community in love, sacramental life, service to the needy, dialogue and openness to the world and sharing the gifts which the Lord has given to each. Where these characteristics are present in the community, the special ministry is also in a real sense apostolic. [p.11]

The apostolic succession of the whole Church is an expression of the permanence and, therefore, continuity of Christ's own mission in which the Church partakes. In insuring this participation and succession to which it is bound, the ordained ministry — to-

Geneva/73 [p. 8]

The primary manifestation of apostolic succession is to be found in the life of the church as a whole. This succession is an expression of the permanence and, therefore, continuity of Christ's own mission in which the church partakes. This participation is rooted in the sending of the apostles and will find its completion in the all-embracing realization of God's kingdom.

The fullness of the apostolic succession of the whole church involves continuity in the permanent characteristics of the church of the apostles: witness to the apostolic faith, proclamation and fresh interpretation of the apostolic gospel, transmission of ministerial responsibility, sacramental life, community in love, service for the needy, unity among local churches, and sharing the gifts which the Lord has given to each.

Accra/74

27. The primary manifestation of apostolic succession is to be found in the life of the Church as a whole. This succession is an expression of the permanence and, therefore, continuity of Christ's own mission in which the church participates. This participation is rooted in the gift of the Holy Spirit, in the sending of the Apostles and their successors, and will find its completion in the all-embracing realization of God's kingdom.

28. The fullness of the apostolic succession of the whole Church involves continuity in the permanent characteristics of the Church of the apostles: witness to the apostolic faith, proclamation and fresh interpretation of the apostolic gospel, transmission of ministerial responsibility, sacramental life, community in love, service for the needy, unity among local Churches, and

Louvain/71 [pp. 81-82 cont.]
tinued this tradition, and opened the door to the conception of a called and set-apart ministry. That is to say, the existence of a set-apart ministry is fully consistent with God's *modus operandi* in calling, sending, and empowering individuals for special responsibilities.

Marseille/72 [p. 11 cont.]
gether with Scriptures and creeds, plays an important role:

(1) constantly to recall the Church to its apostolic origin and task through a fresh interpretation and concretization of the apostolic witness and mission;

(2) serving all members of the Church in order to equip them to participate in the apostolic mission and service of the Church;

(3) serving and signifying the unity of the local churches with one another through time and in space.

Accra/74 [cont.]
sharing the gifts which the Lord has given to each.

Marseille/72 [cont.]
[p. 11]

Accordingly the ordained ministry is instrumental to the preservation and actualization of the apostolicity of the Church. The orderly transmission of the apostolic ministry in ordination is normally an essential part of the means by which the Church is kept from generation to generation in the apostolic faith. (Cf. Montreal, para. 95).

Where this ministry is lacking a community must ask itself whether its apostolicity can be maintained. On the other hand, where this ministry does not adequately subserve the Church's apostolicity, the Church is under permanent obligation to renew, and if need be, to change its ministerial structures.

Geneva/73 [cont.]
[p. 8]

The ordained ministry is related in various degrees to all of these characteristics. It serves as an authorized and responsible instrument for their preservation and actualization. The orderly transmission of the ministry is, therefore, both a visible sign of this succession of the whole church and of the effective participation of the ministry in it and contribution to it. Where this orderly transmission is lacking a community must ask itself whether its apostolicity can be maintained in its fullness. On the other hand, where this ministry does not adequately subserve the Church's apostolicity, the church is under obligation to renew, and if need be, to change its ministerial structures.

Accra/74 [cont.]

29. The ordained ministry is related in various degrees to all of these characteristics. It serves as an authorized and responsible instrument for their preservation and actualization. The orderly transmission of the ministry is, therefore, both a visible sign of the continuity of the whole Church and of the effective participation of the ministry in it and contribution to it. Where this orderly transmission is lacking a church must ask itself whether its apostolicity can be maintained in its fullness. Or, where this ministry does not adequately subserve the Church's apostolicity, a church must ask itself whether or not its ministerial structures should continue with not alteration.

What should be noted is the change from the word "essential" to the word "permanent." Thus some technical metaphysical language is avoided. The later text adds the phrases, "proclamation and fresh interpretation of the apostolic gospel," and "unity among local churches." The former addition seems to replace the following deleted phrase, "dialogue and openness to the world." Thus there is evidenced a tendency to be less and less sociological and more and more theological in the use of terminology. The latter addition is evidence of a more and more ecumenical emphasis. The addition of the phrase, "transmission of ministerial responsibility," gives added emphasis to the importance of the issue of succession of apostolic ministry in relationship to the broader issue of succession of apostolic tradition.

B. SUCCESSION OF THE APOSTOLIC MINISTRY.

As regards the content of this section of the textual material Accra/74 (the final text of this time period being studied in this chapter) is here rooted in Geneva/73 and Marseille/72. In all three texts the issue of apostolic succession is not clearly contextualized in that of apostolic tradition. A movement is noted toward endorsing episcopal succession "as an efficacious sign, not a guarantee, of the continuity of the Church in apostolic faith and mission." (Marseille/72, pp. 11-12)

Churches without the historic episcopate are urged to be open to its acceptance for the sake of church unity. In fact "the episcopal functions and reality have been preserved in many of these churches with or without the title 'bishop'." (Marseille/72, p. 12)

Montreal/63

95. This confirmation is given in ordination. According to the New Testament, this ordination consists in prayer with the laying on of hands. The orderly transmission of authority in ordination is normally an essential part of the means by which the Church is kept from generation to generation in the apostolic faith. All of us regard this continuity in the apostolic faith as essential to the Church. Some of us, including the Orthodox, believe that the unbroken succession of episcopal ordination from the apostles is a necessary guarantee of a valid ministry and of the safeguarding of the true faith, and that ordination is itself a sacrament. Others among us believe that it is the work of the Holy Spirit not only to preserve order in the Church but also to create new forms of order when existing forms have ceased to safeguard the true faith. Some

Louvain/71 [p. 84]

Today all Churches, whatever the inherited pattern of their ministry may be, are having to face the question as to the extent to which the ministry can be changed or adapted. Must it be maintained in its present form? What are the changes or adaptations required? There is a growing recognition that changes in both the understanding and practice of the ministry are possible and that they are called for if the needs of the present situation are to be met. The following factors contribute to this recognition:

[pp. 84-85]
2. Study concerning the various Councils of the Church is leading to a growing recognition of and sophistication about the historical nature of the Councils of the Church. It is recognized that sociological and psychological factors influenced conciliar deci-

Geneva/73 [p. 9]

Today there is growing agreement among scholars that the New Testament presents diverse types and even several principles of organization of the Christian communities, according to the difference of authors, places and times. While, e.g., in the local churches, founded by apostles like Paul there were persons in authority, very little is said about how they were appointed in about the requirement for presiding at the eucharist. On this basis, there have been developed, in the course of history, multiple forms of church order, each with its own advantages and disadvantages: episcopal, presbyterl, congregational, among others.

There is further agreement among scholars that although ordination of ministers of the eucharist by bishops was the almost universal

Accra/74

31. Today there is growing agreement among scholars that the New Testament presents diverse types organization of the Christian communities, according to the difference of authors, places and times. While, in the local churches, founded by apostles like Paul, there were persons in authority, very little is said about how they were appointed and about the requirements for presiding at the eucharist. On this basis, there have been developed, in the course of history, notably since the 16th century, multiple forms of church order, each with its own advantages and disadvantages: episcopal, presbyteral, congregational, among others.

32. There is further agreement among many scholars that although ordination of ministers by bishops was the almost universal practice in

114

Montreal/63 [cont.]
believe that there is not sufficient authority in the New Testament to warrant the practice of ordination in the sense of setting men apart for a life-ministry in the Church. We recognize the gravity of these differences. At the same time we are all agreed in accepting the statement of the Third Assembly that the unity which we seek includes a ministry accepted and acknowledged by all. There are differences of belief and practice among us on what constitutes the special ministry. Some churches recognize seven orders in the special ministry, some three, some only one. But the threefold pat-

Louvain/71 [pp. 84-85 cont.]
sions; there is greater sensitivity to the probability that the intentions of those who framed conciliar statements may have been more modest than subsequent generations believed. For example, development in biblical theology has necessitated a calling into question of Trent's basing its treatment of holy orders on the Epistle to the Hebrews. The historical self-understanding of the Church as a pilgrim people, in via, allows the decisions of the Councils to be seen in more dynamic, historical terms. Such sensitivity seems to make possible and necessary the acceptance, by each, of a variety of church orders.

Geneva/73 [p. 9 cont.]
practice in the Church very early, it is impossible to show that such a church order existed everywhere in the Church from the earliest times. In fact, there is evidence that in the sub-apostolic age even this practice did not become uniform until after some time. Further, there have been well-documented cases later in the history of the Western Church in which priests — not bishops — have ordained other priests to serve at the altar.

Accra/74 [cont.]
the Church very early, it is impossible to show that such a church order existed everywhere in the Church from the earliest times. In fact, there is evidence that in the sub-apostolic age even this practice did not become uniform until after some time. Further, there have been well-documented cases later in the history of the Western Church in which priests, not bishops, have with papal dispensation ordained other priests to serve at the altar.

Montreal/63
[95. cont.]

term (bishop, presbyter, deacon) is also found (e.g. in the form of pastor, elder, deacon) in churches which normally speak of only one order in the special ministry. There is need both for discussion between the churches about these differing traditions, and also for self-examination within our churches about the way in which we have received and used the gift of ministry. For example, we must ask ourselves such questions as the following:

(a) Granted that there is an essential ministry given to the Church by the Lord, does the traditional pattern of ministry in our churches do justice to the variety of the gifts of the Spirit?

(b) Have churches which follow the pattern "bishop, priest, deacon" in fact preserved the specific character of each of these orders of

Louvain/71 [cont.]
[p. 84]

1. There is today a greater awareness of the historical character of the patterns of ministry within the New Testament. Biblical scholarship has come to the conclusion that it is not possible to ground *one* conception of church order in the New Testament to the exclusion of others. It appears that in New Testament times differing forms coexisted and differing forms developed simultaneously in various geographical areas. Furthermore, it is increasingly realized that the forms of ministry in the apostolic period were historically, socially, and culturally conditioned and that it is, therefore, justifiable and even necessary in the present time to seek to adapt the patterns of the ministry to the needs of the current situation.

[p. 85]
4. The experience of differ-

Geneva/73
[p. 9 cont.]

These observations do not imply a devaluation of the emergence and wide acceptance of the historic episcopate. They only indicate that the Church has been able to respond to the needs of particular historical situations in the development of its ministerial structures. It follows, therefore, that faithfulness to the basic task and structure of the apostolic ministry can be combined with an openness to diverse and complementary expressions of this apostolic ministry. Such insights, together with a more comprehensive understanding of the apostolicity of the Church and the means of its preservation and actualization, have led to certain modifications of previously held positions:

Accra/74 [cont.]

33. These observations do not imply a devaluation of the emergence and general acceptance of the historic episcopate. They only indicate that the Church has been able to respond to the needs of particular historical situations in the development of its ministerial structures. It follows, therefore, that faithfulness to the basic task and structure of the apostolic ministry can be combined with an openness to diverse and complementary expressions of this apostolic ministry. Such insights, together with a more comprehensive understanding of the apostolicity of the Church and the means of its preservation and actualization, have led to certain modifications of previously held positions:

Montreal/63 [cont.]
ministry as taught in their formularies? Do churches which have the pattern "pastor, elder, deacon" (or some similar pattern) preserve the ministerial character of each? On what theological principles are elders (presbyters) or deacons included in, or excluded from, the special ministry?

(c) While in all our churches men and women are set aside for limited periods for some forms of ministry, ordination to the special ministry is almost universally regarded as being for life. What are the grounds for this?

Louvain/71 [p. 85 cont.]
ent cultural settings and their needs as well as ecumenical contacts have helped relativise claims of permanence which once were attached to certain patterns of ministry. There is also the experience that imaginative changes have contributed to the overcoming of impasse in mission and in the carrying out of pastoral responsibility in the Churches. This experience calls for openness which permits constantly renewed creativity.

Montreal/'63
[95 cont.]
(d) The following qualifications for the special ministry have by no means always been regarded as indispensable: academic training, full-time service, salary. Are they treated as indispensable in our churches today, and if so, on what grounds? How are these aspects of the ministry related to the fundamental theology of the ministry?

Louvain/71 [cont.]
[p. 85]
Thus all Churches are being confronted with new, and to some extent, similar problems. And it may be said that more and more of them are becoming aware of the need, and the freedom with which they are able to develop their traditional patterns of ministry. But they still differ to a large extent in their ways of realizing adaptations. This is due to their difference in understanding the place of ministry in the tradition and continuous life of the Church. They are all of the conviction that the Church is apostolic, i.e. that at all times it is and has to be in communion with the apostolic community and ministry. Though it changes in the course of history it must not lose the identity which it has been given by Christ. But in what way does the ministry assure this identity? Is it enough to assure the continuity of content

Marseille/72
[pp. 11-12]
Today a growing tendency is noticeable in these Churches to interpret episcopal succession as an efficacious sign, not a guarantee, of the continuity of the Church in apostolic faith and mission, which is manifested in doctrine, proclamation, sacraments, worship, life and service. They value this succession as a gift of God, which they should preserve.

[p. 12]
On the other hand, these new insights enable those in churches without the historic episcopate to appreciate an episcopal succession as a valuable sign of the continuity and unity of the Church. This, therefore, should make them open to acceptance of the historic episcopate, especially where it serves the unity of the Church and where a denial of the apostolic character of their own ministry is not

Geneva/73 [cont.]
[p. 10]
1. A growing tendency is noticeable in churches which have preserved the historic episcopate to interpret episcopal succession as an effective sign, not a guarantee, of the continuity of the Church in apostolic faith and mission, which is manifested in doctrine, proclamation, sacraments, worship, life and service. They value this sign as a gift of God, which they must preserve.

The importance of the historic episcopate has not been diminished by the above-mentioned findings. On the contrary, these new insights are enabling churches without the historic episcopate to appreciate it as a sign of the continuity and unity of the Church. More and more churches, including those in church union negotiations, are expressing willingness to see episcopacy as a pre-

Accra/74 [cont.]
34. (a) A growing tendency is noticeable among theologians in certain churches which have preserved the historic episcopate to interpret episcopal succession as an effective sign, not a guarantee, of the continuity of the Church in apostolic faith and mission, which is manifested in doctrine, proclamation, sacraments, worship, life and service. They value the succession of ministries that have the fullness of *episcope* as a gift of God, which they must preserve.
37. The importance of the historic episcopate has not been diminished by the above-mentioned findings. On the contrary, these new insights are enabling churches without the historic episcopate to appreciate it as a sign of the continuity and unity of the Church. More and more churches, including those in church union negotiations, are expressing willingness

Louvain/71 [p. 85 cont.] and functions? Or can identity be assured only through certain obligatory patterns?

Marseille/72 [p. 12 cont.] implied.

Geneva/73 [p. 10 cont.] eminent sign of the apostolic succession of the whole church in faith, life, and doctrine, and as such, something that ought to be striven for if absent. The only thing they hold as incompatible with contemporary historical and theological research is the notion that the episcopal succession is identical with and comprehends the apostolicity of the whole Church.

Accra/74 [cont.] to see episcopacy as a preeminent sign of the apostolic succession of the whole Church in faith, life and doctrine, and as such, something that ought to be striven for if absent. The only thing they hold as incompatible with contemporary historical and theological research is the notion that the episcopal succession is identical with and comprehends the apostolicity of the whole Church.

Marseille/72 [p. 12]

At the same time, the more comprehensive understanding of the apostolicity of the Church and the means of its preservation and actualization makes it possible to recognize a continuity in apostolic faith, mission and ministry also in churches without the historic episcopate. This recognition finds additional support in the fact that the episcopal functions and reality have been preserved in many of these churches with or without the title "bishop".

Geneva/73 [p. 10]

2. Many find it possible today to recognize a continuity in apostolic faith, mission and ministry also in churches which have not retained the form of historic episcopacy. This recognition finds additional support in the fact that the episcopal functions and reality have been preserved in many of these churches, with or without the title "bishop". Ordination, for example, is always done in them by persons in authority, with the intention of transmitting ministerial commission and authority.

Accra/74

35. (b) Many find it possible today to recognize a continuity in apostolic faith, mission and ministry also in churches which have not retained the form of historic episcopacy. This recognition finds additional support in the fact that the episcopal functions and reality have been preserved in many of these churches, with or without the title "bishop". Ordination, for example, is always done in them by persons in whom the church recognizes the authority to transmit ministerial commission.

Marseille/72 [p. 11]

Under the particular historical circumstances of the growing Church in the sub-apostolic age the instrumentality of the ordained ministry for the preservation of the Church's apostolicity came to be expressed *inter alia* in the form of episcopal succession. This succession was understood as serving, symbolizing and guarding the continuity of the apostolic deposit of faith. Certain Christian traditions view themselves as having preserved this form of ministerial succession. There have been different and changing interpretations of this succession among and within these traditions. They have often thought that the ministries of those Churches which lack this episcopal succession are defective.

Geneva/73 [p. 9]

Under the particular historical circumstance of the growing Church in the sub-apostolic age, the succession of bishops came to be the predominant form of ministry (among others) in which the apostolicity of the Church was expressed. This succession was understood as serving, symbolizing and guarding the continuity of the apostolic faith and communion. Some Christian traditions believe this faith and communion to have been preserved uniquely in this form of ministerial succession, even though there have been varying interpretations and understandings of this succession among these same traditions.

Accra/74

30. Under the particular historical circumstance of the growing Church in the sub-apostolic age, the succession of bishops became one of the ways in which the apostolicity of the Church was expressed. This succession was understood as serving, symbolizing and guarding the continuity of the apostolic faith and communion. Some Christian traditions believe this faith and communion to have been preserved uniquely in this form of ministerial succession, even though there have been varying interpretations and understandings of this succession among these same traditions.

The Montreal text in several places refers to the issue of the continuity of the apostolic ministry. In one place it says that the mission of the apostles "is continued by the Church in its ministry."[18] In another place that text states that "the orderly transmission of authority in ordination is normally an essential part of the means by which the Church is kept from generation to generation in the apostolic faith."[19] And in another place the text states that "the minister, like the apostle, is sent to the world to show forth by word and deed the dying and resurrection of Jesus Christ, and is also given to the Church to remind it of that dying and rising by which it lives, and which it has to communicate to the world."[20]

Accra/74 §s 27-29 (cf. above in the previous subsection) find their specific textual roots in Geneva/73 (p. 8) and Marseille/72 (pp. 10-11). It should be noted, however, that the Accra text addresses the issue primarily in terms of apostolic *succession* and not primarily in terms of apostolic *tradition* (as later texts do). The Accra text titles its Part II, "Apostolic Succession" (§s 27-37).

The Accra text (§s 30-37) can be traced most clearly to its predecessor (Geneva/73, pp. 9-10, in the section entitled, "Episcopal Succession). It can be traced less and less clearly backward to Marseille/72 (pp. 11-12, in the section also entitled, "Episcopal succession); to Louvain/71 (pp. 84-86, in its section entitled, "Tradition and Change"). Finally it can be traced to Montreal/63:

> All of us regard this continuity in the apostolic faith as essential to the Church. Some of us, including the Orthodox, believe that the unbroken succession of episcopal ordination from the apostles is a necessary guarantee of a valid ministry and of the safeguarding of the true faith.[21]

This earlier acknowledgement of the value of episcopal succession alongside other views of how to insure valid ministry and true faith is superseded by an emphasis on episcopal succession outweighing other emphases. As already mentioned above the Marseille/72 text introduces a separate treatment entitled, "Episcopal succession." In it the following observation is noted:

> Today a growing tendency is noticeable in these Churches (which have preserved episcopal succession) to interpret episcopal succession as an efficacious sign, not a guarantee, of the continuity of the Church in apostolic faith and mission, which is manifested in doctrine, proclamation, sacraments, worship, life and service.

---

[18]Montreal/63, §85.

[19]Montreal/63, §95.

[20]Montreal/63, §96.

[21]Montreal/63, §95, pp. 65-66.

They value this succession as a gift of God, which they should preserve.[22]

Thus a movement toward endorsing episcopal succession, along with some flexibility, is reported and endorsed. The Geneva/73 text makes an even stronger endorsement by stating that these same churches "value this sign as a gift of God, which they *must* preserve."[23] In fact the earlier Marseille text itself stated as follows:

New insights enable those in churches without the historic episcopate to appreciate an episcopal succession as a valuable sign of the continuity and unity of the Church. This, therefore, should make them open to acceptance of the historic episcopate, especially where it serves the unity of the Church and where a denial of the apostolic character of their own ministry is not implied.[24]

As a matter of fact in the same text another ecumenical development is reported which acknowledges the following:

The more comprehensive understanding of the apostolicity of the Church and the means of its preservation and actualization makes it possible to recognize a continuity in apostolic faith, mission and ministry also in churches without the historic episcopate. This recognition finds additional support in the fact that the episcopal functions and reality have been preserved in many of these churches with or without the title "bishop".[25]

A giant ecumenical advance has been made among churches which have maintained episcopal succession since earlier "they have often thought that the ministries of those Churches which lack this episcopal succession are defective."[26]

---

[22]Marseille/72, pp. 11-12.

[23]Geneva/73, p. 9. Emphasis added.

[24]Marseille/72, p. 12.

[25]Marseille/72, p. 12.

[26]Marseille/72, p. 11.

V. ORDINATION

A. THE MEANING OF ORDINATION.

There is noted here the binding relationship of ordination to the Jesus of history as well as the Christ of faith. Ordination is also clearly related to the mission and teaching of the apostles. And there is added a reference to the role of the Spirit. As the evolution of the text unfolds it is stated that ordination is an action both by God and the community. An analysis is provided of the etymological roots of the word, "ordination." Etymology reflects sociology; a caution is given regarding the various sociological settings to which "ordination" is used. In this connection what must be especially noted is the growing rift between clergy and laity over the centuries.

Louvain/71 [p. 82]

That is to say, through the commissioning of apostles Jesus bound the church to the revelation of himself which occurred during his ministry. It may be said that the Church in ordaining new persons to ministry in Christ's name, is attempting to follow the mission of the apostles and remain faithful to their teaching; ordination as an act attests the binding of the Church to the historical Jesus and the historical Revelation, at the same time recalling that it is the Risen Lord who is the true Ordainer, who bestows the gift. In ordaining the Church attempts to provide for the faithful proclamation of the Gospel and humble service in Christ's name. The laying on of hands in ordination can be seen as the sign witnessing to the connection of the Church and its ministry with Christ, binding the ministry to a conscious awareness of its anchorage and roots in the revelation accomplished in Him, reminding it to look to Him as the source of its commission.

Marseille/72 [p. 13]

"It may be said that the Church, in ordaining new persons to ministry in Christ's name, is attempting to follow the mission of the Apostles and remain faithful to their teaching; ordination as an act attests the binding of the Church to the historical Jesus and the historical Revelation, at the same time recalling that it is the Risen Lord who is the true ordainer, who bestows the gift. In ordaining the Church attempts to provide for the faithful proclamation of the Gospel and humble service in Christ's name. The laying on of hands in ordination can be seen as the sign witnessing to the connection of the Church and its ministry with Christ, binding the ministry to a conscious awareness of its anchorage and roots in the revelation accomplished in Him, reminding it to look to Him as the source of its commission."

Geneva/73 [pp. 10 11]

"It may be said that the Church, in ordaining new persons to ministry in Christ's name, is attempting to follow the mission of the Apostles and remain faithful to their teaching; ordination as an act attests the binding of the Church to the historical Jesus and the historical Revelation, at the same time recalling that it is the Risen Lord who is the true ordainer, who bestows the gift. In ordaining the Church attempts to provide for the faithful proclamation of the Gospel and humble service in Christ's name. The laying on of hands in ordination can be seen as the sign witnessing to the connection of the Church and its ministry with Christ, binding the ministry to a conscious awareness of its anchorage and roots in the revelation accomplished in Him, reminding it to look to Him as the source of its commission".
[* Louvain 1971, p. 82]

Accra/74

38. The Church, in ordaining some of its members to the ministry in the name of Christ, attempts to follow the mission of the Apostles and to remain faithful to their teaching. Ordination as an act attests the bond of the Church with Jesus Christ and the apostolic witness, recalling that it is the risen Lord who is the true ordainer, who bestows the gift. In ordaining, the Church provides, under the inspiration of the Holy Spirit, for the faithful proclamation of the Gospel and humble service in Christ's name. The laying-on of hands can be seen as the sign of the gift of the Spirit, rendering visible the ordering of this ministry in the revelation accomplished in him, and reminding the Church to look to him as the source of its commission.

Marseille/72 [pp. 13-14]

Properly speaking, then, ordination denotes an action by God and by the community which inaugurates a relationship in which the ordinand is strengthened by the Spirit for his or her task and is upheld by the acknowledgment and prayers of the congregation. The word ordination refers to the liturgical act of laying-on hands, accompanied by prayer for the Holy Spirit. The term is the common translation of the Greek word *cheirotonia* which literally describes the action done. Necessarily, however, the public marking of this spiritual relationship has been expressed in social structures and understood in terms of social metaphors available to the Church at any given time or place. The Latin term *ordo*, with the concept of legally defined status that went with it, not only served as a conceptual vehicle for the relation-to-community of one on whom hands had been laid, but lent itself for common use in translating *cheirotonia* in several Western languages. Similarly the distinction between "clergy" and "laity" arose as a means of putting words to this relationship at a time, when the ability to read and write, status as "cleric" or "clerk" was a notable distinguishing mark of the one set apart. The hardening of "clerical" status into one of the "estates" of medieval society further emphasized the element of social stratification that had crept into the usage, and powerfully influenced the assumptions associated with ordination. Even the Reformation and post-Reformation habit of calling only ordained people "ministers", thus dis-

Geneva/73 [p. 11]

Properly speaking, then, ordination denotes an action by God and by the community which inaugurates a relationship in which the ordinand is strengthened by the Spirit for his or her task and is upheld by the acknowledgment and prayers of the congregation.

Extensive study has already been devoted to the contexts and meanings of the Hebrew, Greek, and Latin words connected with ordination.** [**Recent research is summarized in the Faith and Order document *Ordination A Working Paper*, FO/68:7, March 1968, Chapter II.] It is evident that there is considerable difference between the unspoken cultural setting of the Greek *cheirotonein* and that of the Latin *ordo* or *ordinare*. The New Testament use of the former term borrows its basic secular meaning of "appointment" (Acts 14:23; II Cor. 8:19), which is, in turn, derived from the original meaning of extending the hand, either to designate a person or to cast a vote. Some scholars see in *cheirotonein* a reference to the act of laying-on of hands, in view of the literal description of such action in such seemingly parallel instances as Acts 6:6, 8:17, 13:3, 19:6; I Tim. 4:14; II Tim. 1:6. But the actual use of *cheirotonein* need mean no more than "appoint" without reference to the theory or means of the action. *Ordo* and *ordinare*, on the other hand, are terms derived from Roman law where they convey the notion of the special status of a group distinct from the

Accra/74

39. Properly speaking, then, ordination denotes an action by God and by the community which inaugurates a relationship in which the ordained is strengthened by the Spirit for his or her task and is upheld by the acknowledgment and prayers of the congregation.

41. Extensive study has already been devoted to the contexts and meanings of the Hebrew, Greek, and Latin words connected with ordination. It is evident that there is considerable difference between the unspoken cultural setting of the Greek *cheirotonein* and that of the Latin *ordo* or *ordinare*. The New Testament use of the former term borrows its basic secular meaning of "appointment" (Acts 14:23; II Cor. 8:19), which is, in turn, derived from the original meaning of extending the hand, either to designate a person or to cast a vote. Some scholars see in *cheirotonein* a reference to the act of laying-on of hands, in view of the literal description of such action in such seemingly parallel instances as Acts 6:6, 8:17, 18:19, 13:3, 19:6; I Tim. 4:14; II Tim. 1:6. But the actual use of *cheirotonein* need mean no more than "appoint" without reference either to the theory or means of the action. *Ordo* and *ordinare*, on the other hand, are terms derived from Roman law where they convey the notion of the special status of a group distinct from the plebs, as in the term *ordo clarissimus* for the Roman senate. The starting point of any conceptual construction using these terms will

Marseille/72 [pp. 13-14 cont.]
qualifying the term for reference to the ministry shared by all Christians, tended to have an impact on Protestant habits of thought and action. Most New Testament terms for ministerial leadership are, by contrast, functional. But even these words involve a borrowing of social imagery. The *dia-konos* is a waiter, the *episcopus* an overseer or foreman, and the *presbyteros* an old man!

Geneva/73 [p. 11 cont.]
plebs, as in the term *ordo clarissimus* for the Roman senate. The starting point of any conceptual construction using these terms will strongly influence what is taken for granted in both the thought and action which result.

Accra/74 [cont.]
strongly influence what is taken for granted in both the thought and action which result.

This section of the Accra/74 text is not reflected in that of Montreal/63. The earliest text which serves as antecedent is that of Louvain/71. The content is essentially the same for both texts. The latter adds a reference to the Holy Spirit. Another text which serves as antecedent to Accra/74 in this section is that of Marseille/72. It can be contrasted with that of Geneva/73 which is virtually the same in content as that of Accra/74 §41.

B. THE ACT OF ORDINATION.

Here we have a continuous effort to clarify the three elements that constitute the act of ordination, the invocation of the Holy Spirit in a liturgical context, the "sacramental" sign of the laying on of hands and the acknowledgement by the Church of God's call to the ordained ministry.

The Accra text clarifies the first element, the invocation of the Holy Spirit, by broadening the scope of the ministry beyond that of the local community to that of the Church universal and the whole world. The initiative of God is again pointed out as well as the Church's absolute dependence on the outcome of ordination, which outcome is not predictable.

The second element, the sign of ordination, is again called sacramental. The Marseille text adds this. God's freedom is acknowledged but faith, based on God's (the Father's) faithfulness to promises made in Christ, is the assurance that the act of ordination will bring about the effect signified, namely, the *spirit*ual relationship between the Church and the one ordained.

To the third element, the acknowledgement by the Church of the one ordained, is added discernment of the gifts of the Spirit received by the one to be ordained prior to the Church's acknowledgement. The mutual responsibilities of the Church and the one ordained toward one another are stated. Again, it is the Marseille text which introduces this content. The Accra text adds a more charismatic flavor to the content by its reference to the acknowledgement of the gifts found in the one ordained.

Louvain/71 [pp. 83-84]

Therefore ordination is at one and the same time:

— an invocation to God that he bestow the power of the Holy spirit upon a new minister;

— a sign of the granting of this prayer by the Lord who gives the gift of ministry;

— an offering by the Church to God, of the minister consecrated to his service (cf. I Tim. 4:14 and II Tim. 1:6).

[pp. 88-89]

A long and early Christian tradition placed ordination in the context of worship and especially of the eucharist. Such a place for the service of ordination preserves the understanding of ordination as an *act* of the *whole* community, and not of a certain order within it or of the individual ordained. Even if one believes that the act of ordaining belongs to a special order within the Church, it is always important to remember that the entire community is involved in the act. Ordination in association with the eucharist keeps before the Church the truth that it is

Marseille/72 [p. 14]

The act of ordination is at one and the same time three things: *invocation of the Holy Spirit, sacramental sign, and commitment.* It is:

[pp. 15-16]

A long and early Christian tradition placed ordination in the context of worship and especially of the eucharist. Such a place for the service of ordination preserves the understanding of ordination as an *act* of the *whole* community, and not of a certain order within it or of the individual ordained. Even if one believes that the act of ordaining belongs to a special order within the Church, it is always important to remember that the entire community is involved in the act. Ordination in association with the eucharist keeps before the Church the truth that it is

Geneva/73 [p. 12]

The act of ordination is at one and the same time three things: invocation of the Holy Spirit (*epiklesis*); sacramental sign; acknowledgment of gifts and commitment.

It is:

[p. 13]

A long and early Christian tradition placed ordination in the context of worship and especially of the eucharist. Such a place for the service of ordination preserves the understanding of ordination as an *act* of the *whole* community, and not of a certain order within it or of the individual ordained. Even if one believes that the act of ordaining belongs to a special order within the Church, it is always important to remember that the entire community is involved in the act. Ordination in association with the eucharist keeps before the Church the truth that it is

Accra/74

44. The act of ordination is at one and the same time: invocation of the Holy Spirit (*epiklesis*); sacramental sign; acknowledgment of gifts and commitment. It is:

49. A long and early Christian tradition places ordination in the context of worship and especially of the eucharist. Such a place for the service of ordination preserves the understanding of ordination as an *act* of the *whole* community, and not of a certain order within it or of the individual ordained. Even if one believes that the act of ordaining belongs to a special order within the Church, it is always important to remember that the entire community is involved in the act. Ordination, in association with the eucharist, keeps before the Church the truth that it is

Louvain/71 [pp. 88-89 cont.]
an act which initiates a person to a *service of the "koinonia"*, a service both to God and to fellow man. It is this *"koinonia"* that the eucharist expresses *par excellence* and by continuing to related ordination to the eucharist this dimension of ministry is called to mind. Ordination within the service of the eucharist also reminds the Church that the ordained ministry is set apart to point to Christ's own ministry and not to some other. By placing ordination in the context of worship and especially the eucharist, this act is referred to God Himself and the ordained person is dedicated to the service of "His Servant" who offers Himself for the salvation of the world.

Marseille/72 [pp. 15-16 cont.]
an act which initiates a person to a *service of the "koinonia"*, a service both to God and to fellow man. It is this *"koinonia"* that the eucharist expresses *par excellence* and by continuing to relate ordination to the eucharist this dimension of ministry is called to mind. Ordination within the service of the eucharist also reminds the Church that the ordained ministry is set apart to point to Christ's own ministry and not to some other. By placing ordination in the context of worship and especially the eucharist, this act is referred to God Himself and the ordained person is dedicated to the service of "His Servant" who offers Himself for the salvation of the world."

Geneva/73 [p. 13 cont.]
an act which initiates a person to a *service of the "koinonia"*, a service both to God and to fellow man. It is this *"koinonia"* that the eucharist expresses *par excellence* and by continuing to relate ordination to the eucharist this dimension of ministry is called to mind. Ordination within the service of the eucharist also reminds the Church that the ordained ministry is set apart to point to Christ's own ministry and not to some other. By placing ordination in the context of worship and especially the eucharist, this act is referred to God Himself and the ordained person is dedicated to the service of "His Servant" who offers Himself for the salvation of the world."* [*Louvain 1971, pp. 88, 89]

Accra/74 [cont.]
an act which initiates a person to a *service of the "koinonia"* (the fellowship), a service both to God and to the fellow man. It is this *koinonia* that the eucharist expresses *par excellence* and by continuing to relate ordination to the eucharist this dimension of ministry is called to mind. Ordination within the service of the eucharist also reminds the Church that the ordained is set apart to point to Christ's own ministry and not to some other. By placing ordination in the context of worship and especially the eucharist, this act is referred to God himself and the ordained person is dedicated to the service of "his Servant" who offers himself for the salvation of the world.

Louvain/71 [p. 83]

Therefore ordination is at one and the same time:

— an invocation to God that he bestow the power of the Holy spirit upon a new minister;

— a sign of the granting of this prayer by the Lord who gives the gift of ministry;

— an offering by the Church to God, of the minister consecrated to his service (cf. I Tim. 4:14 and II Tim. 1:6).

Marseille/72 [pp. 1415]

(1) (Louvain) "An invocation to God that he bestow the power of the Holy Spirit upon the new minister" and upon the community to which he is related. The otherness of God's initiative of which the ordained ministry is a symbol is here acknowledged in relation to ordination itself. The Spirit blows where it wills, and invocation of the Spirit involves risk. The epiclesis is at once indispensable to the act of ordination and a reminder that what takes place in this act may not be wholly contained within the limits of the community performing the act.

Geneva/73 [p. 12]

1. An invocation to God that He bestow the power of the Holy Spirit upon the new minister in his or her new relation to the local Christian community, to the Church universal and to the world. The otherness of God's initiative, of which the ordained ministry is a symbol, is here acknowledged in the act of ordination itself. "The Spirit blows where it wills" (John 3:3), and invocation of the Spirit implies an absolute dependence on God for the outcome of the Church's prayer. This means that the Spirit may set new forces in motion and open new possibilities "far more abundantly than all that we ask or think'. (Eph. 3:20).

Accra/74

45. (a) An invocation to God that he bestow the power of the Holy Spirit upon the new minister in his new relation to the local Christian community, to the Church universal and to the world. The otherness of God's initiative, of which the ordained ministry is a symbol, is here acknowledged in the act of ordination itself. "The Spirit blows where it wills" (John 3:3), and invocation of the Spirit implies an absolute dependence on God for the outcome of the Church's prayer. This means that the Spirit may set new forces in motion and open new possibilities "far more abundantly than all that we ask or think" (Eph. 3:20).

Louvain/71 [p. 83]

a sign of the granting of this prayer by the Lord who gives the gift of ministry;

Marseille/72 [p. 15]

(2) (Louvain) "A sign of the granting of this prayer by the Lord who gives the gift of ministry. "The community ordains in the confidence that — free as the Spirit is — God enters sacramentally into historical forms of human relationship and imagination and uses them for his purpose. Thus the sign of ordination is performed in faith that the spiritual relationship signified is present in, with and through the words, acts and churchly forms in use.

Geneva/73 [p. 12]

2. A sign of the granting of this prayer by the Lord who gives the gift of ministry. Although the outcome of the Church's epiklesis depends on the freedom of God, the Church ordains in confidence that God, being faithful to His promises in Christ, enters sacramentally into contingent, historical forms of human relationship and uses them for His purpose. Ordination is a sign performed in faith that the spiritual relationship signified is present in, with and through the words spoken, the gestures made and the ecclesiastical forms employed.

Accra/74

46. (b) A sign of the granting of this prayer by the Lord who gives the gift of ministry. Although the outcome of the Church's *epiklesis* depends on the freedom of God, the Church ordains in confidence that God, being faithful to his promise in Christ, enters sacramentally into contingent, historical forms of human relationship and uses them for his purpose. Ordination is a sign performed in faith that the spiritual relationship signified is present in, with and through the words spoken, the gestures made and the ecclesiastical forms employed.

Louvain/71 [p. 83]

Ordination, then, in this context, necessarily means commitment to a community — not only to certain ideals or a vague "human unity" but to concrete human beings in whose particular circumstances the ordained person is to be unreservedly involved. Thus the ordinand contributes especially to the communion between Christ and His people, and the relation of these people to one another. The ordinand's role is to minister to this community, to mediate its interior divisions and conflicts through his awareness of, and concern for, the oneness of all. Thus ordination also points to the safeguarding of the unity of the Church which is bound up with the responsibility of the one who presides at the eucharist.

[p. 88]

In order to experience and demonstrate the truth that setting apart is not to some superior level of discipleship, but rather to service *within* the Church, it is important that the entire process of ordination involve the whole body of the people. There needs to be continual emphasis on the fact that ordination is

Marseille/72 [p. 15]

(3) A commitment by the community and the one ordained to the testing and service required in the new relationship. By receiving the minister in the act of ordination, the community commits itself to responsibility and openness toward this new ministry. Likewise the one ordained commits himself or herself to the responsibilities of this new relationship.

(4) (Louvain) "In order to experience and demonstrate the truth that setting apart is not to some superior level of discipleship, but rather to service *within* the Church, it is important that the entire process of ordination involve the whole body of the people. There needs to be continual emphasis on the fact that

Geneva/73 [p. 13]

3. An acknowledgment by the Church of its discernment of gifts of the Spirit in the one ordained, and a commitment by both Church and ordinand, to the testing and the service implied in the new relationship. By receiving the new minister in the act of ordination, the congregation acknowledges this minister's gifts and commits itself to responsibility for an openness toward him or her. Likewise the one ordained offers his or her gifts to the Church and commits himself or herself to the burden and opportunity of new authority and responsibility.

[p. 14]

2. The ordinand should be one whom the church can confidently expect to commit himself to the task for which he is called and ordained. This task has to bear a clear relation to the church's mission, however innovative the proposed patterns of activity. It will largely consist in gathering and building up some form of missioning Christian Community, and in aiding thereby and enabling members of the community to exercise ever more fully their own ministry, each in his or her res-

Accra/74

47. (c) An acknowledgment by the Church of its discernment of gifts of the Spirit in the one ordained, and a commitment by both Church and ordinand, to the tests and opportunities implied in the new relationship. By receiving the new minister in the act of ordination, the congregation acknowledges this minister's gifts and commits itself to responsibility for an openness toward him. Likewise the one ordained offers his gifts to the Church and commits himself to the burden and opportunity of new authority and responsibility.

52. (ii) The ordinand should be one whom the church can confidently expect to commit himself to the task for which he is called and ordained. This task has to bear a clear relation to the Church's mission, however innovative the proposed patterns of activity. It will largely consist in gathering and building up some form of missioning Christian Community, and in aiding thereby and enabling members of the community to exercise ever more fully their own ministry, each in his or her respective sphere of activity.

Louvain/71 [p. 88 cont.]
neither "over-against" or *vis-à-vis* the congregation, but rather, that a person is addressed in the midst of the people. It is also important that the congregation have a part in the calling, choosing, and training of an ordinand. thus preserving the basic significance of the *rite vocatus*. This means more than the inclusion of a sentence or two in the liturgy and ordaining in the *presence* of the laity, important as that may be.

Marseille/72 [p. 15 cont.]
ordination is neither "over-against" nor *vis-à-vis* the congregation, but rather, that a person is addressed in the midst of the people. It is also important that the congregation have a part in the calling, choosing, and training of an ordinand, preserving the basic significance of the *rite vocatus*. This means more than the inclusion of a sentence or two in the liturgy and ordaining in the *presence* of the laity, important as that may be.

Geneva/73 [p. 14 cont.]
pective sphere of activity.

5. The ordinand should be one who, in fulfilling his appointed task as ordained minister, will be able to live and act in a relationship of mutual accountability and concern, both within the people of God, and among his or her brothers and sisters in the ministry.

Accra/74 [cont.]
55. (v) The ordinand should be one who, in fulfilling his appointed task as ordained minister, will be able to live and act in a relationship of mutual accountability and concern, both within the People of God and among his or her brothers and sisters who have also been called to ministries.

Geneva/73 [cont.]

[p. 13]

"In order to experience and demonstrate the truth that setting apart is not to some superior level of discipleship, but rather to service *within* the Church, it is important that the entire process of ordination involve the whole body of the people. There needs to be continual emphasis on the fact that ordination is not only "over-against" nor *vis-à-vis* the congregation, but rather, that a person is addressed in the midst of the people. It is also important that the congregation have a part in the calling, choosing, and training of an ordinand, preserving the basic significance of the call to the ministry. This means more than the inclusion of a sentence or two in the liturgy and ordaining in the presence of the laity, important as that may be."

Accra/74 [cont.]

48. In order to experience and demonstrate the truth that setting apart is not to some superior level of discipleship, but rather to service within the Church, it is important that the entire process of ordination involve the whole body of the people. There needs to be continual emphasis on the fact that ordination is not only "over against" nor *vis-à-vis* the congregation, but rather, that a person is addressed in the midst of the people. It is also important that the congregation have a part in the calling, choosing, and training of an ordinand, preserving the basic significance of the call to the ministry. This means more than the inclusion of a sentence or two in the liturgy and ordaining in the presence of the laity, important as that may be."

The paragraphs of this section of the Accra/74 text (§s 44-49) find their textual origin in the text of Louvain/71 in various places. There are no textual parallels in the Montreal/63 text.[27]

Accra 49 is a direct quote from Louvain/71.[28] Accra 44 is found virtually in Louvain with some significant textual changes. There is the addition of the liturgical term from the Greek, *epiklesis*.[29] There is the use of the phrase, *sacramental* sign.[30] And there is the addition of the phrase, acknowledgement of gifts,[31] which puts the emphasis on God's prior offering and call to ministry.

The other paragraph of the Accra text dealing with this topic is §45 which treats the specific issue of the invocation of the Holy Spirit. It finds its first parallel in the text of Marseille/72. The later text introduces the idea of the relationship of the minister not only "to the community" (unspecified and presumably the local community) but also "to the Church universal and to the world." This addition broadens the scope of the ministry.

The word, "risk," in the earlier text is defined in the later text in terms of "an absolute dependence on God for the outcome of the Church's prayer." Thus a more spiritual dimension is given to an otherwise common human task and human risk-taking is directly linked with the Spirit's unpredictability.

The next paragraph of the Accra text dealing with this topic is §46 which treats of the *sign* of ordination. It likewise finds its first parallel in the text of Marseille/72. These parallel texts are virtually the same in content. The later text, however, demonstrates a greater Trinitarian awareness.

The next paragraph of the Accra text dealing with this topic is §47 which treats of the acknowledgement by the community of the one ordained and the commitment of the one ordained to the community. Again, the first parallel to this paragraph is found in Marseille/72. The content of the latter is virtually contained in the former. The emphasis on the phrase, "acknowledgement . . . of gifts," gives

---

[27]This is not to say, however, that there are no roots at all in the Montreal text. In that text, §s 93, 94 and 95 evince an awareness of the context of these later texts without taking the same careful and organized approach which they eventually do.

[28]Louvain/71, pp. 88-89.

[29]Added in Geneva/73, p. 12.

[30]Added in Marseille/72, p. 14.

[31]Added in Geneva/73, p. 12.

a more charismatic flavor to the ministry of the ordained.

Accra 48 is a direct quote from Louvain/71. Again, it finds no parallel in Montreal/63. The paragraph speaks for itself.

C. THE CONDITIONS FOR ORDINATION.

As these texts evolve in this section the content is shorter and more theological (rather than sociological). Emphasis is placed on the call to service in the ministry being from God; discernment of the call is required by the community as well as by the one to be ordained. Those called can live a married or a celibate life-style. Questions of ecclesiastical or non-ecclesiastical sources of income, full-time or part-time exercise of ministry and being ordained for service within or outside the visible organization of the Church are treated. Again, as the evolution of the texts proceeds the emphasis is less sociological, more theological. Some of the other issues considered here are the compatibility of ordination with leave of absence from ministry and there being no need to re-ordain with the resumption of ministry.

Louvain/71 [pp. 91-92]
V. Who is to be Ordained?

The New Testament suggests two criteria for determining who in particular should be ordained: a) an inward and personal call of God to the individual (cf. Gal. 1:15), b) a ratification and authentication of that call by the Church, which discerns the individual to have the gifts and potentialities for the ministry in question (cf. I Tim. 3). These two criteria have usually appeared in that order in the tradition of most of our Churches. The reverse order should also be considered; that is a) that a person should be sought out, selected and called by the Church to fulfil the ministry in question, and b) that he himself should inwardly assent to this call as a call from God.

So in Acts 6:3 the Church was commanded to find men with gifts appropriate to a particular ministry, upon whom hands could then be laid (and the searching out of such men is one meaning of *episkopein*). The call of God to ordination comes through the Church.

Appointment and Discipline

When a person is to be ordained the determining factor is the discernment by the Church that the person in question has the capacity to fulfil the responsibility which is to be put upon him. What the Church looks for in a person to be ordained is

Geneva/73 [p. 14]

1. The ordinand should be one who has a call from the Lord to dedicate himself to the particular style of ministry implied in ordination. This call will be discerned by the ordinand himself, by the Christian community and by its spiritual leaders. It is discerned through personal prayer and reflection, as well as through suggestion, example, encouragement, guidance coming from family, friends, teachers, the school, the congregation, the seminary. It will be tested and fostered and confirmed or perhaps modified particularly through the years of training.

a. Both celibacy and marriage are vocations from God and gifts of the Spirit. Either of these can be used by God to bless the ordained minister and enrich his ministry.

Accra/74

51. (i) The ordinand should be one who has a call from the Lord to dedicate himself to the particular style of ministry implied in ordination. This call will be discerned by the ordinand himself, by the Christian community and by its spiritual leaders. It is discerned through personal prayer and reflection, as well as through suggestion, example, encouragement, guidance coming from family, friends, teachers, the school, the congregation, the seminary. It will be tested and fostered and confirmed or perhaps modified, particularly through the years of training.

57. Both celibacy and marriage are vocations from God and gifts of the Spirit. Either of these can be used by God to bless the ordained minister and enrich his ministry.

Louvain/71 [pp. 91-92 cont.]

evident spiritual and personal maturity of Christian character, together with a particular aptitude or competence for the performance of the ministry itself, whatever it may be. The Church attempts to identify those to whom the necessary gifts have been given. To those with these gifts, who assent to the call of God through the Church, a further gift is spoken of in I Tim. 4:14 and II Tim. 1:6, as bestowed through the laying on of hands.

The process of selecting and ordaining particular persons can be seen *both* as the Church's "natural" activity as a social organism, which must supply to itself the leadership and other roles which it needs for its purposes, *and* (more deeply) as the initiative of God at every point for the fulfillment of his plan for the salvation of the world. Seen in this theological perspective, the selecting of the right person for ordination is a matter of grace at every point.

138

As appointment by the Church, ordination is preceded by preparation, probation and examination. After these responsibilities have been cared for, the Church formally recognizes the gifts and commitments of each ordinand and affirms its belief that he has been chosen and sent by God for ministry in his name and in that of the Church. Because ordination concerns the discernment of spiritual gifts, a risk is involved; thus this discernment must be under constant review. For the ordinand may be mistaken as to his suitability, or on the other hand the Church may not recognize or accept a gift offered to it. This means that ordination is also a testing of the Church, a test of its responsiveness and present openness to new forms of ministry.

Every office of ministry is, therefore, subject to the Church's discipline. The person "in orders" is also "under orders". The Church's responsibility as guardian of the Christian gospel, although vested particularly in those ministerial offices specifically charged with oversight (episkope), is in the last analysis a corporate stewardship. By its very act of granting ordination the Church as a body acknowledges the responsibility of the whole company of the faithful for the continuing guardianship of the apostolic testimony.

Montreal/63 [cont.]

101. Churches faced with rapidly changing situations are struggling to find forms of ministry relevant to their situation, and this not by abandoning traditional forms of the special ministry, but by seeking to give a diversity and flexibility such as we recognize in the New Testament and in the Church of the first centuries.

(a) In many parts of Asia and Africa, in the past, the traditional Western forms of the special ministry have often been preserved in all their institutional rigidity. This has led to the serious results of leaving many congregations in those areas virtually without sacramental life because they cannot support an ordained pastor, and of forming congregations whose energies are more introverted than directed toward strengthening the Church's service and witness in the world. The Church has appeared as an institution centered in a building, rather than as a company moving out into the world.

(b) In many parts of the world, the traditional settled parish-congrega-

140

tion of recent centuries has been changing rapidly. When there is a rapid development of urban and industrial society with its mobility of population and diversity of life, pastors serving within the existing parochial system find it increasingly difficult to minister effectively to the real communities in which men live and make their crucial decisions. In these cases there is need of new patterns of the special ministry; more dynamic, flexible, and relevant to the situation in which the ministry is at work.

Montreal/63

102. There are several possibilities of more flexible forms of ministry in the light of experiments, for example:

(a) The Church may ordain a man who works in a secular employment but has shown pastoral gifts. He will serve the local congregation as a pastor, while continuing his secular work as e.g. farmer or village teacher.

(b) In some sectors of society which are impenetrable to existing forms of ministry (such as certain areas of industrial life, where groups of Christians are learning to work and witness in terms of the conditions of life there), the best way to ensure the full witness of the Gospel may be to ordain members of these groups to the ministry of word and sacraments after appropriate training, so that they may build up the body of Christ without being "professional clergy".

(c) In a frontier situation, where there is not Christian community among the people, the Church may select a minister and send him into

Louvain/71 [pp. 94-95]

Thus at least three sets of educational-economic arrangements respecting ordained ministers can be discerned: (a) employment by the Church of some who have formal theological education, (b) secular employment for some who have such professional education (i.e. worker-priests or other "tent-making ministers"), (c) secular employment for some with other kinds of education or preparation in whom the Church discerns gifts for ordained ministry ("non-professional presbyters").

So long as the Church maintains appropriate discipline or regulations regarding the various forms of ministry, it need not require that all ordained ministers remain dependent upon it financially or give full time to its affairs. Rather, by ordaining to its ministry persons who earn their living in various professions, it may witness more effectively in numerous areas of society and may profit from the insights which these ministers bring to it from their particular disciplines and engagements.

The procedure being discussed

Geneva/73 [p. 15]

c. Ministries need not always be salaried from church sources. Financial support from the church is not essential to ordained ministry, and may, in cases, even diminish its effectiveness. While the Church has a clear duty to make financial provision for its servants, support may come from other sources, not excluding work done by the minister himself, provided this remains subordinate to and serves the purpose for which he was ordained. This possibility is often described as a "tentmaking" ministry, following the example of St. Paul.

d. The exercise of ministry could be full-time or part-time: both possibilities should be accepted. Nothing in Scripture demands that all ministers be full-time and employed by the Church. Full-time ministry has advantages and may be indispensable in some situations. There are, however, other circumstances in which part-time arrangements for ministerial leadership are possible and helpful. The secular experience of the minister, which is implied in these arrangements, could enrich the ministry, and the minister's work in

Accra/74

59. (c) Ministries need not always be salaried from Church sources. Financial support from the Church is not essential to ordained ministry and may, in some cases, even diminish its effectiveness. While the Church has a clear duty to make financial provision for its servants, support may come from other sources, not excluding work done by the minister himself, provided this remains subordinate to and serves the purpose for which he was ordained. This possibility is often described as a "tentmaking" ministry, following the example of St. Paul.

60. (d) The exercise of ministry could be full-time or part-time: both possibilities should be accepted. Nothing in Scripture demands all ministers be full-time and employed by the Church. Full-time ministry has advantages and may be indispensable in some situations. There are, however, other circumstances in which part-time arrangements for ministerial leadership are possible and helpful. The secular experience of the minister, which is implied in these arrangements, could enrich the

Montreal/63 [cont.]

some secular employment so that he becomes a part of the community and within it seeks to witness and to form the community of God's people. the Church.

(d) In highly specialized or diversified societies, the Church may consider the possibility of assigning to the professionally trained ordained minister a specific role to strengthen the witness and service of God's people in a particular sector of society, e.g. among industrial workers or other professional groups.

Louvain/71 [pp. 94-95 cont.]

seems to hold promise of providing ministry for areas of contemporary life now inadequately served by the Church. As examples, the villages of Asia and Africa, where Western standards for ordination have proved unrealistic, can be cited.

Geneva/73 [p. 15 cont.]

the secular world could commend the Gospel. On the other hand, the new problems which can arise for a minister in secular employment require sympathetic study.

e. While a good many will be ordained for service within the church's visible organization, the possibility of ordination for the church's ministry of word and sacrament outside this organization must always remain open. Such ordained persons might then live as bricklayers, as industrial managers, or as TV script writers for example.

ministry and the minister's work in the secular world could commend the Gospel. On the other hand, the new problems which can arise for a minister in secular employment require sympathetic study.

61. (e) While a good many will be ordained for service within the Church's visible organization, the possibility of ordination for the Church's ministry of word and sacrament outside this organization must always remain open. Such ordained persons might then live as bricklayers, as industrial managers or as TV scriptwriters for example.

Montreal/63 [cont.]

102. (e) In many pioneer situations in industrial and urban society a team ministry crossing denominational lines has been formed. Such a group ministry can be, within modern society, a visible manifestation of the solidarity of God's people. Thus the Church can perform a service among the people of today who genuinely seek fellowship in their perplexity and loneliness.

(f) In certain situations an itinerant ministry has enabled the Church to respond effectively to rapidly changing conditions.

Louvain/71 [p. 95 cont.]

There are also many kinds of "extraordinary situations". In parts of the world the church lives "in diaspora", unable to maintain the institutions of mor comfortable times and places and needing all the more a faithful ministry. In some places the Christian community is a tiny minority confronted by a hostile society. Feeling themselves isolated from their neighbours and their fellow believers, the faithful long for a clear witness to the apostolic gospel and regular celebration of the eucharist. Before multiplying the number of denominational ministers in competition with one another, Churches should explore opportunities for ecumenical cooperation and even local union of small congregations. Even so, a part-time or nonprofessional minister will provide the best answer to many a small community of Christians. Again, certain social classes in many societies have not been reached by "professional" ministers coming from the outside, but have responded to the ministries of persons of their own communities. It would seem to be a mistake to insist that such emergent leaders, accepted

Louvain/71 [p. 95 cont.]
by their communities, must be taken
out of their sociocultural *milieu*, to
be formally educated at a school of
theology outside of that context.

Louvain/71 [p. 94]

A person need not have a degree in theology or a salary from the Church in order to administer the eucharist; what he does need is the request of the Christian community and the Church's recognition of him as a minister. Such a person, who qualifies for ordination, even though a "non-professional", may also prove effective in occasional preaching. If theology is indeed the "attempt to relate the truths of God to the torments of the world", then an attorney, an economist, a youth sensitive to injustice, a housewife, a school teacher, a junior executive, or a scientist, none of whom have ever had formal theological education, may bring the word of God with particular power in certain situations. By a careful drafting of its standards for stated posts or types of appointment, and by more varied and imaginative approaches to education for such persons in the meaning of faith, the Church may use their services without compromising its commitment to learning or to theological responsibility.

Geneva/73 [p. 14]

3. The ordinand should be one capable of carrying out the ministry in informed fidelity to the Gospel of Christ and to Christ's lordship over the actual situation within which the service is rendered. He should be able to read and discern the signs of the times. He should, therefore, be appropriately prepared through adequate study of scripture and theology, and through sufficient acquaintance with the social and human realities of the actual situation.

[p. 15]

b. The academic programme should be flexible and considerable elasticity is to be admitted in requirements regarding degrees. To be sure, the ordained minister requires a competence suitable to the style of ministry to be undertaken, and calls for the intellectual training necessary to understand the questions men around are asking and to search along with them for theological answers. It does not, however, follow that such competence and training are achieved only through formal study, or the acquisition of degrees, or prescribed patterns of formation. The variety of situations and of groups to be served demand various types of preparation for the ministry. Team ministries, in particular, will find their capacity to serve greatly enhanced and enriched by diversified formation. What is said here is in no way intended to diminish the importance to the Church of its doctors of theology, its trained interpreters of Scripture, or its experts in other disciplines. It

Accra/74

53. (iii) The ordinand should be one capable of carrying out the ministry in informed fidelity to the Gospel of Christ and to Christ's lordship over the actual situation within which the service is rendered. He should be able to read and discern the signs of the times. He should, therefore, be appropriately prepared through adequate study of Scripture and theology, and through sufficient acquaintance with the social and human realities of the actual situation.

58. (b) The academic programme should be flexible and considerable elasticity is to be admitted in requirements regarding degrees. To be sure, the ordained minister requires a competence suitable to the style of ministry to be undertaken and calls for the intellectual training necessary to understand the questions men around are asking and to search along with them for theological answers. It does not, however, follow that such competence and training are achieved only through formal study or the acquisition of degrees or prescribed patterns of formation. The variety of situations and of groups to be served demand various types of preparation for the ministry. Team ministries, in particular, will find their capacity to serve greatly enhanced by diversified formation. What is said here is in no way intended to diminish the importance to the Church of its doctors of theology, its trained interpreters of Scripture or its experts in other disciplines. It is intended, rather, to emphasize

146

Geneva/73 [p. 15 cont.]
is intended, rather, to emphasize the truth that certain kinds of ministry may need other competences even more, including extensive experience in the "secular" world.

Accra/74 [cont.]
the truth that certain kinds of ministry may need other competences even more, including extensive experience in the "secular" world.

Montreal/63 [cont.]
those who are ordained.
This recovery is one of the
most important facts of recent church history, and we
express our gratitude in this
connection for the work of
the Department on the Laity
of the World Council of
Churches, and especially for
the paper entitled Christ's
Ministry and the Ministry of
the Church (Laity Bulletin
No. 15, available from the
W.C.C.) which has been the
starting point of our discussion.

Louvain/71 [p. 78-79 cont.]
their task *in* the world, they
are beginning to see the
place and ministry of the
ordained person in a new
light also.

Marseille/72 [p. 3 cont.]
men are asking, as they are
taking more seriously the
problem of their task *in* the
world, they are beginning to
see the place and ministry of
the ordained person in a
new light also.

The Accra text provides an entire section entitled, "Conditions for Ordination." [See Appendix, Accra/74, §s 50-63.] In this study we are treating only those paragraphs which eventually effect the Lima text.

The text of Accra, §s 51 and 57, is found exactly in its immediate precursor text, Geneva/73. In a more general way much background material is supplied by the Louvain/71 text in much lengthier fashion. It is important to point out in another place in the Louvain text a reference to theological methodology which touches on the opening ideas of Accra's treatment of the conditions for ordination. This reference states that "scholars have often theologized from Christ to the ministry, and then to the sacraments and the Church, whereas the more appropriate order might be from Christ to Christian community, and then to ministry and sacraments."[32]

The text of Accra, §s 59-61, was first written in its immediate precursor text, Geneva/73. In a more general way the background material is given in both Louvain/71 and Montreal/63 in lengthier fashion. The movement from a more sociological treatment of the matter to a more theological treatment is clear.

The text of Accra, §s 53 and 58, are found in the text immediately preceding. There is one paragraph in the Louvain/71 text which corresponds to this content.

The only other paragraph of this section in Accra/74 to have textual roots before Accra is §62. It treats at length the related topics of time limitations to service in the ordained ministry, e.g., leave of absence as compatible with ordination, and resumption of ministry requiring no re-ordination. Those two parallel treatments are as follows:

Geneva/73 [pp. 15-16]	*Accra/74*
f. While the initial commitment to ordained ministry ought normally to be made without reserve or time limit, leave of absence from service is not incompatible with ordination and should be granted on reasonable grounds. There may also be cases in which an ordained minister wishes to relinquish exercise of his special ministry; a request made for serious reasons to relinquish it should be granted with-out opprobrium or reproach. Such a procedure need not mean in every case that the minister's service was not blessed by the Holy Spirit, or that the initial act of ordination was a mistake, or that one's status as an ordained person and the special relationship to the community constituted by	62. (f) While the initial commitment to or-dained ministry ought normally to be made without reserve or time limit, leave of absence from service is not incompatible with ordination and should be granted on reasonable grounds. There may also be cases in which an ordained minister wishes to relinquish exercise of his special ministry; a request made for serious reasons to relinquish it should be granted without opprobrium or reproach. Such a procedure need not mean in every case that the minister's service was not blessed by the Holy Spirit, or that the initial act of ordination was a mistake, or that one's status as an ordained person and the special relationship to the community constituted by

---

[32]Louvain/71, p. 90.

ordination ceases to exist. Resumption of ministry will require no re-ordination.

ordination ceases to exist. Resumption of ministry will require no re-ordination.

VI. TOWARDS THE MUTUAL RECOGNITION OF THE ORDAINED MINISTRIES.

What is clear here is that the goal of a visible unity (as expressed in the 1961 New Delhi Assembly of WCC) is the controlling principle of the entire effort of Faith and Order in its treatment of baptism, eucharist and ministry.

There is an increasing use of words and phrases theologically rich in meaning. These expressions are as follows: "rite," "intention to transmit the apostolic ministry of the Word of God and of the sacraments," "sacramentality," "invocation (*epiklesis*) of the Holy Spirit," "traditions."

There is an explicit appeal to churches with an episcopal succession and churches without such a succession regarding their attitude toward each other. What is at stake most especially is the possession of apostolic faith and a ministry corresponding to that faith. Even more remarkable here is the ecumenically bold statement, made in the context of the appeal to the churches without an episcopal succession, that they lack the fullness of *the sign of apostolic succession.*

Montreal/63

152. We believe that the Church Universal is manifest in locality only as all Christians in that place fulfil the unity which is described in the statement of the New Delhi Assembly of the World Council of Churches (cp. *New Delhi Speaks*, SCM Press, 1962, p. 55): "We believe that the unity which is both God's will and his gift to his Church is being made visible as all in each place who are baptized into Jesus Christ and confess him as Lord and Savior are brought by the Holy Spirit into one fully committed fellowship, holding one apostolic faith, preaching the one Gospel, breaking the one bread, joining in common prayer, and having a corporate life reaching out in witness and service to all, and who at the same time are united with the whole Christian fellowship in all places and all ages in such wise that ministry and members are ac-

Louvain/71 [p. 96]

The New Delhi Assembly of the World Council of Churches in looking to the future unity of the Church, visualized a concrete vision of Christian unity that would be visible as well as spiritual. It expressed the conviction that the unity which is both God's will and his gift included a ministry accepted by all. [*New Delhi Report* (London: SCM Press, 1962), p. 116.]

Marseille/72 [p. 25]

CHAPTER VI: TOWARDS THE RECOGNITION AND RECONCILIATION OF MINISTRIES

1. The Road to be travelled

(New Delhi statement on unity)

Geneva/73 [p. 23]

C. PROPOSALS FOR ADVANCING ON THE WAY TOWARDS MUTUAL RECOGNITION

In order to advance towards the goal expressed in the New Delhi statement deliberate efforts are required. Discussion can help to clarify the issues but discussion alone will not solve the problem. The churches must ready themselves for actual changes in their approach and their practice.

Accra/74

101. In order to advance towards the goal expressed in the New Delhi statement, deliberate efforts are required. Discussion can help to clarify the issues but discussion alone will not solve the problem. The churches must ready themselves for actual changes in their approach and their practice.

Montreal/63 [cont.]

cepted by all, and that all can act and speak together as occasion requires for the tasks to which God calls his people."

Louvain/71

11. Finally, bi-lateral conversations, Faith and Order studies and statements, and most Plans of Church Union have come close to unanimity in stating that: (a) ordination is regarded as divinely instituted, and (b) that the prayer of the Church connected with ordination is an efficacious invocation of the Holy Spirit for the strengthening of the one ordained. [*See, for example, statements drawn up as a result of Roman Catholic/Reformed and Roman Catholic/Lutheran bilateral conversations.]

Marseille/72 [p. 26]

According to what was said, above, two things are of crucial importance for mutual recognition of ordination practice. First, the rite used must express the intention to transmit the apostolic ministry of the word of God and of the sacraments. Second, the rite must include an invocation (*epiklesis*) of the Holy Spirit and the layingon of hands. The invocation of the Holy Spirit is intended to safeguard and to attest what in some traditions is called the "sacramentality" of ordination.

Geneva/73 [p. 23]

According to what was said above, two things are of crucial importance for mutual recognition of ordination proactice. First, the rite used must express the intention to transmit the apostolic ministry of the word of God and of the sacraments. Second, the rite must include an invocation (epiklesis) of the Holy Spirit and the layingon of hands. The invocation of the Holy Spirit is intended to safeguard and to attest what in some traditions is called the "sacramentality" of ordination.

In order to achieve mutual recognition, different steps are required of different churches:

Accra/74

102. According to what was said above, two things are of crucial importance for mutual recognition of ordination practice. First, the rite used must express the intention to transmit the apostolic ministry of the Word of God and of the sacraments. Second, the rite must include an invocation (*epiklesis*) of the Holy Spirit and the layingon of hands. The invocation of the Holy Spirit is intended to safeguard and to attest what in some traditions is called the "sacramentality" of ordination.

Marseille/72 [pp. 26-27]

1. (a) Churches which have preserved the episcopal succession have to recognize the real content of the ordained ministry that exists in churches that do not have such an episcopal succession. In spite of the mutual separation of both kinds of church, the God who is ever faithful to His promises gives to the communities that lack the episcopal succession but that live in a succession of apostolic faith, a ministry of the Word and Sacraments the value of which is attested by its fruits.

(b) The churches without episcopal succession have to recognize that, while they may not lack a succession in the apostolic faith, they do not have the fullness of the sign of apostolic succession. If full visible unity is to be achieved, the fullness of the sign of apostolic succession ought to be recovered.

2. (a) It is necessary that the value of the episcopal ministry, particularly in its pastoral aspect, should be reasserted, and that its significance as a personally embodied sign of visible unity should be rediscovered.

(b) On the other hand it is necessary to recognize ordained ministries that exist apart from an epis-

Geneva/73 [p. 24]

1. (a) Churches which have preserved the episcopal succession have to recognize the real content of the ordained ministry that exists in churches that do not have such an episcopal succession. In spite of the mutual separation of both kinds of church, the God who is ever faithful to his promises gives to the communities that lack the episcopal succession but that live in a succession of apostolic faith, a ministry of the Word and sacraments the value of which is attested by its fruits. These communities have also, in many cases, developed a vital lay ministry.

(b) The churches without episcopal succession have to realize that churches which value such succession have also retained a ministry of word and sacraments through the centuries, and while the former may not lack a succession in the apostolic faith, they do not have the fullness of the *sign* of apostolic succession. If full visible unity is to be achieved, the fullness of the sign of apostolic succession ought to be recovered.

2. (a) Churches with episcopal succession should reassert the value of episcopal ministry, particularly in its pastoral aspects, and should work in order that others might discover its significance as a personally embodied sign of visible unity.

(b) These churches should also consider the desirability of recognizing some ordained ministries

Accra/74

103. (i) (a) Churches which have preserved the episcopal succession have to recognize the real content of the ordained ministry that exists in churches that do not have such an episcopal succession. In spite of the mutual separation of the two kinds of churches, the God who is ever faithful to his promises gives to the communities that lack the episcopal succession but that live in a succession of apostolic faith, a ministry of the word and sacrament the value of which is attested by its fruits. These communities have also, in many cases, developed a vital lay ministry.

104. (i) (b) The churches without episcopal succession have to realize that churches which value such succession have also retained a ministry of word and sacraments through the centuries and while the former may not lack a succession in the apostolic faith, they do not have the fullness of the *sign* of apostolic succession. If full visible unity is to be achieved, the fullness of the sign of apostolic succession ought to be recovered.

105. (ii) (a) Churches with episcopal succession should reassert the value of episcopal ministry, particularly in its pastoral aspects, and should work in order that others might discover its significance as a personally embodied sign of visible unity.

106. (ii) (b) These churches should also consider the desirability of recognizing some ordained

Marseille/72 [pp. 26-27 cont.]

copal succession but which embody a succession of ordained ministers who combine in their ministries the functions of both bishop and presbyter. It may also be possible to recognize some ministries that do not claim a formal episcopal or episcopal-presbyterial succession in the apostolic faith.

Louvain/71 [p. 100]

Second, it should be noted that church unions already accomplished reveal that ministries of Churches uniting can be brought together, renewed and enlarged in scope as the Churches themselves come before God in repentance, love and acceptance. Some unions already accomplished reveal that ministries of Churches uniting can be brought together, renewed and enlarged in scope as the Churches themselves come before God in repentance, love and acceptance of existing ministry, with all new ordinations to be made b bishops, while others plan a mutual laying on of hands of each, by all. In all union plans, both accomplished and proposed, it is recognized that reordination is not being undertaken, but rather, a unique service, attempting to reconcile and unify ministries of previously divided Churches.

Geneva/73 [p. 24 cont.]

that exist apart from an episcopal succession but which embody a succession of ordained ministers who combine in their ministries the functions of both bishop and presbyter. It may also be possible to recognize some ministries that do not claim a formal episcopal or episcopal-presbyterial succession but that in fact exist with the express intention of maintaining a succession in the apostolic faith.

Geneva/73 [p. 23]

The mutual recognition of the churches and their ministries implied a public act from which point unity would be fully realized. Several forms of such a public act have been worked out or proposed: mutual imposition of hands, eucharistic concelebration, solemn worship without a particular rite, the simple reading of a text of union during the course of a celebration. No one liturgical form would be absolutely required, but in any case it would be necessary to proclaim the accomplishment of such mutual recognition publicly. And the common celebration of the Lord's Supper would certainly be in place in the midst of such a service.

Accra/74 [cont.]

ministries that exist apart from an episcopal succession but which embody a succession of ordained ministers who combine in their ministries the functions of both bishop and presbyter. It may also be possible to recognize some ministries that do not claim a formal episcopal or episcopal-presbyteral succession but that in fact exist with the express intention of maintaining a succession in the apostolic faith.

Accra/74

99. The mutual recognition of the churches and their ministries implied a public act from which point unity would be fully realized. Several forms of such a public act have been proposed: mutual imposition of hands, eucharistic non-celebration (*sic*), solemn worship without a particular rite, the simple reading of a text of union during the course of a celebration. No one liturgical form would be absolutely required, but in any case it would be necessary to proclaim the accomplishment of such mutual recognition publicly. And the common celebration of the Lord's Supper would certainly be the place for such a service.

The Accra/74 text has a long section entitled, "Towards the Recognition of and the Reconciliation of Ministries (§s 88-106). It has three subsections, the third of which is entitled, "Proposals for Advancing on the Way towards Mutual Recognition" (§s 101-106). It is this subsection for the most part which finds its way to the final text at Lima.[33] The only exceptions are one paragraph in an earlier subsection (§99) which deals with the content of the final paragraph at Lima and the paragraphs from the earlier section on "the ordination of women" (§s 64-69) which were considered above in the treatment of "the ministry of men and women in the church."

The Accra text refers to the goal, which is stated in the earlier text, Montreal/63, part of which expresses a being *"united with the whole Christian fellowship in all places and all ages in such wise that ministry and members are accepted by all.*[34] Clearly, this statement, originally from the 1961 New Delhi Assembly of the WCC, sets the tone for this section and the entire treatment of ministry for that matter. A visible unity which can be experienced throughout the world is the controlling principle in this overall effort of Faith and Order.

There are no textual roots in Montreal/63 for the contents of Accra 102. Although Louvain/71 treats the matter, Marseille/72 provides the first rendering of what is contained word for word in Accra 102. It is helpful to compare the Louvain and Marseille texts in order to note the evolution of the text more clearly.

Accra 103 and 104 are paragraphs which directly influence the final Lima text. The earliest textual roots of these two paragraphs are in Marseille/72. It is helpful to see the development of the appropriate paragraphs of the texts (above).

Accra 105 and 106 are also rooted in the Marseille text. They place more obligations on churches with episcopal ministry and were deleted after Accra.

The issue of the ordination of women is considered in this section in the Lima text (and its immediate precursors) and also in an earlier section, "The Ministry of Men and Women in the Church." At this stage of textual evolution (the Accra stage), however, the issue is considered in a special section entitled, "The Ordination of Women." The consideration begins in earnest with the Louvain/71 text. There the bias is clearly in favor of ordination of women as seen in the following:

---

[33]The two subsections of the Accra text which do not, for the most part, find their way to Lima deal explicitly with divisions among the churches and various degrees of recognition of ministries among the churches.

[34]Montreal/63, §152. Emphasis added.

154

Since those who advocate the ordination of women do so out of their understanding of the meaning of the Gospel and ordination, and since the experience of the Churches in which women are ordained has been positive and none has found reason to reconsider its decision, the question must be asked as to whether it is not time for all the Churches to confront this matter forthrightly. Churches which ordain women have found that women's gifts and graces are as wide and varied as men's, and that their ministry is fully as blessed by the Holy Spirit as the ministry of men. But even Churches which already ordain women must guard against discriminatory tendencies, since a real ambiguity can be observed in these Churches — the women ordained have usually been given positions of juridical and pastoral inferiority. The force of nineteen centuries of tradition against the ordination of women cannot be lightly ignored. But traditions have been changed in the Church. This question must be faced, and the time to face it is now.[35]

The text which follows, Marseille/72, adopts a more balanced and ecumenical tone. It can be compared to the Accra/74 text which is substantially the same one written for the text of Geneva/73:

Marseille/72

For most communions, the role of women in the ministry is a matter of discipline and not of doctrine, although there are doctrinal positions relevant to the question. If agreement could be reached that the disciplinary status of the question predominates, the issue could be decided by a future ecumenical council. Short of that differences of opinion on this subject may not, even now, need to be obstacles to the mutual recognition of ministry. Ecumenical considerations need not restrain a full and frank facing of this question.[36]

Accra/74

69. For some churches these problems are not yet alive. While recording a position, they have not yet determined whether the decisive factors are doctrinal and disciplinary factors or about their relation. Differences on this issue could raise possible obstacles to the mutual recognition of ministries. But these obstacles should not be regarded as unsuperable. Openness to each other holds out the possibility that the Spirit may well speak to one Church through the insights of another. Ecumenical awareness and responsibility also demand that once a Church has decided what is timely and right, it should act in obedience to its own conviction. Since the opinion appears to be growing that doctrinal considerations either favour the ordination of women or are neutral, the possibility is open that a future ecumenical council might deal with the question. Ecumenical considerations, therefore, should encourage, not restrain, the full, frank facing of this question.[37]

[35]Louvain/71, p. 93.

[36]Marseille/72, p. 17.

[37]Cf. also Geneva/73, p. 17.

The later text is more nuanced and more clearly recognizes the complexity of the issue. The possibility of an ecumenical council to decide such an issue is put forth as a viable option.

The very last paragraph of the Accra text which directly influenced the Lima text is Accra 99. It was first written in the text of Geneva/73. The only textual precursor is that of Louvain/71. The three texts seen side by side (above) indicate the lines of development. No mention of re-ordination is mentioned in the later text. And the fittingness of the "common celebration of the Lord's Supper" stands out among the several approaches to the public proclamation of mutual recognition.

SUMMARY.

It is difficult to determine the precise influence of individuals in each of these meetings which produced the significant texts under study here. A list of participants (not always possible to find) at each meeting will have to suffice.

Gerald F. Moede (Methodist) was certainly a predominant figure in the group which produced the Louvain/71 text and those of Marseille/72 and Geneva/73 as well. [cf Archives mimeographed material §B-3] Max Thurian (Reformed) was another prominent figure along with Lukas Vischer (Reformed) and Günther Gassmann (Lutheran).

I. THE CALLING OF THE WHOLE PEOPLE OF GOD.

With the Marseille/72 text the christological and pneumatological themes are introduced with some detail. The ministry of both the historical Jesus and the Christ of faith is explicitly stated.

Communion with the Trinity in the Church is explicitly introduced with the text of Geneva/73. The themes of forgiveness, repentance and freedom are major elements of this experience of communion. And the fact that God's purpose for all human beings is membership in the Church is stated.

The Church's (not just Christ's) relationship to the Kingdom of God is clearly introduced with the text of Marseille/72, especially as that relates to the members of the Church struggling alongside the oppressed of this world toward the freedom and dignity promised with the coming of the Kingdom.

Regarding ordained ministry's relationship to other gifts of the Spirit, the note is added in Accra that ordained ministry cannot be carried out independently of the general ministry of the whole people and in some superior mode.

II. THE CHURCH AND THE ORDAINED MINISTRY.
DEFINITION OF TERMS.

None of the texts of these years had introduced such a treatment.

A. THE ORDAINED MINISTRY.

The continuity and necessity of the ministry of the apostles is emphasized. The essential functions of the ordained ministry are specified. And the interdependence of the community and the ordained minister is underscored.

B. ORDAINED MINISTRY AND AUTHORITY.

Geneva/73 is the text most responsible for the material in this section of Accra/74. No material is found in the earliest of the texts of this period, namely, Montreal/63.

The rootedness of authority is christological; the scriptural basis of this authority is cited in the text of Accra/74 with a special emphasis on the commissioning by Christ of the apostles and on the ministry of Paul.

It is a divine authority not given as an individual possession. Thus its exercise involves community participation. And it involves a communion (with the community) which can protect its exercise from being one of domination and insure its being one of genuine service.

C. ORDAINED MINISTRY AND PRIESTHOOD.

The earliest text to treat directly this topic of the priesthood of the ordained ministry is that of Geneva/73. The Montreal and Louvain texts treat only the priesthood of all in the Church.

An acknowledgement of the importance of tradition is made. There is indicated the reluctance on the part of the "churches of the Reformation" to use the word "priesthood" in reference to the ordained ministry. The overriding goal of unity demands the laying aside of this reluctance.

The functions of ordained priests point to the priestly reality of Christ and of the baptized, a reality upon which the reality of ordained priesthood is based and a reality which exceeds that of ordained priesthood. Sacrifice and intercession are noted as characteristic of priesthood. The Accra text notes that the ordained minister "fulfils his particular priestly service in strengthening, building up and expressing the royal and prophetic priesthood of the faithful through the service of the Gospel, the leading of the liturgical and sacramental life of the eucharistic community, and intercession." (Accra 21) It is important for ecumenical dialogue that cultic and intercessory aspects of the priesthood of the ordained are added in the Accra text.

The ordained ministry is "of a completely new and different nature in relation to the sacrificial priesthood of the Old Testament." (Accra 22) This ministry is like that of Paul to the Gentiles, serving the mission in the world for the building up of the Church.

D. THE MINISTRY OF MEN AND WOMEN IN THE CHURCH.

This period of the evolution of the text demonstrates a movement from a mere footnote reference to an entire section devoted to the topic of the ordination of women. Although the arguments for and against women's ordination are given, the impression is that the text favors the arguments for. This is especially evident in the statement in the Louvain text, quoted above, that "traditions have changed in the Church." (Louvain/71, p. 93) It is only with the texts which follow Accra/74 that the issue is placed in the larger context of "the ministry of men and women in the Church."

III. THE FORMS OF THE ORDAINED MINISTRY.

A. BISHOPS, PRESBYTERS AND DEACONS.

In this time period of the evolution of the text there is an acknowledgement of the importance and even divinely given nature of the three-fold ministry (cf. Louvain/71). There is, however, with the Geneva/73 and Accra/74 texts, a willingness to accept a functional approach and to see the three-fold ministry alongside other equally important ecclesial structures.

B. Guiding Principles for the Exercise of the Ordained Ministry in the Church.
C. Functions of Bishops, Presbyters and Deacons.

D. Variety of Charisms.

As was indicated above, these three sections (of the Lima text) are not traceable to the Accra text and those texts which precede it.

IV. Succession in the Apostolic Tradition.

A. Apostolic Tradition in the Church.

This section is marked by the great influence of the Marseille/72 meeting. While there is an effort to avoid heavily laden metaphysical words, e.g., "essential," there is a movement away from the sociological approach of Louvain/71. The aim of achieving ecumenical convergence is clearly becoming the overriding concern of these texts. And, finally, there is a movement toward (although not made entirely clear at this point) the contextualizing of the issue of the succession of apostolic ministry within that of the succession of apostolic tradition. Thus, ecclesiology is seen more and more explicitly as the key to the proper understanding of ministry.

B. Succession of the Apostolic Ministry.

The Accra/74 text is not textually rooted in any clear fashion in that of Montreal/63. It is true, however, that the Montreal text acknowledges the connection between the authority conferred by ordination and the preservation of the apostolic faith.

Textually Accra/74 is here rooted in Geneva/73 and Marseille/72. In all three texts the issue of apostolic succession is not clearly contextualized in that of apostolic tradition. A movement is noted toward endorsing episcopal succession "as an efficacious sign, not a guarantee, of the continuity of the Church in apostolic faith and mission." (Marseille/72, pp. 11-12)

Churches without the historic episcopate are urged to be open to its acceptance for the sake of church unity. In fact "the episcopal functions and reality

have been preserved in many of these churches with or without the title 'bishop'."
(Marseille/72, p. 12)

V. ORDINATION

A. THE MEANING OF ORDINATION.

This section of the Accra/74 text is not reflected in that of Montreal/63.
Louvain/71 provides some of the content, with Marseille/72 and Geneva/73 adding
to that content.

The Louvain text notes the binding relationship of ordination to Christ (both
historical and risen) and to the mission and teaching of the apostles. The Marseille
text is careful to add a reference to the role of the Spirit.

The Marseille and Geneva texts state that ordination is an action both by God
and the community. An analysis is given of the etymological roots of the word,
"ordination," itself with a caution regarding the various sociological settings to which
it owes its origin and development. This is noted especially in regard to the clear
distinction which came to be made between clergy and laity.

B. THE ACT OF ORDINATION.

It is the Louvain/71 and Marseille/72 texts which provide the original content
for this section of the Accra/74 text. The Accra text clarifies the three elements that
constitute the act of ordination: by adding to the invocation of the Holy Spirit a
reference to the liturgical term, *epiclesis*, by referring to the sign of the laying on of
hands as sacramental, and by insisting on God's offer of the call to the ordained
ministry as prior to the Church's offering to God of the one ordained.

The Accra text clarifies the first element, the invocation of the Holy Spirit,
by broadening the scope of the ministry beyond that of the local community to that
of the Church universal and the whole world. The initiative of God is again pointed
out as well as the Church's absolute dependence on the outcome of ordination, which
outcome is not predictable.

The second element, the sign of ordination, is again called sacramental. The
Marseille text adds this. God's freedom is acknowledged but faith, based on God's
(the Father's) faithfulness to promises made in Christ, is the assurance that the act of

ordination will bring about the effect signified, namely, the *spirit*ual relationship between the Church and the one ordained.

To the third element, the acknowledgement by the Church of the one ordained, is added discernment of the gifts of the Spirit received by the one to be ordained prior to the Church's acknowledgement. The mutual responsibilities of the Church and the one ordained toward one another are stated. Again, it is the Marseille text which introduces this content. The Accra text adds a more charismatic flavor to the content by its reference to the acknowledgement of the gifts found in the one ordained.

A paragraph from Louvain/71 emphasizing the involvement of the community in the process of ordination (in the calling, choosing, and training, as well as in the liturgical ceremony) is quoted in its entirety in Accra/74. This is to "experience and demonstrate the truth that setting apart is not to some superior level of discipleship, but rather to service within the Church." (Louvain/71, p. 88 and Accra 48)

C. THE CONDITIONS FOR ORDINATION.

The content of this section of the Accra/74 text is given in a general fashion in the texts of Louvain/71 and even Montreal/63. The treatment is lengthier in the earlier texts; and the emphasis is more sociological and less theological than that of Accra. For the most part the actual textual predecessor of the Accra text is its immediate precursor, Geneva/73.

The ordinand is one who receives a call from the Lord. This call, discerned by the ordinand *himself* (emphasis added), the Christian community and its leaders, is tested, fostered and confirmed. The call may involve either celibacy or marriage for the ordained minister.

Questions of ecclesiastical or non-ecclesiastical sources of income, full-time or part-time exercise of ministry and being ordained for service within or outside the visible organization of the Church are treated. The Accra text gives a briefer and less sociological treatment to these questions. The same is true for the questions of adequate competency and proper training for the ordained ministry. The Accra text seems less caught up with the spirit of activism and social ministry, a spirit more characteristic of the two earlier texts of this period under study here. This seems to correspond to the comments made to this present writer (and reported above in

Chapter I) by Frère Max Thurian.

The only other paragraph of this section in the Accra text (finding its way in some form to the text of Lima) which is rooted in an earlier text (Geneva/73) treats the topics of time limitations to service in the ordained ministry, e.g., leave of absence as compatible with ordination, and resumption of ministry requiring no re-ordination.

VI. TOWARDS THE MUTUAL RECOGNITION OF THE ORDAINED MINISTRIES.

The goal of a visible unity which can be experienced throughout the world (as expressed in the 1961 New Delhi Assembly of WCC) is the controlling principle of the entire effort of Faith and Order in its treatment of baptism, eucharist and ministry. This principle is brought to bear in a practical and concrete way in this section of the Accra text. Only a part of this section finds its way to Lima. What is later left out are Accra's explicit treatment of divisions among the churches and various degrees of recognition of ministries among the churches.

The influence of the Marseille text here is very significant. The Accra text (following the exact wording of Marseille) is characterized here by the explicit use of words and phrases which are theologically rich in meaning. These expressions are as follows: "rite," "intention to transmit the apostolic ministry of the Word of God and of the sacraments," "sacramentality," "invocation (*epiklesis*) of the Holy Spirit," "traditions." It is to be noted that terms such as "divinely instituted" and "efficacious" were not retained.

Again, the Marseille influence is evident in Accra's explicit appeal to churches with an episcopal succession and churches without such a succession regarding their attitude toward each other's possession of apostolic faith and a ministry corresponding to that faith. Even more remarkable is the ecumenically bold statement, made in the context of the appeal to the churches without an episcopal succession, that they lack the fullness of *the sign of apostolic succession*. The guiding principle from the New Delhi statement on visible church unity is again in evidence.

It should be noted that two paragraphs (found in Marseille and Accra) which placed additional obligations on churches with episcopal ministry were deleted after Accra.

The Accra text recognizes the complexity of the issue of the ordination of women. It takes a more nuanced approach than its predecessors, especially the Louvain text, in which the issue is first treated in earnest. The Accra text sees as a viable option the call for an ecumenical council to settle the matter.

Full unity is the aim of mutual recognition although the Accra text admits a partial unity or unity in lesser degrees. (After Accra this treatment of unity by degrees is dropped.) The actual mutual recognition of the churches *and* their ministries implies a public act. To the several forms which that public act might take the Accra text adds (to its precursor's, the Louvain/71's text) several possible approaches, stating the fittingness of the "common celebration of the Lord's Supper."

CHAPTER III

ACCRA/74 TO GENEVA/6-80

The documents which comprise this period in the evolution of the Lima text are the results of the following meetings:

1) Accra, Ghana, July 23-August 4, 1974 meeting of the FO Commission (resulting text heretofore referred to as "Accra/74");

2) Geneva, May 17-20, 1979 meeting of the Steering Group (resulting text heretofore referred to as "Geneva/79");

3) Geneva, January 16-19, 1980 meeting of the Steering Committee under the presidency of Max Thurian
   (*two texts*, one provided at the beginning of the meeting and the other resulting from the deliberations of the meeting, heretofore referred to, respectively, as "Geneva/1-16-80" and "Geneva/1-19-80" or occasionally together as "Geneva/1-80")

4) Geneva, June 3-7, 1980 meeting of the same steering committee which had met the previous January (resulting text heretofore referred to as "Geneva/6-80").

In this chapter many of the same themes discovered already in the preceding chapter are developed. The call to become God's people is clearly issued to all of humanity. The theological themes of the paschal mystery and eschatology are introduced. The treatment of the issues surrounding ministry becomes steadily more theological and less sociological.

A glossary of a few basic terms is introduced during this stage of development in order to help clarify the discussion.

The Twelve are carefully distinguished from the other apostles. The making of this distinction and other such efforts show a great respect which the writers of these texts have for recent scripture and history study. Such insights help to lessen the tendency to claim too much in terms of one's own present church offices and structures.

The authority of the ordained ministry is given a more nuanced treatment especially in terms of its communitarian aspects.

The issue of priesthood receives a more in-depth treatment during this stage, especially the relationship between the priesthood of the ordained and the priesthood of Christ.

More and more unwillingness to face the issue of women's ordination, at least in this particular text of Faith and Order, is detected.

The threefold ministry of bishop, presbyter and deacon, due to the deep influence of the Orthodox churches in Faith and Order, gains greatly in prominence during this stage of the development of the text. And a sharper distinction is drawn between the *ministry* of the ordained and the *service* of all others in the church.

An important distinction is drawn between apostolic tradition and apostolic succession. It will influence greatly the acceptance of non-episcopal church ideas. At the same time the treatment of the ministry of the episcopacy is enhanced and encouraged

Ecumenical considerations cause the issue of ordination to be treated in a more and more inclusive fashion. A call is issued for a more careful investigation into the intentions expressed in the liturgical texts of the various churches.

The text becomes steadily more realistic ecumenically, more precise in its use of terminology and more inviting to dialogue.

As in the previous chapter we use the outline of the Lima text as a guide. That outline is as follows:

I.   THE CALLING OF THE WHOLE PEOPLE OF GOD

II.   THE CHURCH AND THE ORDAINED MINISTRY

    - One paragraph clarifying terminology

    A. The Ordained Ministry

    B. Ordained Ministry and Authority

    C. Ordained Ministry and Priesthood

    D. The Ministry of Men and Women in the Church

III. THE FORMS OF THE ORDAINED MINISTRY

    A. Bishops, Presbyters and Deacons

    B. Guiding Principles for the Exercise of the Ordained Ministry in the Church

    C. Functions of Bishops, Presbyters and Deacons

    D. Variety of Charisms

IV. SUCCESSION IN THE APOSTOLIC TRADITION

I. THE CALLING OF THE WHOLE PEOPLE OF GOD.

The study begins with the call of all humanity, not simply the call of Christ and Christians (the baptized). The trinitarian focus is sharpened with regard to the roles of Father, Son and Spirit in salvation history. The Paschal Mystery of Christ is introduced as a central theme. With regard to the historical Jesus there is a sharpened awareness of the distinction between who he *is* and what he *did*, with an emphasis on the former. There are spiritual bonds that bind members of the Church which are not reducible to institutional realities. A more theological treatment is given as the evolution of the text proceeds. The sociological realities surrounding official ministry are still treated but the emphasis on them is not as heavy as in the earlier stage, especially in the Louvain/71 text. Worship and ministry are closely linked. And, finally, in this first major section, eschatology is introduced as a theological theme.

Accra/74

3. The Lord Jesus Christ, through his Word and Spirit, forgives sins and delivers men from the lordship of the powers of destruction; He continues to gather worshipping communities out of this broken world, the one people of God, coming from the water of baptism; He builds them up through Word and Sacrament.

Geneva/79

A. *The Origin of the Ecclesial Community and the Ordained Ministry*

3. The ecclesial community and the ordained ministry have a common origin:

in the mission of the Father, who sends the Son for the salvation of the world (Jn. 20:21);

in the institution of Christ who sends the apostles to make disciples, evangelize humankind, baptize believers, and celebrate his memorial (Mt. 28:1820; Lk. 22:19);

in the power of the Spirit who distributes his gifts among the baptized so that they may become witnesses and servants of the Word of God, among the ordained ministers so that they may become stewards of the mysteries of God (1 Cor. 4:1).

Geneva/1-16-80

3. In this broken world God has called into being the Church. He has revealed himself in Jesus Christ who gave himself as sacrifice for all. Through the power of the Holy Spirit he has gathered and continues to gather those who believe in Jesus Christ as one people. Through the water of baptism they have been incorporated into his body. The Lord Jesus Christ, present among them in the Spirit, builds them up through the preaching of the Gospel and the administration of the sacraments. Belonging to the Church means having communion with the Father through Jesus Christ in the Holy Spirit. (para. 3)

Geneva/1-19-80

3. In this broken world God has called into being the Church. He has revealed himself in Jesus Christ who gave himself as sacrifice for all. Through the power of the Holy Spirit he has gathered and continues to gather those who believe in Jesus Christ as one people. Through the water of baptism they have been incorporated into his body. The Lord Jesus Christ, present among them in the Spirit, builds them up through the preaching of the Gospel and the administration of the sacraments. Belonging to the Church means having communion with the Father through Jesus Christ in the Holy Spirit. (para. 3)

Geneva/6-80

1. In a broken world God calls the whole of humanity to be his people. He spoke in a unique and decisive way in Jesus Christ, his Son, who identified himself with the human race and gave himself as a sacrifice for all. His life, death and resurrection are the foundation of a new communion which is built up by the good news of the Gospel and the gifts of the sacraments. The Holy Spirit unites those who follow Jesus Christ in a single body and sends them as witnesses into the world. Belonging to the Church means living in communion with God through Jesus Christ and in the Holy Spirit.

Geneva/79 [cont.]

4. In a balanced ecclesiology we must hold together Christ's historical work and the Spirit's present work in the constitution of the Church and the institution of ministries. Sent by the Father, Christ chose his apostles, establishing the community of the New Covenant and endowing it with the necessary ministries for the continuation of its mission. The whole Church community and ministries remains in constant dependence on the Spirit. By the Spirit Christ came, by the Spirit the Body of Christ is constituted and grows, renewed for the strengthening of the royal and prophetic priesthood of the Church in the world. No

Geneva/79 [cont.]

approach to the ministry will be authentic unless we try to keep these two aspects of the mystery of the Church, the christological and the pneumatological aspects, in mind simultaneously.

5. It was following the manifestation of the Spirit at his baptism that Jesus accomplished his ministry: of announcing the Good News, manifesting the coming of the Kingdom, witnessing to the Father. By the power of the same Spirit he sacrificed his own life as the unique priest of the New Covenant, and by the same Spirit he was raised from the dead. So, too, since Pentecost, those who have been charged with the ministry can accomplish the works which lead the Body of Christ to its full stature only in the power of the Holy Spirit. Spirit and ministry are inseparable both in the Head and in the Body. This

Geneva/79
5. [cont.]

On the other hand, this view of the relation between Christ and the Spirit makes it clear that Christ's real presence is by its very nature eschatological. Wherever the Spirit is at work, he transposes history into its last days (cf. Acts 2:17), revealing and bringing to the world the *arrhes* (first-fruits) of its final destiny, which is nothing less than the presence of the Kingdom in creation (cf. Réflexions de théologiens orthodoxes et catholiques, *Episkepsis* 183, 15/2/1978).

Geneva/79 [cont.]

7. Met together in the upper room to celebrate the holy Supper, the disciples represent both the whole community of Christ in the Spirit *and* the ministry called by Christ to edify his Church as a Body, as a temple of the Holy Spirit. In the midst of his disciples, Christ celebrates the holy Supper for them as an ecclesial community which, receiving the body and blood of Christ, is united in the Spirit. He also celebrates it with them and commissions and commands them to celebrate it in memorial of his death and resurrection until he returns

6. The common foundation of the community assembled in the Spirit around Christ as he performs his ministry for the world, and of the ministries ordained by the gift of the Spirit for the edification and service

Geneva/79 [cont.]

9. Christ is often designated Prophet, Priest and King; as such he continues his ministry in the world through

Geneva/79 [cont.]
view of Christ in the Spirit has many implications which may be summarized, however, in two points which govern all the rest:

On the one hand, this view of Christ and the Spirit rules out any idea of Christ as an isolated individual. In reality, whenever he is present in the Spirit he is accompanied by his Body, the community of believers from whom he cannot be separated. For he is the firstborn among many brothers and sisters.

Geneva/79 [cont.]
of the Body of Christ, is the community and ministry of the Twelve, instituted by Christ in the power of the Spirit. The apostolic character of the Church and of the ministries is understood in this light.

Geneva/79 [cont.]
(1 Cor. 11:2326).

8.   After his resurrection, Christ bestows the Holy Spirit on the disciples as he entrusts to them the ministry of reconciliation within the ecclesial community: 'Receive the Holy Spirit. If you forgive anyone's sins, they stand forgiven; if you pronounce them unforgiven, unforgiven they remain' (Jn. 20:21f.).

Geneva/79 [cont.]
the ecclesial community which is a royal and prophetic priesthood. In communion with Christ the Prophet and in the power of the Spirit, the ecclesial community bears witness to the Good News of liberation; in communion with Christ the Priest and by its prayer, obedience and the martyrdom of some of its members, it offers spiritual sacrifices; in communion with Christ the King, it gives signs of the power of the resurrection to transform humanity and anticipates the Kingdom of God.

Accra/74

4. Membership in the community of the Church involves fellowship with God the Father through Jesus Christ, in the Holy Spirit. It means being in a relationship of mutual indwelling with Jesus Christ. This fellowship makes possible a unique experience of community, based as it is upon communion with God and repentance, upon mutual forgiveness and acceptance; it results in freedom and new life. God's purpose is that all men should be brought into this community.

Geneva/79

12. Membership in the community of the Church involves fellowship with God the Father through Jesus Christ, in the Holy Spirit. This fellowship makes possible a unique experience of community, based as it is upon communion with God and repentance, upon mutual forgiveness and acceptance; it results in freedom and new life. God's purpose is that all men and women should be brought into this community. (no 4)

Geneva/1-16-80

4. The communion made possible in the Church is based on Christ's victory over the powers of evil and death. He offers forgiveness to those who repent and delivers them from destruction. He opens a new future and enables people to turn in praise to God and in service to their neighbours. He is the source of new life in freedom and mutual forgiveness and love. God's purpose is that, in Jesus Christ all people should share in this communion (para. 4).

Geneva/1-19-80

4. The communion made possible in the Church is based on Christ's victory over the powers of evil and death. He offers forgiveness to those who repent and delivers them from destruction. He opens a new future and enables people to turn in praise to God and in service to their neighbours. He is the source of new life in freedom and mutual forgiveness and love. God's purpose is that, in Jesus Christ, all people should share in this communion. (para. 4)

Geneva/6-80

2. The life of the Church is based on Christ's victory over the powers of evil and death, accomplished once for all. Christ offers forgiveness, invites to repentance and delivers from destruction. He enables people to turn in praise to God and in service to their neighbours. He is the source of new life in freedom and mutual forgiveness and love. He directs hearts and minds to the expectation of the kingdom where Christ's victory will become manifest and all things will be made new. God's purpose is that, in Jesus Christ, all people should share in this communion.

Accra/74

11. The Church as the communion of the Holy Spirit is called to proclaim and prefigure the Kingdom of God by announcing the Gospel to the world and by being built up as the body of Christ. Within these two commissions each member of the body is called to live his faith and account for his hope. Each stands alongside men and women in their joy and suffering and witnesses among them through loving service; each struggles with the oppressed towards that freedom and dignity promised with the coming of the Kingdom.

70. The Church is the people of God in history. It is part of the world to which it is sent. As human society changes, the Church is called to seek a new obedience to God in the new situation. For instance, if in society new means of communication are developed, they will have their effect

Geneva/79

15. The Church as the communion of the Holy Spirit is called to proclaim and prefigure the Kingdom of God by announcing the Gospel to the world and by being built up as the body of Christ. Within these two commissions each member of the body is called to live his faith and account for his hope. Each stands alongside men and women in their joy and suffering and witnesses among them through loving service; each struggles with the oppressed towards that freedom and dignity promised with the coming of the Kingdom. (no 11)

Geneva/1-16-80

5. The Church is the people of God in history. It is part of the world to which it is sent. In order to remain faithful to this mission the Church is called, therefore, to seek relevant forms of obedience in each situation. The promise of the Kingdom of God makes the body of Christ and each individual member a witness to the Gospel and the hope which has become manifest in it, in the midst of the joys and sufferings of people; and it encourages the participation in the struggle of all who are oppressed.

Geneva/1-19-80

5. The Church is the people of God in history. It lives in the world to which it is sent. In order to remain faithful to this mission the Church is called, therefore, to seek relevant forms of obedience in each situation. The promise of the Kingdom of God makes the body of Christ and each individual member a witness to the Gospel and to the hope which has become manifest in it, in the midst of the joys and sufferings of people; and it encourages the participation in the struggle of all who are oppressed.

Geneva/6-80

4. The Church is called to proclaim and prefigure the kingdom of God by announcing the Gospel to the world and by being built up as the body of Christ. Christ came to proclaim the nearness of the kingdom. He opened a new access to the Father. He preached good news to the poor and release to the captives (Lk 4:18). All members of the body are called to share in this proclamation and to give account of their hope. They will tell the story of Jesus Christ, the teacher and healer, the brother who gave his life, the Lord who is present today. They will stand alongside men and women in their joys and sufferings and seek to witness in caring live. They will struggle with the oppressed towards that freedom and dignity promised with the coming of the kingdom. The same mission needs to be carried out in varying political, social

172

Geneva/6-80 [cont.]
and cultural contexts. In order to fulfil the mission faithfully, they will seek relevant forms of witness and service in each situation.

Accra/74 [cont.]
upon the ministry of the Word. For example, if in a society there is a great movement of population from countryside to city, a church whose structures are wholly adapted to a rural situation is challenged to change them. Such manifestation is required in order that the Church may do in the world what it exists to do: which is, by the power of Christ, to proclaim and show in its own life the breaking in of the Kingdom.

Accra/74

12. This proclamation of the Gospel, service to the world and edification of the community require a variety of activities, both permanent and provisional, spontaneous and institutional. To fulfil these needs the Holy Spirit gives diverse and complementary gifts to the Church. These gifts are given by God to individuals for the common good of his people and their service and manifest themselves in acts of service within the Christian community and to the world. They are all gifts of the same Spirit. The ordained ministry, therefore, cannot be understood or carried out in isolation from the general ministry of the whole people.

Geneva/79

16. This proclamation of the Gospel, service to the world and edification of the community require a variety of activities, both permanent and provisional, spontaneous and institutional. To fulfil these needs the Holy Spirit gives diverse and complementary gifts to the Church. These gifts are given by God to individuals for the common good of his people and their service and manifest themselves in acts of service within the Christian community and to the world. They are all gifts of the same Spirit (1 Cor. 12:4ff). The ordained ministry, therefore, cannot be understood or carried out in isolation from the general ministry of the whole people. (no 12)

Geneva/1-16-80

6. The Church is a charismatic communion. The Holy Spirit bestows on the members of the body diverse and complementary gifts; they are given for the common good of the whole people and manifest themselves in acts of service within the community and to the world. All members are called to discover, with the help of the community, the charisms which they have received and to relate them to the calling of the Church. For the building up of the body and the sharing of the Gospel a multiplicity of ministries is required. It is one of the marks of a truly charismatic communion that members are encouraged and supported in fulfilling their particular ministries. (Para 12)

Geneva/1-19-80

6. The Church is a charismatic communion. The Holy Spirit bestows on the members of the body diverse and complementary gifts; they are given for the common good of the whole people and manifest themselves in acts of service within the community and to the world. All members are called to discover, with the help of the community, the charisms which they have received and to relate them to the calling of the Church. For the building up of the body and the sharing of the Gospel a multiplicity of ministries is required. It is one of the marks of a truly charismatic communion that members are encouraged and supported in fulfilling their particular ministries. (para. 12)

Geneva/6-80

5. The Holy Spirit bestows on the community diverse and complementary gifts. They are given for the common good of the whole people and manifest themselves in acts of service within the community and to the world. They may be gifts of communicating the Gospel in word and deed, gifts of praying, gifts of teaching, learning and serving, gifts of guiding and following, gifts of inspiration and vision. The proclamation of the Gospel, the service to the world and the edification of the community require a multiplicity of gifts. All members are called to discover, with the help of the community, the gifts they have received and to relate them to the calling of the Church.

174

Accra/74

2. The ordained ministry is to be understood as part of the community. An understanding of the ministry must therefore start from the nature of the Church, the community of believers. This conviction is now shared by most of the Churches. Thus the following considerations start from the Christian community; they then try to define the nature and functions of the ordained ministry in the light of this community.

Geneva/1-16-80
Preamble.

1. The considerations on baptism and the eucharist inevitably lead to the issue of the ministry in the Church (cf. para.). Today, the churches are seriously divided both in their understanding and in their practice of the ministry. Therefore, they need to ask the question: how, according to the will of Jesus Christ, and under the guidance of the Spirit, is the ministry to be understood and ordered in the Church? De facto, some kind of order exists in all churches. The question therefore arises what agreement in understanding and practice is required for the mutual recognition by the churches.

Geneva/1-19-80
Preamble

1. The considerations on baptism and the eucharist inevitably lead to the issue of the ministry in the Church (cf. Baptism, para. Eucharist, para. 29). Today, the churches are seriously divided both in their understanding and in their practice of the ministry. Therefore, they need to ask the question: how, according to the will of Jesus Christ, and under the guidance of the Spirit, is the ministry to be understood and ordered in the Church? De facto, some kind of order exists in all churches. The question therefore arises what agreement in understanding and practice is required for the mutual recognition by the churches.

Geneva/6-80

6. Today, the churches are divided in their understanding and their practice of the ministry. As they engage in the effort of overcoming their differences, they need to take their starting point from the calling of the whole people of God. The ministry is to serve the witness and the service of the whole community. Therefore, the churches need to seek a common answer to the following question: How, according to the will of Jesus Christ and under the guidance of the Spirit, is the ministry to be understood and ordered, so that the Gospel may be spread and the community built up in love?

Geneva/1-16-80

16. In what form is the ordained ministry to be exercised in the Church? Though the churches generally agree on the need of some kind of ordained ministry, they differ on the issue of its appropriate form. Is there a diversity of ordained ministries? Or is there only the ordained ministry of Word and Sacrament? How is the ordained ministry to be exercised? What variety of ministries is necessary to reflect the richness and fullness of communion in Christ? These questions can be answered only in the light of the larger question: How, according to the will of Jesus Christ and under the guidance of the Spirit, is the Church to be shepherded?

Geneva/1-19-80

17. In what form is the ordained ministry to be exercised in the Church? Though the churches generally agree on the need of some kind of ordained ministry, they differ on the issue of its appropriate form. Is there a diversity of ordained ministries? Or is there only *the* ordained ministry of Word and Sacrament? How is the ordained ministry to be exercised? What variety of ministries is necessary to reflect the richness and fullness of communion in Christ? These questions can be answered only in the light of the larger question: How, according to the will of Jesus Christ and under the guidance of the Spirit, is the Church to be shepherded?

Geneva/6-80

6. Today, the churches are divided in their understanding and their practice of the ministry. As they engage in the effort of overcoming their differences, they need to take their starting point from the calling of the whole poeple of God. The ministry is to serve the witness and the service of the whole community. Therefore, the churches need to seek a common answer to the following question: How, according to the will of Jesus Christ and under the guidance of the Spirit, is the ministry to be understood and ordered, so that the Gospel may be spread and the community built up in love?

Accra/74 begins with "all ministry in the Church"[1] and ministry's rootedness in Christ; whereas Geneva/6-80 begins with God's call to "the whole of humanity to be his people"[2] even prior to the historical Jesus. The above title, The Calling of the Whole People of God," becomes in Geneva/6-80, for the first time, the title of an independent major section of the document. In Geneva/1-80 it was the heading of a subsection. These structural shifts indicate a major ecclesiological and christological shift in the context of which the ordained ministry is to be considered. God (the Father) calls all human beings, one of whom is the historical Jesus; the call is to humanity, part of which is the Church. Accra/74 does not speak to the issue of such a call to humanity; Geneva/1-80 says that "God has called into being the Church."[3]

The first paragraph of Geneva/1-80 indicates the third paragraph of Accra/74 as its predecessor. The earlier text uses the phrase, "the water of baptism," in reference to ecclesiological membership. The later text drops the phrase. Perhaps the notion of "baptism of desire" is acknowledged with a broader ecclesiological meaning intended. Another contrast may help. Accra/74 states that "an understanding of the (ordained) ministry must therefore start from the nature of the Church, the community of believers."[4] Geneva/6-80 states that "they (the churches) need to take their starting point from the calling of the whole people of God."[5] The latter text seems more inclusive.

Geneva/6-80 adds the words, "his life, death and resurrection are the foundation of a new communion." Thus the Paschal Mystery is seen as the basis for ecclesiology. This is the first mention of the Paschal Mystery in these texts. A few months previously, however, Geneva/1-80 had stated that "the communion made possible in the Church is based on Christ's victory over the powers of evil and death."[6] Geneva/6-80 adds the phrase, "accomplished once for all."[7] Earlier the

---

[1]FO Paper No. 73, *One Baptism, One Eucharist and a Mutually Recognized Ministry: Three Agreed Statements*, Geneva: World Council of Churches, 1975, "The Ministry," § 1.

[2]Geneva/6-80, § 1.

[3]Geneva/1-80, §3.

[4]Accra/74, §2.

[5]Geneva/6-80, §6.

[6]Geneva/1-80, §4; Geneva/6-80, makes a similar statement.

[7]Geneva/6-80, §2.

phrase, "the power of the resurrection," found its way into the evolution of texts.[8]

The last sentence of Accra/74, §4 states, "God's purpose is that all men should be brought into this community." In Geneva/1-80, the word, "community," is changed to the word, "communion."[9] The latter term has the connotation of spiritual bonds which transcend specific institutional bonds. Further, the term, "all men," becomes "all men and women" in Geneva/79 [10] and "all people" in Geneva/1-80.[11] An effort to be more inclusive is in evidence with each succeeding text.

In this ecclesiology there is a lessening of a clerical emphasis and a lessening of a mechanical notion of the sacraments. Thus, "preaching of the Gospel"[12] becomes simply, "the good news of the Gospel."[13] And "the administration of the sacraments"[14] becomes "the gifts of the sacraments."[15]

In this ecclesiology there is an increasing emphasis on the fact that "*all* members are *called to discover*, with the help of the community, the gifts they have received and to relate them to the calling of the Church." (Emphasis added)[16] In Geneva/6-80 these gifts are spelled out: "They may be gifts of communicating the Gospel in word and deed, gifts of praying, gifts of teaching, learning and serving, gifts of guiding and following, gifts of inspiration and vision."[17]

Geneva/6-80, §4 treats much of the same material treated in the Accra text[18] with some alterations and additions. One alteration consists in making a more brief, summary statement about the Church carrying out the mission of Christ "in varying political, social and cultural contexts."[19] In the report on the replies of the churches

---

[8]Geneva/79, §9

[9]Geneva/1-80, §4.

[10]Geneva/79, §12.

[11]Geneva/1-80, §4.

[12]Geneva/1-80, §3.

[13]Geneva/6-80, §1.

[14]Geneva/1-80, §3.

[15]Geneva/6-80, §1.

[16]Geneva/6-80, §5. Also cf. Geneva/1-80, §6.

[17]Geneva/6-80, §5.

[18]Cf. Accra/74, §s 11, 70 and 7-10. Also cf. Geneva/79, §15 and Geneva/1-80, §5.

[19]Geneva/6-80, §4.

to the Accra text it is noted:

> The effort to link the traditional concerns in the reflection on ministry (apostles, community) to the concrete changing context in which it functions is not picked up in the replies; on the contrary, many plead for clear separation of levels of argument. The whole section on the "ministry in practice" does not play a significant role in the debate.[20]

This response by the churches seems to account for the virtual elimination of the entire section of the Accra text in Geneva/6-80. That section was entitled "The Ministry in Practice Today."[21]

Geneva/6-80 adds an emphasis on the historical Jesus which does not fail to speak to what he did:

> Christ came to proclaim the nearness of the kingdom. He opened a new access to the Father. He preached good news to the poor and release to the captives (Lk. 4:18). All members of the body are called to share in this proclamation and to give account of their hope. They will tell the story of Jesus Christ, the teacher and healer, the brother who gave his life, the Lord who is present today.[22]

The christological/ecclesiological nuances become more pronounced in the Geneva/6-80 document. In this regard Geneva/79 states that "no approach to the ministry will be authentic unless we try to keep these two aspects of the mystery of the Church, the christological and the pneumatological aspects, in mind simultaneously."[23] Geneva/6-80 adds an entirely new paragraph on the role of the Holy Spirit *vis-à-vis* Christ and the Church.[24] It should be noted, however, that the statement, "the Church is a charismatic communion," appears only in Geneva/1-80 text.[25]

The focus of the Accra/74 document is on the direct action of Christ who "forgives sins and delivers men from the lordship of the powers of destruction."[26] The succeeding documents drop that phrase altogether. The initiative is placed on God (the Father) who "spoke in a unique and decisive way in Jesus Christ, his Son."[27]

---

[20]FO/77:33, April 1977 (Revised June 1944), p. 282.

[21]In the Accra text that section is Part IV., comprised of §s 70-87.

[22]Geneva/6-80, §4.

[23]Geneva/79, §4.

[24]Geneva/6-80, §3.

[25]Geneva/1-80, §6.

[26]Accra/74, §3.

[27]Geneva/6-80, §1.

Thus Jesus' identity as *the* Word of God is emphasized while his title of "Lord" is dropped in this context.[28] In the process of doing so what seems to be a theological inaccuracy in Accra/74 is eliminated.[29] The precise role of the historical Jesus is clarified in Geneva/6-80 with the addition of the phrase, "who identified with the human race."[30] This introduction of the incarnational principle places the emphasis on who Jesus was or is more than on what he did.

In another place the Geneva/6-80 text maintains the emphasis on the initiative of Christ by asking, "How, according to the will of Jesus Christ and under the guidance of the Holy Spirit, is the ministry to be understood and ordered?"[31]

Sacrificial language in relationship to Christ is introduced with Geneva/79.[32] Thus, in Geneva/1-80 the phrase is added, "who gave himself as sacrifice for all."[33]

The trinitarian focus becomes more precise with each succeeding text. It is Geneva/79 which first gives explicit expression to this need.[34] In Accra/74 "the Lord Jesus Christ . . . continues to gather worshipping communities out of this broken world, the one people of God."[35] In Geneva/1-80 "through the power of the Holy Spirit he (God) has gathered and continues to gather those who believe in Jesus Christ as one people."[36] In Geneva/6-80 "the Holy Spirit unites those who follow Jesus Christ in a single body and sends them as witnesses into the world."[37] The initiating action is attributed first, to Jesus Christ, next, to God (presumably, the Father), and next, to the Holy Spirit who, in addition to gathering, also "sends." Further, it is not clear why the final sentence in Geneva/1-80, §3 needed to be altered

---

[28]Accra/74, §3.

[29]Accra/74, §3 begins with the phrases, "The Lord Jesus Christ, through his Word and Spirit."

[30]Geneva/6-80, §1.

[31]Geneva/6-80, §6. Cf. Geneva/1-80, §s 1 and 17.

[32]Geneva/79, §s 5 and 9.

[33]Geneva/1-80, §3.

[34]cf. Geneva/79, §3.

[35]Accra/74, §3.

[36]Geneva/1-80, §3.

[37]Geneva/6-80, §1.

in the precise way that it was in the final sentence of Geneva/6-80, §1.[38] The term, "Father," is replaced by the term, "God," although earlier in the same paragraph of Geneva/6-80 the phrase, "his Son," is added, thus implying that "God" in this context refers precisely to "the Father." There seems to be an ever stronger emphasis on pneumatology. This emphasis was first made in Geneva/79.[39] As mentioned above, Geneva/6-80 adds a new paragraph on the role of the Spirit to the text of Geneva/1-80.[40]

One other theological theme which is given greater emphasis in Geneva/6-80 than in Accra/74 is that of eschatology. The later text adds the sentence, "He (Christ) directs hearts and minds to the expectation of the kingdom where Christ's victory will become manifest and all things will be made new."[41] The text directly preceding this one stated simply that "he (Christ) opens a new future."[42] The textual predecessor of this "new future" was Accra/74's "unique experience of community (and) . . . new life."[43] This stress on eschatological thinking was advanced by Geneva/79.[44]

There are a few other words and phrases added with each succeeding text which offer a more nuanced theological meaning. A more dynamic terminology is evidenced when "having communion" yields to "living in communion."[45] In a similar vein, "God has called," yields to "God calls."[46] In another instance, this phrase is added to the Accra/74 text, "(Christ) enables people to turn in praise to God and in service to their neighbours."[47] Thus worship and ministry are intimately joined.

---

[38]The language of the earlier text seems more precise to this author than that of the later text. Is there some ecumenical consideration at work here?

[39]cf. Geneva/79, §s 4-8.

[40]Geneva/6-80, §3.

[41]Geneva/6-80, §2.

[42]Geneva/1-80, §4.

[43]Accra/74, §4.

[44]Geneva/79, §5.

[45]Geneva/1-80, §3 and Geneva/6-80, §1.

[46]Ibid.

[47]Geneva/1-80, §4 which purports to parallel Accra/74, §4.

II. THE CHURCH AND THE ORDAINED MINISTRY.

DEFINITION OF TERMS.

The definition of terms is introduced to clarify the subsequent treatment. The attempt is to be inclusive, e.g., by eliminating from the description of Church the explicit references to baptism and confirmation.

182

Geneva/79

2. Three terms are used with a quite precise meaning in this text:

a *charism* is a gift bestowed by the Holy Spirit on Christians for their particular service within the community;

a *ministry* is the use made of a charism, the service which a Christian can be called upon to perform within the community in virtue of his or her consecration by baptism and confirmation; we can also speak of the ministry of the whole people of God, which is the service which the Church performs within humankind as a whole, either as a local community or as the universal Church;

the *ordained ministry* is a permanent service of the Church in response to a special call from God and it implies ordination by the imposition of hands and the authority of the person to whom the Church entrusts a specific mission; this ordained ministry corresponds to what the Church has often called "priesthood"; there is no need, therefore, to distinguish between or oppose ordained ministry and priesthood; it is

Geneva/1-16-80

2. In order to avoid confusion, note needs to be taken of the meaning of the following four terms:

charisms are the gifts bestowed by the Holy Spirit on any members of the body of Christ for the up-building of the unity and the fulfilment of its calling

ministry has a wide meaning. It can refer to the service which the whole people of God is called to perform, either as a local community or as the universal Church. Normally, it means the service which Christians perform within and for the community in virtue of their baptism and confirmation, and according to the particular charisms they have received.

ordained ministry refers to services for which the church practises ordination by the invocation of the Spirit and the imposition of hands. These services are normally considered to be constitutive for the life of the Church.

priest and priesthood are used by some churches to designate what is

Geneva/1-19-80

2. In order to avoid confusion, note needs to be taken of the meaning which the following four terms have in this document:

Charisms are the gifts bestowed by the Holy Spirit on any members of the body of Christ for the up-building of the community and the fulfilment of its calling.

Ministry has a wider meaning. It can refer to the service which the whole people of God is called to perform, either as a local community or as the universal Church. Normally, it means the service which Christians perform within and for the community in virtue of their baptism and according to the particular charisms they have received.

Ordained ministry refers to services for which the church practises ordination by the invocation of the Spirit and the imposition of hands. These services are normally considered to be constitutive for the life of the Church.

Priest and priesthood are used by some churches to designate what is

Geneva/6-80

7. In order to avoid confusion in the discussions on the ministry in the Church it is necessary to delineate clearly how various terms are used in the following paragraphs.

The word *charism* refers to the gifts bestowed by the Holy Spirit on any member of the body of Christ for the up-building of the community and the fulfilment of its calling.

The word *ministry* in its broadest sense refers to the service which the whole people of God is called to perform, as individuals, as a local community, or as the universal Church. It can also refer to more regular particular, institutional forms which this service takes.

The term *ordained ministry* refers to services for which the Church practices ordination by the invocation of the Spirit and the imposition of hands.

The term *priesthood* is used by some churches to designate what is called "ordained ministry". The two terms "ordained ministry" and "priesthood" must not be taken as

Geneva/79 [cont.]
often simply a question of translation into a given culture.

Geneva/1-16-80 [cont.]
here called "ordained ministry". The churches stemming from the Reformation generally avoid the term priesthood while the churches of the catholic tradition employ it in diverse forms: priestly ministry, ministerial priesthood, or, more recently, ministry of priesthood. The two terms must not be taken as referring to two different realities. Both designate the ministry which is constitutive for the life of the Church.

The following considerations are primarily concerned with the understanding and ordering of the ordained ministry.

Geneva/1-19-80 [cont.]
here called "ordained ministry". Churches stemming from the Reformation generally avoid the term priesthood in this context, while the churches of the catholic tradition employ it in diverse forms: priestly ministry, ministerial priesthood, or ministry of priesthood. The two terms "ministry" and "priesthood" must not be taken as referring to two different realities. Both designate the ministry which is constitutive for the life of the Church.

The following considerations are primarily concerned with the understanding and ordering of the ordained ministry.

Geneva/6-80 [cont.]
referring to two different realities.

The first attempt to define the significant terms which relate directly to the study of the ministry in the Church is made in Geneva/79.[48] This defining of terms anticipated by only a few days the suggestion made by the Consultation of Orthodox Theologians on the revision of the Accra statements on Baptism, Eucharist and Ministry, held at Chambésy (near Geneva), May 31-June 2, 1979. That Consultation "was of the opinion that the terms used in the agreed statements were open to misunderstanding and should be clarified; possibly, a new section 'vocabulary' could be included."[49]

In defining "ministry" in the widest sense in reference to the Church the text of Geneva/79 explicitly includes a mention of baptism and confirmation, Geneva/1-80 explicitly mentions baptism, and Geneva/6-80 eliminates an explicit reference to both.[50] This may indicate an increasing attempt to be more inclusive with regard to membership in the Church.

In defining the term, "priesthood," Geneva/1-80 includes an explicit reference to "churches stemming from the Reformation . . . (and) churches of the catholic tradition."[51] This reference is entirely eliminated in the corresponding paragraph of Geneva/6-80.

---

[48]Geneva/79, §2.

[49]FO Paper No. 98, pp. 82-83.

[50]Geneva/79, §2; Geneva/1-80, §2; and Geneva/6-80, §7. Interestingly, the text used as a working draft in meeting which produced Geneva/1-80 still included a reference to confirmation.

[51]Geneva/1-80, §2.

A. THE ORDAINED MINISTRY.

In this section "the Twelve" are carefully differentiated from "the apostles" and the uniqueness of those groups are indicated. While there is an emphasis added on the priestly role of the ordained and while there is an emphasis added on the guiding and teaching role of the ordained as rooted in Christ's own role, there is a clear effort to avoid making the ordained ministry too special, too exclusive, too far removed from the ministry of others in the Church. A more careful and nuanced reference is made to eucharistic presiding and *episkopé*. The same care can be seen in a deeper sense of historical and biblical accuracy, e.g., the difficulty of attributing specific forms of ordained ministry to the will and institution of Jesus Christ himself. And, again, a keener awareness of trinitarian roles (e.g., Christ being sent by the Father) is evinced as the text evolves.

Accra/74

13. In order that his redemptive work might be proclaimed and attested to the ends of the earth, and that its fruits might be communicated to man, Christ chose apostles and committed to them the word of reconciliation. Within the first Christian communities the apostles exercised a unique and fundamental function, which could not be handed on. However, in so far as they bore special (but not exclusive) responsibility for proclaiming the message of reconciliation, establishing churches and building them up in the apostolic faith, their ministry had to be continued. Although there was a variety of gifts in the Early Church, the New Testament reports a setting apart to special ministry. This special ministry was essential in all times and circumstances. Such a

Geneva/79

17. In order that his redemptive work might be proclaimed and attested to the ends of the earth, and that its fruits might be communicated to man, Christ chose apostles and committed to them the word of reconciliation. Within the first Christian communities the apostles exercised a unique and fundamental function, which could not be handed on. However, in so far as they bore special (but not exclusive) responsibility for proclaiming the message of reconciliation, establishing churches and building them up in the apostolic faith, their ministry had to be continued. Although there was a variety of gifts in the Early Church, the New Testament reports a setting apart to special ministry. This special ministry was essential in all times and circumstances. Such a ministry is exercised by persons who are called within

Geneva/1-16-80

7. Within the charismatic community the ordained ministry is essential and has to fulfil an essential role. It has its origin in Christ's choosing and sending of his disciples to be witnesses of his kingdom (......).. The word apostle refers to this mission.

8. Within the communities of the first generations a unique role is attributed to the Twelve. They are described as witnesses of the Lord's life and resurrection, as patriarchs and judges of the New Israel, and as leaders of the community in prayer, teaching and service. (Acts 2:4227 ; 6:24). The very existence of the Twelve among the other disciples means that there was never a totally undifferentiated Church. Nor was the Church ever without a special ministry. This was essential in the beginning, and it remains so at all times

Geneva/1-19-80

7. Within the charismatic community the ordained ministry is essential and has to fulfil an essential role. It has its origin in Christ's choosing and sending of his disciples to be witnesses of his kingdom (Mt. 10:13). The word apostle refers to this mission.

8. Within the communities of the first generations a unique role is attributed to the Twelve. They are described as witnesses of the Lord's life and resurrection, as patriarchs and judges of the New Israel, and as leaders of the community in prayer, teaching and service (Acts 2:4247; 6:26). The very existence of the Twelve among the other disciples means that there was never a totally undifferentiated Church. Nor was the Church ever without a special ministry. This was essential in the beginning, and it remains so at all times

Geneva/6-80

8. The ordained ministry is constitutive for the life and witness of the Church. In order to fulfill its mission, the Church needs persons pointing to its fundamental dependence on Jesus Christ and providing, within the multiplicity of gifts, a focus of its unity.

9. The Church was never without persons holding special authority and responsibility. Christ chose and sent the disciples to be witnesses of the kingdom (Mt 10: 18); and a special role is attributed to the Twelve within the communities of the first generations. They are described as patriarchs and judges of the renewed Israel, as witnesses of the Lord's life and resurrection as leaders of the community in prayer, teaching, proclamation and service (acts 2: 4247; 6: 26, etc.). The very existence of the Twelve shows that, from

Accra/74 [cont.]	*Geneva/79* [cont.]	*Geneva/1-16-80* [cont.]	*Geneva/1-19-80* [cont.]	*Geneva/6-80* [cont.]
ministry is exercised by persons who are called within the community and given gifts and authority to transmit the living testimony of the apostles.	the community and given gifts and authority to transmit the living testimony of the apostles. (no 13)	and in all circumstances.	and in all circumstances.	the beginning, there were differentiated roles in the community.

Geneva/1-16-80 [cont.]
8-Commentary:

One must be careful to preserve the fullness of the New Testament usage in relation to "apostles". Without attempting to be exhaustive, we note that "apostle" is a term clearly applied in the New Testament to the Twelve chosen by Jesus during his lifetime as representatives of the community of the renewed Israel. In that moment they are the community and they are also those who play a special role in the community. "Apostle" is also applied to Paul, and to others as they are sent out by the risen Christ to proclaim the Gospel. So the roles of the Apostles cover both foundation and mission.

Geneva/1-19-80 [cont.]
8-Commentary:

One must be careful to preserve the fullness of the New Testament usage in relation to "apostles". Without attempting to be exhaustive, we note that "apostle" is a term clearly applied in the New Testament to the Twelve chosen by Jesus during his lifetime as representatives of the community of the renewed Israel. In that moment they represent the community and they are also those who play a special role in the community. "Apostle" is also applied to Paul, and to others as they are sent out by the risen Christ to proclaim the Gospel. So the roles of the apostles cover both foundation and mission.

Geneva/6-80
9-Commentary. In the NT the term "apostle" has a wide meaning. It is used for the Twelve but also for a wider circle of disciples. It is applied to Paul and others as they are sent out by the risen Christ to proclaim the Gospel. The roles of the apostles cover both foundation and mission.

Obviously, there is a fundamental difference between the apostles and the ordained ministers. The role of the apostles as witnesses of the risen Christ is unique and unrepeatable. But there is lasting significance in the fact that they were chosen. Jesus called the Twelve during his lifetime as representatives of the renewed Israel. At that moment they represent the whole people of God and at the same time exercise a special role in the midst of that people. After the resurrection they are leaders of the community. It can be said, therefore, that

Geneva/6-80 [cont.]
the Twelve prefigure both the Church and the persons entrusted with special authority and responsibility in the Church.

Accra/74

2. The ordained ministry is to be understood as part of the community. An understanding of the ministry must therefore start from the nature of the Church, the community of believers. This conviction is now shared by most of the Churches. Thus the following considerations start from the Christian community; they then try to define the nature and functions of the ordained ministry in the light of this community.

14. Christ, through the Holy Spirit, stirs up, strengthens and sends those whom he has called for this special ministry making them ambassadors of his message and work. Persons called to this ministry are commissioned to serve the work of the Lord by following him, being conformed to him and by announcing his name. The presence of this ministry in the community signifies the priority of divine

Geneva/79

19. The following are the basic and permanent characteristics of the ordained ministry:

it is a *mission* from Christ for the training of Christians to serve the growth of the Body of Christ in the unity of the faith (Eph. 4:1113);

it is an *ambassadorship* on Christ's behalf so that God's Word should be heard by all human beings, calling them to be reconciled to him (II Cor. 5:20);

it is a *pastoral function*, the role of a shepherd, whereby the flock of God is to be assembled, fed and led in communion with Christ the chief Shepherd, and in the expectation of his coming (1 Peter 5:14).

18. Christ, through the Holy Spirit, stirs up, strengthens and sends those whom he has called for this special ministry, making them am-

Geneva/1-16-80

9. Christ, through the Holy Spirit, continues to choose and to call persons for this special ministry. They serve the community by pointing to its fundamental dependence on Christ who is the source of its mission and the foundation of its unity. The special ministry has the following characteristics:

It is a *mission* from Christ for the training of Christians to serve the growth of the body of Christ in the unity of the faith (Eph. 4:1113);

It is an *ambassadorship* on Christ's behalf so that God's Word should be heard by all human beings, calling them to be reconciled to him (1 Cor. 5:20);

It is a *pastoral function*, the role of a shepherd, whereby the flock of God is to be assembled, fed and led in communion with Christ the chief shepherd, and in the

Geneva/1-19-80

9. Christ, through the Holy Spirit, continues to choose and to call persons for this special ministry. They serve the community by pointing to its fundamental dependence on Christ who is the source of its mission and the foundation of its unity. The ordained ministry has characteristics such as the following: It is an ambassadorship and a mission, related to Christ's being sent by the Father, and directed towards the reconciliation of all human beings to God (John 20:21, II Cor. 5:20). It is an office of guiding and teaching, related to Christ's prophetic and teaching ministry, and to the fulfilment of law and prophets in him (Mt. 5:17, Eph. 4:1113). It is a pastorate, related to Christ the chief shepherd, and directed towards the assembling of the dispersed people of God, in the expectation of his coming (John 11:52, I Peter 5:14).

Geneva/6-80

10. ... As Christ chose and sent the apostles, he continues through the Holy Spirit to choose and call persons into the ordained ministry.

8. The ordained ministry is constitutive for the life and witness of the Church. In order to fulfill its mission, the Church needs persons pointing to its fundamental dependence on Jesus Christ and providing, within the multiplicity of gifts, a focus of its unity.

10. The ordained ministers recall and represent Jesus Christ to the community. They are ambassadors and missionaries. They point to Christ's being sent by the Father and work for the reconciliation of all human beings to God (Jn 20:21; II Cor 5:20). As leaders and teachers they call the community to submit to the authority of Jesus Christ, the teacher and prophet, in

Accra/74 [cont.]
initiative and authority in the Church's existence. Thus, whatever the diversity of functions in a Christian community may be, the specific service of the ordained minister is to assemble the community and to serve it by pointing to its fundamental dependence on Jesus Christ — Christ who is the source of its mission and the foundation of its unity.

Geneva/79 [cont.]
bassadors of his message and work. Persons called to this ministry are commissioned to serve the work of the Lord by following him, being conformed to him and by announcing his name. The presence of this ministry in the community signifies the priority of divine initiative and authority in the Church's existence. Thus, whatever the diversity of functions in a Christian community may be, the specific service of the ordained minister is to assemble the community and to serve it by pointing to its fundamental dependence on Jesus Christ — Christ who is the source of its mission and the foundation of its unity. (no 14)

Geneva/1-16-80 [cont.]
expectation of his coming (I Peter 5:14)

Geneva/6-80 [cont.]
whom law and prophets were fulfilled. As pastors, under Jesus Christ the chief shepherd, they will assemble and guide the dispersed people of God, in the expectation of the coming kingdom. As servants they will seek to reflect Christ's priestly ministry and intercede for the community and the world. As Christ chose and sent the apostles, he continues through the Holy Spirit to choose and call persons into the ordained ministry.

Geneva/1-16-80 [cont.]

10. The ordained ministry and the believing community are inextricably related to one another. On the one hand, the community needs the ordained ministry. Its presence reminds the community of the priority of the apostolic message in its life. It serves the community by pointing to Jesus Christ as the source of its faith and love. It provides a focus for maintaining and building up the communion. On the other hand, it cannot be considered in isolation from the community. It exists only in and for the community. The ordained minister needs the recognition, the support and the encouragement of the community. (Paras 14-15).

10-Commentary:

It must be emphasized that, though the basic necessity for an ordained ministry was given from the beginning, its actual forms have evolved in complicated

Geneva/1-19-80 [cont.]

10. The ordained ministry and the believing community are inextricably related to one another. On the one hand, the community needs the ordained ministry. Its presence reminds the community of the priority of the apostolic message in its life. It provides a focus for maintaining and building up the communion. On the other hand, it cannot be considered in isolation from the community. It exists only in and for the community. The ordained minister needs the recognition, the support and the encouragement of the community. (paras 14-15)

10-Commentary:

It must be emphasized that, though the basic necessity for an ordained ministry was given from the beginning, its actual forms have evolved in complicated historical development. The churches must therefore refrain from attributing parti-

Geneva/6-80 [cont.]

11. The ordained ministers and the believing community are inextricably related. On the one hand, the community needs ordained ministers. Their presence reminds the community of the priority of the apostolic message in its life. They serve to build up the communion in Christ and to strengthen its witness. On the other hand, the ordained ministry cannot be considered in isolation from the community. The ordained ministers can fulfil their calling only in and for the community. They need the recognition, the support and the encouragement of the community.

10-Commentary. It must be emphasized that, although the basic necessity for an ordained ministry was given from the beginning, its actual forms have evolved in complicated historical developments. The churches, therefore, must refrain from

Geneva/1-16-80 [cont.]
historical development. The churches must therefore refrain from attributing particular forms of the ordained ministry to the will and institution of Jesus Christ himself. Even the term ordained ministry is anachronistic if it is used without taking into consideration the historical development. An early form of ordination is found only in the later Parts of the New Testament (e.g. II Tim. 1:6f.).

Geneva/1-19-80 [cont.]
cular forms of the ordained ministry to the will and institution of Jesus Christ himself. Even the term ordained ministry is anachronistic if it is used without taking into consideration the historical development. An early form of ordination is found only in the later parts of the New Testament (e.g. II Tim. 1:6ff.).

Geneva/6-80 [cont.]
attributing particular forms of the ordained ministry to the will and institution of Jesus Christ himself. Even the term "ordained ministry" is anachronistic if used without taking into account the historical development. An early form of ordination is found only in the later parts of the New Testament (e.g. II Tim. 1:6ff.).

Accra/74 [cont.]

15. The essential and specific function of the special ministry is: to assemble and build up the Christian community, by proclaiming and teaching the Word of God, and presiding over the liturgical and sacramental life of the eucharistic community. The Christian community and the special ministry are related to one another. The minister cannot exist and fulfil his task in isolation. He needs the support and encouragement of the community. On the other hand, the Christian community needs the special ministry which serves to coordinate and unite the different gifts in the community and to strengthen and enable the ministry of the whole People of God. But above all, this relationship and mutual dependence manifests that the Church is not master of the Word and Sacrament, nor the source of its faith, hope and unity. Christian life as well as the

Geneva/79 [cont.]

23. *The essential and specific function of the ordained ministry is: to assemble and build up the Christian community, by proclaiming and teaching the Word of God, and presiding over the liturgical and sacramental life of the eucharistic community.* The Christian community and the ordained ministry are related to one another. The minister cannot exist and fulfil his task in isolation. He needs the support and encouragement of the community. On the other hand, the Christian community needs the ordained ministry which serves to coordinate and unite the different gifts in the community and to strengthen and enable the ministry of the whole People of God. But above all, this relationship and mutual dependence manifests that the Church is not master of the Word and Sacrament, nor the source of its faith, hope and unity.

Geneva/1-16-80 [cont.]

11. The central and specific function of the ordained ministry is to assemble and build up the community in Christ by proclaiming and teaching the Word of God and by presiding over the liturgical and the missionary and diaconal life of the eucharistic community. In communion with Christ, the ordained minister as president at the Eucharist gathers the ecclesial community together, feeds it with the Word and the Sacraments, strengthens its unity and encourages its expectation of the kingdom of God. The ordained minister is the envoy who signifies God's initiative and the bond between the local community and the other communities of the universal Church.

Geneva/1-19-80 [cont.]

11. The central and specific function of the ordained ministry in communion with Christ is to assemble, build up and guide the community in Christ by proclaiming and teaching the Word of God and by presiding over the liturgical and diaconal life of the eucharistic community.

Geneva/6-80 [cont.]

12. The central and specific function of the ordained minister is to assemble and build up the body of Christ by proclaiming and teaching the Word of God and by celebrating the sacraments, and to guide the life of the community in its liturgical, missionary and diaconal aspects.

Accra/74 [cont.]
ministry are received from the living Christ in the Church.

Geneva/79 [cont.]
Christian life as well as the ministry are received from the living Christ in the Church. (no 15)

11. Both the ecclesial community and the ordained ministry are in communion with Christ in order that each may manifest and exercise in accordance with its charisms the ministry of the unique Prophet, Priest and King in the world, and are therefore mutually interdependent. There is no Church without ordained ministry, no ordained ministry without ecclesial community, in some form or other. The ecclesial community receives the Word of God from the ordained ministry, which is the sign that this Word originates not

Geneva/79 [cont.]

from the Christian community but from God himself. The ordained ministry can only proclaim the Word of God in communion with the ecclesial community; the community of the Church is a reminder to the ordained ministry that it has no autonomous individual power but only the authority of God given in and for his people.

10. In order that the ecclesial community may become ever more truly the royal and prophetic priesthood through which Christ acts in the world, the Holy Spirit chooses members of the Body of Christ and makes them ministers by endowing them with the charisms needed for their service in the ecclesial community. In communion with Christ the Prophet, the ordained ministers Proclaim the Word of God and by doing so assemble and develop the ecclesial com-

Geneva/1-16-80 [cont.]

11-Commentary:

The function is not exercised by the ordained ministry in an exclusive way. Since the ordained ministry and the community are inextricably related to one another all members participate in fulfilling the function. In fact, every charism serves "to assemble and to build up the communion in Christ". Any member of the body may share in proclaiming and teaching the Word of God and in the carrying out of the liturgical and the missionary and diaconal life of the eucharistic community. The ordained ministry fulfils the function in a representative way providing the focus for the unity of its life and witness.

The New Testament says very little if anything about the actual celebration of the eucharist. There is no evidence about the presidence over the eucharist. In later

Geneva/1-19-80 [cont.]

11-Commentary:

The function is not exercised by the ordained ministry in an exclusive way. Since the ordained ministry and the community are inextricably related to one another, all members participate in fulfilling the function. In fact, every charism serves "to assemble, build up and guide the community in Christ". Any member of the body may share in proclaiming and teaching the Word of God and in the carrying out of the liturgical and the missionary and diaconal life of the eucharistic community. The ordained ministry fulfils the function in a representative way, providing the focus for the unity of its life and witness.

12. In presiding over the celebration of the eucharist, the ordained ministry is the visible focus of the deep and all encompassing communion between Christ and the members of his body.

Geneva/6-80 [cont.]

12-Commentary. The function is not exercised by the ordained ministry in an exclusive way. Since the ordained ministry and the community are inextricably related, all members participate in fulfilling the function. In fact, every charism serves "to assemble and build up the body of Christ". Any member of the body may share in proclaiming and teaching the Word of God and in guiding the life of the community. The ordained ministry fulfils the function in a representative way, providing the focus for the unity of the life and witness of the community.

13. It is in the eucharistic celebration that the ordained ministry is the visible focus of the deep and all encompassing communion between Christ and the members of his body.

13-Commentary. The New

Geneva/79 [cont.]

munity; in communion with Christ the Priest, the ordained ministers intercede for every member of the people of God entrusted to them, especially as they preside at the celebration of the Eucharist, and offer their own lives in the service of Christ and his Church; in communion with Christ the King, the ordained ministers lead that portion of the people of God entrusted to them towards unity in love, encouraging the community to look and hope for the coming Kingdom.

Geneva/1-16-80 [cont.]

times, the ordained ministry has clearly the function of presiding over the celebration. If it is true that the ordained ministry is to provide a focus for the unity of the life and witness of the Church, it is natural that it should be given this task.

Geneva/1-19-80 [cont.]
12-Commentary:

The New Testament says very little about the ordering of the eucharist. There is no clear evidence about the presidency of the eucharist. In later times it is clear that an ordained minister has the function of presiding over the celebration. If it is true that the ordained ministry is to provide a focus for the unity of the life and witness of the Church, it is natural that it should be given this task. It is intimately related to the task of guiding the community, i.e. supervising its life (episkopé) and strengthening its vigilance in relation to the truth of the apostolic message and the coming of the kingdom.

Geneva/6-80 [cont.]

Testament says very little about the ordering of the eucharist. There is no clear evidence about the presidency of the eucharist. In later times it is clear that an ordained minister has the function of presiding over the celebration. If it is true that the ordained ministry is to provide a focus for the unity of the life and witness of the Church, it is natural that an ordained minister should be given this task. It is intimately related to the task of guiding the community, i.e. supervising its life (*episkopé*) and strengthening its vigilance in relation to the truth of the apostolic message and the coming of the kingdom.

Between Accra/74 and Geneva/6-80 there is a reordering of material but much of the content and meaning is the same. There are, however, some significant alterations. The word, "apostles," is undifferentiated in Accra/74[52] although it is implied that it means, "the Twelve," in that Christ chose them. Geneva/1-80 and Geneva/6-80 carefully define the meaning of the word, "apostles,"[53] distinguishing between the Twelve and the other apostles. In Accra/74 their uniqueness is described merely in terms of the fact that "Christ chose apostles and committed to them the word of reconciliation."[54] In Geneva/1-80 the uniqueness of the Twelve is identified with their being "witnesses of the Lord's life and resurrection, as patriarchs and judges of the new Israel, and as leaders of the community in prayer, teaching and service."[55] In Geneva/6-80 this uniqueness of the *apostles* (only the Twelve?) is described in terms of their being "witnesses of the risen Christ."

This uniqueness, however, which accounts for "a fundamental difference between the apostles and the ordained ministers,"[56] does not stand in the way of the fact "that the Twelve *prefigure* both the Church and the persons entrusted with special authority and responsibility in the Church."[57]

Geneva/6-80 adds the sentence, "As servants they (the ordained ministers) will seek to reflect Christ's priestly ministry and intercede for the community and the world."[58] Thus an emphasis is placed on the priestly role.

Christ's being "sent by the Father"[59] is added to the Accra/74 text.[60]

What is added here is the statement that the ordained ministry "is an office of guiding and teaching, related to Christ's prophetic and teaching ministry, and to the fulfilment (*sic*) of law and prophets in him."[61] The intervening texts between

---

[52]Accra/74, §13.

[53]Geneva/1-80, §s 8 and 8-Commentary; Geneva/6-80, §s 9 and 9-Commentary.

[54]Accra/74, §13.

[55]Geneva/1-80, §8.

[56]Geneva/6-80, §9.

[57]Idem. Emphasis added.

[58]Geneva/6-80, §10. Cf. Geneva/1-80, §9.

[59]Geneva/1-80, §9.

[60]Accra/74, §14.

[61]Geneva/1-80, §9. This is added to Accra/74, §14.

Accra/74 and Geneva/6-80 had added a paragraph listing the permanent characteristics of the ordained ministry: mission, ambassadorship, and pastoral function.[62] The contents of this paragraph were subsumed into the Geneva/6-80 text.[63]

One sentence significantly was eliminated from Accra/74 in the text of Geneva/1-80. This sentence describes the persons called to the ordained ministry: "Persons called to this ministry are commissioned to serve the work of the Lord by following him, being conformed to him and by announcing his name."[64] The sentence which follows it is revised significantly. The earlier version reads as follows: "The presence of this ministry in the community signifies the priority of divine initiative and authority in the Church's existence."[65] It is revised to read, "Its presence reminds the community of the priority of the apostolic message in its life."[66] The term, "divine initiative," however, reappears in a later text and eventually in the final text of Lima 1/82.[67]

An entire paragraph is added to the Accra/74 text explaining the difficulty of using the term, "ordained ministry," with historical accuracy and the impossibility of attributing actual forms of the ordained ministry to "the will and institution of Jesus Christ himself."[68]

"The ordained ministers and the believing community are *inextricably* related."[69] The addition of the word, "inextricably," seems to be influenced by the Orthodox theologians. For they had suggested in their May/June, 1979 meeting the following:

> The new text should take its starting point from the theme "Christ, the ministry and the community". The ministry/priesthood has been established together with the Church. No ministry without the community; no community without the ministry.

---

[62]Geneva/79, §19 and Geneva/1-80, §9.

[63]Geneva/6-80, §10.

[64]Accra/74, §14. Cf. Geneva/1-80, §s 2-10.

[65]Accra/74, §14.

[66]Geneva/1-80, §10.

[67]November/80, §11; Lima, §12.

[68]Geneva/1-80, §10-Commentary; Geneva/6-80, §10-Commentary.

[69]Geneva/6-80, §11. Emphasis added. The word, "inextricably," is added to Accra/74, §15.

Strong emphasis should be placed on the interaction between the two.[70]

The earlier text stated that the ordained ministry "serves to coordinate and unite the different gifts in the community and to strengthen and enable the ministry of the whole People of God."[71] Later it is revised to read as follows: "Their (the ordained ministers') presence *reminds* the community of the priority of the apostolic message in its life. They serve to *build up* the communion in Christ and *strengthen* its witness."[72] The earlier, "task," becomes, "their calling," in the later text.[73] The "*recognition* . . . of the community" is added in the later text.[74]

"The *essential* and specific function of the ordained ministry," becomes "the *central* and specific function of the ordained minister."[75] And the phrases, "*by . . . presiding over the liturgical and sacramental life of the eucharistic community*," become the phrases, "by celebrating the sacraments, and to guide the life of the community in its liturgical, missionary and diaconal aspects."[76]

An entirely new paragraph (of commentary) is added to the Accra text. It makes clear that even "the central and specific function of the ordained minister" outlined in the body of the text "is not exercised by the ordained ministry in an exclusive way . . . (that) all members participate in fulfilling the function . . . (and that) the ordained ministry fulfils the function in a representative way, providing the focus for the unity of the life and witness of the community."[77]

Another entirely new paragraph and its accompanying paragraph of commentary is added to the Accra text. It focuses on the function of the ordained ministry at the eucharistic celebration.[78] The succeeding texts between Geneva/79 and Geneva/6-80 evince a careful nuancing of the precise functioning of the

---

[70]FO Paper No. 98, p. 83.

[71]Accra/74, §15.

[72]Geneva/6-80, §11. Emphasis added. This change took place in the Geneva/1-80 text, §10.

[73]Accra/74, §15; Geneva/6-80, §12.

[74]Geneva/6-80, §11. Emphasis added.

[75]Geneva/6-80, §12; Accra/74, §15. Emphasis added.

[76]Accra/74, §15; Geneva/6-80, §12.

[77]Geneva/6-80, §12-Commentary.

[78]The appropriate texts are the following: Geneva/79, §10; Geneva/1-16-80, §s 11 and 11-Commentary; 1/19/80, §s 12 and 12-Commentary; Geneva/6-80, §s 13 and 13-Commentary.

eucharistic presiding and of its relationship to *episkopé* in the historical development of the Church.

B. ORDAINED MINISTRY AND AUTHORITY.

The communitarian nature of this authority is emphasized. There is a careful nuancing of the meaning of that authority in relation to the Word of God. And both the ordained and the non-ordained stand under the authority of the Word of God as exercised by Christ.

Accra/74

17. The setting apart for this special ministry implies both consecration to service and authority for its exercise. Since all ministry is rooted in that of Christ, its essential quality is seen in such words as these: "I am among you as one who serves" (Luke 22:27). The commission which Christ gave his apostles is set in this light in such a passage as John 17: 18-18 and is so accepted by St Paul who exalts his ministry as an apostle in terms of a sharing in the suffering of Christ: "Always bearing in the body the death of Jesus so that the life of Jesus may also be manifested in our bodies" (II Cor.4:10).

18. The exercise of such ministry has authority which ultimately belongs to Christ who has received it from the Father (Matt. 28:18); it is in this sense a divine authority. On the other hand, since ordination is essentially a

Geneva/79

41. The setting apart for the ordained ministry implies both consecration to service and authority for its exercise. Since all ministry is rooted in that of Christ, its essential quality is seen in such words as these: "I am among you as one who serves" (Lk 22:27). The commission which Christ gave his apostles is set in this light in such a passage as John 17:18 and is so accepted by St Paul who exalts his ministry as an apostle in terms of a sharing in the suffering of Christ: "Always bearing in the body the death of Jesus so that the life of Jesus may also be manifested in our bodies" (II Cor. 4:10). (no 17)

42. The exercise of such ministry has authority which ultimately belongs to Christ who has received it from the Father (Mt. 28:18); it is in this sense a divine authority. On the other hand, since ordination is essentially a

Geneva/1-16-80

12. To be set apart for the ordained ministry means consecration to service. The ordained ministers will seek to follow the Lord and to be conformed to him. Words such as "I am among you as the one who serves" (Luke 22:27) will govern their life. They will find their inspiration in the model of the apostles. (Para 17)

Geneva/1-19-80

13. To be set apart for the ordained ministry means consecration to service. The ordained ministers will seek to follow the Lord and to be conformed to him. Words such as "I am among you as the one who serves" (Lk. 22:27) will govern their life. They will find their inspiration in the model of the apostles. (para. 17)

14. It is only on this basis that the ordained ministry exercises authority in the community. Authority has its ultimate source in Jesus Christ who has received it from the Father and conferred it on the apostles. It

Geneva/6-80

14. The authority which is exercised by the ordained ministry has its source in Jesus Christ who "came as one who serves" (Mk 10:45; Lk 22:27). To be set apart for the ordained ministry, therefore, means to be consecrated to service. At the same time, authority stems from the recognition given to the ordained minister by the community. Since this act of recognition is essentially a setting apart with prayer for the gift of the Holy Spirit, the authority of the ordained ministry is not to be understood as the possession of the ordained person but as a gift for the continuing edification of the body in and for which the minister has been ordained. Authority has the character of responsibility before God and is exercised with the participation of the whole community.

13. It is only on this basis that the ordained ministry exercises authority in the community. Authority has its ultimate source in Jesus Christ who has received it from the Father and conferred it on the apostles. It

Accra/74 [cont.]

setting apart with prayer for the gifts of the Holy Spirit for the continuing constitution and edification of the body, the authority of the ordained ministry is not to be understood as an individual possession of the ordained person but belongs to the whole community in and for which the minister is ordained. Authority in the exercise must involve the participation of the whole community. The ordained minister manifests and exercises the authority of Christ in the way Christ himself revealed God's authority to the world: in and through *communion.*

Geneva/79 [cont.]

setting apart with prayer for the gifts of the Holy Spirit for the continuing constitution and edification of the body, the authority of the ordained ministry is not to be understood as an individual possession of the ordained person. Authority in the name of God in its exercise must involve the participation of the whole community. The ordained minister manifests and exercises the authority of Christ in the way Christ himself revealed God's authority to the world: in and through *communion.* (no 18)

Geneva/1-16-80 [cont.]

also stems from the recognition given to the ordained minister by the community. But since this act of recognition is essentially a setting apart with prayer for the gift of the Holy Spirit the authority of the ordained ministry is not to be understood as the possession of the ordained person but as a gift for the continuing edification of the body in and for which the minister is ordained. Authority cannot be truly exercised without the participation of the whole community. (Para 18)

Geneva/1-19-80 [cont.]

also stems from the recognition given to the ordained minister by the community. But since this act of recognition is essentially a setting apart with prayer for the gift of the Holy Spirit the authority of the ordained ministry is not to be understood as the possession of the ordained person but as a gift for the continuing edification of the body in and for which the minister is ordained. Authority cannot be truly exercised without the participation of the whole community. (para. 18)

Accra/74 [cont.]

19. This in practice means that the ordained ministry is authoritative only in and through the concrete community to which it belongs. The ordained minister is not an autocrat nor an impersonal functionary. He is bound to the faithful in interdependence and reciprocity, although his role is one of responsible leadership and judgment. Only if the authority of the ordained minister finds genuine acknowledgment in the communion of the community can this authority be protected from the distortion of domination.

Geneva/79

42. [cont.] This in practice means that the ordained ministry is authoritative only in and through the concrete community to which it belongs. The ordained minister is not an autocrat nor an impersonal functionary. He is bound to the faithful in interdependence and reciprocity, although his role is one of responsible leadership and judgment. Only if the authority of the ordained minister finds genuine acknowledgment in the communion of the community can this authority be protected from the distortion of domination. (no 19)

Geneva/1-16-80 [cont.]

14. Therefore, the ordained minister is not an autocrat nor an impersonal functionary. Although he is called to exercise a role of responsible judgment and leadership he is bound to the faithful in interdependence and reciprocity. Only if the ordained minister genuinely seeks the response and the acknowledgement of the community can the authority of the ordained ministry be protected from the distortion of domination. (para 18)

Geneva/1-19-80 [cont.]

15. Therefore, the ordained minister is not an autocrat nor an impersonal functionary. Although he is called to exercise a role of responsible judgment and leadership, he is bound to the faithful in interdependence and reciprocity. Only if the ordained minister genuinely seeks the response and the acknowledgement of the community can the authority of the ordained ministry be protected from the distortion of domination. (para. 18)

Geneva/6-80 [cont.]

15. Therefore, ordained ministers are not autocrats or impersonal functionaries. Although called to exercise a role of responsible judgment and leadership on the basis of the Word of God, they are bound to the faithful in interdependence and reciprocity. Only when they genuinely seek the response and the acknowledgement of the community can their authority be protected from the distortions of isolation and domination. They manifest and exercise the authority of Christ in the way Christ himself revealed God's authority to the world: by committing their life to the community.

The authority of the ordained ministry "has the character of responsibility before God."[79] Thus it is no longer simply stated as "authority in the name of God."[80] The earlier phrase, "in and through *communion*," is clarified in the later text with the words, "by committing their life to the community."[81] What is not so clear in the later text is the precise community to which the reference is made. For the earlier text adds the sentence, "this in practice means that the ordained ministry is authoritative only in and through the concrete community to which it belongs."[82]

An entire paragraph is added in the commentary section of the Geneva/6-80 text. It speaks to the authenticity of the authority of ordained ministers in terms of its being in conformity with the authority exercised by Christ. More importantly, that paragraph, in speaking to the two-fold danger in the exercise of authority, emphasizes that "the authority of the ordained ministers must not be reduced to make them dependent on the common opinion of the community. Their authority lies in their responsibility to recall the Word of God in the community."[83]

C. ORDAINED MINISTRY AND PRIESTHOOD.

Here again there is a more inclusive ecclesiology in evidence, beyond baptism. There is a more expansive leadership role emphasized, beyond the liturgical/sacramental. And there is indicated a difference in nature between the priesthood of the ordained and the priesthood of Christ.

---

[79] Geneva/6-80, §14.

[80] Accra/74, §18.

[81] Accra/74, §18; Geneva/6-80, §15.

[82] Accra/74, §19.

[83] Geneva/6-80, §15-Commentary.

Accra/74

20. Even if the New Testament never uses the terms, "priest-hiereus" or "priesthood-hierateuma" to designate the ordained minister or the ministry, tradition has not been afraid of this usage. Although churches emerging from the Reformation avoid the word priesthood to designate the ordained ministry, churches of the catholic tradition employ this word in diverse forms: priestly ministry, ministerial priesthood, or, more recently, ministry of priesthood. The search for a reconciliation in ministries makes it especially useful to discuss this question of terms.

Geneva/79

38. Even if the New Testament never uses the terms "priest-hiereus" or "priesthood-hierateuma" to designate the ordained minister or the ministry, tradition has not been afraid of this usage. Although churches emerging from the Reformation avoid the word priesthood to designate the ordained ministry, churches of the catholic tradition employ this word in diverse forms: priestly ministry, ministerial priesthood, or ministry of priesthood. (no 20)

Geneva/1-19-80

16. The ordained minister is a priest by virtue of the relation between the ordained ministry to the unique priesthood of Jesus Christ on the one hand and to the priesthood of the Christian community on the other. Christ is the unique priest of the unique sacrifice of the New Covenant. By ordination, a Christian is established in a new relation with Christ-Priest, in order to represent him within the community. The ordained minister participates, as every Christian does, in the priesthood of Christ and of the whole people of God. He fulfils his particular priestly service in building up, strengthening and expressing the royal and prophetic priesthood of the faithful through the service of the Gospel and through the leading of the liturgical and missionary and diaconal life of the eucharistic community. He fulfils also his priestly service by his pastoral prayer of intercession. (para 21)

Geneva/6-80

16. Jesus Christ is the unique priest of the new covenant. He gave his life as sacrifice for all. In a secondary way, the Church as a whole can be described as a priesthood. All members are called to offer their being "as a living sacrifice" and to intercede for the Church and the salvation of the world. The ordained ministers are related, like all Christians, to both the priesthood of Christ and the priesthood of the Church. They may be called priests because they fulfil a particular priestly service by strengthening and building up the royal and prophetic priesthood of the faithful through their prayers of intercession, their service of the Gospel and their pastoral guidance of the community.

Accra/74 [cont.]

21. This manner of expression always refers the function of the priests to a priestly reality upon which theirs is based, but which exceeds it — that is, the unique priesthood of Christ and the royal and prophetic, common and universal priesthood of the baptized (I Peter 2:9; Rev. 1:6, 3:10, 20:6). The priesthood of Christ and the priesthood of the baptized community is a function of sacrifice and intercession. As Christ offers himself for all men, the Christian offers his whole being "as a living sacrifice" (Rom. 12:1). As Christ intercedes to the Father for all men, the Christian prays for the liberation of his human brothers. The minister, who participates, as every Christian does, in the priesthood of Christ, and of all the People of God, fulfils his particular priestly service in building up, strengthening and expressing the royal and prophetic priest-

Geneva/79 [cont.]

39. This manner of expression always refers the function of the priests to a priestly reality upon which theirs is based, but which exceeds it that is, the unique priesthood of Christ and the royal and prophetic, common and universal priesthood of the baptized (I Peter 2:9; Rev. 1:6, 3:10, 20:6). The priesthood of Christ and the priesthood of the baptized community is a function of sacrifice and intercession. As Christ offers himself for all men, the Christian offers his whole being "as a living sacrifice" (Rom. 12:1). As Christ intercedes to the Father for all men, the Christian prays for the liberation of his human brothers. The minister, who participates, as every Christian does, in the priesthood of Christ, and of all the People of God, fulfils his particular priestly service in building up, strengthening and expressing the royal and prophetic

Geneva/1-16-80

15. Commentary:

The New Testament never uses the term "Priesthood-hierateuma" or "priest-hiereus" to designate the ordained ministry or the ordained minister. This is the main reason for the churches of the Reformation to avoid the term. In the New Testament, the term is reserved on the one hand for the unique priesthood of Jesus Christ and on the other hand for the royal and prophetic priesthood of all baptized. The priesthood of Christ and the priesthood of the baptized community is a function of sacrifice and intercession. As Christ offers himself for everybody Christians offer their whole being "as a living sacrifice" (Rom. 12:1). As Christ intercedes with the Father, Christians pray for the Church and the salvation of the world. In the early Church the terms "priesthood" and "priest" came to be used to designate the

Geneva/1-19-80 [cont.]

16-Commentary:

The New Testament never uses the term "priesthood-hierateuma" or "priest-hiereus" to designate the ordained ministry or the ordained minister. This is the main reason for the churches of the Reformation to avoid the term. In the New Testament, the term is reserved on the one hand for the unique priesthood of Jesus Christ and on the other hand for the royal and prophetic priesthood of all baptized. The priesthood of Christ and the priesthood of the baptized community is a function of sacrifice and intercession. As Christ offers himself for everybody Christians offer their whole being "as a living sacrifice" (Rom. 12:1). As Christ intercedes before the Father, Christians intercede for the Church and the salvation of the world. In the early Church the terms "priesthood" and "priest" came to be used to designate the

Geneva/6-80 [cont.]

16-Commentary. The New Testament never uses the term "priesthood-hierateuma" or "priest-hiereus" to designate the ordained ministry or ordained minister. In the New Testament the term is reserved, on the one hand, for the unique priesthood of Jesus Christ who offered himself once and for all for the sins of all humanity (Heb 7:24), and on the other hand, for the royal and prophetic priesthood of all baptized (I Pet 2:9). The priesthood of Christ and the priesthood of the baptized, in their respective ways, have the function of sacrifice and intercession. In the early Church the terms "priesthood" and "priest" came to be used to designate the ordained ministry and minister. They underline the fact that the ordained ministry is related to the priestly reality of Jesus Christ and the whole community.

Accra/74 [cont.]	*Geneva/79* [cont.]	*Geneva/1-16-80* [cont.]	*Geneva/1-19-80* [cont.]
hood of the faithful through the service of the Gospel, the leading of the liturgical and sacramental life of the eucharistic community, and intercession.	priesthood of the faithful through the service of the Gospel, the leading of the liturgical and sacramental life of the eucharistic community, and intercession. (no 21)	ordained ministry and minister. They underline the fact that the ordained ministry is related to the priestly reality of Jesus Christ and the whole community. The ordained minister, who participates, as every Christian does, in the priesthood of Christ and of the whole people of God, fulfils his particular priestly service in strengthening, building up and expressing the royal and prophetic priesthood of the faithful through the service of the Gospel, the leading of the liturgical and sacramental life of the eucharistic community and intercession. (Para 21)	ordained ministry and minister. They underline the fact that the ordained ministry is related to the priestly reality of Jesus Christ and the whole community.

Accra/74 [cont.]

22. The ordained ministry is then of a completely new and different nature in relation to the sacrificial priesthood of the Old Testament. As He offers his life for the service of the mission in the world and of the edification of the Church, the minister is, as St. Paul says about himself, "a minister of Jesus Christ to the Gentiles in the priestly service of the gospel of God, so that the offering of the Gentiles may be acceptable, sanctified by the Holy Spirit" (Rom.15:16).

Geneva/79 [cont.]

40. The ordained ministry is then of a completely new and different nature in relation to the sacrificial priesthood of the Old Testament. As He offers his life for the service of the mission in the world and of the edification of the Church, the minister is, as St Paul says about himself, " a minister of Jesus Christ to the Gentiles in the priestly service of the gospel of God, so that the offering of the Gentiles may be acceptable, sanctified by the Holy Spirit" (Rom. 15:16). (no 22)

Geneva/1-16-80

15. Commentary [cont.]

If the ordained ministry is called "priesthood" it must be made clear that it is different in nature from the sacrificial priesthood of the Old Testament. The unique sacrifice of Jesus Christ has taken place. Priestly service now means serving the Gospel within and on behalf of the community. Ordained ministers are, as St Paul says about himself, ministers of "Jesus Christ to the Gentiles in the priestly service of the Gospel of God, so that the offering of the Gentiles may be acceptable by the Holy Spirit" (Rom 15:16). (Para. 22)

Geneva/1-19-80

16-Commentary: [cont.]

If the ordained ministry is called "priesthood" it must be made clear that it is different in nature from the sacrificial priesthood of the Old Testament. The unique sacrifice of Jesus Christ has taken place. Priestly service now means serving the Gospel within and on behalf of the community. Ordained ministers are, as St Paul says about himself, ministers of "Jesus Christ to the Gentiles in the priestly service of the Gospel of God, so that the offering of the Gentiles may be acceptable by the Holy Spirit" (Rom. 15:16). (para. 22)

Geneva/6-80

16-Commentary: [cont.]

As one uses the term it must be made clear, however, that the service of the ordained ministry is different in nature not only from the sacrificial priesthood of the Old Testament, but also from the unique propitiatory priesthood of Christ. If we speak today of the priestly service of the ordained ministry, we mean serving the Gospel within and on behalf of the community, as St Paul says about himself: "I am a minister of Jesus Christ to the gentiles in the priestly service of the Gospel of God, so that the offering of the gentiles may be acceptable by the Holy Spirit" (Rom 15:16).

The term, "priesthood," is applied in the later text to "the Church as a whole" whereas the earlier text had referred to "the baptized community."[84] Thus a more expansive ecclesiology with each succeeding revision of the text. The later text in explaining the "particular priestly service" of ordained ministers refers to "their pastoral guidance of the community" whereas the earlier text says, "the leading of the liturgical and sacramental life of the eucharistic community."[85] Thus a more expansive leadership role with the later revision.

The later text, in its commentary section, adds that "the ordained ministry is different in nature . . . from the unique propitiatory priesthood of Christ."[86] The earlier text had stated only that "the ordained ministry is then of a completely new and different nature in relation to the sacrificial priesthood of the Old Testament."[87]

D. THE MINISTRY OF MEN AND WOMEN IN THE CHURCH.

There is more and more reticence to speak to the issue of the question of women in the ministry and especially, the ordination of women, at least in this text, alongside the other issues which concern the ordained ministry.

---

[84]Geneva/6-80, §16; Accra/74, §21.

[85]Ibid.

[86]Geneva/6-80, §16-Commentary.

[87]Accra/74, §22.

Accra/74

64. Both men and women need to discover the full meaning of their specific contribution to the ministry of Christ. The Church is entitled to the style of ministry which can be provided by women as well as that which can be provided by men. Indeed, an understanding of our mutual interdependence needs to be more widely reflected in all branches of ministry. If ministry demands the engagement of the full humanity of those involved in it, may it not also be enriched by the creative interaction of men and women in relationship?

66. It seems clear that, without repudiating the efficacy of their ministries in the past many churches are reading passages such as Genesis 1:27 and Galatians 3:28 with a sensitivity arising from new circumstances and new needs. The implications for the ordained

Geneva/79

47. Both men and women need to discover the full meaning of their specific contribution to the ministry of Christ. The Church is entitled to the style of ministry which can be provided by women as well as that which can be provided by men. Indeed, an understanding of our mutual interdependence needs to be more widely reflected in all branches of ministry. If ministry demands the engagement of the full humanity of those involved in it, may it not also be enriched by the creative interaction of men and women in relationship?

48. It seems clear that, without repudiating the efficacy of their ministries in the past, many churches are reading passages such as Genesis 1:27 and Galatians 3:28 with a sensitivity arising from new circumstances and new needs. The implications for the ministry both

Geneva/1-16-80

24. The new community in Christ has benefited from women and men sharing in a wide variety of Christian ministries. The churches are not agreed, however, on the permissibility of women entering the ordained ministry.

24-Commentary:
Many churches, without repudiating the efficacy of their ordained ministries in the past, are now reading passages such as Genesis 1:27 and Galatians 3:28 with a sensitivity arising from new understanding and new needs. We need to explore more fully, with regard to the implications for ministry, both the relatedness of men and women as created together in the image of God, and the transcending of their separation in the perspective of redemption in Christ. Different traditions read the same text in different ways. Without denying the re- (no 64)

Geneva/1-19-80

25. To be rewritten in June.

Geneva/6-80

51. Some churches ordain both men and women, others ordain only men. Differences on this issue could raise obstacles to the mutual recognition of ministries. But these obstacles must not be regarded as a substantive hindrance for further efforts toward mutual recognition. Openness to each other holds the possibility that the Spirit may well speak to one church through the insights of another. Ecumenical consideration, therefore, should encourage, not restrain, the facing of this question.

17. Where Christ is present, human barriers are being broken. The Church is called to convey the image of a new humanity. In particular, there is in Christ no male or female. Therefore, men and women need to discover the full meaning of their specific contribution to the service of Christ in the

Accra/74 [cont.]

ministry both of the relatedness of men and women as created in the image of God, and of the transcending of the distinction between them in the perspective of redemption in Christ, need to be more fully explored. The different traditions read the same facts in different ways. Without denying the relatedness of the sexes in either creation or redemption, churches which ordain men only tend to see sexual differentiation as requiring a clearly defined separation of social roles. Churches which ordain both men and women, on the other hand, may risk the danger of underestimating the anthropological and social significance of difference between the sexes.

Geneva/79 [cont.]

of the relatedness of men and women as created in the image of God, and of the transcending of the distinction between them in the perspective of redemption in Christ, need to be more fully explored. The different traditions read the same facts in different ways. Without denying the relatedness of the sexes in either creation or redemption, churches which ordain men only tend to see sexual differentiation as requiring a clearly defined separation of social roles. Churches which ordain both men and women, on the other hand, may risk the danger of underestimating the anthropological and social significance of difference between the sexes. (no 66)

Geneva/1-16-80 [cont.]

latedness of the sexes in either creation or redemption, churches which only ordain men tend to see sexual differentiation as requiring a clearly defined separation of ministries and offices in the Church. On the other hand, churches which do ordain both men and women may risk the danger of underestimating the anthropological and social significance of the difference between sexes.

Geneva/6-80 [cont.]

Church. The Church is entitled to the style which can be provided by women as well as that which can be provided by men. A deeper understanding of the mutual interdependence of men and women needs to be more widely reflected in the life of the Church and its ministries.

17-Commentary. Though they agree on this need, the churches draw different conclusions as to the admission of women to the ordained ministry. While some, in fact an increasing number of, churches have decided to ordain women, the majority hold that the unbroken tradition of the Church in this regard should not be changed today.

Accra/74 [cont.]

67. Theological reasoning and church practice on both sides of this debate may be adversely influenced by continuing the predominance of male imagery in the modern social and cultural context. Although contemporary society, particularly in the West, affords greater equality to women than the society of biblical times, both proponents and opponents of the ordination of women are subject to assumptions of male dominance which are part of the fabric of language and custom. Such taken-for-granted conceptual patterns may distort theological reasoning and institutional practice both in churches which ordain women and in those which do not.

Accra/74 [cont.]

69. For some churches these problems are not yet alive. While recording a position, they have not yet determined whether the decisive factors are doctrinal or simply related to a longstanding traditional discipline. Nor are individuals within the different confessions in agreement about the doctrinal and disciplinary factors or about their relation. Differences on this issue could raise possible obstacles to the mutual recognition of ministries. But these obstacles should not be regarded as insuperable. Openness to each other holds out the possibility that the Spirit may well speak to one Church through the insights of another. Ecumenical awareness and responsibility also demand that once a Church has decided what is

Accra/74 [cont.]

65. Since those who advocate the ordination of women do so out of their understanding of the meaning of the Gospel and ordination, and since the experience of the churches in which women are ordained has on the whole been positive and none has found reason to reconsider its decision, the question must be asked as to whether it is not time for all the churches to confront this matter forthrightly. Churches which ordain women have found that women's gifts are as wide and varied as men's, and that their ministry is as fully blessed by the Holy Spirit as the ministry of men. The force of 19

Geneva/79 [cont.]

49. Theological reasoning and church practice on both sides of this debate may be adversely influenced by continuing the predominance of male imagery in the modern social and cultural context. Although contemporary society, particularly in the West, affords greater equality to women than the society of biblical times, both proponents and opponents of the ministry of women are subject to assumptions of male dominance which are part of the fabric of language and custom. Such taken-for-granted conceptual patterns may distort theological reasoning and institutional practice both in churches which ordain women and in those which do not. (no 67)

50. For some churches these problems are not alive. Within the different confessions the theologians are not in agreement about doctrinal and disciplinary factors or

Geneva/1-16-80

24-Commentary: [cont.] On both sides of this debate theological reasoning and church practice may be adversely influenced by continuing the predominance of male imagery in the modern social and cultural context. Such conceptual patters, that are taken for granted, may distort theological reasoning and institutional practice both in those churches which ordain women and in those which do not.

Accra/74 [cont.]

timely and right, it should act in obedience to its own conviction. Since the opinion appears to be growing that doctrinal considerations either favour the ordination of women or are neutral, the possibility is open that a future ecumenical council might deal with the question. Ecumenical considerations, therefore, should encourage, not restrain, the full, frank facing of this question.

Accra/74 [cont.]

centuries of tradition against the ordination of women cannot be lightly ignored. It cannot be dismissed as lack of respect for the role of women in the Church. It raises theological as well as sociological questions which must be faced. The discussion of these questions within several churches and Christian traditions should be complemented by joint study and reflection within the ecumenical fellowship of all churches.

Geneva/79 [cont.]

about their relation. Differences on this issue could raise possible obstacles to the mutual recognition of ministries. But these obstacles should not be regarded as insuperable. Openness to each other holds out the possibility that the Spirit may well speak to one Church through the insights of another. (no 69)

The later text chooses to simplify and shorten the longer treatment of Accra/74. In fact, Accra/74 devoted a distinct section of its text to the topic of "The Ordination of Women." The Geneva/6-80 text chooses the title, "The Ministry of Men and Women in the Church." In its treatment the later text comments only briefly on the fact of the ordination of women in its commentary section[88] stating that "the churches draw different conclusions as to the admission of women to the ordained ministry . . . (and) the majority (of churches) hold that the unbroken tradition of the Church in this regard should not be changed today."[89]

In the body of its text Geneva/6-80 introduces the topic by adding three short sentences to previous texts: "Where Christ is present, human barriers are being broken. The Church is called to convey the image of a new humanity. In particular, there is in Christ no male or female." Later in the same text, under the title, "Towards the Mutual Recognition of the Ordained Ministries," one paragraph is devoted to the fact that "some churches ordain both men and women, others ordain only men."[90] This paragraph goes on to encourage the facing of this question for ecumenical reasons much like the Accra text had.[91] These few statements in the Geneva/6-80 text summarize the many paragraphs cited in the Accra/74 text on the topic of women's ordination.[92]

In the August 1978 meeting of the FO Commission at Bangalore the subject of the ordination of women was discussed at length:

> Members of the group recognized that the matter was for many a matter of inescapable importance and relevance and that discussion must go on. All were agreed that women have a vital and proper role in the ministry of the Church and some support was expressed for the ordination of women to the diaconate. The chapter in (the Accra text's) BEM (section D, p.45) was felt by some to be too short to be able to deal with the matter as the subject deserves and too long for its present purpose of simply making a comment on the question. The passage, it was suggested, sat somewhat uneasily in its present context. Two possibilities were put forward: one was to shorten the section and the other was to make it section (9) under Section C "Conditions of Ordination" in the statement.

---

[88]The texts of 1/80 are the first efforts to provide a Commentary section as distinct from the body of the document.

[89]Geneva/6-80, §17-Commentary.

[90]Geneva/6-80, §51.

[91]Geneva/6-80, §51; Accra/74, §65.

[92]Interestingly, the Accra/74 text does not treat the matter of women's ordination in its section, "Towards the Recognition of and the Reconciliation of Ministries."

> Members agreed that there should be a working group to consider the subject of the ordination of women in collaboration with those engaged in the study on The Community of Women and Men in the Church. . . . Importance was attached to the preparation of material on this issue to be fed into the International Consultation on the Community of Women and Men in the Church planned for 1980.[93]

The Consultation of Orthodox Theologians in 1979 made the following suggestion:

> The ordination of women should not be included in the consensus affirmations. There can be a common affirmation that women should be given a more prominent place in the wide range of ministries in the Church, but the present debate on the ordination should be referred to only in the commentary.[94]

This view is the one which prevailed in the text of Geneva/6-80 and in the final Lima text. M. Thurian related to the present writer in an interview that it was the influence of the Orthodox theologians which was crucial.[95]

Finally, the later text in this section (in the second column above) strives to keep the treatment of the topic of ministry in more general terms. So much is that effort in evidence that the word "ministry" itself is twice changed to "service."[96] In the same vein, the phrase, "reflected in all branches of ministry," is altered to read, "reflected in the life of the Church and its ministries."[97]

---

[93]FO Paper No. 93, p. 255.

[94]FO Paper No. 98, p. 83.

[95]Thurian related to the present writer in interviews (April 29-30, 1985 at the Headquarters of The World Council of Churches in Geneva) that "the Orthodox simply refused to allow a discussion of the question of the ordination of women. The Orthodox agreed only to the descriptive paragraph about it in the Lima text."

[96]Accra/74, §64; Geneva/6-80, §17.

[97]Ibid.

III. THE FORMS OF THE ORDAINED MINISTRY.

A. BISHOPS, PRESBYTERS AND DEACONS.

In this section is seen the development of a whole new emphasis on the role of the bishop and on the three-fold ministry of bishop, presbyter and deacon as the paradigm in the theological and ecumenical discussion of the ordained ministry. A recognition is given to the historical development of the three-fold ministry in the early Church, beyond what is evidenced in the New Testament. Finally, a distinction is drawn between the "ministry" of the ordained and the "service" of all others in the Church.

Accra/74

24. When the diversity of ordained ministry among the various churches is examined, it is evident that this diversity is bound up with the history and cultural particularity of those churches. Each case reveals what might be called a particular "theological-ecclesial culture", that is, a coherence of theology, piety, liturgical tradition, community life, geographical origin, law and jurisprudence. So the diversity of ministerial structures is part of a more complex ecclesial diversity of styles and types, reflecting weighty differences of a theological, sociological and psychological nature. But the limits of ministerial diversity are determined by the apostolic commission, the action of the Holy Spirit and the fact that major patterns of leadership in society are not infinitely variable.

Geneva/79

20. The New Testament attests a great diversity of charisms and ministries distributed for the good of all in accordance with the will of the one Spirit (1 Cor. 12:4-11). A wide range of titles is found there indicative of the ministries exercised in the early Church: prophets, doctors, evangelists, pastors, presbyters, bishops, deacons (Acts 13:1; Eph. 4:11; Acts 20:17; 1 Tim. 3:1-13 etc.). While preserving what is basic and permanent in the ordained ministry, the Church has accepted and can accept a variety of forms of ministry.

20-Commentary:

When the diversity of ordained ministry among the various churches is examined, it is evident that this diversity is bound up with the history and cultural particularity of those churches. Each case reveals what might be called a particular "theological-ecclesial culture", that is, a coherence of theology, piety, liturgical tradition, community life, geographical origin, law and jurisprudence. So the diversity of ministerial structures is part of a more complex ecclesial diversity of styles and types, reflecting differences of a theological, sociological and psychological nature. But the limits of ministerial diversity are determined by the apostolic commission, the action of the Holy Spirit and the fact that major patterns of leadership in society are not infinitely variable. (no 24)

Accra/74 [cont.]

25. The plurality of ecclesial cultures and ministerial structures does not diminish the one ministerial reality found in Christ and constituted by the Holy Spirit in the commission of the Apostles. Among the various ministerial structures the threefold ministry of bishop, presbyter-priest and deacon predominates. But it would be wrong to exclude other patterns of ministry which are found among the churches. Within the same community of faith it is possible to have, side by side, various styles of ecclesial life and ministerial structures, without making the one the model for all the others.

26. There is unity in the diversity of ministerial structures, in that the essential elements of ministry can always be identified in the very plurality and multiformity of essential styles and structures. It would be difficult to imagine any structure of ministry which did not incorporate *episcope*, as that oversight of the Church and of the celebration of the Christian mystery which belongs to the Gospel, and *presbyteral* function understood as the proclamation of the Gospel and administration of the sacraments. Both the epis-copal and presbyteral functions of the Church must be understood as a sharing in the *diakonia*, that is, as costly service to the community of the Church and to the world through the proclamation and actualization of the Gospel. In the course of history, the function of *diakonia* has found expression in the office of deacon and the dea-

Geneva/79 [cont.]

21. The plurality of ecclesial cultures and ministerial structures does not diminish the one ministerial reality found in Christ and constituted by the Holy Spirit in the commission of the Apostles. Among the various ministerial struc-tures the threefold ministry of bishop, presbyter-priest and deacon predominate. But it would be wrong to exclude other patterns of ministry which are found among the churches. Within the same community of faith it is possible to have, side by side, various styles of ecclesial life and ministerial structures, without making the one the model for all the others. (no 25)

22. There is unity in the diversity of ministerial structures, in that the essential elements of ministry can always be identified in the very plurality and multiformity of essential styles and structures. It would be difficult to imagine any structure of ministry which did not incorporate *episcope*, as that oversight of the Church and of the celebration of the Christian mystery which belongs to the Gospel, and *presbyteral* function understood as the proclamation of the Gospel and administration of the sacraments. Both the epis-copal and presbyteral functions of the Church must be understood as a sharing in the *diakonia*, that is, as costly service to the community of the Church and to the world through the proclamation and actualization of the Gospel. In the course of history, the function of *diakonia* has found expression in the office of deacon and deaconess.

Geneva/6-80

19. Though other forms of the ordained ministry have been blessed with the gifts of the Holy Spirit there are good reasons for accepting the threefold form of bishops, presbyters and deacons as a basis for establishing a common form of the ordained ministry today. On the other hand, it has been the generally accepted pattern in the Church of the early centuries and has been retained by the majority of churches up to the present day. In some churches it functions even if different names are used. On the other hand, it provides a valid framework within which the functions of the ordained ministry can be carried out.

22. How can this threefold form be adapted for the Church today? In fact, the question must be asked by all churches. The primary issue is not that some churches, for the sake of unity, should return to the inherited pattern but rather that all churches are called upon to give the fullest possible expression to its potential with a view to a more effective witness of the Church in the world.

22-Commentary:

The pattern stands in need of reform in all churches. In some, the college of elders in the local eucharistic community has disappeared. In others, the functions of deacons have been re-duced to an assistant role in the celebration of the liturgy; they have ceased to fulfil any function with regard to the diaconal witness of the Church.

Accra/74 [cont.]

coness. For about 20 years now, many churches, independently from one another, have been giving attention to the possible renewal of this office.

(no 26)

Geneva/6-80 [cont.]

In some cases, churches which have not formally kept the threefold form have, in fact, better maintained certain of its original intentions.

Geneva/1-16-80

17. Although the New Testament is clear about the ethos of the early Christian community, it does not give a clear and unambiguous answer on the form which the ordained ministry should take in the Church. It is therefore not possible to derive conclusively from the New Testament the appropriate form of the ordained ministry. As soon as local churches had been established, the issue of the form of the ordained ministry arose. Different answers were possible and have, in fact, been given. The New Testament refers to a variety of forms which existed at different places and times. The New Testament points to a historical development which took place as the Holy Spirit led the Church in life, worship and mission. In the second and third centuries, a threefold pattern of bishop, presbyter and deacon eventually emerged.

Commentary:

The New Testament reflects a certain tension between the local church leaders and missionaries like Paul, sent out to the Greek-Roman world. There might have been different organizational patterns at the local level according to hellenist or jewish circumstances. We meet in fact a variety of names and functions by which the original content of the Gospel was transmitted and safeguarded, the faith and discipline of the new Christian communities fed and strengthened, the unity among them protected. In Jerusalem it is the Twelve and the Server, later Jacob and the

Geneva/1-19-80

18. Although the writings of the New Testament are clear about the ethos of the early Christian community, they do not give a clear and unambiguous answer on the form which the ordained ministry should take in the Church. It is therefore not possible to derive conclusively from the New Testament the appropriate form of the ordained ministry. As soon as local churches had been established, the issue of the form of the ordained ministry arose. Different answers were possible and have, in fact, been given. The writings of the New Testament refer to a variety of forms which existed at different places and times. They point to historical developments which took place as the Holy Spirit led the Church in life, worship and mission. In the second and third centuries, a three-fold pattern of bishop, presbyter and deacon eventually emerged.

Commentary:

The New Testament reflects a certain tension between the local church leaders and missionaries such as Paul, sent out to the Greek-Roman world. There might have been different organizational patterns at the local level according to Hellenist or Jewish circumstances. We meet in fact a variety of names and functions by which the original content of the Gospel was transmitted and safeguarded, the faith and discipline of the new Christian communities fed and strengthened, the unity among them protected. The Acts of the Apostles mention for Jerusalem the Twelve and

Geneva/6-80

18. The New Testament does not describe a single pattern of ministry which might serve as a blueprint or continuing norm for all future ministry in the Church. The New Testament writings refer rather to a variety of forms which existed at different places and times. As the Holy Spirit continued to lead the Church in life, worship and mission, certain elements from this early variety became settled into a more universal pattern of ministry. By the second and third centuries, a threefold pattern of bishop, presbyter and deacon became established as the pattern of ordained ministry throughout the Church. In succeeding centuries, the ministry by bishop, presbyter and deacon underwent considerable changes in its practical exercise. At some points of crisis in the history of the Church, the continuing functions of ministry were in some places and communities distributed according to structures other than the predominant threefold pattern. Sometimes appeal was made to the New Testament in justification of these other patterns. In other cases, the restructuring of ministry was held to lie within the competence of the Church as it adapted to changed circumstances.

18-Commentary:

The earliest Church knew both the travelling ministry of such missionaries as Paul and the local ministry of leadership in places where the Gospel was received. At local level, organizational patterns appear to have varied according

Geneva/1-16-80 [cont.]

elders who perform such a function. In Antioch we meet prophets and teachers, in Corinth apostles, prophets and teachers, as well as in Rome, where they have also deacons or assistants. In Philippi there are recorded to be supervisors and helpers. Several of these functions are ascribed to women as well as to men. Together they build up the body of Christ in faithfulness to the one paradosi given to them through Jesus Christ and the disciples sent by him.

Geneva/1-19-80 [cont.]

the Seven, later James and the elders as the performers of such a function; and for Antioch prophets and teachers (Acts 6:1-6; 15:13-22; 13:1). The letters to Corinth speak of apostles, prophets and teachers as well as the letter to the Romans, which also speaks of deacons or assistants (I Cor. 12:28; Rom. 16:1). In Philippi there are recorded to be supervisors and helpers (episkopoi and diakonoi) (Phil. 1:1). Several of these functions are ascribed to women as well as to men. Together they build up the body of Christ in faithfulness to the one paradosis given to them through Jesus Christ and the disciples sent by him.

Geneva/6-80 [cont.]

to circumstances. The Acts of the Apostles mention for Jerusalem the Twelve and the Seven, and later James and the elders; and for Antioch, prophets and teachers (Acts 6: 1-6; 15: 13-22; 13:1). The letters to Corinth speak of apostles, prophets and teachers (I Cor 12: 28); so too does the letter to the Romans, which also speaks of deacons or assistants (Rom 16: 1). In Philippi, the secular terms *episkopoi* and *diakonoi* were together used for Christian ministers (Phil 1:1). Several of these ministries are ascribed to both women and men. While some were appointed by the laying on of hands, there is no indication of this procedure in other cases. Whatever their names, the purpose of these ministries was to proclaim the Word of God, to transmit and safeguard the original content of the Gospel, to feed and strengthen the faith, discipline and service of the Christian communities, and to protect and foster unity within and among them. These have been the constant duties of ministry throughout the developments and crises of Christian history.

Geneva/1-16-80

19. Though the threefold ministry cannot claim to be absolutely binding on the Church, there are good reasons for considering the development leading to its general acceptance as guided by the Holy Spirit. Though other forms have been blessed with the gifts of the Spirit, the use of the threefold ministry as a starting point for seeking a common form of the ordained ministry presents itself as a real possibility for the churches. especially if one considers the variety which is possible within it and the variety of ways in which it actually functions even under different terms.

Geneva/1-19-80

20. Though the threefold ministry of bishop, presbyter and deacon cannot claim to be absolutely binding on the Church, there are good reasons for considering the development leading to its general acceptance as guided by the Holy Spirit. Though other forms have been blessed with the gifts of the Spirit, the use of the threefold ministry as a starting point for seeking a common form of the ordained ministry presents itself as a real possibility for the churches, especially if one considers the variety which is possible within it and the variety of ways in which it actually functions even under different terms.

Geneva/6-80

19. Though other forms of the ordained ministry have been blessed with the gifts of the Holy Spirit there are good reasons for accepting the threefold form of bishops, presbyters and deacons as a basis for establishing a common form of the ordained ministry today. On the other hand, it has been the generally accepted pattern in the Church of the early centuries and has been retained by the majority of churches up to the present day. In some churches it functions even if different names are used. On the other hand, it provides a valid framework within which the functions of the ordained ministry can be carried out.

Geneva/6-80

20. In order to arrive at a common view on the threefold ministry, it is important to be aware of the changes it underwent at an early stage in the history of the Church. The earliest evidence refers to the threefold ministry as the pattern of the ordained ministry in the local eucharistic community. The bishop was the leader of the community. He proclaimed the Word and presided over the celebration of the eucharist. He was surrounded by a college of presbyters who shared in his tasks. Deacons fostered the diakonia of the community.

21. Soon, however, the functions were modified. Bishops began increasingly to exercise *episkopé* over several local communities at the same time. In the first generation, apostles had exercised *episkopé* in the wider Church. Later Timothy and Titus are recorded to have fulfilled a function of oversight in a given area. Now this apostolic task is carried out in a new way by the bishops. They provide a focus for unity in life and witness within areas comprising several eucharistic communities. As a consequence, presbyters and deacons are assigned new roles. The presbyters become the leaders of the local eucharistic community, and as assistants of the bishops deacons receive responsibilities in the larger area.

Geneva/1-16-80

21. As the Gospel spread and the local churches grew in size and number, need for a new form of the ordained ministry arose. Episcope has to be exercised not only over one local church but over several local churches at the same time. For assembling and building up the communion in Christ a focus for unity in life and witness was required not only within each local community but within larger areas comprising several communities. Bishops were increasingly called to fulfil this task. As was the case in apostolic times (Paul), the episcope over several churches acquired new importance. In a certain sense, it can be regarded as an apostolic task.

Geneva/1-19-80

22. As the Gospel spread and the local churches grew in size and number, need for a new form of the ordained ministry can be discerned. Episkopé had to be exercised not only over one local church but over several local churches at the same time. For assembling and building up the communion in Christ a focus for unity in life and witness was required not only within each local community but within larger areas comprising several communities. Bishops were increasingly called to fulfil this task. As was the case in apostolic times (Paul), the episkopé over several churches acquired new importance. In a certain sense, it can be regarded as an apostolic task.

There are only a few paragraphs which parallel one another in this treatment. The documents of the Steering Committee which met at Geneva, January 15-19, 1980, added several paragraphs which are entirely new. And most of the material which appeared as the text emerging from this Steering Committee meeting had been written by Lukas Vischer.[98] Four months prior to that meeting the Consultation entitled, "Episkopé and Episkopos in the ecumenical debate," was convened. The Introduction to the proceedings of that Consultation stated:

> In their responses, several churches expressed their dissatisfaction with the way in which the text on the ministry dealt with the issue of the forms of the ministry and especially with the episcopate. They felt that paragraph 26 was insufficient and that a new approach was required. Some suggested that the Faith and Order Commission convene a consultation on this subject. At its meeting in Bangalore (1978), the Faith and Order Commission made this recommendation its own. The consultation was held in Geneva, August 13-16, 1979.[99]

The new paragraphs in the Geneva/1-80 texts reflect the proceedings of this Consultation.

One paragraph, with its accompanying Commentary, treats the topic under the heading, "The New Testament evidence."[100] Here a more historical treatment of the topic is evident and it is made clear in the subsequent text that "the New Testament does not describe a single pattern of ministry which might serve as a blueprint or continuing norm for all future ministry in the Church."[101] Other historical references are made describing "a threefold pattern of bishop, presbyter and deacon (becoming established) by the second and third centuries, . . . (changing in terms of practical exercise) in succeeding centuries, . . . (and being restructured) at some points of crisis in the history of the Church."[102] Here is evidenced the direct influence of the Consultation of Orthodox theologians of May/June, 1979. Its report states that "in the second and third centuries, the threefold structure of bishop,

---

[98]The text, "Geneva/1-16-80," is the one written by Vischer whereas the text emerging from the meeting of the Steering Committee itself is the one entitled, "Geneva/1-19-80."

[99]FO Paper No. 102, *Episkopé and Episcopate in Ecumenical Perspective*, p. v.

[100]This is Geneva/1-16-80, §17 and §17-Commentary which correspond to Geneva 1-19-80, §18 and §18-Commentary. Much of this material appears next in Geneva/6-80, §18 and §18-Commentary. The Commentary paragraph eventually becomes the Commentary of a later paragraph in the Lima text (Lima 1/82, §21). It remains, however, in the same section of the text.

[101]Geneva/6-80, §18.

[102]Ibid.

presbyter and deacon became dominant."[103]

What is also added in the texts of the January, 1980 meeting of the Steering Committee is an emphasis on the relationship of the bishop (accompanied by his presbyters and deacons) to the local eucharistic community and with the passage of time to many local communities all at once.[104] The 1979 Consultation of Orthodox theologians had stated:

> As the churches grew in size and number, bishops began to exercise *episkopé* over several eucharistic communities and later even over larger areas. Today, in most cases, bishops are in charge of a diocese.[105]

Also added in this Consultation was a reference to the exercise of *episkopé* having "three dimensions — personal, collegial and communal (and to the fact that) the bishop exercising personal *episkopé* is surrounded by the presbyters acting as a college."[106]

A further treatment of the historical development of ministries in the early church is given in a Commentary paragraph.[107] The Geneva/6-80 text uses as its reference point "the earliest Church" rather than "the New Testament." The point is made explicit that the terms, *episkopoi* and *diakonoi* are "secular terms." A more positive note is struck with the elimination of the reference to "tension between the local church leaders and missionaries such as Paul." The later text substitutes the word, "ministries," for the more general term, "functions," in reference to those activities engaged in by both women and men. In the same connection a new sentence is added in the later text, "While some were appointed by the laying on of hands, there is no indication of this procedure in other cases." The word, "service (performed by the Christian communities)," is later added to the list of those aspects of the communities served by the ordained ministry. Thus the service of the ordained is distinguished from that of the community. And the later text adds at the end of the Commentary paragraph the sentence which reads, "These have been the constant

---

[103]FO Paper No. 102, p. 3.

[104]The parallel texts are as follows: Geneva/6-80, §s 20 and 21; Geneva/1-19-80, §s 21 (sentences 1-5a), 22, and 23; Geneva/1-16-80, §s 20 (sentences 1-5a), 21 and 22.

[105]FO Paper No. 102, p. 7.

[106]Ibid., p. 6.

[107]The parallel passages are as follows: Geneva/1-16-80, §17-Commentary; Geneva/1-19-80, §18-Commentary; Geneva/6-80, §18-Commentary; Lima 1/82, §21-Commentary.

duties of *ministry* throughout the developments and crises of Christian history."[108]
Thus it is clear that it is ordained ministry that is being treated here.

The threefold ministry of bishop, presbyter and deacon as the "starting point for seeking a common form of the ordained ministry" was first incorporated in the text with the onset of the Steering Committee meeting of January, 1980.[109] The May/June, 1979 Consultation of Orthodox theologians had stated:

> In the early Church unity could only be preserved by developing common structures. The issue is therefore what kind of common structure of ministry is required today to express the unity of the Church. On the basis of this consideration the question might be raised, in the light of long tradition and of present need for greater unity within and among the churches, whether an adoption of some form of the threefold ministry might not best serve the churches separately and together in the furtherance of their God-given mission. The task is not to debate the irrevocability of the past, but to respond to the way in which the Spirit may be calling the churches to unity today.[110]

The Accra/74 text had devoted a section of its text to "The Diversity of Ministry."[111] In its treatment, however, even though it states that "among the various ministerial structures the threefold ministry of bishop, presbyter-priest and deacon predominates"[112] it refrains from making it the paradigm or starting point in seeking a common form of the ordained ministry. For "within the same community of faith it is possible to have, side by side, various styles of ecclesial life and ministerial structures, without making the one the model for all the others."[113] At the same time the Accra text devotes a paragraph in which it stresses the need for ordained ministry to reflect in some fashion the threefold reality of *episkope*, the *presbyteral* function, and *diakonia*.[114] This paragraph was repeated in the Geneva/79 text.[115] Subsequent texts, however, do not repeat it. One assumes that a more highly nuanced treatment of the topic finds it irrelevant.

---

[108]Emphasis added.

[109]The parallel texts are as follows: Geneva/1-16-80, §19; Geneva/1-19-80, §20; Geneva/6-80, §19; Lima 1/82, §22.

[110]FO Paper No. 102, p. 4.

[111]Accra/74, §s 23-26.

[112]Accra/74, §25.

[113]Ibid.

[114]Accra/74, §26.

[115]Geneva/79, §22.

It is interesting to note this summary statement in reference to the replies of the churches to the Accra text:

> The effort to explain and defend the place of *episcope* and of the so-called "predominant triad" on the basis of a fresh approach to the special ministry is apparently not convincing to all participants: there is fear of an implicit tendency towards a hierarchical ministerial structure.[116]

Notwithstanding such a report the subsequent texts reflect a greater and greater emphasis on the "pre-dominant triad."

Another example of the influence of the 1979 Consultation of Orthodox theologians on the evolution of the Lima text is in answer to the question it poses to itself:

> What are the functions of the bishop in exercising *episkopé* over several churches?
>
> The bishop's basic function remains to assemble the community and to strengthen its witness by proclaiming the Gospel and presiding over the liturgical and sacramental life of the eucharistic community. *Episkopé* at the level of area is an extension of this function. It would be a mistake to regard *episcopé* at the level of an area as merely administrative function. The ministry needs to remain rooted in the basic functions for whose fulfillment the ordained ministry has been given to the Church.
>
> The responsibility for an area involves new functions. The bishop has to be the visible link between the local eucharistic communities; he will represent them to the wider community. He will strengthen the communion by exercising pastoral care together with the leaders of local communities. He will be attentive to issues which arise for the Church in the wider context, etc.
>
> As an expression of the unity among the local eucharistic communities it is legitimate that the bishop is responsible for the ordination of the presbyter/bishops of the local church.[117]

The text introduced by Lukas Vischer uses the ideas expressed in the above Consultation and expands it beyond the functioning of bishops to that of presbyters and deacons. So the text for which he is responsible states the following:

> The threefold ministry represented originally the form of the ordained ministry in the local church. Only as the leader of the local church can the bishop really fulfil the function of "assembling the community by proclaiming the Word of God and presiding over the liturgical and sacramental life of the community". In some churches, the threefold ministry has been maintained but bishops, presbyters and deacons have been attributed new functions. Though such changes might be justified it must be recognized that they modify, in fact, the form of the ordained ministry in the local church. If bishops become the leaders of an area presbyters

---

[116]FO/77:3, April 1977 (Revised June 1977), p. 282.

[117]FO Paper 102, pp. 8-9.

> have to fulfil the role which was formerly reserved for the bishops; as a
> consequence, the collegial dimension in the exercise of the ordained ministry in the
> local church easily suffers. In many churches, deacons have ceased to fulfil any
> function with regard to the diaconal witness of the Church. In some cases,
> churches which have not formally kept the threefold ministry have, in fact, better
> maintained certain of its original intentions in ordering the life of the local church.

> The issue is therefore not that some churches, for the sake of unity, should accept
> again the threefold ministry, but rather that all churches are called upon to restore
> it in its fulness with a view to a more effective witness in today's world.[118]

It seems clear that although he was influenced by previous formulations L. Vischer
was placing a new emphasis on the threefold ministry of bishop, presbyter, and
deacon as a paradigm for the whole discussion of ordained ministry among the
churches.

In its Commentary section the text of Geneva/6-80 refers to "the college of
elders in the local eucharistic community."[119] The phrase in the earlier text, "the
collegial dimension in the exercise of the ministry in the local church," was
dropped for the time being but later found its way into subsequent texts and the final
text at Lima.[120] The remainder of this same paragraph in the Commentary of
Geneva/6-80 was first introduced in the body of the texts of Geneva/1-80. Again, the
final text at Lima reflects the work of the Geneva/1-80 texts.[121]

One sentence in Geneva/1-80 regarding the role of the threefold ministry in
achieving ecumenical unity leads to a paragraph in the Geneva/6-80 text.[122] The
Lima text itself takes a more carefully nuanced approach which ends with a greater
emphasis on the need for all the churches not having the threefold ministry "to ask
themselves whether the threefold pattern *as developed* (through ecumenical dialogue)
does not have a powerful claim to be accepted by them."[123]

---

[118]Geneva/1-16-80, §20 (sentences 1-8). These sentences are reflected in the Lima text,
§s 20, 21, 24, and 25.

[119]Geneva/6-80, §22-Commentary.

[120]Lima 1/82. §24.

[121]Ibid.

[122]Geneva/1-80, §21, sentence no. 8; Geneva/6-80, §22.

[123]Lima 1/82. §25.

B. Guiding Principles for the Exercise of the Ordained Ministry in the Church.

The two paragraphs which comprise this section in the final text of this period in the evolution of the Lima text have no antecedents in the first text of the period (the Accra text). The exercise of the three-fold ministry is outlined. The influence of Orthodox thought is much in evidence.

Geneva/1-16-80

18. For the exercise of the ordained ministry three considerations are of the utmost importance. The ordained ministry needs to be exercised in a personal way. The presence of the Lord Jesus Christ among his people can most effectively be pointed to by one person proclaiming the Gospel and calling the community to serve the Lord in unity of life and witness. The personal ordained ministry needs to be exercised in a collegial way , i.e. there is need for a college of ordained ministers sharing in the common task and representing the concerns of the community. Finally, the intimate relationship between the ordained ministry and community must find expression in a communal dimension, i.e. the exercise of the ordained ministry must be rooted in the life of the community and requires its effective participation in the discovery of God's will and the guidance of the Spirit.

18-Commentary:

The three aspects need to be kept together. In the various churches, one or the other has been overemphasized at the expense of the others. In some churches, the personal dimension of the ordained ministry tends to diminish the collegial and communal dimensions. In other churches, the collegial or communal dimension takes so much importance that the ordained ministry loses its personal dimension. Each church needs to examine itself in what way, in its midst the exercise of the ordained ministry has suffered in

Geneva/1-19-80

19. For the exercise of the ordained ministry three consideration are of the utmost importance. The ordained ministry needs to be exercised in a personal way. The presence of the Lord Jesus Christ among his people can most effectively be pointed to by one person proclaiming the Gospel and calling the community to serve the Lord in unity of life and witness. The personal ordained ministry needs to be exercised in a collegial way, i.e. there is need for a college of ordained ministers sharing F in the common task and representing the concerns of the community. Finally, the intimate relationship between the ordained ministry and community must find expression in a communal dimension, i.e. the exercise of the ordained ministry must be rooted in the life of the community and requires its effective participation in the discovery of God's will and the guidance of the Spirit.

19-Commentary:

The three aspects need to be kept together. In various churches, one or the other has been overemphasized at the expense of the others. In some churches, the personal dimension of the ordained ministry tends to diminish the collegial and communal dimensions. In other churches, the collegial or communal dimension takes so much importance that the ordained ministry loses its personal dimension. Each church needs to ask itself in what way the exercise of the ordained ministry in its midst has suffered in the course of

Geneva/6-80

23. Three considerations are important in this respect. The ordained ministry should be exercised in a personal way. The presence of Christ among his people can most effectively be pointed to by one person proclaiming the Gospel and calling the community to serve the Lord in unity of life and witness. The ordained ministry needs to be exercised in a collegial way, i.e. there is need for a college of ordained ministers sharing in the common task of representing the concerns of the community. Finally, the intimate relationship between the ordained ministry and the community must find expression in a communal dimension, i.e. the exercise of the ordained ministry must be rooted in the life of the community and requires its effective participation in the discovery of God's will and the guidance of the Spirit.

23-Commentary:

These three aspects need to be kept together. In various churches, one or the other has been overemphasized at the expense of the others. In some churches, the personal dimension of the ordained ministry tends to diminish the collegial and communal dimensions. In other churches, the collegial or communal dimension takes so much importance that the ordained ministry loses its personal dimension. Each church needs to ask itself in what way the exercise of the ordained ministry in its midst has suffered in the course of history.

Geneva/1-16-80 [cont.]
the course of history.

The recognition of these three dimensions lies behind a recommendation made by the first World Conference on Faith and Order at Lausanne in 1927: In view of (i) the place which the episcopate, the council of presbyters and the congregation of the faithful, respectively, had in the constitution of the early Church, and (ii) the fact that episcopal, presbyteral and congregational systems of government are each today, and have been for centuries, accepted by great communions in Christendom, and (iii) the fact that episcopal, presbyteral and congregational systems are each believed by many to be essential to the good order of the Church, we therefore recognize that these several elements must all, under conditions which require further study, have an appropriate place in the order of life of a reunited Church .....

Geneva/1-19-80 [cont.]
history.

The recognition of these three dimensions lies behind a recommendation made by the first World Conference on Faith and Order at Lausanne in 1927: "In view of (i) the place which the episcopate, the council of presbyters and the congregation of the faithful, respectively, had in the constitution of the early Church, and (ii) the fact that episcopal, presbyteral and congregational systems of government are each today, and have been for centuries, accepted by great communions in Christendom, and (iii) the fact that episcopal, presbyteral and congregational systems are each believed by many to be essential to the good order of the Church, we therefore recognize that these several elements must all, under conditions which require further study, have an appropriate place in the order of life of a reunited Church. ...."

Geneva/1-16-80 [cont.]

The recognition of these three dimensions lies behind a recommendation made by the first World Conference on Faith and Order at Lausanne in 1927: "In view of (i) the place which the episcopate, the council of presbyters and the congregation of the faithful, respectively, had in the constitution of the early Church, and (ii) the fact that episcopal, presbyteral and congregational systems of government are each today, and have been for centuries, accepted by great communions in Christendom, and (iii) the fact that episcopal, presbyteral and congregational systems are each believed by many to be essential to the good order of the Church, we therefore recognize that these several elements must all, under conditions which require further study, have an appropriate place in the order of life of a reunited Church. ..."

Geneva/1-16-80

20. The threefold ministry represented originally the form of the ordained ministry in the local church. Only as the leader of the local church can the bishop really fulfil the function of "assembling the community by proclaiming the Word of God and presiding over the liturgical and sacramental life of the community". In some churches, the threefold ministry has been maintained but bishops, presbyters and deacons have been attributed new functions. Though such changes might be justified it must be recognized that they modify, in fact, the form of the ordained ministry in the local church. If bishops become the leaders of an area presbyters have to fulfil the role which was formerly reserved for the bishops; as a consequence, the collegial dimension in the exercise of the ordained ministry in the local church easily suffers. In many churches, deacons have ceased to fulfil any function with regard to the diaconal witness of the Church. In some cases, churches which have not formally kept the threefold ministry have, in fact, better maintained certain of its original intentions in ordering the life of the local church.

The issue is therefore not that some churches, for the sake of unity, should accept again the three-fold ministry, but rather that all churches are called upon to restore it in its fulness with a view to a more effective witness in today's world. The bishop and the presbyters represent, in the local church, the personal and the collegial dimensions

Geneva/1-19-80

21. In the ancient Church, the threefold ministry represented the original form of the ordained ministry in the local church. Only as the leader of the local church can the bishop really fulfil the function of "assembling, building up and guiding the community in Christ by proclaiming and teaching the Word of God and by presiding over the liturgical and missionary and diaconal life of the eucharistic community". In some churches, the threefold ministry has been maintained but bishops, presbyters and deacons have been attributed new functions. Though such changes might be justified it must be recognized that they modify, in fact, the form of the ordained ministry in the local church. If bishops become the leaders of an area presbyters have to fulfil the role which was formerly reserved for the bishops; as a consequence, the collegial dimension in the exercise of the ordained ministry in the local church easily suffers. In many churches, deacons have ceased to fulfil any function with regard to the diaconal witness of the Church. In some cases, churches which have not formally kept the threefold ministry have, in fact, better maintained certain of its original intentions in ordering the life of the local church.

The issue is therefore not that some churches, for the sake of unity, should accept again the three-fold ministry, but rather that all churches are called upon to restore it in its fulness with a view to a more effective witness in today's world.

Geneva/680

20. In order to arrive at a common view on the threefold ministry, it is important to be aware of the changes it underwent at an early stage in the history of the Church. The earliest evidence refers to the threefold ministry as the pattern of the ordained ministry in the local eucharistic community. The bishop was the leader of the community. He proclaimed the Word and pre-sided over the celebration of the eucharist. He was surrounded by a college of presbyters who shared in his tasks. Deacons fostered the diakonia of the community.

21. Soon, however, the functions were modified. Bishops began increasingly to exercise *episkopé* over several local communities at the same time. In the first generation, apostles had exercised *episkopé* in the wider Church. Later Timothy and Titus are recorded to have fulfilled a function of oversight in a given area. Now this apostolic task is carried out in a new way by the bishops. They provide a focus for unity in life and witness within areas comprising several eucharistic communities. As a consequence, presbyters and deacons are assigned new roles. The presbyters become the leaders of the local eucharistic community, and as assistants of the bishops deacons receive responsibilities in the larger area.

22. How can this threefold form be adapted for the Church today? In fact, the question must be asked by all churches. The primary issue is not

234

Geneva/1-16-80 [cont.]

of the exercise of the ordained ministry. The bishop, surrounded by the presbyters, provides for the local church the focus of its unity in life, worship and witness. The deacons are mandated to remind the local church of its diaconal witness and to strengthen its service both among its members and in society.

Geneva/1-19-80 [cont.]

The bishop and the presbyters represent, in the local church, the personal and the collegial dimensions of the exercise of the ordained ministry. The bishop, surrounded by the presbyters, provides for the local church the focus of its unity in life, worship and witness. The deacons are mandated to remind the local church of its diaconal witness and to strengthen its service both among its members and in society.

Geneva/6-80 [cont.]

that some churches, for the sake of unity, should return to the inherited pattern but rather that all churches are called upon to give the fullest possible expression to its potential with a view to a more effective witness of the Church in the world.

22-Commentary:

The pattern stands in need of reform in all churches. In some, the college of elders in the local eucharistic community has disappeared. In others, the functions of deacons have been reduced to an assistant role in the celebration of the liturgy; they have ceased to fulfil any function with regard to the diaconal witness of the Church. In some cases, churches which have not formally kept the threefold form have, in fact, better maintained certain of its original intentions.

Geneva/1-16-80

22. The episcope over several churches needs also to be exercised in a personal, collegial and communal way. The bishop needs to be surrounded by a college representing the communities and their need to be ways of securing the participation of the communities in deliberations and in decision-making. Councils are essential for the appropriate shepherding of the Church.

Geneva/1-19-80

23. The episkopé over several churches needs also to be exercised in a personal, collegial and communal way. The bishop needs to be surrounded by a college representing the communities and there need to be ways of securing the participation of the communities in deliberations and in decision-making. Councils are essential for the appropriate shepherding of the Church.

Geneva/6-80

20. In order to arrive at a common view on the threefold ministry, it is important to be aware of the changes it underwent at an early stage in the history of the Church. The earliest evidence refers to the threefold ministry as the pattern of the ordained ministry in the local eucharistic community. The bishop was the leader of the community. He proclaimed the Word and presided over the celebration of the eucharist. He was surrounded by a college of presbyters who shared in his tasks. Deacons fostered the diakonia of the community.

21. Soon, however, the functions were modified. Bishops began increasingly to exercise *episkopé* over several local communities at the same time. In the first generation, apostles had exercised *episkopé* in the wider Church. Later Timothy and Titus are recorded to have fulfilled a function of oversight in a given area. Now this apostolic task is carried out in a new way by the bishops. They provide a focus for unity in life and witness within areas comprising several eucharistic communities. As a consequence, presbyters and deacons are assigned new roles. The presbyters become the leaders of the local eucharistic community, and as assistants of the bishops deacons receive responsibilities in the larger area.

24. At all levels of the Church's life the ordained ministry needs to be exercised in such a way that these three dimensions can find adequate

Geneva/6-80 [cont.]

expression. At the level of the local eucharistic community there is need for an ordained minister acting within a college of elders. Strong emphasis will be placed on the active participation of all members in the life and the decision-making of the community. Deacons will stimulate its diaconal witness. At the level of an area there is again need for an ordained minister exercising a service of unity. The collegial and communal dimensions will find expression in regular representative synodal gatherings. Deacons will foster the cohesion of the common witness of the communities.

The two paragraphs in the Geneva/6-80 text which comprise this section have no antecedents in the Accra text. Only the texts of Geneva/1-80 provide any previous treatment of the same material. Lukas Vischer, as the architect of the Geneva/1-16-80 text, is the one responsible for these additions.[124] He borrowed heavily, however, from the May/June, 1979 Consultation which, while focusing especially on *episkopé*, stated the following:

> The exercise (of *episkopé*) has three dimensions - personal, collegial and communal. *Episkopé* requires the authority and the commitment of single persons within the community. The presence of Jesus Christ in the midst of the people can best be witnessed to by one person proclaiming the Gospel and calling the community to witness and service. One person can provide an effective focus within the community and keep it in unity of life, worship and witness. . . . The personal dimension needs to be accompanied by the collegial dimension. Personal *episkopé* can only be carried out in a collegial way. The authority of the one to provide the focus of the community needs to be tested by a group. The discovery of the will of God requires the insights and the interaction of several people. . . . Finally, *episkopé* has a communal dimension. It is exercised not over the community but with the collaboration and participation of the community. . . .
>
> The threefold ministry is potentially a faithful mirror of the three requirements. The bishop exercising personal *episkopé* is surrounded by the presbyters acting as a college. They are acting together in the same eucharistic community. The deacons have the task to remind the community of its diaconal witness and to provide a link with the bishop and the presbyters. . . .
>
> In the course of history the three dimensions have not been kept together. One or the other has been overemphasized at the expense of the others. The separate churches tend to reflect this one-sidedness. In some traditions, the personal dimension of *episkopé* eclipses the collegial and communal dimensions. In other traditions, the personal ministry tends to be drowned in collegial and communal processes. In this respect, the ecumenical movement could be described as the effort to restore the balance between the dimensions.[125]

What follows in the report of the Consultation is the quotation incorporated in the Geneva/1-16-80 text by L. Vischer from the First World Conference on Faith and Order at Lausanne (1927).

The first paragraph of the Geneva/6-80 text and its Commentary paragraph

---

[124]WCC Archive File, "BEM Steering Group Meetings (1979/1980), Correspondence/Documents," in WCC Archive Box, "Baptism - Eucharist - Ministry, After Bangalore (1978), Detailed replies to some comments by churches (1978); Steering Group (1979/80)."

[125]FO Paper 102, pp. 6-7.

are almost identical to their antecedents.[126] The second paragraph of the Geneva/6-80 text is only partially reflected in the previous texts[127] which at that particular point of their evolution were restricting themselves to the ministry of *episkopé*.

C. FUNCTIONS OF BISHOPS, PRESBYTERS AND DEACONS.

The same summary statement can be made here as was made in reference to the previous section. Here the ideas of the four or five paragraphs in the section are "offered in a tentative way."

---

[126]Geneva/6-80, §s 23 & 23-Commentary; Geneva/1-19-80, §s 19 and 19-Commentary; Geneva/1-16-80, §s 18 and 18-Commentary.

[127]Geneva/6-80, §24; Geneva 1/19/80, §23; Geneva 1/18/180, §22.

Geneva/6-80 [cont.]

23. Three considerations are important in this respect. The ordained ministry should be exercised in a *personal* way. The presence of Christ among his people can most effectively be pointed to by one person proclaiming the Gospel and calling the community to serve the Lord in unity of life and witness. The ordained ministry needs to be exercised in a *collegial* way, i.e. there is need for a college of ordained ministers sharing in the common task of representing the concerns of the community. Finally, the intimate relationship between the ordained ministry and the community must find expression in a *communal* dimension, i.e. the exercise of the ordained ministry must be rooted in the life of the community and requires its effective participation in the discovery of God's will and the guidance of the Spirit.

25. What can then be said about the functions of bishops, presbyters and deacons? Obviously, a uniform answer to this question is not required for the mutual recognition of the ordained ministry. As long as there is agreement on the nature and basic form of the ordained ministry, the precise assignment of functions may vary from place to place. The following considerations are therefore offered in a tentative way.

26. *Bishops* preach the Word, preside at the sacraments, and administer discipline in such a

Geneva/6-80 [cont.]

way as to be representative pastoral ministers of oversight, continuity and unity in the Church. They have pastoral oversight of the area to which they are called. They maintain the apostolicity and unity of the Church's worship and sacramental life. They, in communion with the presbyters and deacons and the whole community, are responsible for the orderly transfer of ministerial authority in the Church.

27. *Presbyters* serve as pastoral ministers of Word and sacraments in a local eucharistic community. They are preachers and teachers of the faith and bear responsibility for the discipline of the congregation to the end that the world may believe and that the entire membership of the Church may be renewed, strengthened and equipped in ministry. Presbyters have particular responsibility for the preparation of members for Christian life and ministry. They preside at acts of the Church such as marriage, declaration of the forgiveness of sin, anointing of the sick and dying, and announcing God's blessing and other rites of the Church.

Geneva/6-80 [cont.]
27-Commentary:

As stated above, at the level of the local eucharistic community the collegial dimension will find expression in a group of elders exercising, together with the presbyter, oversight and pastoral guidance. Elders may be ordained to their ministry.

28. *Deacons* represent to the Church its calling as servant in the world to exemplify the interdependence of worship and service in the Church's life. They will exercise some responsibility in the worship of the congregation and promote its diaconal service. They will fulfil certain administrative tasks.

Although the *functions* of the ordained ministry had been treated in various places in the Accra/74 text[128] the text of Geneva/6-80 offers for the first time a distinct and orderly treatment of the functions of each of the three traditional forms of the ordained ministry. So new is such a treatment that the "considerations are . . . offered in a tentative way."[129] Further the considerations are made in the context of a belief that precise agreement on the functions of each of the three forms is "not required for the mutual recognition of the ordained ministry."[130]

The Consultation of Orthodox Theologians (Chambésy, May/June, 1979) called for an extensive treatment of the episcopacy and suggested a textual structure for the document on ministry. That structure included the following suggestion:

> Among the diversity of charisms, there are some *permanent functions*, or some ministries which structure the ecclesial community; the Lord gives to his Church the ministries which she needs to be in continuity with the apostolic ministry instituted by Christ; ministers are called, set apart and ordained to receive the gifts of the Spirit which are necessary for their service in the Church; to the traditional ministries of the episcopate, the presbyterate and the diaconate can be added others in keeping with the needs of the service of the Church in a changing world.[131]

The content of the treatment of the functions of bishops in Geneva/6-80 is new precisely in its talking of *persons* with specific functions. Also new with reference to bishops are the statements: "They have pastoral oversight of the area to which they are called. They maintain the apostolicity and unity of the Church's worship and sacramental life."[132] In this same treatment some of the content is reflected in various places in the Accra/74 text.[133]

---

[128]Cf. Accra/74, the section entitled, "The Basis and Function of the Ordained Ministry," (§s 13-16) and §s 21, 26, and 35.

[129]Geneva/6-80, §25.

[130]Ibid.

[131]Parmi la diversité des charismes, il y a des *fonctions permanentes*, ou des ministères qui structurent la communauté ecclésiale; le Seigneur donne à son Eglise les ministères dont elle a besoin pour exister dans la continuité avec le ministère apostolique institué par le Christ: les ministres dont appelés, mis à part et ordonnés pour recevoir les dons de l'Esprit nécessaires à leur service dans l'Eglise; aux ministères traditionnels de l'épiscopat, du presbytérat, et du diaconat peuvent s'ajouter d'autres selon les nécessités du service de l'Eglise dans un monde qui change. FO Paper No. 98, pp. 86-87.

[132]Geneva/6-80, §26; Geneva/1-19-80, §21; Geneva/1-16-80, §20. These last two documents which precede the Geneva/6-80 text state that "the bishop surrounded by the presbyters, provides for the local church the focus of its unity in life, worship and witness."

[133]Geneva/6-80, §26; Accra/74, §s 26, 28, 29, and 37.

In regard to presbyters the Geneva/6-80 text[134] adds much content to an earlier short reference in the Accra/74 text which sees the presbyteral function in terms of "the proclamation of the Gospel and administration of the sacraments."[135]

In regard to deacons the Geneva/6-80 text[136] adds a considerable amount of content to the earlier brief treatment of the Accra/74 text.

Accra/74	*Geneva/6-80*
26. Both the episcopal and presbyteral functions of the Church must be understood as a sharing in the *diakonia*, that is, as costly service to the community of the Church and to the world through the proclamation and actualization of the Gospel. In the course of history, the function of *diakonia* has found expression in the office of deacon and the deaconess. For about 20 years now, many churches, independently from one another, have been giving attention to the possible renewal of this office.	28. *Deacons* represent to the Church its calling as servant in the world to exemplify the interdependence of worship and service in the Church's life. They will exercise some responsibility in the worship of the congregation and promote its diaconal service. They will fulfil certain administrative tasks.
	28-Commentary. In many churches there is today considerable uncertainty about the need, the rationale, the status and the functions of deacons. In what sense can the diaconate be considered part of the ordained ministry? What is it that distinguishes it from other ministries in the Church (catechists, musicians, etc.)? Why should deacons be ordained while these other ministries do not receive ordination? If they are ordained do they receive ordination in the full sense of the word or is their ordination only the first step towards ordination as presbyters? Today, there is a strong tendency in many churches to restore the diaconate as an ordained ministry with its own dignity and meant to be exercised for life. Differences in ordering the diaconal ministry should not be regarded as a hindrance for the mutual recognition of the ordained ministries.

It should be noted that in its Commentary section the Geneva/6-80 text echoes the questioning of the meaning of the diaconate by many churches and insists that "differences in ordering the diaconal ministry should not be regarded as a hindrance for the mutual recognition of the ordained ministries."[137]

---

[134]Geneva/6-80, §s 27 and 27-Commentary.

[135]Accra/74, §26.

[136]Geneva/6-80, §s 28 and 28-Commentary.

[137]Geneva/6-80, §28-Commentary.

D. VARIETY OF CHARISMS.

Again, there are no antecedents in the Accra/74 text for what is given in the Geneva/6-80 text. These charisms are called "ministries" in the Geneva/6-80 text. The Lima text will later refer to them as "charisms."

Geneva/1-16-80

23. Often in the history of the Church new impulses of the Holy Spirit could only find their way into the life of the Church through charismatic leaders. Episkopé should encourage the charisms and interpret them to the Church in order that they might contribute to the witness and service of the Church in the world.

Geneva/1-19-80

24. Often in the history of the Church new impulses of the Holy Spirit could only find their way into the life of the Church through charismatic leaders. Episkopé should encourage the charisms and interpret them to the Church in order that they might contribute to the witness and service of the Church in the world.

Geneva/6-80

30. Often in the history of the Church the truth of the Gospel could be preserved only through prophetic and charismatic leaders. Often new impulses could find their way into the life of the Church only in unusual ways. Often reforms required a special ministry. The ordained ministers and the whole community will need to be attentive to the challenge of such special ministries.

The Geneva/6-80 text titles this section, "Variety of ministries." It is an entirely new section. There is no corresponding material in the Accra/74 text. One other paragraph from the Geneva/6-80 text is pertinent:

> 29. The community which lives in the power of the Spirit will be characterized by a variety of ministries. The Spirit is the giver of diverse gifts which enrich the life of the community. In order to enhance their effectiveness, the community will recognize certain of these gifts as ministries. It will, for instance, give recognition to ministries of readers, catechists, musicians, church wardens. While some of these ministries fulfil services permanently required in the life of the community, others will be temporary. Men and women in religious communities fulfil a ministry which is of particular importance for the life of the Church. The ordained ministry must not become a hindrance for the variety of these ministries. On the contrary, it will help the community to discover the gifts bestowed on it by the Holy Spirit and will equip members of the body to serve in a variety of ways.[138]

The texts of 1/80 contributed only two sentences to the content, which sentences were included in their section, entitled, "Episkopé over several local churches".

IV. SUCCESSION IN THE APOSTOLIC TRADITION.

The Geneva/6-80 text names this section, "Succession in the Apostolic Tradition," with two subdivisions whereas the corresponding material in the Accra text is given the single title, Apostolic Succession."[139]

A. APOSTOLIC TRADITION IN THE CHURCH.

Here an important distinction is introduced, between the apostolic tradition of the whole Church and the apostolic succession of the ministry.

---

[138]Geneva/6-80, §29.

[139]The section title and its divisions (reflected in the later text) were first evidenced in the texts of 1/16/80, §25 ff. and 1/19/80, §26 ff. Both these texts introduce the section with the one sentence, "There is division among the churches as to the relation between ordained ministers and the apostles of the New Testament." This sentence is deleted in the text of Geneva/6-80.

Accra/74

28. The fullness of the apostolic succession of the whole Church involves continuity in the permanent characteristics of the Church of the apostles: witness to the apostolic faith, proclamation and fresh interpretation of the apostolic gospel, transmission of ministerial responsibility, sacramental life, community in love, service for the needy, unity among local Churches, and sharing the gifts which the Lord has given to each.

27. The primary manifestation of apostolic succession is to be found in the life of the Church as a whole. This succession is an expression of the permanence and, therefore, continuity of Christ's own mission in which the church participates. This participation is rooted in the gift of the Holy Spirit, in the sending of the Apostles and their successors, and will find its

Geneva/79

32. The fullness of the apostolic succession of the whole Church involves continuity in the permanent characteristics of the Church of the apostles: witness to the apostolic faith, proclamation and fresh interpretation of the apostolic gospel, transmission of ministerial responsibility, sacramental life, community in love, service for the needy, unity among local Churches and sharing the gifts which the Lord has given to each. (no 28)

31. The primary manifestation of apostolic succession is to be found in the life of the Church as a whole. This succession is an expression of the permanence and, therefore, continuity of Christ's own mission in which the Church participates. This participation is rooted in the gift of the Holy Spirit, in the sending of the Apostles and their successors, and will find its

Geneva/1-16-80

26. The Creed confesses the Church to be apostolic. The Church lives in continuity with the apostles and their proclamation. The same Lord who sent the apostles continues to be present in the Church. The Spirit keeps it in the apostolic tradition until the day of the completion of history in the kingdom of God. The apostolicity of the Church involves continuity in the permanent characteristics of the Church of the apostles: witness to the apostolic faith, proclamation and fresh interpretation of the Gospel, celebration of baptism and the eucharist, the transmission of ministerial responsibilities, communion in love and suffering, service to the needy, unity among the local churches and sharing the gifts which the Lord has given to each. (Paras 27-28)

Geneva/1-19-80

27. The Creed confesses the Church to be apostolic. The Church lives in continuity with the apostles and their proclamation. The same Lord who sent the apostles continues to be present in the Church. The Spirit keeps it in the apostolic tradition until the day of the completion of history in the kingdom of God. Apostolic tradition in the Church involves continuity in the permanent characteristics of the Church of the apostles: witness to the apostolic faith, proclamation and fresh interpretation of the Gospel, celebration of baptism and the eucharist, the transmission of ministerial responsibilities, communion in love and suffering, service to the needy, unity among the local churches and sharing the gifts which the Lord has given to each. (paras 27-28)

Geneva/6-80

31. The Creed confesses the Church to be apostolic. The Church lives in continuity with the apostles and their proclamation. The same Lord who sent the apostles continues to be present in the Church. The Spirit keeps the Church in the apostolic tradition until the fulfilment of history in the Kingdom of God. Apostolic tradition in the Church involves continuity in the permanent characteristics of the Church of the apostles: witness to the apostolic faith, proclamation and fresh interpretation of the Gospel, celebration of baptism and the eucharist, the transmission of ministerial responsibilities, communion in love and suffering, service to the needy, unity among the local churches and sharing the gifts which the Lord has given to each.

Accra/74 [cont.]
completion in the all-embracing realization of God's kingdom.

Geneva/79 [cont.]
completion in the all-embracing realization of God's kingdom. (no 27)

Geneva/1-16-80 [cont.]
26-Commentary:

When speaking of the apostolic succession, we must take due note that the term "apostle" must be strictly limited to those disciples of the first generation who are reliable witnesses of the Lord, Crucified and Risen, and who were commissioned by him.

Geneva/1-19-80 [cont.]
27-Commentary:

The apostles, unique witnesses of the life and resurrection of Christ and sent by him, are the original transmitters of the Gospel, of the tradition of the words and acts of Christ which constitute the life of the Church. This apostolic tradition continues through history and links the Church to its origins in Christ and in the college of the apostles. Within this apostolic tradition is an apostolic succession of the ministry which serves the continuity of the Church in its life in Christ and its faithfulness to the words and acts of Jesus transmitted by the apostles. The ministers appointed by the apostles, and then the episkopoi of the churches, were the first guardians of this transmission of the apostolic tradition; they were the first witnesses of the apostolic succession of the ministry which was continued through the bishops

Geneva/6-80 [cont.]
31-Commentary:

The apostles, as witnesses of the life and resurrection of Christ and sent by him, are the original transmitters of the Gospel, of the tradition of the words and acts of Jesus Christ which constitute the life of the Church. This apostolic tradition continues through history and links the Church to its origins in Christ and in the college of the apostles. Within this apostolic tradition is an apostolic succession of the ministry which serves the continuity of the Church in its life in Christ and its faithfulness to the words and acts of Jesus transmitted by the apostles. The ministers appointed by the apostles, and then the episkopoi of the churches, were the first guardians of this transmission of the apostolic tradition; they testified to the apostolic succession of the ministry which was continued through the bishops of the

Geneva/6-80 [cont.]
32. The primary manifestation of apostolic succession is to be found in the apostolic tradition of the Church as a whole. The succession is an expression of the permanence and, therefore, of the continuity of Christ's own mission in which the Church participates. Within the Church the ordained ministry has a particular task of preserving and actualizing the apostolic truth. The orderly transmission of the ordained ministry is therefore a powerful expression of the continuity of the Church throughout history; it also underlines the calling of the ordained minister as guardian of the truth. Where churches neglect the importance of the orderly transmission, they must ask themselves whether they

248

Geneva/1-19-80 [cont.]
of the early Church in collegial communion with the presbyters and deacons within the Christian community. A distinction should be drawn, therefore, between the apostolic tradition of the whole Church and the apostolic succession of the ministry.

Geneva/6-80 [cont.]
early Church in collegial communion with the presbyters and deacons within the Christian community. A distinction should be made, therefore, between the apostolic tradition of the whole Church and the succession of the apostolic ministry.

Geneva/6-80 [cont.]
pay sufficient attention to the continuity in the apostolic tradition. On the other hand, where the ordained ministry does not adequately serve the proclamation of the apostolic truth, churches must ask themselves whether their ministerial structures are not in need of alteration.

The first three sentences of Geneva/6-80, §31 (including the title of the section which that paragraph introduces, namely, "Apostolic tradition in the Church") are not reflected in the Accra/74 text: "The Creed confesses the Church to be apostolic. The Church lives in continuity with the apostles and their proclamation. The same Lord who sent the apostles continues to be present in the Church." This material first appeared in the text of Geneva/1-16-80.[140] The remaining sentences of Geneva/6-80, §31 have direct roots in the Accra text.[141]

The Commentary of Geneva/6-80, §31 is not found in the Accra text. This material first took shape in the Geneva/1-80 texts. The later of the two 1/80 texts is much more complete.

The Geneva/6-80 text deletes the word "unique" in reference to "the apostles, as witnesses of the life and resurrection of Christ."[142]

B. SUCCESSION OF THE APOSTOLIC MINISTRY.

In this section the important point is made regarding the episcopal succession as the fullness of the sign of apostolic succession. The paragraph of commentary in the text outlines the two approaches to this matter in the early Church, that of Clement of Rome and Ignatius of Antioch.

---

[140]Geneva/1-16-80, §26.

[141]Sentence §3 of Accra/74, §27 and the entire contents of Accra/74, §28.

[142]Geneva/6-80, §31-Commentary; Geneva/1-19-80, §27-Commentary.

Accra/74

29. The ordained ministry is related in various degrees to all of these characteristics. It serves as an authorized and responsible instrument for their preservation and actualization. The orderly transmission of the ministry is, therefore, both a visible sign of the continuity of the whole Church and of the effective participation of the ministry in it and contribution to it. Where this orderly transmission is lacking a church must ask itself whether its apostolicity can be maintained in its fullness. Or, where this ministry does not adequately subserve the Church's apostolicity, a church must ask itself whether or not its ministerial structures should continue with not alteration.

Geneva/79

33. The ordained ministry is related in various degrees to all of these characteristics. It serves as an authorized and responsible instrument for their preservation and actualization. The orderly transmission of the ministry is, therefore, both a visible sign of the continuity of the whole Church and of the effective participation of the ministry in it and contribution to it. Where this orderly transmission is lacking a church must ask itself whether its apostolicity can be maintained in its fullness. Or, where this ministry does not adequately subserve the Church's apostolicity, a church must ask itself whether or not its ministerial structures should continue with no alteration. (no 29)

Geneva/1-16-80

27. The ordained ministry serves as an authorized and responsible instrument for the preservation and actualisation of these characteristics. The orderly transmission of the ordained ministry is, therefore, both a visible sign of the continuity of the whole Church and of the effective participation of the ordained ministry in it. Where this orderly transmission is lacking a church must ask itself whether its apostolicity has been maintained in its fullness. (Para 29) Or where this ministry does not adequately subserve the Church's apostolicity, a church must ask itself whether or not its ministerial structures should continue with no alteration.

Geneva/1-19-80

28. The ordained ministry serves as an authorized and responsible instrument for the preservation and actualization of the apostolic tradition. The orderly transmission of the ordained ministry is an expression of the permanence and, therefore, of the continuity of Christ's own mission in which the Church participates. Within the Church the ordained ministry has a particular task of preserving and actualizing the apostolic truth. The orderly transmission of the ordained ministry is therefore a powerful expression of the continuity of the Church throughout history; it also underlines the calling of the ordained minister as guardian of the truth. Where churches neglect the importance of the orderly transmission, they must ask themselves whether they pay sufficient attention to the continuity in the apostolic tradition. On the other hand, where the ordained ministry does not adequately serve the procla-

Geneva/6-80 [cont.]
mation of the apostolic
truth, churches must ask
themselves whether their
ministerial structures are not
in need of alteration.

Accra/74

30. Under the particular historical circumstance of the growing Church in the subapostolic age, the succession of bishops became one of the ways in which the apostolicity of the Church was expressed. This succession was understood as serving, symbolizing and guarding the continuity of the apostolic faith and communion. Some Christian traditions believe this faith and communion to have been preserved uniquely in this form of ministerial succession, even though there have been varying interpretations and understandings of this succession among these same traditions.

31. Today there is growing agreement among scholars that the New Testament presents diverse types of organization of the Christian communities, according to the difference of authors, places and times. While, in the local churches, founded by

Geneva/79

34. Under the particular historical circumstance of the growing Church in the subapostolic age, the succession of bishops became one of the ways in which the apostolicity of the Church was expressed. This succession was understood as serving, symbolizing and guarding the continuity of the apostolic faith and communion. Some Christian traditions believe this faith and communion to have been preserved uniquely in this form of ministerial succession, even though there have been varying interpretations and understandings of this succession among these same traditions. (no 30)

34-Commentary:
Today there is growing agreement among scholars that the New Testament presents diverse types of organization of the Christian communities, according to the difference of authors,

Geneva/1-16-80

28. Under the particular historical circumstances of the growing Church in the early centuries, the succession of bishops (episkopoi, presbyteroi), especially those occupying "apostolic sees", became one of the ways in which the apostolic tradition of the Church was expressed. This succession was understood as serving, symbolizing and guarding the continuity of the apostolic faith and communion.

Geneva/1-19-80

29. Under the particular historical circumstances of the growing Church in the early centuries, the succession of bishops (*episkopoi, presbyteroi*), especially those occupying "apostolic sees", became one of the ways in which the apostolic tradition of the Church was expressed. This succession was understood as serving, symbolizing and guarding the continuity of the apostolic faith and communion.

Geneva/6-80

33. Under the particular historical circumstances of the growing Church in the early centuries, the succession of bishops became one of the ways in which the apostolic tradition of the Church was expressed. This succession was understood as serving, symbolizing and guarding the continuity of the apostolic faith and communion.

Accra/74 [cont.]
apostles like Paul, there were persons in authority, very little is said about how they were appointed and about the requirements for presiding at the eucharist. On this basis, there have been developed, in the course of history, notably since the 16th century, multiple forms of church order, each with its own advantages and disadvantages: episcopal, presbyteral, congregational, among others.

Geneva/79 [cont.]
places and times. While, in the local churches, founded by apostles like Paul, there were persons in authority, very little is said about how they were appointed and about the requirements for presiding at the eucharist. On this basis, there have been developed, in the course of history, notably since the 16th century, multiple forms of church order: episcopal, presbyteral, congregational, among others. (no 31)

Accra/74 [cont.]

32. There is further agreement among many scholars that although ordination of ministers by bishops was the almost universal practice in the Church very early, it is impossible to show that such a church order existed everywhere in the Church from the earliest times. In fact, there is evidence that in the subapostolic age even this practice did not become uniform until after some time. Further, there have been well-documented cases later in the history of the Western Church in which priests, not bishops, have with papal dispensation ordained other priests to serve at the altar.

33. These observations do not imply a devaluation of the emergence and general acceptance of the historic episcopate. They only indicate that the Church has been able to respond to the needs of particular historical situations in the develop-

Geneva/79 [cont.]

34-Commentary [cont.]

There is further agreement among many scholars that although ordination of ministers by bishops was the almost universal practice in the Church very early, it is impossible to show that such a church order existed everywhere in the Church from the earliest times. In fact there is evidence that in the subapostolic age even this practice did not become uniform until after some time. Further, there have been well-documented cases in the history of the Western Church in which priests, not bishops, have with papal dispensation ordained other priests to serve at the altar. (no 32)

Accra/74 [cont.]

ment of its ministerial structures. It follows, therefore, that faithfulness to the basic task and structure of the apostolic ministry can be combined with an openness to diverse and complementary expressions of this apostolic ministry. Such insights, together with a more comprehensive understanding of the apostolicity of the Church and the means of its preservation and actualization, have led to certain modifications of previously held positions:

256

Geneva/79
34-Commentary [cont.]

In the early life of the Church, this bond between the episcopate and the apostolic community was understood in two ways. Clement of Rome (Cor. 44) linked the mission of the bishop with the sending of the apostles by Christ and the sending of Christ by the Father. This made the bishop a successor of the apostles, ensuring the permanence of the apostolic mission in the Church. For Ignatius of Antioch (Magn. 6:1; Trall. 3:12) it is Christ surrounded by the Twelve who is permanently in the Church in the person of the bishop surrounded by his presbyters. Ignatius regards the Christian community assembled around the bishop in the midst of the presbyters as the manifestation in the Spirit of the apostolic community. Clement is primarily interested in thc means whereby the continuity of Christ's

Geneva/1-16-80
28-Commentary:

In the early Church the bond between the episcopate and the apostolic community was understood in two ways. Clement of Rome linked the mission of the bishop (presbyteros) with the sending of Christ by the Father and the sending of the apostles with Christ. This made the bishop a successor of the apostles, ensuring the permanence of the apostolic mission in the Church. Clement is primarily interested in the means whereby the continuity of Christ's presence is ensured in the Church thanks to the apostolic succession. For Ignatius of Antioch (Magn. 6:1; 3:12? Trall 3:12) it is Christ surrounded bv the Twelve who is permanently in the Church in the person of the bishop surrounded by the presbyters. Ignatius regards the Christian community assembled around the bishop (episkopos) in the midst

Geneva/1-19-80
29-Commentary:

In the early Church the bond between the episcopate and the apostolic community was understood in two ways. Clement of Rome linked the mission of the bishop with the sending of Christ by the Father and the sending of the apostles by Christ (Cor. 42,44). This made the bishop a successor of the apostles, ensuring the permanence of the apostolic mission in the Church. Clement is primarily interested in the means whereby the continuity of Christ's presence is ensured in the Church thanks to the apostolic succession. For Ignatius of Antioch (Magn. 6:1; 3:12; Trall. 3:1) it is Christ surrounded by the Twelve who is permanently in the Church in the person of the bishop surrounded by the presbyters. Ignatius regards the Christian community assembled around the bishop in the midst of the presbyters and the deacons

Geneva/6-80 [cont.]
33-Commentary:

In the early Church the bond between the episcopate and the apostolic community was understood in two ways. Clement of Rome linked the mission of the bishop with the sending of Christ by the Father and the sending of the apostles by Christ (Cor. 42,44). This made the bishop a successor of the apostles, ensuring the permanence of the apostolic mission in the Church. Clement is primarily interested in the means whereby the *historical* continuity of Christ's presence is ensured in the Church thanks to the apostolic succession. For Ignatius of Antioch (Magn. 6:1; 3:12; Trall. 3:1) it is Christ surrounded by the Twelve who is permanently in the Church in the person of the bishop surrounded by the presbyters. Ignatius regards the Christian community assembled around the bishop in the midst of the presbyters and the deacons

Geneva/79 [cont.]

Presence is ensured in the Church thanks to the apostolic succession. Ignatius prefers to contemplate the mystery of this presence of Christ in the Church thanks to the person of the bishop. Only when these two views are combined can the figure and function of the bishop be fully comprehended. The necessary complementarity of the two views of the link earlier stressed between Christ and the Spirit is operative here (cf. Réflexions des théologiens orthodoxes et catholiques....)

Geneva/1-16-80 [cont.]

of the presbyters as the manifestation in the Spirit of the apostolic community. Ignatius contemplates the mystery of Christ's presence in the Church thanks to the person of the bishop. Only when these two views are seen together can the figure and function of the bishop be fully discerned in the early Church.

Geneva/1-19-80 [cont.]

as the manifestation in the Spirit of the apostolic community. Ignatius contemplates the mystery of God's presence in the Church thanks to the person of the bishop. Only when these two views are seen together can the figure and function of the bishop be fully discerned in the early Church.

Geneva/6-80 [cont.]

as the *actual* manifestation in the Spirit of the apostolic community. The sign of apostolic succession, therefore, must not be taken as a guarantee for *historical* continuity only, but also as an *actual* manifestation of a spiritual reality.

Geneva/6-80 [cont.]

34. In recent times, churches which practise the succession through the episcopate, increasingly recognize that a continuity in apostolic faith, worship and mission has been preserved in churches which have not retained the form of historic episcopate. This recognition finds additional support in the fact that the reality and function of the episcopal ministry have been preserved in many of these churches, with or without the title "bishop". Ordination, for example, is always done in them by persons in whom the Church recognizes the authority to transmit the ministerial commission.

35. These considerations do not diminish the importance of the episcopal ministry. On the contrary, they enable churches which have not retained the episcopate to appreciate the episcopal succession as a sign of the

Geneva/1-19-80 [cont.]

30. In recent times, churches which practise the succession through the episcopate increasingly recognize that a continuity in apostolic faith, worship and mission has been preserved in churches which have not retained the form of historic episcopacy. This recognition finds additional support in the fact that the reality and the function of the episcopal ministry have been preserved in many of these churches, with or without the title "bishop". Ordination, for example, is always done in them by persons in whom the church recognizes the authority to transmit the ministerial commission. (para. 35)

31. These considerations do not diminish the importance of the episcopal ministry. On the contrary, they enable churches which have not retained the episcopate to appreciate the episcopal succession as a sign of the

Geneva/1-16-80 [cont.]

29. Increasingly churches which practise the succession through the episcopate recognize that a continuity in apostolic faith, worship and mission has been preserved in churches which have not retained the form of historic episcopacy. This recognition finds additional support in the fact that the reality and the function of the episcopal ministry have been preserved in many of these churches, with or without the title "bishop". Ordination, for example, is always done in them by persons in whom the church recognizes the authority to transmit ministerial commission. (no 35)

30. These considerations do not diminish the importance of the episcopal ministry. On the contrary, they enable churches which have not retained the threefold ministry to appreciate the episcopal succession as a sign of the continuity and unity of the

Geneva/79 [cont.]

34-Commentary [cont.]

Many find it possible today to recognize a continuity in apostolic faith, mission and ministry in churches which have not retained the form of historic episcopacy. This recognition finds additional support in the fact that the episcopal functions and reality have been preserved in many of these churches, with or without the title "bishop". Ordination, for example, is always done in them by persons in whom the church recognizes the authority to transmit ministerial commission.

The importance of the historic episcopate has not been diminished by the above-mentioned findings. On the contrary, these new insights are enabling churches without the historic episcopate to appreciate it as a sign of the continuity and unity of the Church. More and more churches, including those in

Accra/75 [cont.]

35. (b) Many find it possible today to recognize a continuity in apostolic faith, mission and ministry also in churches which have not retained the form of historic episcopacy. This recognition finds additional support in the fact that the episcopal functions and reality have been preserved in many of these churches, with or without the title "bishop". Ordination, for example, is always done in them by persons in whom the church recognizes the authority to transmit ministerial commission.

37. The importance of the historic episcopate has not been diminished by the above-mentioned findings. On the contrary, these new insights are enabling churches without the historic episcopate to appreciate it as a sign of the continuity and unity of the Church. More and more churches, including those in

Accra/74 [cont.]

church union negotiations, are expressing willingness to see episcopacy as a pre-eminent sign of the apostolic succession of the whole Church in faith, life and doctrine, and as such, something that ought to be striven for if absent. The only thing they hold as incompatible with contemporary historical and theological research is the notion that the episcopal succession is identical with and comprehends the apostolicity of the whole Church.

Geneva/79 [cont.]

church union negotiations, are expressing willingness to see episcopacy as a pre-eminent sign of the apostolic succession of the whole Church in faith, life and doctrine, and as such, something that ought to be striven for if absent. The only thing they hold as incompatible with contemporary historical and theological research is the notion that the episcopal succession is identical with and comprehends the apostolicity of the whole Church. (no 37)

Geneva/1-16-80 [cont.]

the Church. More and more churches, including those engaged in union negotiations, are expressing willingness to accept episcopal succession as a sign of the apostolicity of the life of the whole Church. (Para 37)

30-Commentary:
More and more, churches without the historical episcopate seem to deepen their awareness and appreciation of it as a sign of the continuity and unity of the Church. Yet, at the same time, they often express reluctance to state that episcopal succession is identical with and comprehends the apostolicity of the whole Church.

Geneva/1-19-80 [cont.]

continuity and unity of the Church. More and more churches, including those engaged in union negotiations are expressing willingness to accept episcopal succession as a sign of the apostolicity of the life of the whole Church. (para. 37)

31-Commentary:
Today, churches without the historical episcopate seem to deepen their awareness and appreciation of it as a sign of the continuity and unity of the Church. Yet, at the same time, they resent any suggestion that the ministry exercised in their own particular tradition should be invalid until the moment that it enters into an existing line of episcopal succession.

Geneva/6-80 [cont.]

continuity and unity of the Church. Today churches, including those engaged in union negotiations, are expressing willingness to accept episcopal succession as a sign of the apostolicity of the life of the whole Church. Yet, at the same time, they cannot accept any suggestion that the ministry exercised in their own tradition should be invalid until the moment that it enters into an existing line of episcopal succession.

260

Accra/74 [cont.]

34. (a) A growing tendency
is noticeable among theologians in certain churches
which have preserved the
historic episcopate to interpret episcopal succession as
an effective sign, not a
guarantee, of the continuity
of the Church in apostolic
faith and mission, which is
manifested in doctrine,
proclamation, sacraments,
worship, life and service.
They value the succession
of ministries that have the
fullness of *episcope* as a gift
of God, which they must
preserve.

36. (c) Many are also in-
creasingly aware of the fact
that the traditional ways of
transmitting ministerial
commission, whether in
churches with episcopal
structures or not, are not
necessarily exhaustive. In
particular situations, for
example, a ministry may
emerge which, because of
its authenticity, is accepted
by the particular community

Accra/74 [cont.]
and receives only afterwards a form of official recognition. Or, in other situations, new forms of ministry are raised by the Holy Spirit. In responding to these ministries the Church should not quench the Spirit, but rather welcome them as an enrichment of its life and service.

The first paragraph of this section in the Geneva/6-80 text is substantially rooted in the Accra text.[143] The second paragraph of Geneva/6-80 is reflected almost word for word in Accra as well.[144] Added to this second paragraph, however, is a paragraph of Commentary. It is not reflected in the Accra text; it first appeared in the text of Geneva/79.[145] This paragraph from Geneva/79 has as its source the Groupe des Dombes,[146] which had drawn a distinction of considerable ecumenical importance. The Faith and Order Advisory Group of the Church of England put it this way:

> The distinction drawn by the Groupe between the *apostolic succession of the whole Church* and the *fullness of the sign* of this succession (viz. an episcopal order of succession) is one which might commend itself especially to the Church of England. It treads a *via media* between two views of the ministry which find themselves in tension, if not in conflict.[147]

In this same connection Lewis S. Mudge says,

> On the one hand, "sign" and "reality" are two different things. On the other hand, where social reality is concerned, the "reality" is actually made present "in, with and through" the sign, for such is the nature of sociality.[148]

The last two paragraphs of this section in Geneva/6-80 are substantially rooted in the Accra/74 text.[149]

---

[143]Geneva/6-80, §32; Accra/74, §27, sentences 1-2 and §29.

[144]Geneva/6-80, §33; Accra/74, §30.

[145]Geneva/79, §34-Commentary. Cf. also Geneva/1-16-80, §28-Commentary and Geneva/1-19-80, §29-Commentary.

[146]The Groupe des Dombes is an ecumenical theological group which, in the understanding of the present writer, based on his discussions with Frère Max Thurian, met occasionally at Taizè, France. The results of these discussions were published and made available to the FO Commission of WCC.

[147]*The Reconciliation of Ministries: A Report by The Faith and Order Advisory Group of The Board for Mission and Unity.* General Synod (GS) 307, Kent, England: The Wickham Press Ltd., Blackfen Road, Sideup, 1976, p. 11.

[148]"The New Ministry Text: Some Tough Questions," a paper delivered by Lewis S. Mudge, at the Forum on Baptism, Eucharist and Ministry, sponsored by the National Council of Churches in the USA, Baltimore, May 19-22, 1980.

[149]Geneva/6-80, §s 34 and 35; Accra/74, §s 35 and 37.

V. ORDINATION

A. THE MEANING OF ORDINATION.

The most recent text is more inclusive ecumenically in that the act of ordaining is seen as being performed by bishops and by those without the title, "bishop." And it calls for a careful investigation of liturgical texts in order to determine the intentions and meaning of ordination in the various churches. A gender reference is made general thus avoiding the need to address the ordination of women. And a more ecumenical tone is struck with the deletion of references to catholic and protestant positions.

Accra/74

38. The Church, in ordaining some of its members to the ministry in the name of Christ, attempts to follow the mission of the Apostles and to remain faithful to their teaching. Ordination as an act attests the bond of the Church with Jesus Christ and the apostolic witness, recalling that it is the risen Lord who is the true ordainer, who bestows the gift. In ordaining, the Church provides, under the inspiration of the Holy Spirit, for the faithful proclamation of the Gospel and humble service in Christ's name. The layingon of hands can be seen as the sign of the gift of the Spirit, rendering visible the ordering of this ministry in the revelation accomplished in him, and reminding the Church to look to him as the source of its commission.

Geneva/79

24. The Church ordains certain of its members for ministry in Christ's name by the invocation of the Spirit and the imposition of hands (I Tim. 4:14; 2 Tim. 1:6); in this way it seeks to continue the mission of the apostles and to remain faithful to their teaching. The act of ordination attests the bond of the Church with Jesus Christ and the apostolic witness, recalling that it is the risen Lord who is the true ordainer, who bestows the gift. In ordaining, the Church provides, under the inspiration of the Holy Spirit, for the faithful proclamation of the Gospel and humble service in Christ's name. The laying-on of hands is the sign of the gift of the Spirit, rendering visible the ordering of this ministry in the revelation accomplished in him, and reminding the Church to look to him as the source of its commission.

Geneva/1-16-80

38. The Church ordains certain of its members for the ministry in the name of Christ by the invocation of the Spirit and the imposition of hands (I Tim. 4:14; II Tim. 1:6); in doing so it seeks to continue the mission of the apostles and to remain faithful to their teaching. The act of ordination attests the bond of the Church with Jesus Christ and the apostolic witness, recalling that it is the risen Lord who is the true ordainer and bestows the gift. In ordaining, the Church Provides, under the inspiration of the Holy Spirit, for the faithful proclamation of the Gospel and humble service in Christ's name. The laying-on of hands is the sign of the gift of the Spirit, rendering visible the ordering of this ministry in the revelation accomplished in him, and reminding the Church to look to him as the source of its commission. (no 38)

Geneva/1-19-80

38. The Church ordains certain of its members for the ministry in the name of Christ by the invocation of the Spirit and the imposition of hands (I Tim. 4:14; II Tim. 1:6); in so doing it seeks to continue the mission of the apostles and to remain faithful to their teaching. The act of ordination by those who are appointed for this ministry attests the bond of the Church with Jesus Christ and the apostolic witness, recalling that it is the risen Lord who is the true ordainer and bestows the gift. In ordaining, the Church provides, under the inspiration of the Holy Spirit, for the faithful proclamation of the Gospel and humble service in the name of Christ. The laying-on of hands is the sign of the gift of the Spirit, rendering visible the ordering of this ministry in the revelation accomplished in him, and reminding the Church to look to him as the source of its commission. (Para 38)

Geneva/6-80

36. The Church ordains certain of its members for the ministry in the name of Christ by the invocation of the Spirit and the imposition of hands (I Tim 4:14; II Tim 1:6); in so doing it seeks to continue the mission of the apostles and to remain faithful to their teaching. The act of ordination by those who are appointed for this ministry attests the bond of the Church with Jesus Christ and the apostolic witness, recalling that it is the risen Lord who is the true ordainer and bestows the gift. In ordaining, the Church, under the inspiration of the Holy Spirit, provides for the faithful proclamation of the Gospel and humble service in the name of Christ. The laying-on of hands is the sign of the gift of the Spirit, rendering visible the ordering of this ministry in the revelation accomplished in him, and reminding the Church to look to him as the source of its commission.

Geneva/1-19-80 [cont.]
Church to look to him as the source of its commission. (para. 38)

38-Commentary:
It is clear that churches have different practices of ordination, and that it would be wrong to single out one of those as exclusively valid. On the other hand, if churches are increasingly able to recognize each other in the sign of apostolic succession, as described above, it would follow that the old tradition according to which it is the bishop who ordains will be recognized and respected as well.

Geneva/6-80 [cont.]
This ordination, however, can have different intentions according to the specific tasks of bishops, presbyters and deacons as indicated in the liturgies of ordination.

36-Commentary.
It is clear that churches have different practices of ordination, and that it would be wrong to single out one of those as exclusively valid. On the other hand, if churches are increasingly able to recognize each other in the sign of apostolic succession, as described above, it would follow that the old tradition according to which it is the bishop who ordains will be recognized and respected as well.

Accra/74

39. Properly speaking, then, ordination denotes an action by God and by the community which inaugurates a relationship in which the ordained is strengthened by the Spirit for his or her task and is upheld by the acknowledgment and prayers of the congregation.

43. The original New Testament terms for ordination tend to be simple and descriptive. The fact of appointment is recorded. The laying-on of hands is described. There seems to be no warrant for building any particular theory — whether "catholic" or "protestant" — on the New Testament evidence alone. Thus when the theory and practice of ordination are worked out, as they must be, to meet new conditions and opportunities, care must be taken to be aware of the intellectual process involved. Ecumenical dialogue may well

Geneva/79

25. Properly speaking, then, ordination denotes an action by God and by the community which inaugurates a relationship in which the ordained is strengthened by the Spirit for his task and is upheld by the acknowledgment and prayers of the congregation. (no 39)

Geneva/1-16-80

39. Properly speaking, then, ordination denotes an action by God and the community which inaugurates a relationship in which the ordained is strengthened by the Spirit for his task and is upheld by the acknowledgement and prayers of the congregation. (Para 39)

39-Commentary:
The original New Testament terms for ordination tend to be simple and descriptive. The fact of appointment is recorded. The laying-on of hands is described. There seems to be no warrant for building any particular theory whether "catholic" or "protestant" on the New Testament evidence alone. Thus when the theory and practice of ordination are worked out, as they must be, to meet new conditions and opportunities, care must be taken to be aware of the intellectual process involved. Ecumenical dialogue may well include a mutual effort

Geneva/1-19-80

39. Properly speaking, then, ordination denotes an action by God and the community which inaugurates a relationship in which the ordained are strengthened by the Spirit for their task and are upheld by the acknowledgement and prayers of the congregation. (para. 39)

39-Commentary:
The original New Testament terms for ordination tend to be simple and descriptive. The fact of appointment is recorded. The laying-on of hands is described. Different interpretations on the basis of these data. Thus when the theory and practice of ordination are worked out, as they must be, to meet new conditions and opportunities, care must be taken to be aware of the intellectual process involved.

Geneva/6-80

37. Properly speaking, then, ordination denotes an action by God and the community which inaugurates a relationship in which the ordained are strengthened by the Spirit for their task and are upheld by the acknowledgement and prayers of the congregation.

37-Commentary:
The original New Testament terms for ordination tend to be simple and descriptive. The fact of appointment is recorded. The laying on of hands is described. Prayer is made for the Spirit. Different traditions have built different interpretations on the basis of these data.

Accra/74 [cont.]
include a mutual effort to uncover the implicit, the unconscious, the unspoken dimensions of what we think and do. Such effort could both break down barriers and enhance our appreciation of the symbolic and experiential riches we have in common.

Geneva/1-16-80 [cont.]
to uncover the implicit, the unconscious, the unspoken dimensions of what we think and do. Such effort could both break down barriers and enhance our appreciation of the symbolic and experiential riches we have in common.

Accra-4 [cont.]

41. Extensive study has already been devoted to the contexts and meanings of the Hebrew, Greek, and Latin words connected with ordination. It is evident that there is considerable difference between the unspoken cultural setting of the Greek *cheirotonein* and that of the Latin *ordo* or *ordinare*. The New Testament use of the former term borrows its basic secular meaning of "appointment" (Acts 14:23; II Cor. 8:19), which is, in turn, derived from the original meaning of extending the hand, either to designate a person or to cast a vote. Some scholars see in *cheirotonein* a reference to the act of laying-on of hands, in view of the literal description of such action in such seemingly parallel instances as Acts 6:6, 8:17, 18:19, 13:3, 19:6; I Tim. 4:14; II Tim. 1:6. But the actual use of *cheirotonein* need mean no more than "appoint" without

Geneva/1-19-80 [cont.]

It is evident that there is considerable difference between the unspoken cultural setting of the Greek *cheirotonein* and that of the Latin *ordo* or *ordinare*. The New Testament use of the former term borrows its basic secular meaning of "appointment" (Acts 14:23; II Cor. 8:19), which is, in turn, derived from the original meaning of extending the hand, either to designate a person or to cast a vote. Some scholars see in *cheirotonein* a reference to the act of layingon of hands, in view of the literal description of such action in such seemingly parallel instances as Acts 6:6, 8:17, 13:3, 19:6; I Tim. 4:14; II Tim. 1:6. But the actual use of *cheirotonein* need mean no more than "appoint" without reference either to the theory or means of the action. (para.41)

Geneva/6-80 [cont.]

It is evident that there is a certain difference between the unspoken cultural setting of the Greek *cheirotonein* and that of the Latin *ordo* or *ordinare*. The New Testament use of the former term borrows its basic secular meaning of "appointment" (Acts 14:23; II Cor 8:19), which is, in turn, derived from the original meaning of extending the hand, either to designate a person or to cast a vote. Some scholars see in *cheirotonein* a reference to the act of laying on of hands, in view of the literal description of such action in such seemingly parallel instances as Acts 6:6; 8:17; 13:3; 19:6; I Tim 4:14; II Tim 1:6. But the actual use of *cheirotonein* need mean no more than "appoint" without reference either to the theory or means of the action.

Accra/74 [cont.]

reference either to the theory or means of the action. *Ordo* and *ordinare*, on the other hand, are terms derived from Roman law where they convey the notion of the special status of a group distinct from the plebs, as in the term *ordo clarissimus* for the Roman senate. The starting point of any conceptual construction using these terms will strongly influence what is taken for granted in both the thought and action which result.

The first paragraph of this section in the Geneva/6-80 text is reflected for the most part in the first paragraph in Accra/74's section entitled, "Ordination." The text of Geneva/6-80 adds a sentence to the end of the above paragraph: "This ordination, however, can have different intentions according to the specific tasks of bishops, presbyters and deacons as indicated in the liturgies of ordination." This makes explicit the need to investigate closely the liturgical texts as indicative of the meaning of ordination in the churches.

A paragraph of commentary is added at this point in the Geneva/6-80 text. It appears first in the text of Geneva/1-19-80.[150] This paragraph of commentary, while attempting to walk a middle course ecumenically in regard to various practices of ordination, emphasizes the important and traditional role of the bishop.

The second paragraph of this section in the Geneva/6-80 text reflects the content of a paragraph in the Accra text.[151] The later text uses the more general pronoun, "their," in reference to the ordained vis-à-vis the phrase, "his or her." Thus is avoided any explicit treatment here of the issue of the ordination of women.

A commentary paragraph is added here to the Geneva/6-80 text. It is contained substantially in Accra text.[152] The later text shortens its treatment, removing any explicit references to "catholic" and "protestant" theories which the earlier text had made. The same is true of the earlier text's spelling out of the influence of Roman law on the use of the Latin terms, *ordo* and *ordinare*.

B. THE ACT OF ORDINATION.

Again, gender references are avoided and the question of the ordination of women is kept open but not discussed at any length in this study. And the later text adds that the ordained take on a collegial relationship with other ordained ministers.

---

[150]Geneva/6-80, §36-Commentary; Geneva/1-19-80, §38-Commentary.

[151]Geneva/6-80, §37; Accra/74, §39.

[152]Geneva/6-80, §37-Commentary; Accra/74, §s 43 and 41 in that order.

Accra/74

49. A long and early Christian tradition places ordination in the context of worship and especially of the eucharist. Such a place for the service of ordination preserves the understanding of ordination as an *act of* the *whole* community, and not of a certain order within it or of the individual ordained. Even if one believes that the act of ordaining belongs to a special order within the Church, it is always important to remember that the entire community is involved in the act. Ordination, in association with the eucharist, keeps before the Church the truth that it is an act which initiates a person to a *service of the "koinonia'* (the fellowship), a service both to God and to the fellow man. It is this *koinonia* that the eucharist expresses *par excellence* and by continuing to relate ordination to the eucharist this dimension of ministry is called to

Geneva/79

30. A long and early Christian tradition places ordination in the context of worship and especially of the eucharist. Such a place for the service of ordination preserves the understanding of ordination as an *act of* the *whole* community, and not of a certain order within it or of the individual ordained. Even if one believes that the act of ordaining belongs to a special order within the Church, it is always important to remember that the entire community is involved in the act. Ordination, in association with the eucharist, keeps before the Church the truth that it is an act which initiates a person to a *service of the "koinonia'* (the fellowship), a service both to God and to the fellow man. It is this *koinonia* that the eucharist expresses *par excellence* and by continuing to relate ordination to the eucharist this dimension of ministry is called to

Geneva/1-16-80

40. A long and early Christian tradition places ordination in the context of worship and especially of the eucharist. Such a place for the service of ordination preserves the understanding of ordination as an act of the whole community, and not of a certain order within it or of the individual ordained. The act of ordination by the laying-on of hands is at one and the same time: invocation of the Holy Spirit (epiklesis); sacramental sign; acknowledgement of gifts and commitment. (Para 44)

Geneva/1-19-80

40. A long and early Christian tradition places ordination in the context of worship and especially of the eucharist. Such a place for the service of ordination preserves the understanding of ordination as an *act of* the *whole* community, and not of a certain order within it or of the individual ordained. The act of ordination by the laying-on of hands is at one and the same time: invocation of the Holy Spirit (epiklesis); sacramental sign; acknowledgement of gifts and commitment. (para. 44)

Geneva/6-80

38. A long and early Christian tradition places ordination in the context of worship and especially of the eucharist. Such a place for the service of ordination preserves the understanding of ordination as an *act of* the *whole* community, and not of a certain order within it or of the individual ordained. The act of ordination by the laying on of hands is at one and the same time: invocation of the Holy Spirit (epiklesis); sacramental sign; acknowledgement of gifts and commitment.

Geneva/79 [cont.]

mind. Ordination within the service of the eucharist also reminds the Church that the ordained ministry is set apart to point to Christ's own ministry and not to some other. By placing ordination in the context of the eucharist, this act is referred to God himself and the ordained person is dedicated to the service of 'his Servant' who offers himself for the salvation of the world. (no 49)

26. The act of ordination by the laying-on of hands is at one and the same time: invocation of the Holy Spirit (*epiklesis*); sacramental sign; acknowledgment of gifts and commitment. (no 44)

It is:

Accra/74 [cont.]

mind. Ordination within the service of the eucharist also reminds the Church that the ordained is set apart to point to Christ's own ministry and not to some other. By placing ordination in the context of worship and especially the eucharist, this act is referred to God himself and the ordained person is dedicated to the service of "his Servant" who offers himself for the salvation of the world.

44. The act of ordination is at one and the same time: invocation of the Holy Spirit (*epiklesis*); sacramental sign; acknowledgment of gifts and commitment. It is:

Accra/74

45. (a) An invocation to God that he bestow the power of the Holy Spirit upon the new minister in his new relation to the local Christian community, to the Church universal and to the world. The otherness of God's initiative, of which the ordained ministry is a symbol, is here acknowledged in the act of ordination itself. "The Spirit blows where it wills" (John 3:3), and invocation of the Spirit implies an absolute dependence on God for the outcome of the Church's prayer. This means that the Spirit may set new forces in motion and open new possibilities "far more abundantly than all that we ask or think" (Eph. 3:20).

Geneva/79

27. (a) An invocation to God that he bestow the power of the Holy Spirit upon the new minister in his new relation to the local Christian community, to the Church universal and to the world. The otherness of God's initiative, of which the ordained ministry is a symbol, is here acknowledged in the act of ordination itself. "The Spirit blows where it wills" (John 3:3), and invocation of the Spirit implies an absolute dependence on God for the outcome of the Church's prayer. This means that the Spirit may set new forces in motion and open new possibilities "far more abundantly than all we ask or think" (Eph. 3:20). (no 45)

Geneva/1-16-80

41. a) An invocation to God that he bestow the power of the Holy Spirit upon the new minister in his new relation to the local Christian community, to the Church universal and to the world. The otherness of God's initiative, of which the ordained ministry is here acknowledged in the act of ordination itself. "The Spirit blows where it wills" (Jn. 3:3); the invocation of the Spirit implies the absolute dependence on God for the outcome of the Church's prayer. This means that the Spirit may set new forces in motion and open new possibilities "far more abundantly than all that we ask or think" (Eph. 3:20). (Para 45)

Geneva/1-19-80

41. a) An invocation to God that he bestow the power of the Holy Spirit upon the new minister in the new relation which is established between this minister and the local Christian community, the Church universal and the world. The otherness of God's initiative, of which the ordained ministry is the symbol, is here acknowledged in the act of ordination itself. "The Spirit blows where it wills" (Jn 3:3); the invocation of the Spirit implies the absolute dependence on God for the outcome of the Church's prayer. This means that the Spirit may set new forces in motion and open new possibilities "far more abundantly than all that we ask or think" (Eph. 3:20). (para. 45)

Geneva/6-80

39. a) Ordination is an invocation to God that he bestow the power of the Holy Spirit upon the new minister in the new relation which is established between this minister and the local Christian community, the Church universal and the world. The otherness of God's initiative, of which the ordained ministry is the symbol, is here acknowledged in the act of ordination itself. "The Spirit blows where it wills" (Jn 3:3); the invocation of the Spirit implies the absolute dependence on God for the outcome of the Church's prayer. This means that the Spirit may set new forces in motion and open new possibilities "far more abundantly than all that we ask or think" (Eph 3:20).

Accra/74

46. (b) A sign of the granting of this prayer by the Lord who gives the gift of ministry. Although the outcome of the Church's *epiklesis* depends on the freedom of God, the Church ordains in confidence that God, being faithful to his promise in Christ, enters sacramentally into contingent, historical forms of human relationship and uses them for his purpose. Ordination is a sign performed in faith that the spiritual relationship signified is present in, with and through the words spoken, the gestures made and the ecclesiastical forms employed.

Geneva/79

28. (b) A sign of the granting of this prayer by the Lord who gives the gift of ministry. Although the outcome of the Church's *epiklesis* depends on the freedom of God, the Church ordains in confidence that God, being faithful to his promise in Christ, enters sacramentally into contingent, historical forms of human relationship and uses them for his purpose. Ordination is a sign performed in faith that the spiritual relationship signified is present in, with and through the words spoken, the gestures made and the ecclesiastical forms employed. (no 46)

Geneva/1-16-80

42. b) A sign of the granting of this prayer by the Lord who gives the gift of the ordained ministry. Although the outcome of the Church's epiklesis depends on the freedom of God, the Church ordains in confidence that God, being faithful to his promise in Christ, enters sacramentally into contingent, historical forms of human relationship and uses them for his purpose. Ordination is a sign performed in faith that the spiritual relationship signified is present in, with and through the words spoken, the gestures made and the forms employed. (Para 46)

Geneva/1-19-80

42. b) Ordination is a sign of the granting of this prayer by the Lord who gives the gift of the ordained ministry. Although the outcome of the Church's epiklesis depends on the freedom of God, the Church ordains in confidence that God, being faithful to his promise in Christ, enters sacramentally into contingent, historical forms of human relationship and uses them for his purpose. Ordination is a sign performed in faith that the spiritual relationship signified is present in, with and through the words spoken, the gestures made and the forms employed. (para. 46)

Geneva/6-80

40. b) Ordination is a sign of the granting of this prayer by the Lord who gives the gift of the ordained ministry. Although the outcome of the Church's epiklesis depends on the freedom of God, the Church ordains in confidence that God, being faithful to his promise in Christ, enters sacramentally into contingent, historical forms of human relationship and uses them for his purpose. Ordination is a sign performed in faith that the spiritual relationship signified is present in, with and through the words spoken, the gestures made and the forms employed.

Accra/74

47. (c) An acknowledgment by the Church of its discernment of gifts of the Spirit in the one ordained, and a commitment by both Church and ordinand, to the tests and opportunities implied in the new relationship. By receiving the new minister in the act of ordination, the congregation acknowledges this minister's gifts and commits itself to responsibility for an openness toward him. Likewise the one ordained offers his gifts to the Church and commits himself to the burden and opportunity of new authority and responsibility.

48. In order to experience and demonstrate the truth that setting apart is not to some superior level of discipleship, but rather to service within the Church, it is important that the entire process of ordination involve the whole body of the people. There needs to be continual emphasis on

Geneva/79

29. (c) An acknowledgment by the Church of its discernment of gifts of the Spirit in the one ordained, and a commitment by both Church and ordinand, to the tests and opportunities implied in the new relationship. By receiving the new minister in the act of ordination, the congregation acknowledges this minister's gifts and commits itself to responsibility for an openness toward him. Likewise the one ordained offers his gifts to the Church and commits himself to the burden and opportunity of new authority and responsibility. (no 47)

29-Commentary:
In order to experience and demonstrate the truth that setting apart is not to some superior level of discipleship, but rather to service within the Church, it is important that the entire process of ordination involve the whole body of the people. There needs to be continual emphasis on

Geneva/1-16-80

43. c) An acknowledgment by the Church of its discernment of the gifts of the Spirit in the one ordained, to the tests and opportunities implied in the new relationship. By receiving the new minister in the act of ordination, the congregation acknowledges this minister's gifts and commits itself to responsibility for an openness towards him. Likewise the one ordained offers his gifts to the Church and commits himself to the burden and opportunity of new authority and responsibility. (Para 47)

Geneva/1-19-80

43. c) Ordination is an acknowledgement by the Church of its discernment of the gifts of the Spirit in the one ordained, and a commitment by both the Church and the ordinand, to the tests and opportunities implied in the new relationship. By receiving the new minister in the act of ordination, the congregation acknowledges this minister's gifts and commits itself to responsibility for an openness towards him. Likewise the one ordained offer their gifts to the Church and commit themselves to the burden and opportunity of new authority and responsibility. (para. 47) At the same time, they accept the collegial relationship with other ordained ministers into which they enter.

Geneva/6-80

41. c) Ordination is an acknowlegement by the Church of its discernment of the gifts of the Spirit in the one ordained, and a commitment by both the Church and the ordinand, to the tests and opportunities implied in the new relationship. By receiving the new minister in the act of ordination, the congregation acknowledges this minister's gifts and commits itself to responsibility for an openness towards these gifts. Likewise those one ordained offer their gifts to the Church and commit themselves to the burden and opportunity of new authority and responsibility. At the same time, they accept the collegial relationship with other ordained ministers into which they enter.

276

Accra/74 [cont.]
fact that ordination is not only "over against" nor *vis-à-vis* the congregation, but rather, that a person is addressed in the midst of the people. It is also important that the congregation have a part in the calling, choosing, and training of an ordinand, preserving the basic significance of the call to the ministry. This means more than the inclusion of a sentence or two in the liturgy and ordaining in the presence of the laity, important as that may be."

Geneva/79 [cont.]
the fact that ordination is not only "over against" nor *vis-à-vis* the congregation, but rather, that a person is addressed in the midst of the people. It is also important that the congregation have a part in the calling, choosing, and training of an ordinand, preserving the basic significance of the call to the ministry. (no 48)

Virtually all of the content in the later text is contained in the earlier one. Of course there is much material deleted from the earlier text. The last paragraph cited in the Geneva/6-80 text adds the sentence, "At the same time, they (the ordained) accept the collegial relationship with other ordained ministers into which they enter.[153] In this same paragraph the gender inclusive pronouns, "their" and "themselves," are used instead of the earlier ones, "he" and "himself."

C. THE CONDITIONS FOR ORDINATION.

The later text abbreviates its treatment of the conditions for ordination. The resulting text provides less sociology, more theology.

Accra/74	Geneva/6-80
51. The ordinand should be one who has a call from the Lord to dedicate himself to the particular style of ministry implied in ordination. This call will be discerned by the ordinand himself, by the Christian community and by its spiritual leaders. It is discerned through personal prayer and reflection, as well as through suggestion, example, encouragement, guidance coming from family, friends, teachers, the school, the congregation, the seminary. It will be tested and fostered and confirmed or perhaps modified, particularly through the years of training.	42. People are called in differing ways to the ordained ministry. There is a personal awareness of a call from the Lord to dedicate oneself to the ordained ministry. This call may be discerned through personal prayer and reflection, as well as through suggestion, example, encouragement, guidance coming from family, friends, the congregation, teachers, and other Church authorities. But there is also a recognition of the gifts and graces of a particular person, both natural and spiritually given, needed for the ministry to be performed. The Church's act of ordination is performed without respect of persons.
57. Both celibacy and marriage are vocations from God and gifts of the Spirit. Either of these can be used by God to bless the ordained minister and enrich his ministry.	Both in celibacy and marriage God can use people for the ordained ministry.

The later text adds these two sentences: "But there is also a recognition of the gifts and graces of a particular person, both natural and spiritually given, needed for the ministry to be performed. The Church's act of ordination is performed without respect of persons."

Accra/74	Geneva/6-80
59. (c) Ministries need not always be salaried from Church sources. Financial support from the Church is not essential to ordained ministry and may, in some cases, even diminish its effectiveness. While the Church has a clear duty to ·make financial provision for its servants, support may come from other sources, not ex-	43. Ordained persons may be professional ministers in the sense that they receive their salaries from the Church. The Church may also ordain people who remain in other occupations or employment.

---

[153]This addition was first made in the Geneva/1-19-80 text.

cluding work done by the minister himself, provided this remains subordinate to and serves the purpose for which he was ordained. This possibility is often described as a "tent-making" ministry, following the example of St. Paul.

60. (d) The exercise of ministry could be full-time or part-time: both possibilities should be accepted. Nothing in Scripture demands all ministers be full-time and employed by the Church. Full-time ministry has advantages and may be indispensable in some situations. There are, however, other circumstances in which part-time arrangements for ministerial leadership are possible and helpful. The secular experience of the minister, which is implied in these arrangements, could enrich the ministry and the minister's work in the secular world could commend the Gospel. On the other hand, the new problems which can arise for a minister in secular employment require sympathetic study.

61. (e) While a good many will be ordained for service within the Church's visible organization, the possibility of ordination for the Church's ministry of word and sacrament outside this organization must always remain open. Such ordained persons might then live as bricklayers, as industrial managers or as TV scriptwriters for example.

Here the later text (above) is clearly much abbreviated.

Accra/74

53. (iii) The ordinand should be one capable of carrying out the ministry in informed fidelity to the Gospel of Christ and to Christ's lordship over the actual situation within which the service is rendered. He should be able to read and discern the signs of the times. He should, therefore, be appropriately prepared through adequate study of Scripture and theology, and through sufficient acquaintance with the social and human realities of the actual situation.

58. (b) The academic programme should be flexible and considerable elasticity is to be admitted in requirements regarding degrees. To be sure, the ordained minister requires a competence suitable to the style of ministry to be undertaken and calls for the intellectual training necessary to understand the questions men

Geneva/6-80

44. Candidates for the ordained ministry need appropriate preparation through study of Scripture and theology and through acquaintance with the social and human realities of the present situation. The period of training will be one in which the candidate's call is tested and fostered and confirmed or perhaps modified.

around are asking and to search along with them for theological answers. It does not, however, follow that such competence and training are achieved only through formal study or the acquisition of degrees or prescribed patterns of formation. The variety of situations and of groups to be served demand various types of preparation for the ministry. Team ministries, in particular, will find their capacity to serve greatly enhanced by diversified formation. What is said here is in no way intended to diminish the importance to the Church of its doctors of theology, its trained interpreters of Scripture or its experts in other disciplines. It is intended, rather, to emphasize the truth that certain kinds of ministry may need other competences even more, including extensive experience in the "secular" world.

51. (i) The ordinand should be one who has a call from the Lord to dedicate himself to the particular style of ministry implied in ordination. This call will be discerned by the ordinand himself, by the Christian community and by its spiritual leaders. It is discerned through personal prayer and reflection, as well as through suggestion, example, encouragement, guidance coming from family, friends, teachers, the school, the congregation, the seminary. It will be tested and fostered and confirmed or perhaps modified, particularly through the years of training.

Here the later text (above) is much abbreviated as well.

Accra/74	Geneva/6-80
62. (f) While the initial commitment to ordained ministry ought normally to be made without reserve or time limit, leave of absence from service is not incompatible with ordination and should be granted on reasonable grounds. There may also be cases in which an ordained minister wishes to relinquish exercise of his special ministry; a request made for serious reasons to relinquish it should be granted without opprobrium or reproach. Such a procedure need not mean in every case that the minister's service was not blessed by the Holy Spirit, or that the initial act of ordination was a mistake, or that one's status as an ordained person and the special relationship to the community constituted by ordination ceases to exist. Resumption of ministry will require no re-ordination.	45. Initial commitment to ordained ministry ought normally to be made without reserve or time limit. Yet leave of absence from service is not incompatible with ordination. Resumption of ministry requires no re-ordination. In recognition of the God-given charism of ministry, ordination to any one of the particular ordained ministries is never repeated.

Here the latter text (above) is somewhat abbreviated and contains substantially the material in the former text.

Accra/74

88. For the Church to be one the full mutual recognition of ministries is required. The statement on the unity we seek which was adopted by the New Delhi Assembly (1961) makes this point clearly. As it enumerates the conditions which need to be fulfilled to be able to speak of a fully committed fellowship it also mentions the ministry. Unity will have been achieved only when members and ministers are recognized throughout the Christian community. It is not only necessary that it be possible for the ministers of one church to be admitted to fulfil certain functions in the other church. This would still be only limited recognition. It must be possible, at least in principle, that ministers be able to fulfil their ministry, upon invitation, in any church. Of course, there may be restrictions of an administrative nature which limit the exercise of any ministry to certain areas. Such restrictions can exist within the one Church. But unity requires that the calling to and the fruit of the ministry be recognized everywhere.

50. It follows from what has been

Geneva/1-16-80

44. It follows from what has been said about ordination that certain preconditions and expectations regarding the ordinand are indispensable, while others are not. The discipline assumed by ordinands in one church need not be seen as universally applicable and used as grounds for not recognizing ministries in others. Churches find themselves empoverished when their ministries do not reflect the richness and diversity that constitute their communion in Christ. Therefore, churches should seriously reevaluate their practices, if they now refuse to test those persons who believe themselves called to the ordained ministry of the Church solely on grounds of their identification with one particular group within the Church. It is especially important today to be clear about this in view of the multitude of experiments in new forms of ministry with which the churches are approaching the modern world.

Geneva/1-19-80

44. To be written in June

Geneva/6-80

46. The discipline with regard to the conditions for ordination in one church need not be seen as universally applicable and used as grounds for not recognizing ministries in others.

47. Churches should, however, seriously reevaluate their practices if they now refuse to test candidates for the ordained ministry solely on the grounds of their belonging to one particular group in the church. It is especially important today to be clear about this in view of the multitude of experiments in new forms of ministry with which the churches are approaching the modern world.

Accra/74 [cont.]
said about ordination that certain preconditions and expectations regarding the ordinand are indispensable, while others are not. It is especially important today to be clear about this in view of the multitude of experiments in new forms of ministry with which the churches are approaching the modern world.

The last four sentences in the Accra text quoted (immediately above, §88) are reflected in the text cited parallel to it from Geneva/6-80, §46. The later text, however, applies the notion of universal recognition of ministries to the specific topic of conditions for ordination. This particular emphasis was first made in the text of Geneva/1-16-80.[154] There are two sentences in the other paragraph from Geneva/6-80 (cited immediately above, §47). The first sentence urging the churches to reevaluate their practices of testing candidates for ordination was first written in the text of Geneva/1-16-80.[155] The second sentence is repeated from the Accra/74 text which had not addressed the issue in such a direct and hortatory fashion.

VI. TOWARDS THE MUTUAL RECOGNITION OF THE ORDAINED MINISTRIES.

This final section in the later text more hortatory and less imperative in tone. In addition, it is ecumenically more positive, inviting and realistic in its expectations. And there is, as is evidenced in the earlier sections, a more precise use of terminology, e.g., the term, "episcopal succession," replacing the term, "apostolic succession." The later text shortens the treatment of this topic considerably while attempting to be more concise.

---

[154]Geneva/1-16-80, §44.

[155]Ibid.

Accra/74

101. In order to advance towards the goal expressed in the New Delhi statement, deliberate efforts are required. Discussion can help to clarify the issues but discussion alone will not solve the problem. The churches must ready themselves for actual changes in their approach and their practice.

Geneva/1-16-80

31. In order to advance towards the mutual recognition of ministries, deliberate efforts are required. At times different terms are employed to describe the same reality and the same terms to describe different realities. Ecumenical conversations can help to clarify the issues and to discover convergences but discussion alone will not overcome the division. The churches must be prepared to renew their understanding and their practice of the ordained ministry. (Para 101)

36. All churches need to examine the forms of the ordained ministry and the degree to which they are faithful to the original intentions.

Geneva/1-19-80

32. In order to advance towards the mutual recognition of ministries, deliberate efforts are required. All churches need to examine the forms of the ordained ministry and the degree to which they are faithful to the original intentions. Churches must be prepared to renew their understanding and their practice of the ordained ministry. (para. 101)

Geneva/6-80

48. In order to advance towards the mutual recognition of ministries, deliberate efforts are required. All churches need to examine the forms of the ordained ministry and the degree to which they are faithful to its original intentions. Churches must be prepared to renew their practice of the ordained ministry.

Accra/74

102. According to what was said above, two things are of crucial importance for mutual recognition of ordination practice. First, the rite used must express the intention to transmit the apostolic ministry of the Word of God and of the sacraments. Second, the rite must include an invocation (*epiklesis*) of the Holy Spirit and the laying-on of hands. The invocation of the Holy Spirit is intended to safeguard and to attest what in some traditions is called the "sacramentality" of ordination.

In order to achieve mutual recognition, different steps are required of different churches:

Geneva/79

55. Two things are of crucial importance for mutual recognition of ordination practice. First, the rite used must express the intention to transmit the apostolic ministry of the Word of God and of the sacraments. Second, the rite must include an invocation (*epiklesis*) of the Holy Spirit and the laying-on of hands. The invocation of the Holy Spirit is intended to safeguard and to attest what in some traditions is called the "sacramentality" of ordination. (no 102)

Geneva/1-16-80

32. For the mutual recognition the issue of the apostolic succession is of particular importance. They can recognize the ordained ministry if they are mutually assured of their intention to transmit the apostolic ministry of Word and Sacrament. The rite of transmission must include the invocation of the Spirit and the laying-on of hands. (Para 102)

Geneva/1-19-80

33. For the mutual recognition the issue of the apostolic succession is of particular importance. Partners in ecumenical conversations can recognize the ordained ministry if they are mutually assured of their intention to transmit the apostolic ministry of Word and Sacrament. The rite of transmission includes the invocation of the Spirit and the laying-on of hands. (para. 102)

Geneva/6-80

49. For the mutual recognition of the issue of the apostolic succession is of particular importance. Partners in ecumenical conversations can recognize the ordained ministry if they are mutually assured of their intention to transmit the apostolic ministry. The rite of transmission includes the invocation of the Spirit and the laying on of hands.

Accra/74

105. (ii) (a) Churches with episcopal succession should reassert the value of episcopal ministry, particularly in its pastoral aspects, and should work in order that others might discover its significance as a personally embodied sign of visible unity.

103. (i) (a) Churches which have preserved the episcopal succession have to recognize the real content of the ordained ministry that exists in churches that do not have such an episcopal succession. In spite of the mutual separation of the two kinds of churches, the God who is ever faithful to his promises gives to the communities that lack the episcopal succession but that live in a succession of apostolic faith, a ministry of the word and sacrament the value of which is attested by its fruits. These communities have also, in many cases, developed a vital lay

Geneva/79

53. Churches with episcopal succession should reassert the value of episcopal ministry, particularly in its pastoral aspects, and should work in order that others might discover its significance as a personally embodied sign of visible unity. (no 105)

51. In order to achieve mutual recognition, different steps are required of different churches.

Churches which have preserved the episcopal succession have to recognize the real content of the ordained ministry that exists in churches that do not have such an episcopal succession. In spite of the mutual separation of the two kinds of churches, the God who is ever faithful to his promises gives to the communities that lack the episcopal succession but that live in a succession of apostolic faith, a ministry of the word

Geneva/1-16-80

33. In order to achieve mutual recognition different steps are required of different churches:

34. Churches which have preserved the episcopal succession have to recognize the apostolic content of the ordained ministry which exists in churches which have not maintained such succession. God who is ever faithful to his promises gives to the communities that lack the episcopal succession but that live in faithfulness to the apostolic faith and mission a ministry, the value of which is attested by its fruits (Para 103.)

Geneva/1-19-80

34. In order to achieve mutual recognition different steps are required of different churches:

35. Churches which have preserved the episcopal succession will need to recognize the apostolic content of the ordained ministry which exists in churches which have not maintained such succession. God who is ever faithful to his promises gives to the communities that lack the episcopal succession but that live in faithfulness to the apostolic faith and mission a ministry of Word and Sacrament the value of which is attested by its fruits. (para. 103)

Geneva/6-80

50. In order to achieve mutual recognition, different steps are required of different churches:

a. Churches which have preserved the episcopal succession will need to recognize the apostolic content of the ordained ministry which exists in churches which have not maintained such succession. The churches without the episcopal succession but living in faithfulness to the apostolic faith and mission have a ministry of Word and Sacrament, as is evident from the life of these churches.

Accra/74 [cont.]
ministry.

106. (ii) (b) These churches
should also consider the
desirability of recognizing
some ordained ministries
that exist apart from an
episcopal succession but
which embody a succession
of ordained ministers who
combine in their ministries
the functions of both bishop
and presbyter. It may also
be possible to recognize
some ministries that do not
claim a formal episcopal or
episcopal presbyteral succession but that in fact exist
with the express intention of
maintaining a succession in
the apostolic faith.

Geneva/79 [cont.]
and sacrament the value of
which is attested by its
fruits. These communities
have also, in many cases,
developed a vital lay ministry. (no 103)

Accra/74 [cont.]
104. (i) (b) The churches without episcopal succession have to realize that churches which value such succession have also retained a ministry of word and sacraments through the centuries and while the former may not lack a succession in the apostolic faith, they do not have the fullness of the *sign* of apostolic succession. If full visible unity is to be achieved, the fullness of the sign of apostolic succession ought to be recovered.

Geneva/79 [cont.]
54. These churches should also consider the desirability of recognizing some ordained ministries that exist apart from an episcopal succession but which embody a succession of ordained ministers who combine in their ministries the functions of both bishop and presbyter. It may also be possible to recognize some ministries that do not claim a formal episcopal or episcopal presbyteral succession but that in fact exist with the express intention of maintaining a succession in the apostolic faith. (no 106)

52. The churches without episcopal succession have to realize that churches which value such succession have also retained a ministry of word and sacraments through the centuries and while the former may not lack a succession in the apostolic faith, they do not have the fullness of the *sign* of apostolic succession. If

Geneva/1-16-80 [cont.]
35. The churches without episcopal succession have to realize that the continuity with the Church of the apostles has found profound expression in the successive layingon of hands by bishops and that, though they may not lack the continuity in the apostolic tradition, this sign will strengthen and deepen that continuity. They may need to recover the sign of the apostolic succession. (Para 104)

Geneva/1-19-80 [cont.]
36. The churches without episcopal succession will need to realize that the continuity with the Church of the apostles finds profound expression in the successive laying-on of hands by bishops and that, though they may not lack the continuity in the apostolic tradition, this sign will strengthen and deepen that continuity. They may need to recover the sign of the apostolic succession. (para. 104)

Geneva/6-80
50. [cont.]
b. The churches without episcopal succession will need to realize that the continuity with the Church of the apostles finds profound expression in the successive laying on of hands by bishops and that, though they may not lack the continuity in the apostolic tradition, this sign will strengthen and deepen that continuity. They may need to recover the sign of episcopal succession.

Geneva/79 [cont.]
full visible unity is to be
achieved, the fullness of the
sign of apostolic succession
ought to be recovered. (no
104)

Accra/74

99. The mutual recognition of the churches and their ministries implied a public act from which point unity would be fully realized. Several forms of such a public act have been proposed: mutual imposition of hands, eucharistic noncelebration (*sic*), solemn worship without a particular rite, the simple reading of a text of union during the course of a celebration. No one liturgical form would be absolutely required, but in any case it would be necessary to proclaim the accomplishment of such mutual recognition publicly. And the common celebration of the Lord's Supper would certainly be the place for such a service.

Geneva/79

56. The mutual recognition of the churches and their ministries implied a public act from which point unity would be fully realized. Several forms of such a public act have been proposed: mutual imposition of hands, eucharistic noncelebration, solemn worship without a particular rite, the simple reading of a text of union during the course of a celebration. No one liturgical form would be absolutely required, but in any case it would be necessary to proclaim the accomplishment of such mutual recognition publicly. And the common celebration of the Lord's Supper would certainly be the place for such a service. (no 99)

Geneva/1-16-80

37. The mutual recognition of the churches and their ministries implies a public act from which point unity would be fully realized. Several forms of such public act have been proposed: mutual imposition of hands, eucharistic concelebration, solemn worship without a particular rite, the reading of a text of union during the course of a celebration. No one liturgical form would be absolutely required, but in any case it would be necessary to proclaim the accomplishment of mutual recognition publicly. The common celebration of the eucharist would certainly be the place for such a service. (Para 99)

Geneva/1-19-80

37. The mutual recognition of the churches and their ministries implies a public act from which point unity would be fully realized Several forms of such public act have been proposed: mutual imposition of hands, eucharistic concelebration, solemn worship without a particular rite of recognition, the reading of a text of union during the course of a celebration. No one liturgical form would be absolutely required, but in any case it would be necessary to proclaim the accomplishment of mutual recognition publicly. The common celebration of the eucharist would certainly be the place for such a service. (para. 99)

Geneva/6-80

52. The mutual recognition of the churches and their ministries implies a public act from which point unity would be fully realized. Several forms of such public act have been proposed: mutual imposition of hands, eucharistic concelebration, solemn worship without a particular rite of recognition. No one liturgical form would be absolutely required, but in any case it would be necessary to proclaim the accomplishment of mutual recognition publicly. The common celebration of the eucharist would certainly be the place for such a service.

Geneva/6-80, §48 adds the important exhortation that "all churches need to examine the forms of the ordained ministry and the degree to which they are faithful to its original intentions."[156] The parallel Accra text, §101, uses the phrase, "solve the problem." The later text places the issue in a more positive ecumenical context.

The parallel texts of Accra, §102 and Geneva/6-80, §49 contain substantially the same content. The later text tends to be more concise and more ecumenically self-conscious. The term, "of the Word of God and of the sacraments," is deleted. The following sentence is eliminated: "The invocation of the Holy Spirit is intended to safeguard and to attest what in some traditions is called the 'sacramentality' of ordination."[157] The phrase, "partners in ecumenical dialogue," is added.[158]

A more ecumenically friendly tone is immediately evident in the parallel paragraphs cited above. Phrases, such as "have to" and "ought to," are replaced by the phrases, "need to," "will need," and "may need."[159]

What is more important theologically is the more precise use of the following phrases: "apostolic content" (replacing "real content"); "episcopal succession" (replacing "apostolic succession"); "apostolic tradition" (replacing "apostolic faith"); and "the successive laying on of hands by bishops" (replacing "the fullness of the sign of apostolic succession").[160]

Accra/74	Geneva/6-80
69. For some churches these problems are not yet alive. While recording a position, they have not yet determined whether the decisive factors are doctrinal or simply related to a longstanding traditional discipline. Nor are individuals within the different confessions in agreement about the doctrinal and disciplinary factors or about their relation. Differences on this issue could raise possible obstacles to the mutual recognition of ministries. But these obstacles should not be regarded as insuperable. Openness to each other holds out the possibility that the Spirit may well speak to one Church through the insights of another. Ecumenical awareness and responsi-	51. Some churches ordain both men and women, others ordain only men. Differences on this issue could raise obstacles to the mutual recognition of ministries. But these obstacles must not be regarded as a substantive hindrance for further efforts toward mutual recognition. Openness to each other holds the possibility that the Spirit may well speak to one church through the insights of another. Ecumenical consideration, therefore, should encourage, not restrain, the facing of this question.

---

[156]This sentence was first introduced in the text of Geneva/1-16-80.

[157]This deletion was made in the text of Geneva/1-16-80.

[158]This addition took place first in the text of Geneva/1-19-80.

[159]These replacements are first made with the Geneva/1-80 texts.

[160]Ibid.

bility also demand that once a Church has decided what is timely and right, it should act in obedience to its own conviction. Since the opinion appears to be growing that doctrinal considerations either favour the ordination of women or are neutral, the possibility is open that a future ecumenical council might deal with the question. Ecumenical considerations, therefore, should encourage, not restrain, the full, frank facing of this question.

Above, in the section entitled, "The Ministry of Men and Women in the Church," this topic of the ordination of women was treated. Here in the Geneva/6-80 text it is treated again, albeit briefly, under the rubric of mutual recognition of ministries. The corresponding material in the Accra/74 text, however, is from its distinct and lengthy section on the ordination of women, a section not found in the Geneva/6-80 text (nor indeed in the Lima 1/82 text).

One sentence in the Geneva/6-80 text here bears comment. It states that "these obstacles (raised by the churches' differences on the issue of women's ordination) must not be regarded as a substantive hindrance for further efforts toward mutual recognition."[161] It replaces the sentence which states that "these obstacles should not be regarded as insuperable."[162] The statement of the later text evinces a greater awareness of the difficulties posed by the different positions taken by the churches and a greater awareness of the need for pursuing the process of ecumenical dialogue with no preconceived outcome in mind.

Accra/74	Geneva/6-80
99. The mutual recognition of the churches and their ministries implied a public act from which point unity would be fully realized. Several forms of such a public act have been proposed: mutual imposition of hands, eucharistic non-celebration, solemn worship without a particular rite, the simple reading of a text of union during the course of a celebration. No one liturgical form would be absolutely required, but in any case it would be necessary to proclaim the accomplishment of such mutual recognition publicly. And the common celebration of the Lord's Supper would certainly be the place for such a	52. The mutual recognition of the churches and their ministries implies a public act from which point unity would be fully realized. Several forms of such public act have been proposed: mutual imposition of hands, eucharistic concelebration, solemn worship without a particular rite of recognition, the reading of a text of union during the course of a celebration. No one liturgical form would be absolutely required, but in any case it would be necessary to proclaim the accomplishment of mutual recognition publicly. The common celebration of the eucharist would certainly be the place for such a service.

---

[161]Geneva/6-80, §51, cited in its entirety earlier in this chapter.

[162]Accra/74, §69. Cited earlier in this chapter in its entirety.

service.

There are no substantial differences in these between the text of Accra/74, §99 and Geneva/6-80, §52 (cited immediately above along with the three intervening texts). The substitution of the term, "the eucharist," for that of "the Lord's Supper," may very well indicate a clear positioning of the text on "Ministry" under the same cover as the one on "Eucharist." in the full text of Baptism, Eucharist and Ministry (the whole "Lima document").

SUMMARY.

In the foregoing chapter we have traced the evolution of the Ministry text of the Faith and Order Commission of the World Council of Churches from August,1974 to June, 1980. Two texts define this period of development, the earlier one being the product of the meeting of the FO Commission in Accra, Ghana, July 23-August 4, 1974, the later one the document produced by the Steering Committee of the FO Commission meeting in Geneva, Switzerland, June 3-7, 1980. There were three intervening texts, one from a Steering Group of FO meeting in Geneva, May 17-20, 1979 and the other two connected with a meeting of the Steering Committee under the presidency of Frère Max Thurian, January 15-19, 1980. One of the documents (which we have entitled, "Geneva/1-16-80," was written by Lukas Vischer, the General Secretary of the FO Commission. The other (which we have entitled, "Geneva/1-19-80" or, in some instances, simply "Geneva/1-80," is also attributed to Lukas Vischer (with the help of M. Thurian and the other members of the Steering Committee). The "Geneva/1-16-8-" text, although it is very similar to (and in most instances identical with) the "Geneva/1-19-80" text, is occasionally referred to as independent from the latter only because it is clearly the work of L. Vischer alone.

During this six-year period of the evolution of the text the major influences are Lukas Vischer, Max Thurian, the Committees that produced the documents in question and the Consultation of Orthodox theologians which met, August 13-16, 1979, in Chambésy, near Geneva.

We have conducted this study in terms of the outline of topics provided in the Lima text, the final text on Ministry of January, 1982. This six-year period of the evolution of the text (August, 1974-July, 1980) can be summarized with the use of this outline as follows:

I. THE CALLING OF THE WHOLE PEOPLE OF GOD.

The study begins with the call of all humanity, not simply the call of Christ and Christians (the baptized), to be God's people. The trinitarian focus is sharpened with regard to the roles of Father, Son and Spirit in salvation history. The Paschal Mystery of Christ is introduced as a central theme. With regard to the historical Jesus there is a sharpened awareness of the distinction between who he *is* and what he *did*, with and emphasis on the former. There are spiritual bonds that bind members of the Church which are not reducible to institutional realities. A more theological emphasis is placed and a less sociological one. Worship and ministry are closely linked. And, finally, in this first major section, eschatology is introduced as a theological theme.

II. THE CHURCH AND THE ORDAINED MINISTRY.

The definition of terms is introduced to clarify the subsequent treatment. The attempt is to be inclusive, e.g., by eliminating from the description of Church the explicit references to baptism and confirmation.

A. THE ORDAINED MINISTRY.

In this section "the Twelve" are carefully differentiated from "the apostles" and the uniqueness of those groups are indicated. While there is an emphasis added on the priestly role of the ordained and while there is an emphasis added on the guiding and teaching role of the ordained as rooted in Christ's own role, there is an clear effort to avoid making the ordained ministry too special, too exclusive, too far removed from the ministry of others in the Church. A more careful and nuanced reference is made to eucharistic presiding and *episkopé*. The same care can be seen in a deeper sense of historical and biblical accuracy, e.g., the difficulty of attributing specific forms of ordained ministry to the will and institution of Jesus Christ himself. And, again, a keener awareness of trinitarian roles (e.g., Christ being sent by the Father) is evinced as the text evolves.

B. ORDAINED MINISTRY AND AUTHORITY.

The communitarian nature of this authority is emphasized. There is a careful nuancing of the meaning of that authority in relation to the Word of God. And both the ordained and the non-ordained stand under the authority of the Word of God as exercised by Christ.

C. ORDAINED MINISTRY AND PRIESTHOOD.

Here again there is a more inclusive ecclesiology in evidence, beyond baptism. There is a more expansive leadership role emphasized, beyond the liturgical/sacramental. And there is indicated a difference in nature between the priesthood of the ordained and the priesthood of Christ.

D. THE MINISTRY OF MEN AND WOMEN IN THE CHURCH.

There is more and more reticence to speak to the issue of the question of women in the ministry and especially, the ordination of women, at least in this text, alongside the other issues which concern the ordained ministry.

III. THE FORMS OF THE ORDAINED MINISTRY.

A. BISHOPS, PRESBYTERS AND DEACONS.

In this section is seen the development of a whole new emphasis on the role of the bishop and on the three-fold ministry of bishop, presbyter and deacon as the paradigm in the theological and ecumenical discussion of the ordained ministry. A recognition is given to the historical development of the three-fold ministry in the early Church, beyond what is evidenced in the New Testament. Finally, a distinction is drawn between the "ministry" of the ordained and the "service" of all others in the Church.

B. GUIDING PRINCIPLES FOR THE EXERCISE OF THE ORDAINED MINISTRY IN THE CHURCH.

The two paragraphs which comprise this section in the final text of this period in the evolution of the Lima text have no antecedents in the first text of the period (the Accra text). The exercise of the three-fold ministry is outlined. The influence of Orthodox thought is much in evidence.

C. FUNCTIONS OF BISHOPS, PRESBYTERS AND DEACONS.

The same summary statement can be made here as was made in reference to the previous section. Here the ideas of the four paragraphs in the section are "offered in a tentative way." [Geneva/6-80, §25]

D. VARIETY OF CHARISMS.

Again, there are no antecedents in the Accra/74 text for what is given in the Geneva/6-80 text. These charisms are called "ministries" in the Geneva/6-80 text. The Lima text will later refer to them as "charisms."

IV. SUCCESSION IN THE APOSTOLIC TRADITION.

A. APOSTOLIC TRADITION IN THE CHURCH.

Here an important distinction is introduced, between the apostolic tradition of the whole Church and the apostolic succession of the ministry.

B. SUCCESSION OF THE APOSTOLIC MINISTRY.

In this section the important point is made regarding the episcopal succession as the fullness of the sign of apostolic succession. The paragraph of commentary in the text outlines the two approaches to this matter in the early Church, that of Clement of Rome and Ignatius of Antioch.

V. ORDINATION.

A. THE MEANING OF ORDINATION.

The most recent text in this stage of development is more inclusive ecumenically than earlier texts in that the act of ordaining is seen as being performed by bishops and by those without the title, "bishop." And it calls for a careful investigation of liturgical texts in order to determine the intentions and meaning of ordination in the various churches. A gender reference is made general thus avoiding the need to address the ordination of women. And a more ecumenical tone is struck with the deletion of references to catholic and protestant positions.

B. THE ACT OF ORDINATION.

Again, gender references are more and more avoided and the question of the ordination of women tends to be kept open but not discussed at any length in this particular Faith and Order study. And the most recent text in this stage adds that the ordained take on a collegial relationship with other ordained ministers.

C. THE CONDITIONS OF ORDINATION.

The most recent text of this stage abbreviates its treatment of the conditions for ordination. The result is less sociology, more theology.

VI. TOWARDS THE MUTUAL RECOGNITION OF THE ORDAINED MINISTRIES.

This final section in the most recent text is more hortatory and less imperative in tone. In addition, it is ecumenically more positive, inviting and realistic in its expectations. And there is, as is evidenced in the earlier sections, a more precise use of terminology, e.g., the term, "episcopal succession," replacing the term, "apostolic succession."

CHAPTER IV

FROM GENEVA/6-80 TO LIMA/82

In this chapter the effort will be to trace the theologically significant differences between the text of Geneva/6-80 and the text of Lima/82. This effort will be accomplished using the section and subsection headings of the Lima text (as in the preceding chapters). In this time frame those headings correspond for the most part, but not entirely, with the headings found in the text of Geneva/6-80, as well as in the two intervening texts of Rome/11-80 and Annecy/81. Further, not all of the theological themes will correspond exactly with the discrete headings. There is some overlap. And some less salient theological and ecumenical themes, e.g., hortatory language, are found throughout the final text.

It may prove helpful at the outset to be aware of the various themes which emerge throughout this analysis. In addition to the themes articulated in the major and minor headings of the Lima text itself there are the following theological themes to be noted at the outset: the Trinity; the Twelve; the apostles; and sacramentality. Other characteristics and emphases which have some bearing on the theological meaning of the text are the following: a tone that is more hortatory (including an effort to be less judgmental and less prescriptive); and awareness of the need to make fewer historical claims; a more present-oriented approach; a more personal (less impersonal) tone; a more dynamic and process-oriented spirit; an emphasis on a need for the "official" or the "authorized"; an emphasis on the responsibility of the churches for decision-making which such theological study places upon them; the notion of "being" in ministry placed alongside "doing" in terms of importance; the notion "faith" replacing that of "truth."

As we move through the various divisions of the text some shifts in theological meaning will be clearly recognizable; other shifts are more highly nuanced and nearly defy detection.

The divisions of the Lima text (which divisions control our study) are as follows:

I.   THE CALLING OF THE WHOLE PEOPLE OF GOD

I. THE CALLING OF THE WHOLE PEOPLE OF GOD.

The trinitarian emphasis is deepened. A greater recognition is given to the historical Jesus, especially as he is situated in the flow of salvation history beginning with the divine choice of Israel. Jesus' complete identification with the human race is highlighted. Eschatology and ecclesiology are developed; the former in terms of a "realized eschatology" in order to distinguish more clearly between the church and the kingdom. To be noted is a greater respect for the canons of scientific history study; more care is exercised in making historical claims. The list of gifts bestowed on the church as a whole is amplified. And a more process-oriented, dynamic terminology is utilized as distinct from a more static approach to the writing of the text.

Geneva/6-80

1. In a broken world God calls the whole of humanity to be his people. He spoke in a unique and decisive way in Jesus Christ, his Son, who identified himself with the human race and gave himself as a sacrifice for all. His life, death and resurrection are the foundation of a new communion which is built up by the good news of the Gospel and the gifts of the sacraments. The Holy Spirit unites those who follow Jesus Christ in a single body and sends them as witnesses into the world. Belonging to the Church means living in communion with God through Jesus Christ and in the Holy Spirit.

Rome/11-80

1. In a broken world God calls the whole of humanity to become God's people. For this purpose God chose Israel and then spoke in a unique and decisive way in Jesus Christ. God's Son. Jesus identified with the whole human race giving himself as a sacrifice for all. Christ's life of service, death and resurrection are the foundation of a new community which is built up continually by the good news of the Gospel and the gifts of the sacraments. The Holy Spirit unites in a single body those who follow Jesus Christ and sends them as witnesses into the world. Belonging to the Church means living in communion with God through Jesus Christ in the Holy Spirit.

Annecy/81

1. In a broken world God calls the whole of humanity to become God's people. For this purpose God chose Israel and then spoke in a unique and decisive way in Jesus Christ, God's Son. Jesus identified with the whole human race giving himself as a sacrifice for all. Jesus's life of service, his death and resurrection, are the foundation of a new community which is built up continually by the good news of the Gospel and the gifts of the sacraments. The Holy Spirit unites in a single body those who follow Jesus Christ and sends them as witnesses into the world. Belonging to the Church means living in communion with God through Jesus Christ in the Holy Spirit.

Lima/82

1. In a broken world God calls the whole of humanity to become God's people. For this purpose God chose Israel and then spoke in a unique and decisive way in Jesus Christ, God's Son. Jesus made his own the nature, condition and cause of the whole human race, giving himself as a sacrifice for all. Jesus' life of service, his death and resurrection, are the foundation of a new community which is built up continually by the good news of the Gospel and the gifts of the sacraments. The Holy Spirit unites in a single body those who follow Jesus Christ and sends them as witnesses into the world. Belonging to the Church means living in communion with God through Jesus Christ in the Holy Spirit.

Geneva/6-80

2. The life of the Church is based on Christ's victory over the powers of evil and death, accomplished once for all. Christ offers forgiveness, invites to repentance and delivers from destruction. He enables people to turn in praise to God and in service to their neighbours. He is the source of new life in freedom and mutual forgiveness and love. He directs hearts and minds to the expectation of the kingdom where Christ's victory will become manifest and all things will be made new. God's purpose is that, in Jesus Christ, all people should share in this communion.

Rome/11-80

2. The life of the Church is based on Christ's victory over the powers of evil and death, accomplished once for all. Christ offers forgiveness, invites to repentance and delivers from destruction Through Christ, people are enabled to turn in praise to God and in service to their neighbours. In Christ they find the source of new life in freedom, mutual forgiveness and love Through Christ their hearts and minds are directed to the consummation of the kingdom where Christ's victory will become manifest and all things made new. God's purpose is that, in Jesus Christ, all people should share in this communion.

Annecy/81

2. The life of the Church is based on Christ's victory over the powers of evil and death, accomplished once for all. Christ offers forgiveness, invites to repentance and delivers from destruction. Through Christ, people are enabled to turn in praise to God and in service to their neighbours. In Christ they find the source of new life in freedom, mutual forgiveness and love. Through Christ their hearts and minds are directed to the consummation of the kingdom where Christ's victory will become manifest and all things made new. God's purpose is that, in Jesus Christ, all people should share in this fellowship.

Lima/82

2. The life of the Church is based on Christ's victory over the powers of evil and death, accomplished once for all. Christ offers forgiveness, invites to repentance and delivers from destruction. Through Christ, people are enabled to turn in praise to God and in service to their neighbors. In Christ they find the source of new life in freedom, mutual forgiveness and love. Through Christ their hearts and minds are directed to the consummation of the kingdom where Christ's victory will become manifest and all things made new. God's purpose is that, in Jesus Christ, all people should share in this fellowship.

Geneva/6-80

3. The Church lives through the liberating and renewing power of the Holy Spirit. Christ himself was anointed with the Holy Spirit and by virtue of the same Spirit he is never without his body, the community of believers. The Spirit calls people to the faith, sanctifies them through his gifts and gives them strength to witness to the Gospel and to serve in hope and love. He keeps the Church in the truth and guides it despite the erring and failures of its members.

Rome/11-80

3. The Church lives through the liberating and renewing power of the Holy Spirit. Jesus was anointed with the Holy Spirit, and after the Resurrection that same Spirit was given to those who believed in the Risen Lord in order to make them the body of Christ. The Spirit calls people to faith, sanctifies them through many gifts, gives them strength to witness to the Gospel, and empowers them to serve in hope and love. The Spirit keeps the Church in the truth and guides it despite the error and failures of its members.

Annecy/81

3. The Church lives through the liberating and renewing power of the Holy Spirit. That the Holy Spirit was upon Jesus is evidenced in his baptism, and after the resurrection that same Spirit was given to those who believed in the Risen Lord in order to recreate them as the body of Christ. The Spirit calls people to faith, sanctifies them through many gifts, gives them strength to witness to the Gospel, and empowers them to serve in hope and love. The Spirit keeps the Church in the truth and guides it despite the frailty of its members.

Lima/82

3. The Church lives through the liberating and renewing power of the Holy Spirit. That the Holy Spirit was upon Jesus is evidenced in his bap-tism, and after the resurrection that same Spirit was given to those who believed in the Risen Lord in order to recreate them as the body of Christ. The Spirit calls people to faith, sanctifies them through many gifts, gives them strength to witness to the Gospel, and empowers them to serve in hope and love. The Spirit keeps the Church in the truth and guides it despite the frailty of its members.

Geneva/6-80

4. The Church is called to proclaim and prefigure the kingdom of God by announcing the Gospel to the world and by being built up as the body of Christ. Christ came to proclaim the nearness of the kingdom. He opened a new access to the Father. He preached good news to the poor and release to the captives (Lk 4:18). All members of the body are called to share in this proclamation and to give account of their hope. They will tell the story of Jesus Christ, the teacher and healer, the brother who gave his life, the Lord who is present today. They will stand alongside men and women in their joys and sufferings and seek to witness in caring live. They will struggle with the oppressed towards that freedom and dignity promised with the coming of the kingdom. The same mission needs to be carried out in varying political, social and cultural contexts. In order to fulfil the mission faithfully, they will seek relevant forms of witness and service in each situation.

Rome/11-80

4. The Church is called to proclaim and prefigure the kingdom of God. It accomplishes this by announcing the Gospel to the world and by its very existence as the body of Christ. In Jesus the Kingdom of God came among us. He preached good news to the poor, release to the captives, recovery of sight to the blind, liberation to the oppressed (Lk 4:18). Christ established a new access to the Father. Living in this communion with God, all members of the Church are called to confess their faith and to give account of their hope. They are to stand alongside the universal community of men and women in their joys and sufferings and seek to witness in caring love. The members of Christ's body are to struggle with the oppressed towards that freedom and dignity promised with the coming of the kingdom. This mission needs to be carried out in varying political, social and cultural contexts. In order to fulfil this mission faithfully, they will seek relevant forms of witness and service in each situation. In so doing they bring to the world a foretaste of the joy and glory of God's Kingdom.

Annecy/81

4. The Church is called to proclaim and prefigure the kingdom of God. It accomplishes this by announcing the Gospel to the world and by its very existence as the body of Christ. In Jesus the Kingdom of God came among us. He preached good news to the poor, release to the captives, recovery of sight to the blind, liberation to the oppressed (Lk 4:18). Christ established a new access to the Father. Living in this communion with God, all members of the Church are called to confess their faith and to give account of their hope. They are to identify with the joys and sufferings of all people as they seek to witness in caring love. The members of Christ's body are to struggle with the oppressed towards that freedom and dignity promised with the coming of the Kingdom. This mission needs to be carried out in varying political, social and cultural contexts. In order to fulfil this mission faithfully, they will seek relevant forms of witness and service in each situation. In so doing they bring to the world a foretaste of the joy and glory of God's Kingdom.

Lima/82

4. The Church is called to proclaim and prefigure the kingdom of God. It accomplishes this by announcing the Gospel to the world and by its very existence as the body of Christ. In Jesus the Kingdom of God came among us. He offered salvation to sinners. He preached good news to the poor, release to the captives, recovery of sight to the blind, liberation to the oppressed (Lk 4:18). Christ established a new access to the Father. Living in this communion with God, all members of the Church are called to confess their faith and to give account of their hope. They are to identify with the joys and sufferings of all people as they seek to witness in caring love. The members of Christ's body are to struggle with the oppressed towards that freedom and dignity promised with the coming of the Kingdom. This mission needs to be carried out in varying political, social and cultural contexts. In order to fulfil this mission faithfully, they will seek relevant forms of witness and service in each situation. In so doing they bring to the world a foretaste of the joy and glory of God's Kingdom.

Geneva/6-80

5. The Holy Spirit bestows on the community diverse and complementary gifts. They are given for the common good of the whole people and manifest themselves in acts of service within the community and to the world. They may be gifts of communicating the Gospel in word and deed, gifts of praying, gifts of teaching, learning and serving, gifts of guiding and following, gifts of inspiration and vision. The proclamation of the Gospel, the service to the world and the edification of the community require a multiplicity of gifts. All members are called to discover, with the help of the community, the gifts they have received and to relate them to the calling of the Church.

Rome/11-80

5. The Holy Spirit bestows on the community diverse and complementary gifts. These are for the common good of the whole people and are manifested in acts of service within the community and to the world. They may be gifts of communicating the Gospel in word and deed, gifts of praying, gifts of teaching and learning, gifts of serving, gifts of guiding and following, gifts of inspiration and vision All members are called to discover, with the help of the community, the gifts they have received and to use them for the service of the world to which the Church is sent.

Annecy/81

5. The Holy Spirit bestows on the community diverse and complementary gifts. These are for the common good of the whole people and are manifested in acts of service within the community and to the world. They may be gifts of communicating the Gospel in word and deed, gifts of praying, gifts of teaching and learning, gifts of serving, gifts of guiding and following, gifts of inspiration and vision. All members are called to discover, with the help of the community, the gifts they have received and to use them for the service of the world to which the Church is sent.

Lima/82

5. The Holy Spirit bestows on the community diverse and complementary gifts. These are for the common good of the whole people and are manifested in acts of service within the community and to the world. They may be gifts of communicating the Gospel in word and deed, gifts of healing, gifts of praying, gifts of teaching and learning, gifts of serving, gifts of guiding and following, gifts of inspiration and vision. All members are called to discover, with the help of the community, the gifts they have received and to use them for the building up of the Church and for the service of the world to which the Church is sent.

306

Geneva/6-80

6. Today, the churches are divided in their understanding and their practice of the ministry. As they engage in the effort of overcoming their differences, they need to take their starting point from the calling of the whole people of God. The ministry is to serve the witness and the service of the whole community. Therefore, the churches need to seek a common answer to the following question: How, according to the will of Jesus Christ and under the guidance of the Spirit, is the ministry to be understood and ordered, so that the Gospel may be spread and the community built up in love?

Rome/11-80

6. Though the churches are agreed in their general understanding of the calling of the people of God, they differ in their understanding of how the life of the Church is to be ordered. In particular, there are differences concerning the place and forms of the ordained ministry. As they engage in the effort to overcome these differences, the churches need to work from the perspective of the calling of the whole people of God. A common answer needs to be found to the following question: How, according to the will of God and under the guidance of the Holy Spirit, is the life of the Church to be understood and ordered, so that the Gospel may be spread and the community built up in love?

Annecy/81

6. Though the churches are agreed in their general understanding of the calling of the people of God, they differ in their understanding of how the life of the Church is to be ordered. In particular, there are differences concerning the place and forms of the ordained ministry. As they engage in the effort to overcome these differences, the churches need to work from the perspective of the calling of the whole people of God. A common answer needs to be found to the following question: How, according to the will of God and under the guidance of the Holy Spirit, is the life of the Church to be understood and ordered, so that the Gospel may be spread and the community built up in love?

Lima/82

6. Though the churches are agreed in their general understanding of the calling of the people of God, they differ in their understanding of how the life of the Church is to be ordered. In particular, there are differences concerning the place and forms of the ordained ministry. As they engage in the effort to overcome these differences, the churches need to work from the perspective of the calling of the whole people of God. A common answer needs to be found to the following question: How, according to the will of God and under the guidance of the Holy Spirit, is the life of the Church to be understood and ordered, so that the Gospel may be spread and the community built up in love?

Lima's first major section (the introductory paragraphs, 1 through 6) is entitled, "The Calling of the Whole People of God." The very same title is used in the text from the meeting of June 3-7, 1980, the text which begins this final stage in the evolution of the Ministry section of "The Lima Document." And, unless otherwise noted below, the paragraphs 1 through 6 in Lima correspond to the same numbering of the initial paragraphs in the 1980 meeting.

In this first section the trinitarian emphasis is strengthened and given greater precision. The material in this section "is clearer and better than in the 1974 text. The ecclesiological framework, based on a trinitarian foundation, provides a good and sufficient starting-point."[1] The role of Jesus Christ is more plainly set in the context of the Trinity. Communion with God, the basis of "belonging to the Church"[2] is "through Jesus Christ in the Holy Spirit" and not "through Jesus Christ and[3] in the Holy Spirit." "The will of God" replaces "the will of Jesus Christ."[4] The mediating role of Christ is made explicit with the addition (in §2) of the phrase "through Christ"[5] and "in Christ."

A greater recognition is given to the historical Jesus. His life and ministry are placed in the flow of salvation history begun with God's choice of Israel.[6] This change was effected by Wolfhart Pannenberg who made the following comment on the 6-80 text:

> The particularity of God's election should be respected in that he called first the Jews. The sending of the Son should be connected with the fulfillment of the election of the Jewish people that in Abraham was already destined to benefit the whole of humanity.[7]

More personal references are made to "Jesus" rather than the more formal

---

[1]Günther Gassmann, "Reaction to the revised Faith and Order text on Ministry," November 11, 1981, p. 2, WCC Archives, Archive Box: "Faith and Order Archives, BEM, 79-82 corr. 81, Lima 82."

[2]1/82, §1.

[3]Emphasis added.

[4]§6

[5]Used twice.

[6]§1.

[7]W. Pannenberg, "Comments on the Revised Text of the Agreed Statements on Baptism, Eucharist and Ministry," October 13, 1980, p. 6, WCC Archives, Archive Box: "Faith and Order, Documents 1980-1981, Circular Letters, 1980-1981."

"Jesus Christ" or simply, "Christ."[8] And this very human Jesus is said not simply and formally to have "identified" with but to have "made his own, the nature, condition and cause of the whole human race."[9] Jesus' human life is not simply a "life" or existence but that specific "life of service" which stands clearly alongside his death and resurrection as the foundation of the life of the Church.[10] For it had been observed that a "note of Christ as servant needs to be introduced at beginning, as in 1975 document; sacrifice-victory language is too one-sided."[11] The sentence is added in Lima, "He offered salvation to sinners."[12] This addition along with the phrase, "made his own the nature, condition and cause of,"[13] strengthens the notion of his mission of compassionate identification with the human race. The single word, "identified," (which was changed at Lima in §1) "is quite unable to convey the theological meaning here intended."[14]

Other words and phrases in this first section give evidence of highly nuanced changes of meaning in matters of ecclesiology and eschatology. "Errors and failures" of the members of the Church are downplayed in favor of their "frailty."[15] This willingness to be historically less judgmental will be noted in other sections of the final text as well. It seems to arise out of a growing consciousness of the lot all churches and church members share in common. No ecclesial community is exempt from human weakness. In this particular place in the evolution of the ministry text the wording was influenced by at least one theologian's statement aimed at those who would so exempt their ecclesial body, if not the individual members of that body: "I do not believe that a church-concept which differentiates between unerring church and its erring members is still tenable today — except for those who believe the

---

[8]§1 and §9.

[9]§1.

[10]§1.

[11]Lewis S. Mudge, "Comments on the draft of the 'Ministry' document resulting from the meeting of June 3-7, 1980, Rome," October 27, 1980, p. 2, WCC Archives, Archive Box: "Faith and Order Archives, BEM, 79-82 corr. 81, Lima 82."

[12]§4.

[13]Lima, §1.

[14]J.K.S. Reid, "Comments on the Ministry document of 1/81," Edinburgh, October, 1981, WCC Archives, Archive Box: "Faith and Order Archives, BEM, 79-82 corr. 81, Lima 82."

[15]§3.

church to be invisible and purely spiritual."[16] In addition, it is emphasized that "the life of the Church is to be ordered"[17] not simply the ministry. To the gifts bestowed on all members of the Church "for the common good" is added "gifts of healing"[18] and gifts of teaching and learning are placed *in tandem*.[19] Also a more dynamic terminology is used in reference to Christ and humanity as well as the Church: "become" replaces "be"[20]; "giving" replaces "gave"[21]; "community" replaces "communion"[22]; "fellowship" replaces "communion"[23]; the word "continually" is added.[24] Such terminology, suggested by the Theological Consultation held in Rome, Oct./Nov., 1980, gives a contemporaneity and a down-to-earthness to the message of the text. Finally, a "realized eschatology" is acknowledged in the final text: "consummation" replaces "expectation."[25] This change was influenced by Max Thurian in order "to avoid the misunderstanding of the kingdom already here and yet still to come."[26] Later in the text "anticipation" will replace "expectation."[27]

---

[16]Ellen Flesseman-van-Leer, Correspondence with M. Thurian, October 22, 1980, WCC Archives, Archive Box: "Faith and Order, Documents 1980-1981, Circular Letters, 1980-1981."

[17]§6. This is suggested by U. Kühn in the Consultation held in Rome, October 29 - November 2, 1980 (WCC Archives, "Rom. Nov 2 - 80, Kühn, Archive Box: "Faith and Order Archives, BEM, 79-82 corr. 81, Lima 82) and by W. Pannenberg (October 13, 1980, WCC Archives, Archive Box: "Faith and Order, Documents 1980-1981, Circular Letters, 1980-1981.").

[18]E. Flesseman-van-Leer states that "when the charisms are summed up the gift of healing, so prominent in NT times, should not be forgotten, though this gift will have a different form today." (Oct. 22, 1980 Correspondence, WCC Archives, Archive Box: "Faith and Order, Documents 1980-1981, Circular Letters, 1980-1981.").

[19]§5.

[20]§1.

[21]§1.

[22]§1.

[23]§2.

[24]§1.

[25]§2.

[26]Tanner-Thurian Correspondence, WCC Archives, October 1, 1980, Archive Box: "Faith and Order, Documents 1980-1981, Circular Letters, 1980-1981."

[27]§11.

II. THE CHURCH AND THE ORDAINED MINISTRY.

The second major section of Lima is entitled, "The Church and the Ordained Ministry." That section contains an introductory paragraph (§7) and then is subdivided into four separate topics. These subdivisions exactly parallel the text of 6-80. We will treat each subdivision in turn. The four subdivisions are entitled:

A. The Ordained Ministry

B. Ordained Ministry and Authority

C. Ordained Ministry and Priesthood

D. The Ministry of Men and Women in the Church

INTRODUCTION [GLOSSARY]

The glossary begun in the documents of the previous stage we have studied is refined for the sake of clarity. Being who one is as minister is acknowledged as a rightful focus of ministry. A greater awareness of the importance of "institutionalizing" changes in ministerial forms is in evidence. Depersonalization is avoided in establishing the parameters of the discussion throughout. Use of the term, "priesthood," is clarified.

Geneva/6-80

7. In order to avoid confusion in the discussions on the ministry in the Church it is necessary to delineate clearly how various terms are used in the following paragraphs.

— The word *charism* refers to the gifts bestowed by the Holy Spirit on any member of the body of Christ for the up-building of the community and the fulfilment of its calling.

— The word *ministry* in its broadest sense refers to the service which the whole people of God is called to perform, as individuals, as a local community, or as the universal Church. It can also refer to more regular particular, institutional forms which this service takes.

— The term *ordained ministry* refers to services for which the Church practices ordination by the invocation of the Spirit and the imposition of hands.

— The term *priesthood* is used by some churches to designate what is called "ordained ministry". The two terms "ordained ministry" and "priesthood" must not be taken as referring to two different realities.

Rome/11-80

7. Differences in terminology are part of the matter under debate. In order to avoid confusion in the discussions on the ordained ministry in the Church, it is necessary to delineate clearly how various terms are used in the following paragraphs.

(a) The word *charism* denotes the gifts bestowed by the Holy Spirit on any member of the body of Christ for the up-building of the community and the fulfilment of its calling.

(b) The word *ministry* in its broadest sense denotes the service to which the whole people of God is called, whether as individuals, or as the universal Church. Ministry or ministries can also denote the particular institutional forms which this service may take.

(c) The term *ordained ministry* refers to persons whom the church appoints for service by ordination through the invocation of the Spirit and the imposition of hands.

(d) Many churches use the word *priest* to denote ordained ministers because this usage is not universal, this document will discuss the substantive questions in para 16.

Annecy/81

7. Differences in terminology are part of the matter under debate. In order to avoid confusion in the discussions on the ordained ministry in the Church, it is necessary to delineate clearly how various terms are used in the following paragraphs.

(a) The word charism denotes the gifts bestowed by the Holy Spirit on any member of the body of Christ for the building up of the community and the fulfilment of its calling.

(b) The word ministry in its broadest sense denotes the service to which the whole people of God is called, whether as individuals, as a local community, or as the universal Church. Ministry or ministries can also denote the particular institutional forms which this service may take.

(c) The term *ordained ministry* refers to persons who have received a charism and whom the church appoints for service by ordination through the invocation of the Spirit and the laying on of hands.

(d) Many churches use the word priest to denote ordained ministers. Because this usage is not universal,

Lima/82

7. Differences in terminology are part of the matter under debate. In order to avoid confusion in the discussions on the ordained ministry in the Church, it is necessary to delineate clearly how various terms are used in the following paragraphs.

(a) The word *charism* denotes the gifts bestowed by the Holy Spirit on any member of the body of Christ for the building up of the community and the fulfilment of its calling.

(b) The word *ministry* in its broadest sense denotes the service to which the whole people of God is called, whether as individuals, as a local community, or as the universal Church. Ministry or ministries can also denote the particular institutional forms which this service may take.

(c) The term *ordained ministry* refers to persons who have received a charism and whom the church appoints for service by ordination through the invocation of the Spirit and the laying on of hands.

(d) Many churches use the word *priest* to denote ordained ministers. Because this usage is not universal,

312

Rome/11-80 [cont.]
Meanwhile the two terms *ordained ministry* and *priesthood* should not be taken as referring to two different realities.

Annecy/81 [cont.]
this document will discuss the substantive questions in para. 16. Meanwhile the two terms ordained ministry and priesthood should not be taken as referring to two different realities.

Lima/82 [cont.]
this document will discuss the substantive questions in paragraph 17.

First, there is the introductory paragraph (§7).[28] When "ministry in its broadest sense" is described the phrase "(service) to perform" is deleted thus acknowledging the importance of forms of ministry in which *being* is considered at least as important as *doing*.[29] In addition, by the deletion of the term, "more regular," the text seems to withhold a favoring of institutionalized forms of ministry over temporary or less common charisms.[30] When the term, "ordained ministry," is described the referents in its final text are *persons* rather than *services* performed by persons.[31] In reference to the denotation of the term, "priest," the word, "certain," is prefixed to the phrase, "ordained ministers."[32] M. Tanner had noted that "in churches which have 'priesthood,'" it is only *part* of 'the ordained ministry.'"[33] A. Dulles, noted that "deacons, even though ordained, are not called priests. The term 'priest' usually corresponds to 'presbyter' (of which it is an abbreviation), but can be extended to bishops as 'high priests' (sacerdotes)."[34] W. Pannenberg stated that the term, priest, defined here "does not seem acceptable in a Lutheran perspective, because the term, 'priesthood' is used by Luther as referring to all Christians, in distinction from the ordained ministry."[35]

---

[28]G. Gassmann notes re: the revision of the 1/81 text that "the terminological clarification at the beginning of section II is very much to be welcomed. This is also a concern of the LWF (Lutheran World Federation) study. Both face, however, the problem of adequate rendering into other languages. English has, in this case, a natural advantage by covering with the term 'ministry' both service (*Dienst*) and office (*Amt*)." [G. Gassmann, Reaction of November 11, 1981, WCC Archives, Archive Box: "Faith and Order Archives, BEM, 79-82 corr. 81, Lima 82."].

[29]This change took place in the Theological Consultation, Rome, Oct/Nov, 1980.

[30]E. Flesseman-van-Leer had criticized the phrase as "unclear." [Flesseman-van-Leer - M. Thurian Correspondence, WCC Archives, October 22, 1980, Archive Box: "Faith and Order, Documents 1980-1981, Circular Letters, 1980-1981."].

[31]Cf. Conway-Thurian Correspondence, September 5, 1980 and the Moede-Thurian Correspondence, September 30, 1980, WCC Archives, Archive Box: "Faith and Order, Documents 1980-1981, Circular Letters, 1980-1981."

[32]Finally added at Lima.

[33]G.W. Comments, October 26, 1980, WCC Archives, Archive Box: "Faith and Order, Documents 1980-1981, Circular Letters, 1980-1981.", p. 1.

[34]A. Dulles Correspondence, May 3, 1981, WCC Archives, Archive Box: "Faith and Order Archives, BEM, 79-82 corr. 81, Lima 82." Dulles suggested the following textual change: ". . . to denote a certain grade or certain grades of the ordained ministry."

[35]Oct. 13, 1980, p. 6, WCC Archives, Archive Box: "Faith and Order, Documents 1980-1981, Circular Letters, 1980-1981."

A. THE ORDAINED MINISTRY.

The ongoing and essential need for ordained ministry in the church becomes more nuanced. It is seen in relationship to the bible, the apostolic message and to Christ himself. Qualities of holiness in ordained ministers are stressed. The indispensable need of the ordained ministers for the support and encouragement of the church community is noted. The careful avoidance of the adjective, "special," in reference to the ordained ministry avoids overtones of superiority. The limited retention of that adjective in the text, however, is still problematic for some. The Twelve and the other apostles are carefully distinguished. This distinction may help to provide a broader base for the churches to be considered apostolic. Eucharistic presiding for the ordained minister is emphasized by reference to the Twelve and to Christ as eucharistic presiders. The issue of the apostolic witnessing to the resurrection is highly nuanced. Surely apostleship and ordained ministry are closely related but the issue of their precise relationship, while increasingly nuanced, in the texts, is not finally resolved. The priestly role of the ordained is, in the final text, no longer discussed in this particular section. There is some downplaying of that priestly role in evidence here. Again, respect for the canons of history study is highly visible in the text as it evolves. While clarifying the chief responsibility of the ordained ministry the final text appears to discourage the possibility of non-ordained members of the church functioning in governing roles in the church.

Geneva/6-80

8.   The ordained ministry is constitutive for the life and witness of the Church. In order to fulfill its mission, the Church needs persons pointing to its fundamental dependence on Jesus Christ and providing, within the multiplicity of gifts, a focus of its unity.

Rome/11-80

8. In order to fulfil its mission, the Church needs persons who are publicly and continually responsible for pointing to its fundamental dependence on Jesus Christ, and thereby provide, within a multiplicity of gifts, a focus of its unity. The ministry of such persons, who since very early times have been ordained, is constitutive for the life and witness of the Church.

Annecy/81

8. In order to fulfil its mission, the Church needs persons who are publicly and continually responsible for pointing to its fundamental dependence on Jesus Christ, and thereby provide, within a multiplicity of gifts, a focus of its unity. The ministry of such persons, who since very early times have been ordained, is constitutive for the life and witness of the Church.

Lima/82

8. In order to fulfil its mission, the Church needs persons who are publicly and continually responsible for pointing to its fundamental dependence on Jesus Christ, and thereby provide, within a multiplicity of gifts, a focus of its unity. The ministry of such persons, who since very early times have been ordained, is constitutive for the life and witness of the Church.

316

Geneva/6-80

9. The Church was never without persons holding special authority and responsibility. Christ chose and sent the disciples to be witnesses of the kingdom (Mt 10: 18); and a special role is attributed to the Twelve within the communities of the first generations. They are described as patriarchs and judges of the renewed Israel, as witnesses of the Lord's life and resurrection and as leaders of the community in prayer, teaching, proclamation and service (Acts 2: 4247; 6: 26, etc.). The very existence of the Twelve shows that, from the beginning, there were differentiated roles in the community.

9-Commentary. In the NT the term "apostle" has a wide meaning. It is used for the Twelve but also for a wider circle of disciples. It is applied to Paul and others as they are sent out by the risen Christ to proclaim the Gospel. The roles of the apostles cover both foundation and mission.

Obviously, there is a fundamental difference between the apostles and the ordained ministers. The role of

Rome/11-80

9. The Church has never been without persons holding special authority and responsibility. Jesus chose and sent the disciples to be witnesses of the Kingdom (Mt 10:118). The Twelve were promised that they would "sit on thrones judging the tribes of Israel" (Lk 22:30). A special role is attributed to the Twelve within the communities of the first generation. They are witnesses of the Lord's life and resurrection (Acts 1:2126), they lead the community in prayer, teaching, the breaking of bread, proclamation and service (Acts 2:4247; 6:26, etc.). The very existence of the Twelve and other apostles shows that, from the beginning, there were differentiated roles in the community.

Commentary

In the New Testament the term "apostle" has a wide meaning. It is used for the Twelve but also for a wider circle of disciples. It is applied to Paul and others as they are sent out by the risen Christ to proclaim the Gospel. The roles of the apostles cover both foundation and mission.

Annecy/81

9. The Church has never been without persons holding special authority and responsibility. Jesus chose and sent the disciples to be witnesses of the Kingdom (Mt 10: 18). The Twelve were promised that they would "sit on thrones judging the tribes of Israel" (Lk 22:30). A special role is attributed to the Twelve within the communities of the first generation. They are witnesses of the Lord's life and resurrection (Acts 1:2126), they lead the community in prayer, teaching, the breaking of bread, proclamation and service (Acts 2:4247; 6:26, etc.). The very existence of the Twelve and other apostles shows that, from the beginning, there were differentiated roles in the community.

Commentary:

In the New Testament the term "apostle" has a wide meaning. It is used for the Twelve but also for a wider circle of disciples. It is applied to Paul and others as they are sent out by the risen Christ to proclaim the Gospel. The roles of the apostles cover both foundation and mission.

Lima/82

9. The Church has never been without persons holding specific authority and responsibility. Jesus chose and sent the disciples to be witnesses of the Kingdom (Mt 10: 18). The Twelve were promised that they would "sit on thrones judging the tribes of Israel" (Lk 22:30). A particular role is attributed to the Twelve within the communities of the first generation. They are witnesses of the Lord's life and resurrection (Acts 1: 2126), they lead the community in prayer, teaching, the breaking of bread, proclamation and service (Acts 2: 4247; 6: 26, etc.). The very existence of the Twelve and other apostles shows that, from the beginning, there were differentiated roles in the community.

Commentary:

In the New Testament the term "apostle" is variously employed. It is used for the Twelve but also for a wider circle of disciples. It is applied to Paul and to others as they are sent out by the risen Christ to proclaim the Gospel. The roles of the apostles cover both foundation and mission.

Geneva/6-80 [cont.]

the apostles as witnesses of the risen Christ is unique and unrepeatable. But there is lasting significance in the fact that they were chosen. Jesus called the Twelve during his lifetime as representatives of the renewed Israel. At that moment they represent the whole people of God and at the same time exercise a special role in the midst of that people. After the resurrection they are leaders of the community. It can be said, therefore, that the Twelve prefigure both the Church and the persons entrusted with special authority and responsibility in the Church.

Lima/82 [cont.]

10. Jesus called the Twelve to be representatives of the renewed Israel. At that moment they represent the whole people of God and at the same time exercise a special role in the midst of that community. After the resurrection they are among the leaders of the community. It can be said that the apostles prefigure both the Church as a whole and the persons within it who are entrusted with the specific authority and responsibility. The role of the apostles as witnesses to the resurrection of Christ is unique and unrepeatable. There is therefore a difference between the apostles and the ordained ministers whose ministries are founded on theirs.

Geneva/6-80

9-Commentary (cont.)

Obviously, there is a fundamental difference between the apostles and the ordained ministers. The role of the apostles as witnesses of the risen Christ is unique and unrepeatable. But there is lasting significance in the fact that they were chosen. Jesus called the Twelve during his lifetime as representatives of the renewed Israel. At that moment they represent the whole people of God and at the same time exercise a special role in the midst of that people. After the resurrection they are leaders of the community. It can be said, therefore, that the Twelve prefigure both the Church and the persons entrusted with special authority and responsibility in the Church.

10. The ordained ministers recall and represent Jesus Christ to the community. They are ambassadors and missionaries. They point to Christ's being sent by the Father and work for the reconciliation of all human beings to God (Jn 20:21; II Cor 5:20). As leaders and teachers they call the community to submit to the authority of Jesus Christ, the

Rome/11-80

10. Jesus called the Twelve as representatives of the renewed Israel. At that moment they represent the whole people of God and at the same time exercise a special role in the midst of that community. After the resurrection they are among the leaders of the community. It can be said, therefore, that the Twelve prefigure both the Church as a whole and the persons within it who are entrusted with the special authority and responsibility. The role of the apostles as witnesses of the risen Christ is unique and unrepeatable. There is therefore a difference between the apostles and the ordained ministers whose ministries are founded on theirs. As Christ chose and sent the apostles, Christ continues in the Holy Spirit to choose and call persons into the ordained ministry. As heralds and ambassadors, ordained ministers are representatives of Jesus Christ to the community, and proclaim his message of reconciliation. As leaders and teachers they call the community to submit to the authority of Jesus Christ, the teacher and prophet, in whom law and prophets were fulfilled. As pastors, under

Annecy/81

10. Jesus called the Twelve as representatives of the renewed Israel. At that moment they represent the whole people of God and at the same time exercise a special role in the midst of that community. After the resurrection they are among the leaders of the community. It can be said that the apostles prefigure both the Church as a whole and the persons within it who are entrusted with the special authority and responsibility.

The role of the apostles as witnesses of the resurrection of Christ is unique and unrepeatable. There is therefore a different (*sic*) between the apostles and the ordained ministers whose ministries are founded on theirs.

As Christ chose and sent the apostles, Christ continues through the Holy Spirit to choose and call persons into the ordained ministry. As heralds and ambassadors, ordained ministers are representatives of Jesus Christ to the community, and proclaim his message of reconciliation. As leaders and teachers they call the community to submit to the authority of Jesus Christ, the teacher and

Lima/82

10. Jesus called the Twelve to be representatives of the renewed Israel. At that moment they represent the whole people of God and at the same time exercise a special role in the midst of that community. After the resurrection they are among the leaders of the community. It can be said that the apostles prefigure both the Church as a whole and the persons within it who are entrusted with the specific authority and responsibility. The role of the apostles as witnesses to the resurrection of Christ is unique and unrepeatable. There is therefore a difference between the apostles and the ordained ministers whose ministries are founded on theirs.

11. As Christ chose and sent the apostles, Christ continues through the Holy Spirit to choose and call persons into the ordained ministry. As heralds and ambassadors, ordained ministers are representatives of Jesus Christ to the community, and proclaim his message of reconciliation. As leaders and teachers they call the community to submit to the authority of Jesus Christ, the teacher

Geneva/6-80 [cont.]

teacher and prophet, in whom law and prophets were fulfilled. As pastors, under Jesus Christ the chief shepherd, they will assemble and guide the dispersed people of God, in the expectation of the coming kingdom. As servants they will seek to reflect Christ's priestly ministry and intercede for the community and the world. As Christ chose and sent the apostles, he continues through the Holy Spirit to choose and call persons into the ordained ministry.

Rome/11-80 [cont.]

Jesus Christ the chief shepherd, they assemble and guide the dispersed people of God, in anticipation of the coming kingdom. As servants, they seek to reflect Christ's priestly ministry and intercede for the community and the world.

10-Commentary

The basic reality of an ordained ministry was present from the beginning (cf. para. 8). The actual forms of ordination and of the ordained ministry, however, have evolved in complex historical developments (cf. para. 18). The churches, therefore, need to avoid attributing their particular forms of the ordained ministry to the will and institution of Jesus Christ.

Annecy/81 [cont.]

prophet, in whom law and prophets were fulfilled. As pastors, under Jesus Christ the chief shepherd, they assemble and guide the dispersed people of God, in anticipation of the coming Kingdom. As intercessors they seek to reflect Christ's priestly ministry and pray for the community and the world.

10-*Commentary:*

The basic reality of an ordained ministry was present from the beginning (cf. para 8). The actual forms of ordination and of the ordained ministry, however, have evolved in complex historical developments (cf. para 18). The churches, therefore, need to avoid attributing their particular forms of the ordained ministry to the will and institution of Jesus Christ.

Lima/82 [cont.]

and prophet, in whom law and prophets were fulfilled. As pastors, under Jesus Christ the chief shepherd, they assemble and guide the dispersed people of God, in anticipation of the coming Kingdom.

Commentary:

The basic reality of an ordained ministry was present from the beginning (cf. para. 8). The actual forms of ordination and of the ordained ministry, however, have evolved in complex historical developments (cf. para. 19). The churches, therefore, need to avoid attributing their particular forms of the ordained ministry directly to the will and institution of Jesus Christ.

320

Geneva/6-80

10-Commentary.

It must be emphasized that, although the basic necessity for an ordained ministry was given from the beginning, its actual forms have evolved in complicated historical developments. The churches, therefore, must refrain from attributing particular forms of the ordained ministry to the will and institution of Jesus Christ himself. Even the term "ordained ministry" is anachronistic if used without taking into account the historical development. An early form of ordination is found only in the later parts of the New Testament (e.g. II Tim 1:6ff.).

Geneva/6-80

11. The ordained ministers and the believing community are inextricably related. On the one hand, the community needs ordained ministers. Their presence reminds the community of the priority of the apostolic message in its life. They serve to build up the communion in Christ and to strengthen its witness. On the other hand, the ordained ministry cannot be considered in isolation from the community. The ordained ministers can fulfil their calling only in and for the community. They need the recognition, the support and the encouragement of the community.

Rome/11-80

11. Ordained ministers and the rest of the believing community are essentially interrelated. On the one hand, the community needs ordained ministers. Their presence reminds the community of the divine initiative, and of the dependence of the Church on Jesus Christ, who is the source of its mission and the foundation of its unity. They serve to build up the community in Christ and to strengthen its witness. This calls for the minister to set an example in holiness and compassion. On the other hand, the ordained ministry has no existence apart from the community. Ordained ministers can fulfil their calling only in and for the community. They cannot dispense with the recognition, the support, and the encouragement of the community.

Annecy/81

11. All members of the believing community, ordained and lay, are interrelated. On the one hand, the community needs ordained ministers. Their presence reminds the community of the divine initiative, and of the dependence of the Church on Jesus Christ, who is the source of its mission and the foundation of its unity. They serve to build up the community in Christ and to strengthen its witness. The minister must set an example of holiness and loving concern. On the other hand, the ordained ministry has no existence apart from the community. Ordained ministers can fulfil their calling only in and for the community. They cannot dispense with the recognition, the support, and the encouragement of the community.

Lima/82

12. All members of the believing community, ordained and lay, are interrelated. On the one hand, the community needs ordained ministers. Their presence reminds the community of the divine initiative, and of the dependence of the Church on Jesus Christ, who is the source of its mission and the foundation of its unity. They serve to build up the community in Christ and to strengthen its witness. In them the Church seeks an example of holiness and loving concern. On the other hand, the ordained ministry has no existence apart from the community. Ordained ministers can fulfil their calling only in and for the community. They cannot dispense with the recognition, the support, and the encouragement of the community.

Geneva/6-80

12. The central and specific function of the ordained minister is to assemble and build up the body of Christ by proclaiming and teaching the Word of God and by celebrating the sacraments, and to guide the life of the community in its liturgical, missionary and diaconal aspects.

12-Commentary. The function is not exercised by the ordained ministry in an exclusive way. Since the ordained ministry and the community are inextricably related, all members participate in fulfilling the function. In fact, every charism serves "to assemble and build up the body of Christ". Any member of the body may share in proclaiming and teaching the Word of God and in guiding the life of the community. The ordained ministry fulfils the function in a representative way, providing the focus for the unity of the life and witness of the community.

Rome/11-80

12. The central service of the ordained ministry is to assemble and build up the body of Christ by proclaiming and teaching the Word of God, by celebrating the sacraments, and by guiding the life of the community in its liturgical, missionary and diaconal aspects.

Commentary

These services are not exercised by the ordained ministry in an exclusive way. Since the ordained ministry and the community are inextricably related, all members participate in fulfilling these functions. In fact, every charism serves "to assemble and build up the body of Christ". Any member of the body may share in proclaiming and teaching the Word of God, may contribute to the sacramental life of that body. The ordained ministry fulfils these functions in a representative way, providing the focus for the unity of the life and witness of the community.

Annecy/81

12. The chief responsibility of the ordained ministry is to assemble and build up the body of Christ by proclaiming and teaching the Word of God, by celebrating the sacraments, and by guiding the life of the community in its worship, its mission and its caring ministry.

Commentary:

These tasks are not exercised by the ordained ministry in an exclusive way. Since the ordained ministry and the community are inextricably related, all members participate in fulfilling these functions. In fact, every charism serves to assemble and build up the body of Christ. Any member of the body may share in proclaiming and teaching the Word of God, may contribute to the sacramental life of that body. The ordained ministry fulfils these functions in a representative way, providing the focus for the unity of the community.

Lima/82

13. The chief responsibility of the ordained ministry is to assemble and build up the body of Christ by proclaiming and teaching the Word of God, by celebrating the sacraments, and by guiding the life of the community in its worship, its mission and its caring ministry.

Commentary:

These tasks are not exercised by the ordained ministry in an exclusive way. Since the ordained ministry and the community are inextricably related, all members participate in fulfilling these functions. In fact, every charism serves to assemble and build up the body of Christ. Any member of the body may share in proclaiming and teaching the Word of God, may contribute to the sacramental life of that body. The ordained ministry fulfils these functions in a representative way, providing the focus for the unity of the community.

Geneva/6-80

13. It is in the eucharistic celebration that the ordained ministry is
the visible focus of the deep and all-
encompassing communion between
Christ and the members of his body.

13-Commentary. The New Testament says very little about the
ordering of the eucharist. There is
no clear evidence about the presidency of the eucharist. In later
times it is clear that an ordained
minister has the function of presiding over the celebration. If it is
true that the ordained ministry is to
provide a focus for the unity of the
life and witness of the Church, it is
natural that an ordained minister
should be given this task. It is
intimately related to the task of
guiding the community, i.e.
supervising its life (*episkopè*) and
strengthening its vigilance in
relation to the truth of the apostolic
message and the coming of the
kingdom.

Rome/11-80

13. It is especially in the eucharistic
celebration that the ordained ministry is the visible focus of the deep
and all-embracing communion between Christ and the members of his
body. In the eucharist Christ
gathers, teaches, and nourishes the
Church. It is Christ who invites to
the meal and who presides at it. In
most of the churches this presidency
is signified by an ordained minister.

Commentary

The New Testament says very little
about the ordering of the eucharist.
There is no explicit evidence about
the presidency of the eucharist.
Very soon it is clear that an
ordained minister presides over the
celebration. If the ordained ministry
is to provide a focus for the unity of
the life and witness of the Church, it
is appropriate that an ordained
minister should be given this task.
It is intimately related to the task of
guiding the community, i.e.
supervising its life (*episkopè*) and
strengthening its vigilance in
relation to the truth of the apostolic
message and the coming of the
kingdom.

Annecy/81

13. It is especially in the eucharistic
celebration that the ordained ministry is the visible focus of the deep
and all-embracing communion between Christ and the members of his
body. In the eucharist Christ
gathers, teaches, and nourishes the
Church. It is Christ who invites to
the meal and who presides at it. In
most of the churches this presidency
is signified by an ordained minister.

Commentary:

The New Testament says very little
about the ordering of the eucharist.
There is no explicit evidence about
the presidency of the eucharist.
Very soon it is clear that an
ordained ministry presides over the
celebration. If the ordained ministry
is to provide a focus for the unity of
the life and witness of the Church, it
is appropriate that an ordained
minister should be given this task.
It is intimately related to the task of
guiding the community, i.e.
supervising its life (*episkopè*) and
strengthening its vigilance in
relation to the truth of the apostolic
message and the coming of the
Kingdom.

Lima/82

14. It is especially in the eucharistic
celebration that the ordained ministry is the visible focus of the deep
and all-embracing communion between Christ and the members of his
body. In the celebration of the
eucharist Christ gathers, teaches,
and nourishes the Church. It is
Christ who invites to the meal and
who presides at it. In most of the
churches this presidency is signified
by an ordained minister.

Commentary:

The New Testament says very little
about the ordering of the eucharist.
There is no explicit evidence about
who presided at the eucharist. Very
soon however it is clear that an
ordained ministry presides over the
celebration. If the ordained ministry
is to provide a focus for the unity of
the life and witness of the Church, it
is appropriate that an ordained
minister should be given this task.
It is intimately related to the task of
guiding the community, i.e.
supervising its life (*episkopè*) and
strengthening its vigilance in
relation to the truth of the apostolic
message and the coming of the
Kingdom.

The Lima text explicitly notes the fact that persons have been ordained "since very early times."[36] The ministry of ordained ministers (or a ministry that is its equivalent) corresponds to the Church's need for a *responsible* witness that is both *public* and *continual*.[37] The actual wording had been suggested by G. Moede and was incorporated in the text of Rome/80.[38] Regarding the ordained ministry being constitutive for the life and witness of the Church, the first sentence of the 6/80 text was placed at the end of the paragraph in the succeeding text of Rome/80. U. Kühn suggested this alteration because the sentence is "to (*sic*) absolute and needs some introduction."[39] Besides reminding the believing community of the dependence of the Church on Jesus Christ the final text stresses the fact that ordained ministers serve as a reminder of "the divine initiative."[40] This latter reminding service replaces an earlier stress on the service of reminding "the community of the priority of the apostolic message in its life."[41] As one theologian put it,

> I would say that it is primarily the bible who (*sic*) reminds the community of the priority of the message. Instead of 'apostolic message' I would, even stronger, say that the ministry represents in a special way Christ in the life of the Church.[42]

Qualities of holiness and loving concern are to be sought by the Church in ordained ministers.[43]

Ordained ministry not only is not to be isolated from the community[44] but also does not even exist apart from the community.[45] Ordained ministers not only

---

[36]§8.

[37]§8.

[38]Moede-Thurian Correspondence, Sept. 30, 1980, WCC Archives, Archive Box: "Faith and Order, Documents 1980-1981, Circular Letters, 1980-1981."

[39]U. Kühn's "Proposals," Nov. 2, 1980, WCC Archives, Archive Box: "Faith and Order Archives, BEM, 79-82 corr. 81, Lima 82."

[40]Lima, §12.

[41]6/80, §11.

[42]E. Flesseman-van-Leer - M. Thurian correspondence, Oct. 22, 1980, WCC Archives, Archive Box: "Faith and Order, Documents 1980-1981, Circular Letters, 1980-1981."

[43]§12.

[44]6/80, §11. Milton suggested the addition of the phrase, "the rest of," in the text of 11/80 in order to insure the avoidance of such isolation. [G.W. Comments, Oct. 26, 1980, WCC Archives, Archive Box: "Faith and Order, Documents 1980-1981, Circular Letters, 1980-1981."]

[45]Lima, §12.

"*need* the recognition, the support and the encouragement of the community"[46] but also "*cannot dispense with*" such recognition, support and encouragement from the community.[47]

The "specific" and "particular" (as opposed to "special") role of the Twelve is treated within the context of the topic of the ordained ministry.[48] This careful use of adjectives avoids a hierarchical placing of ordained ministry *above* others in the Church. D. Fraser refers to "the Anglican Doctrine Report's phrase, '*distinctive* ministry'. But the roles of believers and ministers are interdependent and co-equal."[49] The phrase, "special role," however, is retained in one place.[50] So the tension caused by their specialness (not necessarily to be considered a negative reality) is not entirely removed from the text. Great care is taken in the final text itself (not just the Commentary) to be precise in distinguishing "the Twelve" from "other apostles."[51] For example, one theologian pointed out that in the 6/80 text the "word 'apostle' (is) not introduced in (the) main text."[52] Great care is taken to treat the role of the Twelve in a more precise historical way. W. Pannenberg urges the simple deletion of an "s" in order to be clear about the reference to that role in the first *generation* of the church.[53] The final text omits calling the Twelve "patriarchs."[54] And at Lima to the roles attributed to the Twelve is added that of leading the community in "the breaking of the bread."[55] This eucharistic theme is continued in this same subdivision. The

---

[46]6/80, §11. Emphasis added.

[47]Lima, §12. Emphasis added.

[48]§9.

[49]Fraser-Lazareth Correspondence, Oct. 26, 1981, WCC Archives, Archive Box: "Faith and Order Archives, BEM, 79-82 corr. 81, Lima 82."

[50]§10.

[51]§9.

[52]Mudge Comments, Oct. 27, 1980, WCC Archives, Archive Box: "Faith and Order Archives, BEM, 79-82 corr. 81, Lima 82."

[53]Pannenberg Comments, Oct. 13, 1980, p. 7, WCC Archives, Archive Box: "Faith and Order, Documents 1980-1981, Circular Letters, 1980-1981."

[54]6/80, §9.

[55]§9.

notion of the ordained minister presiding at eucharist is strengthened[56] and even Christ's role in the Eucharist is spelled out and made more explicit.[57]

The Twelve are clearly *not* the *only* leaders of the community for they are said to be "among the leaders."[58] As was mentioned above, the phrase "special role" is retained in one place in the final text[59] in relation to the Apostles. Does the phrase refer in some precise way to their call by Jesus to be representative of the new Israel? T.F. Torrance emphasized the need to "bring out more clearly the *constitutive* nature of the original apostles, their *foundational* character. Otherwise there will (continue to) be confusion between apostles and later bishops."[60] Another theologian, however, stated his reservations concerning the use of this terminology. He stated: "I judge the word 'special' to be an exceedingly difficult and awkward one in contexts like this and would ask for it to be replaced by either 'specific' or 'particular'."[61]

In this same paragraph of the final text, however, there is an abrupt movement from talk of "the Twelve" who are "among the leaders" to talk of "the apostles." The meaning of this abrupt switch is not entirely clear. It appears that the text of 1980 June[62] which clearly referred to the Twelve was not carefully integrated into the body of the Lima text.[63] M. Conway made the following remark which seems to have influenced the final version: "The commentary here should surely belong in the main text, since all discussion of apostleship is central to the debate around the ministry."[64]

---

[56]§14-Commentary. Reservations were expressed by E. Flesseman-van-Leer [Oct. 22, 1980, p. 3, WCC Archives, K-6] and by L.E. Mudge [Oct. 27, 1980, WCC Archives, Archive Box: "Faith and Order Archives, BEM, 79-82 corr. 81, Lima 82.".

[57]§14. G. Gassmann had stated that "the emphasis on the eucharist in §13 of the 1/81 text (Lima, §14) will not, I am afraid, be shared by all Lutherans." [G. Gassmann, Nov. 11, 1981, WCC Archives, Archive Box: "Faith and Order Archives, BEM, 79-82 corr. 81, Lima 82."]

[58]§10. This is a phrase suggested by M. Conway [Sept. 5, 1980, WCC Archives, Archive Box: "Faith and Order, Documents 1980-1981, Circular Letters, 1980-1981."].

[59]§10.

[60]G.W. Notes, Oct. 26, 1980, WCC Archives, Archive Box: "Faith and Order, Documents 1980-1981, Circular Letters, 1980-1981."

[61]M. Conway Comments. Sept. 5, 1980, WCC Archives, Archive Box: "Faith and Order, Documents 1980-1981, Circular Letters, 1980-1981."

[62]Especially §9-Commentary.

[63]§10.

[64]Conway-Thurian Correspondence, Sept. 5, 1980, WCC Archives, Archive Box: "Faith and Order, Documents 1980-1981, Circular Letters, 1980-1981."

This sentiment was voiced also by W. Pannenberg.[65]

The apostles (no longer just the Twelve) are "witnesses *to* the resurrection of Christ" not "*of* the resurrection of Christ"[66] nor *of the Risen Christ*.[67] The wording here may indicate an attentiveness to the precision of the witness, namely, not that of eye-witnesses of the event of the resurrection but rather, the situation of a faith encounter the exact nature of which cannot be determined.

In the final text the difference between the apostles and the ordained ministers whose ministries are *founded* on the apostles is no longer called "fundamental."[68] And the apostles (not simply the Twelve) "prefigure both the Church as a whole and the persons within it who are entrusted with the *specific*[69] authority and responsibility."[70] Here the influence of M. Conway, whose comments were referred to above, is clear.[71] This change was not fully incorporated in the text until Lima. It is important to note that the second paragraph of paragraph §9-Commentary of 6/80 eventually found its way into the *main body* of the Lima text, paragraph §10. The larger topic of apostolicity requires the distinction, clearly drawn here, between the apostles and the Twelve.

The Lima text omits an earlier reference to ordained ministers seeking "to reflect Christ's *priestly* ministry and *intercede* for the community and the world."[72] This priestly role of the ordained is restricted exclusively to a later paragraph in Lima[73] where its *appropriateness* rather than its inherent *necessity* is emphasized.

The reordering of the 6/80 text's paragraph in the third paragraph of the 11/80 text eventually shows up as a separate paragraph number in the Lima text.[74] The

---

[65]Pannenberg Comments, Oct. 13, 1980, WCC Archives, Archive Box: "Faith and Order, Documents 1980-1981, Circular Letters, 1980-1981."

[66]/81, §10, Emphasis added.

[67]6/80, §9-Commentary, Emphasis added.

[68]6/80, §9-Commentary.

[69]Not "special." Emphasis added.

[70]Lima, §10.

[71]M. Conway Comments, Sept. 5, 1980, WCC Archives, Archive Box: "Faith and Order, Documents 1980-1981, Circular Letters, 1980-1981."

[72]6/80, §10. Emphasis added. The omission is made in Lima, §11.

[73]§17.

[74]Lima, §11.

material is reordered in the light of W. Pannenberg's extended comment on the fact "that the 'ordained ministers call (*sic*) and represent Jesus Christ to the community' can only be explained in the context of the topic of apostolic succession. This should not be mentioned first in No. 31 ff. (the section on, 'Succession in the Apostolic Succession')."[75] Pannenberg goes on to state that the fact "that the ordained ministers represent Jesus Christ to the community and are directly chosen and sent by himself like the apostles notwithstanding the mediation of their service through the authority of the apostles, should be treated in close connection with the treatment of apostolic succession."[76]

The word "necessity" in reference to the ordained ministry itself is omitted in the commentary of the 11/80 text. The dropping of the word seems to have been influenced by E. Flesseman-van-Leer who had claimed that "it is overstated to say that the necessity for an ordained ministry was given from the beginning. Church order might have developed differently, though as a matter of fact it didn't."[77]

The Lima text omits the strongly worded reference in 6/80 to the term "ordained ministry" as "anachronistic."[78] Thus it avoids judgmental and inflammatory language.

In commenting on the historical development of the forms of the ordained ministry the text which follows that of 6/80, namely 11/80, distinguishes between forms of ordination and forms of the ordained ministry. U. Kühn had proposed the change in wording thus: "The churches, therefore must refrain from attributing *the action of ordination* as such and particular forms of the ordained ministry to the will and institution of the historic Jesus Christ himself."[79] In the same vein another theologian influenced the addition, in the Lima text, of the word "directly" before the phrase, "to the will and institution of Jesus Christ."[80]

---

[75]Pannenberg Comments, Oct. 13, 1980, p. 7, Archives, Archive Box: "Faith and Order, Documents 1980-1981, Circular Letters, 1980-1981."

[76]Pannenberg, Oct. 13, 1980, pp. 7-8.

[77]Correspondence, Oct 22, 1980, Archives, Archive Box: "Faith and Order, Documents 1980-1981, Circular Letters, 1980-1981."

[78]6/80, §10-Commentary.

[79]U. Kühn Proposals, Rome, Nov 2, 1980, WCC Archives, Archive Box: "Faith and Order Archives, BEM, 79-82 corr. 81, Lima 82." Emphasis added.

[80]J.K.S. Reid, October, 1981, WCC Archives, Archive Box: "Faith and Order Archives, BEM, 79-82 corr. 81, Lima 82." He had suggested the word "immediately."

The chief responsibility of the ordained ministry (rather than of the ordained minister) is clarified grammatically in the final text with the careful use of the preposition "by." The overall responsibility is clearly "to assemble and build up the body of Christ."[81] However the Commentary of the same paragraph omits and replaces a reference to non-ordained members "guiding the life of the community."[82] The phrase which replaces it states that they "may contribute to the sacramental life of that body."[83] It seems that the final text (albeit in its Commentary) wishes to exclude non-ordained members from the function of governance of the Church.[84] G. Gassmann states that "the definitions of function and responsibilities of ordained ministers in II. A. seems to me wholly acceptable to a Lutheran position. The extension of the central definition in para. 12 (Lima, §13) over against the 1974 text is to be welcomed.[85] The phrase, "its liturgical, missionary and diaconal aspects," is changed in the 1/81 text to the phrase, "its worship, its mission and its caring ministry."[86] M. Tanner had stated, "I doubt whether 'diaconal aspects' is very clear here — some more transparent word might be better."[87]

---

[81]§13.

[82]6/80, §12-Commentary.

[83]Lima, §13-Commentary.

[84]If not exclude at least not explicitly include them!

[85]G. Gassmann's Reaction, Nov. 11, 1981, WCC Archives, Archive Box: "Faith and Order Archives, BEM, 79-82 corr. 81, Lima 82.", p. 2.

[86]11/80, §12 and 1/81, §12.

[87]M. Tanner Correspondence , Oct. 1, 1980, p. 2., WCC Archives, Archive Box: "Faith and Order, Documents 1980-1981, Circular Letters, 1980-1981."

B. Ordained Ministry and Authority.

The trinitarian emphasis clarifies the internal "chain of command" in reference to Christ's unique authority. The historical Jesus and the Paschal mystery are highlighted. There is less concern shown about the use of the term, "ordination," as the means of official recognition of ministers/leaders. The origin of the ordained's authority in reference to Christ and the Holy Spirit and in reference to the community is clarified, but perhaps not completely. Certainly the spirit of the exercise of authority involves avoiding extremes. And, finally, the use of the phrase, "the will of God," in place of "the Word of God" presents an interesting question about the extent of the ordained's authority.

Geneva/6-80

14. The authority which is exercised by the ordained ministry has its source in Jesus Christ who "came as one who serves" (Mk 10:45; Lk 22:27). To be set apart for the ordained ministry, therefore, means to be consecrated to service. At the same time, authority stems from the recognition given to the ordained minister by the community. Since this act of recognition is essentially a setting apart with prayer for the gift of the Holy Spirit, the authority of the ordained ministry is not to be understood as the possession of the ordained person but as a gift for the continuing edification of the body in and for which the minister has been ordained. Authority has the character of responsibility before God and is exercised with the participation of the whole community.

Rome/11-80

14. The authority of the ordained minister is rooted in Jesus Christ, who has received it from the Father (Mt 28:18), and who confers it in the Holy Spirit through the act of ordination. This act takes place within a community which accords public recognition to a particular person. Because Jesus "came as one who serves" (Mk 10:45; Lk 22:27), to be set apart means to be consecrated to service. Since ordination is essentially a setting apart with prayer for the gift of the Holy Spirit, the authority of the ordained ministry is not to be understood as the possession of the ordained person but as a gift for the continuing edification of the body in and for which the minister has been ordained. Authority has the character of responsibility before God and is exercised with the cooperation of the whole community.

Annecy/81

14. The authority of the ordained minister is rooted in Jesus Christ, who has received it from the Father (Mt 28:18), and who confers it by the Holy Spirit through the act of ordination. This act takes place within a community which accords public recognition to a particular person. Because Jesus came as one who serves (Mk 10:45; Lk 22:27), to be set apart means to be consecrated to service. Since ordination is essentially a setting apart with prayer for the gift of the Holy Spirit, the authority of the ordained ministry is not to be understood as the possession of the ordained person but as a gift for the continuing edification of the body in and for which the minister has been ordained. Authority has the character of responsibility before God and is exercised with the cooperation of the whole community.

Lima/82

15. The authority of the ordained minister is rooted in Jesus Christ, who has received it from the Father (Mt 28:18), and who confers it by the Holy Spirit through the act of ordination. This act takes place within a community which accords public recognition to a particular person. Because Jesus came as one who serves (Mk 10:45; Lk 22:27), to be set apart means to be consecrated to service. Since ordination is essentially a setting apart with prayer for the gift of the Holy Spirit, the authority of the ordained ministry is not to be understood as the possession of the ordained person but as a gift for the continuing edification of the body in and for which the minister has been ordained. Authority has the character of responsibility before God and is exercised with the cooperation of the whole community.

Geneva/6-80

15. Therefore, ordained ministers are not autocrats or impersonal functionaries. Although called to exercise a role of responsible judgment and leadership on the basis of the Word of God, they are bound to the faithful in interdependence and reciprocity. Only when they genuinely seek the response and the acknowledgement of the community can their authority be protected from the distortions of isolation and domination. They manifest and exercise the authority of Christ in the way Christ himself revealed God's authority to the world: by committing their life to the community.

15-Commentary. Christ's authority is unique. "He spoke as one who has authority (*exousia*), not as their scribes" (Mt 7:29). His authority is an authority governed by love for the "sheep who have no shepherd" (Mt 9:36). It is confirmed by his service and in a supreme way by his death on the cross. Authority in the Church can only be authentic as it seeks to conform to this model. Two dangers need to be avoided. Authority can not be exercised

Rome/11-80

15. Therefore, ordained ministers are not autocrats or impersonal functionaries. Although called to exercise discernment, judgment and leadership on the basis of the Word of God, they are bound to the faithful in interdependence and reciprocity. Only when they seek the response and acknowledgement of the community can their authority be protected from the distortions of isolation and domination. They manifest and exercise the authority of Christ in the way Christ himself revealed God's authority to the world: by committing their life to the community

Commentary
Christ's authority is unique. "He spoke as one who has authority (*exousia*), not as the scribes" (Mt 7:29). This authority is an authority governed by love for the "sheep who have no shepherd" (Mt 9:36). It is confirmed by his life of service and, supremely, by his death and resurrection. Authority in the Church can only be authentic as it seeks to conform to this model. Two dangers must be avoided. Authority cannot be exercised

Annecy/81

15. Therefore, ordained ministers must not be autocrats or impersonal functionaries. Although called to exercise wise and loving leadership on the basis of the Word of God, they are bound to the faithful in interdependence and reciprocity. Only when they seek the response and acknowledgement of the community can their authority be protected from the distortions of isolation and domination. They manifest and exercise the authority of Christ in the way Christ himself revealed God's authority to the world: by committing their life to the community.

Commentary:
Christ's authority is unique. "He spoke as one who has authority (*exousia*), not as the scribes" (Mt 7:29). This authority is an authority governed by love for the "sheep who have no shepherd" (Mt 9:36). It is confirmed by his life of service and, supremely, by his death and resurrection. Authority in the Church can only be authentic as it seeks to conform to this model. Two dangers must be avoided. Authority cannot be exercised

Lima/82

16. Therefore, ordained ministers must not be autocrats or impersonal functionaries. Although called to exercise wise and loving leadership on the basis of the Word of God, they are bound to the faithful in interdependence and reciprocity. Only when they seek the response and acknowledgement of the community can their authority be protected from the distortions of isolation and domination. They manifest and exercise the authority of Christ in the way Christ himself revealed God's authority to the world; by committing their life to the community. Christ's authority is unique. "He spoke as one who has authority (*exousia*), not as the scribes" (Mt 7:29). This authority is an authority governed by love for the "sheep who have no shepherd" (Mt 9:36). It is confirmed by his life of service and, supremely, by his death and resurrection. Authority in the Church can only be authentic as it seeks to conform to this model.

Commentary:
Here two dangers must be avoided. Authority cannot be exercised with-

Geneva/6-80 [cont.]

without regard for the community. Even the apostles were attentive to the experience and the judgment of the believers. On the other hand, the authority of the ordained ministers must not be reduced to make them dependent on the common opinion of the community. Their authority lies in their responsibility to recall the Word of God in the community.

Rome/11-80 [cont.]

without regard for the community. The apostles paid heed to the experience and the judgment of the faithful. On the other hand, the authority of ordained ministers must not be so reduced as to make them dependent on the common opinion of the community. Their authority lies in their responsibility to express the will of God in the community.

Annecy/81 [cont.]

without regard for the community. The apostles paid heed to the experience and the judgment of the faithful. On the other hand, the authority of ordained ministers must not be so reduced as to make them dependent on the common opinion of the community. Their authority lies in their responsibility to express the will of God in the community.

Lima/82 [cont.]

out regard for the community. The apostles paid heed to the experience and the judgment of the faithful. On the other hand, the authority of ordained ministers must not be so reduced as to make them dependent on the common opinion of the community. Their authority lies in their responsibility to express the will of God in the community.

The trinitarian emphasis noted above is evidenced again in this section. Jesus Christ received his authority "from the Father (and) confers it by the Holy Spirit."[88] Emphasis is placed on the unique authority of Christ as a model of the exercise of authority. In this regard what had earlier appeared in the Commentary section finds its way into the body of the final text.[89] As noted above there is a greater emphasis placed on the historical Jesus' *life* of service and on his *resurrection* and not solely on his death on the cross. And the entire reference is moved from the Commentary to the body of the text.[90] Both L.S. Mudge and J.A. Powers had suggested this incorporation into the text with Powers noting that "the drafters are not consistent with their criteria as to what is in the body of the document and what becomes 'commentary.'"[91]

The term, "ordination," is used explicitly in the Lima text. Earlier it was studiously avoided, being referred to as "this act of recognition."[92]

The ordained minister's authority is exercised not "with the *participation*[93] but "with the *cooperation* of the whole community."[94] For the ordained minister's authority clearly does not come "from the recognition given to the ordained minister by the community"[95] but from Jesus Christ "who confers it by the Holy Spirit through the act of ordination."[96] E. Flesseman-van-Leer had asked, "who is it, who sets apart for the ministry, Christ or the congregation? It should be expressed more explicitly."[97] And G. Moede had noted that "what is meant is 'public' recognition

---

[88]Lima, §15.

[89]§16.

[90]§16.

[91]L.S. Mudge, Oct. 27, 1980, WCC Archives, Gr.L; J.A. Powers, Aug. 14, 1980, WCC Archives, Archive Box: "Faith and Order, Documents 1980-1981, Circular Letters, 1980-1981."

[92]6/80, §14.

[93]6/80, §14. Emphasis added.

[94]Lima, §15. Emphasis added.

[95]6/80, §14.

[96]Lima, §15.

[97]Oct. 22, 1980, Archives, Archive Box: "Faith and Order, Documents 1980-1981, Circular Letters, 1980-1981."

given. It is verifiable by all, and thus accountable."[98] So the participants at the Rome Consultation, Oct/Nov, 1980, dropped the phrase, "at the same time authority stems (from the recognition given by the community)," from the 6/80 text.[99] Even so, just prior to the Lima meeting, G. Gassmann noted that this section "on authority still lacks, to my mind, in clarity. The line between the authority of Christ and its application through the service of the minister, expressed in proclamation, celebration of sacraments and episkope, could be spelled out more clearly."[100]

That ordained ministers seek the community's response and acknowledgement is seen as the expected thing.[101] To bolster this point it is indicated that even the apostles were, as a rule, attentive to the experience and judgment of other believers.[102]

In regard to the exercise of authority *vis-à-vis* the community, two dangers, two opposite extremes *must* (not merely *need* to) be avoided.[103] The tone is clearly more than hortatory.

The leadership of the ordained is to be "wise and loving"[104] with the note of "judgment"[105] eliminated as a parallel responsibility.

Their authority lies, in the final text, in their responsibility "to express *the will of God* in the community."[106] The phrase, "the will of God," interestingly replaces "the Word of God." Is this an expansion of the authority of the ordained?

---

[98]Sept. 30, 1980, p. 2, Archives, Archive Box: "Faith and Order, Documents 1980-1981, Circular Letters, 1980-1981."

[99]6/80, §14.

[100]G. Gassmann, Nov. 11, 1981, p. 2, WCC Archives, Archive Box: "Faith and Order Archives, BEM, 79-82 corr. 81, Lima 82."

[101]§16.

[102]§16-Commentary.

[103]§16-Commentary. The change was made at the Oct/Nov, 1980 Consultation.

[104]§16. This was changed in the 1/81 text, §15.

[105]6/80, §15 and 11/80, §15.

[106]§16-Commentary. Emphasis added. The full change in the 11/80 text, §15-C, is from the phrase, "to recall the Word of God," to the phrase, "to express the will of God."

C. Ordained Ministry and Priesthood.

Significant advances are made regarding priesthood in the church. The priesthood of the laity is clearly not a secondary kind of priesthood. Ordained ministers are appropriately called priests. The sacramental ministry of ordained ministers is included alongside ministry of the word. The priesthood of the baptized is carefully described in relationship to the priesthood of Christ. Also carefully described are the relationships between the priesthood of the Christian ordained ministry and the priesthood of the Old Testament and between the priesthood of the Christian ordained ministry and the priesthood of Christ. More emphasis is placed on the priesthood of the whole people of God.

Geneva/6-80

16. Jesus Christ is the unique priest of the new covenant. He gave his life as sacrifice for all. In a secondary way, the Church as a whole can be described as a priesthood. All members are called to offer their being "as a living sacrifice" and to intercede for the Church and the salvation of the world. The ordained ministers are related, like all Christians, to both the priesthood of Christ and the priesthood of the Church. They may be called priests because they fulfil a particular priestly service by strengthening and building up the royal and prophetic priesthood of the faithful through their prayers of intercession, their service of the Gospel and their pastoral guidance of the community.

Rome/11-80

16. Jesus Christ is the unique priest of the new covenant. Christ's life was given as a sacrifice for all. Derivatively, the Church as a whole can be described as a priesthood. All members are called to offer their being "as a living sacrifice" and to intercede for the Church and the salvation of the world. Ordained ministers are related, as are all Christians, both to the priesthood of Christ and to the priesthood of the Church. But they may be called priests in an appropriate way because they fulfil a particular priestly service by strengthening and building up the royal and prophetic priesthood of the faithful through word and sacraments, through their prayers of intercession, and through their pastoral guidance of the community.

Annecy/81

16. Jesus Christ is the unique priest of the new covenant. Christ's life was given as a sacrifice for all. Derivatively, the Church as a whole can be described as a priesthood. All members are called to offer their being "as a living sacrifice" and to intercede for the Church and the salvation of the world. Ordained ministers are related, as are all Christians, both to the priesthood of Christ and to the priesthood of the Church. But they may be called priests in an appropriate way because they fulfil a particular priestly service by strengthening and building up the royal and prophetic priesthood of the faithful through word and sacraments, through their prayers of intercession, and through their pastoral guidance of the community.

Lima/82

17. Jesus Christ is the unique priest of the new covenant. Christ's life was given as a sacrifice for all. Derivatively, the Church as a whole can be described as a priesthood. All members are called to offer their being "as a living sacrifice" and to intercede for the Church and the salvation of the world. Ordained ministers are related, as are all Christians, both to the priesthood of Christ and to the priesthood of the Church. But they may appropriately be called priests because they fulfil a particular priestly service by strengthening and building up the royal and prophetic priesthood of the faithful through word and sacraments, through their prayers of intercession, and through their pastoral guidance of the community.

Geneva/6-80

16-Commentary. The New Testament never uses the term "priesthood-hierateuma" or "priesthiereus" to designate the ordained ministry or ordained minister. In the New Testament the term is reserved, on the one hand, for the unique priesthood of Jesus Christ who offered himself once and for all for the sins of all humanity (Heb 7:24), and on the other hand, for the royal and prophetic priesthood of all baptized (I Pet 2:9). The priesthood of Christ and the priesthood of the baptized, in their respective ways, have the function of sacrifice and intercession. In the early Church the terms "priesthood" and "priest" came to be used to designate the ordained ministry and minister. They underline the fact that the ordained ministry is related to the priestly reality of Jesus Christ and the whole community. As one uses the term it must be made clear, however, that the service of the ordained ministry is different in nature not only from the sacrificial priesthood of the Old Testament, but also from the unique propitiatory

Rome/11-80

16-Commentary

The New Testament never uses the term "priesthood" or "priest" (*hiereus*) to designate the ordained ministry or the ordained minister. In the New Testament the term is reserved, on the one hand, for the unique priesthood of Jesus Christ and, on the other hand, for the royal and prophetic priesthood of all baptized. The priesthood of Christ and the priesthood of the baptized have in their respective ways the function of sacrifice and intercession. As Christ has offered himself, Christians offer their whole being "as a living sacrifice". As Christ intercedes before the Father, Christians intercede for the Church and the salvation of the world. Nevertheless, the differences between these two kinds of priesthood cannot be overlooked. While Christ offered himself as a unique sacrifice once and for all for the salvation of the world, believers have to receive as a gift of God what Christ has done for them.

In the early Church the terms "priesthood" and "priest" came to be

Annecy/81

16-Commentary:

The New Testament never uses the term "priesthood" or "priest" (*hiereus*) to designate the ordained ministry or the ordained minister. In the New Testament, the term is reserved, on the one hand, for the unique priesthood of Jesus Christ and, on the other hand, for the royal and prophetic priesthood of all baptized. The priesthood of Christ and the priesthood of the baptized have in their respective ways the function of sacrifice and intercession. As Christ has offered himself, Christians offer their whole being "as a living sacrifice". As Christ intercedes before the Father, Christians intercede for the Church and the salvation of the world. Nevertheless, the differences between these two kinds of priesthood cannot be overlooked. While Christ offered himself as a unique sacrifice once and for all for the salvation of the world, believers need to receive continually as a gift of God that which Christ has done for them.

In the early Church the terms "priesthood" and "priest" came to be

Lima/82

17-Commentary:

The New Testament never uses the term "priesthood" or "priest" (*hiereus*) to designate the ordained ministry or the ordained minister. In the New Testament, the term is reserved, on the one hand, for the unique priesthood of Jesus Christ and, on the other hand, for the royal and prophetic priesthood of all baptized. The priesthood of Christ and the priesthood of the baptized have in their respective ways the function of sacrifice and intercession. As Christ has offered himself, Christians offer their whole being "as a living sacrifice". As Christ intercedes before the Father, Christians intercede for the Church and the salvation of the world.' Nevertheless, the differences between these two kinds of priesthood cannot be overlooked. While Christ offered himself as a unique sacrifice once and for all for the salvation of the world, believers need to receive continually as a gift of God that which Christ has done for them.

In the early Church the terms "priesthood" and "priest" came to be

Geneva/6-80 [cont.]
priesthood of Christ. If we speak today of the priestly service of the ordained ministry, we mean serving the Gospel within and on behalf of the community, as St Paul says about himself: "I am a minister of Jesus Christ to the gentiles in the priestly service of the Gospel of God, so that the offering of the gentiles may be acceptable by the Holy Spirit" (Rom 15:16).

Rome/11-80 [cont.]
used to designate the ordained ministry and minister as presiding at the eucharist. They underline the fact that the ordained ministry is related to the priestly reality of Jesus Christ and the whole community. When the terms are used in connection with the ministry, their meaning differs in appropriate ways from the sacrificial priesthood of the Old Testament, from the unique propitiatory priesthood of Christ and from the corporate priesthood of the people of God. St Paul could call his ministry "a priestly service of the gospel of God, so that the offering of the Gentiles may be acceptable by the Holy Spirit" (Rom 15:16).

Annecy/81 [cont.]
used to designate the ordained ministry and minister as presiding at the eucharist. They underline the fact that the ordained ministry is related to the priestly reality of Jesus Christ and the whole community. When the terms are used in connection with the ordained ministry, their meaning differs in appropriate ways from the sacrificial priesthood of the Old Testament, from the unique propitiatory priesthood of Christ and from the corporate priesthood of the people of God. St Paul could call his ministry "a priestly service of the gospel of God, so that the offering of the Gentiles may be acceptable by the Holy Spirit" (Rom 15:16).

Lima/82 [cont.]
used to designate the ordained ministry and minister as presiding at the eucharist. They underline the fact that the ordained ministry is related to the priestly reality of Jesus Christ and the whole community. When the terms are used in connection with the ordained ministry, their meaning differs in appropriate ways from the sacrificial priesthood of the Old Testament, from the unique propitiatory priesthood of Christ and from the corporate priesthood of the people of God. St Paul could call his ministry "a priestly service of the gospel of God, so that the offering of the Gentiles may be acceptable by the Holy Spirit" (Rom 15: 16).

340

In the body of the text there are three significant advances made in the final version of this section on the priesthood which consists of one paragraph and its Commentary. These advances were made at the Rome Consultation of Oct/Nov, 1980. First, the priesthood of the Church is clearly *derivative* from Christ but no longer called priesthood "in a secondary way."[107] Secondly, the *appropriateness* of calling ordained ministers priests is explicitly acknowledged. E. Fleeseman-van-Leer notes in this regard that "it is not clear what point exactly is intended to be made in this paragraph — or is it merely to argue that the word 'priesthood,' though not biblical, is acceptable?"[108] Thirdly, the priestly service of the ordained ministers includes service through *sacraments*, actually "through word and sacraments"[109] rather than simply "service of the Gospel."[110]

In the Commentary section the priesthood of Christ is more fully and carefully described as truly different from the priesthood of the baptized. This careful description is eventually refined, especially in its reference to the fact that "believers *need* to receive *continually* . . . that which Christ has done for them."[111] This description also includes an explicit reference to Christ's interceding "before the Father." Thus the final text continues its trinitarian emphasis which has been cited elsewhere.

No longer is the difference between the priesthood of the Christian ordained ministry and that of the Old Testament and of Christ said to be a difference "in nature"[112] but "in appropriate ways."[113] And to the comparison with the priesthood of the ordained ministry is added "the corporate priesthood of the people of God."[114]

---

[107]6/80, §16.

[108]Oct. 22, 1980, Archives, Archive Box: "Faith and Order, Documents 1980-1981, Circular Letters, 1980-1981."

[109]§17.

[110]6/80, §16.

[111]§17-Commentary. Emphasis added. The alteration was made in the 1/81 text.

[112]6/80, §16-Commentary.

[113]Lima, §17-Commentary. W. Pannenberg had suggested that "in the commentary it should at least be mentioned that the terminology of priesthood in relation to the ordained ministry developed in connection with the typological application of the Old Testament." [Oct. 13, 1980, p. 8, WCC Archives, Archive Box: "Faith and Order, Documents 1980-1981, Circular Letters, 1980-1981."]

[114]§17-Commentary.

J.R. Wright had suggested this addition to M. Thurian, the President of the Steering Committee for the BEM Documents, explaining,

> I know that many today would wish to suggest that there is *no* difference between the ordained ministerial priesthood and the general priesthood of the faithful, but that there *is* such a difference was already asserted in the famous passage of Vatican II, *Lumen Gentium* 10, and has emerged anew, I think, in the ARCIC dialogues . . . and perhaps in other ecumenical dialogues as well. If your committee can *not* agree to such a clarification/emendation, however, I would prefer to see a clear admission that there is disagreement on this point rather than the implication . . . that the ordained priestly ministry is *not* different from the priesthood of the Church.[115]

D. THE MINISTRY OF MEN AND WOMEN IN THE CHURCH.

Although not treating the issue of the ordination of women in thoroughgoing fashion the Lima text at least faces it squarely. The strength of theological argumentation in favor of the ordination of women is acknowledged. The movement among the churches toward the acceptance of women's ordination is noted. In the final analysis, however, the Lima text does not take a stand one way or another. On the other hand, ministry (not just pastoral service) by women, alongside men in the church, seems to be presumed in the text. The use of more inclusive language fosters the interdependence and the common qualities of women and men's ministry. And, with each succeeding text, language which encourages those on both sides of this and similar issues replaces partisan and inflammatory language.

---

[115]Sept. 8, 1980 Archives material, pp. 1-2, Archive Box: "Faith and Order, Documents 1980-1981, Circular Letters, 1980-1981."

Geneva/6-80

17. Where Christ is present, human barriers are being broken. The Church is called to convey to the world the image of a new humanity. In particular, there is in Christ no male or female. Therefore, men and women need to discover the full meaning of their specific contribution to the service of Christ in the Church. The Church is entitled to the style which can be provided by women as well as that which can be provided by men. A deeper understanding of the mutual interdependence of men and women needs to be more widely reflected in the life of the Church and its ministries.

Rome/11-80

17. Where Christ is present, human barriers are being broken. The Church is called to convey to the world the image of a new humanity. There is in Christ no male or female. Therefore, men and women need to discover the full meaning of their particular, as well as their shared, contributions to the service of Christ in the Church. The Church is entitled to the style of service which can be provided by women as well as that which can be provided by men, and also to that which can be provided by women and men in cooperation. A deeper understanding of the interdependence of men and women needs to be more widely reflected in the life of the Church and its ministries. Though they agree on this need, the churches draw different conclusions as to the admission of women to the ordained ministry. An increasing number of churches have decided that there is no theological or biblical reason against ordaining women, and many of them have subsequently proceeded to do so. Yet most churches still hold that the tradition of the Church in this regard shall not be changed.

Annecy/81

17. Where Christ is present, human barriers are being broken. The Church is called to convey to the world the image of a new humanity. There is in Christ no male or female. (Gal 3: 28). Both women and men must discover together their contributions to the service of Christ in the Church. The Church must discover the ministry which can be provided by women as well as that which can be provided by men. A deeper understanding of the comprehensiveness of ministry which reflects the interdependence of men and women needs to be more widely manifested in the life of the Church.

Though they agree on this need, the churches draw different conclusions as to the admission of women to the ordained ministry. An increasing number of churches have decided that there is no biblical or theological reason against ordaining women, and many of them have subsequently proceeded to do so. Yet most churches hold that the tradition of the Church in this regard must not be changed.

Lima/82

18. Where Christ is present, human barriers are being broken. The Church is called to convey to the world the image of a new humanity. There is in Christ no male or female. (Gal 3: 28). Both women and men must discover together their contributions to the service of Christ in the Church. The Church must discover the ministry which can be provided by women as well as that which can be provided by men. A deeper understanding of the comprehensiveness of ministry which reflects the interdependence of men and women needs to be more widely manifested in the life of the Church.

Though they agree on this need, the churches draw different conclusions as to the admission of women to the ordained ministry. An increasing number of churches have decided that there is no biblical or theological reason against ordaining women, and many of them have subsequently proceeded to do so. Yet many churches hold that the tradition of the Church in this regard must not be changed.

Geneva/6-80
17-Commentary.

Though they agree on this need, the churches draw different conclusions as to the admission of women to the ordained ministry. While some, in fact an increasing number of, churches have decided to ordain women, the majority hold that the unbroken tradition of the Church in this regard should not be changed today.

Rome/11-80
17-Commentary

Those churches which practice the ordination of women do so out of their understanding of the ministry and the Gospel. They read passages such as Genesis 1:27 and Galatians 3:28 with a sensitivity arising from new circumstances and new needs. They have found that women's gifts are as wide and varied as men's and that their ministry is as fully blessed by the Holy Spirit as the ministry of men. None has found reason to reconsider its decision.

Yet the force of nineteen centuries of tradition against the ordination of women cannot be lightly ignored. It cannot be dismissed as lack of respect for the role of women in the Church. There are questions concerning the theological understanding of humanity, and concerning Christology which need investigation.

The discussion of these questions within the various churches and Christian traditions should be complemented by joint study and reflection within the ecumenical fellowship of all churches. Openness to

Annecy/81
17-Commentary:

Those churches which practice the ordination of women do so because of their understanding of the Gospel and of the ministry. It rests for them on the deeply held theological conviction that the ordained ministry of the Church is defective when it is limited to one sex. This theological conviction has been reinforced by their experience during the years in which they have included women in their ordained ministries. They have found that women's gifts are as wide and varied as men's and that their ministry is as fully blessed by the Holy Spirit as the ministry of men. None has found reason to reconsider its decision.

Those churches which do not practise the ordination of women consider that the force of nineteen centuries of tradition against the ordination of women must not be lightly ignored. They believe that such a tradition cannot be dismissed as a lack of respect for the role of women in the Church. They believe that there are theological issues concerning the nature of humanity

Lima/82
18-Commentary:

Those churches which practise the ordination of women do so because of their understanding of the Gospel and of the ministry. It rests for them on the deeply held theological conviction that the ordained ministry of the Church lacks fullness when it is limited to one sex. This theological conviction has been reinforced by their experience during the years in which they have included women in their ordained ministries. They have found that women's gifts are as wide and varied as men's and that their ministry is as fully blessed by the Holy Spirit as the ministry of men. None has found reason to reconsider its decision.

Those churches which do not practise the ordination of women consider that the force of nineteen centuries of tradition against the ordination of women must not be set aside. They believe that such a tradition cannot be dismissed as a lack of respect for the participation of women in the Church. They believe that there are theological issues concerning the nature of humanity and concerning Christology which

344

Rome/11-80 [cont.]
each other holds out the possibility that the Spirit may speak to one church through the insights of another.

Annecy/81 [cont.]
and concerning Christology which lie at the heart of their convictions and understanding of the role of women in the Church.

The discussion of these practical and theological questions within the various churches and Christian traditions should be complemented by joint study and reflection within the ecumenical fellowship of all churches. Openness to each other holds out the possibility that the Spirit may speak to one church through the insights of another.

Lima/82 [cont.]
lie at the heart of their convictions and understanding of the role of women in the Church.

The discussion of these practical and theological questions within the various churches and Christian traditions should be complemented by joint study and reflection within the ecumenical fellowship of all churches.

The Lima document takes the Commentary paragraph of 6/80 into the body of its text. It thereby faces squarely the dilemma facing the churches, namely, to ordain or not to ordain women. L. Mudge seems to be the one most responsible for the rewriting of this paragraph, especially the placing of the commentary section of the 6/80 text into the main body of the subsequent text (11/80).[116] That there is no theological or biblical evidence against ordaining women is stated. And the word, "unbroken," which modifies "tradition" is deleted. The wording which influenced the wording of the 11/80 text regarding the lack of evidence and the deletion of the word "unbroken" comes from J.A. Powers.[117] Thus there is acknowledged the strength of the argumentation in favor of the ordination of women. The same is true of the use of the word, "many,"[118] in reference to those churches which choose not to ordain women. Previously (in the 6/80 text) the word, "majority," and then the word, "most,"[119] was used. Thus there is acknowledged the movement toward acceptance of the ordination of women. M. Conway suggested "that it would be better to avoid a numerical reference. A position does not become either right or wrong because a larger or smaller number hold it."[120] Furthermore, as M. Tanner points out, "there is some confusion here over the use of ordained. We in the C of E (Church of England) *ordain* women to be deaconesses (as I think the Orthodox do?); the Church of Wales now *ordaining* women to the diaconate, though not to priesthood or episcopate!"[121] In the final text, however, the issue is held in abeyance and a mutual respect for opposing positions of the churches is carefully maintained.

---

[116]Oct. 27, 1980, p. 1, Archives, Archive Box: "Faith and Order Archives, BEM, 79-82 corr. 81, Lima 82.": "The 'commentary' contains what ought to be the main subject-matter of the text."

[117]Aug. 14, 1980, p. 2, Archives, WCC Archives, Archive Box: "Faith and Order, Documents 1980-1981, Circular Letters, 1980-1981." [Also found in G.W. Notes, Oct. 26, 1980, p. 3, WCC Archives, Archive Box: "Faith and Order, Documents 1980-1981, Circular Letters, 1980-1981."]

[118]Lima, §18.

[119]11/80, §17.

[120]Sept. 5, 1980, p. 4, WCC Archives, Archive Box: "Faith and Order, Documents 1980-1981, Circular Letters, 1980-1981." The same point is made by E. Flesseman-van-Leer [Oct. 22, 1980, p. 4, WCC Archives, Archive Box: "Faith and Order, Documents 1980-1981, Circular Letters, 1980-1981."]

[121]Oct. 1, 1980, p. 2, WCC Archives, Archive Box: "Faith and Order, Documents 1980-1981, Circular Letters, 1980-1981."

In the final section of the text, "Towards the Mutual Recognition of the Ordained Ministries," there is a clear affirmation of the obstacle that the ordination of women poses to such recognition. There M. Tanner[122] urged the deletion of the word, "could,"[123] so that the hard facts be faced forthrightly.

The process of *mutual discovery* replaces the notion of *entitlement* in regard to "the *ministry*," not simply "the style of service" which women along with men can provide in the Church. In fact H. Russell stated that the word "styles" is a term that is "cheap for the richness of the 'grace-gifts' of God."[124] The specificity or particularity of male and female contributions to ministry is de-emphasized. Words, like "specific,"[125] and "particular,"[126] are dropped from the final text of Lima so that this more inclusive stance can be taken in the discovery of the interdependence of women and men in the ministry.

A new commentary section is added to the paragraph in the Oct/Nov 80 text. It is further refined in 1/81 and 1/82 (Lima). After briefly fleshing out the reasons for the opposing stances on the question of the ordination of women there is a plea for "joint study and reflection within the ecumenical fellowship of all churches" to augment the discussions going on within each church and within each church tradition. M. Conway had asked, "Could there not be in the commentary here a reference to the continuing dialogue and studies of this issue and to ways in which churches can share in that?"[127] J.R. Wright had observed that "in view of the disagreements that do exist, I do think it (6/80, §17) could be expanded a bit with a view towards clarifying *where* the differences lie and what possible questions might

---

[122]Oct. 1, 1980, p. 3, Archive Box: "Faith and Order, Documents 1980-1981, Circular Letters, 1980-1981."

[123]Lima, §54; 6/80, §51. The change was made in the 1/81 text.

[124]Comments, Sept. 15, 1980, p. 1, WCC Archives, Archive Box: "Faith and Order, Documents 1980-1981, Circular Letters, 1980-1981." [Restated in G.W. Comments, Oct. 26, 1980, p. 2, WCC Archives, Archive Box: "Faith and Order, Documents 1980-1981, Circular Letters, 1980-1981."]

[125]6/80, §17.

[126]Oct/Nov 80, §17.

[127]Sept. 5, 1980, p. 4, WCC Archives, Archive Box: "Faith and Order, Documents 1980-1981, Circular Letters, 1980-1981."

be asked towards future reconciliation."[128] G. Moede had commented: "I think this section needs more meat. At the very least it needs to be mentioned that an increasing number of churches ordain women, and find their pastoral gifts and fruits equal to those of men. Can we set limits as to where the Holy Spirit will lead the Church?"[129] The wording used in this Commentary section to clarify each of the opposing views is highly nuanced in order that dialogue be encouraged. Less inflammatory and more open-ended, respectful terminology is in evidence, e.g., as 1/82 is compared to 1/81: "lacks fullness" replaces "is defective"[130]; "set aside" replaces "lightly ignored"[131]; "participation of women" replaces "role of women".

In the final section of the Lima document, namely, "Towards the Mutual Recognition of the Ordained Ministries," this same issue of the ordination of women is taken up. No significant changes are made, however, between the texts of 6/80 and 1/82. G. Gassmann later pointed out in reference to this topic in the 1/81 text that "the question should be pushed whether differences with regard to the ordination of women are or are not an insuperable barrier to mutual recognition of ministries (taken up rather late, in §50)."[132]

---

[128]Sept. 8, 1980, p. 2, WCC Archives, Archive Box: "Faith and Order, Documents 1980-1981, Circular Letters, 1980-1981."

[129]Sept. 30, 1980, p. 2, WCC Archives, Archive Box: "Faith and Order, Documents 1980-1981, Circular Letters, 1980-1981."

[130]J.K.S. Reid Comments, Oct., 1981, WCC Archives, Archive Box: "Faith and Order Archives, BEM, 79-82 corr. 81, Lima 82."

[131]Idem.

[132]Nov. 11, 1981, pp. 2-3, WCC Archives, Archive Box: "Faith and Order Archives, BEM, 79-82 corr. 81, Lima 82."

III. The Forms of the Ordained Ministry.

A. Bishops, Presbyters and Deacons.

There is acknowledged the overwhelming predominance of the threefold ministry of bishops, presbyters and deacons, in the development of ministerial offices in the early days of the church. There is, however, an appreciation of historical developmental processes at work always in the church. These processes are at times difficult to determine with satisfactory precision. The work of the Spirit is noted in terms of adaptation to human needs. More leeway is thus given to further adaptations today under the aegis of the Spirit. The problem of the precise role of the deacon today is taken into account as well as the problem of the exact distinction between bishop and presbyter. While canonical needs are acknowledged people are still preferred to structures in these texts. And "being" as well as "doing" in ministry is deemed important. While the threefold pattern of ministry is emphasized, its reform is called for. Judgments about the meaning of historical facts are avoided, for example, in reference to the ministerial effectiveness of churches which have not retained the threefold pattern of ministry. The challenge of the threefold ministry is indeed a challenge for *all* the churches.

Geneva/6-80

18. The New Testament does not describe a single pattern of ministry which might serve as a blueprint or continuing norm for all future ministry in the Church. The New Testament writings refer rather to a variety of forms which existed at different places and times. As the Holy Spirit continued to lead the Church in life, worship and mission, certain elements from this early variety became settled into a more universal pattern of ministry. By the second and third centuries, a threefold pattern of bishop, presbyter and deacon became established as the pattern of ordained ministry throughout the Church. In succeeding centuries, the ministry by bishop, presbyter and deacon underwent considerable changes in its practical exercise. At some points of crisis in the history of the Church, the continuing functions of ministry were in some places and communities distributed according to structures other than the predominant threefold pattern. Sometimes appeal was made to the New Testament in justification of these other patterns. In other cases, the restructuring of ministry was

Rome/11-80

18. The New Testament does not describe a single pattern of ministry which might serve as a blueprint or continuing norm for all future ministry in the Church. In the New Testament there appears rather a variety of forms which existed at different places and times. As the Holy Spirit continued to lead the Church in life, worship and mission, certain elements from this early variety were further developed and became settled into a more universal pattern of ministry. During the second and third centuries, a threefold pattern of bishop, presbyter and deacon became established as the pattern of ordained ministry throughout the Church. In succeeding centuries, the ministry by bishop, presbyter and deacon underwent considerable changes in its practical exercise. At some points of crisis in the history of the Church, the continuing functions of ministry were in some places and communities distributed according to structures other than the predominant threefold pattern. Sometimes appeal was made to the New Testament in justification of these other patterns. In other cases, the restructuring of

Annecy/81

18. The New Testament does not describe a single pattern of ministry which might serve as a blueprint or continuing norm for all future ministry in the Church. In the New Testament there appears rather a variety of forms which existed at different places and times. As the Holy Spirit continued to lead the Church in life, worship and mission, certain elements from this early variety were further developed and became settled into a more universal pattern of ministry. During the second and third centuries, a threefold pattern of bishop, presbyter and deacon became established as the pattern of ordained ministry throughout the Church. In succeeding centuries, the ministry by bishop, presbyter and deacon underwent considerable changes in its practical exercise. At some points of crisis in the history of the Church, the continuing functions of ministry were in some places and communities distributed according to structures other than the predominant threefold pattern. Sometimes appeal was made to the New Testament in justification of these other patterns. In other cases, the restructuring of

Lima/82

19. The New Testament does not describe a single pattern of ministry which might serve as a blueprint or continuing norm for all future ministry in the Church. In the New Testament there appears rather a variety of forms which existed at different places and times. As the Holy Spirit continued to lead the Church in life, worship and mission, certain elements from this early variety were further developed and became settled into a more universal pattern of ministry. During the second and third centuries, a three-fold pattern of bishop, presbyter and deacon became established as the pattern of ordained ministry throughout the Church. In succeeding centuries, the ministry by bishop, presbyter and deacon underwent considerable changes in its practical exercise. At some points of crisis in the history of the Church, the continuing functions of ministry were in some places and communities distributed according to structures other than the predominant threefold pattern. Sometimes appeal was made to the New Testament in justification of these other patterns. In other cases, the restructuring of

350

Geneva/6-80 [cont.]
held to lie within the competence of the Church as it adapted to changed circumstances.

Rome/11-80 [cont.]
ministry was held to lie within the competence of the Church as it adapted to changed circumstances.

Because there is no single New Testament pattern, and because the Spirit has many times led the Church to adapt its ministries to contextual needs, the threefold ministry of bishop, priest, and deacon may serve today as expression, and means for the realization, of the unity we seek. Other forms of the ordained ministry have also been blessed with the gifts of the Holy Spirit. But the threefold ministry was the generally accepted pattern in the Church of the early centuries. It has been retained by the majority of churches up to the present day. In some churches it functions even if different names are used. It provides an appropriate framework within which the functions of the ordained ministry can be carried out.

Annecy/81 [cont.]
ministry was held to lie within the competence of the Church as it adapted to changed circumstances.

Lima/82 [cont.]
ministry was held to lie within the competence of the Church as it adapted to changed circumstances.

Geneva/6-80

20. In order to arrive at a common view on the threefold ministry, it is important to be aware of the changes it underwent at an early stage in the history of the Church. The earliest evidence refers to the threefold ministry as the pattern of the ordained ministry in the local eucharistic community. The bishop was the leader of the community. He proclaimed the Word and presided over the celebration of the eucharist. He was surrounded by a college of presbyters who shared in his tasks. Deacons fostered the diakonia of the community.

Rome/11-80

20. It is important for this purpose to be aware of the changes the threefold ministry underwent at an early stage in the history of the Church. In the earliest instances, where threefold ministry is mentioned, the reference is to the local eucharistic community. The bishop was the leader of the community. He proclaimed the Word and presided over the celebration of the eucharist. He was surrounded by a college of presbyters and by deacons who assisted in his tasks. Deacons fostered the diakonia of the community.

Annecy/81

19. It is important for this purpose to be aware of the changes the threefold ministry underwent at an early stage in the history of the Church. In the earliest instances, where threefold ministry is mentioned, the reference is to the local eucharistic community. The bishop was the leader of the community. He proclaimed the Word and presided over the celebration of the eucharist. He was surrounded by a college of presbyters and by deacons who assisted in his tasks. Deacons fostered the diakonia of the community.

Lima/82

20. It is important to be aware of the changes the threefold ministry has undergone in the history of the Church. In the earliest instances, where threefold ministry is mentioned, the reference is to the local eucharistic community. The bishop was the leader of the community. He was ordained and installed to proclaim the Word and preside over the celebration of the eucharist. He was surrounded by a college of presbyters and by deacons who assisted in his tasks. In this context the bishop's ministry was a focus of unity within the whole community.

Geneva/6-80

21. Soon, however, the functions were modified. Bishops began increasingly to exercise *episkopé* over several local communities at the same time. In the first generation, apostles had exercised *episkopé* in the wider Church. Later Timothy and Titus are recorded to have fulfilled a function of oversight in a given area. Now this apostolic task is carried out in a new way by the bishops. They provide a focus for unity in life and witness within areas comprising several eucharistic communities. As a consequence, presbyters and deacons are assigned new roles. The presbyters become the leaders of the local eucharistic community, and as assistants of the bishops deacons receive responsibilities in the larger area.

Rome/11-80

21. Soon, however, the functions were modified. Bishops began increasingly to exercise *episkopé* over several local communities at the same time. In the first generation, the apostles had exercised *episkopé* in the whole Church. Later Timothy and Titus are recorded to have fulfilled a function of *episkopé* in a given area. Now this apostolic task is carried out in a new way by the bishops. They provide a focus for unity in life and witness within areas comprising several eucharistic communities. As a consequence, presbyters and deacons are assigned new roles. The presbyters become the leaders of the local eucharistic community, and as assistants of the bishops deacons receive responsibilities in the larger area.

Annecy/81

20. Soon, however, the functions were modified. Bishops began increasingly to exercise *episkopé* over several local communities at the same time. In the first generation, apostles had exercised *episkopé* in the wider Church. Later Timothy and Titus are recorded to have fulfilled a function of *episkopé* in a given area. Later again this apostolic task is carried out in a new way by the bishops. They provide a focus for unity in life and witness within areas comprising several eucharistic communities. As a consequence, presbyters and deacons are assigned new roles. The presbyters become the leaders of the local eucharistic community, and as assistants of the bishops deacons receive responsibilities in the larger area.

Lima/82

21. Soon, however, the functions were modified. Bishops began increasingly to exercise *episkopé* over several local communities at the same time. In the first generation, apostles had exercised *episkopé* in the wider Church. Later Timothy and Titus are recorded to have fulfilled a function of *episkopé* in a given area. Later again this apostolic task is carried out in a new way by the bishops. They provide a focus for unity in life and witness within areas comprising several eucharistic communities. As a consequence, presbyters and deacons are assigned new roles. The presbyters become the leaders of the local eucharistic community, and as assistants of the bishops deacons receive responsibilities in the larger area.

Geneva/6-80
18-Commentary:

The earliest Church knew both the travelling ministry of such missionaries as Paul and the local ministry of leadership in places where the Gospel was received. At local level, organizational patterns appear to have varied according to circumstances. The Acts of the Apostles mention for Jerusalem the Twelve and the Seven, and later James and the elders; and for Antioch, prophets and teachers (Acts 6: 16; 15: 1322; 13:1). The letters to Corinth speak of apostles, prophets and teachers (I Cor 12: 28); so too does the letter to the Romans, which also speaks of deacons or assistants (Rom 16: 1). In Philippi, the secular terms *episkopoi* and *diakonoi* were together used for Christian ministers (Phil 1:1). Several of these ministries are ascribed to both women and men. While some were appointed by the laying on of hands, there is no indication of this procedure in other cases. Whatever their names, the purpose of these ministries was to proclaim the Word of God, to transmit and safeguard the original content of the Gospel, to feed and strengthen the faith, discipline and

Rome/11-80
18-Commentary:

The earliest Church knew both the travelling ministry of such missionaries as Paul and the local ministry of leadership in places where the Gospel was received. At local level, organizational patterns appear to have varied according to circumstances. The Act of the Apostles mentioned for Jerusalem the Twelve and the Seven, and later James and the elders; and for Antioch prophets and teachers (Acts 6:16; 15: 1322; 13:1). The letters to Corinth speak of apostles, prophets and teachers (I Cor 12:28); so too does the letter to the Romans, which also speaks of deacons or assistants (Rom 16:1). In Philippi, the secular terms *episkopoi* and *diakonoi* were together used for Christian ministers (Phil 1:1). Several of these ministries are ascribed to both women and men. While some were appointed by the laying on of hands, there is no indication of this procedure in other cases. Whatever their names, the purpose of these ministries was to proclaim the Word of God, to transmit and safeguard the original content of the Gospel, to feed and strengthen the faith, discipline and

Annecy/81
20-Commentary:

The earliest Church knew both the travelling ministry of such missionaries as Paul and the local ministry of leadership in places where the Gospel was received. At local level, organizational patterns appear to have varied according to circumstances. The Acts of the Apostles mentioned for Jerusalem the Twelve and the Seven, and later James and the elders; and for Antioch, prophets and teachers (Acts 6: 16; 15: 1322; 13:1). The letters to Corinth speak of apostles, prophets and teachers (I Cor 12: 28); so too does the letter to the Romans, which also speaks of deacons or assistants (Rom 16: 1). In Philippi, the secular terms *episkopoi* and *diakonoi* were together used for Christian ministers (Phil 1:1). Several of these ministries are ascribed to both women and men. While some were appointed by the laying on of hands, there is no indication of this procedure in other cases. Whatever their names, the purpose of these ministries was to proclaim the Word of God, to transmit and safeguard the original content of the Gospel, to feed and strengthen the faith, discipline and

Lima/82
21-Commentary:

The earliest Church knew both the travelling ministry of such missionaries as Paul and the local ministry of leadership in places where the Gospel was received. At local level, organizational patterns appear to have varied according to circumstances. The Acts of the Apostles mentioned for Jerusalem the Twelve and the Seven, and later James and the elders; and for Antioch, prophets and teachers (Acts 6: 16; 15: 1322; 13:1). The letters to Corinth speak of apostles, prophets and teachers (I Cor 12: 28); so too does the letter to the Romans, which also speaks of deacons or assistants (Rom 16: 1). In Philippi, the secular terms *episkopoi* and *diakonoi* were together used for Christian ministers (Phil 1:1). Several of these ministries are ascribed to both women and men. While some were appointed by the laying on of hands, there is no indication of this procedure in other cases. Whatever their names, the purpose of these ministries was to proclaim the Word of God, to transmit and safeguard the original content of the Gospel, to feed and strengthen the faith, discipline and

Geneva/6-80 [cont.]

service of the Christian communities, and to protect and foster unity within and among them. These have been the constant duties of ministry throughout the developments and crises of Christian history.

Geneva/6-80

19. Though other forms of the ordained ministry have been blessed with the gifts of the Holy Spirit there are good reasons for accepting the threefold form of bishops, presbyters and deacons as a basis for establishing a common form of the ordained ministry today. On the other hand, it has been the generally accepted pattern in the Church of the early centuries and has been retained by the majority of churches up to the present day. In some churches it functions even if different names are used. On the other hand, it provides a valid framework within which the functions of the ordained ministry can be carried out.

Rome/11-80 [cont.]

service of the Christian communities, and to protect and foster unity within and among them. These have been the constant duties of ministry throughout the developments and crises of Christian history.

Rome/11-80

Annecy/81 [cont.]

service of the Christian communities, and to protect and foster unity within and among them. These have been the constant duties of ministry throughout the developments and crises of Christian history.

Annecy/81

21. Although there is no single New Testament pattern, although the Spirit has many times led the Church to adapt its ministries to contextual needs and although other forms of the ordained ministry have been blessed with the gifts of the Holy Spirit, nevertheless the threefold ministry of bishop, presbyter and deacon may serve today as an expression of the unity we seek and also as a means for achieving it. The reasons for this suggestion are historical, pastoral and systematic. Historically, it is true to say, the threefold ministry became the generally accepted pattern in the Church of the early centuries and is still retained today by many churches. Another reason is more pastoral and systematic. In the fulfilment of their mission and service the churches need people

Lima/82 [cont.]

service of the Christian communities, and to protect and foster unity within and among them. These have been the constant duties of ministry throughout the developments and crises of Christian history.

Lima/82

22. Although there is no single New Testament pattern, although the Spirit has many times led the Church to adapt its ministries to contextual needs, and although other forms of the ordained ministry have been blessed with the gifts of the Holy Spirit, nevertheless the threefold ministry of bishop, presbyter and deacon may serve today as an expression of the unity we seek and also as a means for achieving it. Historically, it is true to say, the threefold ministry became the generally accepted pattern in the Church of the early centuries and is still retained today by many churches. In the fulfilment of their mission and service the churches need people who in different ways express and perform the tasks of the ordained ministry in its diaconal, presbyteral and episcopal aspects

Geneva/6-80 [cont.]

22. How can this threefold form be adapted for the Church today? In fact, the question must be asked by all the churches. The primary issue is not that some churches, for the sake of unity, should return to the inherited pattern but rather that all churches are called upon to give the fullest possible expression to its potential with a view to a more effective witness of the Church in the world.

Geneva/6-80
22-Commentary:
The pattern stands in need of reform in all churches. In some, the college of elders in the local eucharistic community has disappeared. In others, the functions of deacons have been reduced to an assistant role in the celebration of the liturgy; they have ceased to fulfil any function with regard to the diaconal witness of the Church. In some

---

Rome/11-80 [cont.]

19. How can this threefold form be adapted for the Church today? In fact, the question must be asked by all the churches. The primary issue is not that some churches, for the sake of unity, should return to the traditional pattern but rather that all churches are called upon to give the fullest possible expression to its potential with a view to a more effective witness of the Church in the world.

Rome/11-80
19-Commentary:
The pattern stands in need of reform in all churches. In some, the collegial dimension of leadership in the local eucharistic community has suffered. In others, the functions of deacons have been reduced to an assistant role in the celebration of the liturgy; they have ceased to fulfil any function with regard to the diaconal witness of the Church. In some

---

Annecy/81 [cont.]

who in different ways express and perform the tasks of the ordained ministry in its diaconal, presbyteral and episcopal aspects and functions. Indeed, in some churches, these ministerial functions are performed in this threefold fashion even if the traditional names are not used.

How can this threefold ministry be adapted for the Church today? In fact, the question must be asked by all the churches. The primary issue is not that some churches, for the sake of unity, should return to the traditional pattern but rather that all churches are called upon to give the fullest possible expression to its potential with a view to a more effective witness of the Church in the world.

Annecy/81
21-Commentary:
The pattern stands in need of reform in all churches. In some, the collegial dimension of leadership in the local eucharistic community has suffered. In others, the functions of deacons have been reduced to an assistant role in the celebration of the liturgy; they have ceased to fulfil any function with regard to the diaconal witness of the Church. In

---

Lima/82 [cont.]

and functions.

23. The Church as the body of Christ and the eschatological people of God is constituted by the Holy Spirit through a diversity of gifts or ministries. Among these gifts a ministry of *episkope* is necessary to express and safeguard the unity of the body. Every church needs this ministry of unity in some form in order to be the Church of God, a sign of the one body of Christ, a sign of the unity of all in the Kingdom.

Lima/82
24. The threefold pattern stands evidently in need of reform. In some churches the collegial dimension of leadership in the eucharistic community has suffered diminution. In others, the function of deacons has been reduced to an assistant role in the celebration of the liturgy: they have ceased to fulfil any function with regard to the diaconal witness of the Church. In general, the

356

Geneva/6-80 [cont.]
cases, churches which have not formally kept the threefold form have, in fact, better maintained certain of its original intentions.

Rome/11-80 [cont.]
some cases, churches which have not formally kept the threefold form have, in fact, maintained certain of its original intentions.

Annecy/81 [cont.]
some cases, churches which have not formally kept the threefold form have, in fact, maintained certain of its original intentions.

Lima/82 [cont.]
relation of the presbyterate to the episcopal ministry has been discussed throughout the centuries, and the degree of the presbyter's participation in the episcopal ministry is still for many an unresolved question of far-reaching ecumenical importance. In some cases, churches which have not formally kept the threefold form have, in fact, maintained certain of its original patterns.

25. The traditional threefold pattern thus raises questions for all the churches. Churches maintaining the threefold pattern will need to ask how its potential can be fully developed for the most effective witness of the Church in this world. In this task churches not having the threefold pattern should also participate. They will further need to ask themselves whether the threefold pattern as developed does not have a powerful claim to be accepted by them.

The Lima text eliminates the *title* of the first subsection in the 6/80 text (consisting of one opening paragraph and its commentary), entitled, "Historical beginnings and developments." U. Kühn was among those who were proposing both the changing of the headings and the reordering of the contents of part III of the 6/80 text.[133] It uses, however, the *content* of the subsection as the initial content of its own first subsection, entitled, "Bishops, presbyters and deacons." Thus is acknowledged outright the overwhelming predominance of the threefold office in the very early development of office in the Church. A more developmental phrase, "during the second and third centuries,"[134] instead of the phrase, "by the second and third centuries,"[135] is used. This newer phrase, along with the one, "were further developed," in the same paragraph of the Lima text, indicates a deepening of an appreciation for historical development even though it is acknowledged that the threefold pattern was settled relatively early on in Christian times. W. Pannenberg was the one who had suggested the addition of this phrase, "were fully developed." He explained that "this is necessary in order to do justice to the fact that e.g. the episcopacy in the form it was developed since the second century was not even present as an element in the NT."[136] No final historical judgment is made, however, as to exactly when the pattern was universally set. This is indicated by the elimination[137] of the phrase, "at an early stage"[138] in reference to changes which the threefold ministry had undergone. Thus is left open-ended any determination of exactly when any developments took place.

There is clear acknowledgement of the work of the Holy Spirit in leading the Church "to adapt its ministries to contextual needs" with the threefold ministry serving "*today* as an expression of the unity we seek and also as a means for

---

[133]Cf. Kühn Proposals, Nov 2, 1980, p. 1, WCC Archives, Archive Box: "Faith and Order Archives, BEM, 79-82 corr. 81, Lima 82."

[134]§19.

[135]6/80, §18.

[136]W. Pannenberg Comments, Oct. 13, 1980, p. 8, WCC Archives, Archive Box: "Faith and Order, Documents 1980-1981, Circular Letters, 1980-1981.". This particular comment was made in regard to the 6/80 text, §18.

[137]In Lima §20.

[138]6/80, §20.

achieving it."[139] Thus the need for the threefold ministry escapes the narrower context of merely serving "as a basis for establishing a common form of the ordained ministry today."[140] M. Conway had questioned the earlier wording stating that "this could be taken as a requirement of uniformity."[141] G. Gassmann, a Lutheran, observed "that the distinction between bishop and presbyter certainly poses an ecumenical problem, but not the threefold structure as such which has become a problem even for Roman Catholics and Anglicans themselves."[142] Although M. Tanner, an Anglican, finds "it difficult to find *good* reasons for keeping the diaconate,"[143] another Anglican, D. Fraser, states that "England is less happy than the continent on the minimal role of deacons."[144] An important emphasis is placed on the need for the ordained ministry, and therefore the threefold ministry, "to be constitutionally or canonically ordered."[145] Yet the Lima text prefers people to structures. For the phrase, "it provides a valid framework,"[146] is replaced by the phrase, "the churches need people."[147] And these people "*express*" as well as "perform the tasks of the ordained ministry in its diaconal, presbyteral and episcopal *aspects* and functions."[148] Thus "being" as well as "doing" or "functioning" is deemed important and sacramentality is emphasized.

At Lima less imposing a claim is made regarding the numbers of churches generally accepting and retaining the threefold pattern: "the majority of churches"

---

[139]§22. Emphasis added.

[140]6/80, §19.

[141]Sept. 5, 1980, Archives, Archive Box: "Faith and Order, Documents 1980-1981, Circular Letters, 1980-1981."

[142]Nov. 11, 1981, Archives, Archive Box: "Faith and Order Archives, BEM, 79-82 corr. 81, Lima 82."

[143]Oct. 1, 1980, p. 2, Archives, Archive Box: "Faith and Order, Documents 1980-1981, Circular Letters, 1980-1981."

[144]Oct. 26, 1981, p. 4, Archives, Archive Box: "Faith and Order Archives, BEM, 79-82 corr. 81, Lima 82."

[145]§27.

[146]6/80, §19. Cf. M. Conway, Sept. 5, 1980, p. 4, Archives, Archive Box: "Faith and Order, Documents 1980-1981, Circular Letters, 1980-1981."

[147]§22.

[148]§22. Emphasis added.

becomes "many churches."[149] Furthermore at Lima an emphasis is placed on the threefold pattern standing clearly in need of reform. This emphasis is accomplished by placing a paragraph previously located in the Commentary section[150] into the body of the text.[151] L. Mudge contended that the earlier commentary material "contains assertions which, from the 'protestant' point of view, are needed to balance assertions in the main text."[152] In that same paragraph the Lima text deletes the word, "better," in describing the fact that "in some cases, churches which have not formally kept the threefold form have, in fact, maintained certain of its original patterns."[153] That deletion avoids a judgment being made on such churches regarding their effectiveness in maintaining original "intentions" as well as "patterns."[154]

Lima, however, revises some earlier material and thereby expresses the challenge which the threefold pattern presents "to all the churches."[155] In the case of those who do not have it the threefold pattern may "have a powerful claim to be accepted by them."[156] In the case of both those who have it and those who do not there is the task of developing the threefold pattern so that its recognized potential can be realized "for the most effective witness of the Church in this world."[157] In any case the development of that potential is paramount.

---

[149]6/80, §19; Lima, §22.

[150]6/80, §22-Commentary.

[151]Cf. Lima, §24.

[152]Oct. 27, 1980, p. 1, Archives, Archive Box: "Faith and Order Archives, BEM, 79-82 corr. 81, Lima 82."

[153]Lima, §24.

[154]The Lima text substitutes "patterns" for "intentions." Thus it betrays its tendency to prefer structures and signs to unspecified spiritual realities.

[155]§25 which corresponds to Geneva 6/80, §22 (and earlier in Geneva 1/80, §21, sentence no. 8).

[156]Lima 1/82, §25.

[157]Ibid.

B. GUIDING PRINCIPLES FOR THE EXERCISE OF THE ORDAINED MINISTRY IN THE CHURCH.

Public appointment to ministry and accountability in ministry are emphasized here. A more hortatory and less prescriptive tone is accomplished, with each succeeding text, by the careful use of language. That is especially in evidence here in reference to an appreciation of the personal, collegial and communal dimensions of the ordained ministry. The two church polities, presbyterial (governed by a council of elders) and episcopal (governed by a monarchical bishop), are carefully balanced by use of the phrase, "collegial body," in place of the phrase, "college of elders."

Geneva/6-80

23. Three considerations are important in this respect. The ordained ministry should be exercised in a *personal* way. The presence of Christ among his people can most effectively be pointed to by one person proclaiming the Gospel and calling the community to serve the Lord in unity of life and witness. The ordained ministry needs to be exercised in a *collegial* way, i.e. there is need for a college of ordained ministers sharing in the common task of representing the concerns of the community. Finally, the intimate relationship between the ordained ministry and the community must find expression in a *communal* dimension, i.e. the exercise of the ordained ministry must be rooted in the life of the community and requires its effective participation in the discovery of God's will and the guidance of the Spirit.

Rome/11-80

22. Three considerations are important in this respect. The ordained ministry should be exercised in a *personal* way, i.e. the presence of Christ among his people can most effectively be pointed to by the person ordained to proclaim the Gospel and to call the community to serve the Lord in unity of life and witness. The ordained ministry needs to be exercised in a *collegial* way, i.e. there is need for a college of ordained ministers sharing in the common task of representing the concerns of the community. Finally, the intimate relationship between the ordained ministry and the community must find expression in a *communal* dimension, i.e. the exercise of the ordained ministry must be rooted in the life of the community and requires its effective participation in the discovery of God's will and the guidance of the Spirit.

Annecy/81

22. Three considerations are important in this respect. The ordained ministry should be exercised in a personal, collegial and communal way. *Personal* in that the presence of Christ among his people can most effectively be pointed to by the person ordained to proclaim the Gospel and to call the community to serve the Lord in unity of life and witness. *Collegial*, for there is need for a college of ordained ministers sharing in the common task of representing the concerns of the community. Finally, the intimate relationship between the ordained ministry and the community must find expression in a *communal* dimension where the exercise of the ordained ministry must be rooted in the life of the community and requires its effective participation in the discovery of God's will and the guidance of the Spirit.

Lima/82

26. Three considerations are important in this respect. The ordained ministry should be exercised in a personal, collegial and communal way. It should be *personal* because the presence of Christ among his people can most effectively be pointed to by the person ordained to proclaim the Gospel and to call the community to serve the Lord in unity of life and witness. It should also be *collegial*, for there is need for a college of ordained ministers sharing in the common task of representing the concerns of the community. Finally, the intimate relationship between the ordained ministry and the community should find expression in a *communal* dimension where the exercise of the ordained ministry is rooted in the life of the community and requires the community's effective participation in the discovery of God's will and the guidance of the Spirit.

Geneva/6-80

23-Commentary:

These three aspects need to be kept together. In various churches, one or the other has been over-emphasized at the expense of the others. In some churches, the personal dimension of the ordained ministry tends to diminish the collegial and communal dimensions. In other churches, the collegial or communal dimension takes so much importance that the ordained ministry loses its personal dimension. Each church needs to ask itself in what way the exercise of the ordained ministry in its midst has suffered in the course of history.

The recognition of these three dimensions lies behind a recommendation made by the first World Conference on Faith and Order at Lausanne in 1927: "In view of (i) the place which the episcopate, the council of presbyters and the congregation of the faithful, respectively, had in the constitution of the early Church, and (ii) the fact that episcopal, presbyteral and congregational systems of government are each today, and have been for centuries, accepted by great commu-

Rome/11-80

22-Commentary

The three aspects need to be kept together. In various churches, one or the other has been over-emphasized at the expense of the others. In some churches, the personal dimension of the ordained ministry tends to diminish the collegial and communal dimensions. In other churches, the collegial or communal dimension takes so much importance that the ordained ministry loses its personal dimension. Each church needs to ask itself in what way the exercise of the ordained ministry in its midst has suffered in the course of history.

An appreciation of these three dimensions of all ordained ministry lies behind a recommendation made by the first World Conference on Faith and Order at Lausanne in 1927: "In view of (i) the place which the episcopate, the council of presbyters and the congregation of the faithful, respectively, had in the constitution of the early Church, and (ii) the fact that episcopal, presbyteral and congregational systems of government are each today, and have been for centuries, accepted by

Annecy/81

22-Commentary:

These three aspects need to be kept together. In various churches, one or the other has been over-emphasised at the expense of the others. In some churches, the personal dimension of the ordained ministry tends to diminish the collegial and communal dimensions. In other churches, the collegial or communal dimension takes so much importance that the ordained ministry loses its personal dimension. Each church needs to ask itself in what way its exercise of the ordained ministry in its midst has suffered in the course of history.

An appreciation of these three dimensions lies behind a recommendation made by the first World Conference on Faith and Order at Lausanne in 1927: "In view of (i) the place which the episcopate, the council of presbyters and the congregation of the faithful, respectively, had in the constitution of the early Church, and (ii) the fact that episcopal, presbyteral and congregational systems of government are each today, and have been for centuries, accepted by great commu-

Lima/82

26-Commentary:

These three aspects need to be kept together. In various churches one or another has been overemphasized at the expense of the others. In some churches, the personal dimension of the ordained ministry tends to diminish the collegial and communal dimensions. In other churches, the collegial or communal dimension takes so much importance that the ordained ministry loses its personal dimension. Each church needs to ask itself in what way its exercise of the ordained ministry has suffered in the course of history.

An appreciation of these three dimensions lies behind a recommendation made by the first World Conference on Faith and Order at Lausanne in 1927: "In view of (i) the place which the episcopate, the council of presbyters and the congregation of the faithful, respectively, had in the constitution of the early Church, and (ii) the fact that episcopal, presbyteral and congregational systems of government are each today, and have been for centuries, accepted by great communions in Christendom, and (iii) the

Geneva/6-80 [cont.]

nions in Christendom, and (iii) the fact that episcopal, presbyteral and congregational systems are each believed by many to be essential to the good order of the Church, we therefore recognize that these several elements must all, under conditions which require further study, have an appropriate place in the order of life of a reunited Church ..."

Rome/11-80 [cont.]

great communions in Christendom, and (iii) the fact that episcopal, presbyteral and congregational systems are each believed by many to be essential to the good order of the Church, we therefore recognize that these several elements must all, under conditions which require further study, have an appropriate place in the order of life of a reunited Church ...".

Annecy/81 [cont.]

nions in Christendom, and (iii) the fact that episcopal, presbyteral and congregational systems are each believed by many to be essential to the good order of the Church, we therefore recognize that these several elements must all, under conditions which require further study, have an appropriate place in the order of life of a reunited Church ..."

Lima/82 [cont.]

fact that episcopal, presbyteral and congregational systems are each believed by many to be essential to the good order of the Church, we therefore recognize that these several elements must all, under conditions which require further study, have an appropriate place in the order of life of a reunited Church ..."

Geneva/6-80

24. At all levels of the Church's life the ordained ministry needs to be exercised in such a way that these three dimensions can find adequate expression. At the level of the local eucharistic community there is need for an ordained minister acting within a college of elders. Strong emphasis will be placed on the active participation of all members in the life and the decision-making of the community. Deacons will stimulate its diaconal witness. At the level of an area there is again need for an ordained minister exercising a service of unity. The collegial and communal dimensions will find expression in regular representative synodal gatherings. Deacons will foster the cohesion of the common witness of the communities.

Rome/11-80

23. At all levels of the Church's life the ordained ministry needs to be exercised in such a way that these three dimensions can find adequate expression. At the level of the local eucharistic community there is need for an ordained minister acting within a collegial body. Strong emphasis will be placed on the active participation of all members in the life and the decision-making of the community. Deacons will stimulate its diaconal witness. At the level of an area there is again need for an ordained minister exercising a service of unity. The collegial and communal dimension will find expression in regular representative synodal gatherings. Deacons will foster the cohesion of the common witness of the communities.

Annecy/81

23. At all levels of the Church's life the ordained ministry needs to be exercised in such a way that these three dimensions can find adequate expression. At the level of the local eucharistic community there is need for an ordained minister acting within a collegial body. Strong emphasis will be placed on the active participation of all members in the life and the decision-making of the community. At the level of an area there is again need for an ordained minister exercising a service of unity. The collegial and communal dimensions will find expression in regular representative synodal gatherings.

Lima/82

27. The ordained ministry needs to be constitutionally or canonically ordered and exercised in the Church in such a way that each of these three dimensions can find adequate expression. At the level of the local eucharistic community there is need for an ordained minister acting within a collegial body. Strong emphasis should be placed on the active participation of all members in the life and the decision-making of the community. At the regional level there is again need for an ordained minister exercising a service of unity. The collegial and communal dimensions will find expression in regular representative synodal gatherings.

The phrase, "by one person proclaiming the Gospel and calling the community,"[158] is replaced by the phrase, "by the person ordained to proclaim the Gospel and to call the community."[159] G. Moede influenced the revision with his "point that the public appointment and accountability is important."[160] As mentioned above, an addition is made in this section asserting the need for the ordained ministry "to be constitutionally or canonically ordered" as well as exercised in such a way that its personal, collegial and communal dimensions be adequately expressed.[161]

Also, terms, such as, "must," "must be," and "will," are replaced by the terms, "should," "is," and "should," respectively, in order to give a more hortatory, less prescriptive tone to the expression of the personal, collegial and communal dimensions of ordained ministry.[162] In this same vein, the phrase, "an *appreciation* of these three dimensions," replaces the phrase, "the *recognition* of these three dimensions."[163]

In keeping with the change in wording earlier in the text[164] the phrase, "college of elders,"[165] is changed to the phrase, "collegial body."[166] E. Flesseman-van-Leer contends that the change is required because there is being followed "here a particular church tradition in opposition to the reformed tradition where elders = presbyters form the pivotal ordained ministry."[167] L. Mudge stated that, "as a Presbyterian I feel a certain gratification to read that the earliest settled order we know had a minister-episcopos surrounded by elders. But I am confused by the intention . . . of introducing 'elders' in the light of the bishop-priest-deacon ordering for which this document . . . opts. These 'elders' could not be ordained, and that

---

[158]6/80, §23.

[159]11/80, §22.

[160]Sept. 30, 1980, p. 2, Archives, Archive Box: "Faith and Order, Documents 1980-1981, Circular Letters, 1980-1981."

[161]§27.

[162]6/80. §s 23-24; Lima, §s 26-27.

[163]6/80. §23-Commentary; Lima, §26-Commentary. Emphasis added.

[164]6/80. §22-C and 1/82, §24.

[165]6/80. §24.

[166]11/80, §23; 1/82, §27.

[167]Oct. 22, 1980, p. 1, Archive Box: "Faith and Order, Documents 1980-1981, Circular Letters, 1980-1981."

would *not* please Presbyterians."[168] M. Conway notes that here "there is considerable potential confusion about deacons and elders."[169]

C. FUNCTIONS OF BISHOPS, PRESBYTERS AND DEACONS.

BISHOPS.

The ministry of *episkopé*, as an indispensable ministry of unity in the church, is strongly endorsed. Bishops serve the apostolicity and unity of the church's teaching, worship and sacramental life. A brief mention of this service of unity at the wider (regional) and even universal level gives some, but not much, importance to the needs of the church beyond each local eucharistic community. No mention is made of the petrine ministry or of the papacy. The unwillingness of the architects of these texts to face this issue may indicate much lingering fear that such universal church structures tend to be accompanied by the misuse of power and authority.

---

[168]Oct. 27, 1980, p. 2, Archive Box: "Faith and Order Archives, BEM, 79-82 corr. 81, Lima 82."

[169]Sept. 5, 1980, p. 5, Archive Box: "Faith and Order, Documents 1980-1981, Circular Letters, 1980-1981."

Geneva/6-80

25. What can then be said about the functions of bishops, presbyters and deacons? Obviously, a uniform answer to this question is not required for the mutual recognition of the ordained ministry. As long as there is agreement on the nature and basic form of the ordained ministry, the precise assignment of functions may vary from place to place. The following considerations are therefore offered in a tentative way.

Rome/11-80

24. What can then be said about the functions of bishops, presbyters and deacons? A uniform answer to this question is not required for the mutual recognition of the ordained ministry. As long as there is agreement on the nature and basic form of the ordained ministry, the precise assignment of functions may vary from place to place. The following considerations are therefore offered in a tentative way.

Annecy/81

24. What can then be said about the functions and even the titles of bishops, presbyters and deacons? A uniform answer to this question is not required for the mutual recognition of the ordained ministry. The following considerations on functions are, however, offered in a tentative way.

Lima/82

28. What can then be said about the functions and even the titles of bishops, presbyters and deacons? A uniform answer to this question is not required for the mutual recognition of the ordained ministry. The following considerations on functions are, however, offered in a tentative way.

Geneva/6-80

26. *Bishops* preach the Word, preside at the sacraments, and administer discipline in such a way as to be representative pastoral ministers of oversight, continuity and unity in the Church. They have pastoral oversight of the area to which they are called. They maintain the apostolicity and unity of the Church's worship and sacramental life. They, in communion with the presbyters and deacons and the whole community, are responsible for the orderly transfer of ministerial authority in the Church.

Rome/11-80

25. *Bishops* preach the Word, preside at the sacraments, and administer discipline in such a way as to be representative pastoral ministers of oversight, continuity and unity in the Church. They have pastoral oversight of the area to which they are called. They serve the apostolicity and unity of the Church's teaching, worship and sacramental life. They have responsibility for leadership in the Church's mission. They relate the Christian community in their area to the wider Church, and the universal Church to their community. They, in communion with the presbyters and deacons and the whole community, are responsible for the orderly transfer of ministerial authority in the Church.

Annecy/81

25. *Bishops* preach the Word, preside at the sacraments, and administer discipline in such a way as to be representative pastoral ministers of oversight, continuity and unity in the Church. They have pastoral oversight of the area to which they are called. They serve the apostolicity and unity of the Church's teaching, worship and sacramental life. They have responsibility for leadership in the Church's mission. They relate the Christian community in their area to the wider Church, and the universal Church to their community. They, in communion with the presbyters and deacons and the whole community, are responsible for the orderly transfer of ministerial authority in the Church.

Lima/82

29. *Bishops* preach the Word, preside at the sacraments, and administer discipline in such a way as to be representative pastoral ministers of oversight, continuity and unity in the Church. They have pastoral oversight of the area to which they are called. They serve the apostolicity and unity of the Church's teaching, worship and sacramental life. They have responsibility for leadership in the Church's mission. They relate the Christian community in their area to the wider Church, and the universal Church to their community. They, in communion with the presbyters and deacons and the whole community, are responsible for the orderly transfer of ministerial authority in the Church.

Earlier in the major section, of which this subsection is a part, there are several references to the bishop's ministry or to *episkopé*. A new paragraph is added in that earlier subsection in the Lima text.[170] That paragraph strongly emphasizes the necessity of the ministry of *episkopé* as the ministry of unity. Without some form of that ministry the Church cannot "be the Church of God, the one body of Christ, a sign of the unity of all in the Kingdom."[171] This ringing endorsement of the ministry of *episkopé* as essential to the nature of the Church today canonizes a comment made about early evidence of the threefold ministry in the history of the Church. That comment noted that "the bishop's ministry was a focus of unity within the whole community."[172]

In that same paragraph it is noted that the earliest historical evidence points to the fact that the bishop not only proclaimed the Word and presided over the celebration of the eucharist but also "was ordained and installed"[173] to do so. There is a whole new emphasis on the ministry of the bishop in the Lima text. This emphasis is evinced again in the very subsection under consideration here. Bishops now "serve" rather than merely "maintain" the "apostolicity and unity of the Church's *teaching* (added at Lima), worship and sacramental life."[174] In another place it is noted that "a service of unity" is needed from an ordained minister (presumably a bishop) "at the regional level."[175] In earlier texts the geographical or jurisdictional reference was less technical, namely, "the level of an area."[176]

The same emphasis on the ministry of bishops is shown with the addition of these two sentences: "They (Bishops) have responsibility for leadership in the Church's mission. They relate the Christian community in their area to the wider Church, and the universal Church to their community."[177] This change was directly

---

[170] §23.

[171] Idem.

[172] §20.

[173] Idem.

[174] Lima, §29; 6/80, §26.

[175] §27.

[176] 6/80, §24.

[177] Lima, §29.

influenced by M. Conway[178] and perhaps indirectly influenced by P. Ricca who noted regarding the paragraphs in this section that "the personal dimension of ministry received greater emphasis than the communal dimension."[179] It is to be noted, however, that it is precisely here that the issue of the papacy is simply not faced in the text. M. Thurian related to the present writer in personal interviews that "in Accra the emphasis is on ordained ministry in general, then, subsequent to Accra, the focus shifted to the three-fold ministry and not on the structure of the Church *per se*."[180] Furthermore on the same occasion Thurian affirmed that the issue of overall church structure was not faced in these texts because the question of structure is too much a question of power and not enough a question of service! It should be noted here as well what the Consultation of Orthodox Theologians had concluded in their meeting of May 31-June 2, 1979 at Chambésy:

> Though it was recognized that the issue of primacy among the churches was an important problem and needs to be taken up in ecumenical discussion, doubts were expressed whether it should be included in a text on the ministry. Perhaps the text could state that primacy is an issue arising from the relationship between the local churches and, therefore strictly speaking, goes beyond the theme of priesthood.

Even this minimal reference to primacy (and therefore, papacy) was avoided in all the texts on ministry.

PRESBYTERS.

The Lima text faces but does not resolve the theological controversy about the precise relationship between the presbyterate and the episcopacy. Also left unresolved is the relationship between presbyters and elders This unresolvedness keeps open-ended various options in regard to church polity. Left unresolved as well are the defining the term, "local church," and naming the specific tasks of presbyters.

---

[178]Sept. 5, 1980, p. 5, Archive Box: "Faith and Order, Documents 1980-1981, Circular Letters, 1980-1981."

[179]Sept. 25, 1980, p. 1, Archives, Archive Box: "Faith and Order, Documents 1980-1981, Circular Letters, 1980-1981.": "La dimension personnelle du ministère reçoit un poids plus grand que celle communautaire."

[180]Personal interviews with Frère Max Thurian, at the Headquarters of the World Council of Churches, Geneva, Switzerland, April 29-30, 1985.

Geneva/6-80
27. *Presbyters* serve as pastoral ministers of Word and sacraments in a local eucharistic community. They are preachers and teachers of the faith and bear responsibility for the discipline of the congregation to the end that the world may believe and that the entire membership of the Church may be renewed, strengthened and equipped in ministry. Presbyters have particular responsibility for the preparation of members for Christian life and ministry. They preside at acts of the Church such as marriage, declaration of the forgiveness of sin, anointing of the sick and dying, and announcing God's blessing and other rites of the Church.

27-Commentary:
As stated above, at the level of the local eucharistic community the collegial dimension will find expression in a group of elders exercising, together with the presbyter, oversight and pastoral guidance. Elders may be ordained to their ministry.

Rome/11-80
26. *Presbyters* serve as pastoral ministers of Word and sacraments in a local eucharistic community. They are preachers and teachers of the faith, exercise pastoral care, and bear responsibility for the discipline of the congregation to the end that the world may believe and that the entire membership of the Church may be renewed, strengthened and equipped in ministry. Presbyters have particular responsibility for the preparation of members for Christian life and ministry.

Annecy/81
26. *Presbyters* serve as pastoral ministers of Word and sacraments in a local eucharistic community. They are preachers and teachers of the faith, exercise pastoral care, and bear responsibility for the discipline of the congregation to the end that the world may believe and that the entire membership of the Church may be renewed, strengthened and equipped in ministry. Presbyters have particular responsibility for the preparation of members for Christian life and ministry.

Lima/82
30. *Presbyters* serve as pastoral ministers of Word and sacraments in a local eucharistic community. They are preachers and teachers of the faith, exercise pastoral care, and bear responsibility for the discipline of the congregation to the end that the world may believe and that the entire membership of the Church may be renewed, strengthened and equipped in ministry. Presbyters have particular responsibility for the preparation of members for Christian life and ministry.

The Lima text adds a new sentence which acknowledges the uncertain relationship between the presbyterate and the episcopacy. It states that "in general, the relation of the presbyterate to the episcopal ministry has been discussed throughout the centuries, and the degree of the presbyter's participation in the episcopal ministry is still for many an unresolved question of far-reaching ecumenical importance."[181] W. Pannenberg, a Lutheran, had pointed out that in the 6/80 text "the adoption of the notion of the threefold office (bishop, presbyter and deacon) seems questionable . . . (and) it seems especially deplorable that this strategy precludes the possibility of treating the equivalence of bishops and presbyters in terms of their ordination that lasted until this century."[182] G. Gassmann, also a Lutheran, observed "that the distinction between bishop and presbyter certainly poses an ecumenical problem, but not the threefold structure as such."[183] Torrance, in reference to the role of presbyters, as well as bishops, presiding at eucharist[184] noted that the text's treatment of the topic "seems unaware how historically and theologically controversial this is."[185] This addition in the Lima text faces the controversy without resolving it.

References to "the collegial dimension of leadership in the (local) eucharistic community"[186] and "an ordained ministry acting within a collegial body"[187] indicate some ambivalence in the final text. Earlier references to "elders" have been dropped.[188] Are they distinct from presbyters? It seems so in the 6/80 text.[189] By using the term, "collegial dimension," in place of the term, "college of elders," a

---

[181]§24.

[182]Oct. 13, 1980, p. 8, Archive Box: "Faith and Order, Documents 1980-1981, Circular Letters, 1980-1981."

[183]Nov. 11, 1981, p. 3, Archive Box: "Faith and Order Archives, BEM, 79-82 corr. 81, Lima 82."

[184]6/80, §s 26-27.

[185]G.W. Comments, Oct. 26, 1980, p. 4, Archive Box: "Faith and Order Archives, BEM, 79-82 corr. 81, Lima 82."

[186]Lima, §24; 11/80, §19-Commentary.

[187]Lima, §27; 11/80, §23.

[188]6/80, §s 22, 24, and 27-Commentary.

[189]6/80, §27-Commentary. This Commentary paragraph is dropped entirely in the next revision, up to and including the Lima text.

statement about its total disappearance is avoided.[190] A reference to "the collegial dimension of leadership"[191] is made in a more general fashion than "the college of elders."[192] Thus an absolute statement is avoided regarding its total disappearance.[193] This amended statement eventually makes its way into the main text at Lima.[194]

Furthermore the dropping of the word, "local," in the final text of Lima leaves the "eucharistic community" undefined.[195] The total disappearance of 6/80's Commentary paragraph for §27 is an indication that the whole issue of elders has been subsumed under the rubric, "presbyters." And less mandatory and more hortatory is the call for "active participation of all members in the life and the decision-making of the community."[196]

Specific tasks of presbyters are deleted. This is another indication of the intention of the final redactors to keep the question open-ended. Although the phrase, "exercise pastoral care," is added to the overall description of the role of presbyters.[197]

---

[190]Lima, §24; 6/80, §22-Commentary.

[191]1/82, §24. This wording had been introduced in the 11/80 text.

[192]6/80, §22-C.

[193]G. Moede made this commentary on the 6/80 text: "The term college of elders appears without warning or interpretation. Who are they? I find this commentary paragraph (6/80, §22-C) out of place." [G. Moede, Sept. 30, 1980, p. 2, Archives, Archive Box: "Faith and Order, Documents 1980-1981, Circular Letters, 1980-1981."] T.F. Torrance also questions the reference to elders. [G.W. Comments, Oct. 26, 1980, p. 3, Archives, Archive Box: "Faith and Order, Documents 1980-1981, Circular Letters, 1980-1981."]

[194]§24.

[195]Lima, §24, 6/80, §22-Commentary.

[196]Lima, §27.

[197]Lima, §30; 6/80, §27.

DEACONS.

The discussion of the diaconate as such is more and more restricted as these texts evolve. The issue of the office of deacon, however, is used in the texts to discuss other issues facing the church: the reform of the threefold ministry as the inherited pattern, the church's struggling to meet the needs of the world, and the church's struggling to give due recognition, even official status, to a variety of ministries which continue to emerge but which are not easily classified in the threefold scheme.

Geneva/6-80

28. *Deacons* represent to the Church its calling as servant in the world to exemplify the interdependence of worship and service in the Church's life. They will exercise some responsibility in the worship of the congregation and promote its diaconal service. They will fulfil certain administrative tasks.

28-Commentary:

In many churches there is today considerable uncertainty about the need, the rationale, the status and the functions of deacons. In what sense can the diaconate be considered part of the ordained ministry? What is it that distinguishes it from other ministries in the Church (catechists, musicians, etc.)? Why should deacons be ordained while these other ministries do not receive ordination? If they are ordained do

Rome/11-80

27. *Deacons* represent to the Church its calling as servant in the world. By struggling in Christ's name with the myriad needs of societies and persons, deacons exemplify the interdependence of worship and service in the Church's life. They exercise responsibility in the worship of the congregation: for example by reading the Scriptures, preaching and leading the people in prayer. They carry on a ministry of love within the community. They may fulfil certain administrative tasks, or be elected to responsibilities for congregational governance.

27-Commentary.

In many churches there is today considerable uncertainty about the need, the rationale, the status and the functions of deacons. In what sense can the diaconate be considered part of the ordained ministry? What is it that distinguishes it from other ministries in the Church (catechists, musicians, etc.)? Why should deacons be ordained while these other ministries do not receive ordination? If they are ordained do

Annecy/81

27. *Deacons* represent to the Church its calling as servant in the world. By struggling in Christ's name with the myriad needs of societies and persons, deacons exemplify the interdependence of worship and service in the Church's life. They exercise responsibility in the worship of the congregation: for example by reading the Scriptures, preaching and leading the people in prayer. They help in the teaching of the congregation. They exercise a ministry of love within the community. They fulfil certain administrative tasks and may be elected to responsibilities for congregational governance.

27-Commentary:

In many churches there is today considerable uncertainty about the need, the rationale, the status and the functions of deacons. In what sense can the diaconate be considered part of the ordained ministry? What is it that distinguishes it from other ministries in the Church (catechists, musicians, etc.)? Why should deacons be ordained while these other ministries do not receive ordination? If they are ordained do

Lima/82

31. *Deacons* represent to the Church its calling as servant in the world. By struggling in Christ's name with the myriad needs of societies and persons, deacons exemplify the interdependence of worship and service in the Church's life. They exercise responsibility in the worship of the congregation: for example by reading the Scriptures, preaching and leading the people in prayer. They help in the teaching of the congregation. They exercise a ministry of love within the community. They fulfil certain administrative tasks and may be elected to responsibilities for governance.

31-Commentary:

In many churches there is today considerable uncertainty about the need, the rationale, the status and the functions of deacons. In what sense can the diaconate be considered part of the ordained ministry? What is it that distinguishes it from other ministries in the Church (catechists, musicians, etc.)? Why should deacons be ordained while these other ministries do not receive ordination? If they are ordained do

Geneva/6-80 [cont.]
they receive ordination in the full sense of the word or is their first step towards ordination only the first step towards ordination as presbyters? Today, there is a strong tendency in many churches to restore the diaconate as an ordained ministry with its own dignity and meant to be exercised for life. Differences in ordering the diaconal ministry should not be regarded as a hindrance for the mutual recognition of the ordained ministries.

Rome/11-80 [cont.]
they receive ordination in the full sense of the word or is their ordination only the first step towards ordination as presbyters? Today, there is a strong tendency in many churches to restore the diaconate as an ordained ministry with its own dignity and meant to be exercised for life. As the churches move closer together there may be united in this office ministries now existing in a variety of forms and under a variety of names. Differences in ordering the diaconal ministry should not be regarded as a hindrance for the mutual recognition of the ordained ministries.

Annecy/81 [cont.]
they receive ordination in the full sense of the word or is their ordination only the first step towards ordination as presbyters? Today, there is a strong tendency in many churches to restore the diaconate as an ordained ministry with its own dignity and meant to be exercised for life. As the churches move closer together there may be united in this office ministries now existing in a variety of forms and under a variety of names. Differences in ordering the diaconal ministry should not be regarded as a hindrance for the mutual recognition of the ordained ministries.

Lima/82 [cont.]
they receive ordination in the full sense of the word or is their ordination only the first step towards ordination as presbyters? Today, there is a strong tendency in many churches to restore the diaconate as an ordained ministry with its own dignity and meant to be exercised for life. As the churches move closer together there may be united in this office ministries now existing in a variety of forms and under a variety of names. Differences in ordering the diaconal ministry should not be regarded as a hindrance for the mutual recognition of the ordained ministries.

In two different places in this section of the Lima text an explicit reference to deacons is eliminated.[198] As H. Russell contends, "'deacons' seem to be dragged in. . . . My suggestion is that the 'deacon' ought to be treated in his or her own right, as part of the sacramental life of the World, made manifest in the Church. It is not therefore 'function', which is the criterion for the diaconate but the reconciliation of the world by Christ, through the Church."[199] The role of deacons, however, is given prominence in the context of the call for the reform of the threefold pattern of ministry. In fact, what had formerly been said in the Commentary section is moved up to the main text.[200]

In the Lima text more explicit references are made to what deacons do and may do. M. Tanner had called the "description of diaconate not convincing. Find something better, or stop insisting on diaconate."[201] Earlier it was reported that Tanner "questions whether there are *good* reasons for keeping the diaconate."[202] At Lima the role of deacons is placed in the overall context of "struggling in Christ's name with the myriad needs of societies and persons."[203] They read the scriptures, preach, lead the people in prayer, "help in the teaching of the congregation. They exercise a ministry of love within the community. They . . . may be elected to responsibilities for governance."[204]

In the Commentary section there is added this note about the office of the diaconate: "As the churches move closer together there may be united in this office ministries now existing in a variety of forms and under a variety of names."[205]

---

[198]Lima, §s 20 and 24; 6/80, §s 20 and 24.

[199]Sept. 15, 1980, p. 2, Archive Box: "Faith and Order, Documents 1980-1981, Circular Letters, 1980-1981."

[200]Lima, §24, 6/80, §22-Commentary.

[201]Re: 6/80, §28. G.W. Comments, Oct. 26, 1980, p. 4, Archive Box: "Faith and Order, Documents 1980-1981, Circular Letters, 1980-1981."

[202]Re: 6/80, §19. G.W. Comments, Oct. 26, 1980, p.3, Archive Box: "Faith and Order, Documents 1980-1981, Circular Letters, 1980-1981."

[203]Lima, §31, 6/80, §28.

[204]Idem. Cf. U. Kühn, Nov 2, 1980, p. 2, Archive Box: "Faith and Order Archives, BEM, 79-82 corr. 81, Lima 82."

[205]§31-Commentary.

D. VARIETY OF CHARISMS.

Here the Lima text gets very technical. A clear distinction is drawn between "ministry" (meaning "ordained ministry") and "service"; between "ministry" and "charism," the latter to be taken as the more generic term. Respect for the canons of scientific history study, which we have observed in various times and places during the course of the evolution of texts, is again in evidence here with the result that historical claims are less formidable with each succeeding text.

Geneva/6-80

29. The community which lives in the power of the Spirit will be characterized by a variety of ministries. The Spirit is the giver of diverse gifts which enrich the life of the community. In order to enhance their effectiveness, the community will recognize certain of these gifts as ministries. It will, for instance, give recognition to ministries of readers, catechists, musicians, church wardens. While some of these ministries fulfil services permanently required in the life of the community, others will be temporary. Men and women in religious communities fulfil a ministry which is of particular importance for the life of the Church. The ordained ministry must not become a hindrance for the variety of these ministries. On the contrary, it will help the community to discover the gifts bestowed on it by the Holy Spirit and will equip members of the body to serve in a variety of ways.

Rome/11-80

28. The community which lives in the power of the Spirit will be characterized by a variety of ministries. The Spirit is the giver of diverse gifts which enrich the life of the community. In order to enhance their effectiveness, the community will recognize certain of these gifts as ministries. It will, for instance, give recognition to ministries of readers, catechists, musicians, church wardens. While some of these ministries fulfil services permanently required in the life of the community, others will be temporary. Men and women in religious communities fulfil a ministry which is of particular importance for the life of the Church. The ordained ministry must not become a hindrance for the variety of these ministries. On the contrary, it will help the community to discover the gifts bestowed on it by the Holy Spirit and will equip members of the body to serve in a variety of ways.

Annecy/81

28. The community which lives in the power of the Spirit will be characterized by a variety of charisms. The Spirit is the giver of diverse gifts which enrich the life of the community. In order to enhance their effectiveness, the community will recognize publicly certain of these charisms. While some serve permanent needs in the life of the community, others will be temporary. Men and women in religious communities fulfil a service which is of particular importance for the life of the Church. The ordained ministry, which is itself a charism, must not become a hindrance for the variety of these charisms. On the contrary, it will help the community to discover the gifts bestowed on it by the Holy Spirit and will equip members of the body to serve in a variety of ways.

Lima/82

32. The community which lives in the power of the Spirit will be characterized by a variety of charisms. The Spirit is the giver of diverse gifts which enrich the life of the community. In order to enhance their effectiveness, the community will recognize publicly certain of these charisms. While some serve permanent needs in the life of the community, others will be temporary. Men and women in the communities of religious orders fulfil a service which is of particular importance for the life of the Church. The ordained ministry, which is itself a charism, must not become a hindrance for the variety of these charisms. On the contrary, it will help the community to discover the gifts bestowed on it by the Holy Spirit and will equip members of the body to serve in a variety of ways.

Geneva/6-80

30. Often in the history of the Church the truth of the Gospel could be preserved only through prophetic and charismatic leaders. Often new impulses could find their way into the life of the Church only in unusual ways. Often reforms required a special ministry. The ordained ministers and the whole community will need to be attentive to the challenge of such special ministries.

Rome/11-80

29. Often in the history of the Church the truth of the Gospel could be preserved only through prophetic and charismatic leaders. Often new impulses could find their way into the life of the Church only in unusual ways. Often reforms required a special ministry. The ordained ministers and the whole community will need to be attentive to the challenge of such special ministries.

Annecy/81

29. In the history of the Church there have been times when the truth of the Gospel could only be preserved through prophetic and charismatic leaders. Often new impulses could find their way into the life of the Church only in unusual ways. At times reforms required a special ministry. The ordained ministers and the whole community will need to be attentive to the challenge of such special ministries.

Lima/82

33. In the history of the Church there have been times when the truth of the Gospel could only be preserved through prophetic and charismatic leaders. Often new impulses could find their way into the life of the Church only in unusual ways. At times reforms required a special ministry. The ordained ministers and the whole community will need to be attentive to the challenge of such special ministries.

There is consciousness here of the use of technical terminology in reference to the whole topic of ministry. First, the word, "ministry," is restricted to "the ordained ministry."[206] The ordained ministry is itself acknowledged as a charism, thereby making the latter word a more generic one.[207] Secondly, members of "communities of religious orders"[208] fulfil "a service" rather than "a ministry."[209]

Various charisms, named explicitly in earlier texts and dubbed "ministries" there, are dropped in the Lima text. They are "readers, catechists, musicians, church wardens."[210]

And, as has occurred elsewhere in the final redacting, careful wording contributes to an attitude of desiring to make less claims and less explicit claims historically. The word, "often," is dropped as part of the phrase "in the history of the Church;" the phrase, "there have been times when," is added; and the word, "often," is replaced by the phrase, "at times."[211]

---

[206]Lima, §32; 6/80, §29.

[207]Idem.

[208]Earlier (in 6/80, §29) they were simply members of "religious communities."

[209]Lima, §32.

[210]6/80, §29. The alterations of this paragraph in the 6/80 text, made in the text of 1/81, are apparently influenced by M. Conway whose remarks are reported by M. Thurian as incorporated in the latter text. ["Remarques sur para 29 incorporés," Sept. 5, 1980, p. 5, Archive Box: "Faith and Order, Documents 1980-1981, Circular Letters, 1980-1981."]

[211]Lima, §33; 6/80, §30.

IV. SUCCESSION IN THE APOSTOLIC TRADITION.

A. APOSTOLIC TRADITION IN THE CHURCH.

Here the term, "continuity," is stressed as crucial to this issue. This continuity goes far beyond maintaining an unbroken line of bishops throughout history. It is noted that continuity in the transmission of the gospel should predominate over the transmission of ministry. This is a dialectic between the two which should be maintained. Some characteristics of the theological writing found more and more prominently as the text evolves are in evidence here, namely, the valuing of "being" alongside "doing" in ministry, the preferring of the personal over the structural and impersonal, and the stressing of the present reality of ecclesial life alongside past traditions.

Geneva/6-80

31. The Creed confesses the Church to be apostolic. The Church lives in continuity with the apostles and their proclamation. The same Lord who sent the apostles continues to be present in the Church. The Spirit keeps the Church in the apostolic tradition until the fulfilment of history in the Kingdom of God. Apostolic tradition in the Church involves continuity in the permanent characteristics of the Church of the apostles: witness to the apostolic faith, proclamation and fresh interpretation of the Gospel, celebration of baptism and the eucharist, the transmission of ministerial responsibilities, communion in love and suffering, service to the needy, unity among the local churches and sharing the gifts which the Lord has given to each.

Rome/11-80

30. In the Creed the Church confesses itself to be apostolic. The Church lives in continuity with the apostles and their proclamation. The same Lord who sent the apostles continues to be present in the Church. The Spirit keeps the Church in the apostolic tradition until the fulfilment of history in the kingdom of God. Apostolic tradition in the Church means continuity in the permanent characteristics of the Church of the apostles: witness to the apostolic faith, proclamation and fresh interpretation of the Gospel, celebration of baptism and the eucharist, the transmission of ministerial responsibilities, communion in prayer, love, joy and suffering, service to the needy, unity among the local churches and sharing the gifts which the Lord has given to each.

Annecy/81

30. In the Creed the Church confesses itself to be apostolic. The Church lives in continuity with the apostles and their proclamation. The same Lord who sent the apostles continues to be present in the Church. The Spirit keeps the Church in the apostolic tradition until the fulfilment of history in the Kingdom of God. Apostolic tradition in the Church means continuity in the permanent characteristics of the Church of the apostles: witness to the apostolic faith, proclamation and fresh interpretation of the Gospel, celebration of baptism and the eucharist, the transmission of ministerial responsibilities, communion in prayer, love, joy and suffering, service to the needy, unity among the local churches and sharing the gifts which the Lord has given to each.

Lima/82

34. In the Creed the Church confesses itself to be apostolic. The Church lives in continuity with the apostles and their proclamation. The same Lord who sent the apostles continues to be present in the Church. The Spirit keeps the Church in the apostolic tradition until the fulfilment of history in the Kingdom of God. Apostolic tradition in the Church means continuity in the permanent characteristics of the Church of the apostles: witness to the apostolic faith, proclamation and fresh interpretation of the Gospel, celebration of baptism and the eucharist, the transmission of ministerial responsibilities, communion in prayer, love, joy and suffering, service to the sick and needy, unity among the local churches and sharing the gifts which the Lord has given to each.

384

Geneva/6-80
31-Commentary:

The apostles, as witnesses of the life and resurrection of Christ and sent by him, are the original transmitters of the Gospel, of the tradition of the words and acts of Jesus Christ which constitute the life of the Church. This apostolic tradition continues through history and links the Church to its origins in Christ and in the college of the apostles. Within this apostolic tradition is an apostolic succession of the ministry which serves the continuity of the Church in its life in Christ and its faithfulness to the words and acts of Jesus transmitted by the apostles. The ministers appointed by the apostles, and then the episkopoi of the churches, were the first guardians of this transmission of the apostolic tradition; they testified to the apostolic succession of the ministry which was continued through the bishops of the early Church in collegial communion with the presbyters and deacons within the Christian community. A distinction should be made, therefore, between the apostolic tradition of the whole Church and the succession of the apostolic ministry.

Rome/11-80
30-Commentary

The apostles, as witnesses of the life and resurrection of Christ and sent by him, are the original transmitters of the Gospel, of the tradition of the words and acts of Jesus Christ which constitute the life of the Church. This apostolic tradition continues through history and links the Church to its origins in Christ and in the college of the apostles. Within this apostolic tradition is an apostolic succession of the ministry which serves the continuity of the Church in its life in Christ and its faithfulness to the words and acts of Jesus transmitted by the apostles. The ministers appointed by the apostles, and then the *episkopoi* of the churches, were the first guardians of this transmission of the apostolic tradition; they testified to the apostolic succession of the ministry which was continued through the bishops of the early Church in collegial communion with the presbyters and deacons within the Christian community. A distinction should be made, therefore, between the apostolic tradition of the whole Church and the succession of the apostolic ministry.

Annecy/81
30-Commentary:

The apostles, as witnesses of the life and resurrection of Christ and sent by him, are the original transmitters of the Gospel, of the tradition of the words and acts of Jesus Christ which constitute the life of the Church. This apostolic tradition continues through history and links the Church to its origins in Christ and in the college of the apostles. Within this apostolic tradition is an apostolic succession of the ministry which serves the continuity of the Church in its life in Christ and its faithfulness to the words and acts of Jesus transmitted by the apostles. The ministers appointed by the apostles, and then the *episkopoi* of the churches, were the first guardians of this transmission of the apostolic tradition; they testified to the apostolic succession of the ministry which was continued through the bishops of the early Church in collegial communion with the presbyters and deacons within the Christian community. A distinction should be made, therefore, between the apostolic tradition of the whole Church and the succession of the apostolic ministry.

Lima/82
34-Commentary:

The apostles, as witnesses of the life and resurrection of Christ and sent by him, are the original transmitters of the Gospel, of the tradition of the saving words and acts of Jesus Christ which constitute the life of the Church. This apostolic tradition continues through history and links the Church to its origins in Christ and in the college of the apostles. Within this apostolic tradition is an apostolic succession of the ministry which serves the continuity of the Church in its life in Christ and its faithfulness to the words and acts of Jesus transmitted by the apostles. The ministers appointed by the apostles, and then the *episkopoi* of the churches, were the first guardians of this transmission of the apostolic tradition; they testified to the apostolic succession of the ministry which was continued through the bishops of the early Church in collegial communion with the presbyters and deacons within the Christian community. A distinction should be made, therefore, between the apostolic tradition of the whole Church and the succession of the apostolic ministry.

In this major section of the Lima document on Ministry the changes and additions in the text reflect many of the themes already noted in earlier major sections. They will be noted here again. G. Gassmann commented that "Section IV is the crucial section of the whole document."[212]

Regarding the issue of the apostolic tradition itself the strongest possible emphasis is placed on the word, "continuity." For apostolic tradition not only "involves continuity"[213] but "*means* continuity in the permanent characteristics of the Church of the apostles."[214] Thus continuity is taken to be essential to the notion of the apostolic tradition. The Lima text adds the phrase, service to the sick,"[215] as one of the permanent characteristics.

Later in this same section the Lima document makes explicit that continuity is not only expressed in the succession of bishops but also in "the transmission of the Gospel and the life of the community."[216] In fact, P. Ricca had pointed out a need for a more critical attentiveness to factual history and had stated his reservations about the text of Geneva/6-80 (§s 31-35):

> The topic of the transmission of ministry predominates (wrongly) over that of the transmission of the Gospel. The two topics are not identical nor are they superimposed. The transmission of the Gospel, which is the essential reality, is a more comprehensive, more complex and more fascinating phenomenon than the transmission of the ministry. Before all else one may need to describe in broad outline the reality of the transmission of the Gospel, to state that it had been accomplished especially by innumerable witnesses to Christ who are unknown (but not to God) and to stress the fact that this transmission is a veritable miracle of history, often accomplished *in spite of* the failures of the ordained minister. Then it can be said that the ordained too have played a positive part, according to the broad outlines of the promise of Jesus in regard to his useless servants. In summary: in these paragraphs the dialectic between apostolic succession and

---

[212]Nov. 11, 1981, p. 3, Archive Box: "Faith and Order Archives, BEM, 79-82 corr. 81, Lima 82." He goes on in the same place to state: "My personal conviction is that this comprehensive statement on apostolic tradition and apostolic succession can be acceptable to Lutherans. It is on the same line as the recent LWF - Roman Catholic statement. The problem is that on the Lutheran side there has not yet been sufficient discussion and clarification on episcopacy and episcopal succession within Lutheranism."

[213]6/80, §31.

[214]Lima, §34. Emphasis added.

[215]§34. This addition was urged by E. Flesseman-van-Leer [July, 1981, p. 2, Archive Box: "Faith and Order Archives, BEM, 79-82 corr. 81, Lima 82."].

[216]Lima, §36.

evangelical transmission is neither as present nor as clear as it ought to be.[217]

When listing the permanent characteristics of the Church of the apostles the Lima text adds the words, "prayer," and "joy."[218] Thus as was noted above in the tracing of the earlier paragraphs of the text *being* as well as doing is valued and there is an effort to strike a positive note in describing the life of the Church.

The Lima text tends to use more personal expressions instead of the more impersonal. Thus the phrase, "The Creed confesses the Church to be," is replaced by the phrase, "In the Creed, the Church confesses itself to be."[219]

And in the Commentary there is added the word, "saving," to the phrase, "words and acts of Jesus Christ." Thus the *present* reality of the apostolic tradition is emphasized.

---

[217]G.W. Comments, Oct. 26, 1980, p. 4, Archive Box: "Faith and Order, Documents 1980-1981, Circular Letters, 1980-1981." Also in P. Ricca, Sept. 25, 1980, p. 2, Archive Box: "Faith and Order, Documents 1980-1981, Circular Letters, 1980-1981.", emphasis added. The original text: "Le thème de la transmission du ministère prend le dessus sur celui de la transmission de l'Evangile. Les deux ne s'identifient pas ni se superposent. La transmission de l'Evangile, qui est le fait essentiel, est un phénomène bien plus vaste, bien plus complèxe et aussi bien plus fascinant que la trasmission (*sic*) du ministère. Il faudrait avant tout decrire à grandes lignes le fait de la trasmission de l'Evangile, dire qu'elle a été faite surtout par d'innombrables témoins du Christ inconnus (non pas auprès de Dieu), insister sur le fait que cette trasmission est un vrai miracle historique, qui s'est souvent réalisé malgré les défaillances du ministère ordonné. Ensuite on pourrait dire que celui-ci a aussi joué un rôle positif, dans le cadre de la parole de Jésus sur les serviteurs inutiles. Ensomme: dans ces paragraphes la dialectique entre succession apostolique et transmission évangélique n'est ni présente ni évidente comme elle devrait l'être."

[218]§34. P. Ricca suggested: "La communion dans la prière devrait être mentionée." [Sept. 25, 1980, p. 1, Archive Box: "Faith and Order, Documents 1980-1981, Circular Letters, 1980-1981."] The same was stated in another place. [G.W. Comments, Oct. 26, 1980, p. 4, Archive Box: "Faith and Order, Documents 1980-1981, Circular Letters, 1980-1981."]

[219]Lima, §34; 6/80, §31. The change is suggested by M. Conway [Sept. 5, 1980, p. 5, Archive Box: "Faith and Order, Documents 1980-1981, Circular Letters, 1980-1981."].

B. SUCCESSION OF THE APOSTOLIC MINISTRY.

Contextualizing this topic of succession of the apostolic ministry is an important approach adopted as the text evolves. Efforts by episcopal churches to achieve church unity is one such context. The text is unclear regarding the "sacramental" implications of episcopal succession as well as its necessity as a "sign" of apostolicity for the church. The continuous introduction of hortatory language in place of imperative language, here, as in other places in the text, heightens the appeal to dialogue among the churches. And, more importantly from a theological point of view, the term, "faith," comes to replace the term, "truth," thus broadening the meaning of what is handed down in the churches from apostolic times.

Geneva/6-80

32. The primary manifestation of apostolic succession is to be found in the apostolic tradition of the Church as a whole. The succession is an expression of the permanence and, therefore, of the continuity of Christ's own mission in which the Church participates. Within the Church the ordained ministry has a particular task of preserving and actualizing the apostolic truth. The orderly transmission of the ordained ministry is therefore a powerful expression of the continuity of the Church throughout history; it also underlines the calling of the ordained minister as guardian of the truth. Where churches neglect the importance of the orderly transmission, they must ask themselves whether they pay sufficient attention to the continuity in the apostolic tradition. On the other hand, where the ordained ministry does not adequately serve the proclamation of the apostolic truth, churches must ask themselves whether their ministerial structures are not in need of alteration.

Rome/11-80

31. The primary manifestation of apostolic succession is to be found in the apostolic tradition of the Church as a whole. The succession is an expression of the permanence and, therefore, of the continuity of Christ's own mission in which the Church participates. Within the Church the ordained ministry has a particular tssk of preserving and actualizing the apostolic faith. The orderly transmission of the ordained ministry is therefore a powerful expression of the continuity of the Church throughout history; it also underlines the calling of the ordained minister as guardian of the faith. Where churches see little importance in orderly transmission, they should ask themselves whether they have not to change their conception of continuity in the apostolic tradition. On the other hand, where the ordained ministry does not adequately serve the proclamation of the apostolic faith, churches must ask themselves whether their ministerial structures are not in need of essential reform.

Annecy/81

31. The primary manifestation of apostolic succession is to be found in the apostolic tradition of the Church as a whole. The succession is an expression of the permanence and, therefore, of the continuity of Christ's own mission in which the Church participates. Within the Church the ordained ministry has a particular task of preserving and actualizing the apostolic faith. The orderly transmission of the ordained ministry is therefore a powerful expression of the continuity of the Church throughout history; it also underlines the calling of the ordained minister as guardian of the faith. Where churches see little importance in orderly transmission, they should ask themselves whether they have not to change their conception of continuity in the apostolic tradition. On the other hand, where the ordained ministry does not adequately serve the proclamation of the apostolic faith, churches must ask themselves whether their ministerial structures are not in need of essential reform.

Lima/82

35. The primary manifestation of apostolic succession is to be found in the apostolic tradition of the Church as a whole. The succession is an expression of the permanence and, therefore, of the continuity of Christ's own mission in which the Church participates. Within the Church the ordained ministry has a particular task of preserving and actualizing the apostolic faith. The orderly transmission of the ordained ministry is therefore a powerful expression of the continuity of the Church throughout history; it also underlines the calling of the ordained minister as guardian of the faith. Where churches see little importance in orderly transmission, they should ask themselves whether they have not to change their conception of continuity in the apostolic tradition. On the other hand, where the ordained ministry does not adequately serve the proclamation of the apostolic faith, churches must ask themselves whether their ministerial structures are not in need of reform.

Geneva/6-80

33. Under the particular historical circumstances of the growing Church in the early centuries, the succession of bishops became one of the ways in which the apostolic tradition of the Church was expressed. This succession was understood as serving, symbolizing and guarding the continuity of the apostolic faith and communion.

33-Commentary:
In the early Church the bond between the episcopate and the apostolic community was understood in two ways. Clement of Rome linked the mission of the bishop with the sending of Christ by the Father and the sending of the apostles by Christ (Cor. 42,44). This made the bishop a successor of the apostles, ensuring the permanence of the apostolic mission in the Church. Clement is primarily interested in the means whereby the *historical* continuity of Christ's presence is ensured in the Church thanks to the apostolic succession. For Ignatius of Antioch (Magn. 6:1; 3:12; Trall. 3:1) it is Christ surrounded by the Twelve who is permanently in the Church in the person of the bishop surrounded

Rome/11-80

32. Under the particular historical circumstances of the growing Church in the early centuries, the succession of bishops became one of the ways, together with the transmission of the gospel and the life of the community, in which the apostolic tradition of the Church was expressed. This succession was understood as serving, symbolizing and guarding the continuity of the apostolic faith and communion.

32-Commentary
In the early Church the bond between the episcopate and the apostolic community was understood in two ways. Clement of Rome linked the mission of the bishop with the sending of Christ by the Father and the sending of the apostles by Christ (Cor. 42,44). This made the bishop a successor of the apostolic mission in the Church. Clement is primarily interested in the means whereby the *historical* continuity of Christ's presence is ensured in the Church thanks to the apostolic succession. For Ignatius of Antioch (Magn. 6:1; 3:1.2; Trall. 3:1) it is Christ surrounded by the Twelve

Annecy/81

32. Under the particular historical circumstances of the growing Church in the early centuries, the succession of bishops became one of the ways, together with the transmission of the Gospel and the life of the community, in which the apostolic tradition of the Church was expressed. This succession was understood as serving, symbolizing and guarding the continuity of the apostolic faith and communion.

32-Commentary:
In the early Church the bond between the episcopate and the apostolic community was understood in two ways. Clement of Rome linked the mission of the bishop with the sending of Christ by the Father and the sending of the apostles by Christ (Cor.42:44). This made the bishop a successor of the apostles, ensuring the permanence of the apostolic mission in the Church. Clement is primarily interested in the means whereby the *historical* continuity of Christ's presence is ensured in the Church thanks to the apostolic succession. For Ignatius of Antioch (Magn. 6:1; 3:1.2; Trall. 3:1) it is Christ surrounded by the Twelve

Lima/82

36. Under the particular historical circumstances of the growing Church in the early centuries, the succession of bishops became one of the ways, together with the transmission of the Gospel and the life of the community, in which the apostolic tradition of the Church was expressed. This succession was understood as serving, symbolizing and guarding the continuity of the apostolic faith and communion.

36-Commentary:
In the early Church the bond between the episcopate and the apostolic community was understood in two ways. Clement of Rome linked the mission of the bishop with the sending of Christ by the Father and the sending of the apostles by Christ (Cor.42:44). This made the bishop a successor of the apostles, ensuring the permanence of the apostolic mission in the Church. Clement is primarily interested in the means whereby the *historical* continuity of Christ's presence is ensured in the Church thanks to the apostolic succession. For Ignatius of Antioch (Magn. 6: 1, 3: 12; Trall. 3:1) it is Christ surrounded by the Twelve

Geneva/6-80 [cont.]

by the presbyters. Ignatius regards the Christian community assembled around the bishop in the midst of the presbyters and the deacons as the *actual* manifestation in the Spirit of the apostolic community. The sign of apostolic succession, therefore, must not be taken as a guarantee for *historical* continuity only, but also as an *actual* manifestation of a spiritual reality.

Rome/11-80 [cont.]

who is permanently in tbe Church in the person of the bishop surrounded by the presbyters. Ignatius regards the Christian community assembled around the bishop in the midst of the presbyters and the deacons as the *actual* manifestation in the Spirit of the apostolic community. The sign of apostolic succession thus not only points to historical continuity; it also manifests an actual spiritual reality.

Annecy/81 [cont.]

who is permanently in the Church in the person of the bishop surrounded by the presbyters. Ignatius regards the Christian community assembled around the bishop in midst of the presbyters and the deacons as the *actual* manifestation in the Spirit of the apostolic community. The sign of apostolic succession thus not only points to historical continuity; it also manifests an actual spiritual reality.

Lima/82 [cont.]

who is permanently in the Church in the person of the bishop surrounded by the presbyters. Ignatius regards the Christian community assembled around the bishop in midst of the presbyters and the deacons as the *actual* manifestation in the Spirit of the apostolic community. The sign of apostolic succession thus not only points to historical continuity; it also manifests an actual spiritual reality.

Geneva/6-80

34. In recent times, churches which practise the succession through the episcopate, increasingly recognize that a continuity in apostolic faith, worship and mission has been preserved in churches which have not retained the form of historic episcopate. This recognition finds additional support in the fact that the reality and function of the episcopal ministry have been preserved in many of these churches, with or without the title "bishop". Ordination, for example, is always done in them by persons in whom the Church recognizes the authority to transmit the ministerial commission.

Rome/11-80

33. In churches which practise the succession through the episcopate, it is increasingly recognized that a continuity in apostolic faith, worship and mission has been preserved in churches which have not retained the form of historic episcopate. This recognition finds additional support in the fact that the reality and function of the episcopal ministry have been preserved in many of these churches, with or without the title "bishop". Ordination, for example, is always done in them by persons in whom the Church recognizes the authority to transmit the ministerial commission.

Annecy/81

33. In churches which practise the succession through the episcopate, it is increasingly recognized that a continuity in apostolic faith, worship and mission has been preserved in churches which have not retained the form of historic episcopate. This recognition finds additional support in the fact that the reality and function of the episcopal ministry have been preserved in many of these churches, with or without the title "bishop". Ordination, for example, is always done in them by persons in whom the Church recognizes the authority to transmit the ministerial commission.

Lima/82

37. In churches which practise the succession through the episcopate, it is increasingly recognized that a continuity in apostolic faith, worship and mission has been preserved in churches which have not retained the form of historic episcopate. This recognition finds additional support in the fact that the reality and function of the episcopal ministry have been preserved in many of these churches, with or without the title "bishop". Ordination, for example, is always done in them by persons in whom the Church recognizes the authority to transmit the ministerial commission.

392

Geneva/6-80

35. These considerations do not diminish the importance of the episcopal ministry. On the contrary, they enable churches which have not retained the episcopate to appreciate the episcopal succession as a sign of the continuity and unity of the Church. Today churches, including those engaged in union negotiations, are expressing willingness to accept episcopal succession as a sign of the apostolicity of the life of the whole Church. Yet, at the same time, they cannot accept any suggestion that the ministry exercised in their own tradition should be invalid until the moment that it enters into an existing line of episcopal succession.

Rome/11-80

34. These considerations do not diminish the importance of the episcopal ministry. On the contrary, they enable churches which have not retained the episcopate to appreciate the episcopal succession as a sign, though not a guarantee, of the continuity and unity of the Church. Today churches, including those engaged in union negotiations, are expressing willingness to accept episcopal succession as a sign of the apostolicity of the life of the whole Church. Yet, at the same time, they cannot accept any suggestion that the ministry exercised in their own tradition should be invalid until the moment that it enters into an existing line of episcopal succession.

Annecy/81

34. These considerations do not diminish the importance of the episcopal ministry. On the contrary, they enable churches which have not retained the episcopate to appreciate the episcopal succession as a sign, though not a guarantee, of the continuity and unity of the Church. Today churches, including those engaged in union negotiations, are expressing willingness to accept episcopal succession as a sign of the apostolicity of the life of the whole Church. Yet, at the same time, they cannot accept any suggestion that the ministry exercised in their own tradition should be invalid until the moment that it enters into an existing line of episcopal succession.

Lima/82

38. These considerations do not diminish the importance of the episcopal ministry. On the contrary, they enable churches which have not retained the episcopate to appreciate the episcopal succession as a sign, though not a guarantee, of the continuity and unity of the Church. Today churches, including those engaged in union negotiations, are expressing willingness to accept episcopal succession as a sign of the apostolicity of the life of the whole Church. Yet, at the same time, they cannot accept any suggestion that the ministry exercised in their own tradition should be invalid until the moment that it enters into an existing line of episcopal succession. Their acceptance of the episcopal succession will best further the unity of the whole Church if it is part of a wider process by which the episcopal churches themselves also regain their lost unity.

There is an acknowledgement of the importance of contextualizing the issue of episcopal succession for non-episcopal churches within the world-wide movement for visible unity and doing so by linking it to the strivings for church unity by episcopal churches. A sentence is added at Lima: "Their (Non-episcopal churches') acceptance of the episcopal succession will best further the unity of the whole Church if it is part of a wider process by which the episcopal churches themselves also regain their lost unity."[220]

The Commentary section gives a strong emphasis and explication to the sacramentality of apostolic succession. The change of language is subtle but significant. Use of the words, "points to," and "manifests,"[221] together makes this emphasis on sacramentality abundantly clear. This change was specifically suggested by W. Pannenberg.[222] It should be noted, however, that by using the phrase, "sign, though not a guarantee," the main text of Lima (as contrasted with its Commentary section) takes back with the left hand what the right hand had given.[223] This had been suggested by W. Pannenberg.[224] P. Ricca had asked whether "episcopal succession is to be understood 'as a sign of the apostolicity of the whole Church'? The hidden question is the following: possible sign or necessary sign?"[225]

As noted in earlier sections a more hortatory tone characterizes the Lima text. The word, "should," replaces the word, "must."[226] When the word, "reform," replaces the word, "alteration," the same hortatory tone prevails because the change advocated

---

[220]§38.

[221]Lima, §36-Commentary; 6/80, §33-Commentary.

[222]Oct. 13, 1980, p. 9, Archive Box: "Faith and Order, Documents 1980-1981, Circular Letters, 1980-1981."

[223]Lima, §38; 6/80, §33-Commentary.

[224]Oct. 13, 1980, p. 9, Archive Box: "Faith and Order, Documents 1980-1981, Circular Letters, 1980-1981."

[225]Sept. 25, 1980, p. 2, Archive Box: "Faith and Order, Documents 1980-1981, Circular Letters, 1980-1981." "La succession épiscopale acceptée 'comme un signe d'apostolicité de toute l'Eglise'? La question ouverte est la suivante: signe possible ou signe nécessaire?" Translation: "Is episcopal succession to be taken as a sign of the apostolicity of the whole Church? The hidden question is the following: possible sign or necessary sign?" A reiteration of the latter question is made in G.W. Comments, Oct. 26, 1980, p. 4, Archive Box: "Faith and Order, Documents 1980-1981, Circular Letters, 1980-1981."

[226]Lima, §35; 6/80, §32.

is less radical and drastic, more continuous with past forms.[227] This same spirit or tone characterizes the final text with the replacement of the phrase, "where churches neglect the importance of the orderly transmission," with the phrase, "where churches see little importance in orderly transmission."[228] This is also true when the phrase, "whether they pay sufficient attention to the continuity," is replaced by the phrase, "whether they have not to change their conception of continuity."[229]

Finally, in this section, it is important to note the replacement of the term, "the apostolic truth," with the term, "the apostolic faith."[230] Less emphasis is thereby placed on specific articulations and on the exclusive emphasis on the intellectual aspects of believing. M. Conway was the one who had remarked, "I wonder if the phrase 'the apostolic truth' could not be taken in too narrow and rationalistic a way — would it be as good to refer to 'the apostolic faith'?"[231]

V. ORDINATION.

A. THE MEANING OF ORDINATION.

In this section of the text we again witness a respect for scientific history study. More and more care is exercised in regard to what can or cannot be attributed directly to the will and action of the historical Jesus. Care is also taken to view ordination as part of a human process and not as a magic conferral of powers. The participation of the community of the church in ordinations is appropriately noted. The churches are more directly and candidly invited to make decisions regarding their mutual acceptance of one another's ordinations. And special care is taken to explain how language influences the very attitudes of church members and the very structures of church polity.

---

[227]Lima, §35; 6/80, §32.

[228]Lima, §35; 6/80, §32.

[229]Lima, §35; 6/80, §32.

[230]Lima, §35; 6/80, §32. The change is first made in the 11/80 text.

[231]Sept. 5, 1980, pp. 5-6, Archive Box: "Faith and Order, Documents 1980-1981, Circular Letters, 1980-1981."

Geneva/6-80

36. The Church ordains certain of its members for the ministry in the name of Christ by the invocation of the Spirit and the imposition of hands (1 Tim 4:14; II Tim 1:6); in so doing it seeks to continue the mission of the apostles and to remain faithful to their teaching. The act of ordination by those who are appointed for this ministry attests the bond of the Church with Jesus Christ and the apostolic witness, recalling that it is the risen Lord who is the true ordainer and bestows the gift. In ordaining, the Church, under the inspiration of the Holy Spirit, provides for the faithful proclamation of the Gospel and humble service in the name of Christ. The laying-on of hands is the sign of the gift of the Spirit, rendering visible the ordering of this ministry in the revelation accomplished in him, and reminding the Church to look to him as the source of its commission. This ordination, however, can have different intentions according to the specific tasks of bishops, presbyters and deacons as indicated in the liturgies of ordination.

Rome/11-80

35. The Church ordains certain of its members for the ministry in the name of Christ by the invocation of the Spirit and the imposition of hands (1 Tim 4:14; II Tim 1:6); in so doing it seeks to continue the mission of the apostles and to remain faithful to their teaching. The act of ordination by those who are appointed for this ministry attests the bond of the Church with Jesus Christ and the apostolic witness, recalling that it is the risen Lord who is the true ordainer and bestows the gift. In ordaining, the Church, under the inspiration of the Holy Spirit, provides for the faithful proclamation of the Gospel and humble service in the name of Christ. The laying on of hands is the sign of the gift of the Spirit, rendering visible the ordering of this ministry in the revelation accomplished in him, and reminding the Church to look to him as the source of its commission. This ordination, however, can have different intentions according to the specific tasks of bishops, presbyters and deacons as indicated in the liturgies of ordination.

Annecy/81

35. The Church ordains certain of its members for the ministry in the name of Christ by the invocation of the Spirit and the laying on of hands (1 Tim 4:14; II Tim 1: 6); in so doing it seeks to continue the mission of the apostles and to remain faithful to their teaching. The act of ordination by those who are appointed for this ministry attests the bond of the Church with Jesus Christ and the apostolic witness, recalling that it is the risen Lord who is the true ordainer and bestows the gift. In ordaining, the Church, under the inspiration of the Holy Spirit, provides for the faithful proclamation of the Gospel and humble service in the name of Christ. The laying on of hands is the sign of the gift of the Spirit, rendering visible the fact that the ministry in the revelation accomplished in him, and reminding the Church to look to him as the source of its commission. This ordination, however, can have different intentions according to the specific tasks of bishops, presbyters and deacons as indicated in the liturgies of ordination.

Lima/82

39. The Church ordains certain of its members for the ministry in the name of Christ by the invocation of the Spirit and the laying on of hands (I Tim 4:14; II Tim 1 : 6); in so doing it seeks to continue the mission of the apostles and to remain faithful to their teaching. The act of ordination by those who are appointed for this ministry attests the bond of the Church with Jesus Christ and the apostolic witness, recalling that it is the risen Lord who is the true ordainer and bestows the gift. In ordaining, the Church, under the inspiration of the Holy Spirit, provides for the faithful proclamation of the Gospel and humble service in the name of Christ. The laying on of hands is the sign of the gift of the Spirit, rendering visible the fact that the ministry was instituted in the revelation accomplished in Christ, and reminding the Church to look to him as the source of its commission. This ordination, however, can have different intentions according to the specific tasks of bishops, presbyters and deacons as indicated in the liturgies of ordination.

Geneva/6-80 [cont.]

36-Commentary. It is clear that churches have different practices of ordination. and that it would be wrong to single out one of those as exclusively valid. On the other hand, if churches are increasingly able to recognize each other in the sign of apostolic succession, as described above, it would follow that the old tradition according to which it is the bishop who ordains will be recognized and respected as well.

Rome/11-80 [cont.]

35-Commentary

It is clear that churches have different practices of ordination, and that it would be wrong to single out one of those as exclusively valid. On the other hand, if churches are increasingly able to recognize each other in the sign of apostolic succession, as described above, it would follow that the old tradition, according to which it is the bishop who ordains, with the participation of the community, will be recognized and respected as well.

Annecy/81 [cont.]

35-Commentary:

It is clear that churches have different practices of ordination, and that it would be wrong to single out one of those as exclusively valid. On the other hand, if churches are increasingly able to recognize each other in the sign of apostolic succession, as described above, it would follow that the old tradition, according to which it is the bishop who ordains, with the participation of the community, will be recognized and respected as well.

Lima/82 [cont.]

39-Commentary:

It is clear that churches have different practices of ordination, and that it would be wrong to single out one of those as exclusively valid. On the other hand, if churches are willing to recognize each other in the sign of apostolic succession, as described above, it would follow that the old tradition, according to which it is the bishop who ordained, with the participation of the community, will be recognized and respected as well.

Geneva/6-80

37. Properly speaking, then, ordination denotes an action by God and the community which inaugurates a relationship in which the ordained are strengthened by the Spirit for their task and are upheld by the acknowledgement and prayers of the congregation.

37-Commentary:
The original New Testament terms for ordination tend to be simple and descriptive. The fact of appointment is recorded. The laying on of hands is described. Prayer is made for the Spirit. Different traditions have built different interpretations on the basis of these data.

It is evident that there is a certain difference between the unspoken cultural setting of the Greek *cheirotonein* and that of the Latin *ordo* or *ordinare*. The New Testament use of the former term borrows its basic secular meaning of "appointment" (Acts 14: 23; II Cor 8: 19), which is, in turn, derived from the original meaning of extending the hand, either to designate a person or to cast a vote. Some scholars see in *cheirotonein* a reference to the act of

Rome/11-80

36. Properly speaking, then, ordination denotes an action by God and the community which inaugurates a relationship in which the ordained are strengthened by the Spirit for their task and are upheld by the acknowledgement and prayers of the congregation.

36-Commentary
The original New Testament terms for ordination tend to be simple and descriptive. The fact of appointment is recorded. The laying on of hands is described. Prayer is made for the Spirit. Different traditions have built different interpretations on the basis of these data.

It is evident that there is a certain difference between the unspoken cultural setting of the Greek *cheirotenein* and that of the Latin *ordo* or *ordinare*. The New Testament use of the former term borrows its basic secular meaning of "appointment" (Acts 14:23; II Cor 8:19), which is, in turn, derived from the original meaning of extending the hand, either to designate a person or to cast a vote. Some scholars see in *cheirotonein* a reference to the act of

Annecy/81

36. Properly speaking, then, ordination denotes an action by God and the community by which the ordained are strengthened by the Spirit for their task and are upheld by the acknowledgement and prayers of the congregation.

36-Commentary:
The original New Testament terms for ordination tend to be simple and descriptive. The fact of appointment is recorded. The laying on of hands is described. Prayer is made for the Spirit. Different traditions have built different interpretations on the basis of these data.

It is evident that there is a certain difference between the unspoken cultural setting of the Greek *cheirotonein* and that of the Latin *ordo* or *ordinare*. The New Testament use of the former term borrows its basic secular meaning of "appointment" (Acts 14: 23; II Cor 8: 19), which is, in turn, derived from the original meaning of extending the hand, either to designate a person or to cast a vote. Some scholars see in *cheirotonein* a reference to the act of laying on of hands, in view of the

Lima/82

40. Properly speaking, then, ordination denotes an action by God and the community by which the ordained are strengthened by the Spirit for their task and are upheld by the acknowledgement and prayers of the congregation.

40-Commentary:
The original New Testament terms for ordination tend to be simple and descriptive. The fact of appointment is recorded. The laying on of hands is described. Prayer is made for the Spirit. Different traditions have built different interpretations on the basis of these data.

It is evident that there is a certain difference between the unspoken cultural setting of the Greek *cheirotonein* and that of the Latin *ordo* or *ordinare*. The New Testament use of the former term borrows its basic secular meaning of "appointment" (Acts 14: 23; II Cor 8: 19), which is, in turn, derived from the original meaning of extending the hand, either to designate a person or to cast a vote. Some scholars see in *cheirotonein* a reference to the act of laying on of hands, in view of the

Geneva/6-80 [cont.]
laying on of hands, in view of the literal description of such action in such seemingly parallel instances as Acts 6: 6; 8: 17; 13: 3; 19: 6; I Tim 4: 14; II Tim 1:6. But the actual use of *cheirotonein* need mean no more than "appoint" without reference either to the theory or means of the action.

Rome/11-80 [cont.]
laying on of hands, in view of the literal description of such action in such seemingly parallel instances as Acts 6:6; 8:17; 13:3; 19:6; I Tim 4:14; II Tim 1:6. *Ordo* and *or-dinare*, on the other hand, are terms derived from Roman law where they convey the notion of the special status of a group distinct from the plebs, as in the term *ordo claris-simus* for the Roman senate. The starting point of any conceptual construction using these terms will strongly influence what is taken for granted in both the thought and action which result.

Annecy/81 [cont.]
literal description of such action in such seemingly parallel instances as Acts 6: 6; 8: 17; 13: 3; 19: 6; I Tim 4: 14; II Tim 1:6. *Ordo* and *or-dinare*, on the other hand, are terms derived from Roman law where they convey the notion of the special status of a group distinct from the plebs, as in the term *ordo claris-simus* for the Roman senate. The starting point of any conceptual construction using these terms will strongly influence what is taken for granted in both the thought and action which result.

Lima/82 [cont.]
literal description of the action in such seemingly parallel instances as Acts 6: 6; 8: 17; 13: 3; 19: 6; I Tim 4: 14; II Tim 1:6. *Ordo* and *or-dinare*, on the other hand, are terms derived from Roman law where they convey the notion of the special status of a group distinct from the plebs, as in the term *ordo claris-simus* for the Roman senate. The starting point of any conceptual construction using these terms will strongly influence what is taken for granted in both the thought and action which result.

Earlier in the text the fact of ordination was made more explicit as belonging to "the person *ordained* to proclaim the Gospel and to call the community to serve the Lord in unity of life and witness."[232]

The phrase, "the laying on of hands . . . rendering visible the ordering of the ministry in the revelation accomplished in him (Christ)," is replaced by the phrase, "the laying on of hands . . . rendering visible the fact that the ministry was instituted in the revelation accomplished in Christ."[233] The word, "ordering," is thus dropped in its close association with what Christ accomplished historically. The emphasis is placed on a process of ministering initiated by Christ but by no means determined in its final form by Christ.

Ordination is part of a process and not merely an isolated action which can be given some magical connotation. This is emphasized by the deletion of the phrase, "ordination . . . which inaugurates a relationship in which," and its replacement with the simple phrase, "by which."[234]

In the Commentary an important phrase is added. To the phrase, "it is the bishop who ordains," is added these words, "with the participation of the community."[235] Thus a misconception about what "the old tradition"[236] holds regarding the meaning of ordination is clarified. P. Ricca had observed the following: "Nothing is said about the forms of participation of the community at the ordination of ministers - even if it is affirmed that ordination is essentially an action accomplished by God and by the community. Here again the episcopal function seems to assume too much prominence."[237]

Also, in this Commentary section on the meaning of ordination, the phrase, "if churches are *increasingly able* to recognize each other in the sign of apostolic

---

[232]Lima, §26; 6/80, §23. Emphasis added.

[233]Lima, §39; 6/80, §36. E. Flesseman-van-Leer had asked, "What is the meaning of the words 'in the revelation'"? [Oct. 22, 1980, p. 4, Archive Box: "Faith and Order, Documents 1980-1981, Circular Letters, 1980-1981."].

[234]Lima, §40; 6/80, §37.

[235]Lima, §39-Commentary; 6/80, §36-Commentary.

[236]Idem.

[237]Sept. 25, 1980, p. 2, Archive Box: "Faith and Order, Documents 1980-1981, Circular Letters, 1980-1981." "Rien n'est dit des formes de participation de la communauté à l'ordination des ministres - même si l'on affirme que l'ordination est essentiellement une action accomplie par Dieu et par la communauté. Ici encore la fonction épiscopale semble prendre trop de relief."

succession," is replaced by the phrase, "if churches are *willing* to recognize each other in the sign of apostolic succession."[238] This alteration was made by M. Thurian.[239] Thus responsibility of the churches for making choices is made clear. An active ecumenical stance is favored over a purely passive one.

The Commentary section here also takes special pains to spell out how the very choice of language (rooted, in this case, in the historical meaning of the Latin, *ordo*) connotes a special status being accorded to those ordained, namely, "a group distinct from the plebs."[240] As the Commentary itself goes on to emphasize, "the starting point of any conceptual construction using these terms will strongly influence what is taken for granted in both the thought and action which result."[241]

B. THE ACT OF ORDINATION.

Here the community's role in ordination is again stressed. The act of ordaining is not restricted to episcopal officers. The relationship of the ordained to the world seems to be precisely *through* the church and not a direct relationship. Unclarity continues to reign over the use of "sacramental" language. And the steady introducing of more positive, inviting language continues to characterize the evolution of the text.

---

[238]Lima, §39-Commentary; 6/80, §36-Commentary. Emphasis added.

[239]"Corrections of BEM for Lima," FO Paper, Nov. 14, 1981, p. 5, Archive Box: "Faith and Order Archives, BEM, 79-82 corr. 81. Lima 82." Also given in printed form in FO/81:18, November 1981.

[240]Lima, §40-Commentary.

[241]Idem.

Geneva/6-80

38. A long and early Christian tradition places ordination in the context of worship and especially of the eucharist. Such a place for the service of ordination preserves the understanding of ordination as an *act* of the *whole* community, and not of a certain order within it or of the individual ordained. The act of ordination by the laying on of hands is at one and the same time: invocation of the Holy Spirit (epiklesis); sacramental sign; acknowledgement of gifts and commitment.

Rome/11-80

37. A long and early Christian tradition places ordination in the context of worship and especially of the eucharist. Such a place for the service of ordination preserves the understanding of ordination as an *act* of the *whole* community, and not of a certain order within it or of the individual ordained. The act of ordination by the laying on of hands of those appointed to do so is at one and the same time: invocation of the Holy Spirit (*epiklesis*); sacramental sign; acknowledgement of gifts and commitment.

Annecy/81

37. A long and early Christian tradition places ordination in the context of worship and especially of the eucharist. Such a place for the service of ordination preserves the understanding of ordination as an *act* of the *whole* community, and not of a certain order within it or of the individual ordained. The act of ordination by the laying on of hands of those appointed to do so is at one and the same time: invocation of the Holy Spirit (*epiklesis*); sacramental sign; acknowledgement of gifts and commitment.

Lima/82

41. A long and early Christian tradition places ordination in the context of worship and especially of the eucharist. Such a place for the service of ordination preserves the understanding of ordination as an act of the whole community, and not of a certain order within it or of the individual ordained. The act of ordination by the laying on of hands of those appointed to do so is at one and the same time invocation of the Holy Spirit (*epiklesis*); sacramental sign; acknowledgement of gifts and commitment.

Geneva/6-80

39. a) Ordination is an invocation to God that he bestow the power of the Holy Spirit upon the new minister in the new relation which is established between this minister and the local Christian community, the Church universal and the world. The otherness of God's initiative, of which the ordained ministry is the symbol, is here acknowledged in the act of ordination itself. "The Spirit blows where it wills" (Jn 3:3); the invocation of the Spirit implies the absolute dependence on God for the outcome of the Church's prayer. This means that the Spirit may set new forces in motion and open new possibilities "far more abundantly than all that we ask or think" (Eph 3:20).

Rome/11-80

38. (a) Ordination is an invocation to God that he bestow the power of the Holy Spirit upon the new minister in the new relation which is established between this minister and the local Christian community, the Church universal and the world. The otherness of God's initiative, of which the ordained ministry is a sign, is here acknowledged in the act of ordination itself. "The Spirit blows where it wills" (Jn 3:3); the invocation of the Spirit implies the absolute dependence on God for the outcome of the Church's prayer. This means that the Spirit may set new forces in motion and open new possibilities "far more abundantly than all that we ask or think" (Eph 3:20).

Annecy/81

38. (a) Ordination is an invocation to God that he bestow the power of the Holy Spirit upon the new minister in the new relation which is established between this minister and the local Christian community and, by intention, the Church universal. The otherness of God's initiative, of which the ordained ministry is a sign, is here acknowledged in the act of ordination itself. "The Spirit blows where it wills" (Jn 3:3): the invocation of the Spirit implies the absolute dependence on God for the outcome of the Church's prayer. This means that the Spirit may set new forces in motion and "far more abundantly than all that we ask or think" (Eph. 3: 20).

Lima/82

42. (a) Ordination is an invocation to God that the new minister be given the power of the Holy Spirit in the new relation which is established between this minister and the local Christian community and, by intention, the Church universal. The otherness of God's initiative, of which the ordained ministry is a sign, is here acknowledged in the act of ordination itself. "The Spirit blows where it wills" (Jn 3:3): the invocation of the Spirit implies the absolute dependence on God for the outcome of the Church's prayer. This means that the Spirit may set new forces in motion and "far more abundantly than all that we ask or think" (Eph. 3: 20).

Geneva/6-80

40. b) Ordination is a sign of the granting of this prayer by the Lord who gives the gift of the ordained ministry. Although the outcome of the Church's epiklesis depends on the freedom of God, the Church ordains in confidence that God, being faithful to his promise in Christ, enters sacramentally into contingent, historical forms of human relationship and uses them for his purpose. Ordination is a sign performed in faith that the spiritual relationship signified is present in, with and through the words spoken, the gestures made and the forms employed.

Rome/11-80

39. (b) Ordination is a sign of the granting of this prayer by the Lord who gives the gift of the ordained ministry. Although the outcome of the Church's epiklesis depends on the freedom of God, the Church ordains in confidence that God, being faithful to his promise in Christ, enters sacramentally into contingent, historical forms of human relationship and uses them for his purpose. Ordination is a sign performed in faith that the spiritual relationship signified is present in, with and through the words spoken, the gestures made and the forms employed.

Annecy/81

39. (b) Ordination is a sign of the granting of this prayer by the Lord who gives the gift of the ordained ministry. Although the outcome of the Church's epiklesis depends on the freedom of God, the Church ordains in confidence that God, being faithful to his promise in Christ, enters sacramentally into contingent, historical forms of human relationship and uses them for his purpose. Ordination is a sign performed in faith that the spiritual relationship signified is present in, with and through the words spoken, the gestures made and the forms employed.

Lima/82

43. (b) Ordination is a sign of the granting of this prayer by the Lord who gives the gift of the ordained ministry. Although the outcome of the Church's epiklesis depends on the freedom of God, the Church ordains in confidence that God, being faithful to his promise in Christ, enters sacramentally into contingent, historical forms of human relationship and uses them for his purpose. Ordination is a sign performed in faith that the spiritual relationship signified is present in, with and through the words spoken, the gestures made and the forms employed.

404

Geneva/6-80

41. c) Ordination is an acknowledgement by the Church of its discernment of the gifts of the Spirit in the one ordained, and a commitment by both the Church and the ordinand, to the tests and opportunities implied in the new relationship. By receiving the new minister in the act of ordination, the congregation acknowledges this minister's gifts and commits itself to responsibility for an openness towards these gifts. Likewise those one ordained offer their gifts to the Church and commit themselves to the burden and opportunity of new authority and responsibility. At the same time, they accept the collegial relationship with other ordained ministers into which they enter.

Rome/11-80

40. (c) Ordination is an acknowledgement by the Church of its discernment of the gifts of the Spirit in the one ordained, and a commitment by both the Church and the ordinand to the tests and opportunities implied in the new relationship. By receiving the new minister in the act of ordination, the congregation acknowledges this minister's gifts and commits itself to responsibility for an openness towards these gifts. Likewise those ordained offer their gifts to the Church and commit themselves to the burden and opportunity of new authority and responsibility. At the same time, they accept the collegial relationship with other ordained ministers into which they enter.

Annecy/81

40. (c) Ordination is an acknowledgement by the Church of its discernment of the gifts of the Spirit in the one ordained, and a commitment by both the Church and the ordinand to the opportunities implied in the new relationship. By receiving the new minister in the act of ordination, the congregation acknowledges this minister's gifts and commits itself to responsibility for an openness towards these gifts. Likewise those ordained offer their gifts to the Church and commit themselves to the burden and opportunity of new authority and responsibility. At the same time, they enter into a collegial relationship with other ordained ministers.

Lima/82

44. (c) Ordination is an acknowledgement by the Church of the gifts of the Spirit in the one ordained, and a commitment by both the Church and the ordinand to the new relationship. By receiving the new minister in the act of ordination, the congregation acknowledges the minister's gifts and commits itself to be open towards these gifts. Likewise those ordained offer their gifts to the Church and commit themselves to the burden and opportunity of new authority and responsibility. At the same time, they enter into a collegial relationship with other ordained ministers.

The Lima text adds the phrase, "of those appointed to do so," to the phrase, "the act of ordination by the laying on of hands."[242] Thus the part played by the whole community is highlighted and episcopacy is not specifically named as an essential qualification of "those appointed" to do the laying on of hands.

The phrase, "the new minister in the new relation (to) . . . the local Christian community, the Church universal and the world," is replaced by the phrase, "the new minister . . . in the new relation (to) . . . the local Christian community and, by intention, the Church universal."[243] Thus the relationship between the ordained and "the world" seems to be derivative from the ecclesial relationship.

It is not clear what is the meaning of the change from the term, "*the* symbol," to the term, "*a* sign,"[244] in reference to the ordained ministry's relationship to the otherness of God's initiative. Is sacramentality enhanced or diminished by the change in terminology?

And, as noted in earlier sections of this analysis, there is an effort in the Lima text to strike a more positive note. Thus the phrase, "a commitment by both the Church and the ordinand *to the tests* and opportunities implied in the new relationship," is replaced by the shorter phrase, "a commitment by both the Church and the ordinand to the new relationship."[245]

C. THE CONDITIONS FOR ORDINATION.

This final stage of textual evolution evidences an emphasis on the public ecclesial process for authorizing the ordination of those called and for authorizing the resumption of those returning from a leave of absence from the ordained ministry. There is an increased awareness that racial grounds are not to be countenanced as barriers to ordination. The same is true of the issue of physical handicaps. Greater and greater scope is granted to the various forms which ordained ministry can take. An increased use of hortatory language is again witnessed as the development of the texts unfolds, and another reference to "being" alongside "doing" in the ministry is in evidence.

---

[242]Lima, §41; 6/80, §38. The addition was made in the 11/80 text.

[243]Lima, §42; 6/80, §39. This change was made in the 1/81 text.

[244]Lima, §42; 6/80, §39. Emphasis added. This change was made in the 11/80 text.

[245]Lima, §44; 6/80, §41. Emphasis added.

Geneva/6-80

42. People are called in differing ways to the ordained ministry. There is a personal awareness of a call from the Lord to dedicate oneself to the ordained ministry. This call may be discerned through personal prayer and reflection, as well as through suggestion, example, encouragement, guidance coming from family, friends, the congregation, teachers, and other Church authorities. But there is also a recognition of the gifts and graces of a particular person, both natural and spiritually given, needed for the ministry to be performed. The Church's act of ordination is performed without respect of persons. Both in celibacy and marriage God can use people for the ordained ministry.

Geneva/6-80

43. Ordained persons may be professional ministers in the sense that they receive their salaries from the Church. The Church may also ordain people who remain in other occupations or employment.

Rome/11-80

41. People are called in differing ways to the ordained ministry. There is a personal awareness of a call from the Lord to dedicate oneself to the ordained ministry. This call may be discerned through personal prayer snd reflection, as well as through suggestion, example. encouragement, guidance coming from family, friends, the congregation, teachers, and other Cburch authorities. This call must be authenticated by the Church's recognition of the gifts and graces of the particular person, both natural and spiritually given, needed for the ministry to be performed. Both in celibacy and marriage God can use people for the ordained ministry.

Rome/11-80

42. Ordained persons may be professional ministers in the sense that they receive their salaries from the Church. The Church may also ordain people who remain in other occupations or employment.

Annecy/81

41. People are called in differing ways to the ordained ministry. There is a personal awareness of a call from the Lord to dedicate oneself to the ordained ministry. This call may be discerned through personal prayer and reflection, as well as through suggestion, example, encouragement, guidance coming from family, friends, the congregation, teachers, and other Church authorities. This call must be authenticated by the Church's recognition of the gifts and graces of the particular person, both natural and spiritually given, needed for the ministry to be performed. Both in celibacy and marriage God can use people for the ordained ministry.

Annecy/81

42. Ordained persons may be professional ministers in the sense that they receive their salaries from the Church. The Church may also ordain people who remain in other occupations or employment.

Lima/82

45. People are called in differing ways to the ordained ministry. There is a personal awareness of a call from the Lord to dedicate oneself to the ordained ministry. This call may be discerned through personal prayer and reflection, as well as through suggestion, example, encouragement, guidance coming from family, friends, the congregation, teachers, and other Church authorities. This call must be authenticated by the Church's recognition of the gifts and graces of the particular person, both natural and spiritually given, needed for the ministry to be performed. God can use people both celibate and married for the ordained ministry.

Lima/82

46. Ordained persons may be professional ministers in the sense that they receive their salaries from the Church. The Church may also ordain people who remain in other occupations or employment.

Geneva/6-80

44. Candidates for the ordained ministry need appropriate preparation through study of Scripture and theology and through acquaintance with the social and human realities of the present situation. The period of training will be one in which the candidate's call is tested and fostered and confirmed or perhaps modified.

Rome/11-80

43. Candidates for the ordained ministry need appropriate preparation through study of Scripture and theology, prayer and spirituality, and through acquaintance with the social and human realities of the present situation. In some situations, this preparation may take a form other than that of prolonged academic study. The period of training will be one in which the candidate's call is tested, fostered and confirmed or its understanding modified.

Annecy/81

43. Candidates for the ordained ministry need appropriate preparation through study of Scripture and theology, prayer and spirituality, and through acquaintance with the social and human realities of the contemporary world. In some situations, this preparation may take a form other than that of prolonged academic study. The period of training will be one in which the candidate's call is tested, fostered and confirmed or its understanding modified.

Lima/82

47. Candidates for the ordained ministry need appropriate preparation through study of scripture and theology, prayer and spirituality, and through acquaintance with the social and human realities of the contemporary world. In some situations, this preparation may take a form other than that of prolonged academic study. The period of training will be one in which the candidate's call is tested, fostered and confirmed or its understanding modified.

Geneva/6-80

45. Initial commitment to ordained ministry ought normally to be made without reserve or time limit. Yet leave of absence from service is not incompatible with ordination. Resumption of ministry requires no reordination. In recognition of the God-given charism of ministry, ordination to any one of the particular ordained ministries is never repeated.

Rome/11-80

44. Initial commitment to ordained ministry ought normally to be made without reserve or time limit. Yet leave of absence from service is not incompatible with ordination. Resumption of ministry requires the assent of the Church, but no reordination. In recognition of the God-given charism of ministry, ordination to any one of the particular ordained ministries is never repeated.

Annecy/81

44. Initial commitment to ordained ministry ought normally to be made without reserve or time limit. Yet leave of absence from service is not incompatible with ordination. Resumption of ordained ministry requires the assent of the Church, but no reordination. In recognition of the God-given charism of ministry, ordination to any one of the particular ordained ministries is never repeated.

Lima/82

48. Initial commitment to ordained ministry ought normally to be made without reserve or time limit. Yet leave of absence from service is not incompatible with ordination. Resumption of ordained ministry requires the assent of the Church, but no reordination. In recognition of the God-given charism of ministry, ordination to any one of the particular ordained ministries is never repeated.

Geneva/6-80

46. The discipline with regard to the conditions for ordination in one church need not be seen as universally applicable and used as grounds for not recognizing ministries in others.

Geneva/6-80

47. Churches should, however, seriously reevaluate their practices if they now refuse to test candidates for the ordained ministry solely on the grounds of their belonging to one particular group in the church. It is especially important today to be clear about this in view of the multitude of experiments in new forms of ministry with which the churches are approaching the modern world.

Rome/11-80

45. The discipline with regard to the conditions for ordination in one church need not be seen as universally applicable and used as grounds for not recognizing ministry in others.

Rome/11-80

46. Churches should, however, seriously reevaluate their practices if they now refuse to test candidates for the ordained ministry solely on the grounds of handicap or of their belonging to one particular group in the church. It is especially important today to be clear about this in view of the multitude of experiments in new forms of ministry with which the churches are approaching the modern world.

Annecy/81

45. The discipline with regard to the conditions for ordination in one church need not be seen as universally applicable and used as grounds for not recognizing ministry in others.

Annecy/81

46. Churches which refuse to test candidates for the ordained ministry on the grounds of handicap or because they belong, for example, to one particular sociological group must reevaluate their practices. This re-evaluation is particularly important today in view of the multitude of experiments in new forms of ministry with which the churches are approaching the modern world.

Lima/82

49. The discipline with regard to the conditions for ordination in one church need not be seen as universally applicable and used as grounds for not recognizing ministry in others.

Lima/82

50. Churches which refuse to consider candidates for the ordained ministry on the ground of handicap or because they belong, for example, to one particular race or sociological group should reevaluate their practices. This reevaluation is particularly important today in view of the multitude of experiments in new forms of ministry with which the churches are approaching the modern world.

The most significant change in this subsection is an added emphasis on the authority or authorization process of the Church. The final text deletes the statement that "there is also a recognition of the gifts and graces of a particular person (called to ordained ministry)" in favor of the much stronger statement that "this call *must be authenticated* by the Church's recognition of the gifts and graces of the particular person."[246] R.G.P. Lamburn had noted that "this is the place to make clear that the outward call of the Church is needed for the ordained ministry and the inward call of the Spirit for the charismatic ministry."[247]

In addition it should be noted here that the final text deletes the sentence in this same context that states that "the Church's act of ordination is performed without respect of persons."[248] M. Conway had observed, "I am not sure what is meant by the second last sentence in its 'without respect of persons', and would ask that that be made clearer."[249] The same emphasis on official authorization, however, is made in connection with the issue of resumption of the ordained ministry after leave of absence. Both texts (6/80 and Lima) state that such resumption requires no re-ordination. The Lima text adds, however, that it does require "the assent of the Church."[250]

The earlier text stated that "churches should, however, seriously re-evaluate their practices if they now refuse to test candidates for the ordained ministry solely on the grounds of their belonging to one particular group in the church."[251] The final text revises that sentence to read that "churches which refuse to consider candidates for the ordained ministry on the ground of handicap or because they belong, for example, to one particular race or sociological group should re-evaluate their practices."[252] R.G.P. Lamburn had asked for a clarification about the earlier reference

---

[246]Lima, §45; 6/80, §42. Emphasis added. This change was made in the 11/80 text.

[247]Mbwana/Thurian Correspondence, Oct. 8, 1980, p. 2, Archive Box: "Faith and Order, Documents 1980-1981, Circular Letters, 1980-1981."

[248]Lima, §45; 6/80, §42. This deletion was made in the 11/80 text.

[249]Sept. 5, 1980, p. 6, Archive Box: "Faith and Order, Documents 1980-1981, Circular Letters, 1980-1981."

[250]Lima, §48, 6/80, §45. This addition was made in the 11/80 text.

[251]6/80, §47.

[252]Lima, §50.

to those belonging to one particular group.[253] The revision makes explicit the racial issue and the handicap issue. Regarding the latter, G. Moede had asked, "Can some mention be made that God also calls persons with handicaps for ministry?"[254] The revision also maintains the hortatory tone ("should") even though the text immediately preceding Lima used the word, "must."[255]

There is another addition found in the final text which shows a sensitivity to various forms which the ordained ministry may take in the churches. It states that "in some situations, this preparation (for the ordained ministry) may take a form other than that of prolonged academic study."[256]

Also the phrase, "prayer and spirituality,"[257] is added. This addition reinforces the previous emphasis made earlier in the final text as noted above, namely, that ministry is important in the realm of being as well as that of doing.

There is possibly some significance in the fact that "Scripture" (capital "S") becomes "scripture" in the final text.[258]

VI. TOWARDS THE MUTUAL RECOGNITION OF THE ORDAINED MINISTRIES

In this final section of the text the notion of the ministry of *episkopé* is broadened to include offices in non-episcopal churches. There is evidenced a greater sensitivity to the issue of the exercise of *official* authority, the issue of liturgical expression in the processes of mutual recognition and the issue of the incompleteness of many ecumenical efforts. Attention to the "continuity" of the apostolic tradition is again prominent in the evolution of the text. Greater and greater sensitivity to the process of ecumenical dialogue is witnessed to by the careful use of language. And, finally, the use of the term, "sacrament," indicates that sacramentology is an important issue to be reckoned with in future ecumenical efforts.

---

[253]Mbwana/Thurian Correspondence, p. 2, Archive Box: "Faith and Order, Documents 1980-1981, Circular Letters, 1980-1981."

[254]Sept. 30, 1980, p. 3, Archive Box: "Faith and Order, Documents 1980-1981, Circular Letters, 1980-1981."

[255]/81, §46.

[256]Lima, §47; 6/80, §44. This addition was made in the 11/80 text.

[257]Lima, §47, 6/80, §44. This addition was made in the 11/80 text.

[258]Lima, §47; 6/80, §44.

Geneva/6-80

48. In order to advance towards the mutual recognition of ministries, deliberate efforts are required. All churches need to examine the forms of the ordained ministry and the degree to which they are faithful to its original intentions. Churches must be prepared to renew their practice of the ordained ministry.

Rome/11-80

47. In order to advance towards the mutual recognition of ministries, deliberate efforts are required. All churches need to examine the forms of ordained ministry and the degree to which they are faithful to its original intentions. Churches must be prepared to renew their understanding and their practice of the ordained ministry.

Annecy/81

47. In order to advance towards the mutual recognition of ministries, deliberate efforts are required. All churches need to examine the forms of ordained ministry and the degree to which they are faithful to its original intentions. Churches must be prepared to renew their understanding and their practice of the ordained ministry.

Lima/82

51. In order to advance towards the mutual recognition of ministries, deliberate efforts are required. All churches need to examine the forms of ordained ministry and the degree to which the churches are faithful to its original intentions. Churches must be prepared to renew their understanding and their practice of the ordained ministry.

Geneva/6-80

49. For the mutual recognition of the issue of the apostolic succession is of particular importance. Partners in ecumenical conversations can recognize the ordained ministry if they are mutually assured of their intention to transmit the apostolic ministry. The rite of transmission includes the invocation of the Spirit and the laying on of hands.

Rome/11-80

48. For the mutual recognition the issue of the apostolic succession is of particular importance. Churches in ecumenical conversations can recognize their respective ordained ministries if the are mutually assured of their intention to transmit the ministry of Word and Sacrament in continuity with apostolic times. The act of transmission should be performed in accordance with the apostolic tradition, which includes the invocation of the Spirit and the laying on of hands.

Annecy/81

48. For the mutual recognition the issue of the apostolic succession is of particular importance. Churches in ecumenical conversations can recognize their respective ordained ministries if they are mutually assured of their intention to transmit the ministry of Word and Sacrament in continuity with apostolic times. The act of transmission should be performed in accordance with the apostolic tradition, which includes the invocation of the Spirit and the laying of hands.

Lima/82

52. Among the issues that need to be worked on as churches move towards mutual recognition of ministries, that of apostolic succession is of particular importance. Churches in ecumenical conversations can recognize their respective ordained ministries if they are mutually assured of their intention to transmit the ministry of Word and sacrament in continuity with apostolic times. The act of transmission should be performed in accordance with the apostolic tradition, which includes the invocation of the Spirit and the laying of hands.

Geneva/6-80

50. In order to achieve mutual recognition, different steps are required of different churches:

a. Churches which have preserved the episcopal succession will need to recognize the apostolic content of the ordained ministry which exists in churches which have not maintained such succession. The churches without the episcopal succession but living in faithfulness to the apostolic faith and mission have a ministry of Word and Sacrament, as is evident from the life of these churches.

b. The churches without episcopal succession will need to realize that the continuity with the Church of the apostles finds profound expression in the successive laying on of hands by bishops and that, though they may not lack the continuity in the apostolic tradition, this sign will strengthen and deepen that continuity. They may need to recover the sign of episcopal succession.

Rome/11-80

49. In order to achieve mutual recognition, different steps are required of different churches:

(a) Churches which have preserved the episcopal succassion will need to recognize the apostolic content of the ordained ministry which exists in churches which have not maintained such succession. The churches without the episcopal succession but living in faithful continuity with the apostolic faith and mission have a ministry of Word and Sacrament, as is evident from the belief, the intention and the life of these churches.

(b) The churches without episcopal succession will need to realize that the continuity with the Church of the apostles finds profound expression in the successive laying on of hands by bishops and that, though they may not lack the continuity in the apostolic tradition, this sign will strengthen and deepen that continuity. They may need to recover the sign of the episcopal succession.

Annecy/81

49. In order to achieve mutual recognition, different steps are required of different churches:

(a) Churches which have preserved the episcopal succession will need to recognize the apostolic content of the ordained ministry which exists in churches which have not maintained such succession. The churches without the episcopal succession but living in faithful continuity with the apostolic faith and mission have a ministry of Word and Sacrament, as is evident from the belief, the intention and the life of these churches.

(b) The churches without episcopal succession will need to realize that the continuity with the Church of the apostles finds profound expression in the successive laying on of hands by bishops and that, though they may not lack the continuity in the apostolic tradition, this sign will strengthen and deepen that continuity. They may need to recover the sign of the episcopal succession.

Lima/82

53. In order to achieve mutual recognition, different steps are required of different churches. For example:

(a) Churches which have preserved the episcopal succession are asked to recognize both the apostolic content of the ordained ministry which exists in churches which have not maintained such succession and also the existence in these churches of a ministry of *episkope* in various forms.

(b) Churches without episcopal succession, and living in faithful continuity with the apostolic faith and mission have a ministry of Word and sacrament, as is evident from the belief, practice, and life of those churches. These churches are asked to realize that the continuity with the Church of the apostles finds profound expression in the successive laying on of hands by bishops and that, though they may not lack the continuity of the apostolic tradition, this sign will strengthen and deepen that continuity. They may need to recover the sign of the episcopal succession.

Geneva/6-80

51. Some churches ordain both men and women, others ordain only men. Differences on this issue could raise obstacles to the mutual recognition of ministries. But these obstacles must not be regarded as a substantive hindrance for further efforts toward mutual recognition. Openness to each other holds the possibility that the Spirit may well speak to one church through the insights of another. Ecumenical consideration, therefore, should encourage, not restrain, the facing of this question.

Rome/11-80

50. Some churches ordain both men and women, others ordain only men. Differences on this issue could raise obstacles to the mutual recognition of ministries. But these obstacles must not be regarded as substantive hindrance for further efforts toward mutual recognition. Openness to each other holds the possibility that the Spirit may well speak to one church through the insights of another. Ecumenical consideration, therefore, should encourage, not restrain, the facing of this question.

Annecy/81

50. Some churches ordain both men and women, others ordain only men. Differences on this issue raise obstacles to the mutual recognition of ministries. But those obstacles must not be regarded as substantive hindrance for further efforts towards mutual recognition. Openness to each other holds the possibility that the Spirit may well speak to one church through the insights of another. Ecumenical consideration, therefore, should encourage, not restrain, the facing of this question.

Lima/82

54. Some churches ordain both men and women, others ordain only men. Differences on this issue raise obstacles to the mutual recognition of ministries. But those obstacles must not be regarded as substantive hindrance for further efforts towards mutual recognition. Openness to each other holds the possibility that the Spirit may well speak to one church through the insights of another. Ecumenical consideration, therefore, should encourage, not restrain, the facing of this question.

Geneva/6-80

52. The mutual recognition of the churches and their ministries implies a public act from which point unity would be fully realized. Several forms of such public act have been proposed: mutual imposition of hands, eucharistic concelebration, solemn worship without a particular rite of recognition, the reading of a text of union during the course of a celebration. No one liturgical form would be absolutely required, but in any case it would be necessary to proclaim the accomplishmnent of mutual recognition publicly. The common celebration of the eucharist would certainly be the place for such a service.

Rome/11-80

51. The mutual recognition of churches and their ministries implies decision by the appropriate authorities and a liturgical act from which point unity would be publically manifest. Several forms of such public act have been proposed: mutual imposition of hands, eucharistic concelebration, solemn worship without a particular rite of recognition, the reading of a text of union during the course of a celebration. No one liturgical form would be absolutely required, but in any case it would be necessary to proclaim the accomplishment of mutual recognition publicly. The common celebration of the eucharist would certainly be the place for such an act.

Annecy/81

51. The mutual recognition of churches and their ministries implies decision by the appropriate authorities and a liturgical act from which point unity would be publicly manifest. Several forms of such public act have been proposed: mutual laying on of hands, eucharistic concelebration, solemn worship without a particular rite of recognition, the reading of a text of union during the course of a celebration. No one liturgical form would be absolutely required, but in any case it would be necessary to proclaim the accomplishment of mutual recognition publicly. The common celebration of the eucharist would certainly be the place for such an act.

Lima/82

55. The mutual recognition of churches and their ministries implies decision by the appropriate authorities and a liturgical act from which point unity would be publicly manifest. Several forms of such public act have been proposed: mutual laying on of hands, eucharistic concelebration, solemn worship without a particular rite of recognition, the reading of a text of union during the course of a celebration. No one liturgical form would be absolutely required, but in any case it would be necessary to proclaim the accomplishment of mutual recognition publicly. The common celebration of the eucharist would certainly be the place for such an act.

Earlier in the text of 6/80 there was a statement regarding mutual recognition which the Lima text deletes: "As long as there is agreement on the nature and basic form of the ordained ministry, the precise assignment of functions may vary from place to place."[259] This deletion makes possible a later addition in the Lima text (in the section under consideration here). It is a request made of churches which have preserved the episcopal succession. They are asked to recognize the existence in churches which have not maintained such succession "a ministry of *episkopé* in various forms."[260] This addition may be made in the light of some earlier remarks by W. Pannenberg calling for a clarification of "the special relation between episcopal succession and ordination of ministers by ministers in view of the originally local character of episcopal office. It should mention that the churches of the Lutheran Reformation did not regard episcopal succession as something lost in their own church."[261]

In the final paragraph of the key texts under consideration here the first sentence is significantly altered. The earlier text states: "The mutual recognition of the churches and their ministries implies *a public act* from which point unity would be *fully realized*."[262] The later (and final) text restates it as follows: "The mutual recognition of churches and their ministries implies *decision by the appropriate authorities* and a *liturgical* act from which point unity would be *publicly manifest*."[263] The final text thus evinces a sensitivity to the issues of: the exercise of official authority, liturgical expression, and the incomplete nature of many ecumenical processes. M. Tanner had expressed a lack of understanding for the earlier phrase, saying, "Do you mean it would be 'organic unity' or just unity of ministries? Clearly the former isn't the case."[264] The change, first made in the 11/80 text, reflects her questioning.

Continuity with the apostolic tradition is an important emphasis in this final

---

[259] 6/80, §25; deleted in Lima, §28.

[260] Lima, §53.

[261] Oct. 13, 1980, p. 10, Archive Box: "Faith and Order, Documents 1980-1981, Circular Letters, 1980-1981."

[262] 6/80, §52. Emphasis added.

[263] Lima, §55. Emphasis added.

[264] Oct. 1, 1980, p. 3, Archive Box: "Faith and Order, Documents 1980-1981, Circular Letters, 1980-1981."

section of the texts under consideration. The very word, continuity, is added in the later text: the phrase, "churches without the episcopal succession, *and* living *in faithful continuity with* the apostolic faith and mission" replaces the phrase, "churches without the episcopal succession *but* living *in faithfulness to* the apostolic faith and mission."[265] And a more precise use of prepositions emphasizes the careful approach taken in the final text toward the issue of this continuity. Thus, the phrase, "the continuity *of* the apostolic tradition," replaces the phrase, "the continuity *in* the apostolic tradition."[266]

The way in which that continuity is evidenced is spelled out in the later text which replaces the word, "life (of these churches)," with the phrase, "the belief, practice, and life of those churches."[267]

Two other phrases are added in the Lima text which make emphatic the effort to keep the apostolic tradition in the forefront of ecumenical dialogue. The phrase, "the ministry of Word and sacrament in continuity with apostolic times," replaces the simpler phrase, the apostolic ministry."[268] And to this is added the words, "should be performed in accordance with the apostolic tradition, which . . ."[269] This addition had been suggested by W. Pannenberg.[270]

As noted above in earlier sections there is in this section as well a special effort to use hortatory language and to resist dictating to the churches what actions they must take. The addition of the phrase, "for example," to introduce steps *required* to achieve mutual recognition relativizes the "requirements" which

---

[265]Lima, §53; 6/80, §50. Emphasis added. The phrase, "faithful continuity with," was inserted in the 11/80 text. The change in conjunctions (made at Lima) indicates a less judgmental attitude toward the non-episcopal churches.

[266]Lima, §53; 6/80, §50. Emphasis added. This change was made in the 1/81 text.

[267]6/80, §50; Lima, §53. The addition of the phrase was first made in the 11/80 text. Within the phrase, the word, "practice," (in the Lima text) replaces the term, "the intention," found in the two intermediary texts of 11/80 and 1/81. This change indicates the effort on the part of the final redactors at Lima to be less judgmental in regard to the churches without the episcopal succession.

[268]Lima, §52; 6/80, §49. This change was made in the 11/80 text.

[269]6/80, §49; Lima, §52. The word, "rite," is changed to the word, "act," in the intermediary (11/80 and 1/81 texts) and the final text, thus achieving a more ecclesiologically inclusive emphasis.

[270]Oct. 13, 1980, p. 10, Archive Box: "Faith and Order, Documents 1980-1981, Circular Letters, 1980-1981."

follow.[271] The phrase, "(churches) are asked," replaces the phrase, "(churches) will need."[272]

Perhaps the replacement of the phrase, "*Word* and *S*acrament," with the phrase, "*W*ord and *s*acrament," has some significance.[273] It may be that ecumenically there is a need to keep a sacramental emphasis in a less formal mode. Perhaps the word, "*S*acrament," implies particular ritual celebrations which one or the other church may or may not accept as Sacraments in the strict and formal sense understood by other churches.

SUMMARY

In this chapter the effort has been to trace the theologically significant differences between the text of Geneva/6-80 and the text of Lima/82. This effort has been accomplished (as in earlier chapters) using the section and subsection headings of the Lima text. Those headings correspond for the most part, but not entirely, with the headings found in the text of Geneva/6-80. Not all of the theological themes have been found to correspond exactly with the discrete headings. There has been some overlap. Some less salient theological and ecumenical themes, e.g., hortatory language, are found throughout the final text. It is hoped that this overall approach has provided a helpful tool for the analysis of all previous stages of the evolution of the Lima text on ministry.

In this period many themes are clarified and developed. And the language becomes more dynamic, less static. The almost complete deletion of the adjective, "special," in reference to the ordained ministry avoids overtones of superiority. The Twelve and the other apostles are carefully distinguished. This distinction may help to provide a broader base for churches to be considered apostolic. Eucharistic presiding for the ordained minister is emphasized by reference to the Twelve and to Christ as eucharistic presiders. The issue of the apostolic witnessing to the resurrection is highly nuanced.

---

[271]Lima, §53; 6/80, §50.

[272]Lima, §53; 6/80, §50. There are two instances of this redaction occurring in this place.

[273]Lima, §s 52 and 53; 6/80, §s 49 and 50. Emphasis added. It is interesting to note that earlier in the text (Lima, §17) the phrase, "through word and sacraments," is used. The same care to capitalize the word, "Word," and to keep the word, "sacrament," in the singular was not present earlier when discussing the issue of the ordained ministry and priesthood.

The trinitarian emphasis clarifies the internal "chain of command" giving Christ his unique authority.

Significant advances are made regarding priesthood in the church. The priesthood of the laity is clearly not secondary. *But* ordained ministers are appropriately called priests.

Although not treating the issue of the ordination of women in thoroughgoing fashion the Lima text at least faces it squarely. The strength of theological argumentation in favor of the ordination of women is acknowledged. In the final analysis, however, the Lima text does not take a stand one way or another. On the other hand, "ministry" (not just pastoral "service") by women, alongside men in the church, seems to be presumed.

There is acknowledged the overwhelming predominance of the threefold ministry of bishops, presbyters and deacons, in the development of ministerial offices in the early days of the church. There is, however, an appreciation of historical developmental processes at work always in the church. These processes are at times difficult to determine with satisfactory precision. The work of the Spirit is noted in terms of adaptation to human needs. More leeway is thus given to further adaptations today under the aegis of the Spirit.

Public appointment to ministry and accountability in ministry are emphasized. The two church polities, presbyterial (governed by a council of elders) and episcopal (governed by a monarchical bishop), are carefully balanced, e.g., by use of the phrase, "collegial body," in place of the phrase, "college of elders."

The ministry of *episkopé*, as an indispensable ministry of unity in the church, is strongly endorsed. A brief mention of the bishop's service of unity at the wider (regional) and even universal level gives some, but not very much, importance to the needs of the church beyond each local eucharistic community. No mention is made of the petrine ministry or of the papacy.

The Lima text faces but does not resolve the theological controversy about the precise relationship between the presbyterate and the episcopacy. Also left unresolved is the relationship between presbyters and elders. This unresolvedness keeps openended questions of church polity. Left unresolved as well are: defining the term, "local church" and naming the specific tasks of presbyters.

The discussion of the diaconate as such is more and more restricted as the text evolves. The issue of the office of deacon, however, is used to discuss other issues facing the church: e.g., the reform of the threefold ministry as the inherited pattern, the church's struggling to meet the needs of the world, and the church's struggling to give due recognition, even official status, to a variety of ministries which continue to emerge but which are not easily classified in the threefold scheme.

In regard to apostolic tradition it is noted that continuity in the transmission of the gospel should predominate over the transmission of ministry. A dialectic between the two should be maintained.

The text is unclear regarding the "sacramental" implications of episcopal succession as well as its necessity as a "sign" of apostolicity for the church. The term, "faith," comes to replace the term, "truth," thus broadening the meaning of what is handed down in the churches from apostolic times.

In regard to ordination more and more care is exercised in regard to what can or cannot be attributed directly to the will and action of the historical Jesus. Care is also taken to view ordination as part of a human process and not as a magical conferral of powers. The participation of the community of the church in ordinations is appropriately noted. The churches are more directly and candidly invited to make decisions regarding their mutual acceptance of one another's ordinations. And special care is taken to explain how language influences the very attitudes of church members and the very structures of church polity.

In the final section of the text, "Towards the Mutual Recognition of the Ordained Ministries," the notion of the ministry of *episkopé* is broadened to include offices in non-episcopal churches. There is evidenced a greater sensitivity to the issue of the exercise of *official* authority, the issue of liturgical expression in the processes of mutual recognition and the issue of the incompleteness of many ecumenical efforts.

CHAPTER V

THE THEOLOGY OF MINISTRY IN THE LIMA TEXT

In this chapter the approach will be fivefold: 1) a comparative analysis of each of the sections of the Lima document with official Roman Catholic theological positions; 2) a consideration of theological positions taken by several Roman Catholic theologians, positions which go beyond the present official positions and which indicate that many of the same tensions which exist between the official teaching of the Roman Catholic Church and the Lima text exist also within Roman Catholicism itself; 3) a consideration of the theological starting points which underlie and actually cause these different conclusions to be drawn and tensions to persist; 4) in the light of the above considerations the particular stand which the present writer takes in advancing toward a theology of ministry; 5) the specific strengths and weaknesses of the Lima text on ministry, the challenges it puts forth and the improvements it must make so that its challenge will be better heeded, and particularly the insights and challenges which the Lima document on ministry offers to any Roman Catholic theology of ministry.

SECTION ONE. A COMPARATIVE ANALYSIS : THE LIMA DOCUMENT ON MINISTRY AND OFFICIAL ROMAN CATHOLIC THEOLOGICAL POSITIONS.

What we will see emerging in this comparative analysis is as follows. In regard to part I of the Lima text, there is first, general agreement about the calling of the whole people of God. There is noted a lack of clarity about the distinction between what is divinely determined for the structuring of the church and what may be of human making. The question will be raised whether such a distinction can be so clearly drawn. The drawing of such a distinction involves preconceived notions about the structuring of authoritative decision-making processes present in the various partner churches engaged in ecumenical dialogue.

In part II of the Lima text there is a consideration of the mission of the Twelve as distinct from the other disciples and the implications for the ordained ministry. Also the concept of representation (of Christ and the Church) is introduced and how it involves the ordained minister's relationship to Christ and the Church. The sequence of representation in the Vatican response is different from that of the Lima text. It is noted that "representation" needs further clarification. Also in this section the Vatican exhibits constant insistence on the presider of the eucharist being an ordained minister.

As regards ordained ministry and authority there is a lack of clarity noted by the Vatican in the Lima text about the precise relationship between the laity and the ordained. In its commenting on participation in the priesthood of Christ the Vatican insists on the essential difference between the ordained and the laity. The Vatican again shows great sensitivity on the issue of presiders at eucharist.

With regard to the ordination of women the Vatican refers to Christological reasons which prevent such ordination but it does not name those reasons. The Vatican response insists that the practice of tradition is beyond its competence to change.

In part III the Vatican states clearly that it considers the threefold structure of the episcopate, the priesthood and the diaconate to be of divine institution and therefore constituting the *esse* of the church. The Lima text is not so clear on the matter while strongly recommending the threefold structure. The Vatican affirms the Lima text's expression of the guiding principles for the exercise of the ordained ministry. The Vatican focuses, as had Vatican Council II, on the functions of bishops, placing less emphasis on those of presbyters and deacons. There is noted the Lima document's neglect of the issue of episcopal collegiality because of its methodological starting-point, the local church. The same neglect is noted in regard to the episcopal magisterium or teaching authority. Also noted is the lack of treatment in the Lima text of the petrine ministry. Thus the church universal and the ministries which directly serve its unity and catholicity are topics not treated by Lima. Finally the Vatican response to Lima expresses overall agreement with its treatment of the variety of charisms in the church.

In part IV the Vatican finds many points of agreement with the Lima text while warning of too unnuanced a treatment of the various elements which constitute apostolic tradition and the relationship of those elements one to the other. And while agreeing with much of Lima's treatment of succession of the apostolic ministry the Vatican insists on the crucial importance of episcopal succession. Its insistence may very well be taken to be too physical and more narrow in a linear-historical sense than need be.

In part V, on ordination, the Vatican's emphasis is more ontological-juridical than that of the Lima text. Again, the Vatican worries about the use of the term, "sign." It asks for greater clarity especially as its use relates to the Catholic understanding of sacrament as effective sign. This is especially apropos in regard to the competent minister of the sacrament of ordination who, for the Vatican, is a bishop standing in the line of authentic apostolic succession.

In part VI, the Vatican response again pinpoints the issue of sacramental ordination by a bishop in authentic apostolic succession as a major stumbling block to mutual recognition of ordained ministries in the churches. It leaves open, however, the possibility of working toward unity by trying to overcome such major ecclesiological issues.

I. THE CALLING OF THE WHOLE PEOPLE OF GOD.

In keeping with the approach of the previous three chapters which traced the evolution of the text this analysis will follow the outline of the Lima text itself. The first theological theme to emerge is that of God's call to the whole of humanity to become God's people. The phrase, "people of God," so common in the texts of Vatican II, indicates the compatibility of this text with Roman Catholic ecclesiology. God is clearly and precisely trinitarian in the Lima text. The Vatican response to BEM states that "we agree with the general understanding of the calling of the people of God as it is stated in the first section."[1]

It is in this same response that the Vatican raises the question of authority in the church. The Lima document seeks a common answer to the question, "How, according to the will of God and under the guidance of the Holy Spirit, is the life of the Church to be understood and ordered, so that the Gospel may be spread and the community built up in love?"[2] Noting that it is a fair question the Vatican grants that it implies an "awareness that church order, at least in its fundamental constitution, is not the result of historical developments and human-made organization."[3] It is not clear to the present writer how such an awareness can be drawn out of the Lima text.

---

[1]*Origins: NC Documentary Service*, November 19, 1987 (Vol. 17: No. 23), p. 412.

[2]Lima 6.

[3]*Origins*, November 19, 1987, p. 412.

Further it is not clear that the will of God and the guidance of the Spirit are realities which are necessarily separate or separable from historical developments and human-made organization. The documents of Vatican Council II evidence a tension between a vision of the Church as an invisible community and as a visible hierarchical structure. A. Grillmeier explains the tension and the Council's attempt to deal with it thus:

> The great exponent of the notion of the Church Visible was Cardinal Bellarmine, who thus formed a contrast to St. Thomas, the latter viewing the Church above all from the aspect of its inner reality but neglecting to some extent the visible which is so clearly given in the New Testament and the Fathers. The first chapter (of *Lumen Gentium*), on the mystery of the Church, is a deliberate effort at a synthesis such as is already implicit in the biblical and patristic notion of *mysterium.*[4]

Some questions had been raised, earlier in the Vatican response to BEM which indicate its recent emphasis on the visible pole of the tension:

> What are the constitutive elements of authority and order in the church? What are the nature and role of decisive authority in the discernment of God's will as to the development of ministry in the church in the past and with regard to the present needs of the church?[5]

To be sure the Vatican's concern that this issue of authority remains unclear in BEM is a legitimate concern. It is true, however, that this issue stands at the very heart of ecumenical dialogue and that such dialogue depends on the willingness of the dialogue partners to reexamine (and perhaps even alter) the very structures and processes of authoritative decision-making which are operative in their respective ecclesial bodies. In other words, any preestablished and unchangeable view of authoritative decision-making itself prevents from the start the whole ecumenical enterprise.

II. The Church and the Ordained Ministry.

A. The Ordained Ministry.

The Vatican response acknowledges that

> in the description of the chief responsibility of the ordained ministry, given in No. 13 (Lima M13), we recognize the framework of a Catholic understanding of the

---

[4] Aloys Grillmeier, "Chapter I, The Mystery of the Church," *Commentary on the Documents of Vatican II*, ed. by Herbert Vorgrimler, vol. I. New York: Herder and Herder, 1967.

[5] *Origins*, Vol. 17, p. 405.

mission of the ordained ministry. We approve of the way this ministry is already related to the mission of the Twelve. We would suggest that this mission should be related further with Christ's own mission by the Father: "As the Father sent me, so I am sending you" (Jn 20:21).[6]

The Scriptural reference here is one whose original context is that of an appearance of the risen Christ to an unspecified group of "disciples," not necessarily the Twelve only. To restrict its application to a mission transmitted to the ordained alone is a less plausible reading of the scriptural text.[7]

Next, the concept of "representation" is acknowledged by the Vatican as a valuable concept which

> needs further qualification in the context of the agreed statement, so that through its relation to the *archetypos* Christ, the ordained ministry is in and for the church an effective and sacramental reality by which a minister acts *in persona Christi*. This view should also help to explain more fully why, according to the Catholic faith, the eucharist must be presided over by an ordained minister, who represents Christ in a personal and sacramental way.[8]

The phrase, *in persona Christi*, is the one used in earlier documentation of the Vatican to describe the "role (this is the original sense of the word *persona*)"[9] which men (not women) can fulfill as presiders at eucharist. In that earlier documentation the Vatican states the following:

> It is true that the priest represents the church, which is the body of Christ. But if he does so, it is precisely because he first represents Christ himself, who is the head and shepherd of the church. The Second Vatican Council[10] used this phrase to make more precise and to complete the expression *in persona Christi*. It is in this quality that the priest presides over the Christian assembly and celebrates the eucharistic sacrifice.[11]

It seems clear that the Lima text sees the role of representation for the ordained minister thus: first, representative of the Church, then, representative of Christ; whereas the Vatican sees it thus: first, representative of Christ, then, representative

---

[6]*Origins*, vol. 17, p. 412.

[7]Bruce Vawter notes the following in reference to John 20: 19-23: "Whether Jn means that only ten were present (the Twelve less Judas and Thomas) or that there was a larger group (cf. Lk 24: 33) is not certain." [*The Jerome Biblical Commentary*, Englewood Cliffs, New Jersey: Prentice-Hall, Inc., 1968, Vol. II, p. 463.]

[8]*Origins*, vol 17, p. 412.

[9]Vatican Congregation for the Doctrine of the Faith, "Declaration on the Question of the Admission of Women to the Ministerial Priesthood," January 27, 1977, *Origins*, vol. 6, p. 522.

[10]L.G., 28; P.O., 2.

[11]*Origins*, vol. 6, p. 523.

of the Church. This is made clear in the first six paragraphs of the M text. As W. Marrevee notes,

> one cannot move immediately from Jesus Christ to the ordained ministry; one is bound to take into account the calling of the whole people of God that actualizes, in the power of the Spirit, Christ's mission of service to the world.[12]

Furthermore the Vatican, in its earlier *Declaration* (on the ordination of women), as well as in its response here to BEM, makes a facile shift in its use of the terms sign and image. As G. Worgul has noted in regard to the great difference between these two terms:

> An effective sign need not necessarily resemble what it signifies, as in the example of smoke and fire. An image, however, does seek as exact a reproduction as possible, as in the case of a portrait or architectural model.[13]

Worgul further notes that

> one might wish to marshal an argument that in an alternative "symbol system" bio-physiological maleness or femaleness are irrelevant to being the image of God, made in the image of Christ and, therefore, possessing the ability to symbolize Christ.[14]

By stressing the eucharist as necessarily presided over by an ordained minister the Vatican response to BEM neglects to mention two sacraments, according to its own tradition, which can be presided over by ordained and non-ordained alike, baptism and marriage.[15] In these sacraments (as in all the sacraments) the unity of the community is focused.[16]

B. ORDAINED MINISTRY AND AUTHORITY.

The Vatican response to BEM commends these paragraphs in the M text while pointing out that "the task remains of reflecting upon the ecclesiological

---

[12]"The Lima Document on Ordained Ministry," *Catholic Perspectives on Baptism, Eucharist and Ministry: A Study Commissioned by the Catholic Theological Society of America,* ed. by Michael A. Fahey, Lanham, MD: University Press of America, 1986, p. 166.

[13]George S. Worgul, Jr., "Ritual, Power, Authority and Riddles: The Anthropology of Rome's Declaration on the Ordination of Women," *Louvain Studies.* Vol. 14, no. 1, Spring 1989, p. 46.

[14]Ibid.

[15]The Orthodox tradition requires an ordained presbyter for the sacrament of marriage.

[16]Worgul, "Ritual, Power, Authority and Riddles," pp. 47-48.

dimension and the peculiar nature of this authority."[17] What is implied here is the matter of spelling out of the precise relationship between the authority of the ordained and the authority of the laity. The word, "authorization," in English may be a good word to keep in mind here. How does the process of authorization take place in the Church? In the past the community delegated much of its power to the ordained ministers. There are indications in Roman Catholicism that now the community is desirous of taking back some of that power, e.g., in regard to the election of bishops.

Actually it is in an earlier paragraph in the M text that a significant reference to authority is made. "As leaders and teachers, they (the ordained) call the community to submit to the authority of Jesus Christ."[18] Again, it requires ecclesiological interpretation to clarify the exact functioning of this task of calling the community to submit.

C. ORDAINED MINISTRY AND PRIESTHOOD.

The Vatican response to BEM reiterates the official teaching given in Vatican Council II stating that

> although the common priesthood of the faithful and the ministerial or hierarchical priesthood are interrelated, each being in its own way a participation in the one priesthood of Christ, they differ from one another in essence and not only in degree (cf. *Lumen Gentium*, 10).[19]

In this regard the absence in the body of the text of M of a reference to the offering of sacrifice by the ordained is noted. Further, the Vatican notes, the reference in M's Commentary to the ordained priest presiding at the eucharist "could have been made correctly in the paragraph itself,"[20] namely the body of the text of M (No. 17). The Vatican response to BEM continues to evince a great sensitivity to the issue of presidency at the eucharist. Perhaps the issue of women's ordination is the unspoken cause of this sensitivity since the Vatican limits the use of the phrase, *in persona Christi*, to eucharist.

---

[17]*Origins*, vol. 17, p. 413.

[18]M11.

[19]*Origins*, Vol. 17, p. 413.

[20]Ibid.

D. THE MINISTRY OF MEN AND WOMEN IN THE CHURCH.

The official Vatican response to BEM acknowledges the "challenge to our position"[21] posed by the experience of churches which ordain women. The response also refers in general terms to

> theological issues rooted not only in the understanding of tradition, but also of the Scriptures concerning Christology which lie at the heart of our convictions and understanding with regard to the admission of women to the ordained ministry.[22]

Those theological issues are not addressed.

Furthermore the Vatican response corrects M's statement (No. 18) that "many churches hold that the tradition of the church in this regard must not be changed." In response the Vatican insists:

> In our view, it would be more accurate to say that we have no authority to change it, since we believe it belongs to the apostolic tradition of the church. Perhaps this nuance also points to a different conception of apostolic tradition.[23]

III. THE FORMS OF THE ORDAINED MINISTRY.

A. BISHOPS, PRESBYTERS AND DEACONS.

Roman Catholic doctrine clearly states:

> Canon 1008. By divine institution some among Christ's faithful are, through the sacrament of order, marked with an indelible character and are thus constituted sacred ministers; thereby they are consecrated and deputed so that, each according to his own grade, they fulfil, in the person of Christ the Head, the offices of teaching, sanctifying and ruling, and so they nourish the people of God.

> Canon 1009. #1. The orders are the episcopate, the priesthood and the diaconate.

Thus it is taught that it is by divine institution and therefore belonging to the *esse* of the Church's constitution. Yet there is a willingness on the part of the Vatican to admit that "an ecumenical discernment is needed to see what belongs to the constitutive structure of the church and what to the contingent social organization."[24]

The Lima text does not make clear what is constitutive and what is not. It

---

[21]*Origins*, Vol. 17, p. 413.

[22]Ibid.

[23]Ibid.

[24]*Origins*, Vol. 17, p. 413.

does, however, strongly state that "the threefold ministry of bishop, presbyter and deacon may serve today as an expression of the unity we seek and also as a means for achieving it." (M22) The text highlights the episcopacy. As W. Marrevee puts it, "acceptance of the episcopacy is not being proposed as a matter of sociological convenience."[25] For the M text states that:

> a ministry of *episkopé* is *necessary* to express and safeguard the unity of the body. Every church *needs* this ministry of unity in some form in order to be the Church of God, the one body of Christ, a sign of the unity of all in the Kingdom.[26]

B. GUIDING PRINCIPLES FOR THE EXERCISE OF THE ORDAINED MINISTRY IN THE CHURCH.

The Vatican response affirms the content of this section of Lima M as being in keeping with its understanding of the historical development of the church.

C. FUNCTIONS OF BISHOPS, PRESBYTERS AND DEACONS.

In this section the Vatican focuses on the functions of bishops and states that "the description (of Lima M29) hardly mentions the very traditional and essential collegial aspect of episcopacy."[27] Indeed this teaching is affirmed in Vatican Council II's statement:

> Just as, in accordance with the Lord's decree, St. Peter and the rest of the apostles constitute a unique apostolic college, so in like fashion the Roman Pontiff, Peter's successor, and the bishops, the successors of the apostles, are related with and united to one another. Indeed, the very ancient discipline whereby the bishops installed throughout the whole world lived in communion with one another and with the Roman Pontiff in a bond of unity, charity and peace. . . points clearly to the collegiate character and structure of the episcopal order.[28]

That same statement continues emphasizing what the Vatican states in its recent response that

> the ecumenical council becomes thus a representative image of the universal church, because it is a meeting of the college of bishops around the bishop of Rome

---

[25]*Catholic Perspectives on BEM*, p. 173.

[26]M23. Emphasis added.

[27]*Origins*, Vol. 17, p. 413.

[28]L.G. 22 (Flannery, pp. 374-76).

who, according to the Catholic Church, is the head of this college.[29]

W. Marrevee contends that the Lima document leaves underdeveloped certain issues of ecclesiology, e.g., this issue of collegiality among bishops, precisely because of the text's methodology:

> The starting point for the document's reflections on the ordained ministry was the place and role of the ordained ministry in the more immediate experience of ecclesial fellowship at the local level. The question is what about the link or bond of a given local community with other local communities? Is the Church not actualized as well in the bond between the local communities and is there not a need for a unique ministry at that level too?[30]

It is at this point that the Vatican response notes that "we miss here the clear expression of the teaching function of the bishops, the magisterium."[31] Vatican Council II states simply that "in order that the full and living Gospel might always be preserved in the Church the apostles left bishops as their successors. They gave them 'their own position of teaching authority'."[32] Here again Lima's silence is probably dictated by its methodology which highlights the local church experience to the neglect of the church universal.

The recent Vatican response to BEM goes on to state as follows:

> We understand that it may not be the purpose, at present, of the Faith and Order Commission to reflect upon the personal expression of a "focus of unity" in the universal church, but one can ask whether that would not be a logical result of the reflections started upon a representative service of oversight, continuity and unity in the church.[33]

Thus is delicately noted the intentional omission from the Lima text of the issue of the papacy. Here again the Lima text is guided by its methodology which neglects issues impacting on the church universal. The text, in its consideration of the functions of bishops, sketches ever so briefly that "they relate the Christian community in their area to the wider Church, and the universal Church to their community." (M29) What W. Marrevee says in reference to that brief allusion is the following:

> It would be difficult to maintain that this brief reference has given sufficient attention to the catholicity of the Church, to which the college of bishops relates in

---

[29]*Origins*, Vol. 17, p. 413.

[30]*Catholic Perspectives on BEM*, p. 173.

[31]Ibid.

[32]D.V. 7, (Flannery, p. 753 f.). Cf. also *The New Code of Canon Law*, §749, 2.

[33]*Origins*, Vol. 17, p. 413.

a significant way. In fact, it is safe to say that the catholic dimension of the Church has been largely ignored in the Lima text. Could the reason for the virtual absence of this dimension be that, if it were to be articulated more extensively, eventually the possibility of a Petrine ministry, with its unique place within the college of bishops with which it is supposed to serve the unity of the universal Church, would have to be considered?[34]

D. VARIETY OF CHARISMS.

The Vatican response to BEM expresses overall agreement with the content of this section of Lima M.

IV. SUCCESSION IN THE APOSTOLIC TRADITION.

A. APOSTOLIC TRADITION IN THE CHURCH.

The Vatican response commends the Lima M text for clearly distinguishing between the apostolic tradition and episcopal succession and approves its understanding of apostolic tradition as "the continuity in the permanent characteristics of the church of the apostles," (Lima M34) which characteristics it goes on to list. Nonetheless the Vatican offers this caveat in the form of a question:

> Is there not the tendency here to be content with a listing and a juxtaposition of items which all have to do with the apostolic tradition without showing sufficiently how they have their own function within the totality and how they are related among themselves?[35]

B. SUCCESSION OF THE APOSTOLIC MINISTRY.

The major response, however, is made to the issue of succession. It agrees with Lima M that "in the early centuries, the succession of bishops became one of the ways, . . . in which the apostolic tradition of the Church was expressed." (M36) It agrees as well that "this succession was understood as serving, symbolizing and guarding the continuity of the apostolic faith and communion." (M36) And it approves of Lima's appreciation of "the episcopal succession as a sign . . . of the

---

[34]*Catholic Perspectives on BEM*, p. 175.

[35]*Origins*, Vol. 17, p. 414.

continuity and unity of the Church." (M38) It insists, however, that "the meaning of 'sign/expression' needs to be clear."[36]

The Vatican response goes on to state the following in regard to the ministry of the bishop in Catholic ecclesiology:

> It is more than a function of oversight next to other functions and ministries. In his very personal ministry, the bishop represents the local church entrusted to him. He is its qualified spokesperson in the communion of the churches. At the same time he is the first representative of Jesus Christ in the community. By his ordination to the episcopacy he is commissioned to exercise leadership in the community, to teach with authority and to judge. All other ministries are linked to his and function in relationship to it. Thus his ministry is a sacramental sign of integration and a focus of communion. Through the episcopal succession the bishop embodies and actualizes both catholicity in time, i.e., the continuity of the church across the generations, as well as the communion lived in each generation. The actual community is thus linked up through a personal sign with the apostolic origins, its teaching and way of living.[37]

Finally in regard to this section of the Lima M text the Vatican disagrees that "the episcopal succession (is) . . . not a guarantee, of the continuity and unity of the Church." (M38) This disagreement lies in the precise area of sacramental theology. W. Marrevee does not emphasize this disagreement but states that:

> the Lima document could find a broader base of support in a more developed communion ecclesiology. The episcopal succession it recommends stands too isolated. This could easily be corrected if the Lima document were to be attentive to a practice of the episcopal churches whereby, in the ordination ceremony, neighboring bishops, as witnesses of the apostolic faith of their own churches, lay hands on a new bishop thereby inserting the latter with his church into the communion of local churches that recognize and affirm each other in the apostolic faith. This orientation would prevent episcopal succession from being understood in a physical and narrowly linear-historical sense and would bring out more forcefully the communion with other apostolic churches.[38]

It seems that the official Roman Catholic perspective on episcopal succession might suffer from the same "physical and narrowly linear-historical sense" that Marrevee points out and that the Roman Catholic perspective has much to gain from looking to its own *praxis* as described by Marrevee here.

---

[36]Ibid.

[37]Ibid.

[38]*Catholic Perspectives on BEM*, pp. 178-179.

V. Ordination

While affirming a general agreement with the content here it is in the area of sacramental theology that the Vatican expresses some reservations in this major section of Lima M.

As W. Marrevee adds, however, in treating this section of the Lima text:

> What must be kept in mind though is that, as may be expected, the Lima statement refrains from approaching this in ontological-juridical categories. Its starting point here, too, is that the Church is to be understood as a christological-pneumatological reality.[39]

A. The Meaning of Ordination.

It is the word, "sign," which the Vatican response wants clarified.

B. The Act of Ordination.

The Vatican acknowledges that the M text describes essential elements for the sacrament of order, that it even uses the word sacrament as an adjective and adverb and that such use "points in the direction of a sacramental understanding"[40] The response points out, however, that ordination is never clearly called a sacrament and that "Catholics would like it to be stated clearly that ordination is not only a sign, but an effective sign."[41]

The Vatican response also considers insufficient M's treatment of the problem of the competent minister of ordination. Again, the issue involves a particular understanding of sacramental theology as well as ecclesiology:

> Our view, however, is that ordination is a sacrament. The competent minister of this sacrament is a bishop who stands in the authentic apostolic succession and who acts in the person of Christ. We therefore ask the Commission on Faith and Order to reflect on the ecclesiological meaning of the episcopal succession for ordination. We believe that its necessity is due to the fact that the episcopal succession signifies and actualizes the sacramental link of the ministry — first of all, of the episcopal ministry itself — with the apostolic origin. It is rooted in the sacramental

---

[39]Ibid., p. 168.

[40]*Origins*, Vol. 17, p. 414.

[41]Ibid.

nature of the church.[42]

C. THE CONDITIONS FOR ORDINATION.

There seems to be no incompatibility between the official teaching of the Roman Catholic Church and the content of this section of the Lima text.

VI. TOWARDS THE MUTUAL RECOGNITION OF THE ORDAINED MINISTRIES.

The crux of the Vatican's response to this section of the Lima text is the following sentence: "We believe that ordained ministry requires sacramental ordination by a bishop standing in the apostolic succession."[43] This response indicates the Vatican's tendency to allow no deviation from the norm of literal episcopal succession as a strict requirement for valid sacramental ordination. On the other hand, the Vatican, in practically the same breath, acknowledges "the many ways in which continuity in apostolic faith, worship and mission has been preserved in communities which have not retained the form of historic episcopate."[44] One is left wondering whether the door for dialogue is still open in this regard. The response ends its "particular comments" on Lima M by stating the following:

> Since, in our view, ordained ministry requires sacramental ordination in the apostolic succession, it is premature to make pronouncements on the form a public act of mutual recognition of churches and their ministries would have (M No.55) Rather, it is necessary now to work toward unity in faith on this central ecclesiological issue.[45]

In summary it can be said that the Vatican, in evaluating the M text, has engaged in a process of comparison rather than dialogue. There has been no questioning of its own positions in terms of the acknowledgement of various theological points of view that exist within Roman Catholicism itself. Positions have been taken without taking into account that many Roman Catholic theologians exhibit a willingness to engage in a common ecumenical search for new articulations of the faith of the church. It is this openness to new formulations of the faith that

---

[42]Ibid.

[43]Ibid., p. 415.

[44]Ibid.

[45]Ibid.

leads us to consider at this juncture the evidence for theological tensions within Roman Catholicism itself, many of the same tensions we have outlined between Lima M and the official Roman Catholic response to BEM.

Section Two: the Tensions Between Lima M and the Official Roman Catholic Tradition Are Also Tensions in Roman Catholicism Itself.

In this section it is the intention of the present writer to isolate three major areas of theological tension already uncovered in the present study between official Roman Catholicism and the contents of Lima M. After naming these three major areas and the various subtopics or issues which each area covers it will be shown how each of these issues is a source of tension within the theological life of Roman Catholicism itself.

The first major area of theological tension is that of structures or offices of the Church. The second major area focuses on the persons holding such offices. The third area is that of sacramentality, the mediation of divine grace and presence by the Church, its structures and persons.

Structures/Offices of the Church: Some Questions.

The specific issues here can be expressed in the form of several questions being asked currently. What pastoral offices of the Church are essential constitutive elements of the reality of the Church's structure, i.e., the *esse* of the Church and not merely its *bene esse*? What is divinely determined? What is sociologically (humanly) determined? What about the following specific issues:

a) the three-fold ministry (of bishop, presbyter, deacon)
b) the episcopal office (and its precise relationship to the office of presbyter)
c) the collegiality of bishops
d) the feasibility of non-episcopal churches
e) episcopal succession *vis-à-vis* apostolic succession
f) the petrine ministry?

How does "authorization" for official functioning take place in the Church? In past ages the community relinquished much of its power of decision-making to ordained ministers. Now there is some willingness on the part of the community to once again assume some of its rightful responsibilities, e.g., in regard to the election of bishops. What are the specific functions of ordained ministry? What does it mean to be authorized to function in the name of the church?

Is the apostolic age to be considered a kind of "golden age" and therefore entirely normative and determinative of the structures of the Church for all ages to come? The NT texts themselves evince a variety of church structures which existed side by side.

Is life essentially symbolic and therefore capable of an infinite variety of expressions? If so, then the proliferation of ministries and church structures, far from detracting from the reality of the continuing ministry of the People of God through history, actually enhances that ministry and brings it to perfection and fulfillment. Should church unity be accomplished in terms of an organic whole or a communion of local churches?

Should there be a clearer distinction between charisms, connoting the Johannine spirit in the church, and gifts, the more common inheritance of all the baptized, and very Pauline in origin? The Lima text itself seems to warrant such a distinction. It might help to clarify the ramifications and the tensions of linking an institutional structure, like ordained ministry (a gift) with a highly personal style of life, like a celibate life-style (a charism). Should there be a greater reappropriation of the spirit of the "Johannine" approach to church life?

PERSONS HOLDING OFFICES IN THE CHURCH: SOME QUESTIONS.

Again, the issues can be expressed in interrogatory form. What is the nature of the distinction between the ministry of ordained ministers in the Church and the ministry of the baptized non-ordained members of the Church? What does it mean to insist that there is an essential difference between the priesthood of the laity and the priesthood of those who are ordained? Is the use of such terminology, "difference of degree" and "essential difference" helpful in the context of the effort today to achieve greater unity among the churches?

What is the precise authority of the ordained *vis-à-vis* the laity. What is more important for salvation, a process of discernment of the Spirit involving all segments of the church or a stronghold of authority exercised by a specific ecclesial group whose jurisdiction must lay outside the challenge of any other group?

Can functions which have been exercised virtually exclusively by those ordained be delegated to those who are not ordained? For example, is ordination a strict requirement for presiding at eucharist? Of what relevance is it that the baptized are automatically authorized to preside at some sacraments, i.e., simply by reason of their being baptized, namely, baptism itself and marriage? In this regard of what relevance is the distinction between mission and ministry?

What prevents women from being apt candidates for ordination? This question itself touches upon several others being asked here in this chapter, especially in regard to the issue of ecclesial structures, divinely/humanly determined, and the issue of acting officially in the name of the Church and *in persona Christi*.

How permanent need the call to ordained ministry be? Is more provision necessary for an "honorable discharge" from such ministry?

SACRAMENTALITY: SOME QUESTIONS.

The term, "sacrament" is used in reference to Christ, to the Church and to the signs used by the church to guarantee the promised action of God on behalf of God's People. How is order a sacrament in relation to Christ and to the Church? What is primary for the ordained, representing Christ or representing the Church?

STRUCTURES/OFFICES OF THE CHURCH: SOME ANSWERS.

What pastoral offices of the Church are essential constitutive elements of the reality of the Church's structure? The NT books evince a variety of church structures which existed side by side. The Pastoral letters attributed to Paul (I and II Timothy and Titus) emphasize a presbyteral structure. The earlier Pauline letters (Colossians and Ephesians) attest to more loosely organized churches. The Pauline heritage of Luke/Acts places emphasis on the Spirit. The Petrine heritage of I Peter highlights the notion of the People of God. The Beloved Disciple in the fourth gospel emphasizes the theme of people personally attached to Jesus while that same disciple in the Johannine epistles highlights the theme of individuals guided by the Paraclete-Spirit. Finally there is the heritage of the Jewish/Gentile Christianity in Matthew's gospel, authority that does not stifle Jesus.

Some have looked at the canon of the scriptures with a predeliction for the books which are the earlier chronologically and therefore closer to the time of Jesus and stemming from Christianity's first generation, the generation of the first disciples of Jesus. It is true that "Jesus was not structuring a society; he did not live in an organized church; the Twelve were selected not as administrators but as eschatological judges of the renewed Israel."[46] The structure which developed out of primitive Christianity because of what some scholars have pejoratively called "early catholicizing" tendencies emphasized sacramentalism, hierarchy and dogma. These emphases were made because, as B. Vawter puts it:

> In a process of development guided by the Spirit, the Church made these features a part of herself, so that what was truly normative was not a group of writings but the Spirit acting with the living Church. It was Church usage that led Trent to determine which books of Scripture should be accepted as canonical; so also it is Church usage that determines the degree of normative authority (canonicity) to be attributed to a NT practice or doctrine.[47]

Yet Vawter qualifies this understanding of Church usage as normative remarking that "we cannot simply equate Church usage with the will of God."[48] He also hints that every development may not be a positive one by noting the following:

> But the structure that was not chosen still has something to teach the Church and can serve as a modifying corrective on the choice that was made. Only thus is the Church faithful to the whole NT. In NT times the Church was ecumenical enough to embrace those who, while sharing the one faith, held very different theological views. The Church of today can be no less ecumenical.[49]

In this same vein K. Rahner makes the following observation:

> There is no doubt that the feeling has grown and become more distinct since the Second Vatican Council that the Church is changeable in all its structures to a far greater extent than people thought during the Pian epoch. The reasons for this change in the Church's concrete self-understanding will not be set out here, particularly since they are obviously many and varied. In exegesis and history of dogma, theology has gradually roused an awareness generally in the Church of the historicity even of dogma and of the dogmatically formulated structures of the Church. It has now become clearer, and the view was sanctioned to a certain extent by Vatican II (despite reactionary trends after the Council in recent years), that the Church, now become a world-Church, must live in a secularized and pluralistic world and yet be engaged in missionary activity and present in quite new cultural fields beyond that of an older Europe; that it cannot simply live on the defensive, in a traditional and merely reactionary way; that — while remaining faithful to its message and to its own nature arising from that message — it needs *aggiornamento*, an adaptation, to the world in which it must live and grow.[50]

Later in the same article Rahner asks:

---

[46]Brown, *The Churches the Apostles Left Behind*, p. 35.

[47]Vawter, JBC, 67:95 (p. 533).

[48]Ibid., 67:96.

[49]Ibid.

[50]T.I., XX, p. 118.

> Must not the question of mutual recognition of ministries be tackled with much
> more theological energy and confidence, while aiming at a generous (and possible)
> solution, than it has been hitherto when there was too much fear and (if we may so
> express it) too little theological imagination? When this sort of thing and so much
> else is appreciated and its realization facilitated, does it not necessitate in the
> Catholic Church very considerable structural changes, which must be seen to be
> possible and must be prepared for the sake of the future society, so that as far as
> possible a *united* Christendom can exist and fulfil its task in this future society?[51]

The above references indicate that there is some tension in the Roman
Catholic church in regard to the issues of interpreting the New Testament evidence
and of making one structure of ordained ministry the paradigm for all. H. Küng goes
further when he states the following:

> In the light of the New Testament therefore — although we should not argue about
> words — terms like "priest," "clergyman," "clergy" or "Church" should be avoided
> as the specific and exclusive designation solely of those who have a ministry in the
> Church, since the New Testament itself regards all believers as "priests," "clerics,"
> "clergy," "Church." The expression "priestly ministry" too, if it is not used of all
> Christians but only of certain people who have a ministry in the Church, obscures
> the real state of affairs in the New Testament.[52]

Going beyond the NT evidence K. Rahner states the following:

> Even if we say that the threefold division of the official ministry into episcopate,
> diaconate and presbyterate is binding upon the Church, and as a prescription is
> irrevocable and *juris divini*, something which has been developed in the apostolic
> age and is already abidingly present at the outset of the post-apostolic age — even
> then, the following point still always remains to be borne in mind: even on this
> showing the precise content of these three offices is still far from clear, and is
> surely capable of modification by the Church.[53]

It is the contention of the present writer that one honors the spirit of apostolic
times by engaging in a creative and flexible attitude toward church structures. The
New Testament itself witnesses to such flexibility. And the very confusion over the
Lima text's use of the term, "ministry," witnesses to the honest refusal of many to
restrict its meaning and its exercise in the church. Furthermore the church structures
themselves, even though they be considered *juris divini*, are far from determined in
regard to their precise content and historical expressions. The functions which were
performed by the persons occupying those offices in the early days of the church
must be evaluated in terms of the essential needs not only of those ancient
communities but also, and equally important, in terms of the abiding needs of

---

[51]Ibid., pp. 127-128.

[52]Küng, *On Being a Christian*, pp. 487-488.

[53]T.I., XIV, p. 210.

Christian communities. The Lima text offers its own principles of evaluation in the section entitled, "Guiding Principles for the Exercise of the Ordained Ministry in the Church." (M26-27).

With regard to the issue of the precise relationship between the presbyteral and episcopal offices R. McBrien summarizes some of the debate as follows:

> A presbyteral tendency is still pressed by some (e.g., Hans Küng and Edward Schillebeeckx), in spite of Vatican II's strongly "episcopal" doctrine. These theologians ask whether the distinction between episcopacy and presbyterate is of divine institution, and whether the episcopacy as it has developed has any real basis at all in the New Testament.[54]

R. Brown urges his readers to

> follow the common scholarly opinion that, where they existed in the post-Pauline churches, presbyters and bishops were for all practical purposes the same, that as a group they were responsible for the pastoral care of those churches, and that we have in the Pastoral Epistles, I Peter, and Acts a picture of their activities in the 80's, if not earlier.[55]

The Lima text states that "the relation of the presbyterate to the episcopal ministry has been discussed throughout the centuries, and the degree of the presbyter's participation in the episcopal ministry is still for many an unresolved question of far-reaching ecumenical importance." (M24) One theologian has summarized the recent Roman Catholic position as follows:

> in the immediate past, in the Tridentine era, the bishop was seen essentially as a priest, but with two additional sacramental powers, the power to ordain and the power to confirm. . . . The post-Vatican II Church no longer tends to see the bishop in terms of the priest but tends rather to see the priest in terms of the bishop. In the Tridentine Church the bishop was a "priest plus." In the post-Vatican II Church, the priest is a "bishop minus."[56]

In light of the theological unresolvedness of this issue this present writer holds that the Roman Catholic tradition is much closer to presbyterally-structured churches than is commonly thought. The Lima text is correct in saying that such unresolvedness is "of far-reaching ecumenical importance." (M24) The gulf between so-called "non-episcopal" and "episcopal" churches may be able to be bridged in relatively simple fashion.

With regard to the collegiality of bishops there is some tension today among

---

[54]*Catholicism*, p. 810.

[55]*Priest and Bishop*, p. 35.

[56]M. Edmund Hussey, "Needed: A Theology of Priesthood," *Origins*, Vol. 17, No. 34 (February 4, 1988), p. 581.

the bishops themselves about the role and precise authority of bishops in international synods of bishops, national episcopal conferences and national advisory boards. Some tension also exists regarding the extent to which curial offices and congregations exercise authority in the church. In short, the fears expressed by some non-episcopal churches with regard to hierarchical bureaucracy in episcopal churches are similar to the fears expressed in some sectors of episcopal churches themselves regarding their own functioning. This concern may account to some extent for the methodology of BEM, namely, using as its point of reference, not the relationship among local churches but "the locally experienced ecclesial fellowship in congregations or parishes."[57]

It should be noted that the decision by the architects of BEM not to consider the issue of the papacy and not to treat more comprehensively the relationship of local churches one to the other in the church universal places great limitations on its dialogue with the Roman Catholic church.

Those built-in limitations, however, need not prevent our attempts to overcome them. And the fears of many Christian churches about the far-reaching implications of episcopal/papal structures can still be addressed. For as one Roman Catholic church historian recently stated:

> The doctrine of a juridical primacy of the pope was overtly formulated in the last century of the Western Roman Empire. The older doctrine of episcopal collegiality survived, however, and both doctrines have persisted down to the present day. The constitutional history of the church is mainly the story of the interplay between them.[58]

Patrick Granfield, a Roman Catholic theologian, has stated the following about the relationship between the Pope and the bishops:

> Papal primacy is not opposed to episcopal collegiality, because it is a primacy of service fostering the unity of the communion of the Churches in faith and love. The Pope should be viewed neither as a dictator arbitrarily imposing his will on the bishops nor as an executor simply carrying out the wishes of the bishops. The bishops, for their part, are not vicars of the Pope but Vicars of Christ who exercise an authority that is proper to them. "Their power, therefore, is not destroyed by the supreme and universal power." (*Lumen gentium*, art. 27).[59]

---

[57]W. Marrevee, *Catholic Perspectives on BEM*, p. 166.

[58]Brian Tierney, "Pope and Bishops: A Historical Survey, "*America*, March 5, 1988, p. 231.

[59]Patrick Granfield, *The Limits of the Papacy: Authority and Autonomy in the Church*, New York: The Crossroad Publishing Company, 1987, p. 85.

Regarding the feasibility of accepting non-episcopal structures or "models" of church one has only to refer to the now famous study by Avery Dulles. R. McBrien, in his treatment of ecclesiology in the Roman Catholic Church since Vatican II, presents the following summary paragraph which pinpoints the many and varied emphases made in recent years:

> Catholic ecclesiology since Vatican II has carried forward the basic theological insights of the council itself. The greatest emphasis is on the sacramentality of the Church ("the universal sacrament of salvation"). This emphasis is seen especially in Rahner, Schillebeeckx, Dulles, and Gutierrez. Secondly, there is a stress on the subordination of the Church to the Kingdom of God and a wider understanding of the Kingdom to include the coming of peace, justice, and freedom (Rahner, Schillebeeckx, Küng, Dulles, Metz, Baum, and Gutierrez). Thirdly, there is renewed attention to the need for ongoing institutional reform as a way of fulfilling the Church's sacramental mission (Rahner, Küng, and Gutierrez). Finally, because of the universality of grace, all the foregoing theologians stress the abiding need for dialogue with others and for collaboration in the task of humanizing the world.[60]

Furthermore Vatican II itself, by referring to other Christian bodies as "churches," has opened the door to accepting non-episcopal church structures of all kinds.[61]

This present writer contends that non-episcopal structures can speak very well to the reform of episcopal structures which, if not balanced by cooperative, and even democratic, processes tend to become unresponsive to the sensus fidelium. No one human structure, it would seem, can exhaust what Vatican II called the "mystery," which is primarily what the Church is.

In regard to the issue of episcopal succession vis-à-vis apostolic succession one may turn to the Lutheran-Catholic Dialogue for evidence of the tension that exists in Roman Catholicism. W. Burghardt sums up much of the discussion among scholars around this topic:

> What is "normative" here? What is binding on later ages? This is as difficult to answer as the question, what is "normative" for Christian ministry in light of the New Testament evidence? Perhaps a restatement of the essential fact as I see it will be sufficient for our purposes in the present dialogue. In the first two centuries of patristic thought, great emphasis is laid on the need of being in the doctrinal succession of the apostles (fidelity to the gospel); for otherwise one is not really a Christian. But this is not simply guaranteed by looking at the doctrine. There is a mutual interplay: doctrinal integrity and an identifiable chain (most often of those in an official position). Put another way: doctrinal communion and legitimate appointment. The manner of appointment is often difficult to determine — more difficult the farther back you go. And, of course, still to be satisfactorily

---

[60]Catholicism, pp. 724-725.

[61]Unitatis Redintegratio, 19ff.

determined is the precise meaning of *episkopoi* and *presbyteroi* in the first two centuries — an issue of vital importance in the quest for the normative.[62]

Again the matter of the relationship between bishops and presbyters is seen as significant in the determination of acceptable church polity as well as authentic church doctrine. This present writer contends that the very concern which the early church addressed is much relativized in our world today. For we are blessed with vehicles of mass communications which are nearly instantaneous and with possibilities for the structuring of dialogue less hampered than in previous ages by wide gaps of geography and culture. Of course these possibilities do not guarantee dialogue and communication nor do they insure that individuals and groups will indeed desire to communicate.

Furthermore the awareness, on the scholarly level at least, of the historicity of all forms of communication, reduces the possibility that doctrinal formulations will be considered frozen products no longer subject to the process of dialogue and development.

In regard to the issue of the petrine ministry, H. Fries and K. Rahner offer a rather extensive commentary from which the following is excerpted:

> If the papacy, both at present and in future, is to gain ecumenical significance, and if it is to serve the Church as a whole better and more effectively, then, so it is said, a renewal of its structure, or rather structures, is necessary. These structures should be oriented to the principles of legitimate diversity, collegiality, and subsidiarity. . . . A renewal in the structures of the papacy should be carried out on the basis of these principles. The differentiation between supreme authority and its use enables the pope to limit the exercise of his jurisdiction voluntarily. This would produce a differentiation with regard to the functions of the papacy which would make a larger "ecumenicity" conceivable. For the same reason, and with reference to the same principles, the result would be that the pope's primacy would be more a preeminence of pastoral care than a juridical primacy with its typical problems of rights, of powers, and of qualifications.[63]

H. Küng echoes this by making a distinction between ministry and power:

> Did not the distortion of the functions of the Petrine ministry come about . . . because this Petrine ministry — for a variety of historical reasons and certainly not because of the evil will of one or several individuals — was presented to men increasingly as Petrine power? It was a long process which turned the papacy into a world power and an absolutist ecclesiastical power.[64]

In bringing his book, *The Limits of the Papacy*, to a conclusion P. Granfield

---

[62]*Eucharist & Ministry: Lutherans and Catholic in Dialogue IV*, p. 177.

[63]*Unity of the Churches*, pp. 71-72.

[64]*On Being a Christian*, p.497.

states the following:

> In examining the ecumenical perspective of the limits of the papacy, we have explored some areas in which the Pope might voluntarily limit his authority. Although significant convergence on the nature of papal authority has been made in the ecumenical dialogues, the papacy remains a major barrier. The road to reunion will be long and difficult. Despite real, unresolved differences among Christians, there is also a genuine communion that binds them together.[65]

Those ecumenical dialogues, including the Lutheran-Catholic dialogues and those of *Le groupe des Dombes*, have involved Roman Catholic theologians. It seems, however, that the very one occupying the chair of Peter must himself voluntarily take many of the first steps if the unity hoped for by many can be achieved. The voluntary limitation of his own power for the sake of the larger goal, unity among the churches, seems, to this present writer at least, a relatively small price to pay.

In regard to the "authorization" for official functioning in the Church the election of bishops "as a new desideratum in Church practice"[66]provides an example of the ecclesial community's effort to resume its rightful place in official decision-making. None of the present forms of selecting leaders (bishops) for the Church can be absolutely obligatory because

> they all have grown out of historical situations, and . . . thus would logically be modifiable by new historical postulates. This conclusion can be clearly verified by looking back to the broader horizons of church history. From the history of the church at the time of the fathers two aspects merit special attention in this context: the participation of the entire body of all ordained Christians and the active role of all the baptized in the appointment of bishops.[67]

As K. Rahner indicates, "there is really no 'divine' law on the exact form in which someone must be selected in practice and appointed to office in the Church."[68]

To this present writer it seems that in matters which clearly involve no divine law there ought to be granted the widest latitude possible for the sake of the larger goal, stated thus, in the Preface of the Lima text, "visible Church unity."

The specific functions of those who are officially authorized to act in the

---

[65]pp. 192-193.

[66]Günter Biemer, "Election of Bishops as a New Desideratum in Church Practice," *Bishops and People*, ed. by Leonard Swidler and Arlene Swidler, Philadelphia: The Westminster Press, 1970, p. 38 ff.

[67]Ibid., p. 39.

[68]*The Shape of the Church to Come*, p. 119.

name of the church are difficult to determine in the light of the NT evidence. R. Brown concludes his study of the biblical background of the Catholic priesthood by stating "the legitimacy of pluralism in priestly work"[69] and by naming only one task common to "all NT forms of what would eventually come together under the heading of priestly activity . . . (namely) bearing witness of Jesus."[70] In the same vein K. Rahner states the following:

> If therefore we seek to determine the task of the priest as official minister on the basis of the New Testament, we should not take as our starting-point the power to celebrate the Eucharist, even though since the apostolic age this has, at least in normal cases, been reserved to the priesthood. The legitimate starting-point in the New Testament for determining the nature of the official priesthood is to be found, rather in the function of official leadership of a Christian community. . . . The preaching of the gospel cannot be excluded from this function of leadership. The "ministry of the word", as an official commission, is certainly to be numbered among the functions of any such official leadership.[71]

In the light of these statements by R. Brown and K. Rahner it is difficult to understand the near fixation exhibited by the Vatican on the eucharist, even the power to confect the eucharistic species, as the locus of the role of the ordained minister. It is in this regard that the exclusion of women from top leadership (priestly) roles is focused. If leadership in the church and witnessing to Christ are as specific as one can get in describing the functioning of ordained ministry, it is difficult to fathom how women, baptized into Christ, simply by being women, can be excluded from that ministry.

Ordination came to be a most important way in which officials of the church were authorized. It is to be noted, however, as E. Schillebeeckx points out:

> Although the laying on of hands at *ordinatio* is a clear fact of the tradition, it is not regarded as the most important thing; what is essential is the church's mandate or the church's sending of the minister, not the specific form in which the calling and sending takes shape. . . . Recognition and sending by the church is the really decisive element. . . . The history of the first millennium therefore leaves completely open the question whether the rite of consecration is absolutely necessary.[72]

Much like the question of the election of bishops, considered above, the question of the ordination rite needs to serve the larger goal of church unity. Granted

---

[69] *Priest and Bishop*, p. 44.

[70] Ibid., p. 45.

[71] T.I. XIV, p. 208.

[72] *Ministry*, p. 47.

that it is more time-honored and laden with the sacredness of ritual behavior. Still there may be ways of expressing a church's recognition or sending of the minister which in fact can purify the ancient ritual of ordination and speak more clearly to the needs of modern believers. Perhaps what is really at stake here is the actual sense of community itself on the part of those who do the recognizing and the sending, ultimately the local church. A clarification of what exactly constitutes a local church is the need which lies hidden in this whole discussion. Lima's methodology involves an interpretation of ministry in terms of the experience of the local church. Roman Catholic experience of local church is the local parish, whereas Roman Catholic theory of local church is the diocese, an experience far removed from most Catholics.

In regard to the question of the apostolic age as normative for the structures of the church for all ages to come K. Rahner makes the following observations:

> Scripture, we are saying, is the objectification of the church of the apostolic age which is normative for us. . . . The church of the apostolic age objectifies itself in scripture. Therefore this scripture has the character and the characteristics which belong to this church in its relationship to future ages of the church.[73]

As has already been noted above the NT texts themselves evince a variety of church structures which existed side by side. R. Brown offers the following pertinent remark:

> Precisely because there is no blueprint, it is not inconceivable . . . that in later ages in the face of new historical circumstances the Church can continue in its discovery of Christ's will — a discovery that may imply change. (But notice that it is a question of discovering Christ's will and not simply of finding the best sociological response.) What can change and what cannot change? There is no hard and fast rule. A sense of apostolicity means that some past decisions made within the Church under the guidance of the Spirit of Christ are thought to be normative for the future, just so that the future will remain in continuity with the past. A sense that Christ's will is not yet fully discovered means that other past decisions can cede to new decisions made under the guidance of the Holy Spirit.[74]

This same portrayal of apostolicity in a dynamic sense (i.e., not purely chronological as in unbroken episcopal succession) is stated by the U.S. Catholic Conference as the "continuing fidelity to Christ's loving and saving work and message, to ministry and service inspired by the evangelical vision and teaching of the original apostles."[75]

The Lima document's pneumatological emphasis is key here. Is the Spirit any

---

[73]*Foundations of Christian Faith*, pp. 371-372.

[74]*Biblical Reflections on Crises Facing the Church*, pp. 58-59.

[75]*Sharing the Light of Faith: National Catechetical Directory for Catholics of the United States* (Washington, D.C.: USCC, 1979), p. 40.

less present in the process of the church structuring itself in response to the needs of people and the demands of the mission entrusted to it by Christ? Continuity with the apostolic age does not imply the continuance of all structures in all their details. Historical investigation reveals that those structures were often modeled on the political and social structures of the apostolic and post-apostolic years.

Further, in the light of the variety exhibited in the New Testament texts themselves, there is much room for variety among churches today. There is no serious denial here of apostolicity itself.

In regard to the question of the symbolic nature of all reality, the contribution of K. Rahner is especially apropos. What may be called his "principle of internal symbolism" states essentially that there is a primordial unity which discloses itself in multiplicity, which multiplicity is the resolution and perfection of that unity.[76] In the view of this present writer such a principle can serve as an ontological basis for any theology of ministry. It will overcome the temptation to think that a more restrictive structuring of official ministry is more ideal. In this view a proliferation of ministries far from detracting from the unity of the church actually enhances that unity.

This still leaves open the question of what kind of church unity is to be favored. Should that unity be organic, demanding one church structure for all? Or should it be a communion (or confederation) of variously structured churches? K. Rahner and H. Fries call for a recognition of offices among the churches in one of their eight theses proposed for making unity "an actual possibility."[77] They are clear about the depth of unity demanded in the following statement:

> We clearly demand a unity of the churches in the faith, even though we think of this unity of faith — on the basis of the spiritual situation of today — as more differentiated than had been supposed in earlier ecumenical reflections. This also means that we do not simply leave the present status quo of the churches unchanged; rather, we speak in favor of their renewal, and we hope for renewal. This signifies a way and a movement. We state conditions for an actual possibility.[78]

K. Rahner and H. Fries also hold that full communion among the churches is possible as long as they accept the teaching of Scripture and the ancient Creeds and do not reject what is binding dogma in a partner church as totally contrary to the substance

---

[76]T.I., IV., "The Theology of the Symbol," pp. 221-252, esp. pp. 227-232.

[77]*Unity of the Churches: An Actual Possibility.* Philadelphia: Fortress Press, 1985.

[78]Ibid., p. 6.

of Christianity.[79]

These theologians go further in proposing a plurality of church structures in keeping with principles expressed in Vatican II documents, particularly *Lumen Gentium* and *Unitatis Redintegratio*.[80] This proposal is especially clear in the case of the Orthodox churches of the East but they go on to say that "the ecclesiological principle of a legitimate pluralism of discipline and life in the individual partner churches can and should be applied not only to the Eastern churches (as the Council does explicitly) but also to the churches of the Reformation."[81]

Thus it seems to this present writer that, considering the actual state of affairs among the churches today (as Rahner and Fries do), a communion of local churches can be accomplished thus creating a new phase in ecumenism. This new phase would enable the lived experience of unity to find its own proper course instead of being determined beforehand by some preconceived plan for a unified Church. The process orientation of the Lima document lends itself to this approach very readily. There is an invitation to *praxis* ecclesiology along with good theoretical ecclesiology. The churches will learn not only from the time-honored experience of the living tradition but also from the lived experience of their striving for unity by their actions which confess the truth in love.

One last issue remains to be considered in this treatment of the structures/offices of the church, namely, the distinction between the charismatic elements and the gifts of order and structure in the church. R. Brown refers to the profit to be gained by the Roman Catholic Church's uniting with less formally structured (non-episcopal) churches:

> There are dangers inherent in the episcopacy precisely because it is an institutionalized form of church government. Inevitably it will tend to become too rigid and too confining, to the point of frustrating the spontaneity of the Christian experience. The impression will be given that the Holy Spirit works only through the hierarchy, from the top down and never from the bottom up. As we read the NT, I think we are right in judging that the strongly charismatic community at Corinth was not a viably structured church. Yet we can learn from Corinth, not only negatively but also positively. If under the guidance of the Spirit, the Church, even in NT times, was led to a more viable, episcopal structure, it still cannot ignore the manifestation of the same Spirit in the charisms of Corinth. A respect

---

[79]Ibid., pp. 25-41. Cf. P. Granfield's summary of various views in his, *The Limits of the Papacy*, pp. 188-193.

[80]*Unity of the Churches*, pp. 43-47.

[81]Ibid., p. 47.

for the charismatic element in Christianity, especially in terms of a willingness to see the movement of the Spirit outside the hierarchical structure, is the best corrective for some of the innate perils of an episcopally structured church.[82]

In another place Brown refers to the hermeneutical decision on the part of the church to place in the same canon of scriptures the Johannine writings and the writings of Mark, Matthew and Luke, "Gospels which implicitly advocate the side opposite to many Johannine positions."[83]   The church thereby has chosen to live with the tension of unresolved positions. Brown goes on to state:

> We Roman Catholics have come to appreciate that Peter's pastoral role is truly intended by the risen Lord, but the presence in our Scriptures of a disciple whom Jesus loved more than he loved Peter is an eloquent commentary on the relative value of the church office. The authoritative office is necessary because a task is to be done and unity is to be preserved, but the scale of power in various offices is not necessarily the scale of Jesus' esteem and love.[84]

Again, Rahner and Fries offer some observations in regard to this question of the priority owed to the charismatic character of the Church. First about the official ministry of the Church:

> The ministerial office of the Church also considers itself a charism of the Spirit and thereby resists the danger of being merely institution. But the Spirit is not confined to the ministerial office, channeled in such a way as to make it subordinate to the ministerial office.[85]

Secondly, about the Church itself Rahner and Fries make the following pertinent remark:

> The Church as creature and *sacrament* of the Spirit thereby confesses that its future — and with it the future in which the partner churches together will represent the one Church of Jesus — is not totally predictable, cannot be manipulated, and in no way runs only according to the norms known heretofore. Instead, the future, without detriment to the binding commitments of all Christians and churches, is a matter of unavailability and freedom of the Spirit of God, who, as Creator Spirit, is also repeatedly capable of new creation.[86]

These observations by Brown, Rahner and Fries prompt the present writer to comment that Lima M32-33, "Variety of Charisms," is a short but very significant section in the text. An acute awareness of the "church of the beloved disciple" is

---

[82]*Priest and Bishop*, pp. 85-86.

[83]*The Community of the Beloved Disciple*, p. 163.

[84]Ibid., p. 164.

[85]*Unity of the Churches*, p. 22.

[86]Ibid.

crucial to any ecclesiology. The pneumatology of BEM, as noted elsewhere, is among the most important contributions it makes to the advance of ecclesiology and the theology of official ministry. The very acknowledgement of the importance of this aspect of Church life and practice creates tensions in that any structure tends by the very fact of being a structure to the taming of the Spirit. Living with the tension of a Spirit-guided Church involves a never-ending process of change and adaptation, of restructuring and even the abandoning of obsolete structures. It does not assume some form of reckless abandon; it does, however, demand many forms of trusting and risky experimentation.

This present writer sees in these observations by theologians an effort to overcome the human penchant to use differences in function as the basis for maintaining positions of power and control. Yet service (the very meaning of ministry) is the hallmark of discipleship of Jesus and membership in the Christian community.

The very need for a separate treatment of ministry in a document such as BEM testifies to the constant need to overcome the will to dominance, which invades every aspect of human life, even the most sacred and religious. Why is it that the very offices which embody the service (*diakonia*) of God's people are at times the biggest stumbling blocks to the service of unity among God's people?

PERSONS HOLDING OFFICES IN THE CHURCH: SOME ANSWERS.

The first question asked here is in regard to the nature of the distinction between the ministry of ordained ministers in the Church and the ministry of the baptized non-ordained members of the Church. *Lumen Gentium*, in article 10, made the following statement:

> Though they differ essentially and not only in degree, the common priesthood of the faithful and the ministerial or hierarchical priesthood are none the less ordered one to another; each in its own proper way shares in the one priesthood of Christ.

As M. Edmund Hussey wrote,

> that difference ought not to be overemphasized and used as the starting point for developing a theology of the priesthood. In fact, I believe that a search for the essential difference between the two as a *starting point* for understanding the

ordained priesthood may complicate the issue unnecessarily.[87]

H. Vorgrimler, in commenting on the history of the text of *Lumen Gentium*, especially as it relates to this distinction between the common priesthood of the faithful and the hierarchical priesthood, states the following:

> The Constitution does not claim to have found the definitive distinction. Its concern is to make a positive statement about the priesthood of the faithful while still keeping it apart from the consecrated priesthood.[88]

E. Schillebeeckx explains it in the following manner:

> At a very early stage after the New Testament, with Clement, a distinction arose between *klerikos* and *laikos*, . . . but this terminology in no way indicates a difference of status between laity and clergy. A *klerikos* is someone who has a *kleros*, i.e. a ministry.   What we have here, therefore, is a distinction of function. . . . In this light, given the whole of the church's tradition, the insertion in *Lumen Gentium* — which is in fact a quotation from an encyclical of Pius XII — in which it is said that the ordained priesthood is "essentially different" (*essentia differunt*) from the priesthood of the believing people of God (the Reformers' phrase "universal ministry" also seems to me to be inappropriate terminology) must be interpreted as the confirmation of a specific and indeed sacramental function and not as a state.[89]

In reference to this matter, K. Rahner makes the following comments:

> In so far as Christ has offered the sacrifice of the Cross as a sacrifice of humanity as a whole and as a consequence it belongs to everyone who is a member of it and so of Him, the universal priesthood of all the faithful is *anterior* to the official priesthood and not merely its weak reflection.[90]

And, in another place, he states:

> The officially ordained priest is not the sacral representative of God who is equipped with celestial powers and set apart from an unholy people by God. Rather he is the bearer of one specific and necessary function within a people that has already been sanctified by God. The universal priesthood is not an entity deduced from the official priesthood by a process of metaphorical refinement. Rather it constitutes the sustaining basis for this official priesthood.[91]

So, differences of function should not be the basis for dominance but, even more so, for disciples of him who emptied himself and took the form of a slave, they are opportunities for greater service.

---

[87]"Needed: A Theology of Priesthood," *Origins*, February 4, 1988, p. 581. Emphasis added.

[88]*Commentary on the Documents of Vatican II*, Vol. I, p. 158.

[89]*Ministry*, p. 70.

[90]T.I., III, p. 249.

[91]T.I., XII, pp. 44-45.

In regard to the question of the precise authority of the ordained *vis-à-vis* the laity it is helpful to keep in mind the distinction drawn by B. Cooke between authority and jurisdiction. He explains that what must be discussed in regard to this whole question is

> an issue that appears to underly all the intertwined and unresolved questions about ecclesiastical authority, namely, is the very notion of "jurisdiction" (i.e., authority that attaches to a societal office and that comes to a person precisely because he or she occupies that office) genuinely applicable to the corporate life of the Christian community?[92]

As Cooke later indicates, "jurisdiction and authority are not identical"[93] and "because it operates in the realm of law, jurisdiction deals with the direction and control of persons' external behavior and not properly with their inner consciousness."[94] He calls jurisdiction "a misleading metaphor"[95] for

> describing the membership of the church by dividing those who possess the power of jurisdiction from those who are subject to this power has tended to obscure the radical freedom of spirit that should characterize each Christian's faith and conscience.[96]

Cooke also observes that the distinction between "power of orders" and "power of jurisdiction" is "a distinction whose validity is widely questioned by theologians today."[97] He concludes that "the entire discussion would probably be helped if we were to drop from usage this distinction between orders and jurisdiction."[98]

It seems to this present writer that discussions of power and authority are hampered by confusion over the use of the terms themselves. Perhaps the use of the Greek words *exousia* and *dynamis* can help to clarify the efforts. The former connotes a right which someone possesses, the latter the power to exercise that right. The right to influence the thoughts, opinions and behavior of others can be accurately called "authority" (*exousia*). The power to exercise that right is accurately called "power" (*dynamis*).

---

[92]*Ministry to Word and Sacraments*, p. 517.

[93]Ibid.

[94]Ibid.

[95]Ibid., p. 518.

[96]Ibid.

[97]Ibid.

[98]Ibid., pp. 518-519.

Authority (*exousia*) can be of at least four types: 1) mystical or autocratic (based on an absolute right, inherent in one's position or coming from God); 2) legislative (a right granted by law); 3) learned (a right based on expertise); 4) charismatic (a right stemming from inherent qualities of one's personhood).

Power (*dynamis*) can be of at least five types: 1) exploitative; 2) manipulative (not necessarily involving a disrespect for the other as in exploitative); 3) competitive (vying with the other); 4) nutrient ("feeding" the other, providing the other with what he/she needs); 5) integrative (treating the other as an equal)

It seems that all the forms of authority described above, as long as they are based on respect for the other and genuine service to the other have a place in the life of the Church. Likewise all the forms of power, except exploitative, have a place as well.

What is important is that authority be carefully distinguished as it is exercised and that no more authority than warranted by its source be claimed. What is equally important is that power be exercised in all of its forms with the aim of constantly seeking its integrative expression characterized by the saying of Jesus, "I no longer speak of you as slaves, . . . instead I call you friends." (Jn 15: 15) Thomas Aquinas noted that friendship is precisely characterized by equality.

As regards the question of the exercise by the non-ordained of functions normally exercised by the ordained in a virtually exclusive way R. McBrien summarizes the evidence from the NT as follows:

> We simply do not know how a certain individual came to preside (over the Eucharist) and whether it came to be a permanent or regular function for that person. As we have already seen, there was a remarkable diversity of structure and form in the New Testament churches. The most that can be said is that those who presided did so with the consent of the local church and that this consent was tantamount, but not always equivalent to ordination.[99]

E. Schillebeeckx states that "the question whether a layman could preside at the eucharist is a modern one. The early church would have found it perverse"[100] for "the decisive element is the acceptance of a president by the church."[101] Schillebeeckx quotes Tertullian who is the sole source of any evidence in the early church in this matter:

---

[99]*Catholicism*, p. 803.

[100]*Ministry*, p. 50.

[101]Ibid., p. 51.

> "But where no college of ministers has been appointed, you, the laity, must celebrate the eucharist and baptize; in that case you are your own priests, for where two or three are gathered together, there is the church, even if these three are lay people."[102]

Schillebeeckx goes on to state the following:

> Tertullian's vision is not so isolated in the early church as one might think. . . . Anyone who in such circumstances was required by the community to preside over the community (and thus at the eucharist) *ipso facto* became a minister by the acceptance of the church. . . . The specific character of the ministry was defended by all, but not a sacral power of consecration or a specific way in which institution to the ministry takes place.

Other Catholic theologians have admitted the possibility of members of the church other than the ordained being delegated or authorized to preside at eucharistic liturgies, especially in communities experiencing a shortage of ordained clergy.[103]

In summary, E. Schillebeeckx notes that "according to the views of the ancient church a shortage of priests was an ecclesiastical impossibility."[104]

R. McBrien sums up much of the recent theological research in the following statement:

> There is no evidence in the New Testament that ordination was required even for presiding over the Eucharist. There *is* evidence in the history of the Church that non-ordained Christians heard confessions, and it is the common teaching of the Church today that the ministers of the sacrament of Matrimony are the two parties to the marriage, not the priest. *In principle*, every baptized Christian is empowered to administer every sacrament. Ordination does not confer a kind of magical power. It is a public act concerned with *order*. It designates someone for particular ministries so that everything will be done properly and the life and mission of the Church will be served.[105]

What was said above regarding the issue of authority, authorization and jurisdiction can lend a proper nuance to the meaning of the above findings.

What McBrien says about the distinction between ministry and mission can

---

[102]Ibid.

[103]*The Future of Catholic Leadership*, Dean R. Hoge. New York: Sheed and Ward, 1987. Hoge quotes Gerald Broccolo who wrote an article in *The Journal of the Catholic Campus Ministry Association*, Vol. I (Spring, 1986), pp. 22-24. In that article Broccolo suggests that bishops delegate deacons or laity to preside at eucharist. He warns that failure to do so may contribute to what he calls "rampant congregationalism" (communities deputing their own leadership), an even more radical departure from the Catholic tradition than the delegation of deacons and laity.

[104]*Ministry*, p. 72.

[105]*Catholicism*, pp. 846-847. It should be noted that in regard to the sacrament of marriage the Orthodox require for validity the action of the priest-celebrant.

also clarify and put in proper perspective the issue of presiding as a specific ministry:

> *Ministry is a service publicly or at least explicitly designated by the Church to assist in the fulfillment of its mission.* Ministry is not the same as mission; it exists for the sake of mission, as means to end.[106]

This present writer contends that many situations in the church today call for radical solutions. These situations are more and more desperate, especially when local communities are being deprived of presiders at eucharist. This deprivation is both quantitative and qualitative. Often it is the latter which is overlooked. There are those present in such communities who have both the talent and the desire to serve the community in its need for nourishment in the eucharist, which K. Rahner rightly insists is primarily (and in some sense entirely) a word-event.[107] It is not enough that the word be "spoken" and presided over in some magical or perfunctory way by those who, albeit officially designated, are not otherwise endowed with qualities of leadership to inspire faith-ful openness and loving decisiveness in the "hearers."[108]

As regards the question of the ordination of women there have been references made to the theological grappling surrounding it in the first section of this chapter, especially in the article by G. Worgul.[109] Many theological arguments in favor of women's ordination have been advanced by committees of learned societies (e.g., The Catholic Biblical Association,[110] The Canon Law Society of America, and The Catholic Theological Society of America), by national associations (e.g., Leadership Conference of Women Religious), and by various theologians (notably,

---

[106]Ibid., p. 848.

[107]*Foundations of Christian Faith*, p.427.

[108]Ibid., pp. 414-415.

[109]Worgul, "Ritual, Power, Authority and Riddles: The Anthropology of Rome's Declaration on the Ordination of Women," *Louvain Studies.* Vol. 14, no. 1, Spring 1989.

[110]Note here especially the report of the Catholic Biblical Association of America's task force on "The Role of Women in Early Christianity." The report appeared in the October 1979 issue of *The Catholic Biblical Quarterly* as part of the official record of the 1979 annual CBA meeting. It was reprinted in *Origins*, Vol. 9: No. 28 (December 27, 1979), pp. 450-454. The concluding paragraph of the report is as follows: "An examination of the biblical evidence shows the following: That there is positive evidence in the New Testament that ministries were shared by various groups and that women did in fact exercise roles and functions later associated with priestly ministry; that the arguments against the admission of women to priestly ministry based on the praxis of Jesus and the apostles, disciplinary regulations, and the created order cannot be sustained. The conclusion we draw, then, is that the New Testament evidence, while not decisive by itself, points toward the admission of women to priestly ministry."

Elisabeth Schüssler Fiorenza and Rosemary Radford Ruether).

R. McBrien summarizes many of these arguments in favor of the ordination of women as follows:

1. The exclusion of women from priesthood violates human dignity and the baptismal mandate to participate in the mission of the Church according to one's qualifications, opportunities, and vocation.

2. Women have in fact served as deaconesses in the early Church.

3. There is nothing in Sacred Scripture which positively excludes the ordination of women.

4. Arguments against the ordination of women are deficient:

   a. To say the tradition of the Church is against it assumes that we are already in the adulthood of the Church. But if the Church is still alive in the year 20,000, the latter part of the twentieth century will look like the "early Church" to those in the two-hundred-first century.

   b. Women are equal to men in human dignity and before God. The exclusion of women on the basis of sex assumes a radical inferiority of women and, therefore, a basic incapacity, if not unworthiness, to act on behalf of the Church in the presence of God.

   c. Jesus, in fact, called no one to *ordained priesthood* (as distinguished from discipleship and the apostolate).[111]

It is already abundantly clear that this present writer accepts the overwhelming *theological* arguments which favor the possibility of ordaining women. On May 30, 1994, however, in his celebrated Apostolic Letter, "Ordinatio Sacerdotalis," Pope John Paul II stated that

in order that all doubt may be removed regarding a matter of great importance, a matter which pertains to the church's divine constitution itself, in virtue of my ministry of confirming the brethren (cf. Lk. 22:32) I declare that the church has no authority whatsoever to confer priestly ordination on women and that this judgement is to be definitively held by all the church's faithful.[112]

In spite of this strong statement the theological controversy rages. The present resistance to even the possibility in the official stance of the Pope (and the Vatican officials in response to BEM) may be evidence of a blindness born of the possession of power, the *power* of jurisdiction (as distinct from the power of orders, as earlier noted in the writings of B. Cooke).

---

[111]*Catholicism*, pp. 852-853.

[112]*Origins*, Vol. 24, p. 51.

In regard to the question of the permanency of the call to ordained ministry E. Schillebeeckx notes the following:

> Another fundamental consequence of the canon of Chalcedon was that a minister who for any personal reason ceased to be the president of a community *ipso facto* returned to being a layman in the full sense of the word. The distinction between jurisdiction, i.e. specific charge over a community, and *ordo*, the power of ordination in itself, did not exist at that time. So at that time the departure of a minister had quite a different significance from the present-day laicization of a priest.[113]

Such historical evidence seems to assume that "honorable discharge" from the ordained ministry is a foregone conclusion. In an ecclesiastical structure which requires jurisdictional processes some positive steps seem mandatory to insure the prizing of past services rendered.

Here again we note the distinction drawn so clearly above by B. Cooke, between the power of order and the power of jurisdiction. And we note the intimate relationship between the minister and the community. One cannot be understood in isolation from the other. Yet the distinction of essential difference which the Vatican continues to emphasize cannot but exacerbate their further isolation. This present writer is cognizant not only of the lack of "honorable discharge" from the official ministry in the Roman Catholic church but also the often punitive process of laicization. That process typically attaches numerous conditions to the granting of official return to the lay state, among which conditions are the prevention of the one laicized from exercising even minimal ministerial services for which he had been trained. One wonders what long-range goods are envisioned by the decision to take such punitive measures against former leaders of local communities of faith.

SACRAMENTALITY: SOME ANSWERS

The roots of much of the continuing tension in Roman Catholic theology in regard to the issue of sacramentality can be located in the fact that "in the Church's consciousness there are two different conceptual models for God's grace as it operates in human history."[114] K. Rahner contrasts these two models thus:

> The *first* way of seeing the operation of divine grace in the world considers that operation first of all and primarily as an intervention of God in the world at a definite point in space and time. The world is regarded in the first place as secular, both because of what we call "nature" and because of the inherited sinful state of this history of the world and humanity. . . .

---

[113]*Ministry*, p. 41.

[114]T.I., XIX, p. 141.

The *second* way of considering the operation of grace starts out from the assumption that the secular world from the outset is always encompassed and permeated with the grace of the divine self-communication. This grace is always and everywhere present in the world.[115]

According to the second model the sacraments "are not really to be understood as successive individual incursions of God into a secular world, but as 'outbursts' . . . of the innermost, ever present gracious endowment of the world with God himself into history."[116]

As G. Worgul has pointed out:

Historical criticism has created a sensitivity to the difficult tasks of understanding the exact historical number of the sacraments, and, more important, the understanding of the general term "sacrament" and the particular meaning of each sacrament within its historical age and context. Christological investigations have finally accepted the full humanity of Christ and viewed him as the *sacrament of God.* Christ is portrayed as the primary sacrament. Any sacramental theology that does not see Christ as the center of sacramentology is judged inadequate. Developments in ecclesiology have underscored the intrinsic and necessary relation of the Church to Christ. The Church is the reality Christ instituted above and beyond any institution of sacraments. The sacraments are meaningful insofar as they are extensions of the Church.[117]

In the context of these historical and theological developments K. Rahner offers the following definition of a sacrament:

Wherever the finality and the invincibility of God's offer of himself becomes manifest in the concrete in the life of an individual through the church which is the basic sacrament of salvation, we call this a Christian sacrament.[118]

When all the foregoing is brought to bear on the sacrament of order in the church and in the history of the church E. Schillebeeckx makes the following remarks:

It has to be conceded that the first Christian millennium — above all in the pre-Nicene period — expressed its view of the ministry chiefly in ecclesial and pneumatological terms, or better pneuma-christologically, whereas the second Christian millennium gave the ministry a directly christological basis and shifted the mediation of the church into the background. In this way a theology of the ministry developed without an ecclesiology, just as in the Middle Ages the so-called treatise on the sacraments followed immediately on christology without the

---

[115]Ibid., pp. 142-143.

[116]Ibid., p. 143.

[117]*From Magic to Metaphor*, p. 15.

[118]*Foundations of Christian Faith*, p. 412.

intervention of an independent ecclesiology (which at that stage had not yet been worked out).[119]

Keeping in mind the separate emphases of each of the first two millennia of the Church's history Schillebeeckx observes further:

> At many points Vatican II deliberately referred back to the theological intuitions of the ancient church, but its view of the church's ministry, above all in the terminology it used, is unmistakably a compromise between these two great blocks of tradition in the church.[120]

He concludes, however, that on the basis of theological criteria "preference must be given to the first Christian millennium as a model for a future shaping of the church's ministry."[121] He explicitly admits that he is taking into account the work done in recent years "by official ecumenical commissions of theologians."[122]

In this regard, B. Cooke refers to the fact that in recent centuries "there has been debate among the Christian confessions as to whether ordination is a genuine sacrament."[123] By contrast he points out the following:

> Today, however, it seems that there is broad acceptance, confessional and theological, of some special Christian sacramentality in the ritual by which the various churches designate ministers to lead their worship services. There is general agreement that the designation and empowering (however one may wish to understand these two notions) are not purely human, that somehow the call from God and the empowering by the Spirit enter into the picture.[124]

Cooke offers the following suggestion which might help clarify the issue of sacramentality as it applies to ecumenical efforts of understanding:

> Perhaps one can avoid some (if not all) of the traditional conflict of opinion by transposing the question to another context. If ministries emerge organically from the church's inner life as specialized agencies to nurture that life, and if the ministry of liturgical leadership emerges from the life of the church *as sacrament* so that the church can become more profoundly sacramental, then the process of that emergence (i.e., the historical sequence of ordinations) must surely be sacramental.[125]

In discussing the possible process for acknowledging the sacramental validity

---

[119]*Ministry*, pp. 66-67.

[120]Ibid., p. 67.

[121]Ibid.

[122]Ibid., p. 68.

[123]*Ministry to Word and Sacraments*, p. 641.

[124]Ibid.

[125]Ibid., p. 642.

of ministerial offices in the Reformation churches K. Rahner and H. Fries note the
following:

> Ordinations are ultimately valid not because it is absolutely certain that, even in
> exceptional cases, they have corresponded to the concept of an almost physical
> norm of effectiveness of the sacraments (which in normal cases ordinations *should*,
> of course). They are valid because they are deemed valid within the one Church,
> and because they must be acknowledged as valid in a variety of situations.
>
> There are analogous cases pertaining to marriage: can one seriously rate a marriage
> "invalid" before God, when there was a "procedural error," for which no one was
> seriously to blame and which was entirely unavoidable under the actual
> circumstances? Or can one say that such a marriage is valid even with *that kind* of
> procedural error, because it is nevertheless a reality in the church and is lived in
> this church as a Christian marriage?[126]

It is clear, then, that in recent decades there have been newer and broader
understandings of sacramentology emerging in Roman Catholic theology and that the
two distinct conceptual models for understanding the meaning of sacraments
described above can cause tension in regard to the interpretation one gives to the term
"sacrament".

This present writer agrees with the statement, albeit negatively cast, made
earlier by Rahner and Fries that

> it is not simply self evident why their (Protestant churches') faithfully given
> testimony to Christ's grace should not be valid sacraments at a time when these
> other Christian churches exist in an undisputed state of security regarding their self-
> understanding.[127]

At some point the vicissitudes of history must be accepted for what they are
— in some way in keeping with divine providence and the divine will. And we must
look forward to possibilities for reconciliation rather than backward to reasons for
recrimination.

SECTION THREE: DIFFERENT THEOLOGICAL STARTING POINTS CAUSING DIFFERENT THEOLOGICAL CONCLUSIONS.

As one views the theological differences which emerge both within Roman
Catholicism itself and in the official Roman Catholic response to the Lima text on
ministry there arises an awareness of various theological (and especially

---

[126]*Unity of the Churches*, pp. 120-121.

[127]Ibid., pp. 116-117.

ecclesiological) starting points which may account for the different conclusions. Some of these starting points have been alluded to above. Here it is the purpose of the author to isolate them for further clarification. They are: the juridical *vis-à- vis* the pastoral; the ontological *vis-à-vis* the phenomenological; and the "five models of the church" (made famous by Avery Dulles) each of which has its positive and negative effects on ecclesiological discourse.

One is the juridical point of view as contrasted with a more pastoral approach to official ministry. In reference to the question of deciding who should preside at eucharist E. Schillebeeckx makes the following comment:

> In the second millennium (of the Church's history) a primarily juridical view of the ministry comes into being, almost exclusively concentrated on the ministry and less concentrated on the church, in which "sacrament" and "law" are detached from each other.[128]

In discussing the shift from the first millennium's emphasis on the pneumatological-christological basis for ordained ministry to the second millennium's directly christological basis Schillebeeckx notes the following:

> Although Thomas, at least, still always talks of "sacraments of the church" (*sacramenta ecclesiae*), the sacrament will later be defined in a technical and abstract sense as *signum efficax gratiae*, in which the ecclesial dimension remains completely unconsidered. Its sacramental power is founded directly on the "sacred" power (*sacra potestas*) which is the priest's personal possession. In this way the ecclesial significance of the ministry with its charismatic and pneumatological dimensions is obscured, and the more time goes on, the more the ministry is embedded in a legalistic cadre which bestows sacred power.[129]

This juridical approach is contrasted with a more pastoral/sacramental one in B. Cooke's treatment of authority held by the ordained ministry in the church:

> The question is how one understands this according to one or other soteriology. If one views Jesus himself as having exercised some form of jurisdiction (or as possessing all jurisdictional authority, but deciding to exercise only that which pertained to the spiritual realm) and then having passed on this jurisdiction to a line of successors who act as his legates until he himself comes in final judgment, this is a fundamentally different viewpoint from that of the person who sees the risen Christ still exercising his redemptive function *sacramentally* through those who fulfill the ministry of governing.[130]

Another set of ecclesiological starting points which account for contrasting conclusions is the ontological/phenomenological one. E. Schillebeeckx

---

[128]*Ministry*, p. 52.

[129]Ibid., p. 67.

[130]*Ministry to Word and Sacraments*, p. 516.

describes it thus:

> The tension between an ontological-sacerdotalist view of the ministry on the one hand and a purely functionalist view on the other must therefore be resolved by a theological view of the church's ministry as a charismatic office, the service of leading the community, and therefore as an ecclesial function within the community and accepted by the community. Precisely in this way it is a gift of God.[131]

This contrast can also be described as deductive/inductive or doctrinal/sociological or structural/experiential. According to W. Marrevee one of the important components of the methodology embraced by the Lima document and by virtually all ecumenical documents on the question of the ordained ministry is the fact that

> the locally *experienced* ecclesial fellowship in congregations or parishes — in other words, not the diocese — serves as a starting point for the articulation of the place and role of the special ministry that functions in such an ecclesial fellowship.[132]

Perhaps the most comprehensive treatment of the various starting points for ecclesiological reflection is A. Dulles' critical assessment tool, the now-famous "models of the church."[133] In this study he isolates five ecclesiological models which are not mutually exclusive but nonetheless the cause of much tension, both healthy and unhealthy, in the church. The five models are: the institutional model, the community model, the sacramental model, the kerygmatic model, and the diaconal model. In his treatment of "ecclesiology and (ordained) ministry" Dulles explores "the relationship between the patterns of ministry and the five basic models of the Church."[134]

> Tensions are quite evident in Dulles's first model, the institutional:

> In defense of the institutional model of priesthood one may say that in a society as large and complex as the Church there is need for officers with a determinate sphere of competence, responsibility, and power. Without administrators designated in some regular way, and acknowledged as having certain well-defined roles, there would be chaos and confusion.

> On the other hand, it must be recognized that there has sometimes been an overemphasis on the institutional element in the Church, to the detriment of effective service. The Church has at times become too much like the secular state

---

[131] *Ministry*, p. 70.

[132] *Catholic Perspectives on BEM*, p. 166. Emphasis added.

[133] *Models of the Church: A Critical Assessment of the Church in All Its Aspects*, Garden City, New York: Doubleday & Company, Inc., 1974.

[134] Ibid., p. 152.

to do justice to the spiritual mission of the Church and its connection with the mystery of Christ. Furthermore, the particular forms of government that have become established in some churches — perhaps especially in Roman Catholicism — owe too much to the political forms inherited from Patristic and medieval times.[135]

Turning to the second model, the community model, Dulles again locates positive and negative features. Here the positive contribution is its emphasis on the priest as leader of the community; the negative side to this model is its subordination of all other functions to this one with a tendency to depreciate the sacramental and mystical dimensions of Christianity.

In regard to the third model, the sacramental model, Dulles contrast the following views:

As a focal center for the community the priest must visibly be a sign and sacrament of Christ. Catholicism has perhaps a special responsibility to keep alive this sacral dimension of priesthood. The idea of the priest as a living symbol of Christian holiness tends to be underplayed in some Protestant traditions.[136]

The negative side to this model is its tendency to exaggerate the sacral aspects of priesthood until it borders on the magical. The priest is so close to the divine in this model that he takes the place of the community almost to the exclusion of the community from its proper sacral roles.

In the application of his fourth ecclesiological model, the kerymatic model, to a fourth paradigm for his consideration of the ordained ministry Dulles draws a sharp contrast between catholic and protestant tendencies in the exercise of the ministry. He offers the following observations for dealing with the contrast:

It may be possible for Protestants and Catholics to get beyond their sterile dispute as to whether word or sacrament is primary. In ministry we are dealing with a presence of God that transcends both, encompasses both, and gives power to both. The word of God is always somehow sacramental, for it symbolically makes God present, and the sacrament, which is the symbol of God's real presence in the assembly, never comes to pass without the word of proclamation.[137]

Dulles treats the fifth model, the diaconal model, mainly in terms of the ordained minister's involvement in movements in society which may lead to the taking of political stances and the taking of political action. Here there is the twofold danger of partisan politics to the detriment of religion and, on the other hand, a

---

[135]Ibid., pp. 153-154.

[136]Ibid., p. 159.

[137]Ibid., p. 162.

dangerous indifference bordering on collusion with an unjust social order.

SECTION FOUR: TOWARD A THEOLOGY OF MINISTRY . . . IN LIGHT OF THE ABOVE ANALYSIS.

Here it is our intention to propose three avenues for developing a theology of official ministry in the life of the Church. The first is experiential and practical. It emphasizes the experience of the practical life of faith, i.e., the experience of faith in *praxis*. The second is ecclesiological and theoretical. It directly concerns the way we think of relationships among ecclesial bodies. The third is philosophical. It sees plurality in ministries and church structures as a blessing and not a curse in human history.

E. Kilmartin comments as follows on the Lima document:

> BEM thinks sacramentally. It stresses the active presence of Christ in the Spirit in the case of baptism, eucharist and ordained ministry. . . . Two theologies of ordained ministry are . . . introduced.

> BEM seems to favor a more functional view of office in the Church. But it recommends the introduction of an episcopal constitution in churches which lack it. I believe that it would be wrong to judge this to be a naive suggestion. The FO Commission undoubtedly does not expect that the mere introduction of . . . an episcopal constitution would solve dogmatic problems on the road to visible communion.

> In my opinion these suggestions reflect the FO Commission's conviction that agreement on the theology of . . . episcopal constitution of the Church can never be attained by theoretical discussion. Rather practice will finally decide what must be done. Practice of the faith is not a mere pragmatic application of pre-established directives. Rather practice arises from a global perception of the faith and is known to be orthopraxis because it corresponds to the experience of the faith which impregnates and structures the lives of believers. Orthopraxis is the discovery of the behaviour which corresponds to the nature of the Church willed by Christ. Practice, not theoretical schemes, decides what must be done.

> . . . Can these churches, which are asked to introduce the episcopacy, come to a correct experience of an episcopally constituted church without experiencing in practice communion with episcopally constituted churches, even before they have accepted this constitution as pertaining to more than the *bene esse* of the Church? Could the Catholic Church go along with the recommendation of episcopal constitution for churches which lack it without supporting their experience by

concrete visible expressions of communion on the way to full communion?[138]

The experience of faith is not easily articulated. Gospel faith is judged by its "fruits," its *praxis*. However, it needs to be articulated, made visible, sacramentalized. This faith defies measurement and predictability. Yet it is an ecclesial reality. And the *ecclesia* is first and foremost, in keeping with the careful deliberations of Vatican II, *mysterion* (sacramentum). One of the commentators on the deliberations of the Council expresses it thus in regard to the first chapter of the Dogmatic Constitution on the Church, *Lumen Gentium*:

> Article 8 now expressly takes up the title of the whole chapter, presenting the Church in its reality as mystery, in its sacramental structure. As such, it forms a totality which is at once visible and invisible. There is a manifold tension here. . . . The point here is merely to characterize the mystery of the Church as a unity full of tension. Visible and invisible Church are not to be understood as two separate, distinct and completely different entities but as one complex reality composed of a divine and a human element (8:1). The whole reality of the Church can never be fully visible on earth, it can only be accepted for the moment in faith.[139]

Keeping in mind the above remarks by Kilmartin and Vorgrimler it is clear to the present writer that the Lima document's invitation (in the Preface to all three texts) is key to a proper ecclesiological vision of faith and a most important emphasis in any theological approach to a development of a theology of the ordained ministry. The Faith and Order Commission asks of each ecclesial body which studies the three documents:

> — the extent to which your church can recognize in this text the faith of the Church through the ages;

> — the consequences your church can draw from this text for its relations and dialogues with other churches, particularly with those churches which also recognize the text as an expression of the apostolic faith;

> — the guidance your church can take from this text for its worship, educational, ethical, and spiritual life and witness.[140]

Theologizing must follow *praxis*. This has been made eminently clear in recent years through the effort of "liberation theology." A theology of ordained ministry must be willing to deal patiently with the rich experience and *praxis* of faith, albeit filled with many unresolved (perhaps unresolvable) tensions. Theology must

---

[138]Edward J. Kilmartin, S.J., "A Catholic Response to Lima 1982," *Bulletin/Centro Pro Unione* (N. 27 — Spring 1985), p. 14.

[139]Herbert Vorgrimler, *Commentary on the Documents of Vatican II*, Vol. I, p. 146.

[140]FO Paper 111, p. x.

work hand in hand with sociology, psychology and anthropology to insure its distinctive contribution to the reflective process which Anselm so succinctly defined as *fides quaerens intellectum.*

The second avenue being proposed here toward the development of a theology of the ordained ministry is ecclesiological and theoretical. Vatican Council II's Decree on Ecumenism states the following:

> The separated Churches and communities as such, though we believe they suffer from the defects already mentioned, have been by no means deprived of significance and importance in the mystery of salvation. For the Spirit of Christ has not refrained from using them as means of salvation.[141]

One commentator on this conciliar statement notes the following:

> The basic statement that is made here undoubtedly represents a decisive step forward in the ecumenical thought of the Catholic Church: the non-Catholic Christian communities, are, as communities, means which the Spirit of Christ uses to lead their members to salvation. Thus it is not sufficient to say, in accordance with the usual thinking hitherto, that non-Catholics can attain salvation, *although* they live outside the Catholic Church. Rather, one must say that Christ gives them salvation through the reality of non-Catholic communities, albeit not in so far as these are separated from the Catholic Church, but in so far as within them the effect is present of the elements of the Church through which Christ effects the salvation of the faithful in the Catholic Church also.[142]

F. Sullivan makes further comments about the history of this text for the sake of exquisite clarity:

> It did not escape the notice of some less ecumenically minded bishops that this text was clearly attributing a salvific role not just to the sacraments that might be found in non-Catholic communities, but to these churches and communities as such. This occasioned a *modus* proposing that the text be amended to say rather: "In these communities means of salvation are preserved which the Holy Spirit has not refrained from using, etc." The response of the (Conciliar Theological) Commission is as follows: "Wherever valid means of salvation are being used, which, as social actions, characterize those communities as such, it is certain that the Holy Spirit is using those communities as means of salvation" (AS III/7,36).[143]

In the context of criticizing the response of the Vatican's Congregation for the Doctrine of the Faith to Leonardo Boff's book, *Church Charism and Power* F. Sullivan emphasizes that

---

[141] *Unitatis Redintegratio*, art. 3, para. 4:

[142] H. Vorgrimler, ed., pp. 75-76.

[143] Francis A. Sullivan, S.J., "The Significance of Vatican II's Decision to Say of the Church of Christ Not That It 'Is' But That It 'Subsists In' the Roman Catholic Church," *Bulletin/Centro Pro Unione* (N. 29 - Spring 1986), p. 7.

> while the Council did not hesitate to speak of the separated Eastern Churches as "particular churches" without qualification, it was the mind of the (Conciliar Theological) Commission that the western communities that lack the full reality of the Eucharist — without attempting to decide which ones these were — still have a truly ecclesial character, and are at least analogous to particular churches of the one Church of Christ.[144]

Sullivan further states and concludes:

> Can it be said that the universal Church in some way also embraces the "ecclesial communities"? If we understand the universal Church as essentially the communion of the particular churches "in which and from which the universal Church has its existence" (cf. LG 23 a), and if one accepts the fact that in the actual state of divided Christianity both of these terms: "communion" and "churches" admit greater or less fullness, I believe that one can think of the universal Church as a communion, at various levels of fullness, of bodies that are more or less fully churches. Such a view is by no means identical with the one excluded by the Declaration *Mysterium Ecclesiae*, which insists rightly that "we cannot imagine that Christ's Church is nothing more than a collection (divided, but still possessing a certain unity) of churches and ecclesial communities" (AAS 65, 1973, 398). The Church of Christ is certainly something more than any such "collection" (*summa*); it is a real communion, realized at various degrees of density or fullness, of bodies, all of which, though some more fully than others, have a truly ecclesial character.

> I am convinced that such a view is consistent with our belief that we belong to that Church in which alone the one true Church of Christ subsists with all those properties and structural elements that are gifts of Christ to his Church, and which, by his enduring grace, it can never lose.[145]

It seems clear from the above careful reading of the documents of Vatican II that Roman Catholic theology can readily admit that other ecclesial communities in Christianity, precisely as communities, are, in various degrees, means of salvation. Because of this, the official ministries of those communities (the very ways they are ordered) are means of salvation. It is true that faith can be informed by greater or lesser degrees of charity. And faith can be expressed with greater or lesser degrees of clarity. Faith, however, does not admit of degrees in terms of its ultimate salvific efficacy. It either *is* or *is not* salvific; it either saves or does not save. One is either alive to God or dead in sin.

The ministry text of the Lima document (BEM) views the ordained ministry as a "sacramental sign." (M41) In light of the salvific efficacy of the faith that informs them the official ministries of the various ecclesial communities or churches can be accepted, in various degrees of clarity of signification, as effective signs and

---

[144]Ibid., p. 7.

[145]Ibid., p. 8.

communities.

The third avenue proposed here for developing a theology of official ministry in the life of the Church is philosophical. It is based on the "principle of internal symbolism" outlined briefly in an earlier section of this chapter. It is a comprehensive and universal principle which aims not to resolve plurality in all facets of existence but actually regards such plurality as the resolution and perfection of the unity of all of reality. It regards tension and even many forms of conflict as desirable.

K. Rahner, in explaining this metaphysical principle, says that "a being is, of itself, independently of any comparison with anything else, plural in its unity."[146] He elaborates on the principle and shows how it applies even to the fundamental doctrine of Christianity on the Trinity:

> A plurality in an original and an originally superior unity can only be understood as follows: the "one" develops, the plural stems from an original "one", in a relationship of origin and consequence; the original unity, which also forms the unity which unites the plural, maintains itself while resolving itself and "disclosing" itself into a plurality in order to find itself precisely there. A consideration of the Trinity shows that the "one" of unity and plurality, thus understood, is an ontological ultimate, which may not be reduced to an abstract and merely apparently "higher" unity and simplicity: it cannot be a hollow, lifeless identity. It would be theologically a heresy, and therefore ontologically an absurdity, to think that God would be really "simpler" and hence more perfect, if there were no real distinction of persons in God. There exists therefore a differentiation which is in itself a "perfectio pura" and which must be taken into consideration from the very start of a theological understanding of being. . . . Being *as* such, and hence *as* one (*ens* as *unum*), for the fulfilment of its being and its unity, emerges into a plurality — of which the supreme mode is the Trinity.[147]

Plurality, then, is not necessarily a detraction from unity. On the contrary, from the metaphysical point of view elaborated by Rahner, plurality may actually enhance unity and bring it to a greater and greater perfection.

Armed with this philosophical viewpoint we turn to Rahner's discussion of the divisions in Christianity, the plurality of structural expressions of the one Church of Christ. Of this plural situation as it actually exists today Rahner states that "the majority of Christians really exist in an interior, positive and guiltless relationship

---

[146]"The Theology of Symbol," T.I., Vol IV, p. 227.

[147]Ibid., pp. 227-228.

to their church and to the other churches."[148] He goes on to state the following:

> At least presupposing that people today are by and large innocent with respect to the divisions in Christianity, we have to ask and demand much more intensively that these facts (historical facts causing the divisions) have and must have a positive meaning in God's salvific providence than we would if these facts were just the objectification of an abysmal guilt on man's part.[149]

Rahner offers the following positive meaning of the plurality of expressions of Christianity in the division of the churches:

> We can say that Christians perceive and experience the really radical and fundamental truths and realities of Christian faith and of Christian existence more clearly than perhaps would be the case if everyone were in the same social and ecclesial situation, and if they all naturally and obviously belonged to one and the same church. The radical question about what Christianity really is, and the constantly critical attitude towards the Christianity which they themselves embody remain present in this division.[150]

Of course, Rahner adds, "we cannot say . . . that this process of salvation may dispense Christians from devoting all of their powers towards striving for the unity of the church."[151] It is in this striving that the Lima document gives strong and admirable witness to a practical unity in diversity. This is clearly stated at the end of its opening section:

> There are differences concerning the place and forms of the ordained ministry. . . . A common answer needs to be found to the following question: How, according to the will of God and under the guidance of the Holy Spirit, is the life of the Church to be understood and ordered, so that the Gospel may be spread and the community built up in love?[152]

Instead of bemoaning the plurality of ecclesial expressions in Christianity these philosophical and practical considerations may be helpful in advancing in a positive way to a deeper and more fruitful unity among the churches. As Rahner succinctly states the matter:

> As long as we are separated, as long as in God's dispensation people's consciences are convinced that their churches have to be separated, we can certainly ask about a positive salvific meaning in this situation and say that we have to make the best of it.[153]

---

[148]*Foundations of Christian Faith*, p. 368.

[149]Ibid., pp. 368-369.

[150]Ibid., p. 369.

[151]Ibid.

[152]M6.

[153]*Foundations*, p. 369.

This approach is the one evinced in the Lima text on ministry.

SECTION FIVE: IN CONCLUSION, THE STRENGTHS AND THE WEAKNESSES OF THE LIMA TEXT ON MINISTRY.

STRENGTHS.

The Lima text on ministry has many strengths. The following seven seem particularly significant. First, its methodology, its approach, its perspective. W. Marrevee, as we have already seen above, has pointed out the importance of Lima's starting-point and primary emphasis on "the locally *experienced* ecclesial fellowship in congregations or parishes."[154] This reference to the experience of ecclesial faith is reminiscent of the phrase *sensus fidelium* in Roman Catholic theology. It also suggests the approach of Latin American liberation theology with its emphasis on *praxis*.

Theological reflection is at the service of faith. St. Anselm has provided us with the simplest yet most profound definition of theology, *fides quaerens intellectum*, faith seeking understanding. Faith exists fundamentally in the lived experience of faith. Faith is not, in its basic roots, a set of beliefs or creeds or articulations of faith, as important and as sacred as they may be. Faith is to be found first and foremost in the creature's encounter with the self-revealing God of creation.

Theologizing most properly follows, not precedes, the experience and the practice of faith. For theologizing is a process of reflecting, of turning back on what has already come to pass. The norm for the full experience of faith is the adult experience, not the infant or the childhood experience. The newly revived Rite of the Christian Initiation of Adults emphasizes the importance of evaluating the celebration of sacraments of faith in terms of such adult experience.

Further, Christian faith is fundamentally communal. The ordinary locus for the experience of faith is the local Christian community, where the scriptural and eucharistic word of God is celebrated. All other expressions and experiences of God's word are derivative from this primary experience. So it is important that the Lima text emphasize this experience before any other. The Lima document does not

---

[154]*Catholic Perspectives on BEM*, p. 166. Emphasis added.

rule out other derivative experiences of the faith of the church, in regions (groups of local eucharistic communities) and in the *oikoumene*, the whole inhabited world. The architects of the text made some decisions to treat some important issues only briefly or not at all, leaving to future study and to the ongoing process of ecumenical dialogue, their resolution. One such matter is that of the petrine ministry. Their decision to not treat it in this text may prove to be unwise. On the other hand, it may be a decision based soundly on prudence, the positive virtue of deciding what can and cannot be accomplished given the present state of affairs among believers.

A second strength of the Lima text is its brevity and succinctness. Its approach reveals a depth of insight expressed with an economy of language. Its compact format makes it an apt tool for dialogue and discussion. Its lack of physical density does not correspond to a lack of theological depth. The commentary format attests to its conscious attempt not to resolve differences and tensions when such a resolution is not warranted.

We have witnessed throughout the chronological textual analysis of the previous chapters of this study an unrelenting refinement of meanings. There has been a concerted effort not to claim too much from historical evidence. At the same time every attempt was made to benefit from current scriptural and patristic scholarship in order to allow for the widest possible accommodation of present church structures and practices. For the various churches in dialogue over these issues claim that their structures and practices are in continuity with the apostolic and subapostolic age. An effort to seek out and appreciate that continuity has been a hallmark of the text.

Further there has been witnessed an effort to benefit from the various insights of the various church structures and practices. At the same time the architects of the document have not refrained from making strong recommendations, e.g., with regard to the possible adoption of some form of episcopal structure by all the churches. There is an awareness of various ecclesiologies but as Max Thurian states it:

> The ecclesiology presupposed by the Lima document and thought of as that of the New Testament (which does not rule out institutional diversity), is definitely a "sacramental" ecclesiology. The church is the sign of God's presence and the instrument of God's work in the world; it is the body of Christ which unites believers by the word and sacraments; it is the temple of the Holy Spirit in which

Christians are sanctified by faith and prayer.[155]

The succinctness of language has not fostered the use of arcane theological terminology nor has it contributed to a lack of nuance of meanings. Great care has been taken to communicate with those who are trained in theological disciplines but not to the neglect of the theologically unrefined members of the churches. The language is simple and straightforward, yet calling for careful study and reflection.

Its reading may be the occasion for more questions to be raised than answers to be given. It is, after all, a tool for ecumenical dialogue, not a catechism of simple definitions to be accepted as the final word. Compared to much of the documentation of Vatican Council II it exhibits a greater simplicity and is more likely to be read and pondered.

The third strength of the Lima text on ministry is that it evinces an openendedness. It issues a call for further study, development, and improvement. The tone is invitational. J. Eagan expresses it thus:

> DM (the ministry text) is not unrealistic for it expects this stage of assimilation, discussion, and refinement to last for a decade or more before mutual recognition may be achieved. BEM and DM in this case are meant to be the "consciousness-raising" catalyst in this process of moving by states toward unity. This may be in fact its greatest achievement![156]

In the Preface of the Lima document the following words exhibit its openendedness and invitational spirit:

> We believe that the Holy Spirit has led us to this time, a *kairos* of the ecumenical movement when sadly divided churches have been enabled to arrive at substantial theological agreements. We believe that many significant advances are possible if in our churches we are sufficiently courageous and imaginative to embrace God's gift of Church unity.
>
> As concrete evidence of their ecumenical commitment, the churches are being asked to enable the widest possible involvement of the whole people of God at all levels of church life in the spiritual process of receiving this text.[157]

Hearkening back to the first strength which we outlined above there is an invitation to listen to the *sensus fidelium*, the actual lived experience of faith among all God's people, not merely the people of a particular church communion and not merely the

---

[155]*Churches Respond to BEM: Official Responses to the "Baptism, Eucharist and Ministry" text*, Vol. I (Faith and Order Paper 129), ed. by Max Thurian, Geneva: WCC, 1986, pp. 6-7.

[156]*Mid-Stream* (July, 1984), p. 302.

[157]FO Paper 111, p. x.

representatives of those people, the official ministers of the churches. Theology depends on a viable and vibrant contact with this, its very life-blood, the faith lived by *all* God's people.

What is demanded is that there be more efficient structures by which the *vox populi* can be heard. Synods must be designed to be more than "synods of bishops" with only token representation from the laity. The teaching church must also become more and more the learning church, the listening church. Authority, in the terms discussed above, must be integrative as well as nutritive. There is an equality among all God's people, an equality which transcends all differentiations of office. Ladislaus Orsy wrote recently, of two hierarchies (two sources of sacred leadership) in the church, the hierarchy of external authority and the hierarchy of internal charity:

> The Spirit has always kept two kinds of teaching authorities alive in the church to balance and to complete each other. One judged doctrines in dispute and bore witness to the evangelical truth in solemn assemblies and through formal definitions, another taught the faithful about the mysteries with a charism that is granted directly by the Holy Spirit. Thus, we have the measured and precise definitions of the great Eastern councils on the doctrine of the Trinity; and we also have the breathtaking descriptions of Teresa of Avila about the presence of the same Trinity in the human spirit. Or, we have the Roman councils of the Middle Ages setting patterns for the reform of the church, and the living example of the *poverello*, the poor man from Assisi, who effectively moved the church to reform.[158]

Orsy admits that "the line between the two hierarchies, of course, should not be drawn so sharply that one person (we might add, *any* baptized person) could not belong to both of them."[159] As was noted above, in principle, any baptized person can exercise leadership in the church, even in regard to all the sacred rituals, the sacraments. What is true in principle, can very well become true in fact. Such is the case especially at a time in human history when so many movements of liberation are afoot in the world. These movements give ample evidence that the Spirit of God is working on many fronts to free groups of people, previously passive in the face of their plight, to assume their rightful adult place as active participants in all of society, most especially the church, *the* sacrament of the Spirit.

In this regard, the Lima text does exhibit an openness to the ever greater participation of women in leadership roles in the church. It is true that for ecumenical reasons the Lima text is sensitive to those traditions, especially the

---

[158]Ladislaus Orsy, "The Two Hierarchies in the Church," *America*, Vol 158, No. 10 (March 12, 1988), p. 272.

[159]Ibid.

Orthodox and the Roman Catholic, which do not permit the ordination of women to roles of official ministry or leadership. There is an openendedness, however, an invitational spirit calling for more dialogue in this matter. No doors are closed.

The fourth strength of the Lima text on ministry is its demonstration of a keen awareness of recent theological and biblical advances in scholarship. In being up to date theologically it opts for more pastoral and practical categories in its approach and depends less on juridical and ontological concepts. G. Moede states the strength of this characteristic as follows:

> The insights of most of the ecumenical agreements on ordained ministry that are most productive of hope are found in their shift away from traditional preoccupation with juridical, or even ontological concepts. One can understand why some of these more materialistic criteria came into the Church at the end of the first millennium, but they inevitably led to distortion and aberration, to legalistic categories of ministry that easily could be controlled and domesticated. They also produced a church rigidly divided between "clerical" and "lay", with the laypersons eventually finding their place as spectators at an activity in which the ordained had all of the responsibility and authority.[160]

In isolating these various strengths of the Lima text there seems to emerge an overlapping which is almost inevitable when describing a project which attempts to be both theoretically sound and practically bound. It is an exercise in theology, but most especially pastoral theology. When sound scriptural and dogmatic scholarship encounter the exigencies of lives lived in close relationship in the local church the juridical and the legalistic and the clerical emphases of a highly structured bureaucracy and an aloof hierarchical system seem more and more irrelevant. For scripture and dogma themselves are rooted in the daily personal encounters of people with people and of those same people with the divine presence which encompasses and embraces all. The beginning and end of biblical religion is religious experience, personal and communal (not to be understood as sheer emotionalism or some form of sacred exclusivism). This same experience, when healthy and authentic, is open to sound theory and the critique of the tradition from which it springs.

The fifth strength of the Lima document on ministry is its hope and optimism. It appears at first that this is not, strictly speaking, a theologically scientific trait. But who can dismiss a theology of hope as unimportant or irrelevant? As J. Egan puts it:

> Its greatest contribution may prove to be its underlying pervading spirit of optimistic faith: the strong belief that the union of Christ's Church is the most

---

[160]Gerald F. Moede, "BEM and COCU's Emerging Consensus: A Reflection on Ministry," *Mid-Stream: An Ecumenical Journal*, Vol. XXIII, No. 3 (July, 1984), p. 315.

important responsibility of all the churches; the unflagging hope despite formidable obstacles, that union is possible; the gut-level sense that now is the acceptable time.[161]

Further the Lima text, as we have pointed out in the analysis of the text above, exhibits an awareness of realized eschatology. The kingdom has already come. There is no doubt about the divine dynamism which has been unleashed in human history with the call of Israel and the cause of the Christ. There is only the vigilance required to be in tune with the music of this symphony of providential action.

The church is not equivalent to the kingdom. The church is at the service of the kingdom's reaching its fullest expression in human history. Official ministry in the church is at the service of the church's straining to know the many forms which that expression can take. It is a straining, however, which is not strained or anxious about the final outcome. The only anxiety is that the church and the various communions in the church see in the very variety of their efforts evidence of the unity in multiplicity which is characteristic of all reality, and especially this richest of all realities, the kingdom of God.

It is the role of official ministry to provide leadership, particularly in terms of keeping vibrant the vision of the goal of the church's mission. The church and the churches will pass away with the passing away of time and history; the goal of the mission, however, will remain forever. It is the recapitulation of all things in Christ. For

> God the Father has let us know the mystery of his purpose, according to his good pleasure which he determined beforehand in Christ, for him to act upon when the times had run their course: that he would bring everything together under Christ, as head, everything in the heavens and everything on earth. (Eph. 1: 9-10)

There is every reason to be filled with hope in the face of this vision, common to all the churches.

The sixth strength of the Lima text we have been analyzing is its grounding of the topic of ordained ministry in trinitarian and especially pneumatological categories. G. Vischer explains it as follows:

> The doctrine of ministry is distorted when the ministries in the Church, which as such belong to the work of the Holy Spirit, are described in christological categories. . . . The work of Christ cannot be described otherwise than as completed once and for all, as all sufficient, valid and effective. From the christological standpoint, there is no cooperation and continuation. From the

---

[161]*Mid-Stream* (July, 1984), p. 306.

> pneumatological standpoint, no less, there is no incarnation, although there is
> certainly indwelling and therefore, cooperation, continuation, continuity, abiding,
> witnessing, contemporanization, representation, obedience and responsibility,
> thankfulness.[162]

Perhaps some of the problems surrounding the issue of representation (acting *in persona Christi*) as discussed above can be obviated by a greater awareness of this pneumatological emphasis in the ministry text.

Yves Congar, in his recent contribution "towards a pneumatological christology,"[163] stated that "it is in fact almost true to say that Christology must be situated *within* soteriology, which embraces it."[164] Congar then distinguished between the ontological (and non-historical) christology of even Aquinas and the realistic theology of the NT (historical) christology. The latter gives a proper role to the Spirit in the unfolding ministry of the incarnate Son of God and *a fortiori* to the unfolding ministry of the church through the ages. Just as the acknowledgement of this proper role of the Spirit contributes to our seeing a gradual dawning of Jesus' consciousness during his earthly ministry so this same acknowledgement can contribute to our seeing a gradual dawning of consciousness during the ongoing ministry of the church. The church only gradually comes to new insights and the development of new approaches (structures of ministry).

Further the emphasis made by the church of the beloved disciple on charism can remind us that the work of the Spirit, the work of peace and *order* (not disorder), is not opposed to the realities of institution, structure or authority. As Nathan Mitchell has pointed out:

> "Charism", as interpreted by Paul, is itself an ordering principle within the
> community. The opposite of charism is neither institution nor structure nor
> authority, but rather chaos and disorder. Apostleship, with its God-given authority
> and broad pastoral responsibility for all the churches, is thus the premier example

---

[162]"Die Amtslehre dort schief wird, wo man die Dienste in der Kirche, die als solche zum Werk des Heiligen Geistes gehören, mit christologischen Kategorien beschreibt. . . . Das Werk Christi kann nicht anders denn als ein für allemal vollbracht, als allgenügsam, gültig und wirksam beschrieben werden. Christologisch gesehen gibt es keine Mitwirkung und Fortführung. Eben sowenig gibt es pneumatologisch eine Inkarnation, wohl aber gibt es da Einwohnung und darum Mitwirkung, Fortführung, Kontinuität, Bleiben, Bezeugen und Vergegenwärtigen, Gehorsam und Verantwortung, Dankbarkeit." Georg H. Vischer, *Apostolischer Dienst: Fünfzig Jahre Diskussion über das kirchliche Amt in Glauben und Kirchenverfassung*, Frankfurt am Main: Verlag Otto Lembeck, 1982, p. 218.

[163]*I Believe in the Holy Spirit*, Volume III: *The River of Life Flows in the East and in the West*, New York: The Seabury Press, 1983, pp. 165-173.

[164]Ibid., p. 165.

of charismatic ministry. Moreover, Paul's insistence that charism manifest itself in concrete deeds of service that build up the body allowed him to check both excessive enthusiasm and divisive individualism within the congregation. Charism thus orders the community by respecting each individual's unique gifts, while linking those gifts to the larger community where all work together for the common good.[165]

As Mitchell also reminded his readers, "according to the Pauline view the entire (Christian) community is thus 'charismatic' and ministry belongs to *all* members rather than to a hierarchically constituted few."[166] The Lima text's emphasis on pneumatology will contribute to a recovery of this Pauline view.

Congar pointed out the evidence of pneumatology in the texts of Vatican II. He added this statement, however, which gives added weight to what we had said earlier about the importance of *praxis* in the development of the theology of ministry:

> The Council provided the texts, but the truth of that pneumatology has to be confirmed in the life of the Church. . . . The Catholic Renewal which began in Pittsburgh in the U.S.A. in 1967 and which has spread throughout the world is clearly part of this living pneumatology, since the Spirit is undoubtedly experienced in that movement. . . . Pneumatology, like ecclesiology and theology as a whole, can only develop fully on the basis of what is experienced and realized in the life of the Church. In this sphere, theory is to a great extent dependent on praxis.[167]

The theorists and practitioners of Liberation Theology have much to teach the whole church in this regard.

The seventh and last strength which we isolate here is one that involves a common theme of ecumenicity that runs through the entire text under study here. F. McManus describes it in the following way:

> It is the refrain that each church should not merely reappraise other churches in the hope of discovering that some long assumed deficiency is not present. It should also reevaluate its own forms and practices in the hope of discovering what may indeed be common ground, once defects are removed, and thus move toward the desired recognition. This certainly has a positive application to the Roman Catholic Church's ecumenical participation.[168]

As we noted above in this present chapter (at the end of section one), the

---

[165]Nathan Mitchell, O.S.B., *Mission and Ministry: History and Theology in the Sacrament of Order*, Wilmington, Delaware: Michael Glazier, Inc., 1982, p. 286.

[166]Ibid., p. 125.

[167]Yves Congar, *I Believe in the Holy Spirit,* Volume I: *The Experience of the Spirit*, New York: The Seabury Press, 1983, p. 172.

[168]Frederick McManus, "Report on the Lima Statement on Ministry," October, 1984 (unpublished mimeographed paper).

recent Vatican response to BEM has exhibited an unwillingness to acknowledge the theological tensions which exist within Catholicism itself thus opening the door to a possible reappraisal of its own official theological positions. It is to be hoped that such unwillingness is not evidence of any arrogance which may accompany the claim of being the "one true church of Christ." For, as we have seen, even the phrase in Vatican II stating that the reality of the Church "subsists in the Catholic Church (*subsistit in Ecclesia catholica*) is not to be interpreted as meaning that the Church "is" the Roman Catholic church.[169]

Furthermore it should be clear from the findings of the sciences of linguistics and hermeneutics that there is an inexhaustibility to truth and that even the most sacred expression of religious truth (dogmas) suffers from "the poverty of language." Semantic studies have distinguished between discourse and text in coming to grips with the ebb and flow of meanings expressed in oral and written forms of language. Even though scientists of language like Naom Chomsky have uncovered abiding structures in all human languages it is difficult to determine with exactitude the precise meanings intended in various contexts, especially when, as historians and scientists of culture have pointed out, texts are separated by long intervals of time and across vast chasms of culture.

What is said of language can be said as well of sociological structures which attempt, in different times and in various cultures, to respond to the need to preserve the truth from past generations and to pass on the truth to generations yet to come. As we have seen, the Lima text preferred the term, "faith," to the term "truth," thus displaying a keen awareness of the richness and complexity of the heritage of biblical, apostolic and subapostolic times.

WEAKNESSES.

One glaring omission is a fuller treatment of the issue of the ordination of women, an issue which has assumed particular poignancy and prominence in recent years. As Frère Max Thurian indicated in an interview with this present writer, the architects of the Lima document decided that it was an issue which could not be given proper treatment within the limited space and scope of the other issues

---

[169]See *Commentary on the Documents of Vatican II*, ed. by Herbert Vorgrimler, Vol. I, pp. 149-150.

surrounding ministry. This is true precisely in the light of the fifty-year history of the text. Recent interest in the this one issue may very well have come to overshadow the entire text on ministry. The Faith and Order Commission promises some further treatment in the context of a separate study.[170]

It is true, however, that no matter how inconvenient it is to treat this issue more extensively in such a document, not to give it more scope is a mistake. The issue has particular poignancy in these days what with the advance of the women's movement, especially in the western world, and the many movements of liberation of oppressed groups throughout the world. No amount of explaining from church leaders who represent male-dominated social structures can adequately convince the readers of this text that it should not be treated here and now.

Theologically speaking its short treatment is not excusable. As a text claiming to argue theologically it simply must be willing to face the overwhelming theological arguments in favor of women assuming positions of authority and responsibility, leadership among God's people. Its credibility as a theological document is at stake. When so much scholarship has been expended on issues like the episcopal office, not to give adequate scope to the scholarly advances in this highly publicized and important matter is a major miscalculation which detracts from the overall effectiveness of the document as a whole. To use the excuse that it is too divisive, if indeed that is the real reason behind its being treated so briefly, is to miss the point of dialogue in the first place. Not to face divisive issues is simply not to engage in honest and forthright dialogue. The issue will be treated whether or not the Lima text chooses to enter the fray.

The second weakness of the Lima text on ministry is what E. Schillebeeckx views as "the greatest deficiency of the Lima Report."[171] It concerns the penchant of the text to look backward to the old, still undivided church and the ministries which accompany it while neglecting to look forward to the new, emerging church and "the practice, even alternative practices, of ministry in the present, in connection with the many new forms of ministry instituted by pastoral workers, ecumenical ministries

---

[170]This is the WCC's study, entitled, "Community of Women and Men in the Church," which has become part of the more comprehensive study, entitled, "The Unity of the Church and the Renewal of Human Community." Actually the statement in the ministry text of BEM is the highest recognition given by the FO Commission to the issue of the ordination of women in a presentation to the churches.

[171]Edward Schillebeeckx, *The Church with a Human Face: A New and Expanded Theology of Ministry*, New York: The Crossroad Publishing Company, 1985, p. 262.

480

and so on."[172]

Schillebeeckx goes on to state the following about these new, emerging forms of ministry:

> Must these forms be excluded from the ministry, or *per se* introduced within the tripartite division of episcopacy, presbyterate and diaconate? In that case does not this church order which, while very old, is nevertheless the result of a historical development, become so important that it can hinder the vitality of churches in the gospel?
>
> Or is the *de facto existence* of a fourth kind of ministry which is now emerging the consequence of historical blockages to be found above all in connection with priesthood and episcopacy in the Roman Catholic Church?[173]

In this connection Schillebeeckx goes on to make the following important observation which is reminiscent of what we stated above about the need to engage in *praxis* theologizing:

> The Lima Report is not a grass-roots working paper but a piece of theoretical theology - a working paper written in studies, not on the basis of practical experience. As such it certainly seems to me to be a good piece of work, in which, in self criticism, every church can to some degree find traces of itself. However, I doubt whether many ecumenical basic communities will recognize themselves in it. Nevertheless, the Lima Report is also a challenge for them, though on the other hand the basic communities are a challenge for the Lima Report.[174]

Although the Lima document seemingly utilizes a methodology of viewing ministry from the experience of the local eucharistic community there is a misleading impression left that its theorizing is almost always from *praxis*. In fact it is the contention of this writer that due to the overwhelming influence of episcopal churches in the Faith and Order movement the Lima document tends, in its theorizing, to favor *a priori* the time-honored tripartite structure of bishop, presbyter, deacon over the experience of the actual functioning of those offices in the churches. The Lima document neglects *a fortiori* the newer emerging offices of leadership, e.g., those of pastoral workers in ecumenical and base communities of the Third World.

The third weakness of the Lima document's ministry text is its failure to treat adequately the relationship between and among the church traditions and local ecclesial communities which make up the Church universal. As J. Eagan states it:

> While it is true that DM (the Lima text on ministry) affirms that one of the functions of bishops is to link the local community and the "wider . . . Universal" Church, (n.29) nonetheless its basic argument for the historical episcopacy does not

---

[172]Ibid.

[173]Ibid.

[174]Ibid.

include the reality of the Universal Church. This significantly weakens the case for episcopacy, not only because its *de facto* concrete form through the centuries included the universal dimension but also because a value that only episcopacy can give is precisely its link function to the Church Universal.[175]

What Eagan says involves the issue of episcopal collegiality and perhaps even more significantly that of the petrine ministry. As he puts it:

In a future united Church this link function will assume prime importance. However, to have introduced this dimension (of the link function to the Church Universal) with its inevitable implication of the papacy would have enormously complicated the document at this stage.[176]

This reference to an "enormous complication" for the document reflects the comments of J.M.R. Tillard and M. Thurian to this present writer.

Here again some remarks by E. Schillebeeckx can prove helpful:

In my view rightly, the Roman Catholic Church cherishes the principle of both unity and catholicity (or intercultural plurality). The Spirit of God is the ultimate source of both principles, and he is the Spirit as he lives throughout the church, which is filled with him. Unity and Catholicity are therefore a task for every believer and for the whole of the believing community.

Nevertheless, here too *ministerial* service is necessary. The ministerial principle of unity is then embodied in the Petrine function in the church, while the ministerial principle of many-coloured and polycentric catholicity is embodied in the episcopal college, spread all over the world.[177]

The principles of unity and catholicity which are so prominent in the Roman Catholic tradition are sorely lacking in the Lima document. Of course the simultaneous presence of these two principles in the life of the church is the source of tension. That tension is evidence of life itself, its fundamental plurality and unity. We treated these ontological realities above in the writings of Karl Rahner. To note the presence of these realities in a particular church and among the churches and to acknowledge their tension-producing character is to testify to the vibrancy of the mission entrusted to the Church of Christ.

One church tradition, the Roman Catholic, speaks eloquently to the others in regard to this particular vibrancy willed by Christ and his Spirit. To neglect these principles is to neglect much of the life of the church. There is tension and there are complications resulting from an emphasis on these life-producing realities. Speaking

---

[175]Joseph F. Eagan, S.J., "Ordained Ministry in BEM: A Theological Critique," *Mid-Stream: An Ecumenical Journal*, Vol. XXIII, No. 3, (July, 1984), p. 296.

[176]Ibid.

[177]E. Schillebeeckx, *The Church with a Human Face*, p. 264.

to the issue of the petrine ministry P. Granfield notes that "the road to reunion will be long and difficult (but) despite real, unresolved differences among Christians, there is also a genuine communion that binds them together."[178] The length and difficulty of a journey must never be an excuse for not facing the unresolved theological differences among the churches of Christianity.

A FINAL APPEAL.

It is endemic to the theological enterprise to name and analyze, to attempt to control and tame. It is this drive that must be constantly monitored lest the divine which suffuses the human be thought to be exhausted by such analyses and lest the divine be limited by the resources of human wisdom. K. Rahner in his "prayer for the reunion of all Christians"[179] expresses the following appeal:

> Make the leaders of the churches clearsighted and courageous so that they feel more of a responsibility to the unity of the churches in the future than to the independence of their churches in the past. Make them daring because in the history of the Church something that is really new and great arises only when it is not completely legitimized by the past alone. Give them the joyous conviction that much more from the past can be gathered into the One Church by all the churches than is thought possible by a vision made shortsighted and fearful by the fact that what is to be gathered in was once the cause of division. Grant those in positions of responsibility in the Church the conviction that unity does not mean uniformity, by which one Church alone becomes the complete law for all the others, but rather reconciled diversity of the churches[180]

In the light of detailed analyses just completed it is the hope and prayer of this present writer that the Lima text on ministry be what a text etymologically ought to be, a fabric of carefully woven strands, each of which adds strength and beauty to the whole cloth, called the kingdom of God.

No expression exhausts the reality and no amount of weaving completes the work of the kingdom here in human history. May the strength and the beauty of the Lima text we have studied help the official ministry to better serve the church in its serving of the kingdom.

---

[178]Patrick Granfield, *The Limits of the Papacy*, pp. 192-193.

[179]Karl Rahner, *Prayers for a Lifetime*, New York: The Crossroad Publishing Company, 1984, pp. 163-165.

[180]Ibid., pp. 164-165.

EPILOGUE

THE PURPOSE OF THIS STUDY

The course of history is shaped by human discourse. The threads of human discourse at times, perhaps not often enough, weave a wonderful pattern which is identifiable as a significant text. In fact the word, text, itself arises from the analogy of weaving. Discourse and text, two important concepts in the art of communication, are key to the weaving of a theology of ministry in the Christian Church and among the churches which comprise it.

Without texts the strands of discourse remain just strands, discrete, disconnected, albeit beautiful in themselves, but never workable, never helpful in the ongoing process of unification through communication. The *Lima Document* is a text comprised of many strands. Like many documents of Vatican II it serves to focus our communication, to refine our speech, to channel our efforts to achieve greater unity.

The ministry text of the *Lima Document* is particularly important as well as difficult in that it touches on the issue of church unity where it sometimes hurts the most — in the area of power and authority, in the area of ordering or coordinating the church to serve the kingdom come in Jesus the Christ.

What precisely does this text say? How, exactly, did this text take shape, how was it weaved, what are the strands of meaning? Is it a text in which the Roman Catholic church can identify the strands of tradition which shape its own church order? To what extent? These are some of the questions I have attempted to answer.

Even more importantly, however, does this ministry text provide a useful pattern of theological themes by which the Roman church, alongside the other churches, can reshape its present church order to better serve the Greater Church's mission of service? Or, in keeping with our master analogy, can we, with the help of this text, loosen some of the strands which bind us to past patterns and reweave the fabric of church order thus making more and more recognizable the face of Christ the Servant, the Minister, and more recognizable the Church as his body?

LOOKING TO THE FUTURE

Scholarship is a never-ending process. This ministry study is intended to deepen and further that process for the benefit of God's people. Like the *Lima Document* it produces more questions than answers. Hopefully they are good questions, questions which lead the churches along the path to greater unity in service of the kingdom of God. Some of those questions, as I see it, fall into the following eight categories:

1) What is "of divine institution" *vis-à-vis* what is "of human making"? How distinct is this distinction in the first place? Or an allied question: Is the Holy Spirit as active *now* as in the early days of the church about which we read in Acts 15, 22-29: "The apostles and elders, with the whole church (at Jerusalem)" wrote in a letter to the church at Antioch the following words, "It has been decided by the Holy Spirit and by ourselves not to impose on you any burden beyond these essentials . . ." In other words exactly how are *those* days to be interpreted as normative for *these* days in which we are living?

2) What is the proper sequence in discussing representative roles in the church: Church, to official minister, to Christ, OR official minister, to Church, to Christ? How does this impact on the issue of presiding at Eucharist? Or, how for that matter, does it impact on the whole issue of the ordination of women?

3) What prevents the term, "sacrament," from being applied to the ministerial offices or structures of many ecclesial bodies besides the Roman Catholic and Orthodox?

4) In what sense does *praxis* always precede *theoria* in theologizing? Or, perhaps better stated, How better insure that the enterprise of speculative theology walk hand in hand with pastoral theology? Or, an allied question, how better integrate the experience of faith with the expression of truth?

5) Does Karl Rahner's principle of internal symbolism provide a reliable basis for a theology of ministry which prizes plurality? This question involves the status of the threefold ministry, its normative character, and the possible expansion of the diaconate to include many emerging forms of ministry.

6) Is there any great value in continuing to stress an "essential" difference between the priesthood of the laity and the priesthood of the ordained? Do

ontological categories serve theology when isolated from phenomenological ones?

7) How can the Roman Catholic emphasis on the church universal (especially in regard to the petrine ministry and episcopal collegiality) serve to enhance the emphasis by other traditions on the local church? And *vice versa*? Further, what precisely is the meaning of "local church"?

8) Can we finally learn from the approach adopted by Lund '52? Can our approach to ecclesiological questions in theology be guided by ecumenicity, that is, reevaluating one's own expressions, forms and practices by a search for common theological ground instead of reappraising positions other than one's own in the hope of discovering that some long assumed deficiency is not present?

May the questioning continue!

BIBLIOGRAPHY

PRIMARY SOURCES

"All Things New: Preparatory Booklet for the Fourth Assembly of the WCC, Uppsala, Sweden, July 4-20, 1968." Geneva: WCC, 1968.

Baptême, Eucharistie, Ministère: Convergence de la foi. Paris: Éditions du Centurion, 1982.

Codex Iuris Canonici. Vatican City: Libreria Editrice Vaticana, 1983. English translation in *The Code of Canon Law.* Grand Rapids Michigan: William B. Eerdmans Publishing Company, 1983.

Delaney, Edmund Francis, SA. *New Catholic Encyclopedia.* Vol. 2. New York: McGraw-Hill Book Company, 1967, pp. 784-785.

Denzinger, Henrici. *Enchiridion Symbolorum: Definitionum et Declarationum De Rebus Fidei et Morum.* Editio 31. Roma: Herder, 1960.

Documents of Vatican Council II. English translation in *Vatican Council II: The Conciliar and Post Conciliar Documents.* Edited by Austin Flannery. Northport, N.Y.: Costello Publishing Company, 1975.

Evanston to New Delhi, 1954-1961: Report of the Central Committee to the Third Assembly of the World Council of Churches, Geneva: WCC, 1961.

Faith and Order Paper No. 59. *Faith and Order: Louvain 1971, Study Reports and Documents.* Geneva: World Council of Churches, 1971.

Faith and Order Paper No. 82. *Lausanne 77: Fifty Years of Faith and Order.* Geneva: The World Council of Churches, 1977.

Faith and Order Paper No. 106. *Minutes of the Meeting of the Standing Commission, 1981, Annecy.* Geneva: WCC, 1981.

Faith and Order Paper No. 111. *Baptism, Eucharist and Ministry.* Geneva: World Council of Churches, 1982.

Fey, Harold E., ed. *A History of the Ecumenical Movement, 1948-1968*, volume 2, Philadelphia: The Westminster Press, 1970.

Flannery, Austin, O.P., ed. "Decree on Ecumenism" (Unitatis redintegratio"). *Vatican Council II: The Conciliar and Post Conciliar Documents.* Page 452ff.

Flannery, Austin, O.P., ed. "Decree on the Ministry and Life of Priests" ("Presbyterorum ordinis"). *Vatican Council II: The Conciliar and Post Conciliar Documents.* Page 863ff.

Flannery, Austin, O.P., ed. *Vatican Council II: The Conciliar and Post Conciliar Documents.* Northport, New York: Costello Publishing Company, Inc., 1975.

Flesseman-van-Leer, Ellen. Correspondence with M. Thurian, October 22, 1980. WCC Archives, Archive Box: "Faith and Order, Documents 1980-1981, Circular Letters, 1980-1981."

FO Mimeograph Paper. FO/65/6, February, 1965.

FO Mimeograph Paper. FO/66:35, June 1966.

FO Mimeograph Paper. FO/66:46, August 1966.

FO Mimeograph Paper. FO/67:4, January 1967.

FO Mimeograph Paper. FO/67:14, March 1967.

FO Mimeograph Paper. FO/67:21, April 1967.

FO Mimeograph Paper. FO/67:42, July 1967.

FO Mimeograph Paper. FO/67:48, August 1967.

FO Mimeograph Paper. FO/68:4, February 1968

FO Mimeograph Paper. FO/68:4, February 1968 (Revised April 1968).

FO Mimeograph Paper. FO/68:7, March 1968, "Ordination — A Working Paper."

FO Mimeograph Paper. FO/68:21, June 1968.

FO Mimeograph Paper. FO/68:21 rev., June 1968 (revised July 1968).

FO Mimeograph Paper. FO/69:1, January 1969.

FO Mimeograph Paper. FO/70:29, Juillet 1970.

FO Mimeograph Paper. FO/70:29, June, 1970.

FO Mimeograph Paper. FO/70:33, June 1970.

FO Mimeograph Paper. FO/70:33 (R), September 1970.

FO Mimeograph Paper. FO/70:39.

FO Mimeograph Paper. FO/70:43.

FO Mimeograph Paper. FO/70:44.

FO Mimeograph Paper. FO/70:45.

FO Mimeograph Paper. FO/70:46.

FO Mimeograph Paper. FO/70:47 (*en français*).

FO Mimeograph Paper. FO/70:47 (in English).

FO Mimeograph Paper. FO/70:48.

FO Mimeograph Paper. FO/70:50, September 1970.

FO Mimeograph Paper. FO/70:55, November 1970.

FO Mimeograph Paper. FO/71:1.

FO Mimeograph Paper. FO/71:1, January 1971.

FO Mimeograph Paper. FO/72:6.

FO Mimeograph Paper. FO/72:6, juin 1972 (*en français*).

FO Mimeograph Paper. FO/72:6, June 1972 (in English)

FO Mimeograph Paper. FO/72:8, June 1972.

FO Mimeograph Paper. FO/72:14, September 1972.

FO Mimeograph Paper. FO/72:15, September 1972.

FO Mimeograph Paper. FO/72:16, September 1972.

FO Mimeograph Paper. FO/72:17, September 1972.

FO Mimeograph Paper. FO/72:18, October 1972.

FO Mimeograph Paper. FO/73:33.

FO Mimeograph Paper. FO/73:33, September 1973.

FO Mimeograph Paper. FO/73:40, November, 1973.

FO Mimeograph Paper. FO/73:40, November 1973.

FO Mimeograph Paper. FO/73:40 (R), January 1974.

FO Mimeograph Paper. FO/73:41, November 1973.

FO Mimeograph Paper. FO/75:4, May 1975.

FO Mimeograph Paper. FO/76:2, March 1976.

FO Mimeograph Paper. FO/76:4.

FO Mimeograph Paper. FO/76:4, April 1976.

FO Mimeograph Paper. FO/76:5, May 1976.

FO Mimeograph Paper. FO/76:8, May 1976.

FO Mimeograph Paper. FO/77:3, April 1977, "Churches on the Way to Consensus:
     A Survey of the Replies to the Agreed Statements, 'One Baptism, One
     Eucharist and a Mutually Recognized Ministry.'"

FO Mimeograph Paper. FO/77:3, April 1977, Revised June 1977. "Churches on the
     Way to Consensus."

FO Mimeograph Paper. FO/77:6, May 1977, "Fifty Years in Quest of Unity," Yves
     Congar.

FO Mimeograph Paper.   FO/77:8, June 1977 (Report of Crêt-Bérard evaluation
     meeting, May-June, 1977).

FO Mimeograph Paper. FO/77:33, April 1977 (Revised June 1977).

FO Mimeograph Paper. FO/78:12, September 1978, "Conspectus of Studies."

FO Mimeograph Paper. FO/78:22, October 1978, "Growing Together in Unity."

FO Mimeograph Paper. FO/79:1, February 1979.

FO Mimeograph Paper. FO/79:1, February 1979, "Consultation on Believers' Baptism in Louisville, Ky.," 28 March-1 April, 1979.

FO Mimeograph Paper. FO/79:7, May 1979, "Authority in the Church."

FO Mimeograph Paper. FO/79:12, June 1979, "Consensus in the Formulation of Doctrine."

FO Mimeograph Paper. FO/79:14, June 1979, "Report from Second Forum on Bilateral Conversations."

FO Mimeograph Paper. FO/79:16, June 1979, "*Episcopé* and *Episcopos.*"

FO Mimeograph Paper. FO/79:17, July 1979, "Episcope - Episcopacy - Episcopate."

FO Mimeograph Paper, FO/79:17, July 1979.

FO Mimeograph Paper. FO/79:18, July 1979.

FO Mimeograph Paper. FO/79:18, July 1979, "Ministry."

FO Mimeograph Paper. FO/79:19, August 1979.

FO Mimeograph Paper. FO/79:19, August 1979, "Notes For Report to Standing Committee."

FO Mimeograph Paper. FO/80:2, February 1980.

FO Mimeograph Paper. FO/80:3, February 1980.

FO Mimeograph Paper. FO/80:6, juillet 1980, "Ministère — Texte révisé de la rencontre du Steering Committee, 3-7 juin, 1980."

FO Mimeograph Paper. FO/80:6, July 1980 (in English).

FO Mimeograph Paper. FO/80:6 (R), Oct./November 1980 (Final draft of Rome meeting of Oct/Nov 1980.).

FO Mimeograph Paper. FO/80:6, September 1980, "*Amt.*" (in German).

FO Mimeograph Paper. FO/81:2, January 1981.

FO Mimeograph Paper. FO/81:4, March 1981.

FO Mimeograph Paper. FO/81:4, March 1981 (Used for "Lima Master Text — Eucharist" and containing Max Thurian's handwritten corrections for Lima of 14 Nov. 81.)

FO Mimeograph Paper. FO/81:6, February 1981 (Used for "Lima Master Text — Baptism" and containing Max Thurian's handwritten corrections for Lima of 14 Nov. 81.)

FO Mimeograph Paper. FO/81:7, March 1981.

FO Mimeograph Paper. FO/81:7, March 1981 (Used for "Lima Master Text — Ministry" and containing Max Thurian's handwritten corrections for Lima of 14 Nov. 81.)

FO Mimeograph Paper. FO/81:15, November 1981.

FO Mimeograph Paper. FO/81:16, November 1981.

FO Mimeograph Paper. FO/81:18, November 1981.

FO Mimeograph Paper. FO/84:5, February 1984.

FO Mimeograph Paper. FOCL/82:24, "Baptism," Changes from FO/81:6, Feb. 1981.

FO Paper No. 36.

FO Paper No. 41.

FO Paper No. 42.

FO Paper No. 44.

FO Paper No. 45.

FO Paper No. 48.

FO Paper No. 50, 1968.

FO Paper No. 53.

FO Paper No. 54.

FO Paper No. 65.

FO Paper No. 71.

FO Paper No. 73. *One Baptism, One Eucharist and a Mutually Recognized Ministry: Three Agreed Statements.* Geneva: World Council of Churches, 1975.

FO Paper No. 83. *Minutes of the Meeting of the Standing Commission, held at Kloster Loccum, Federal Republic of Germany, July 18-25, 1977.* Geneva: WCC, 1977.

FO Paper No. 84. *Towards an Ecumenical Consensus on Baptism, the Eucharist and the Ministry: A Response to the Churches.* Geneva: WCC, 1977.

FO Paper No. 92. *Sharing in One Hope: Commission on Faith and Order, Bangalore 1978.* Geneva: WCC, 1978.

FO Paper No. 97. *Louisville Consultation on Baptism.* A reprint of *Review nd Expositor: A Baptist Theological Journal,* Vol. LXXVII, No. 1 (Winter, 1980).

FO Paper No. 98. *Minutes of the Meeting of the Standing Commission held at Taizé, France, August 20-24, 1979.* Geneva: WCC, 1980.

FO Paper No. 102. *Episkopé and episcopate in Ecumenical Perspective.* Geneva: WCC, 1980.

Fo Paper No. 107. *The Three Reports of the Forum on Bilateral Conversations.* Geneva: WCC, 1981.

Gassmann, Günther. "Reaction to the revised Faith and Order text on Ministry." November 11, 1981. WCC Archives, Archive Box: "Faith and Order Archives, BEM, 79-82 corr. 81, Lima 82."

Hodgson, Leonard. *The Second World Conference on Faith and Order: Held at Edinburgh, August 3-18, 1937.* New York: The Macmillan Company, 1938.

Johnson, David Enderton, ed. *Uppsala To Nairobi, 1968-1975: Report of the Central Committee to the Fifth Assembly of the World Council of Churches.* New York: Friendship Press, 1975.

Mudge, Lewis S. "Comments on the draft of the 'Ministry' document resulting from the meeting of June 3-7, 1980, Rome." October 27, 1980. WCC Archives, Archive Box: "Faith and Order Archives, BEM, 79-82 corr. 81, Lima 82."

Nairobi To Vancouver, 1975-1983: Report of the Central Committee to the Sixth Assembly of the WCC. Geneva: WCC, 1983.

Neuner, J., S.J., and Dupuis, J., S.J., editors. *The Christian Faith in the Doctrinal Documents of the Catholic Church.* Westminster, Md.: Christian Classics, Inc., 1975.

Pannenberg, Wolfhart. "Comments on the Revised Text of the Agreed Statements on Baptism, Eucharist and Ministry." October 13, 1980. WCC Archives, Archive Box: "Faith and Order, Documents 1980-1981, Circular Letters, 1980-1981."

Paton, David M., ed. *Breaking Barriers, Nairobi 1975: The Official Report of the Fifth Assembly of the World Council of Churches, Nairobi, 23 November-10 December, 1975.* Grand Rapids: Wm. B. Eerdmans, 1976.

Proceedings of the World Conference: Lausanne, August 3-21, 1927, ed. by H.N. Bate, New York: George H. Doran Company, 1927.

Reid, J.K.S. "Comments on the Ministry document of 1/81." Edinburgh, October, 1981. WCC Archives, Archive Box: "Faith and Order Archives, BEM, 79-82 corr. 81, Lima 82."

"Report: NCC USA Forum on Baptism, Eucharist and Ministry," May 19 - 22, 1980, pp. 3-4. (From the files of the Commission on Faith and Order of the National Council of Churches of Christ in the U.S.A., 475 Riverside Drive, New York, N.Y. 10027.)

Rodger, P.C. and Vischer, L., eds. *The Fourth World Conference on Faith and Order: Montreal 1963.* FO Paper No. 42. London: SCM Press Ltd., 1964.

Rodger, P.C. and Vischer, Lukas., editors. *The Fourth World Conference on Faith and Order: Montreal 1963.* New York: Association Press, 1964.

Rouse, Ruth and Neill, Stephen Charles, eds. *A History of the Ecumenical Movement, 1517-1948.* Philadelphia: The Westminster Press, 1954.

Synod of Bishops, 1971. "The Ministerial Priesthood and Justice in the World." Washington, D.C.: National Conference of Catholic Bishops, 1971.

Taufe, Eucharistie und Amt. Frankfurt am Main: Verlag Otto Lembeck, 1982. *The First Six Years, 1948-1954: Report of the Central Committee of the WCC.*

Thurian, Frère Max. World Council of Churches, Geneva, Switzerland. Interviews. (15 April 1985 and 29-30 April, 1985.)

Tillard, J.M.R. The Dominican House of Studies, Ottawa, Canada. Interviews. March 26-28, 1985.

van der Bent, Ans, compiler. *Major Studies and Themes in the Ecumenical Movement.* Geneva: World Council of Churches, 1981.

Vatican Congregation for the Doctrine of the Faith. "Vatican Declaration: Women in the Ministerial Priesthood." *Origins: NC Documentary Service.* Washington, D.C.: National Catholic News Service, Vol. 6: No. 33 (February 3, 1977), 517-524.

Vatican Secretariat for Promoting Christian Unity, in consultation with the Congregation for the Doctrine of the Faith, "Baptism, Eucharist and Ministry: An Appraisal." *Origins: NC Documentary Service.* Washington, D.C.: National Catholic News Service, November 19, 1987 (Vol. 17: No. 23).

Vischer, Lukas, ed. *A Documentary History of the Faith and Order Movement 1927-1963.* St. Louis: The Bethany Press, 1963.

Wainwright, Geoffrey. Duke University, Durham, North Carolina. Interview, July 19, 1985.

WCC Archive Box. "Baptism - Eucharist - Ministry, After Bangalore (1978), Detailed replies to some comments by churches (1978); Steering Group (1979/80)."

WCC Archive Box. "Churches on the Way to Consensus: A Survey of the Replies to the Agreed Statements 'One Baptism, One Eucharist and a Mutually Recognized Ministry'."

WCC Archive Box. "Department of Faith and Order IV 1965."

WCC Archive Box. "Dept. of F & O, VII, vom 1967 bis 1968."

WCC Archive Box, "Faith and Order, Archives, BEM, 79-82 corr. 81, Lima 82."

WCC Archive Box. "Faith and Order Archives, BEM, 79-82 corr. 81, Lima 82."

WCC Archive Box. "Faith and Order, Baptism, Eucharist & Ministry, Meeting to evaluate responses of the churches to Faith and Order Paper 73, Crêt-Bérard June 1977, etc."

WCC Archive Box. "Faith and Order Commission, Mimeographed Master File, 1968."

WCC Archive Box. "Faith and Order, consultation on Ordination 1970, Cartigny, September 28 to October 3, 1970, Documentation and Correspondence."

WCC Archive Box. "Faith and Order, Consultation on the Ordained Ministry, Marseille, Sept 1972, Documents."

WCC Archive Box. "Faith and Order, Documents 1980-1981, Circular Letters, 1980-1981."

WCC Archive Box. Faith and Order, Master File: 72: 1-23, Mimeographed Papers, 1972."

WCC Archive Box. "Faith and Order, Mimeographed Documents 1971, Master File."

WCC Archive Box. "Faith and Order, Mimeographed Master File, FO/70: 1-58."

WCC Archive Box. "Faith and Order. Mimeographed Papers FO/66: 1-73 (plus mailing to WCC member churches concerning Instructio on mixed marriages - 1966) vom January 1966 bis December 1966."

WCC Archive Box. "Faith and Order, Mimeographed Papers 1-38, 1969."

WCC Archive Box. "Faith and Order, Mimeographed Papers 1974." It contains the file, "Faith and Order Mimeographed Papers 1974, (FO/74: 23 Missing)"

WCC Archive Box. "Faith and Order, Mimeographed Papers, 1975, 1976 (incl. Circular Letters)."

WCC Archive Box. "Faith and Order, Mimeographed Papers, 1978 (1-27); Mimeographed Papers 1979 (1-20)."

WCC Archive Box. "Faith and Order Mimeographed Papers, June 1967 - FO/67:34, Dec. 1967 - FO 67:59 Plus RCC/WCC/67: 3;4;5;6;7."

WCC Archive Box. "Faith and Order Mimeographed Papers, January 1967 - FO/67:1, May 1967 - FO/67:33 Plus RC/WCC/67: 1;2;and 3."

WCC Archive Box. "Faith and Order Mimeographed Papers, 1977."

WCC Archive Box. "Faith and Order, Number Papers, 1970."

WCC Archive Box. "Faith and Order, Ordained Ministry Documents, Ordination of Women." (Contains file: "Various stages in Ministry Document, 1972-1974.)

WCC Archive Box. "Faith and Order, Replies of Churches to Faith and Order Paper 73, One Baptism, One Eucharist and a Mutually Recognized Ministry, 1976-1977, Replies O-Z, Replies of Roman Catholic Universities & Colleges."

WCC Archive Box. "Mimeographed documents in chronological order, 1970-72."

WCC Archive Box. "Mimeographed documents in chronological order, 1973 - ." It contains WCC File, "Faith and Order, Mimeographed Master File, 1973/1-41."

WCC Archive Box. "Nairobi Follow-up (1976), Section II; Bangalore Follow-up 1978 (Aug. '79), Correspondence; Faith and Order, Standing Commission, Taizé, August, 1979, Correspondence/documents."

WCC Archive Box. "Nairobi Follow-up 1976), Section II; Bangalore Follow-up 1978 Aug. '79, Correspondence; Faith and Order, Standing Commission, Taizé, August 1979, Correspondence/documents."

WCC Archive File. "BEM Steering Group Meetings (1979/1980), Correspondence/Documents."

WCC Archive File, "BEM Steering Group Meetings (1979/1980), Correspondence/Documents."

WCC Archive File. "Mimeographed documents in chronological order, 1970-72."

WCC Archive File No. FO772.MCO, "Mimeographed documents in chronological order, 1970-72."

WCC Archive Memorandum, May 1967, M.B. Handspicker, Archive Box: "Dept. of F and O, VII, vom 1967 bis 1968;" File: "Department of faith and order, 1967."

WCC Archives Box, "Nairobi Follow-up (1976), Section II; Bangalore Follow-up 1978 (Aug. '79), Correspondence; Faith and Order, Standing Commission, Taizé, August 1979, Correspondence/documents."

WCC Mimeograph Paper. RCC/WCC/67:3, November 1967.

WCC Mimeograph Paper. RCC/WCC/67:5.

WCC Mimeograph Paper. RCC/WCC/67:6, December 1967.

WCC Mimeograph Paper. RCC/WCC/68:2, November 1968.

WCC Mimeograph Paper. RCC/WCC/73:1 (R), June 1973.

SECONDARY SOURCES

Anglican/Roman Catholic Agreed Statement, "The Purpose of the Church," *Origins: NC Documentary Service.* Washington, D.C.: National Catholic News Service 5 (1975) 328-34.

Anglican-Roman Catholic International Commission. *The Final Report: Windsor, September, 1981.* Cincinnati: Forward Movement Publications, 1982.

Baptism, Eucharis & Ministry 1982-1990: Report on the Process and Responses. Faith and Order Paper No. 149. Geneva: WCC Publications, 1990.

Bauer, Norman R. "Intercommunion: Possibilities and Practicalities." *Ecumenical Trends* 7, no. 7 (July/August 1978) 97-102.

Baum, Gregory. "The Ministerial Priesthood." *Ecumenist* 4 (1964-66), pp. 4-7.

Bertalot, Renzo. "Risposte al BEM [Review of *Churches Respond to BEM*, 6 volumes]." *Protestantesimo* 44, No.3(1989), 171-177.

Berzonsky, Vladimir. "Baptism, Eucharist and Ministry: A Pastor's View." *St. Vladimir's Theological Quarterly.* Volume 27, 1983, No. 4, pp. 251-256.

Biemer, Günter. "Election of Bishops as a New Desideratum in Church Practice." *Bishops and People.* Edited and translated by Leonard Swidler and Arlene Swidler. Philadelphia: The Westminster Press, 1970, pp. 38-53.

Blenkinsopp, Joseph. *Celibacy, Ministry, Church.* New York: 1968.

502

Board for Mission and Unity of the General Synod of the Church of England. *Towards a Church of England Response to BEM and ARCIC.* London: CIO Publishing, 1985.

Bobosh, Theodore. "A Lutheran Reaction to the Lima Document." *St. Vladimir's Theological Quarterly.* Volume 28, 1984, No. 1, pp. 66-70.

Boulding, Mary Cecily, O.P. "Grass Roots Ecumenism — the Real Situation." *Priests & People* 3 (December 1989), 440-442.

Bowman, David, S.J., ed. *U. S. Catholic Ecumenism — Ten Years Later.* Washington D.C.: USCC, 1975.

Braaten, Carl E. "The Ministry." *Dialog* 27 (Winter 1988), 2-47.

Broccolo, Gerard T. "Can We Have Prayer Without Father?" *The Journal of the Catholic Campus Ministry Association*, Vol. I (Spring, 1986), pp. 22-24.

Brothers, Joan. "Women in Ecclesial Office." *Concilium* 80. New York: Herder and Herder, 1972.

Brown, Raymond E. *Biblical Exegesis and Church Doctrine.* New York: Paulist Press, 1985.

Brown, Raymond E. *Biblical Reflections on Crises Facing the Church.* New York: Paulist Press, 1975.

Brown, Raymond E. "Episkopé and Episkopos: the New Testament Evidence." *Theological Studies*, 41 (1980), p. 322ff.

Brown, Raymond E. *Priest and Bishop: Biblical Reflections.* New York: Paulist Press, 1970.

Brown, Raymond E. *The Churches the Apostles Left Behind.* Ramsey, N.J.: Paulist Press, 1984.

Brown, Raymond E. *The Community of the Beloved Disciple.* New York: Paulist Press, 1979.

Brown, Raymond E. *The Critical Meaning of the Bible.* New York: Paulist Press, 1981.

Brown, Raymond E., and Meier, John P. *Antioch and Rome: New Testament Cradles of Catholic Christianity.* New York: Paulist Press, 1983.

Brown, Robert McAfee. *The Ecumenical Revolution: An Interpretation of the Catholic-Protestant Dialogue.* New York: Doubleday (Anchor Image Book), rev. ed., 1969.

Burgess, Joseph A., ed. *The Role of the Augsburg Confession.* Philadelphia: Fortress Press, 1980.

Burghardt, Walter J. "Apostolic Succession: Notes on the Early Patristic Era." *Eucharist & Ministry: Lutherans and Catholics in Dialogue IV*, edited by Paul C. Empie and T. Austin Murphy. Minneapolis: Augsburg Publishing House, 1979, pp. 173-77.

Bürki, Bruno. "Entre Jean Calvin et le Texte de Lima: Le Fonctionnement des Ministères dans les Eglises Réformées Francophones." *Freiburger Zeitschrift für Philosophie und Theologie* 35, No. 3 (1988), 469-484.

Butler, B.C. *The Church and Unity.* London: Chapman, 1979.

Catholic Biblical Association. "Task Force Report: Women in the Church." *Origins: NC Documentary Service.* Washington, D.C.: National Catholic News Service 9:28 (December 27, 1979), 450-454.

Centro pro Unione. "A Continuing Bibliography for the Study of Interchurch Dialogues." No. 15 (Spring, 1979), 3-24.

504

Chadwick, Henry. "Lima, ARCIC, and the Church of England." *One in Christ.* Volume 20, 1984, No. 1, pp.31-37.

Congar, Ives. *Ministères et communion ecclesiale.* Paris: 1971.

Congar, Yves. *I Believe in the Holy Spirit.* Volume I: *The Experience of the Spirit.* New York: The Seabury Press, 1983.

Congar, Yves. *I Believe in the Holy Spirit.* Volume II: *Lord and Giver of Life.* New York: The Seabury Press, 1983.

Congar, Yves. *I Believe in the Holy Spirit.* Volume III: *The River of Life Flows in the East and in the West.* New York: The Seabury Press, 1983.

Cooke, Bernard. *Ministry to Word and Sacraments: History and Theology.* Philadelphia: Fortress Press, 1976.

Coventry, John. "Baptism, Eucharist and Ministry: A Roman Catholic Response." *One in Christ.* Volume 20, 1984, No. 1, pp. 2-7.

Coventry, John, S.J. "Theological Trends: Intercommunion." *The Way* 18 (1978) 300-309; 19 (1979) 56-65, 144-153.

Cranford, Stephen. "An Overview of Recent Bilateral Interchurch Conversations." *Centro pro Unione.* No. 14 (Fall, 1978), 7-33.

Cunningham, Agnes, S.S.C.M. *The Bishop in the Church: Patristic Texts on the Role of the "Episkopos".* Wilmington, Delaware: Michael Glazier, Inc., 1985.

Daley, Brian E. "Ordination: The Sacrament of Ministry." *America,* December 11, 1982, 365-69.

Dodd, W. "Toward a Theology of Priesthood." *Theological Studies* 28 (1967), pp. 683-705.

Doohan, L. "Contemporary Theologies of the Laity: An Overview Since Vatican II." *Communio* 7 (1980) 255f.

Döring, Heinrich. "Taufe, Eucharistie und Amt im Kontext der Communio-Ekklesiologie: Analysen zur offiziellen römischen Antwort auf das Lima-Dokument." *Catholica* 42, No. 3 (1988), 170-194.

Dorris, Tom. "Deacons: Ecumenical Problem or Possibility? Responses to BEM and the Diaconate." *Mid-Stream* 29 (January 1990) 44-50.

Dorris, Tom. "Steps Towards Unity: What Ever Happened to BEM?" *One World*, No. 150 (November 1989) 10-11.

Dulles, Avery. "Ecumenism: Problems and Opportunities for the Future." *Toward Vatican III: The Work That Needs to be Done*. David Tracy *et al.*, ed. New York: Seabury Press, 1978, pp. 91-101.

Dulles, Avery. *Models of the Church: A Critical Assessment of the Church in All Its Aspects*. Garden City, N.Y.: Doubleday and Company, Inc., 1974.

Dulles, Avery. "The Lima Meeting." *America*. February 20, 1982, pp. 126-129.

Dunn, James, D.G. *Unity and Diversity in the New Testament: An Inquiry Into the Character of Earliest Christianity*. Philadelphia: The Westminster Press, 1977.

Eagan, Joseph F., S. J. "Ordained Ministry in BEM: A Theological Critique." *Mid-Stream: An Ecumenical Journal* XXIII, 3. (July, 1984), 290-307. Also found in *The Ecumenical Review* 36, 3 (July 1984), 263-277.

Ecumenism. No. 70, June 1983.

Ehrenstrom, N. and Gassmann, G. *Confessions in Dialogue: A Survey of Bilateral Conversations among World Confessional Families, 1959-1974*. Third Revised Edition. Geneva: WCC, 1975.

Eijk, A.H.C. van. "Ordained Ministry: Divine Institution and Historical Development: Reflections on a Roman Catholic Response to the Lima Report." *One in Christ* 27, No. 4 (1991), 352-367.

Ellingsen, Mark. "After Lima, The Creation Doctrine and the Way Towards Visible Unity." *One in Christ.* Volume 20, 1984, No. 1, pp. 38-47.

Empie, Paul C. and Murphy, T.Austin, eds. *Eucharist and Ministry: Lutherans and Catholics in Dialogue IV.* Minneapolis: Augsburg Publishing House, 1979.

Empie, Paul C., and Murphy, T. Austin, editors. *Lutherans and Catholics in Dialogue I-III.* Minneapolis: Augsburg Publishing House, 1965.

The Epistles of St. Clement of Rome and St. Ignatius of Antioch. Translated by James A. Kleist, S.J., Ph.D. *Ancient Christian Writers: The Works of the Fathers in Translation,* No. 1. New York: Newman Press, 1946.

Fahey, Michael A. "Before and After the Decree on Ecumenism of Vatican II." *Ecumenical Trends* 18 (November 1989), 157-159.

Fahey, Michael A., ed. *Catholic Perspectives on Baptism, Eucharist and Ministry: A Study Commissioned by the Catholic Theological Society of America.* Lanham, MD: University Press of America, 1986.

Fahey, Michael A., S.J. "Eucharistic Sharing (Intercommunion)." *New Catholic Encyclopedia* (Vol. 17) *Supplement: Changes in the Church* (1979), pp. 215-217.

Faith and Order Commission (WCC). "Report from the Second Forum on Bilateral Conversations to the Participating World Confessional Families and Churches and to the World Council of Churches." *Centro pro Unione.* No. 16 (Fall, 1979).

Feuillet, A. *Le sacerdoce du Christ et de ses ministres.* Paris: 1972.

Fraser, Daphne. "Baptism, Eucharist and Ministry: An Anglican Lay Response." *One in Christ.* Volume 20, 1984, No. 1, pp. 8-11.

Fries, Heinrich, and Rahner, Karl. *Unity of the Churches: An Actual Possibility.* Translated by Ruth C.L. Gritsch and Eric W. Gritsch. New York: Paulist Press, 1985.

Frisque, J. and Congar, Ives. *Les prêtres: Formation, ministère, et vie.* Paris: 1968.

Galadza, Peter. "Eastern Orthodox Responses to the BEM Ministry Section." *One in Christ* 26, No. 1-2 (1990), 94-105.

Galot, Jean, S.J. *Theology of the Priesthood.* San Francisco: Ignatius Press, 1984.

Ganoczy, A. "'Splendours and Miseries' of the Tridentine Doctrine of Ministries." *Concilium* 80 (1972), pp. 75-86.

Gassman, Günther. "Scripture, Tradition, and the Church: The Ecumenical Nexus in Faith and Order Work." *Journal of Ecumenical Studies* 28, No. 3 (Summer 1991), 435-454.

Goldie, R. "Laity: A Bibliographical Survey of Three Decades." *The Laity Today* 26 (1979) 107-43.

Grace, James P. "Symbol and Priesthood." *America* 153, 10 (October 19, 1985), 233-35.

Granfield, Patrick. *The Limits of the Papacy: Authority and Autonomy in the Church.* New York: The Crossroad Publishing Company, 1987.

Grillmeier, Aloys. "The Mystery of the Church." *Commentary on the Documents of Vatican II*, ed. by Herbert Vorgrimler, vol. I. New York: Herder and Herder, 1967.

508

Gromada, Conrad T. "Toward a Theology of Ministry: The Lima Document and Roman Catholic Theology." *Louvain Studies*. Vol. 15, no. 4, Winter 1990, pp. 353-369.

Gros, Jeffrey. "Ordained Ministry: The Ecumenical Climate." *Ecumenical Trends* 20 (October 1991), 139-142.

Gros, Jeffrey, ed. *The Search for Visible Unity: Baptism, Eucharist, Ministry.* New York: The Pilgrim Press, 1984.

Guérin, Nicolas. "La Réception du BEM: Une Évaluation des Réponses des Eglises aux Quatre Questions de sa Préface." *Freiburger Zeitschrift für Philosophie und Theologie* 36, No. 1-2 (1989), 173-192.

Hamer, Jérome. "Réflexions sur les dialogues théologiques interconfessionnels." *Documentation catholique* 70 (1973) 569-73.

Hoge, Dean R. *The Future of Catholic Leadership.* New York: Sheed and Ward, 1987.

Holstein, H. *Hierarchie et peuple de Dieu.* Paris: 1970.

Hopko, Thomas. "The Lima Statement and the Orthodox." *St. Vladimir's Theological Quarterly.* Volume 27, 1983, No. 4, pp. 281-290.

Horgan, Thaddeus. "What is the State of Ecumenism Today?" *Emmanuel* 85 (1979) 11-15.

Hotchkin, John f. "Probing the Possibilities: The Unfolding Debate on Models of Unity." *Interface.* Washington: USCC. Issue no. 2 (Spring 1980) 1-11.

Houtepen, Anton. "Verso Una Visione Ecumenica della Chiesa: L'ecclesiologia Implicita del BEM" [Translated by S. Voicu. English Abstract, p. 171.] *Studi Ecumenici* 7 (April-September 1980), 137-171.

Howell, Leon. *Acting in Faith: The World Council of Churches Since 1975.* Geneva: World Council of Churches, 1982.

Hume, Cardinal George Basil. "The Churches: How Can Visible Unity Begin? Must Full Doctrinal Agreement Come First?" *Origins: NC Documentary Service.* Washington, D.C.: National Catholic News Service 7 (April 27, 1978) 709-13.

Hunter, Harold D. "Reflections by a Pentecostalist on Aspects of BEM." *Journal of Ecumenical Studies* 29, Numbers 3-4 (Summer-Fall 1992), 317-345.

Hussey, M. Edmund. "Needed: A Theology of Priesthood." *Origins: NC Documentary Service.* Washington, D.C.: National Catholic News Service, Vol. 17: No. 34 (February 4, 1988): 577-83.

Huwyler, Christoph. *Das Problem der Interkommunion.* Band I und II. Bad Honnef: Bock und Herchen, 1984.

In Quest of a Church Unity, Princeton, New Jersey: Consultation on Church Union (COCU), [228 Alexander Street, Princeton, N.J. 08540].

Irwin, Kevin. Kilmartin, Edward D. McGuire, Joan M. "The official Vatican Response to BEM." *Ecumenical Trends* 17 (March 1988), 33-43.

Ismail, Andar. "Laity in BEM: A Theological and Educational Critique." *Ecumenical Review* 41 (January 1989), 73-77.

John Paul II, Pope. "Apostolic Letter on Ordination" (*"Ordinatio Sacerdotalis"*). *Origins: CNS Documentary Service,* Vol. 24: No. 4 (June 9, 1994), 49, 51-52.

Jorgenson, James. "Reflections on the Lima Statement." *St. Vladimir's Theological Quarterly.* Volume 27, 1983, No. 4, pp. 239-250.

Kasper, Walter. "A New Dogmatic Outlook on the Priestly Ministry." *The Identity of the Priest. Concilium: Theology in the Age of Renewal*, Vol. 43. New York: Paulist Press, 1969, pp. 20-33.

Kearney, Peter. "New Testament Incentives for a Different Ecclesial Order." *Concilium* 80 (1972).

Kennedy, Eugene C. and Heckler, Victor J. *The Catholic Priest in the United States: Psychological Investigations*. Washington, D.C.: U.S.C.C. Publications, 1972.

Kilmartin, Edward J.,S.J. "A Catholic Response to Lima 1982." *Bulletin/Centro Pro Unione* 27 (Spring 1985), 8-16.

Küng, Hans and Kasper, Walter, eds. *The Plurality of Ministries. Concilium: Religion in the Seventies*, Volume 74. New York: Herder and Herder, 1972.

Küng, Hans. *On Being a Christian*. Translated by Edward Quinn. Garden City, New York: Doubleday & Company, Inc., 1976.

Küng, Hans. *The Church*. New York: Sheed and Ward, 1967.

Küng, Hans. "Vatican III: Problems and Opportunities for the Future." *Toward Vatican III: The Work That Needs to be Done*. David Tracy *et al*., ed. New York: Seabury Press, 1978, pp. 67-90.

Lange, Ernst. *And Yet It Moves: Dream and Reality of the Ecumenical Movement*. Translated by Edwin Robertson. Grand Rapids, Michigan: William B. Eerdmans Publishing Company, 1979.

Lanne, Emmanuel. "La Problematique Oecumenique des Ministères." Personal Papers. [Typewritten.]

Lanne, Emmanuel, O.S.B. "Pluralism and Unity: The Possibility of a Variety of Typoligies within the Same Ecclesial Allegiance." *One in Christ* 6 (1970) 430-51.

Lawler, Michael G. *Symbol and Sacrament: A Contemporary Sacramental Theology.* New York: Paulist Press, 1987.

Lazareth, William H. *Growing Together in Baptism, Eucharist and Ministry.* Faith and Order Paper No. 114. Geneva: World Council of Churches, 1982.

Lazareth, William H. "Holy Trinity and Holy Tradition: Orthodox Contributions to Baptism, Eucharist, and Ministry." *St. Vladimir's Theological Quarterly.* Volume 27, 1983, No. 4, 291-293.

Legrand, Hervé-Marie. "The Presidency of the Eucharist According to the Ancient Tradition." *Worship* 53 (1979), 413-438.

"Le ministère sacerdotal: Rapport de la Commission international de théologie." Paris: Editions du Cerf, 1971.

Limouris, Gennadios, and Vaporis, Nomikos Michael, editors. *Orthodox Perspectives on Baptism, Eucharist, and Ministry.* Faith and Order Paper No. 128. Brookline, Massachusetts: Holy Cross Orthodox Press, 1985.

Macquarrie, John. *Christian Unity and Christian Diversity.* London: SCM Press, 1975.

Macquarrie, John. *Principles of Christian Theology.* Second Edition. New York: Charles Scribner's Sons, 1977.

Marrevee, William. "The Lima Document on Ordained Ministry." *Catholic Perspectives on Baptism, Eucharist and Ministry: A Study Commissioned by the Catholic Theological Society of America*, Michael A. Fahey, ed. Lanham, MD: University Press of America, 1986, pp. 163-185.

May, Melanie A. "The Ordination of Women: the Churches' Responses to Baptism, Eucharist, and Ministry." *Journal of Ecumenical Studies*, 26 (Spring 1989), 251-269.

McBrien, Richard P. *Catholicism.* Minneapolis, MN: Winston Press, Inc., 1980.

McBrien, Richard P. *Catholicism: New Edition.* New York: HarperCollins Publishers, 1994.

McBrien, Richard P. *Church: The Continuing Quest.* New York: Newman Press, 1970.

McBrien, Richard P. *Ministry: A Theological, Pastoral Handbook.* San Francisco: Harper and Row Publishers, 1987.

McGrath, Roger Eugene. "The Theology of Pastoral Office in Ecumenical Dialogue Since Vatican Council II." Ph.D. dissertation, University of Notre Dame, 1982.

McGuire, Joan M. "The Official Vatican Response to BEM: Ministry." *Ecumenical Trends*, 17 (March 1988), 41-43.

McKenzie, John L. *Authority in the Church.* Garden City, New York: Doubleday and Company, Inc., 1966.

McManus, Frederick. "Report on the Lima Statement on Ministry." October, 1984 (Mimeographed.)

Meeking, Basil. "The Dialogue of the Roman Catholic Church With the Member Churches of the World Council of Churches." Lecture delivered 22 April, 1982.

Meyer, Harding, and Vischer, Lukas, editors. *Growth in Agreement: Reports and Agreed Statements of Ecumenical Conversations on a World Level.* Faith and Order Paper No. 108. New York: Paulist Press, 1984.

Mid-Stream: An Ecumenical Journal, Volume XXIII, No. 3 (July, 1984).

Minus, Paul M., Jr. *The Catholic Rediscovery of Protestantism: A History of Roman Catholic Ecumenical Pioneering.* New York: Paulist Press, 1976.

Mitchell, Nathan O.S.B., *Mission and Ministry: History and Theology in the Sacrament of Order.* Wilmington, Delaware: Michael Glazier, Inc., 1982.

Moede, Gerald F. "BEM and COCU's Emerging Consensus: A Reflection on Ministry," *Mid-Stream: An Ecumenical Journal*, XXIII, 3 (July, 1984) 308-317.

Moingt, J. "Nature du sacerdoce ministeriel." *Recherches de science religieuse* 58 (1970), pp. 237-72.

Mudge, Lewis S., "The New Ministry Text: Some Tough Questions." Paper delivered at the Forum on Baptism, Eucharist and Ministry, sponsored by the National Council of Churches in the USA, Baltimore, May 19-22, 1980.

Murphy, Roland and van Iersel, Bas, eds. *Office and Ministry in the Church. Concilium: Religion in the Seventies*, Volume 80. New York: Herder and Herder, 1972.

Murray, John, C.C.S.B. "Ecumenism: The Next Steps." *One in Christ* 25, No. 2 (1989), 163-168.

National Conference of Catholic Bishops. *As One Who Serves: Reflections on the Pastoral Ministry of Priests in the United States.* Washington, D.C.: United States Catholic Conference, 1977.

Nelson, J. Robert. "Convergence, Resurgence and Emergence." *Centro pro Unione.* No. 1 (1969) 29-36.

O'Meara, Thomas Franklin, O.P. *Theology of Ministry.* New York: Paulist Press, 1983.

514

Orsy, Ladislaus. "The Two Hierarchies in the Church." *America* 158, 10 (March 12, 1988), 272.

Parker, David. "An Evangelical Response to BEM." *Colloquium* 22 (October 1989), 28-36.

Puglisi, James F. *A Workbook of Bibliographies for the Study of Interchurch Dialogues.* Rome: Centro pro Unione, 1978.

Puglisi, J.F., and Voicu, S.J. *A Bibliography of Interchurch and Interconfessional Theological Dialogues.* Rome: Centro Pro Unione, 1984.

Putney, Michael. "The Ordained Ministry in the Light of Recent Ecumenical Statements." *Faith and Culture: Challenges to Ministry*, edited by Neil Brown. Manly, N.S.W., Australia: Catholic Institute of Sydney, 1989, pp. 137-154.

Radano, John A. "The Catholic Church and BEM, 1980-1989." *Mid-Stream* 30 (April 1991), 139-156.

Rahner, Karl. *Concern for the Church. Theological Investigations*, Vol. XX. Translated by Edward Quinn. New York: The Crossroad Publishing Company, 1981.

Rahner, Karl. *Ecclesiology, Questions in the Church, the Church in the World. Theological Investigations*, Vol. XX. Translated by David Bourke. New York: The Seabury Press, 1976.

Rahner, Karl. *Faith and Ministry. Theological Investigations*, Vol. XIX. Translated by Edward Quinn. New York: The Crossroad Publishing Company, 1983.

Rahner, Karl. *Foundations of Christian Faith: An Introduction to the Idea of Christianity.* Translated by William V. Dych. New York: The Seabury Press, 1978.

Rahner, Karl. *More Recent Writings. Theological Investigations*, Vol. IV. Translated by Kevin Smyth. New York: The Seabury Press, 1974.

Rahner, Karl. *Prayers for a Lifetime.* New York: The Crossroad Publishing Company, 1984.

Rahner, Karl. *The Priesthood.* Translated by Edward Quinn. New York: Herder and Herder, 1973.

Rahner, Karl. *The Shape of the Church to Come.* Translated by Edward Quinn. New York: The Seabury Press, 1974.

Rahner, Karl. "What Is the Theological Starting Point for a Definition of the Priestly Ministry?" *Concilium: Theology in the Age of Renewal*, Vol. 43. New York: Paulist Press, 1969, pp. 80-84.

Roman Catholic/Lutheran International Commission. "Statement on the Augsburg Confession." *Origins: NC Documentary Service.* Washington, D.C.: National Catholic News Service 9 (April 10, 1980) 685-89.

Root, Michael. "Do Not Grow Weary in Well-doing: Lutheran Responses to the BEM Ministry Document." *Dialog*, 27 (Winter 1988), 23-30.

Ryan, Herbert, S.J. "The Churches: How Can Visible Unity Begin? 2. The Path to Unity." *Origins: NC Documentary Service.* Washington, D.C.: National Catholic News Service 7 (April 27, 1978) 714-19.

Sartori, Luigi. "La 'Receptio' Cattolica del BEM: La Problematica di Fondo." [English Abstract.] *Studi Ecumenici* 7 (O-D 1989), 383-395.

Schelkle, Karl. "Ministry and Minister in the New Testament Church." *The Identity of the Priest*, edited by Karl Rahner, vol. 43 of *Concilium.* New York: Paulist Press, 1969, pp. 6-19.

Schillebeeckx, Edward. *Christ the Sacrament of the Encounter with God.* London: Sheed and Ward, 1963.

Schillebeeckx, Edward, ed. *The Unifying Role of the Bishop. Concilium: Religion in the Seventies*, Volume 71. New York: Herder and Herder, 1972.

Schillebeeckx, Edward. *Ministry: Leadership in the Community of Jesus Christ.* New York: Crossroad, 1981.

Schillebeeckx, Edward. *The Church with a Human Face: A New and Expanded Theology of Ministry.* New York: The Crossroad Publishing Company, 1985.

Schillebeeckx, Edward. *The Mission of the Church.* Translated by N. D. Smith. New York: The Seabury Press, 1973.

Schillebeeckx, Edward. *The Schillebeeckx Reader.* Edited by Robert J. Schreiter. New York: The Crossroad Publishing Company, 1984.

Schoof, T.M. *A Survey of Catholic Theology, 1800-1970.* Translated by N. D. Smith. New York: Paulist Newman Press, 1970.

Schrotenboer, Paul, ed. "An Evangelical Response to Baptism, Eucharist and Ministry." [Prepared by the World Evangelical Fellowship, June 1989.] *Evangelical Review of Theology* 13 (October 1989), 291-313.

Secretariat for Promoting Christian Unity. *Guidelines for Ecumenical Collaboration at the Regional, National and Local Levels.* Washington: NCCB, February 22, 1975.

Sharing the Light of Faith: National Catechetical Directory for Catholics of the United States. Washington D.C.: USCC, 1979.

Skoglund, John E. and Nelson, J. Robert. *Fifty Years of Faith and Order: An Interpretation of the Faith and Order Movement.* New York: The Committee for the Interseminary Movement, 1963.

Song, Choan-Seng, ed. *Growing Together into Unity: Texts of the Faith and Order Commission on Conciliar Fellowship.* Geneva: WCC, 1978.

Stransky, Thomas F., C.S.P., and Sheerin, John B., C.S.P., editors. *Doing the Truth in Charity: Statements of Pope Paul VI, Popes John Paul I, John Paul II, and the Secretariat for Promoting Christian Unity, 1964-1980.* New York: Paulist Press, 1982.

St. Vladimir's Theological Quarterly. Vol. 27, No. 4, 1983.

Stylianopoulos, Theodore, and Heim, S. Mark, editors. *Spirit of Truth: Ecumenical Perspectives on the Holy Spirit.* Brookline, Massachusetts: Holy Cross Orthodox Press, 1986.

Sullivan, Francis A., S.J. *Magisterium: Teaching Authority in the Catholic Church.* Mahwah, N.J.: Paulist Press, 1983.

Sullivan, Francis A., S.J. "The Significance of Vatican II's Decision to Say of the Church of Christ Not That It 'Is' But That It 'Subsists In' the Roman Catholic Church." *Bulletin/Centro Pro Unione* 29 (Spring 1986), 3-8.

Tavard, George H. "A Theological Approach to Ministry and Authority." *The Jurist* 32 (1972).

Tavard, George H. *A Theology For Ministry.* Wilmington, Delaware: Michael Glazier, Inc., 1983.

Tavard, George H. "The Anglican-Roman Catholic Agreed Statements and Their Reception." *Theological Studies* 41 (1980) 74-97.

Tavard, George H. "The Function of the Minister in the Eucharistic Celebration: An Ecumenical Approach." *Journal of Ecumenical Studies* 4 (1967), pp. 629-49.

Taylor, David W.A. "Ordained to the Ministry of the Church: An Ecumenical Perspective." *Insights* 106 (Spring 1991), 25-36.

518

"The Bilateral Consultations between the Roman Catholic Church in the United States and Other Christian Communions: A Theological Review and Critique by the Study Committee of the Catholic Theological Society of America [July 1972]." *Proceedings of the CTSA* 27 (1972) 179-232. An update for 1972-1979 [June 1979], *Proceedings of the CTSA* 34 (1979) 253-85.

The Reconciliation of Ministries: A Report by The Faith and Order Advisory Group of The Board for Mission and Unity. General Synod (GS) 307, Kent, England: The Wickham Press Ltd., Blackfen Road, Sideup, 1976.

Thurian, Max, ed. *Churches Respond to BEM: Official Responses to the "Baptism, Eucharist and Ministry" Text.* Volume I (Faith and Order Paper 129). Geneva: World Council of Churches, 1986.

Thurian, Max, ed. *Churches Respond to BEM: Official Responses to the "Baptism, Eucharist and Ministry" Text.* Volume II (Faith and Order Paper 132). Geneva: World Council of Churches, 1986.

Thurian, Max, ed. *Churches Respond to BEM: Official Responses to the "Baptism, Eucharist and Ministry" Text.* Volume III (Faith and Order Paper 135). Geneva: World Council of Churches, 1987.

Thurian, Max, ed. *Churches Respond to BEM: Official Responses to the "Baptism, Eucharist and Ministry" Text.* Volume IV (Faith and Order Paper 137). Geneva: World Council of Churches, 1987.

Thurian, Max, ed. *Churches Respond to BEM: Official Responses to the "Baptism, Eucharist and Ministry" Text.* Volume V (Faith and Order Paper 143). Geneva: World Council of Churches, 1988.

Thurian, Max, ed. *Churches Respond to BEM: Official Responses to the "Baptism, Eucharist and Ministry" Text.* Volume VI (Faith and Order Paper 144). Geneva: World Council of Churches, 1988.

Thurian, Max, ed. *Ecumenical Perspectives on Baptism, Eucharist and Ministry.* Faith and Order Paper No. 116. Geneva: World Council of Churches, 1983.

Thurian, Max. *Priesthood and Ministry: Ecumenical Research.* Translated by Paula Clifford. London: Mowbray, 1983.

Thurian, Max. *Sacerdoce et ministère.* Taizé: 1970.

Tierney, Brian. "Pope and Bishops: A Historical Survey." *America*, Vol. 158, No. 9 (March 5, 1988): 230-37.

Tillard, J.M.R., O.P. "Eucharist, Baptism, Church Oneness and Unity." *New Blackfriars* 61, no. 716 (1980) 4-15.

Tillard, J.M.R., O.P. *The Bishop of Rome.* Translated by John de Satgé. Wilminton, Delaware: Michael Glazier, Inc., 1983.

Tillard, J.M.R., O.P. "Préparer l'unité: Pour une pastorale oecumenique." *Nouvelle Revue Théologique* 102 (1980) 161-78.

Till, Barry. *The Churches Search for Unity.* London: Penguin, 1972.

Torrance, James B. "The Lima Report — A Church of Scotland Perspective." *One in Christ.* Volume 20, 1984, No. 1, pp. 12-18.

Tripp, David. "Can These Dry Bones Live? One Methodist's Response to the Lima Document." *One in Christ.* Volume 20, 1984, No. 1, pp. 19-23.

Unterkoefler, E.L. and Harsanyi, A. *The Unity We Seek: A Statement by the Roman Catholic/Presbyterian-Reformed Consultation.* New York: Paulist Press, 1977.

Vandervelde, George. "BEM and the 'Hierarchy of Truths': A Vatican Contribution to the Reception Process." *Journal of Ecumenical Studies* 25 (Winter 1988), 74-84.

Vandervelde, George. "Vatican Ecumenism at the Crossroads? The Vatican Approach to Differences with BEM." *Gregorianum* 69, No. 4 (1988), 689-711.

van der Bent, Ans. *Six Hundred Ecumenical Consultations, 1948-1982.* Geneva: World Council of Churches, 1983.

van der Bent, Ans, *et al. Index to the World Council of Churches' Official Statements and Reports, 1948-1978.* Geneva: WCC, 1978.

van Eyden, Rene. "The Place of Women in Liturgical Functions." *Concilium* 72. New York: Herder and Herder, 1972, pp. 68-81.

Vawter, Bruce, C.M. "The Gospel According to John." *The Jerome Biblical Commentary*, Englewood Cliffs, New Jersey: Prentice-Hall, Inc., 1968.

Vischer, Georg H. *Apostolischer Dienst: Fünfzig Jahre Diskussion über das kirchliche Amt in Glauben und Kirchenverfassung.* Frankfurt am Main: Verlag Otto Lembeck, 1982.

Visser 't Hooft, W.A. *Memoirs.* Geneva: WCC Publications, 1973.

Visser 't Hooft, W.A. "The Task of the World Council of Churches." Report, Amsterdam, 1948.

Vorgrimler, Herbert, ed. *Commentary on the Documents of Vatican II.* 5 volumes. Translated by Lalit Adolphus, Kevin Smyth and Richard Strachan. New York: Herder and Herder, 1966.

Wainwright, Geoffrey. "Word and Sacrament in the Churches' Responses to the Lima Text." *One in Christ* 24, No. 4 (1988), 304-327.

WCC Archive File. "Faith and Order, Master File: 72:1-23, Mimeographed Papers, 1972."

West, W.M.S. "Baptism, Eucharist, Ministry: A Baptist Comment." *One in Christ.* Volume 20, 1984, No. 1, pp. 24-30.

Willebrands, Cardinal Jan.   Address of January 18, 1970, *Documents on Anglican/Roman Catholic Relations.* Vol. I. Washington D.C.: USCC, 1972, 32-41.

Worgul, George S., Jr. *From Magic to Metaphor: A Validation of the Christian Sacraments.* New York: Paulist Press, 1980.

Worgul, George S., Jr. "Ritual, Power, Authority and Riddles: The Anthropology of Rome's Declaration on the Ordination of Women." *Louvain Studies.* Vol. 14, no. 1, Spring 1989, pp. 38-61.

INDEX

A

apostolic age, (as normative) 446

apostolic succession, 112-121, 156, 158-159, 249-262, 296, 297, 386-394, 422-423, 431-433, 434, 435

apostolic tradition, 107-112, 158, 244-249, 296, 382-386, 417, 419, 431-432, 446-447

authority, 156, 295, 423-424

authority (of ordained ministry), 85-89, 156, 201-205, 330-335, 426-427, 452-455, *See* priesthood

authoritative decision-making, 424

authorization, 427, 435-436, 444-445, 452-455

B

biblical scholarship, openness to, 474

bishops, selection of, 427

C

charisms, variety of, 106, 242-244, 296, 378-381, 422, 431, 436, 448-450

christological emphasis, 16, 155, 156, 294, 458-459, 461

church, local, 422, 430-431, 470-471, 480-481

church structure, 423-424, 428-429, 435-436, 478

church polity (presbyterial and/or episcopal), 418, 419, 440

church unity (1961 definition), 60, *See* unity (church)

churches, non-episcopal, 8-10, 42, 60, 158-159, 419, 435, 442

collegiality (episcopal), 418, 429-431, 440-441

D

deacons, *See* three-fold ministry

definition of terms, 181-184, 310-313

Dulles' models of the church, 442, 461, 462-464

E

ecclesiological avenue (for developing a theology of ministry), 466-468

ecumenical movement

    Anglican influence, 3ff.

    Orthodox participation, 8

ecumenicity, 477-478

ecumenism (methodological shift), *See* methodology

episcopal office (as relating to that of the presbyter), 435, 440, 442-443

episcopal succession, 296, 297, 435, 442-443, *See* apostolic succession

episcopate, *See* three-fold ministry